ALPHONSO T. CLEARWATER

The History of Ulster County New York

Volume 1

Edited by

Alphonso T. Clearwater, LL.D.

MEMBER OF THE NEW YORK HISTORICAL SOCIETY; OF THE ULSTER HISTORICAL SOCIETY; OF THE HISTORICAL SOCIETY OF NEWBURGH BAY AND THE HIGHLANDS; OF THE MINNISINK HISTORICAL SOCIETY; ETC.

HERITAGE BOOKS
2007

HERITAGE BOOKS
AN IMPRINT OF HERITAGE BOOKS, INC.

Books, CDs, and more—Worldwide

For our listing of thousands of titles see our website
at
www.HeritageBooks.com

A Facsimile Reprint
Published 2007 by
HERITAGE BOOKS, INC.
Publishing Division
65 East Main Street
Westminster, Maryland 21157-5026

Originally published by
W. J. Van Deusen
Kingston, New York
1907

— Publisher's Notice —
In reprints such as this, it is often not possible to remove blemishes from the original. We feel the contents of this book warrant its reissue despite these blemishes and hope you will agree and read it with pleasure.

International Standard Book Number: 978-0-7884-1943-9

INTRODUCTION

BY THE EDITOR

No County in the State has annals of more striking interest than Ulster. Second only to New York and Albany in antiquity Ulster from the earliest period was the theatre of important and romantic events. Traversed by the great Indian trails which formed the aboriginal highways between the Hudson, the Delaware and the Susquehanna, the strategic importance of its situation was known for centuries to the red men and from their first acquaintance with it acknowledged by the whites. Upon its soil the first constitution of the State was framed, the first constitutional Governor was inaugurated and the first Grand Jury under the constitution empaneled by the State's first Chief Justice. Its history never has been adequately written because an exhaustive work would fill many royal octavo volumes, and never can be prepared or published without governmental aid. The Republic is too young for Americans to regard local history with the veneration accorded it in older lands. Our people look forward, not backward, and so little are they interested in the lives and achievements of their ancestors that they are reluctant to contribute to governmental expenditure the sole object of which is to preserve the account of them.

Nearly twenty-seven years have passed since the publication of Judge Sylvester's History of the County. Since that time Marius Schoonmaker's History of Kingston, Benjamin M. Brink's History of Saugerties. Ralph LeFevre's History of New Paltz, Dr. Van Santvoord's History of the One Hundred and Twentieth Regiment, General Gates's History of The Ulster Guard in the War of the Rebellion, a Commemorative Biographical Record of the Men of the County, the Records of the First Dutch Church of Kingston, by the Reverend Roswell Randall Hoes, the Records of the Huguenot Church of New Paltz, Dr. Anjou's Probate

Records and Mr. Brink's Olde Ulster have been published, and the early Dutch Records of the County have been translated into English under the supervision of the editor of this work by Mr. Dingman Veersteg, the official translator of the Holland Society. All of these are invaluable contributions to the early history of Ulster, but many generations will pass before a complete and authoritative history of the County will appear. It follows that this modest work makes no pretense to that rank. It is a collation of data by a staff of contributors consisting of the most accurate and brilliant writers in their respective fields in the County, who here crystallize and preserve the material they have gathered from many sources. Never so far as I am aware, has any local history in any county been prepared as this has been. Each writer is in a position to speak with absolute authority upon the subject of which he treats, and it was the intention of the editor that each should present in the most attractive and concise form such material relative to the matter of which he writes as had not appeared in previous publications. How far that hope has been realized the gentle and critical reader will judge. It is the habit of many to deride those biographical sketches without which it is impossible to publish any local history. For the future historian the sketches of the men whose names appear in this volume will be of great value. Some of their contemporaries will read them in that censorious spirit which always finds satiric expression when others are spoken of. It has been the aim of the editor to limit the sketches to a statement of such facts as will be of interest to the reader of to-day and of importance to those of the years to come. That the work contains many errors is inevitable. The orthography of proper names will be, as always it has been, a source of criticism, but to those familiar with the subject the changes in spelling in the course of centuries is an interesting study. In extracts from ancient documents and official records the spelling there found usually has been retained. No attempt has been made to give uniformity to names as that is an impossible and thankless task. Everyone knows that different families known to be descended from a common ancestry, frequently insist on a different mode of spelling. There are for instance seventeen different methods of spelling the name of the editor of this work, and thirty-two different ways of spelling the much simpler name of one of his ancestors, Deyo.

The greater part of the material of this volume appears in print for the first time. There are two omissions. No account of Methodism or of the Baptist Faith appears. To none will this be a matter of greater regret than it is to the editor of this work. The most prominent Methodist and Baptist Clergymen in the County agreed that they would write for the work an historical account of their respective denominations, and the matter was entrusted to them. Both re-considered their promise, and in consequence the great branches of the Christian Church they so admirably adorn fail of representation here.

If my colleagues and myself have helped to perpetuate the memory of the heroism, the fortitude, the sufferings and the achievements of the men and women who placed Ulster in the foremost rank of the Counties of America, we shall be content.

Kingston, February 22, 1907. A. T. Clearwater.

CONTENTS

PART I.

E. M. Ruttenber

THE COUNTY OF ULSTER

By E. M. RUTTENBER

CHAPTER I

LOCATION AND TOPOGRAPHY.

THE County of Ulster, in the State of New York, is located on the west bank of Hudson's River along which it extends for a distance of forty miles, beginning about sixty-two miles north from New York City. Its County Seat, the City of Kingston, its largest and most populous town, is in longitude 74 degrees west from Greenwich, and latitude 41 degrees 55 minutes north. It is one of the original, or "Mother Counties" of the State, and has, at different times, had portions of its territory taken for the creation of new counties required for the more convenient transaction of official business in outlying districts.

Situated to a considerable extent between the Catskill Mountains on the northwest, the Shawangunk Mountains on the southwest and the Highlands on the south, the county viewed from a commanding elevation presents the appearance of a great basin, with mountains and high hills on nearly every side, with the lower portion cut up into smaller sloping hills and gently undulating lowlands, through the valleys of which streams and streamlets take their way.

In the northern part of the county extending from northeast to southwest, is one of the main ranges of the Catskill Mountains, the most southerly of that system. Their lofty peaks, lifting their majestic heads high in air, present an aspect of grandeur rarely equalled. In some places the ascent of the mountain sides is easy and gradual, while in others it is rocky and broken and steep, and covered with boulders; in still other places sheer cliffs, impossible of ascent, a thousand to two thousand feet in height. In these mountains arise innumerable streams, some of which rush down the steep sides, and some through the beds of ravines hundreds of feet deep, having almost vertical sides. These ravines are locally called "cloves," as though, through some mighty convulsion of nature, the "huge mountain had been cloven asunder, as by the Almighty stroke of an Eternal sword."

About the same formation is found in the Shawangunk Mountains. These mountains extend from northeast to southwest in the southwestern part of the county, and are the most northerly range of the Alleghanys. These are not quite so high as the Catskills, but are of the same general formation. On the northwest and merging in the Catskill range or Blue Hills, so called from the reflected color of the rocks, which stand at the head of the Esopus Valley and spread over Sullivan County.

The Shawangunk range takes that name from a particular place in the present town of Shawangunk, from which it was extended to the hills * which were otherwise known of record as the High Hills, and the Steep Rocks. The highest elevation in the range is known as High Point, in New Jersey, better known in some connections as Hawk's Nest. The second in elevation is known as Sam's Point, in the present town of Wawarsing, about seven miles south of the Village of Ellenville. It takes its familiar name from Samuel Gonsaulus, an early settler and owner. Gertruyd's Nose, so called from the fancied resemblance of the shadows of some of the massive rocks that stand on its brow to the nose of the wife of Jacobus Bruin who held the ownership of the patent, and who was succeeded in that relation by his widow, Gentruyd Bruin. North, the third highest elevation is now called Mohonk—historically, Moggonck, or Paltz Point. The elevation is divided from Gertruyd's Nose by what is known as The Traps, a pass or clove some six hundred and fifty feet wide, extending through the range and presenting the appearance of the hill having slipped apart. The name was primarily given on the presumption that the rocks on either side of the pass were Trapean, which, however, is not the fact. The pass is the purely natural result of a fault in the rocks from which the softer material was washed away leaving rugged clear-cut banks, which invite not only geological study, but the study of chronology. The three surviving Indian names that may be regarded

* The name is of record first in a deed to Governor Dongan in 1684, as that of a certain piece or tract, which was later conveyed by patent to Thomas Lloyd. It was never spoken as the name of the mountain or of the Indian fort until later. It means "at or on the hillside," and aptly described Lloyd's land in part. It adjoined Col. Rutsen's tract called Nescotack, later Guilford.

as names of particular elevations are Aioskawasting, Pitkiskaker, and Moggonck. It may be stated here that the Indians had no names for continuous ranges; where there were hills grouped they said Adchué Kontu, "Where there are many hills," or plenty of hills.

About three-quarters of a mile west of Sam's Point is supposed to be, but is not, the original historic pond referred to in early land papers as Maretange. The name is English, not Indian, as some suppose. It means simply a pond the water of which is sour or offensive to the taste. The water of the pond or lake is in evidence that the name never belonged to it. About one mile north of Sam's Point lies what was called in local records The Great Salt Pond, so called it is said from the effervescent salt which was found on the rocks which formed "Deer Licks." The pond is now called Lake Minniewaska. Still further north lies what is now known as Lake Mohunk, on the historic elevation called Moggonck above noted. Beyond Moggonck is the clove or cleft which bears the Indian name of Tawarataque, now fancifully written Tower-a-tauch. The elevation known as the Sandberg, or Zand-berg, is the boundmark of the great Minnisink and the Hardenburgh patents. With the exception of Maretange the lakes named now form attractive features of summer resorts. In the town of Gardiner are the famed Verkeerde Falls, a cataract of about seventy feet, now called Awosting Falls.

On the west side of the Shawangunk range the rocks are precipitous; on the east side in many large districts the land has the appearance of having been shaved off and the rocks pulverized as by the slipping of an iceberg during the Ice Age, and the valley of the Wallkill, near the base of the range, bears the evidence of the path through which the bergs passed to the ocean. These hillsides are generally very fertile, particularly in grasses, from which the ancient milk and butter of this and original southern Ulster was famous. As a basin for the wash of the hills on its three borders its three valleys, the Esopus, the Groot Esopus and the Wallkill, had primarily no equal in the province for production.

Probably no locality within the whole Appalachian system of mountains presents more interesting phases than Ulster County, from a geological standpoint. The rocks are those of the very earliest periods, those of the newer era being unknown. There are no indications of the carboniferous period; the highest points in the county show on their tops the white pebbly conglomerate which, in some other parts of the Appalachian system, underlie the coal deposits. It almost seems as though this particular section was subjected to greater upheaval than some others during the cataclysms by which the surface was buckled into mountains, and, the tops of those of this locality, being higher than those surrounding, became the "snag" on which great glaciers stuck, which ground the mountains into valleys which, on the subsidence of the waters, were left filled with the alluvium of the erosion. The break in the continuity of the mountain ranges, as well as the rock formations, which underlie the soils of the valleys, and the scratched and broken sides of some of the mountains, give standing, if not actual value to this view.

The more ancient rocks in Ulster County belong to the Silurian and Devonian periods of the Palaeozoic era, and are covered deep with drift and alluvium. They lie in their respective series, and extend across the county from the southeast to the northwest. The oldest lie in the town of Marlborough.

The limestone is highly magnesian, and probably belongs to the Calciferous or Primordial epoch of the Silurian age. Some of its layers make cement.

The slates of the Hudson River period of the lower Silurian age underlie the towns of Lloyd, Plattekill, Shawangunk, Gardiner and New Paltz, except that the lower rocks of the Niagara period of the upper Silurian age are found along the northwestern borders of Shawangunk, Gardiner and New Paltz, while in the northwestern part of Esopus are found some of the upper strata of the Niagara period, and the lower strata of the Helderberg period of the upper Silurian. The slates have been in demand for many years for sidewalk, hearth and flooring purposes, and the sandstones are extensively quarried for buildings, and other commercial uses.

Along the northwest portion of Shawangunk, Gardiner and New Paltz, overlying the slates, is what is locally known as the "Shawangunk grits," but is properly the Oneida conglomerate. It has been extensively used for millstones since very early days, being fully equal, it is said, to the best imported stones. They are called the Esopus Millstones, but the principal production has been in the Town of Rochester.

"The Ellenville lead mines," says Hon. James G. Lindsley, of Rondout, who prepared a most able article on the subject about a quarter of a century ago, "belong to this formation, and there are other like deposits of ore. The overlying Medina sandstone is not found in many places, but there are points about High Falls, in the town of Marbletown, where it shows considerable thickness."

"Rocks representing the Niagara epoch are those coralline limestones lying above and below the stone known as dark cement stone, and of which it also constitutes a part. They lie above and conformably to the Medina and Clinton as far east as the town of Rosendale, through the southeasterly portions of the towns of Wawarsing, Rochester and Marbletown; but to the north and east of this, through the town of Ulster, City of Kingston, and town of Saugerties, they lie upon and conformably to the Hudson River slates."

There are immense quarries of these rocks, which are used for the manufacture of cement, a prominent industry in the towns of Marbletown, Rosendale and at Rondout, in the City of Kingston.

"Above these Niagara rocks, and conforming to them, are the water limestones of the lower Helderberg." "These water limestones, known as light cement, also form an important part of the material in the manufacture of cement, being added in due proportion to the dark cement of the Niagara."

"Rising above the water-line, we find nearly or quite all of the series of the lower Helderberg running the whole length of the County, the first being the Tentaculite, which is a fine building stone. It is crowned by rocks known as the Stromatopora limestone, — a very coarse stratum of corals and sponges."

"Above this comes the lower Pentamerous limestone, a heavy blue limestone." "Then we have the Catskill or shaly limestone, the encrinial limestone, and the upper Pentamerous limestone." "This latter contains a layer of fossiliferous limestone excellent for making lime and fluxing iron." "This series of rocks of the lower Helderberg can be recognized at almost all the points where cement stone is quarried, but notably at the Vleight Bergh at Rondout, the Fly Mountain, at Eddyville, and the Yoppen Bergh in Rosendale." "The later rocks of the Silurian age, known as the Oriskany sandstone, has few exposures, though it may be seen in places between Rondout and Wilbur along the bank of the Rondout kill, at Glen Erie, and at points in the town of Rosendale."

"The rocks of the Devonian age all lie to the southwest of those just described, and the lower series of them extend through the towns of Wawarsing, Rochester, Marbletown, Hurley, Kingston (City and town), Ulster and Saugerties. The first of them is known as the Canda Galla grit. It is a rather soft shale and where exposed crumbles by action of the weather. It is generally called slatestone, but it is not true slate." The high ridge above Rondout and extending northward to Saugerties, is of this formation, which also underlies most of the old Lucas Turnpike which extends southwest from Kingston.

"The Carniferous limestones, lying above these grits, are a marked feature of the county, extending as they do, through its entire length and often much exposed." These have been extensively quarried for construction purposes where great solidity is required. Many of the lock stones of the canal, and much of the heavy foundations of the Brooklyn bridge are of this stone, as are also many of the fine historic mansions along the Esopus Creek road.

"The Marcellus shale rises in a bluff along the left bank of Esopus Creek, in its northwest course through Marbletown, Hurley, Ulster and Saugerties. The lower layers are soft and friable.

"The Hamilton beds lying above the Marcellus shale, is the formation from which the product known as bluestone is obtained." "Quarries of this stone are found in the towns of Hurley, Kingston, Ulster, Saugerties, Woodstock, Shandaken, Olive, Marbletown, Rochester and Wawarsing." It also exists in Denning and Hardenburgh.

"It is now conceded that the higher layers of the mountains belong to the Chemung Period, with traces of the subcarniferous on some of the loftiest peaks."

"Coming down to the later deposits belonging to the Quaternary age, we find in this county long stretches of alluvial beds bordering the streams which flow beside or make their course through it. The high banks along the Hudson and the Esopus, like that upon which the older part of Kingston is built, are fair representatives of the higher benches, while the fertile intervales which border the Wallkill, the Rondout and the Esopus are as fine specimens as can be met with anywhere of the lower terraces of this formation; while all the hillsides are covered with the drift of the glacial period, and there are many evidences of the action of the glaciers abounding in the erosion and scratching of the

Alton B. Parker

surface of the rocks where the drift has protected them from the effects of the atmosphere."

Ralph S. Tarr, Professor of Geology at Cornell University, published a work in 1902 in which he states that the Catskills are not true mountain ranges, but are pseudo or imitation mountains. His account of their formation is interesting and is here reproduced in part:

"During the Devonian Period, just before the uplift of the great interior Paleozoic Sea which accompanied the development of the Appalachians, the site of the Catskills was the shore line of a sea-bottom that was gradually sinking. The land side of the shore was occupied by the Taconic Mountains from which sediment entered the sea, where it was strewn over the bottom in the region where the Catskill Mountains now rise. Here, near the coast, coarse beds of sandstone and conglomerate were accumulated, while further west shales and sandy shales were being deposited. The sinking of the sea-bottom permitted these beds to gather to great depth. Then, when the reverse process of elevation had commenced, the sea-bottom was raised to dry land, and eventually uplifted to the condition of a plateau. Possibly the uplift in the Catskill region was greater than in Central New York, although of this there is no direct proof. But in both places the elevation was accompanied by very little disturbance of the strata, so that in the two parts of the state the upper Paleozoic beds are still nearly horizontal." * * * "In the Catskill Mountains the topography is much more rugged and more mountainous than elsewhere. Denudation, operating upon hard rocks of nearly horizontal position, has carved out a complex of peaks, which, because of the superior hardness of their rocks, rise higher than the rest of the plateau."

The principal streams of the county, those whose function it is to perform the office of the leaders in the drainage arrangement, are three in number. They are the Esopus, the Rondout and the Wallkill. Of these the most important is the Esopus. It rises in the extreme northwestern corner of the county, and takes a southeasterly course until it reaches a point near the center of the town of Marbletown, not more than 12 miles from the Hudson; then it turns in an abrupt elbow and flows northward, bearing a trifle easterly, and discharges its waters into the Hudson at Saugerties. The stream is more than sixty miles in length.

The Rondout has its rise in the Town of Denning, but soon gets beyond the Ulster line into Sullivan County. After making a wide circuit in that county, it re-enters Ulster across its southern boundary just at the western base of the Shawangunk Mountains and flows northeasterly along their base discharging into the Hudson at Rondout. The present name of the stream is from Dutch *Rondhout,* "standing timber," the reference being to the palisaded "Fort" which Stuyvesant erected at Ponckhockie, which the English called a Redout.

The Wallkill, or more properly the "Waalkil," has its rise in New Jersey, flows thence north through eastern Orange County on a course almost due north along the foot of the eastern slope of the Shawangunk Mountains, and westward of the ridge of bluffs which border the Hudson, empties into Rondout Creek a few miles above its mouth.

There are a great variety of smaller streams tributaries to those above mentioned. Of these the more historic are the ancient Peakadasink, so called in 1684, now the Shawangunk, which skirts the mountain base through Orange County, and becomes a tributary of the Wallkill in Shawangunk. The Zandberg, the Fantine * Kill, the Wawarsing, the Plattekill, Sawyer's Kill, Green Kill, Mother (Modder, "Mud") Kill, the Little Esopus, Old Man's Kill, Rochester Creek (the ancient Mombaccus), etc. The principal falls on the Rondout are Honk Falls, near Ellenville, and High Falls in Marbletown. The former descend two hundred feet of which sixty is in a single cataract; the latter has a fall of about fifty feet; and are supposed to have been "the Second Fall," so named in the treaty deed of 1677; to which reference will be made in a subsequent chapter. There are five principal ponds which the Dutch called Binnen-water (inland water). A small lake in the town of Rochester retains the name of Mombaccus. In the town of Woodstock a small body of water now bears the unattractive name of Shues Lake, illustrating what an English speaking people can do with a Dutch name when they get fairly hold of it. The original Dutch was Schoon Meer, a very pleasant name. It means "a fine, handsome, clear, pure lake." The vulgar "Shue" should be obliterated from maps. The overflow of the lake goes to the Esopus. On Old Man's Kill, where it unites with the Hudson in Marlborough, is a picturesque waterfall and

* The name is from Fontaine (French) meaning "a spring of water." There seems to have been two springs and two streams bearing the name, one on the hills near Mamakating, the Fantine Kill of local history, and the other near the Catskills which formed the head of Sawyer's or Sawkill. The former is referred to.

ravine. Coxing Kill, in Rosendale, has one of the most remarkable Indian names of the series — Koghksuhk-sing, "Near a high place." On map of U. S. Geological Survey the stream is marked as the outlet of Minniewaska Lake, which lies in a basin of hills 1650 feet above the level of the Hudson. Other local streams will probably be noted in town histories. Generally speaking the water of the principal streams is pure, and limpid, and to its excellence is attributed in a great measure the remarkable longevity and the uniform health of the people of this region.

The land was originally covered with forests, except strips of lowland along the streams where the Indians planted their maize and other crops. These were kept clear of new growths by fires which were set by the natives after harvesting the crops in the fall.

The trees with which the land was covered were remarkable for their great variety. A writer of that period names among others Oak, Hickory (Nutwood), White and Yellow Pine, Chestnut, several kinds of Beech (among them Water-beech, which grows very largely along the streams, larger than most of the trees of the country — evidently meaning the Buttonwood), Maple, Whitewood—which grew very large, two kinds of Ash, Birch, Linden, and some others. Of the fruit bearing trees there are given as growing wild the Mulberry, Wild Cherry, several kinds of Plum, Juniper and Apple (bearing small fruit, but of several varieties). Of the fruits there are mentioned, in addition to those named, Hazel Nuts, Black Currants, Gooseberries, Blue Indian Figs, and Strawberries (which ripen continuously from "half May until July") Raspberries, Black Caps, etc., with Artichokes, Ground Acorns, Ground Beans, Wild Onions, Leeks, and several others.

Among the most prolific and plentiful of the vegetable growths found in the county by the early settlers, were the endless varieties of grape vines. They are said to have grown everywhere. The woods were full of them, their great stems denoting great age "being often as thick as a man's leg," and their long vines climbing through and over trees in their search for sunlight. The fact that the fruit, while beautiful to look upon, was "sour, harsh, fleshy, and strong," was attributed solely to the fact that neither the growing grapes nor the roots of the vines were ever visited by the sun's rays, the former being shaded by the foliage of the trees, and the latter by the density of the forest growth.

In some parts of New Netherland, in the early days of settlement, cuttings were brought from Holland of some of the finest varieties of grapes, and at the proper season grafted into some of the old stems and properly trained and cultivated with more than satisfactory results. There do not seem to be any verified instances of this, however, in Ulster County, though it is very probable that it was done, as the early population was composed of persons above the average in intelligence and education.

Among the native flowers were the sunflower, red and yellow lillies, mountain lillies, morning stars, red, white and yellow maritoffles and several species of bell-flowers. The very earliest Dutch settlers brought an almost infinite variety of flowers, which grew and still grow luxuriously in almost every portion of the county, but the above named are the native ones, found growing spontaneously.

Of the garden vegetables, it is difficult to determine in many instances which are native and which of European origin. Among those which seem to be purely native are the different varieties of squashes (the cucurbita) which are described as being delicious in flavor, easy to digest, and nutritious. Tomatoes, also, are said to be indigenous to the soil, as are some varieties of beans.

Melons of several varieties were found here by the Dutch settlers, also cucumbers; but Indian legend traced them to Spanish or Portuguese origin, seeds having been brought from the south by migratory savages. The soil accommodated itself so readily to every sort of garden vegetable that in the very earliest years of the settlement every variety known to Holland was grown here.

The maize or Indian corn, or Turkey wheat, which the first traders found here growing in abundance, and forming one of the principal food staples, has long been supposed to be native. It was cultivated on the benches and along the creeks of what is now Ulster County, and grew "to great heighth, and with enormous bearing." Investigation seems to show, however, that instead of being primogenial here, it was transplanted from a foreign shore. The oldest Indians stated that neither their fathers nor grandfathers could remember when it was not grown, but that there were old legends which indicated that it came from the south — handed from tribe to tribe as the years succeeded each other — and was changed from what may have been an original Spanish corn by the variation of soil and climatic conditions.

Wheat, barley, oats and buckwheat grew profusely when planted by the early settlers, but care had to be used in selecting the proper location for various crops, as otherwise the strength of the soil would produce such enormous growths of stalk as to practically destroy the value of the crop. Some of the grains, however, like rye and barley, would produce enormously, "with stalks six or seven feet tall."

Of the wild animals at the date of the first settlement of the county, (the Esopus Valley) they do not vary from the general rule in this climate in America. That there were lions here was proven by the fact that the Indians had lion's (probably panther's) skins, and brought them for sale. Bears were plentiful, but always the black species, which were not dangerous unless attacked; there were also buffalo, and even at the early date of 1652 efforts were made to cross them with domestic cows, brought from Holland bred animals. The plan does not seem to have been successful. There were deer in abundance, moose, wolves, wild cats, foxes, raccoons, mink, hares and rabbits. The latter were easily tamed. There were beavers, otters, muskrats, lynxes, squirrels, etc., and the streams were filled with fishes of many different varieties.

The feathered tribe, the birds of native origin were numerous, and some of them gorgeous in the coloring of their plumage. The birds of prey, like the eagle, the hawk, the crow and others seem to have decreased with the advance of civilization, but are still found. Swans were abundant in all the coves of the Hudson. One early writer states that they were white with them. From their presence about Kingston, in 1673, the name of that settlement was changed to Swanandale.

Ulster County is bounded, according to the revised statutes of the State of New York, as follows:

"Beginning in the middle of Hudson's River, opposite to the north end of Wanton Island, and running thence in a direct line to the said north end; then north forty-eight degrees west four hundred and forty-five chains, to the west bounds of the patent granted to Johannes Hollenbeck; then along the same south eight degrees west seventy-one chains to or near the end of a stone wall in the forks of the road between the houses now or heretofore of Hezekiah Wynkoop, and Daniel Drummond; then north eighty-nine degrees west, eighty-seven chains to stones near a chestnut tree cornered and marked, being the corner of lots numbered one and two in the subdivision of great lot number twenty-six of the Hardenburgh patent; then along the division line between the said lots north fifty-nine degrees and thirty minutes west, seventy-eight chains to a rock-oak tree, being the corner of the land now or heretofore of Gilbert E. Palen and Jonathan Palen; thence south twenty-four degrees west four hundred and eleven chains to the line run by Jacob Trumpbour in the year one thousand eight hundred and eleven, for the division line between the counties of Ulster and Greene; thence along the said line until it intersects the northeasterly bounds of Great lot number eight in said patent; then along said bounds to the easterly bounds of the county of Delaware; then along the same southwesterly to the bounds of the county of Sullivan; then southeasterly along the same to the county of Orange; then easterly along the northerly bounds of the county of Orange to the middle of Hudson's River, and then up along same to the point of beginning." The area included in these limits is 1,204 square miles, or 760,560 acres.

A S Staples

CHAPTER II.

THE ABORIGINAL PEOPLE.

THE aboriginal people of Ulster differed in no essential respect from their contemporaries in other parts of the once great wilderness. Untouched by demoralization from contact with rude European civilizations, they were a fine people. In speaking of them reference must, in justice, be had to their character and personal appearance at the time of the discovery of the continent. Verazzano, who sailed along the coast of North America in 1524, wrote of those whom he met in the bay of New York as being of middle stature, broad across the breast, strong in the arms, and well formed; that in clothing they were "dressed out with the feathers of birds of various colors." Among those who came on board his vessel in Narragansett Bay he noted particularly "two Kings more beautiful in form and stature than can possibly be described. One was about forty years old, the other about twenty-four." "They were dressed," he added, "in the following manner: The oldest had a deer's skin around his body, artificially wrought in damask figures, his head was without covering, his hair was tied back in various knots; around his neck he wore a large chain ornamented with many stones of different colors." The young man was "similar in his general appearance." The persons described were types of the race. The former was possibly the historic Sachem Caunounicus, and the latter his nephew Miantunnonmu, the men who welcomed Roger Williams as a friend. The visitors who accompanied the chiefs, he writes, "in size exceeded us; their complexion tawny, inclining to white; their faces sharp, their hair long and black, their eyes black and sharp, their expression mild and pleasant, greatly resembling the antique." The women were "of the same form and beauty, very graceful, of fine countenances and pleasing appearance in manner and modesty." They wore no clothing "except a deer skin ornamented like those of the men." Some had "very rich lynx skins upon their arms, and various ornaments upon their heads, composed of braids of hair which hung upon their breasts on each side." The older and the married people, both men and women, "wore many ornaments in their ears, hanging down in the oriental manner." In disposition they were generous, giving away whatever they had; of their wives they were careful, always leaving them in their boats when they came on shipboard, and their general deportment was such that with them, he says, "we formed a great friendship."

Similar is the picture drawn by Hendrick Hudson, in 1609, of those whom he met on the waters of the stream now bearing his name. "This day," he wrote, "Many of the people came abroad, some in mantles of feathers, and some in skins of divers sorts of good furs. Some women also came to us with hemp. They had red copper tobacco pipes, and other things of copper they did wear about their necks."

These pictures are good to look upon in contrast with those of which many have been drawn of the Indian in later years, the civilization which he had wrought out for himself turned back in the presence of the new civilization which had been thrust upon him — his ancient lessons worthless, his new lessons a mystery —

"His heraldry a broken bow;
His very name a blank;"

a man — a wreck.

Notwithstanding the efforts of theologians to connect the race through Adam with other races, the fact remains that they were a native people; a creation of the Quartenary Age, or age of man, that indefinable period which we dismiss with a name; a race that was wholly indigenous, had borrowed nothing — absolutely nothing — from either Europe, Asia or Africa; a race as distinct in type as any other race and from its isolation probably the purest of all native races in its social traits.

When they were discovered the race had wrought out unaided a development far in advance of any of the old barbaric races of Europe. They were still in the age of stone, but entering upon the age of iron. Their implements were mainly of stone and flint and bone, yet they had learned the art of making copper pipes and ornaments. This would rank their civilization as about with that of the Germans in the days of Tacitus (about the year 200 A. D.) They had, unaided by the civilizations of Europe — for to the Europeans they were never known prior to Columbus — made great progress. They had learned to weave cloth from wild hemp and other grasses; had learned to extract dyes from vegetable substances; how to make earthen pots and kettles; how to make large water casks from the bark of trees, as well as the lightest and fleetest canoes; had passed from the cave to the dwelling-house; had established the family relation and democratic forms of government; their wives were the most faithful, their young women the most brilliant in paint and garments of feathers and robes of furs; they carved figures on stone and wrote the story of their lives in hieroglyphics of which some of the finest specimens in America are preserved in the Senate House in Kingston, and most remarkable of all, and that which carries their chronology back to a period that cannot be defined, they had developed spoken languages that were rich in grammatical forms, differing radically from any of the ancient and modern languages of the old hemisphere, languages which were surely indigenous and of which it was said by the most expert philologists of Europe that they were among "the most expressive languages dead or living." A native race than whom no superior was ever discovered; a race pure from creative hands, unmixed, original, and which may well command our reverence, and lead us to more careful study. They were savages, or barbarians as you may please to call them, men who wrote their vengeance in many scenes of blood, the recital of which around the firesides of the pioneers became more terrifying by repetition; nevertheless they were representatives of a race whose civilization, though it was twelve hundred years behind our own, had no faults greater than were found in the races from which we boast our lineage.

As the aborigines came to be classed from language, at a later date, they were included in two general divisions known as the Algonquins and the Iroquois, terms conferred by the French in Canada as the languages were there met by the Jesuit missionaries especially. The Algonquins were by far the most numerous and were mainly seated on the Atlantic coast, including eastern Canada, Maine, the New England States, eastern New York, New Jersey, Pennsylvania, Maryland, Delaware, Virginia, etc. The Iroquois occupied particularly central and western New York, where they had their principal seat, including the Mohawk River, the head waters of the Delaware, the Great Lakes, and the St. Lawrence, and were known as the Five Confederated Nations. The most eastern nation was the Mohawk, called by the Dutch Maquas, a branch of which on the lower Delaware was called the Minquas. Of the same linguistic stock were the Tuscaroras of North Carolina, who later removed to New York, and became the sixth nation of the Confederacy, and the Cherokees and some other southern people. The Algonquins, whose principal seat was on the lower Delaware at Philadelphia, called themselves Lenape, or "original people" and came to be known familiarly as the Delawares. Both the Lenape and the Iroquois were divided in totemic tribes, as the tribe of the Turtle, the tribe of the Turkey, and the tribe of the Wolf, among the Delawares, and the tribes of the Turtle, the Bear, and the Wolf among the Mohawks. These tribes were again divided in sub-tribes or families each with a principal head, father or founder of a family. A number of these families combining for mutual defense and interests, the several sachems or heads of families elected one of their number as chief sachem, and was regarded as a nation, i. e. a political division that made its own laws, treaties, etc., and engaged in wars with other nations similarly constituted, but mainly with antagonistic Iroquoian stocks. The nations were not necessarily composed entirely of one primary totemic tribe; on the contrary they were mixed more or less. In the Delaware combinations the Minsi, or Wolf tribe, and the Unalachtigo, or Turkey tribe, spread over New Jersey, eastern New York and eastern Pennsylvania, and extended in sub-tribes or nations north along the Hudson to the Katskills, those dwelling between the Dans Kamer and Zager's Kil, appearing of record first, in 1614-16, as the Waronawanka, "People of the cove or bay," which became local at what is now the cove or bay south of Kingston Point, "where a creek comes in, and the river becomes more shallow," as described by De Laet, but contemporaneously, from a companion term on the same map record, as Esopus, from Sepuus (generic Alonquin), "A small river," or small by comparison, from which it was extended to the people in occupation as the Esopus Indians, by which they were known and are still known historically, who represented a combination of four sub-tribes or families whose names are of record as the Amangarickan, the Kettyspowy, the Mahou, the Katatawis, whose Chief Sachem was Sewakenamo, successor of Pruemaker, "the oldest and the best" of the Esopus Chiefs, who gave deed to the English government, April 27, 1677, for all the lands between the mouth of the Esopus (now Saugerties) Creek and the mouth of the Groot Esopus (now Rondout) Creek, as defined in general terms, thence west to the Blue Hills, including the sites of the forts called Kahanesing, and Shawangunk, which they admitted in previous treaty with the Dutch (1664) to have been "conquered" by the "sword" — a belt of country running from the Hudson west to the Rochester hills. The precise district which each of the families named occupied cannot now be ascertained, if they were ever known to the Dutch or to the English authorities. It is only known that their forts or palisaded villages were amid the mountains on the west, that their fields included the Esopus Valley, and to a certain point the Wallkill Valley, that their war dances were held on the Dans Kamer, and their blazing brands waved over the most fertile fields of our now Ulster County. No doubt their territory was much larger, as represented by other families in the combination, but the particular territory which the families named, owned and occupied, and which they admitted to have been "conquered by the sword," was the Esopus Valley. Whatever strength the Esopus combination had outside of the families immediately interested as owners was made up of recruits from kindred families, particularly the Minnisinks on the Delaware, and from the Wappingers on the east side of the Hudson. The Katskill Indians on the north were Mohicans in alliance with the Dutch at Fort Orange and hence neutrals — the Tappans on the south were their intercessors, the grantors of the New Paltz lands were classed as Esopus Indians, the grantors of lands up to the south line of the Katskills were classed as Esopus Indians. The only break in the chain is in Dongan's purchase, in 1684, from the Murderers' Creek Indians who certainly were not on the Esopus watershed.

While it may be conceded that the aborigines on Hudson's River or some of them, may have seen European ships and Europeans sent to American waters for trade during the hundred years that preceded Hudson's explorations, we know certainly that they visited Hudson's ship at several points where he anchored, particularly in what is now known as Newburgh Bay, in part primarily in the original limits of Ulster, on the evening of September 14th, 1609, on his upward course, and again on the 29th of September on his return, and that "the people of the mountains" visited his ship. Of certain date also is it that a Dutch trading vessel was at Kingston Point in 1613, and that Dutch traders left there some boats in 1621-22. While other nationalities may have had part in the early trade, it is clear that the Dutch traders conducted traffic along the river, and particularly at the mouths of creeks which were the pathways of aboriginal commerce, and on which Indian families lived. Kingston Point obviously became a permanent trading post contemporaneously with that at Manhattan and at Tawalsontha, our present New York and Albany. From that point, or perhaps more particularly from the cove on the south side of the point, which the Dutch called Punthoekje, meaning "Point of a small hook," now corrupted to Ponkhockie, radiates the aboriginal history of Ulster County.

No trouble with the aboriginal owners of the trading posts is of record, nor is any manuscript prior to the advent of a colony of settlers who came down from the Manor of Rensselaerswyck in 1652, under the lead of Thomas Chambers, an Englishman by birth, and began permanent occupation, presumably by consent or by purchase of farms. No doubt whatever can there be that the traders of the previous years had made the aborigines familiar with intoxicants, nor that they had through that medium fully inaugurated the work of their demoralization, when Chambers and Kit Davids, and their comrades pitched their tents on the Groot Esopus "about a league west of the Hudson," and one Jacob Andrieson located at the Strand now Rondout. Although the Dutch authorities had forbidden the sale of brandy and other liquors to the aborigines, Chambers reported to Director Stuyvesant, May 28, 1658, that "great trouble" had occurred at the Strand "through the fearful intoxication of the barbarians." They had obtained "an anker of brandy" (about five gallons), and, lying under a tree at the tennis-court, had, in their "madness," fired at and killed one "Harmen Jacopsen, who was standing on the yacht of William Maer, and during the night had set fire to the house of Jacob Andrieson, so that the people were compelled to fly." The cause of the outbreak was no doubt correctly stated by Chambers — "fearful intoxication" — men crazed by the "strong water" which the settlers or the traders had supplied, or as one sachem said in an interview with Director Stuyvesant, "they sold the *boison* that is brandy, to his people," and were consequently responsible for the result. The trouble did not end here. Under the same influence the Red Men became quarrelsome and compelled the settlers, under threats of arson, to plough their lands for them, killed some hogs and a horse or two that seemed to have strayed on their plantations, and used "great violence every day" in the estimation of their white neighbors.

On appeal to Director Stuyvesant for assistance he went up from Man-

John B. Alliger.

hattan to the scene of disturbance, and, after looking over the ground, told the settlers that the time was not favorable for engaging in war on account of the murder of Jacopsen and "the burning of two small houses"; that the alternative of war had better be "deferred to a better time and chance"; that the first business of the settlers should be to gather their scattered dwellings in one place and enclose them in palisades. Reluctantly the settlers consented, and the Director marked out for them the site of a village on the north part of the Groot Plat, to which he gave the name of Wildwijk, now the oldest part of the City of Kingston. The Red Men were not altogether pleased, and complained that the land which had been taken had not been paid for. Stuyvesant talked with them and accused them of many breaches of good neighborhood, and the sachems finally came forward and gave him the land "to grease his feet with, because he had made such a long journey to come and see them." So it was that Wildwijk marked the first aggressive step for the occupation of the fertile fields of the Groot Plat by the Red Men called Atkarkarton by some translators and Atharhacton by Dr. E. H. Corwin.

On the 15th October following Stuyvesant held another conference with the sachems of Esopus at Wildwijk, with a view to ascertain what they were willing to do in regard to the land which he wanted. He restated to the sachems the complaints which had been made to him against them "or their tribe," and asserted that "the land from the Esopus" as far as he had viewed it, was demanded "for the expenses and troubles incurred" by him in visiting the settlement. The doctrine of indemnity was new to the sachems, and they withdrew for consultation. On the 16th they returned and submitted to the Director the counter-proposition that they would "desist from their claims for payment as to one half of the land." The conference closed without definite result beyond an exchange of prisoners, but on the 28th the sachems visited Jacob Jansen Stoll, an early settler, whose name is frequently met in the narrative, who reported to Stuyvesant that "the Esopus sachems or right owners" of the "certain piece of land, namely the large tract" which the Director coveted, they proposed to give to him (Stoll) one half "in recompense" for any wrong that they had done. "Then," wrote Stoll, "we went, three of us, to the land, and, on the 20th had them show us how much and which part they intended to keep for themselves";

that "there were some plantations, but of little value"; that it was "a matter of one or two pieces of cloth, then they (the owners) would surrender the whole piece and remove." The parties who had visited the land were Jacob Jansen Stoll, Thomas Chambers and Derick Smith, Ensign, the latter the commander of the Dutch guard. No payment in cloth was made, but arrangements were considered for forcing the owners to give up possession, and for the employ of "some allied savages" on Long Island to assist in the subjugation of "the rightful owners."

Matters drifted along with more or less friction until the 29th of September, 1659, when a party of eight (not eighteen) "Esopus Savages" who "had broken off corn for Thomas Chambers," were "at dark," given some brandy by him. They went with it "to a place at no great distance from the fort," i. e., where the guard was stationed, and sat down and "drank there until about midnight." When the supply of brandy became exhausted they "began to yell, being drunk." One of the number went for more brandy, and obtained it from a soldier. Asked where he drank the brandy, they replied "close by, near the little Kil," presumed to have been the small stream known later as the Twaalfs Kil. The debauch continued. In the midst of it Ensign Smith, the commandant of the guard, sent out a company of eight men with a view to suppress the boisterousness and "get the savages into the fort." The sergeant in command of the company sent back one of his men who reported "that a crowd of savages was there." Jacob Jansen Stoll came to the Ensign saying, "I will go, give me four or five men." "He thereupon took," says the narrative, "four or five men, namely Jacob Jansen van Stoutenburgh, Thomas Higgens, Gisbert Philips, Evert Pells, Jan Artsen and Berent Hermsen," who with himself (Stoll) constituted a force of seven men who are all classed as "inhabitants" in the record. Certain "soldiers" are named as having "all been with the sergeant and Jacob Jansen Stoll," namely, Martin Hofman, Gillis de Necker, Abel Dircksen, Dirck Hendricksen, Michael Vreegh (Ferch), and Jooris Metser. The "crazed savages" were fired upon; the fire was returned; one Indian was killed; Jacob Jansen Stoll was wounded; the Indians ran away with the exception of one who was found asleep near the fire, and was awakened by "a cut into the head with a sword or hanger," when he "jumped up and ran away," and the posse "ran back to the fort," which seems to have been the guard-house in the northeast corner of the palisaded village.

The attack upon the "drunken savages" was cowardly and unprovoked.* Retaliation followed quickly. The account of what followed is a little confused in the dates, one writer giving the occurrence of the attack on the Indians as on the night of September 20th, and the capture of a company of Dutch as occurring on the afternoon of the same day, and another writer giving the date as the 21st, which is probably correct. Whatever the precise fact, the substance of the narrative is that the Indians immediately set on fire Stoll's grain-stacks and barn, and committed other devastations. "Jacob Jansen Stoll and Thomas Chambers went to the strand and hired a yacht to go up the river to make their report. Returning to the fort the party numbered thirteen "the sergeant, Andries Laurens, with five men, Thomas Chambers, Jacob Jansen Stoll (Jacob Hal), a carpenter Abraham by name, Pieter Dircks and his man, Evert Pells' boy, and Lewis the Frenchman," who, "at the tennis court near the Strand" supposed to be at about the site of the present City Hall, "allowed themselves to be taken prisoners. Thomas Chambers was exchanged for a savage, one soldier escaped during the night and ten are still in captivity." What became of them? Schoonmaker writes that they were compelled to "run the gauntlet and that those who survived the ordeal were burned alive." Sergeant Laurens, one of the number, sent a letter by one of the Indians, apparently written three or four days later, in which he wrote: "I am a prisoner with nine men. Jacob Jansen is dead with three others." Another writer says: "Thomas Chambers is free again; five have been cut in the head; one has been shot dead; the sergeant is still living with two others." The Jacob Jansen spoken of was Jacob Jansen Stoll, not Jacob Jansen Stoutenburgh, as has been stated by a local writer. Stoutenburgh was living and in service in 1663, while Stoll was certainly dead prior to January 25th, 1661, as appears by an affidavit quoted in a subsequent page. The only prisoner who is known to have escaped was the son of Evert Pells, who was saved from death by an Indian maiden, in accordance with the Indian custom so frequently quoted in the rescue of Captain John Smith by Pocahontas. Pells and the maiden were married, and later he refused to be exchanged. We shall meet him again.

The occurrences narrated inaugurated the Esopus War of 1659-60.

* The question of the responsibility for the attack upon the Indians gave rise to a heated discussion. The narrative places it on Stoll, but Ensign Smith was certainly guilty of permitting Stoll to go out with his posse of "burghers" for whose acts he became responsible.

"The savages besieged and surrounded the place during twenty-three days; fired with brand-arrows one dwelling house and four grain stacks"; killed and wounded a number of the settlers and took others prisoners as already quoted. The record narrative of the events of the period is complete in Colonial History, Volume XIII, which is available to every one who may be interested. The student especially should not be guided by any other relation.

Peace was concluded July 15th, 1660. By its terms the Esopus sachems "promised to convey as indemnification all the territory of the Esopus, and to remove to a distance from there, without ever returning again to plant." In other words, they promised to give up the Groot Plat which Director Stuyvesant wanted, and which the settlers hoped to obtain without paying for it. On that Plat a settlement was soon commenced which was called the Nieuw Dorp, or New Village, about three miles west of Wildwijk, or the Old Village. The sachems protested. They "were willing to allow the erection of dwellings," but would have no fortifications made, and claimed positively "that the second large piece of land was not included in the treaty of peace made with them in the year 1660," and they would not, therefore, allow it to be plowed, sowed, planted or pastured, "before they were paid for it," with many threats to burn and destroy what had been done. The two large pieces of land spoken of in the narrative are supposed to have been east of and at what is now known as Old Hurley. They were obviously clear, open river bottoms or meadows.

The storm broke on the settlements on the morning of the 7th of June, 1663. The "barbarians" as they were called, attacked the New Village when the male settlers were at work in the fields, "burned twelve dwelling houses, murdered eighteen persons (men, women and children), and carried away as prisoners ten persons more." "The New Village has been burned to the ground," continues the narrative, "and its occupants are mostly taken prisoners or killed, only a few of them have come safely to this place," i. e., to Wildwijk. The disaster did not stop here. The attacking "barbarians" had planned the destruction of both villages, had penetrated the Old Village ostensibly for trading and at a given signal struck down inhabitants and set dwellings on fire. Eighteen settlers were killed, eight wounded, and twenty-six made prisoners. Total destruction by fire was averted by a change in the wind, and by the rallying of men who were in the fields by whom the invaders were driven out. Within its palisades and around its ruined homes the settlers gathered when night came on and kept mournful watch.

Now began the Esopus War of 1663. Martin Kregier was placed in command of the Dutch forces, and with the aid of sixty-five Marsapequa Indians from Long Island, carried sword and cannon into the heart of the Esopus country, burned the Indian villages in the more immediate vicinity of Wildwijk, crossed the hills and destroyed the Indian palisaded towns of Kerhanksen and Shawangunk, killed a large number, and destroyed wigwams and plantations. Peace came May 15, 1664. In the Council Chamber at Fort Amsterdam Esopus sachems and sachems of friendly tribes assented to the terms which Stuyvesant proposed. All the land which had been previously given to the Dutch in compensation of damages, as well as that over which the Dutch forces had passed and possessed themselves of "as far as the two captured forts," was surrendered to the Dutch as having "been conquered by the sword." Of the beautiful Esopus valley was left to them permission to plant around their former forts for one year. Amid the many fertile fields of the Blue Hills many of them found new homes, while others remained on adjacent lands that had not been surrendered.

With the advent of the English Government in 1665, a different policy than that which had been pursued under Director Stuyvesant was inaugurated. On the 7th of October of that year a new treaty of peace and friendship was made with the Esopus sachems. The lands which the Dutch had conquered by the sword remained in the possession of the English, but the sting of conquest was removed from it by the payment for it of forty blankets, twenty pounds of powder, twenty knives, six kettles, and twelve bars of lead. Whatever criticism may be made on the action of Director Stuyvesant in the manner of obtaining, it remains a fact that ultimately all the lands in Ulster County were paid for, and no title is handed down to-day tainted by unjust primary acquisition. For several years, or until 1674, when the Court of Sessions of Ulster County was given charge, the treaty of 1665 was renewed annually at Fort Amsterdam (New York). In 1732, the original manuscript and the treaty belt by which it was accompanied in 1665, were passed over to the Court of Sessions and are now carefully preserved in the office of the Clerk of Ulster County. The treaty belt is the oldest treaty belt that has been preserved in any part of this broad land — a belt, the touch of which awakens in the thoughtful a narrative of untold ages, a romance of history of more interest than any which has been written by man or woman. With the deepest interest we trace the footprints of the perished race, mindful ever that they are marked by barbaric excesses, but nevertheless a race of many virtues, its enemies being judges.

Crushed and broken by the war of 1663, and by later conflict with the Senecas, as allies of the Minquas, we hear little more of the "Esopus Indians." As rapidly as they could they sold their unconquered lands and fell back to the East Branch of the Delaware where they were known as the Papagoncks, while others became incorporated with the Minnisinks, whose battle cries as Monseys were heard in the Great West. Except in stone implements and in spear and arrow points, many of which were thrown away when they became possessed of fire arms, no trace of them remains other than in records written by their enemies of an opposing civilization and in the singularly quaint but expressive geographical names which have come down to us badly mangled in orthography in the course of their transmission. While not remarkable in significance—while only an approximation to the sounds of the names as originally spoken—there is that about them that attracts and invites study and preservation as the only names that are strictly American. Esopus, Waronawanka, Atkarkarton, Kahankson, Shawangunk, Mogonck, Magaat, Ramis, will remain with us indelibly blended with the history of our own race—indelibly sharing the geographical terms of a Dutch ancestry—as a priceless inheritance.

Eugene R. Durkee.

CHAPTER III.

PIONEER SETTLEMENTS AND PATENTS.

PIONEER history is eminently a history of individuals, the periods of their immigration, their privations, sacrifices, and accomplishments, and the results following their footsteps. In the aboriginal history of the county we have been introduced to the conditions under which early settlement was made, and to many of the pioneers, who located on the banks of the Groot Esopus, and have learned something of their baptism of blood. It seems to be clear from official records that the resident settlement dates from 1652, when Thomas Chambers came down from Troy, presumably accompanied by servants, obtained lands from the Indians and located his "Bowerie" on the north side of the Groot Esopus about three miles — the record says "about one league" — inland from the Hudson.* He was of English birth, and came to this country as a farmer under the first Patroon of Rensselaerswyck and had a farm where the City of Troy now stands. He was young, unmarried, and ambitions, and presumably his removal to the Esopus country was under the charter of "Freedoms and Exemptions" of 1640, which gave to certain classes of immigrants the rank of "master colonists," and the privilege of holding for ten years without tax two hundred acres of land, which was about the extent of his first holding. He was soon joined in his new home by Mattys Hendricks, to whom there is no patent record, and by Johan de Hulter (1604), who made purchase from the Indians of five hundred morgens (a little over one thousand acres) of land adjoining Christopher Davidson, on the south side of the Groot Esopus. Christopher Davids (Davidson), who had first located at Rens-

* The deed to Thomas Chambers bears date June 5th, 1652, and recites the conveyance to him by "Kawachhikan and Sowappekat, aboriginees of this country living in the Esopus, situated on the North river," empowered by other Indians whose names are given in the deed, "Certain parcels of land situated in the Esopus above named, extending southwest and northeast, named Machstapacick, Naranmapeth, Wiwisowachkick, with a path from the said lands to the river." The sale was confirmed by one "Anckrup, an Indian, called then in this Bill of Sale Kawachijkan" (Kawachhikan). Anckrup was still living in 1722, when he gave testimony of the Paltz Patent boundmark. He was then "a very old man," certainly.

selaerswyck, was granted in 1656 a patent for about seventy acres on the south side of the Groot Esopus "opposite the farm of Thomas Chambers"; by Jurian van Westphalen, who was in the same neighborhood in 1657; by Evert Pels van Steltyn, who sailed a yacht but was a brewer by occupation, and had lived at the Mill Creek, Greenbush, and by Jacob Jansen Hap, otherwise known as Jacob Jansen Stol, who had been ferry master at Beaverswyck, and who had purchased from Christopher Davids his farm, sold by Davids in August, 1657, in consequence of the death of his wife.* The man of wealth among the pioneers was Johan de Hulter. His father was at one time a director in the West India Company, while he himself was the holder of one-fifth share of the common stock of the Killian Van Rensselaer Company, which came to him from his wife, Johanna de Laet, daughter of Captain Johannes de Laet, whose explorations of the Hudson in 1625 are historic. Dying in 1657, he is not particularly known in Esopus history beyond his purchase and later residence, and the experiences and residence of his wife, who later became the wife of Johannes Ebbinck, a Shepen of Manhattan and a man of substantial character. Previous to her marriage with Ebbinck she had established by proof in 1659, that her husband had purchased five hundred morgens of land, November 5th, 1654, and asked and was granted a patent for it. The official record in this and in the patents of Christopher Davids, and Jacob Jansen Stoll, supply evidence of the first location of the permanent settlement as distinguished from a trading post. There were two contemporary residents in the vicinity of "the landing," presumably Ponkhockie as now written. They were Jacob Andrieson and Andries van der Sluys, whose dwellings were burned by the Indians in 1658. To the enumeration must be added Cornelius Barentse Slecht, an immigrant of 1655. Others names which appear in 1658 are Peter Dircksen, Jan Broersen and Jan Jansen.

In response to an appeal for help in the trouble with the Indians in 1658, Director Stuyvesant visited the settlement May 28th, of that year, and in reply to his advice the colonists agreed to concentrate their dwellings at one place and enclose it with palisades. The consent was signed by Jacob Jansen Stoll, Thomas Chambers, Cornelius Barentsen Slecht,

*Stoll was a leading spirit in the colony. In his notes of his visit to the Esopus in 1658, Director Stuyvesant wrote: "Jacob Jansen Stoll's house, which is the nearest to most of the habitations and plantations of the savages, where we had appointed to meet the Sachems, and where on Sundays and the other usual feasts the Scriptures are read."

William Jansen, Pieter Dircksen, Jan Jansen, Jan Braersen, Dirck Hendrickson Graaf, and Jan Lootman. Stuyvesant marked out a site for enclosure by palisades of about two hundred feet square, and gave to the inchoate village the name of Wildwijk, "Wild retreat" or refuge, now anglicised to Wiltwyck, and for additional protection directed the construction of a Rondhout, substantially a palisaded Redout at Ponkhockie. Soldiers who had accompanied Stuyvesant aided the settlers in the work of removing their log houses and in palisading the village, and within its limits were gathered under the first assignment of lots the dwellings of sixteen families, viz: Lot No. 1, Thomas Chambers; 2 Evert Pels; 3 Balthasar Laser; 4 The Dominie's House (or lot for it, it had not been built); 5 Mrs. Johanna de Hulter*; 6 Jacob Hap's little bowery (printed Jacob Grovier by Schoonmaker); 7 Jacob Hap's second bowery (printed Jacob Jansen by Schoonmaker and otherwise as Jacob Jansen Stoll); 8 Henry Zewant Ryger (printed Hendrick Sewan Stringer by Schoonmaker); 9 Andries, the weaver; 10 Jan, the Brabanter; 11 Jan Brouwersen (Broersen); 12 Michael the first; 13 Michael Verre; 14 Jan, the smith (printed Jan Depuit by Schoonmaker); 15 Andries van der Sluys, precentor and schoolmaster (printed Annetje Vandersluys by Schoonmaker); 16 House and lot of Ger (printed "Gertwig" by Schoonmaker). No assignment was made for a church; there was none; what religious services there were were at the house of Jacob Jansen Stoll; the "Dominie's House" after it was built, was the church and the public building. Some of the residents were given the name of their occupation — "Jan the Smith," was probably a blacksmith; "Henry Sewant Ryger," was a stringer of Sewan, the Indian shell money, which had more value when strung on cord — "strings of wampum," they were called. "Jan, the Branabter" should perhaps read Jan Janse Van Osterhoudt," who was sometimes called Brabanter." (Schoonmaker.)

Director Stuyvesant soon learned that he had not made the enclosure of the village sufficiently large, and on the 5th of May, 1661, went up to Esopus and marked out an additional number of lots, the receivers of which were required to enclose "with good, stout and dutiable palisades" the full breadth on the outside. The addition was over double the size of the first enclosure, thirty-one lots being numbered and assigned: No. 1 Hendrick Jochemsen (Hendrick, the smith); 2 Hendrick Mastersen; 3

* "Johannes Ebbinck, and his wife, the widow of Honorable Johan de Hulter." April 16, 1660.

Harmen Hendricksen (Harmanus Hendrix Bleu); 4 Jan Jansen Timmerman (Jan Jansen, carpenter); 5 Jacob Barentsen (Slecht); 6 Jan de Backer (Jan, the baker, otherwise entered "Jan Lootman, the baker at the Esopus); 7 Jan Joosten (Jacob Joosten); 8 Willem Jansen (William Pauli); 9 Pieter van Alen; 10 Mattys Roeloffsen; 11 Jacob Boerhans (Burhans); 12 Gerrit van Campen; 13 Anthony Cruepel (Crispel); 4 Albert Gerretsen (wheelwright); 15 Meerten Gysbert (Dr. Gysbertsen van Imborch); 16 Dirck Adriaen (Floriaen); 17 Mattys Capito; 18 Jan Lammersen; 19 Carsten de Noorman (Caster the Norman); 20 Barent Garretson (Brandy distiller); 21 The Church Yard (i. e. Burial ground as shown by the proceedings of the Commissioners); 22 Jan Barensen; 23 Not assigned (Schoonmaker wrote "the Church." It may have been the lot on which the first church stood later, but the evidence is not clear); 24 Albert Hymansen Roosa; 25 Jurian Westval; 26 Nicholas William Stuyvesant; 27 Albert Gysbertsen (Gysberts); 28 Tejerick Classen (de Witt); 29 Aert Jacobsen (Peter); 30 Jan Schoon (Jan R.); 31 Aert Pietersen Tack (Evert Petersen). "Jan Schoon" may stand for Jochem Schoonmaker, who had been appointed Lieutenant under Captain Thomas Chambers.* Quite a village had Wildwijk become in 1663. It had a minister, physician, a skilled midwife, a precentor or schoolmaster, a smith, a weaver, a wheelwright and thrifty farmers.

Pending the development of the village other immigrants had pushed

* Some of the names are uncertain. In May, 1662, Jan Thomassen and Volckart Jansen leased No. 4 to Gerrit Toocke, or Tocken, and Jan Gerritsen, the latter identified by "from Oldenburgh." One Jan Jansen's may have been Jacob Jansen van Stoutenberg, who was a subscriber in 1661 to the minister's salary. Schoonmaker may have been at the Rondhout. Judge Clearwater, in his introduction to "Anjou's American Records," writes: "A novice always experiences difficulty in tracing the ancestry of Dutch families in examining documents signed by Dutchmen, and in following the proceedings of Dutch Courts in America, arising from the fact that while the French invariably used their surnames, the Dutch as a rule were indifferent about this, and usually are designated by their Christian names even in important legal documents, and proceedings. This answered every purpose in primitive and small communities where every one was known, but now leads to much confusion. For instance, Lambert Huyberts always is Lambert Huyberts Brink; Tirick Classen is Tjrick Classen de Witt; Jan Wilhelsen is Jan Wilhelsem Houghtaling; Jan Mattys is Jan Mattys Jansen; Teunis Jacobse or Jacobsen is Teunis Jacobsen Klaarwater (Clearwater); Peter Cornellis is Peter Cornellis Lowe; Albertse Heymans is Albertse Heymans Roosa; Hendrick Jochemsen is Hendrick Jochemsen Schoonmaker; Aert Jacobsen is Aaert Jacobsen Van Wagonen." Frequently all of these names appear in Ulster records, but where there are several apparently of the same name other identification is necessary in tracing genealogies. Identification by occupation was very frequent, and in many cases the occupation became the surname, and so of the name of the place from which the immigrant came, of which the instances are not infrequent.

on further west and founded a Nieuw Dorp, (New Village) principally under the lead of Louis du Bois, a Huguenot, and his brother-in-law Matthew Blanshan. Presumably there were residents roundabout the two centres of settlement — unmarried farmers, laborers, and servants, soldiers at the Rondhout, etc. In the distribution of house lots in Wildwijk only heads of families were provided for. The New Village was not palisaded.

Looking in upon the old Village of Wildwijk on Thursday June 7th, 1663, "between the hours of eleven and twelve in the morning," we see Indians entering through all the gates of the palisades, dividing and scattering themselves among the houses and dwellings in a friendly way with a little corn to sell, just as they had done on many previous occasions. The men of the village, or most of them, were abroad or at work in the fields, the women busy in their household duties, the children playing around their homes. A "short quarter of an hour" passed when a horseman rushed in through the Mill Gate crying out, "The Indians have destroyed the New Village!" An Indian fires a gun; it is a signal to his confederates. Forthwith men are struck down with axes and tomahawks, and shot with guns and pistols, women and children in some number killed and others carried away captive, and houses plundered and set on fire, the peaceful homes of the morning converted to scenes of carnage and death and terror. At this point the narrative tells us the wind changed to the west and the firing of guns alarmed some of those who were working in the fields. "Near the Millgate were Albert Gysbertson with two servants, and Tejerck Classen de Witt; at the Sheriff's, himself, and two carpenters, two clerks and one thresher; at Cornelius Barentsen Sleight's, himself and his son; at the Dominie's, himself, and two carpenters and one laboring man; at the guard-house a few soldiers; at the gate towards the river, Hendrick Jochemsen, and Jacob the Brewer, but Jochemsen was very severely wounded in his house by two shots at an early hour. By these men, most of whom had neither guns nor side arms, were the Indians chased and put to flight.* * After these few men had been collected, by degrees others arrived from the fields, and we found ourselves, when mustered in the evening, including those who had escaped from the Nieuw Dorp and taken refuge among us, in number sixty-nine effective men." Add to this number fifteen men who had been killed, two who had been mortally wounded and could not be classed as effective, two who had been taken prisoners, and the total number of male settlers in the Esopus villages was less than one hundred men. Further than the narrative shows their names cannot be given — perhaps there were some at the Redout at the landing — perhaps some were from home. The narrative is signed by Roelof Swartwout, Sheriff, Albert Gysbertsen, Tjerck Classen de Witt, Thomas Chambers, Gysbert van Imbroch, Christian Nyssen and Hendrick Jochemsen, who composed the Court at Wildwijk, the names of some of whom have already been given.

Passing from the description of the attack to its results the official report shows that at Wildwijk nine men, three soldiers, four women, and two children, had been killed; four women and five children taken prisoners, and twelve houses and barns burned, viz: Garent Gerretsen, killed in front of his house; Jan Alberts, killed in his house; Lechen Dirreck, killed on the farm; William Jansen Seba, killed opposite his door; Willem Jansen Hap, killed in Peter van Hall's house; Jan the smith, killed in his house; Hendrick Jansen Looman, killed on his farm; Thomas Chambers' negro, killed on the farm; Hey Olferts, killed in the gunner's house; Hendrick Martensen (soldier) killed on the farm; Dominicus (soldier), killed in Jan Alberts' house; Christian Andriesen (soldier), killed on the street; Lichten Dirrack's wife, burnt, behind Barent Garritsen's house; Mattys Capito's wife, killed and burned in the house; Jan Albertsen's wife, big with child, killed in front of her house; Pieter van Hall's wife, shot and burned in her house; Jan Alberts' little girl, murdered with her mother; Willem Hap's child burned alive in the house. Prisoners taken: Master Gysbert's wife; Hester Douwe (blind Hester); Sara, daughter of Hester Douwe; Grietje, Dominie Laer's wife; Femmetje, sister of Hilletje, recently married to Joost Ariaens; Tjerck Classen de Witt's oldest daughter; Dominie Laer's * child; Ariaen Gerretsen's daughter; two little boys of Mattys Roeloffsen. Houses burned of Michael Frer, Willem Hap, Mattys Roeloffsen, Albert Gerretson, Lichten Derrick, Hans Carolusen, Pieter van Hael, Jacob Boerhans (two), Barent Gerretsen (two), Mattys Roloffsen. Wounded in Wildwijk: Thomas Chambers, shot in the woods; Hendrick Frere, shot in front of his house (died of his wound); Albert Gerretsen, shot in front of his house; Andries Barents, shot in

* Adriaen van Laer and servant emigrated from Amsterdam in the ship Gilded Otter, May, 1658. He married later. He was a Lutheran minister who happened to be at Wildwijk.

ADAM NEIDLINGER.

1831 – 1904.

front of his house; Jan du Parck, shot in the house of Aert Pietersen Tack; Hendrick, the Herr Director-general's servant; Paulus Noorman, shot in the street. Killed in the Nieuw Dorp: Marten Harmensen, found dead and stript behind his wagon; Jacques Tyssen, found dead beside Barent's house; Derrick Ariaeson, shot on his horse. Taken prisoners: Jan Gerritsen on Volckert's bouwery; wife and three children of Louis du Bois; two children of Matthew Blanchan; wife and child of Antoni Crispel; wife and four children of Marten Harmensen; wife and three children of Lambert Huybertsen; wife and two children of Jan Joosten; wife and child of Barent Harmensen; wife and three children of Grietje Westercamp; wife and child of Jan Barents; two children of Michael Frere; child of Hendrick Jochems; child of Hendrick Martensen; two children of Albert Heymans. The Nieuw Dorp was entirely destroyed except, says the report, "a new uncovered barn, one rick and a little stack of reed." *

A dark day in Esopus was that Thursday, June 7th, 1663—that day of terror, of murder, of fire, which has few equals in pioneer history—that day on which names were written in imperishable record. Among the actors in the scenes which have been referred to was the interesting Dutch Minister Hermanus Bloom who wrote to his Classis, "We have escaped, with most of the inhabitants," and in his description of the scene: "There lay the burnt and slaughtered bodies, together with those who were wounded by bullets and axes. The last agonies and the moans and lamentations of many were dreadful to hear. The houses were converted into heaps of stones, so that I may say with Micah, We are made desolate."

Dominie Bloom wrote that twenty-four persons had been killed, and forty-five taken prisoners. (Letter of Sept. 13, 1663.)

The surrender of the Province of New Netherlands to the English in September, 1664, brought with it no immediate material change in the settlement of the Esopus country, the most material being in the manner

* Schoonmaker in his "History of Kingston" wrote: "All the captives were returned except Barent Slecht's daughter. She had married a young warrior and remained with him." Her name is not in the list of prisoners of June 7th; she may have been captured in 1658-9. The story of her marriage is given as traditional. It is of record that a son of Evart Pels was taken prisoner in 1658-9, and was condemned to death, but saved from execution by an Indian maiden, that he married her and refused to return to his Dutch friends. The record may be found in Colonial History, N. Y., Vol. XIII, p. 143. The story of Slecht's daughter may be true.

of obtaining title to real estate, the change of the name of Wildwijk village to Kingston, that of the Nieuw Dorp to Hurley, and the laying out of a new village under the name of Marbletown, primarily for the purpose of assigning lands to the disbanded soldiers at the Rondhout with a view to induce them to become permanent residents. The manner in which titles to land had been obtained by the pioneers under the Dutch administration was by individual purchases from the Indians, in some cases by gifts from them, sometimes from grant by the local court, in the village, by assignment. Under the new or English rule all titles by whatever authority, were required to be surrendered to the Governor and new titles obtained from him, and purchases from the Indians, except by license was forbidden. No previous title was held to be invalid, but legal order was introduced. By the renewal in 1665 of the treaty of peace with the Esopus Indians, Deputy Governor Richard Nicolls, the English successor of Director-general Stuyvesant, found himself in possession of the large district of country which the Indians admitted to have been "conquered by the sword," but for which they were compensated later, and wrote: "The lands which I intend shall be first planted are those upon the west side of Hudson's River, at or adjoining to the Sopes, which is ready now to put the plow into, being clear ground." Under the Governor's encouragement and the reputation which the Esopus lands had acquired for fertility, immigrants began to come in a large number compared with the then total volume of immigration. Presumably the titles of the early settlers were returned to the Governor and renewed and new patents granted, though no doubt the largest proportion of immigrants became tenants, or made purchases from proprietors. In Colonial History, and in the record of land papers at Albany are the following entries:

1656—Sept. 25—Patent issued by Director Stuyvesant to Christoffel Davids for a tract of thirty-six morgens of land (about seventy-five acres) "situate about a league inland from the North River, opposite to the land of Thomas Chambers, running west and northeast half way to a small pond on the border of a valley which divides this parcel and the land of Johan de Hulter, deceased, with as much hay land (meadow) as shall pro rata be allowed to the other bouweries." *

1657—March 27—Patent issued by Director Stuyvesant to Johanna de Hulter, widow of Johan de Hulter, for 500 morgens (about 1,200 acres) of land purchased from the Indians, and for which her late husband had petitioned for a patent No-

* Christoffle Davids' son, David, with his family, perished in the massacre at Schenectady in 1690. In records Davids is written "Kit Davitsen," "Kit Davits," etc. The correct spelling would seem to be Christoffle Daavis.

vember 5th, 1654, "contiguous to the land of Thomas Chambers and Christoffel Davits, where the boundary is formed by a large Kil, and is divided at the north from the land on which Jurian van Westphalen lives now (1653) by a small Kil."

1661—Jan. 25—Jan ver Beek and Francis Pietersen (probably of Fort Orange) made declaration that they were present "in the spring of 1654, when Evert Pels and the late Jacob Jansen Stoll divided the land bought by them together from the Indians at the Esopus." Stoll purchased Christopher Davids tract in 1657, but seems to have been contemporary with him and with Evert Pels and Chambers, De Hulter and Juriaen van Westphalen.

1663—April 25—Deed from Director Stuyvesant to Hendrick Cornelissen from Holstein, for a "piece of land at the Esopus," bounded "on the east by the Kil, on the west and south by the meadow lying under the village." Also a small parcel of land adjoining."

1664—June 18—Deed of confirmation from Governor Nicolls to Matthew Blanchan for a house and lot of ground lying and being at Wildwyck.

1664—June 23—Deed of confirmation from Governor Nicolls to Roeloffe Swartwout for land in Wildwyck.

1664—July 23—Deed of confirmation from Governor Nicolls to Cornelijs Barents Slecht for between forty and fifty acres of land at Esopus.*

1669—April 9—Tjerck Claus de Witt and William Montania represented to the Commissioners that the Governor had given to them a grant for the setting up of a sawmill about five miles north of Kingston, and asked that the commissioners would recommend the further grant by the Governor of a piece of land about one mile further north called Dead Men's Bones, containing about seventy acres. At the same session John Oosterhout, Jan Burhans and Cornelius Vernoy, "husbandmen" of Kingston, asked for "a certain neck of land five miles distant from Kingston, over the Kill near the footpath leading to Albany, containing about fifty-four acres clear and good land. De Witt, Montania and the other parties named obliged themselves to build their houses all together on the other side of the Kill due north from the land of Thomas Chambers, and intended the same for a township within the precinct of Kingston. In the same neighborhood Thomas Chambers desired to build a house for a tenant, and also one for his son-in-law. The commissioners passed the recommendation as requested. The mill was erected and the settlement formed at what is now the bridge over the Plattekill between the towns of Saugerties and Ulster, writes Mr. Brink in his "History of Saugerties." The place called "Dead Men's Bones," was about a mile further north, but why so called awaits satisfactory explanation.

1670—April 13—Deed from Governor Lovelace to Christopher Bersford for a lot and a half in the new town laid out at Esopus called Marbletown.

1670—Aug. 18—Deed from Governor Lovelace to Richard Cage for a house lot in Marbletown.

1671—Oct. 11—Deed of confirmation from Governor Lovelace to John Joesten for a lot of ground in Marbletown, containing 30 acres.

* "Deed of confirmation" shows that the party receiving it had previously received title from Director Stuyvesant or other authority. Matthew Blanchan, for example, was an immigrant of 1660. Cornelis Barentsen Slecht was given the land in his confirmatory deed named from Stuyvesant in 1662. He described it in 1663 as "lying near the new village"; that he had found it "too far for his convenience" as himself and his wife were "now old people" and "would prefer living near the church," the more so as his wife was "the midwife of the village of Wildwijk." He asked deed for land which he had "formerly purchased" from the Indians, and for which he had been obliged to pay the tax to build the Minister's house, a little piece of land lying close to it, called in the savage tongue Wichquanis."

1672—April 1—Minute of a grant from the Court at Kingston to Cornelius Hoogeboom of a lot of ground for a brickyard.

1672—June 25—Deed from Governor Lovelace to Tjerck Classen de Witt for a parcel of bush land, together with a house lot, orchard and calves' pasture lying near Kingston, in Esopus.

1673—Feb. 18—Minute of a grant from the Court at Kingston to Jan Mattyson of a lot of ground.

1673—April 14—Minute of a grant from the Court at Hurley of a lot of ground to Albert Hymans. In minutes of the commissioners, Sept. 20, 1669, "Albert Heymans (Roosa)," who asked permission to "set up a brew-house and tan-vats at Hurley." He was an immigrant of 1660.

1673—June 7—Deed of confirmation from Governor Lovelace to Matthias Blanchan for 36 acres of land in the town of Hurley.

1675—March 1—Minute of a grant from the Court at Marbletown to Jan Bigs of a small piece of land.

1675—March 9—Minute of a grant from the Court at Kingston to George Hall, of a small piece of land.

1675—Sept. 10—Minute of a grant from the Court at Hurley to Hyman Albertsen Roosa, of a small piece of land.

1675—Oct. 13—Deed from Governor Andros confirming to Cornelius Hogeboom the lot of ground granted him by the Corporation of Kingston for a brickyard. (See 1672, April 1.)

1676—April 15—Minute of a grant by the Court at Kingston to William Trophagen for 20 acres of land.

1676—April 20—Description of a survey of 40 acres of land lying at the Esopus, laid out for Paulus Paulessen.

1676—Aug. 4—Description of survey of land belonging to Marbletown "called ye third stuck" (piece) containing by estimation about 100 acres to be patented to William Ashfordby. Deed from Andros Oct. 2, 1676.

1676—Sept. 4—Description of a survey of 40 acres of land "at ye Mumbackers lying at ye Round Doubt Kill," laid out for Charrat Clausa. (Q. Tjerck Classen de Witt.)

1676—Sept. 4—Description of survey of 40 acres of land "at ye Esopus lying at ye Mombackers at ye Roundoubt River, laid out for Thomas Quicke."

1676—Sept. 4—Description of survey of 32 acres of land "at ye Esopus, at ye Mumbackers, lying by ye Roundout Kill, laid out for Aron ffranse."

The three grants above named are the first of record in the present town of Rochester. The name is from a Mascaron (Dutch Mumbackers) painted on a tree by an Indian commemorative of himself—not of "a place of death" or "a place of battle." Trees and rocks so marked were frequently met.

1676—Sept. 5—Minute of a grant from the Court at Kingston to Tjerck Classen (de Witt), for a tract of wild land.

1676—Sept. 5—Minute of a grant from the Court of Kingston to Mattys Mattison and Dirck Jansen Skipmouse of a piece of land "near that village."

1676—Sept. 15—Minute of a grant from the Corporation of Kingston "to Captain Chambers for a piece of land lying on the Great Kill."

Thomas Chambers located (1652-3) on the Groot Esopus. He secured several parcels of land which were included in a manorial charter issued to him by Governor Lovelace, Oct. 16th, 1672, under the title of the "Lordship and Manor of Foxhall." Although his manor was within the bounds of Kingston, it had independent manorial powers and was so recognized in the organization of the county in 1685, and was given a supervisor in the Board of Supervisors.

1676—Sept. 15—Minute of a grant from the Court at Kingston to Wessel Ten Broeck of a certain marsh containing 11 acres.

1676—Sept. 25—Minute of a grant from the Court at Kingston to William Ashfordby, of 104 acres of land in Marbleton, situated behind the Kaelbergh (Bald Hill), and called the fifth stuck, and 4 acres at the same place near a tract called the sixth stuck. (See description of survey above. Aug. 4, 1676.)

1676—Oct. 1—Conveyance from Frederick Hussey to Claes Tunison of a lot of land of about 50 acres, in Marbletown.

1676—Oct. 2—Deed from Governor Andros to Anthony Addison for a certain parcel of land above Marbletown in Esopus, lying over against the Kaelberg "called by the name of Brookeboome Hook," containing 20 acres.

1676—Oct. 2—Deed from Governor Andros to William Trophagen for a certain piece of land at Esopus lying northeast from Captain Thomas Chambers' farm, containing about 10 acres, "lying north and south along the great creek or Kill to the Water Kolch." (Kolk, Dutch, "gulf, abyss.")

1676—Nov. 13—Description of a survey of 20 acres of land being part of a tract upon ye towne of Kingston, laid out by order of ye Magistrates of Esopus for Wessel Ten Broeck." (See 1676, April 15.)

1676—Nov. 13—Description of a survey of about seven acres of ffly "before ye towne of Kingston at Esopus," laid out for Mathas Matison and Derricke Jonson Schapmos. (See 1676, Sept. 5.)

1676—Nov. 15—Description of a survey of eight acres of ffly lying before ye towns of Kingston at Esopus, "laid out for ye troopers of Esopus." (Granted on petition of Jan Andriansen, Michael Mott and other troopers for the pasturage of their horses.)

1676—Nov. 13—Description of a survey of 20 acres of lang being part of a tract known as the Butterfield, lying to the southwest of Marbletown, laid out for George Hall.

1676—Nov. 13—Description of a survey of 20 acres of land, being part of a tract known as the Butterfield, lying to the southwest of Marbletown, laid out for Samuel Leetee.

Same date—22 acres of the Butterfield laid out for Thomas Kerton.

Same date—28 acres of the Butterfield, laid out for John Kerton.

Governor Lovelace wrote the commissioners in 1669: "There is a tract of land by ye Cale Berg which I purpose to improve for a breeding ground which I wish you to survey and give me. It is called the Butterfield."

1676—Dec. 28—Description of a survey of an Island in Roundout River "called by the Indians Assincke" (i. e. stony land or place), with 16½ acres "near the same," laid out for Henry Bateman (Beekman) and Thomas Hendricks.

1677—April 25—Minutes of a grant from the Court at Kingston to Albert Geretsen of a tract of land on the opposite side of the Kill which runs through the Esopus land.

Same date—Minute of a grant from the Court at Kingston to Joost Adriansen for six acres over the Mill Kill.

1677—May 26—Deed from the Esopus Indians to Louis du Bois and associates, of a tract of land over the Rondout Kill, "beginning at the high hill called Moggonck, thence southeast to Juffrous Hook in the Long Reach, on the Great River called in Indian Magaat Ramis, thence north along the river to the island called Raphoes lying in Kromme Elebow, at the commencement of the Long Reach, thence west to the High Hill at a place called Waracahaes and Tawaretaque, along the High Hill southwest to Moggonck, with free access to the Rondout Kill."

For this purchase a patent was granted by Governor Andros, Sept. 29th, of the same year, on which was founded the settlement known as New Paltz. The patentees were "Louis du Bois, Christian Doyou, Abraham Hasbroucq, Andrié le Fevre, Jean Hasbroucq, Pierre Doyou, Louis Bevier, Antonie Crespel, Abraham du Bois, Hugo Freer, Isaac du Bois and Simon le Fevre, their heirs and others." They were all French Huguenots. The government of the patent was intrusted to the care of twelve trustees known colloquially as "the Duzine," who continued by succession until the formation of the town. It was the first of the large patents issued in the county, and covered, by later survey, 92,126 acres, on which are now the towns of New Paltz, Lloyd and part of Esopus. Descendants of the patentees now constitute a large quota of the inhabitants of Ulster, Orange and Dutchess counties, and are widely scattered over the country.

1677—June 9—Draught of Roeloffe Hendrick's patent at Esopus.

1677—Sept. 24—Petition of John Garton to build a house on his land in the fourth stuck (Marbletown). Presumably the father of Thomas Garton, Judge of Common Pleas of Ulster, 1692.

Same date—Anthony Addison, of Marbletown, asked for permission to "live over the Kill" and for the grant of twenty acres of land.

1677—Sept. 25—Minute of a grant of land from the Court at Kingston to John Rutgerson. He presented a deed from the Indians for the land.

1677—Sept. 27—Jan Borhans conveyed to Joost Andrianson his house and lot in Kingston.

1677—Oct. 8—Deed from Governor Andros to Tjerck Claessen for a piece of woodland containing about 50 acres, lying to the west of the town of Kingston. Granted to Tjerck Claessen de Witt by the Court of Kingston, Sep. 4 of the same year. See above.

1677—no date—Petition of Henry Pawling for a grant of a piece of land "under Hurley, joining to Wassmaker's land," being about 20 acres.

Wasmaker's (Dutch) probably stands for Wax-chandler's land. Governor Stuyvesant had an interest in this tract. Ex-Governor Lovelace asked the commissioners to treat "Mr. Stuyvesant with all the honor

NICHOLAS R. GRAHAM.

so that it prejudice not ye town." The commissioners recommended that "one moiety of the tract be granted to Mr. Petrus Stuyvesant pursuant to his Royal Highnesses's directions." Stuyvesant had a warm place in the hearts of the Dutch colonists of Esopus.

1679—April 11—Description of the bounds of a parcel of woodland lying on ye south side of Kingston, and a small meadow lying and being by the Mill Creek, to the west of a rocky hill, containing in all 16 acres, with a house in Kingston, granted to William de Miere, otherwise written Wilhelmus DeMyer.

1680—July 18—Description of a survey of an island at the rocky point of the Rondout Kill (See Dec. 28, 1676), about the quantity of six acres; also a parcel of meadow land at the west side of Rondout Kill, containing about forty acres, with a parcel of woodland, commonly called Pamahaky (slanting land) and Bartman's Hoeke, containing about 100 acres, laid out for Michael Gorton.

1680—Aug. 13—Minute of a grant from the Court at Kingston to John and William De Meyer and Matthias Mattison of about six acres of land under the fall of the Platte Kill; also woodland as far as they have need to cut wood for the sawmill.

1680—Sept. 16—Minute of a grant from the Court at Kingston to William De Meyer of a lot of land over the Mill Kill, south of Kingston, contain 16 acres, with 3 acres of valley; also a house lot.

1680—Nov. 2—Certificate of the Corporation of Kingston to the effect that William De Meyer is the right owner of half of the mill and Kill called by the name of Platte Kill, in company with Matias and John Mattison.

1683—Minute of a grant from the Court at Kingston to Henry Alberts for a parcel of woodland "by ye south side of ye great creek."

1684—Oct. 25—Deed from the Indians to Governor Dongan for lands extending along Hudson's River to the lands belonging to the Murderer's Creek Indians, thence westward to the foot of the high hills called Pitkiskaker and Aioskawasting (now known as the Shawangunk Mountains), thence southwest all along the said hills and the river called Peakadasank (now Shawangunk Kill) to a water pond lying upon said hills called Maretange, comprehending all those lands, meadows and woods called Nescotack, Chawangon, Memorasink, Kakogh, Gitawanuck and Ghittawagh.

This purchase was included in a patent Sept. 12, 1694, to Captain John Evans. The grant was set aside by the Colonial Assembly in 1698, approved by Queen Ann in 1709, and the immense tract thrown open for settlement by small patents, the first one granted being that on which the City of Newburgh now stands. For nearly one hundred years that portion of the territory lying north of Murderer's Creek, continued a part of Ulster County, and many of the early patents adjoining or more immediately south of the New Paltz Patent, remain in that connection.

1685—May 25—Description of a survey of 200 acres of land lying upon the north side of Esopus Kill or river, butting upon the land of Captain Thomas Chambers and known by the name of Upton. Laid out for Edward Whittaker.

1685—May 26—Description of a survey of 672 acres of land lying upon both sides of Rondout Kill including part of the Paltz River, and known by the name of Hardick, laid out for William Fisher.

1685—May 27—Description of a survey of 830 acres of land, lying on both sides of the Rondout Kill or river, and known by the name of Moggewarsinck, laid out for Henry Beakman.

Beekman sold this patent to Peter Lowe, Nov. 2, 1708, who included it in a grant to himself March 8, 1722, as appears by survey abstract, Land Papers 89, 158. The limits of the new patent are described as within the then town of Rochester, and as "beginning at the great fall called Honeck, from thence up the creek northerly to the high mountains, including several pieces of land** and also all the land that lies on Mombaccus Kill within the bounds belonging to the Indians, i. e. not conveyed by the deed of 1677, excepting 300 acres of land which had been granted to Warnear Koornbeck. Moggewarsink, otherwise on record Moggew-assin-k, means "At (on or to) a great rock," and refers to the great rock lying in Rondout Creek above its junction with the Sandberg.

1685—May 28—Description of a survey of 963 acres of land lying upon the south side of Rondout Kill, or river, and known by the name of Rosendale, laid out for Jacob Rutsen.

1685—May 29—Description of a survey of 400 acres of land lying upon Rondout Kill, and known by the name of Wawarasinke, laid out for Anne Beak.

On this patent was founded the old village of Wawarsing, and the name of the boundmark became the name of the present town. The name was from that of the southeast boundmark of the patent where Rondout Kill bends abruptly to the north which it describes as a point, a stone or corner "where the current bends, winds, or eddies around." The precise point is a large stone lying on the bank of the stream which has been identified by surveys of the patent.

1685—June 6—Description of a survey of a 160 acres of land "lying upon both sides of the Mumbackehouse Kill or brook (now Rochester Creek), in the rear of the land of Tjrk Claus de Witt, laid out for Tunis Jacobsen Klaarwater.

1685—June 6—Description of a survey for 290 acres upon the north side of Mumbackhous Kill, laid out for Tjerck Claus de Witt.

1685—June 6—Description of a survey of 212 acres lying on the south side of Rondout Kill, and known by the name of Mumbackhouse, laid out for Philip Coale.

1685—June 8—Description of a survey of 212 acres of land lying upon the south side of Rondout Kill, and known by the name of Mumbackhous, laid out for Leonard Coale.

1685—June 8—Description of a survey of 344 acres upon the south side of Rondout Kill, being known by the name of Mumbackhouse, laid out for Nicholas Antonia.

1685—June 8—Description of 208 acres of land lying upon the south side of Rondout Kill, and known by the name of Mumbackhouse, laid out for Claud Loeter.

1685—June 8—Description of a survey of 222 acres lying upon the north side of Rondout Kill, and known by the name of Mumbackhouse, laid out for Garret Daker.

1685—June 9—Description of a survey of 176 acres lying on the north side ot Rondout Kill, laid out for Peteer Cole.

1685—June 9—Description of a survey of 366 acres on the north side of Rondout Kill, laid out for Peter Holebrand.

1685—June 9—Description of a survey of 100 acres of land lying on the north side of Rondout Kill, laid out for Gisbert Alerts.

All the preceding tracts of land were in the district known as Mumbackhouse (Mumbakers). The several orthographies are given as they appear of record.

1685—June 12—Description of survey of 2900 acres of land lying upon Hudson's River betwixt the Rondout Kill and the Cline Esopus, and known by the name of Hussey's Hill, including the Cline Esopus ffly and Sunken ffly at the mouth of Rondout Kill with the two lakes. Laid out for Frederick Hussey and others.

1685—June 16—Description of a survey of 259 acres of land lying on the south side of Esopus Kill, laid out in two parcels for Waldron Du Mont.

1685—June 16—Description of two pieces of land containing together 83 acres, lying on the south side of Esopus Kill, together with a house and lot in Kingston, bounded on the northeast by the house-lot of Wessel Tenbrooge, laid out for Matice Matison.

1685—June 17—Description of a survey of 324 acres upon the north side of Rondout Kill, and known by the name of Mumbackhouse, laid out for Roeliffe Hendrick Infelt.

1685—June 17—Description of a survey of 100 acres of land lying at Esopus, being near and on the east side of Esopus Kill, and in the rear of the lands of Captain Thomas Chambers and William Traphagen, laid out for Derricke Henderson.

1685—June 20—Description of survey of 327 acres of land lying on the south side of Esopus Kill or river bear the dividing line between Kingston and Hurley, laid out for Tjerke Clause de Witt.

1685—June 20—Description of a survey of four acres of land lying by Kingston to the northward of the Mill lot; also a house-lot in Kingston, laid out for Cornelius Hogeboom.

1685—July 7—Description of a survey of 290 acres of land lying upon the north side of Rondout Kill, and known by the name of Mumbackus, laid out for Leonard Beckwith.

1686—April 4—Description of a survey of 2000 acres of land lying upon both sides of the Well's River, in the town of New Pauls, beginning on the east side of the river, and at the south end of a small island in the river at the mouth of the river Chauwangung, laid out for James Graham.

This tract was at the junction of the Shawangunk and the Wallkill, on the east side or slope of the ridge or hill called Nescotack.

1686—April 5—Description of a tract of 83 acres on the north side of the Esopus Kill, within the bounds of Hurley, and known by the name of the Old Bowery, laid out for Garret Cornelius.

1686—April 9—Description of survey of a ffly or meadow ground upon the great Binnewater (inland water), lying to the northeast of Kingston, containing about 38 acres, laid out for Henry Clauson and Yochum Englebert Van Nauman.

1686—April 10—Description of a survey of 69 acres upon the south side of Esopus Kill, laid out for John Hamell.

1686—April 12—Description of a survey of 19 acres within the limits of Hurley, laid out for John Ewenson.

1686—April 13—Description of a survey of 200 acres upon the south side of Esopus Kill, within the limits of Marbletown, laid out for John Post.

1686—April 13—Description of a survey of 158 acres of land upon the south side of Esopus Kill, within the limits of Marbletown, laid out for Gisbert Cron.

1686—April 13—Description of two parcels of land on the south side of Esopus Kill, one lying entirely in Marbletown and the other partly in Hurley, laid out for Garrat Gisbertson.

1686—April 15—Description of a survey of a certain tract known as "Primaker's Land," lying upon the Esopus in the limits of Hurley, and some other lands in the vicinity, containing 321 acres laid out for Venike Rosen.

Primaker or Pruemaker, from whom the land was named, was the aged Indian sachem who was killed by the Dutch troops in the Esopus war of 1660. "The oldest and best of the Esopus chiefs," is his record.

1686—April 20—Description of 80 acres in Marbletown, upon the south side of Esopus Kill, touching a hill called the Calibar (Kaleberg), laid out for William Johnson.

1686—April 23—Description of 30 acres to the northeast of Maudlin (?) Island, in Kingston, laid out for William Haines.

1686—April 13—Description of survey of two lots, in all about 130 acres on the south side of Esopus Kill, in Marbletown, laid out for John Coke.

1686—April 26—Description of a survey of about 169 acres on the north side of Esopus Creek, in Marbletown, laid out for Henrik Cornelius Bogart.

1686—April 26—Description of several tracts of land within the limits of Hurley adjoining the Mother Kill on the west, laid out for Derick Skipmouse.

1686—April 26—Description of a tract "within the limits of Kingston, by the Roundout Kill, known by ye name of ye Plain Fields, together with swamp land, in all 144 acres," laid out for Thomas Chambers.

1686—April 29—Description of three pieces of land, in all about 90 acres in Marbletown, laid out for John Bigges.

1686—April 29—Description of eight acres in Kingston, also a house-lot lying upon ye west street in Kingston, laid out for Jacob Aretson.

1686—April 28—Description of three acres in Kingston, "westward by ye Mill Pond," laid out for Jacobus Elmindorf.

1686—May 1—Survey of 47 acres on the north side of Esopus Kill, in Kingston, together with an island called Pearl Island, containing about 21 acres, laid out for William Legg.

1686—May 1—Survey of 600 acres lying upon Hudson's River to the northward of Callicoone Hooke (Turkey Hook), in Kingston, laid out for John Tyson.

1686—May 3—Survey of 87 acres in Kingston, upon ye north side of Esopus Kil, and "fronts on ye Platte Kill," laid out for Peter Winne.

1686—May 4—Description of survey of 201 acres about two miles south of Kingston, laid out for Cornelius Sleght and Cornelius Hoghboom.

1686—May 4—Survey of 55 acres of swamp and "about seven acres of land in ye valley, to the eastward of the southwest gate," laid out for Jan Tyson.

1686—May 4—Description of survey of 100 acres on the south side of Esopus Kill, beginning at the falls, laid out for Arian Tunisson.

1686—May 4—Survey of 25 acres lying at the Green Kill in the bounds of Hurley, also six acres of upland by the Wagon Path on the south side of Esopus Creek, laid out for Corns. Elmendorf.

1686—May 4—Description of survey of about 216 acres lying upon Esopus Kill, within the bounds of Kingston, laid out for Henry Alburts.

1686—May 4—Survey of 27 acres on the east side of the Kline ffly, on the west side of Kingston, together with a garden lot at Kingston, containing five acres, and a piece of woodland on the south side of Esopus Creek, near Kingston, containing 25 acres, laid out for Girth Artson.

1686—May 7—Survey of about 442 acres at the mouth of Esopus Kill, being part of the tract called "the Sagiers," laid out for George Meales.

1686—May 7—Description of survey of 252 acres lying about three miles westward from the mouth of Esopus Kill, beginning at the side of a run called the Beaver Kill, being part of the tract called Sagiers, laid out for George Meales, and others.

1686—May 8—Survey of 300 acres lying northward from the mouth of Esopus Creek, being part of the tract called Sagiers, laid out for George Meales and others.

Sagier was a pioneer of date prior to 1660. He obtained lands from the Indians and is said to have built a small sawmill at the mouth of the creek which still bears his name. The tradition is of doubtful value. He did not perfect his title by patent, and the land reverted to the government. Zager (Dutch) means Sawyer, and Zagerij means Sawmill. The latter is not met of record.

1686—May 8—Survey of 201 acres crossing the run called Sawyer's Kill, about a mile north of the mouth of Esopus Creek, being part of the tract called Sagiers, laid out for George Meales and others.

1686—May 14—Description of a survey of 797 acres in the county of Ulster, in the neighborhood of Wanton Island, laid out for himself by Ro. Fulerton, surveyor.

Wanton Island (Lenape Wanquon), is now the northeast bound of Ulster County. The Indian name means "Heel," heel-shaped, protuberant.

1686—May 28—Survey of about 63 acres "being part of Hurley great piece" on the north side of Esopus Kill, laid out for Matthew Blanjohon.

1686—May 28—Description of a house-lot in Kingston "on ye north side of the Bridge Street," together with another small lot "without Kingston by the Mill," laid out for Matice Slight.

1686—May 28—Survey of 47 acres "being part of Hurley great piece," lying on the north side of Esopus Kill; likewise a house-lot in Hurley, and two lots of Hurley ffly or meadow ground, known as Nos. 11 and 13, laid out for Rowliffe Swartwood (Swartwout).

1687—March 9—Survey of a house-lot in Kingston, containing about ten acres, laid out for Henry Denyke.

A survey implies title previously obtained from some authority or individual—not record patents.

1686—May 31—Description of a survey of 64 acres on the north side of Esopus Creek within the limits of Marbletown, laid out for Thos. Van de Marke.

1686—June 3—Description of a house-lot in the Church Street, in Kingston, laid out for Mart Hoffman.

Hoffman was a soldier in the war of 1663. He was the father of Zachariah Hoffman of Shawangunk.

1686—May 7—Survey of sundry lots in Hurley, in all about 30 acres, laid out for John Elta.

1686—June 8—Survey of 100 acres "lying on both sides of the Mother Kill, and known by the name of Otford, being within the limits of Kingston," laid out for John Hall.

1686—June 16—Survey of 400 acres in Kingston, laid out for John Spragg.

1686—Dec. 9—Survey of two pieces of meadow or fly, in all 89 acres, lying north of Kingston, laid out by request of Wm. de Myre.

1687—Jan. 20—Description of a survey of 410 acres "known by the Indian name of Chauwangung," laid out for Thomas Lloyd.

This tract was at the settlement known later as Tuthiltown. The survey was based on a prior grant. It was the specific tract or place called Chawangon in the Indian deed to Governor Dongan in 1684, from which the name was extended to the mountain, the stream, and the town. All subsequent grants in the vicinity were located by it, as "at" or "near" Skawongung. Severyn Tenhout, Benjamin Smedis, Jacobus Bruyn, Matthias Mort, John McClean, located in the same vicinity. The tract was on the north side of the abrupt bend in the stream and extended from the bottom lands on the creek up the hill or ridge called Nescotack. The name means "On the hill's side." It was never the name of the mountain except by extension to it. Every place round about was called at or near "Shawongunk," or "ung," after Lloyd's settlement.

1687—May 17—Patent granted by Governor Dongan, approved by Council May 17th, 1688, to Dirick Shepmous, William de Meyer, Jacob Ruttsen, Wessell Tenbrooge, Barrett Aertze, Tunis Jacobsen, Benjamin Provoost, Wm. Legge, Jacob Aertson, Mattyze Mattise, Wm. Haines and John Wm. Hooghteen, "one body corporate and politique to be called by the name of The Trustees of the Freeholders and Commonality of the Town of Kingston," and defining the bounds of their jurisdiction, "beginning at the southward of Little Esopus Creek, thence west to the bounds of the Town of Hurley, thence along the bounds of Hurley to a certain creek called Motthar Creeke, thence northerly to another creek called Preenaker's Creek; thence upon a north line three miles into the woods, thence on the same course as the mountains range to the bounds of Albany County, and from thence along the said bounds to Hudson's River." Under this charter the town was governed, from 1688 to 1816, by trustees elected annually.

1688—July 30—On representation of having purchased from the Indians by consent, Governor Dongan issued patent to Joochim Staats for a tract of land "lying and being above the village called Mombackus, extending from the land of Anna Beake southwesterly," etc., including the now most valuable portion of the valley of Sandberg Kill in the present town of Wawarsing.

John D. Fratsher.

1693—May 10—Draught of two pieces of land, in all 130 acres on the west side of Esopus Creek, laid out for Hendrick Cornelius.

1695—April 5—Deed from two Indian women to the children of Nicholas Anthony for land lying to the south of Rondout Kill.

1697—May 27—Joost van Metren asked for "a tract of stoney woodland in Marbletown," and Humphrey Davenport asked for land upon Mumbackhous Kill.

1697—Oct. 14—William West asked patent for a piece of land "on which he had erected a corne mill"; also the vacant land adjoining, the whole being bounded south and east by lands of Col. Beekman, the Rondout Kill, and a direct line over the hills to the bounds of Hurley.

1697—Oct. 14—Patent to Thomas Swartwout, Jacob Coddeback, Peter Gumaer, Anthony Swartwout, Bernardus Swartwout, Jan Tys, and David Jamis, for lands on the Neversink River known as Machagh-Kameck, Paenpach, etc., now in part in Orange County, and in part in Sullivan County, primarily in Ulster and known on the Tax roll of 1714 as the "Neighborhood of Wackemeck."

1700—April 10—Indian deed to Engeltie, wife of Stephen Gasherie, lands on the south side of Rondout Kill, at a small run of water, to the west of the land of Rochsinck, called by the Indian name of Wiggewappog; thence along Rondout Kill to a small run of water called by the Indian name of Warramick, together with a certain fall named Sanchatisinck.

1701—Dec. 10—Survey of 710 acres of land, "at a place called Maschabeneer Shawengonck, laid out for Matthias Mott, with affidavit by Jacob Rutsen concerning its purchase from the Indians. Survey and affidavit filed with application for a patent.

1701—Sept. 22—Petition of Matthias Mott for a patent of about 400 acres "at a place called Shawangung," which was given him by the Indians when he was a child.

1702—June 10—Remonstrance by Sovereyn Tenhout against granting to Matthias Mott the land which he had petitioned for, accompanied by an extract from the minutes of the Court at Kingston showing that the land had been granted to Tenhout in 1683. He asked for a patent for 300 acres (apparently additional) "called by the Indians Masseecks" or Massecks, a name which describes low wet lands, a marsh or meadow.

No date—John Smedes and James Greeyer asked for 300 acres "lying on the south side of Nesquatalk, otherwise written Nescotack," on both sides of the Paltz River, for which a patent had been promised by Governor Bellmont.

No date—John Middagh "of Ulster County" asked for 300 acres on the south side of Esopus Creek "commonly called or known by the Indian name of Aquameeck," which the name probably described as "a fishing place on the other side" serving to locate the tract.

1702—March 12—John Hardenbergh, "of ye County of Ulster," asked license to purchase 300 acres "called by the Indians Wenachsink, lying over ye Shawengonck Kill on both sides of ye Wallkill." The place was in Shawangunk, and the Indian name described it as "at or on the fine, rich lands."

1702—March 12—Albert Rosa, "of ye county of Ulster," asked for a license to purchase about 300 acres of land "called by the Indians Anguagekonk," northward of Kingston upon a certain creek called Sawkill, "westerly above Wm. Legg's new Sawmill, and near ye high mountains."

1702—March 12—John Hardenbergh, "of ye county of Ulster" asked for license to purchase from the Indians 250 acres on the Sawkill.

1702—April 18—Robert Sanders asked for a patent for a tract of "2000 acres of profitable land, besides waste land and woodland in Ulster County, at a place called by the Indians Oghgotacton." The patent seems to have been granted, but there is no trace of its location.

1702—Sept. 12—Petition of William Nottingham, "an inhabitant of ye county of Ulster," for a piece of land "on ye second piece of ye towne of Marbletown." Granted July 1, 1703.

1703—May 8—Petition of Claes Clase Sluyter for land on Rondout Kill containing 400 acres, "between ye land of widow Pawling and ye widow Dirck Kyser." Court at Kingston reported favorably.

1703—June 16—Petition of Captain Thomas Garton for and on behalf of ye inhabitants of the town of Marbletown, praying for the appointment of Trustees for said town and the issuing of letters patent.

This was the beginning of the organization of the town of Marbletown. The patent was issued June 25, 1703, and Col. Henry Beekman, Capt. Thomas Gaston (Garton) and Capt. Chas. Brodhead named as Trustees, whose successors continued to be elected annually until 1808.

1703—June 16—Petition of Colonel Henry Beekman "for and on behalf of the inhabitants of the town of Mumbackus," praying the appointment of Trustees for said town, and the issuing of letters patent.

The petition was granted June 25, 1703, and Colonel Henry Beekman, Joachim Schoonmaker and Moses de Puy named as the first trustees. The early and familiar name Mumbackus was exchanges for Rochester, as a compliment to the Earl of Rochester.

1703—Nov. 4—Petition of Arian Garretson and others in behalf of themselves and the rest of the inhabitants of Hurley praying for a patent and the appointment of trustees. Not acted on.

1704—Aug. 28—Patent to Philip French, Ebenezer Wilson and others, for lands "Beginning at a place in Ulster County called the Hunting House or Yagh House, lying to the northeast of land called Bashe's Land, thence to run west by north until it meets the Fishkill or main branch of Delaware River, thence to run southerly to the south end of Great Minnisink Island, thence due south to the land lately granted to John Bridges & Co." i. e., to the Wawayanda Patent.

This was the Great Minnisink Patent covering lands now in Orange County and as far south as Great Minnisink Island nine miles south of Port Jervis, and as far north as about Mamakating, Sullivan (then Ulster) County, near which the Hunting House stood. Its boundaries were materially enlarged in 1764 under an order granting unoccupied lands to parties who were willing to pay taxes thereon, the line being extended north to Sandberg and east to Middletown, Orange County, and the Minnisink angle formed. A considerable portion of southwestern Ulster is still on this immense grant.

1704—Oct. 24—Petition of Cornelius Cool for and on behalf of the freeholders and inhabitants of Hurley for survey of a tract "lying between the north bounds of Kingston and the Great Mountains, commonly called the Blue Hills."

The "Blue Hills" referred to bound Esopus Valley on the west, spread over Western Ulster and mingle with the Katskills on the north. Their name is from the reflection of the color of the rocks. The survey asked for was made and the tract described: "Bounded N. W. by the mountains, N. E. and east by Kingston, S. E. and S. W. by New Paltz, and Marbletown."

1706—July 16—Petition of Johannes Hardenbergh and Company for permission to purchase "a small tract of vacant land in the County of Ulster."

1707—March 22—Indian Deed to Johannes Hardenbergh for a tract of land in Ulster County "extending from the west bounds of Marbletown to a certain place called Kawienesink (Kawanesink), and northeast to a certain Kill called by the Indians Anquathkonck, and southerly to the town of Marbletown."

1708—Feb. 4—Petition of Johannes Hardenbergh and others for a patent for lands "beginning at ye Sandberg or hill" at ye N. E. corner of ye lands of Ebenezer Wilson & Co. (Minnisink Patent) thence northwesterly to ye Fish Kill River, and west to the headwaters thereof, including the same, thence to a small river called Cartwright's Kill, and so by ye said Kill to ye northwesternmost bounds of Kingston, on said Kill, thence by ye bounds of Kingston, Hurley, Marbletown and Rochester, and other patented lands to the beginning.

This was the historic Hardenbergh Patent which covered northwestern Ulster and mainly the County of Sullivan and part of Delaware. The patent was granted in 1709.

1708—Oct. 12—Petition of Cornelius Cool and others of the town of Hurley, for a patent for a tract of land adjoining the town of New Paltz, Report thereon by Rip van Dam and other members of the Council recommending the issue of the patent, with the saving clause admitting the rest of the town of Hurley to share in its benefits.

The patent was issued Oct. 19, 1708. Its issue was to Cornelius Kool, Adrien Garretsie, Matthew Ten Eyck, Jacob du Bois, Johannes Schepmose, Roeloff Swartwout, Cornelius Lammerse, Peter Petersies, Lawrence Osterhout and Jannetie Newkirk, trustees of Hurley.

1708—Nov. 2—Deed from Hendricus (Henry) Beekman and Johanna his wife, to Pieter Louw (Lowe) for a tract in Rochester, including several small pieces, within the bounds belonging to the Indians, from the bounds of Kahansick to the bounds of the High Mountains. The survey began at Honk Falls. The patent to Lowe has been noted.

1709—Aug. 18—Petition of Alexander Griggs, of the County of Ulster, for 600 acres of land on the south side of Old Man's Creek, and running up the Hudson's River to a point called the Old Man's Hook, at a certain place called the Dans Kamer.

The patent was the second granted on the resumed lands patented to Capt. John Evans. The lands asked for were in the present Town of Marlborough. Old Man's Creek and Old Man's Hook were so called from Old Dennis Reljie, now Relyea, whose place of residence is described in official papers at Albany. He was the first settler at Juffrow's Hook. His name is on the tax roll of 1714.

1709—Nov. 1—Petition of Peter Barbarre for 2000 acres of the Evans Patent. Now in Marlborough.

1709—Nov. 8—Description of a survey of 400 acres in Shawangunk on the south side of the land of John van Camp, laid out for Evart Derwilighe (Terwilliger).

1709—Nov. 12—Description of survey of 200 acres of the Evans Patent lying on Shawangunk Kill, laid out for Severeyn Tenhout. Described as woodland on Shawangunk Kill, and Crum Kill.

1709—Nov. 14—Petition of Jacobus Bruin and Benjamin Smedes, of Shawangunk, for 400 acres of the Evans Patent. Surveyor's description: "Lying near a small hill called in ye Indian tongue Wecbqu-atenn-onck," meaning literally "at the end of a hill." Surveyed Nov. 15, 1709.

1709—Nov. 18—Petition of John McLean, of Shawangunk for 300 acres of the Evans Patent, described in survey: "Lying on the northward side of the Paltz Kill at Shawangunk."

1709—May 11—Petition of Zacharias Hoffman of Shawangunk, for 330 acres of the land formerly granted to Captain John Evans. Described in survey Dec. 2, 1709: "Lying on the east side of Shawangunk River."

1709—Nov. 28—Petition of Matthias Mott that the 300 acres of land which had "been granted to Sovereign Tenhout be so divided that he (Mott) may have a proportionate share of the good land upon said river, i. e. on Shawangunk Kill.

1709—Nov. 28—Petition of Hugo Frere and others, inhabitants of ye Paltz for "a reasonable quantity of the resumed land formerly granted to Capt. John Evans. 1200 acres granted and surveyed May 3rd, 1714. Adjoining New Paltz.

1709—May 11—Petition of Peter Matthews and others for 2000 acres of the Evans Patent, lying near the New Paltz, about twenty miles backward in the woods from Hudson's River, upon or near Paltz Creek." A part of this tract was owned by Jacobus Bruin in 1744, and described, "called the Gerbrande Vly, or the Burned Meadows." Burned over to clear it of bushes and coarse grass.

1709—May 11—Petition of Evart Derwillighe of Shawangunk, for 400 acres of the Evans Patent.

1709—Feb. 29—Petition of Augustine Graham, surveyor, and Alex. Griggs, for 1200 acres of the Evans Patent, "at ye Old Man's Creek," now in Marlborough.

1709—March 4—Anne of Greatt Brittaine, France and Ireland, Queene defender of the Ffaith, to William Peartree, Rip Van Dam, Adolph Phillipse, Geradus Beekman, Hendrick Vernooye, Abraham Dilijoe, Teunis Jacobson Klaarwater and Jacob Klaarwater, grant by patent of a certaine parcell of land situate on the west side of Hudson's River, and beginning at the southeast corner of a small island lying in the Paltz Creeke, and on the southwest side of the land granted to Capt. Mathews and Company, and is in breadth on the Paltz River on a straight line one hundred and eighty-six chains, and runs by the line of Capt. Peter Mathews and Company two hundred and two chains west twenty-four degrees north and on the south side of the said land at the termination of one hundred and eightysix chains it runs west twenty-four degrees north two hundred and fifty-seven chains containing four thousand acres.

1710—March 2—Petition of Peter Barbarie for 2000 acres of the Evans Patent, "lying on the southeast side of Paltz Creek."

1710—March 7—Petition of John Barbarie for 2000 acres of the Evans Patent, "beginning on the west side of Hudson's River at the south bounds of the Paltz

Patent, running along the Hudson in a straight line southerly one hundred chains," southerly from Juffrouw's Hook in Marlborough.

1710—March 7—Petition of Gerardus Beekman and others for 3000 acres of the Evans Patent adjoining the lands of William Peartree and Company, in town of Shawangunk.

1710—March 24—Petition of Obadiah Hunt and others for 2500 acres of the Evans Patent, "beginning at a small brook called Tent Brook, and extends along the said brook to the Paltz River, sixty chains on each side." In Plattekill.

1710—March 24—Petition of John Thomas for 2500 acres of the Evans Patent.

1710—March 24—Petition of William Provost for 2500 acres of the Evans Patent.

1710—March 24—Petition of Dirck Benson for 1000 acres of the Evans Patent.

1710—March 24—Petition of Abraham de Peyster for 8000 acres of the Evans Patent.

1711—March 29—Warrant for a patent to Mindert Scutt for 300 acres at Sawyer's Creek.

1712—May 3—Warrant to Wm. Bond for 600 acres of the Evans land "adjoining John Barbarie's on Hudson's River." In Marlborough.

1712—May 30—Petition of John McLean and Richard Winfield praying patents for their lands in Ulster County, being part of the tract formerly granted to Capt. John Evans. In Shawangunk.

The land at Guilford, "by the Indians called Nescotsck," was known for many years as "Guilford Church." The actual location of the Indian name is claimed for a village now known as Libertyville, which was long known as Nescotack. The name describes a hill or ridge. The hill runs north from Lloyd's tract called Shawangunk.

1712—June 6—Petition of Hugo Frere and others for 2000 acres of the Evans tract, "near adjoining to the Paltz River at a place called the Platte Kill, six miles west of Hudson's River, on both sides of the Platte Kill. Surveyed May 3, 1714.

1712—June 25—Petition of Jacob Ruttsen of Ulster County, for 2000 acres "near the land of which he is already possessed," i. e. near Guilford. Surveyed June 12, 1712.

1712—June 5—Petition of John Ruttsen and Jacob Bruin of Ulster County, on behalf of themselves and Company, for 3000 acres of the Evans tract, "contiguous to their improved lands." Surveyed June 13, 1712. In Shawangunk.

1713—June 11—Petition of Solomon du Bois and Lewis du Bois, "of ye county of Ulster" for 2000 acres of the Evans Patent near New Paltz.

1714—Aug. 20—Warrant to the Surveyor general to lay out for Lewis Morris and others, 5000 acres of the Evans tract, "lying on both sides of Old Man's Creek, near Hudson's River." In Marlborough

1714—Aug. 19—Warrant of survey for 1500 acres of the Evans tract, granted to Robert Milward, "pursuant to a grant from Governor Ingolsby." On north side of land of Francis Harrison & Co. Now in Marlborough.

1715—May 30—Grant of 300 acres to John Macklain, "lying on the north side of Shawangunk Creek, bounded on the southwest by the land of Severeigne Tenhout, south by the creek aforesaid, east by a small run which flows into Shawangunk Creek, and northwest by land not yet laid out.

Here, at the lands not yet laid out, a region of many acres, the enumeration of patents may be suspended, and later grants remanded to the history of the Towns in which they came to be included, a sufficient number having been quoted from which to trace the evolution of the county and the persons by whom that evolution was wrought in the pioneer era along the lines of the Groot Esopus, the Esopus and the Wallkill, and from Wanton Island to the Dans Kamer on the Hudson, and from the Dans Kamer west to the Blue Hills, and south to Pachanassink, where Sam's Point lifts its wall of rock. The enumeration is panoramic. As it passes it presents the location of the homes of the pioneers, in some cases the precise location of their dwellings, as well as chronologically the flow of the tide of immigration. A more democratic policy than that which was pursued in the early stages of settlement of apportioning lands in homestead parcels to actual residents is not met in pioneer history. In some few cases the parties to whom the homestead grants were issued did not remain in their occupation, death came to them from exposures and privations and from the tomahawk and scalping knife, but as a whole the homesteads became permanent and were cherished for generations — homes and graves in the wilderness, what more deserving of monumental remembrance? Large patents, especially of later eras, were taken up by non-residents, as well as by prosperous residents for speculative purposes; land was cheap; a few shillings annual rent gave many acres to be sold for a price. To the record of names given in the early grants, others can be gathered from military rolls, road lists, church records, etc., and as an incident of the "Leisler Rebellion." A list of residents of the country who subscribed to the oath of allegiance to Prince William and Mary, in 1689, may be found in available documentary histories, most of the orthographies requiring expert reading. The majority and a large majority, of the people of Ulster were undoubtedly favorably disposed to the success of the Prince of Orange and when Leisler requested it, 190 promptly took the oath of allegiance; four refused to do so, and thirty absented themselves. Presumably the list does not represent all the male inhabitants of the county, but the general temper of the people was in that direction. A much more satisfactory list of inhabitants is to be found in the original tax roll of the county in 1715.

Zadoc P. Boice.

CHAPTER IV.

EARLY FREEHOLDERS AND INHABITANTS.

THE freeholders, inhabitants, residents and sojourners in County of Ulster, theire Reale & Personal Estates are Rated as Assessed by the Assessors (on their oath) chosen for the same on the 20th day of January 171 4/5, and are to-
the rate of one penny half Pr L, to discharge this..................
of said County's quota, Layd by an Act of Assembly Intitled an Act for Levying the sume of Ten thousand pounds, viz:

CORPORATION OF KINGSTON.

John Wood
Nicolaas Dermeyer
Jan Oosterhout
Howd Alberse Pleogh
Pieter Oosterhout
Hellena Burhans
Susana Legg
John Legg
Joh's Traphagen
Willen Traphagen
James Whittaker
Edward Whitaker
Jan Mattyson
Egbert Schoonmaker
Gurtray Schoonmaker
Evert Wynkoop
Collo Henrieus Beekman
Phillyp Hoogtylingh
Samuel Hooghtyling
Dina Hooghtyling, alias Fysen
Willem Hooghtylingh
Kesia Hooghtylingh
Jacomyntie Stynhout
Estate of Grelie Elmendorf, dec'd
Dirck Schepmoes
Teunis Ellisten
Gerritt Aartsen
Elizabeth Masten
House of M Anthony
Gysbert Vandenbergh
Jan f- Heermans
Evert Bogardus
Estate of Wyntie Bogardus, deced.
Major Joh'o Hardenbergh
Petrus Bogardus
Anthony Slecht
Theunis Swart
Barent Van Wagenin
Phillyp Vielle
Dowd Nucella
Humphry Davenport
Kryn Oosterhout
Nicholas Hofman
Hillegonda Van Slichtenhorst
Arien Van Vliet
Cornelis Vernooy, Jun.
Mattys Pearce
——es De Graaf
———— Baptista Du Mont
—hn Davenport
Bastian De Witt
Henricus Heermans
Stephanus Gacherie
Willem Eltinge
Roelogg Eltinge
Keeper the Negro
Mattys Mattysen Jun.
Aardt Van Wagenin
Cornelis Louis
Cornelis De La Matter
Claas Schoonhoven
John Pearce
Jean Frere
——rick Kip

CORPORATION OF KINGSTON.—*Continued.*

—enncke Lagransie
Tjirck Mattysen
Teunis Tappen
—ter Tappen
Thomas Van Steenbergen
Abraham De La Metter
—llart Kiersteden
—thony Dilpha
——— Du Mont
—erand Du Mont
Mattys Mattisen, L. D.
Estate of Tjirck DeWitt, deced.
——— Van Aken
———mertie Winne
———n Cottin
——h's Tenbroeck
—col Tenbroeck
—arent Burhans
Major Joh's Wynkoop
Doctor Hans Kiersteden
A— metie Hoogenboom
Matthys Slecht
Dirck Valck
Thomas Hoxon
Jan La Chaire
Samuel Bayard
Amerentie Hofman
Pieter —ambornnsel
Barent Nieuwkerk
Bruyn Bresser
Gusie Peer
John Viello
Barent Van Benthuisen
Annavan Vliet
Cornelis Swart
Moses Contain
Pieter Pielle
Hendrick Pruyn
Evert Bogardus
Hendrick Traphagen
Elsie Smedes
Ffredrick Clute
Mattys Jansen
Omie Lagransie
Jan Past
Pieter Dubois
Teunis Pier
Dowd Ffreeman
Mattys Dubois
Coenraate Elmendorf
Mattys Van Steenbergen
Major Dirck Wessellis

——sen van Eagenin
Jacob Cool
Jan Pleogh
Willem Schepmoes
Jan Degraaf
Johannes Turck
—arbara Wynkoop
—hanns Louw
—ndries Heermans
——— Crook
—hannis Burhans
Gysbert Pielle
—achel Bogardus
Christopher Tappen
Manuel Gunsalis Duck
Autie Van Bunschooten
Arien Neimskorck
Thomas Beekman
Hendrick Jansen
Jacobus Dubois
Arent Stynhout
Jno Rutsen
Thomas Pearce
Arien Hendrickse
Thomas Mattysen
Tobias Van Beuren
Allart Ariense Roosa
Evert Roosa
House of Wessel Tenbroecks heirs
Tjerck Dewitt
Nathaniel Davenport
William Harris
Ragel Pleogh
Geesie Winne
Henricus Beekman Jun.
Willem Burhans
John Fortune
John Chambers
Estate of Collo Wm. De Myer, deced.
John Pawling
Cornelis Lange Dyck
Benjamin De Mes
Jacob Loun
Ephraim Bogardus
Henekel Rou
Valentyn Bender
Henrich Beam
Kahaneman De Wever
Chrystofel Moul
Johan Klyn
Johan Willem Snyder
Hermanus De hoogduytser

	Assessment.	Tax.
Total sume	L.9176,	L. 57—7—0.

MANNOR OF FOXHALL.

	Assessment.	Tax.
Collo Abraham Gaasbeen Chambers	L.900	L 5—12—6
Capt Wessel Tenbroeck	330	2— 2—3
Francis Salisbury	80	00—10—0
Pieter Ploegh	12	00— 1—6
Total sume	L1322	08—05—3

TOWN OF HURLEY.

	Assessment.	Tax.
Cornelius Lambertsen	L200	L1— 5— 0
William West	140	00—17— 6
Albert and Nicholas Roosa	175	1—11—10
Pieter Oostrander Sen.	85	00—10—17
Andries Bratt	15	00— 2—10
Arma Vanetten	200	1— 5— 0
Marya Roosa	150	00—18— 0
Mattys Ten Eyck	280	1—15— 0
Arian Gerrittsen	655	4— 1—10
Jan Roosa Sen.	125	00—15— 7½
Junne he Niewkerck	130	00—16— 3
Roeloff Swartwout	170	1— 1— 3
Cornelly Cool	952	5—19—00
Charley Wilei	50	00— 6— 3
Jacob Dubois	260	1—12— 6
Egbert Gerritsen	15	00— 1—10
Huybert Suyland	40	00— 5—00
Johannis Schepmoes	225	1— 8— 1½
Jan Crespel	85	00—10— 7½
Willem Van Vredenburgh	15	00— 1—10
Heirs of Griete DeHooges	8	00— 1—00
Barnardus Swartwout	30	00— 3— 9

	Assessment.	Tax.
Pieter Oostrander Jun.	L20	00— 2—06
Pieter Van Etten	35	00— 4— 4½
children of Pieter Crispel	40	00— 5—00
Dirck De Duytser	40	00— 5—00
Jacobus Van Etten	25	00— 3— 1
Willem Roosa	10	00— 1— 3
Arien Roosa	20	00— 3— 9
Allart Janse Roosa	25	00— 3— 1½
Gerritt Neiuekerk	70	00— 8— 9
Jacobus Elmendorf	36	00— 4— 4½
Cornelius Wynkoop	30	00— 3— 9
Arent Oostrander	15	00— 1—10½
Jan Roosa Jun.	8	00— 1—00
Jan Terwillige	10	00— 1— 3
Jacobus Terwillige	5	00—00— 7½
Lowrens Cortreght	5	00—00 —7½
Lambert Cool	10	00— 1— 3
Totall Sume	L4398	27 9 d9

TOWNE OF MARBLETOWNE.

	Assessment.	Tax.
Collo. Jacob Rutsen	1020	6— 7— 6
Major Jacob Aartsen	290	1—16— 3
Mattys Blanchan	310	1—18— 9
Wm. Nottingham	140	00—17— 0
Jno. Beatty	60	00— 7— 6
Jno. Joosten of Raretans	110	00—13— 9
Cornelis Eltinge	160	1—00—00
Mrs. N. Pawling	200	1— 5—00
Gysbert Krom	150	00—18— 9
Richard Brodhead	155	00—19— 4
Peter Van Luven	100	00—12— 6
Engeltie Mourits	80	00—10—00
Pieter Mourits	25	00— 3— 1⊥
Heirs to Jno. Bigges	15	00—11—10
Cornelis Flack	25	00—00— 7½
Joris Middagh	125	00—15— 7⊥
Widow Keetell	5	00—00— 1
Huybert Lambertse	70	00— 8— 9
Thomas Vandermarke	60	00— 7— 6
Charles Broadhead	185	1— 3— 1⊥
Nicolaas Sluyter	2	00—00— 3
Hendrick Clasen	65	00—00— 1-'
Thomas Cock	65	00— 8— 1⊥
Catherine Ashfordbie	35	00— 4— 4⊥
Thomas Garton	390	2— 8— 9
John Cock	125	00—15— 7⊥
Jannetie Davies	25	00— 3— 1⊥
Cornelia Ennis	10	00— 1— 4
Jeremiah Keetell	15	00— 1—10
Hendrick Boss	3	00—00— 4⊥
Claas Keator	15	00— 1—10⊥
Arie Vandermarke	20	00— 2— 6
Jacob Vandermarke	15	00— 1—10⊥
Frederick Vandermarke	5	00—00— 7⊥
Augustinno Vandermarke	5	00—00— 7⊥
Thomas Jansen	45	00— 5— 7⊥
Jacob Keyser	5	00—00— 7⊥
Jan Van Campen Sen.	140	00—17— 6
Nicolaas Dapuis	110	00—13— 9
Gysbert Roosa	30	00— 3— 9
Hendrick Bogart	380	2— 7— 6
Jno. Brigges	15	00— 1—10⊥
Cornelis Keyser	6	00—00— 0
Jacobus Boss	5	00—00— 7⊥
Johannis Cool	10	00— 1— 3
Nicholas Blanchan	15	00— 1— 9
Jannetie De Witt	190	1— 3— 9
James Robinsone	8	00— 1—00
Johannis Van Luven	5	00—00— 7⊥
Lambert Dolderbrinck	50	00— 6— 3
Marten Bogart	8	00— 1—00
Henricus Krom	5	00—00— 7⊥
Roeloft Dolderbrinck	5	00—00— 7⊥
Henry Pawling	15	LL— 1—10⊥

TOWNE OF MARBLETOWNE.—*Continued.*

	Assessment.	Tax.
Hartman Heyn	5	00—00— 7½
Jurian Best	5	00—00— 7½
Johannis Tack	5	00—00— 7½
Totall Sume	L5142	L22 s 2 d 9

TOWN OF ROCHESTER.

Dirck Krom	15	00— 1—10½
Cornelis Vernooy Sen.	410	2—11— 3
Teunis Oosterhout	125	00—15— 7½
David Du bois	85	00—10— 7½
Geertruy Van Cortland	45	00— 5— 7½
Pieter Lambertsen	110	00—13— 9
Moses Dupuis	450	2—15— 3
Marynus Van Aken	60	00— 7— 6
Jochem Shoonmaker	285	1—15— 7½
Gerrit Decker	105	00—13— 1½
Gysert Van Garden	20	00— 3— 9
Jan Van Vliet	15	00— 1—10½
Hendrick Jansen Cortrecht	55	00— 6—10½
Grietie Hoornbeck	25	00— 3— 1½
Lodewyck Hoornbeck	80	00—10—00
Cornelis Switts	220	1— 7— 6
Cornelis De Duyser	25	00— 1—10
Magdalena Rosenkrans	110	00—13— 9
Dirck Rosenkrans	130	00—16— 3
Jacob De Witt	150	00—18— 9
Simon Westphaalen	20	00— 2— 6
Harmanus Decker	60	00— 7— 6
Hendrick Rosenkrans	40	00— 5—00
Jan Cort Recht	20	00— 2— 6
Cornelis Cortrecht	55	00— 6—10
Jan Van Etten	30	00— 3— 9
Leendert Cool Sen.	150	00—18— 9
Barent Harmense	3	00—00— 4½
Johannes Westbroeck	35	00— 4— 4½
Pieter Louw	40	00— 5—00
Dirck Westbroeck	30	00— 3— 9
Allexander Rosenkrance	60	00— 7— 6
Andries Van Luven	15	00— 1—10½
Jurian Quick	120	00—15—00
Albert Van Garden	5	00—00— 7½
Cornelius Schoonmaker	30	00— 3— 9
Harmanus Cool	15	00— 1—10½
Johannis Vernooy	40	00— 5—00
Jean Beveire	15	00— 1—10
Abraham Beviere	20	00— 2— 6
Samuell Beviere	10	00— 1— 3
Jacob Vernooy	55	00— 6—10½
Wm. Cool	10	00— 1— 3
Johannis Hoornbeck	5	00—00— 7½
Jacobus Wynkoop	15	00— 1—10½
Thomas Quick	10	00— 1— 3
Willem Decker	5	00—00— 7½
Frederick Shoonmaker	10	00— 1— 3

TOWN OF ROCHESTER.—*Continued.*	Assessment.	Tax.
Jan Van Campen Jun.	15	00— 1—10½
Jan Gerritsen Decker Jun.	10	00— 1— 3
Cornelius Dupuis	10	00— 1— 3
Pieter Van Garden	5	00—00— 7½
Mattys Louw	15	00— 1— 7½
Anthony Westbroeck	5	00—00— 7½
Cornelis Van Aken	5	00—00— 7½
Sara Rosenkrans	15	00— 1—10½
Totall Sume	3523	L22 00 4½

TOWN OF NEW PALLES.

Name	Assessment	Tax
Abraham Doyo	L 55	L10—s6—d10½
Christian Doyo	50	00— 6— 3
Peter Doyo	35	00— 4— 4½
Henry Doyo	50	00— 6— 3
Abraham Hasbrouck	230	1— 8— 9
Louis Bevier	350	2— 3— 9
Jacob Hasbrouck	150	00— 8— 9
Mary Du bois	165	1—00— 7½
Abraham Du bois	280	1—15— 00
Arien Le fevre & Comp.	250	1—11— 3
Hugo Frere	90	00—11— 3
Abraham Frere	90	00— 3— 1½
Jacob Frere	25	00— 3— 1½
Elias Uim	35	00— 4— 4½
Solomon Du Bois	100	00—12— 6
Louis Du bois	80	00—10— 00
Joseph Hasbrouck	35	00— 4— 4
Hendrick Van Weye	15	00— 1— 10½
Jacob Claarwater	10	00— 1— 3
Jan Teerpenningh	5	00—00— 7½
Louis Bevier	20	00— 2— 6
Teunis Claarwater Jun.	5	00—00— 7½
Hart Claarwater	5	00—00— 7½
Hendrik Jochense Schoonmaker	10	00— 1— 3
Totall Sume	L2075	L12 s19 d4½

PRECINCTS OF SHAWANGONCK.

Name	Assessment	Tax
Severyn Ten hout	L240	L1—s10—d00
Zacharias Hofman	130	00— 16— 3
Jacobus Bruyn	120	00— 15— 00
Benjamin Smedes	150	00— 18— 9
John Macklaine	5	00— 00— 7½
Richard Winfield	5	00— 00— 7½
Jacob Decker Sen.	15	00— 1— 10½
Abraham Schutt	35	00— 4— 4½
Jacob Gerretsen Decker	50	00— 6— 3
Evert Terwillige	60	00— 7— 6
Leendert Coal Jun.	10	00— 1— 3
Collo. Peter Matthews & Comp.	15	00— 1— 10½
Johannes Terwillige	3	00— 00— 4½
Phillip Miller		1— 1— 3
Totall Sume	L848	L5 s 6 00

Henry A. Reynolds

A. W. Reynolds

NEIGHBORHOOD OF WACKEMECK.

	Assessment.	Tax.
Thomas Swartwout	L25	Loo..s3..d1½
Harmen Barentsen	15	00— 1—10½
Jacob Coddeberg	10	00— 1— 3
Peter Guymard	50	00— 6— 3
Jacobus Swartwout	5	00—00— 7½
Totall Sume	L 105	L 00 s13 d 1½

PRECINCT OF THE HIGHLANDS.

Peter Magregory	L 30	L 00—s3—d9
Swerver	5	00—00— 7½
William Southerland	45	00— 5— 7½
Michael Wygant	15	00— 1—10½
Burger Myndertsen	10	00— 1— 3
Jacob Weber	15	00— 1—10½
Peter La Ross	10	00— 1— 3
John fisher	10	00— 1— 3
Andrew Volck	12	00— 1— 6
George Lockste .	10	00— 1— 3
Pieter Jansen	10	00— 1— 3
Henry Rennau	25	00— 3— 1½
William Elsworth's widow	5	00—00— 7½
Dennis Relje	3	00—00— 4½
Thomas Harris	5	00—00— 4½
Capt. Bond	15	00— 1—10½
Melgert the Joyner	13	00— 1—10½
Christian Henneke	3	00—00—14½
Jacob Decker Jun.	10	00—10— 3
Cornelis Decker	5	00—00— 7½
	L293	L1 s16 d7½

	Assemt.	
Kingston	L9176	L7—s7—doo
foxhall	1322	8— 5— 3
Hurley	4398	27— 9— 9
Marbletown	5142	32— 2— 9
Rochester	3523	22—00— 4½
Showongonck	848	5— 6— 00
Wagachkemeck	105	0—13— 1½
High-lands	293	1—16— 7½
Totall Sume	L 26882	L168 00 3

(Signatures)

Henr Beekman
Avidn Yornlaeu
A. Gaasbeek Chambers
Egbert Schoonmaker
Cornelis Cool
Mattys Jansen

(Endorsed.) "Kings tax—
1715.
Justices signed.

Peek de Witt L 25)
) Assessors.

Jean frere L 25)
Mattys Van Keuren) Assessor.

Note—The Precinct of the Highlands then embraced the territory lying between the mouth of Murderers' Creek and the southeast line of the Paltz Patent, west to the Precinct of Shawangunk. It covered the present towns of Newburgh, New Windsor, Montgomery and Crawford in Orange County, and Marlborough and Plattekill in Ulster.

CHAPTER V.

CIVIL ORGANIZATIONS AND DIVISIONS.

PRIMARILY the settlement in the Esopus country was without local government other than that which was conferred by the general laws and customs of Holland; it was simply a dependency of Fort Orange (Albany). Brought to the special attention of Director Stuyvesant by the difficulties with the Indians in what is known as the war of 1660, and the enclosure of the village of Wildwijk, he appointed (May 5th, 1661), what he called "A small bench of Justices as commissaries," consisting of Evert Pels, Cornelius Barentsen Slecht and Albert Heymse Roosa to "administer good care and justice" according to the best of their knowledge; "prevent all mutiny, strife and disorder, and assist in preventing them; "maintain and exercise the Reformed Church service, and no other," and "do everything which good and faithful magistrates are bound to do."* The directors of the West India Company, Department at Amsterdam, had recommended to him (April 15, 1660), the appointment of Roeloff Swartwout as Schout (Sheriff) at Wildwijk, but Stuyvesant held that appointment in abeyance until May 11th, 1661, when by formal charter or patent he decreed that the "place called Esopus" should be given a more extended municipal form of government, by the addition of a Schout (Sheriff) who should with the justices (Shepens) form a Board of Magistrates over which the Schout should preside, to which was given the title of "The Court at Wildwijk," and which should hold its sessions at Wildwijk every fortnight — harvest time excepted. The organization of the Court was completed May 23d by the appointment of Roeloff Swartwout as Schout.* It was the third of the similar charters issued in the Province—Fort Amsterdam (New York) being first, and Fort Orange (Albany) second. At the same time Stuyvesant appointed Thomas Chambers captain of the

* Cornelis Barentsen Slecht was an immigrant of 1661; Albert Heymes (or Heymanes) Roosa, an immigrant of 1660, and Evert Pels of 1642. Roosa located first at Fort Orange, from whence he removed to Esopus in 1654. He assumed the name of Roose (now Roosa). Swartwout came from Holland for the second time in April, 1660.

militia; Hendrick Jochem Schoonmaker,* lieutenant, and Roeloff Swartwout, Hendrick Jansen, Cornelius Barentsen Slecht and Peter Jacobsen, minor officers. Thereafter the village of Wildwijk and the Esopus country became a dependency of Fort Amsterdam, and directly under the charge of the Director-general. So far as is known the Board of Magistrates, and the militia organization were in full power under the charter on June 7th, 1663, when the settlements were surprised by the Indians. The first meeting of the Board or Court was held July 12, 1661.

The civil government conferred by Director Stuyvesant continued for only a few years; substantially it was only the beginning. The English captured Fort Amsterdam Aug. 27th, 1664, and successively all the principal towns were surrendered. No immediate change in civil government at Esopus followed, English laws not being introduced until June 12, 1673. The Duke of York, into whose hands the Province had fallen, deemed it wise to permit the Dutch settlements to grow into the new order of things. Even under the Dutch had Wildwijk been asked to send representatives to a convention at New Amsterdam. That was in April, 1664, when Thomas Chambers and Dr. Gysbert Van Imbrocht went there for the purpose of considering a proposition to send a delegate to Holland to lay before the States General and the West India Company the condition of affairs. The first change that came about was the appointment by the English Governor Nicolls, in 1665, of Daniel Brodhead as Sheriff, vice Roeloff Swartwout, and the adding to the Sheriff's duties those of chief officer of the militia, Captain Chambers being continued in a subordinate relation. Swartwout was not a very superior man. Brodhead was a captain in the regular service of England; his effort to "boss" the Dutch at Esopus was not regarded with special favor to say the least. He died at Esopus in 1669.

In September, 1669, after making personal inspection of affairs at Esopus, Governor Lovelace, the successor of Governor Nicolls, directed the dismissal of the garrison at Rondout, and the granting to the disbanded soldiers of lands on which to establish homes, and appointed a commission, consisting of Ralph Whitfield as President, and Captain John Manning, Captain Jaques Cortelyou, Captain Thomas Chambers,

* Schoonmaker was a native of Hamburg, Germany. He came to this country in the military service of the West India Company, about 1654, and was stationed at Esopus with his company in 1660, and settled there on the expiration of his term of enlistment. He died about 1681. His descendants are still numerous in Ulster County, and are widely scattered over the country.

William Beeckman, Schout, Henry Pawling, and Christopher Berrisford, to regulate affairs at Wildwijk, and Nieuw Dorp. The action of this commission has been stated in part in connection with the change in the name of Wildwijk to Kingston, and of Nieuw Dorp to Hurley, and the organization of the new town of Marbletown. In addition, the commission abrogated the laws and customs of Holland, and proclaimed the "Duke's Laws" which had been promulgated at Hempstead, L. I., March 1, 1665, by Governor Nicolls. In general terms this code was very good, and remained, with some amendments, as the laws of the Province of New York until the rebellion of 1776, and the adoption of the State Constitution of 1777. As the code required the placing of towns under the care of commissioners, Christopher Beresford was appointed Chief Magistrate of Hurley and Marbletown; Henry Pawling officer over the Indians; Louis du Bois and Albert Heymans, overseers of Hurley; John Biggs and Frederick Hussey, overseers of Marbletown, and Thomas Chambers and William Beeckman overseers for Kingston. Justices of the Peace appointed by the Governor and continuing during his pleasure, and constables to execute public whippings, apprehend thieves and drunken men, vagrants, Sabbath breakers, and other offenders, make up assessment rolls for confirmation by the overseers, and do a great many other things for the promotion of good order and good government were introduced and continued after the inchoate towns had been organized under trustees. Beresford, who was appointed Chief Magistrate of Hurley and Marbletown, was ranked by the commissioners as "above a High Constable and short of a Justice of the Peace."

The proceedings of the commissioners as stated of record are of no little interest to students of the civil history of the county. Order was brought out of the chaos which had grown out of the conditions under which the settlements had been laboring; a military system established; provision made for the opening and repair of roads, and English laws and customs introduced though not fully proclaimed until 1673. The Chief Magistrates were required to give speedy decision in all cases coming before them, "not regarding parties but ye merritt of ye cause"; to see that the overseers of the towns performed their duties; to preserve the peace as much as possible between individuals; to remove all obstructions from trade or correspondence with the Indians, and permission given to freely debate anything that might conduce to the advantage of the public. The towns were given up to the newly constituted authorities April 11th, 1669.

Under "An Act to divide this Province into Shires and Countyes," passed by the Governor and his Council, November 1, 1683, the County of Ulster came into being in the terms of the act described, "the County of Ulster to contayn the towns of Kingston, Hurley and Marbletowne, Fox Hall and the New Paltz, and all the villages, neighborhoods, and Christian habitacions on the west side of Hudson's River from the Murderers Creeke neare the high lands to the Sawyers Creeke." There may have been at that date (1683) settlements and habitations north of New Paltz and west of Marbletown, but further than is shown in the list of patents they are not of record. South of the south line of the New Paltz patent the only one known of about that time was that of Captain Patrick MacGregorie at the mouth of Murderers' Creek. Substantially the district was *Ghittatawagh,* the Great Wilderness.

The prior organization of the towns included in the county is sufficiently stated in the list of patents in a previous chapter. In 1684-5, as has been stated, Governor Dongan purchased from the Indians the lands lying south of the line of the New Paltz Patent, including the lands of the Murderers' Creek Indians and as far south as Haverstraw. In 1694 the entire district was covered by patent granted by Governor Lovelace to Captain John Evans. In 1698 the Assembly abrogated this grant, but as the act required the approval of the Queen, which was not given until 1709, the district was not opened for settlement at an earlier date. On the approval of the act by the Queen came into being the settlement at the mouth of Quassaick Creek, a few miles north of the mouth of Murderers' Creek, the south bound of the county, by a company of immigrants from the Palatinate of the Rhine, and the establishment by order of the Court, of *the Precinct of the Highlands,* with territory extending from Murderers' Creek to the New Paltz line at Juffrouw's Hook on the Hudson, and west to the Shawangunk range of hills, a dependency of New Paltz to which it was attached for government. About the same time, and by similar order *the Precinct of Shawangunk* was created and attached to New Paltz. From the Precinct of the Highlands was evolved the precincts of New Windsor, Newburgh, Marlborough, Hanover and Wallkill now including the towns and cities of Newburgh, New Windsor, Crawford, Wallkill, Middletown, Marlborough and Plattekill, the two last

Jacob Rice.

named now in the county of Ulster, the others now in Orange, the whole forming a group of settlements that gave honor in the sons to Ulster County for nearly a century, and whose connection with the parent stem in the colonial and revolutionary eras cannot be eliminated by boundary lines or passing notice. As well eliminate the name of Washington of Virginia from the history of the nation, as that of George Clinton of New Windsor from the history of Ulster County.

The act of the Legislature passed April 3d, 1801, gave the bounds of the county as south by the north bounds of the county of Orange, easterly by the middle of Hudson's River, west by the Delaware River at the most southerly corner of lot number twenty-eight in the sub-division of great lot number two in the Hardenbergh patent; north, sixty-two degrees east, to the southwesterly bounds of great lot number eight in said patent, east to the north end of Schoon Lake (now in the town of Woodstock), continuing east along the northwest line of the town of Kingston to Hudson's River; thence due east to the middle of said river, the land limit now forming the northeast corner of the town of Saugerties. The south line of the county has not been changed since 1798. The line—the north line of Orange County—was very irregular from its bounds on the north by the lines of certain patents. Very few know precisely its point of beginning on Hudson's River, and fewer still could possibly trace it its entire length. The description of it in the act reads: "From a point in the middle of Hudson's River, opposite the northeast corner of a tract of land granted to Francis Harrison and Company (now the northeast corner of the town of Newburgh); thence westerly along the north bounds of said tract and the north bounds of another tract granted to the said Francis Harrison to the tract of land commonly called Wallace's tract, then along the same northerly and westerly to the northeasterly bounds of a tract of land granted to Jacobus Kip, John Cruger and others, then westerly along the northeasterly and northerly bounds thereof to the northwest corner thereof, and then westerly to the northeast corner of a tract granted to Rip van Dam and others, thence southerly along the same to the northeast corner of a tract granted to Henry Wileman, thence along the north bounds thereof to Paltz River, then southerly up the said river to the southeast corner of a tract granted to Gerardus Beekman and others, then westerly and northerly along the southerly and westerly bounds thereof to the northeast corner thereof, then northwesterly and westerly along the north bounds of the land granted to Jeremiah Schuyler and Company to the Shawangunk Kill, thence southerly along said Kill to the north part of the farm now or late in the occupation of Joseph Wood, junior, thence west to the river Mongaap." Though now not easily traced, there is a volume of local history along that old boundary line. By the erection of Sullivan County in 1809, the Mongaap River is now the boundary between Sullivan and Orange counties. It has a beautiful Dutch name, primarily the name of the mouth of the stream.

The act of 1801, defining the bounds of the county also defined the limits of the several towns which were included in those bounds, viz: Marlborough, Plattekill, Shawangunk, Kingston, Marbletown, New Paltz, Woodstock, Mamakating, Neversink, Lumberland and Rochester. From the original county (1798) had then been taken part of Orange County, part of Delaware County (1797), and the towns of Mamakating, Neversink and Lumberland went off into Sullivan County, November 27, 1809. As now constituted the county is divided in the town and city of Kingston, the towns of Denning, Esopus, Gardiner, Hardenbergh, Hurley, Lloyd, Marbletown, Marlborough, New Paltz, Olive, Plattekill, Rochester, Rosendale, Saugerties, Shandaken, Shawangunk, Wawarsing, and Woodstock—18.

By the general law of 1683, the judicial arrangement of 1669, was changed by the organization of four distinct Courts, viz: Town Courts for the trial of small causes, to be held each month; County Courts, or Courts of Sessions, to be held at certain times, quarterly or half yearly; Courts of Oyer and Terminer, with original and appellate jurisdiction, to sit twice in every year in each county, and a Court of Chancery, to be the "Supreme Court of the Province," composed of the Governor and Council, with power in the Governor to depute a Chancellor in his stead, and appoint clerks and other officers. The Court of Oyer and Terminer replaced more particularly the Court of Assizes as known under Dutch laws. This system continued until 1691, when courts of Justices of the Peace were organized in every town, and one of Common Pleas in every county. Of the first Court of Common Pleas of Ulster County, Thomas Garton was appointed Judge, February 27, 1692. He seems to have been a resident of Marbletown, as he was one of the signers of the petition for a patent for that town in 1703. Of early date (1677) John Garton of Marbletown, asked permission to build a house on his lot there.

Some changes necessarily followed in the classification of the duties of Sheriffs and of Constables. Every county had its High Sheriff and every town its High Constable. A recapitulation of those changes is not necessary. The first Sheriff of record after the organization of the county was William Ashfordby, who, like Judge Garton, appears in the record of patents. In the matter of granting probates of wills, the law of Nov. 11, 1692, directed that all probates and letters of administration should thenceforth be granted by the Governor or his delegate, and that two freeholders should be elected or appointed in each town to have charge of the estates of intestates, which duty had been performed by the Constables, Overseers, and Justices. All wills relating to estates in New York, Orange, Richmond, Westchester, and Kings, were to be proved in New York; in more remote counties, the Court of Common Pleas was authorized to take the proof and transmit the papers to the record office for probate. Subsequently, under the law of 1750, Surrogates with limited powers were appointed. Of Surrogates the first appointee of record was John Elting, of the early New Paltz stock of Eltings, March 14th, 1760.

In 1701, the General Assembly, by act of October 18, provided that the Justices of the Peace of the several counties, "or any five or more of them, two to be a quorum," should, once in each year, at a court of general or special sessions, "supervise, examine and allow the public and necessary charge of their respective county, and of every town thereof," including the "allowance made by law to their representative or representatives," *i. e.*, in the General Assembly who drew their pay from the counties. For the assessment and collection of the accounts allowed by them they were "empowered to issue their warrant to the several towns for the election of two assessors and one collector in each town." The act further provided that the "Justices at the representative general sessions," should, "once in the year, make provision for maintenance and support of the poor" in their several towns or precincts.

This law continued in force until June, 1703, when it was enacted that there should be "elected and chosen, once every year, in each town, by the freeholders and inhabitants thereof, one of their freeholders and inhabitants to compute, ascertain, examine, oversee and allow the contingent public and necessary charge of each county, and that each and every inhabitant, being a freeholder in any manor, liberty, jurisdiction, precinct, and out-plantation" should "have liberty to join his or her vote with the next adjacent town in the county, where such inhabitants shall dwell, for the choice of a supervisor." The law further authorized the election in each town or precinct of "two assessors and one collector." In general terms, the law constituted what is now, with some modifications, the present Board of Supervisors. It was a more democratic law than that which now prevails, in this, that it provided for minority representation, and gave to females the right to vote as the representatives of property. The noble old principle of "no taxation without representation" was firmly intrenched in the hearts of the Dutch.

Representation in the General Assembly did not come to the county under its organization in 1683. The Duke of York, bound hand and foot to the prerogatives of royalty, would only permit a council of advisors to the person whom he should appoint as Deputy Governor. His determination was not satisfactory. In 1669, the taxation of the people was decreed to pay the expense of repairing the palisades of Fort James (Fort Amsterdam) at New York. Several towns on Long Island refused to respond, substantially because under the British Constitution no taxes could be levied on them except by their own Representatives. The temporary reoccupancy of the Province by the Dutch, in 1673, carried the question over to 1680, when several merchants in New York refused to pay customs duties. The collector of the port of New York was arrested for detaining goods on which duties had not been paid, and sent over to England for trial. Coming directly under the eyes of the Duke of York, he sent Colonel Thomas Dongan over as Deputy Governor with instructions to convene a General Assembly, in which Esopus was given two representatives. The Assembly met at Fort James, New York, October 17, 1683. The accession of the Duke of York to the throne of his brother James, led him to reconsider the proposition for a General Assembly, and in its stead to authorize the Deputy Governor, with the advice and consent of his council, to enact such laws as he deemed best, and to forward them to England. This arbitrary form of government continued until June 9, 1689, when Captain Jacob Leisler seized the Fort in the name of William and Mary, and, as acting governor, directed the election of Members of Assembly. This assembly held two sessions. Governor Sloughter came over in 1691, drove Leisler out and hung him.

The representative Assembly which had been proposed by Governor Dongan was brought together. In that Assembly, the first representative Assembly in the Province, April 9th, 1691, Ulster and Duchess, the latter then being attached to Ulster, was represented by Henry Beekman, William de Mire, and Thomas Garton, whose names as settlers in Ulster have already been met. The issue, "No taxation without representation," was carried forward for a hundred years, and became, at the opening of the Revolution, the "Battle Cry of Freedom." What connection the people of Ulster County had with the issue which had been raised cannot be stated; what connection they had with its final determination is not uncertain. Baptized with the best blood of pioneers and sons of liberty, they stand before us to-day not wholly demoralized by the conditions by which they are surrounded.

The organization of the village of Wildwijk, under the patent given to it by Director Stuyvesant, May 16th, 1661, providing, among other things, for the holding there once in every two weeks of a Court of Justice, the jurisdiction of which extended over "all the inhabitants of Esopus," gave it, substantially, the rank of the county seat, a relation which has not been taken from it. The holding of the court and the detention of prisoners implies a place for the holding of the court and a place for the detention of prisoners. Where the latter was is not clear; the former was pretty certainly the building called "the Dominie's house and lot," assigned to lot No. 4 in the first allotment. In the instructions issued to the Commissioners appointed by Governor Lovelace, September 11th, 1669, "that they take some order for ye reparation of ye house next to Mr. Beekman's, called ye Dominie's or ye State House," reference was made to this building. It had been erected by Director Stuyvesant, and final bills rendered in 1662; was apparently a stone structure of two stories with a tile roof, a description inferable from the bills rendered * and from the reply to the Commissioners that they "would retile the house when wanted," and particularly from their reference to its location under the Governor's instruction "to impale the place for Burryal, as likewise the place for a Towne-House," which the Commissioners "conceived to be

* The building was erected under an ordinance of Director Stuyvesant, and its cost paid by a land tax on the town. Its cost was 3,007.8 florins, or something over twelve hundred dollars of our present standard. The bills included 5,000 brick, tiles, lime, boards, wainscoting, slating, iron, hinges, locks, and nails, and wages of carpenters, masons, and hod-carriers. It was a substantial and for its times a very fine building. It was literally the Town-House, paid for by the town.

a mistake," as they had a Town-House already standing conveniently within the town," *i. e.* within the palisade; that it was "absolutely necessary" that it should be kept in good repair from its frequent use "both for religious duties and civil affairs," and that they would proceed with the work as "soon as pan-tiles and other materials" could be procured. In stating a fact in regard to the house, they seem to have misunderstood the Governor's instructions in the matter of "impaleing" the burial ground and the place reserved for a town-house, which obviously referred to lots 21 and 23 of the second allotment which had not been palisaded or "paled" as had been ordered by Director Stuyvesant.

Possibly a jail was built soon after the house was repaired. The only trace that we have of it is in an act of the General Assembly of 1715 requiring the Justices of the County to repair "the County-House and Prison in the said county of Ulster now being." In 1732, the Assembly authorized "the Justices of the Peace of the county of Ulster" to build "a Court House and Prison and to sell the old one. The new building on a new site was repaired in 1745, 1750, 1765, 1773 and 1775, and in 1777 it was burned by the invading army of England under Vaughan and Wallace, and soon after a lottery was granted to provide two thousand pounds for rebuilding on the site occupied by the structure of 1732. It is said that the building of 1782, was "set back in the lot about the same distance of the present one," and that in front of it "were the public stocks and whipping post," the latter especially an ancient method, for the punishment of minor offenses, in those times very often employed for the whipping of slaves, and in a few instances for the whipping of white men as well as women. Primarily the constable was the whipping master. The old court house was the scene of many famous trials and rang with many eloquent appeals in the early days of the Revolution; the old jail was crowded with political prisoners—King's men—"Tories," as they were called. It was a cold bleak prison, the annals of which await the pen of an ABBOT. Compared with the "Old Sugar-House," New York, in which the British confined their prisoners, the latter was a palace. The existing Court House, a spacious and handsome edifice, of fine Colonial design, was erected upon the site of the ancient building in 1818, and was greatly enlarged in 1898. In addition to the Court and Jury rooms, the building contains the chambers of the resident Justice of the Supreme Court, those of the County Judge, the offices of the District

David Kennedy M.D.

Attorney, the County Treasurer, the Sheriff, Clerk of the Board of Supervisors, and the Supervisors' assembly room. Its walls are adorned with the portraits of those Justices of the Supreme Court who have been residents of the County and with the portraits of the County Judges from an early period. A unique and remarkable feature of the Court House is the cornice of its northern façade which is classical in design, of carved wood, and is regarded as the finest cornice of any public building in America. It frequently has been copied by architects who have in part reproduced it in public buildings, in different parts of the Union.

At the time of the enlargement of the Court House in 1898, the County erected a large and thoroughly modern jail which has served as a model for similar structures in various counties in the State.

CHAPTER VI.

COLONIAL MILITARY ORGANIZATIONS.

THE military organizations of the county had their beginning in the appointment by Director Stuyvesant (April 23d, 1660) of Thomas Chambers as Captain of the inchoate militia — the Trainband of Wildwijk and Esopus; Hendrick Jochem Schoonmaker, Lieutenant, and Roelof Swartwout, Hendrick Jansen, Cornelius Barentsen Slecht, and Peter Jacobsen, minor officers. As noted in another connection, Schoonmaker had had some previous military training. In official signatures his name is written Hendrick Jochemsen. The officers named evidently understood their responsibilities, but seem to have aroused some opposition from the wording of the Ordinance which they adopted January 2d, 1663, posted it on the door of the Town House in Wildwijk, and had the mortification of seeing it torn down by order of the Court at Wildwijk because therein was not acknowledged the authority of the Magistrates. The authority of the Court must be respected even in those primitive times. The real "hitch," however, seems to have been that any one appearing on parade with borrowed fire-arms should forfeit the same and also be liable to a fine of twelve guilders. The Ordinance recited several facts that are of interest aside from its general purpose. It reads:

"1. Whoever appears for training at the appointed place of gathering without proper side and handarms, powder and lead, shall be fined and pay the first time twelve guilders, the second time double that sum, and the third time he shall be punished according to the judgment of the court-martial. Everybody must be provided with at least ten charges of powder, and lead, in the cartridge box besides his full side and handarms.

"2. Whoever does not appear unless excused, or comes too late, shall pay a fine of two guilders; who remains away from contumacy or willfullness without sufficient excuse, shall be fined and corrected arbitrarily by the court-martial in addition to the above fine of two guilders.

"3. Sergeants, corporals and lancepesades (privates), who are too late or remain away, shall pay a double fine.

"4. In case of alarm of fire the members of the Captain's squad shall assemble at the place near Barent Gerritsen, the brandy distiller; the members of the Lieutenant's squad near the wheelwright's Albert Gysbertson; the third squad under Pieter Jacobsen Molenear at Hendrick Jochemsen's under a penalty of five and twenty guilders.

"5. All officers are forbidden to exchange with others, every one must appear personally under a penalty of four and twenty guilders.

"6. It is ordered, that every one who mounts guard or reports at the place of rendezvous, must have *his own* side and handarms, under penalty of confiscation of the arms, which he may have borrowed from another, and he shall besides pay a fine of twelve guilders.

"7. Nobody shall in being relieved from our mounting guard, or marching, be allowed to load his musket with ball, wadding or paper, nor to discharge it at any window, gable or weathervane, under a penalty of six guilders and reparation of the damage done; but in discharging their muskets they shall raise it above man's height, under a like penalty, to prevent all mishaps.

"8. If anybody desires to remove from here to do his business elsewhere, either at Manhattans, Fort Orange or some other place, he shall notify the Mustermaster of his departure, under penalty of twenty-five stuyvers.

"9. Nobody shall be allowed to mount guard, or appear at the rendezvous, when intoxicated, and having reported; nobody shall curse or swear or profane God's holy name and sacraments, under a penalty of twenty-five guilders.

"Thus enacted at the meeting of the Citizen's Council of War in the Village of Wildwijk the first day of January, Anno 1663." *Thomas Chambers, Hendrick Jochemsen, the mark X of Pieter Jacobsen, Cornelis Barentsen Slecht.*

This was also published:

"Everybody is hereby informed that muskets, powder and lead, may be bought at *Wouter* the baker's, and further, if no more is to be had, at *Wouter* the baker's, people may come to the officers of the trainband, who will inform them where they may buy it for money. Done at Wildwyck, the 2d of January, 1663.

"Signed: By order of the officers of the trainband of Wildwyck Village.

"MATHEWS CAPITO-MUSTERMASTER."

Very sensible rules indeed even judged from the standpoint of modern discipline. The fines, perhaps, were heavy. A guilder was about forty cents of our money — twenty-five guilders $10. In reporting them to Director Stuyvesant, Captain Chambers wrote, "After the savages have had several gatherings here with their *Kinte Kaying,* while we did not know what they might attempt, we have not dared to omit calling together the people on the 1st of January of this year and tried to keep good order to the best of our knowledge," adding that unless the officers were not sustained in the matter of their ordinances, "we shall not be able in time of need to acquit ourselves of our duties."

In and around the little village of Wildwijk was held, as stated in the narrative quoted, on the New Year's Day, 1663, the first general training, or the first assembly of "the trainband." "They were well entertained by some citizens, but everything went well." The inference which may probably be drawn from the word "but" in the sentence is suggestive to those who in years ago attended a general training. The reader can easily change the word to "and." Did either the officers or the privates appear in uniforms? Did they have drums? Probably "Yes," two dozen drums were sent to them in 1659. Did they float the flag of Holland?

That the men of that trainband were brave and efficient in dealing with the Indians on the 7th of June following we have ample evidence. Rallied from their labors in the fields to meet the Indian band who had entered the village and were murdering their wives and devastating and burning their homes, they fell upon the invaders without arms and drove them out, says the book. There were some regular soldiers at the Rondout, but we do not read that they came to the aid of the trainband; presumably they did not for the first inquiry sent out was to ascertain what fate had befallen the post where they were stationed. From that disastrous day, however, by order of Director Stuyvesant who had hastened to the relief of the settlement, the commander of the military company, Christiaen Niessen; the commander of the trainband, Thomas Chambers, Roelof Swartwout, the Schout, and Hendrick Jochemsen, Lieutenant of the trainband, and the commissaries, were placed in full charge, and the inhabitants "commanded and directed" to obey them. The order was changed a little when, on the 30th of June, Captain Marten Kregier and his Council of War came upon the scene, and the guns of the last war with the Indians of Esopus rang out in the wilderness. The results of that war have been summarized in another connection; the students of local history will find its incidents completely narrated in the original documents in Colonial History of New York, volume XIII. In connection with the colonial militia the only incident that may properly be referred to there is the imperfect account of the action of Louis du Bois and his neighbors who accompanied Kregier's forces in their attack on the Shawangunk Indian fort where were held the wife of Du Bois and his children and most of the prisoners captured by the Indians in June, of whom twenty-three were recovered, not even a hair of their heads injured.

In 1669, April 4th, the commissioners appointed by Governor Lovelace formally organized the militia of Hurley and Marbletown under the following commissioned officers, viz: Henry Pawling, Captain; Christopher Beresford, Lieutenant; John Biggs, Ensign. Most if not all of these men had been in regular employ as soldiers. Henry Pawling came over as a soldier under Colonel Richard Nicolls in 1664, had "behaved himself well," so stated on his certificate of discharge, (April 18, 1670), and became an honored resident of Ulster. His company will be met later. Tuesday, April 1st, 1669, Captain Chambers and his company were out for their annual review. The commissioners commanded them "to remove the East Gate of Kingston to the middle of the curtaine." The company "was mustered and exercised," and the artillery was drawn into the ffield and ffyred," says the record. The commissions of Captain Chambers and Lieutenant Hendrick Jochemsen were renewed April 18th, 1670, and Mathys Mattysysen commissioned as Ensign. On the same date commissions were issued to Pawling, Beresford and Biggs of the new Hurley and Marbletown company. The company was "mustered and exercised in their arms." The laws relating to military affairs were read before them, and "Then marched with flying colors to the town of Hurley and there dismissed. The colors were lodged with a guard at the Town Hall in Kingston, where the soldiers were commanded to appear next day in court to draw their lots," i. e. house lots which were assigned to all soldiers who had been in the employ of the Government at Kingston. The following is the roll:

Henry Pawling, Captain,
Christopher Berisford, Lieutenant,
John Biggs, Ensign,
Samuel Oliver, Sergeant,
Albert Heymensen, Sergeant,
Richard Cage, Drummer.

MARBLETOWN SOLDIERS.

Thomas Quynell,
William Fisher,
John Hendrick,
Geor: Porter,
Joh: Pound,
Edw: Whitacre,
Thom. Mathews,
George Hall,
Antho: Cooke,
Fredr. Hussey,
Antho: Addyson,
Evart Price,
Thom: Edgar,
Edwar: Ffrench,
Wm: Horton,
Robt. Bickerstaffe,
Robt. Peacock,
John Reynolds,
John Joesten,
——— Joesten,
Jacob de Wael,
Henry Crump,
Fredr. Pietersen,
Cornel. Ffenehold,
Gisbert Crump,
Garret Johnson,

HURLEY SOLDIERS.

Paulus Paulenson,
Jacob Johnson,
Leuys De Boys,
Aaron Tunys,
Lambert Hyberts,
Wardener Hornbeck,
Garret Fokar,
Garret Corneliuson,
Ffrancois Le Shiere,
John Albertson,
Arian Albertse,
Jacob Carte,
Robert Goldsberry,
John Diboth,
Arian Ffrancis,
Allard Rose,
Arian Rose,
John Rose,
Pieter the Negro,
Mathias Blanchan,

In all 54.

During the few months that the Dutch repossessed the Province (1673), the Governor, Clove, appointed Captain Mathys Mathysen, Lieutenant Jan Willensen, and Ensign Mathys Barentsen, officers of the Kingston, or as it was then named by the Dutch, Swaenenburg, company, and Albert Heymansen, Captain; Jan Braersen, Lieutenant, and Gerrit Andriaensen Ensign of the Hurley and Marbletown company, but no service appears under the appointments. The old order was soon restored.

In 1685, Aug. 30, Thomas Chambers was appointed Major of the foot and horse forces in the County of Ulster, and on the same date a troop of horse was constituted under Hendrick Beekman, Captain; Wessel Ten Broek, Lieutenant; Daniel Brodhead, Cornet, and Anthony Addison, Quartermaster. On the same date "a foot company for Kingston and New Paltz was formed — Matthias Mattheysen, Captain, Abraham Hasbrouck, Lieutenant, and Jacob Rutgers, Ensign. A company of foot was also organized for Hurley, Marbletown and Mombaccus—Thomas Garton, Captain, John Biggs, Lieutenant, and Charles Brodhead, Ensign. In 1700 the county had (including one from Duchess) seven companies of infantry, and a troop of horse, together numbering three hundred and twenty men. Further than that Jacob Rutsen was Lieutenant Colonel, the Field Officers are not of record.

Peace reigned around the habitations of Ulster County for three quarters of a century after the close of the war of 1663; the "dark and bloody" ground of the province was transferred to the northern frontiers and the country of the Iroquoians, more particularly to the valley of the Mohawk. Between the tribe occupying that valley and the French in Canada there was an irrepressible hostility springing primarily from the alliance of the French with the Huron-Iroquoi and the Algonquians who were seated in proximity to the French settlements, fanned by the conflicting interest of the civilizations of France and England, the former largely influenced by the efforts of the Jesuit missionaries for the conversion of the Indians to the Catholic faith. For nearly one hundred years the Mohawks and their confederates devastated the French plantations in Canada, and in retaliation the armies of France scourged the Iroquoian country. In 1687, wearied by the repeated devastations of the Iroquoi, who were furnished with the munitions of war by the English, Count de Frontenac, the Governor-general of Canada, or New France as it was known, determined to attack the English plantations as the allies of the

Jacob Van Gelder

Iroquoi. Planning three aggressive divisions of his forces, one to attack Fort Albany (old Fort Orange), one to attack New England, and one to attack Fort James (old Fort Amsterdam), the former, under the lead of the Count himself, came down from Quebec in the winter of 1690, attacked and destroyed Schenectady (Feb. 10th), and massacred most of its inhabitants, and then retreated. Presumably the English had made some preparation for the defense of Fort Albany, they had repaired and strengthened the palisades of the fort, and ordered the assembling there of one-tenth of the militia of the counties. Presumably the militia of Ulster responded to this call, as they did to others, but records of names have not been handed down. The order reads:

"* * * These are therefore in his Mag'ties name to will and require you and every of you forthwith upon receipt hereof to select out of the County of Ulster one hundred or eighty at least good able men, compleet in armes, which shall be transported to Albany for his Mag'ties service at upon the first day of January next, and that at all times before, uppon notice of the Commiss's at Albany of the enemies approaching you send the number of men or as many as can be obtained without thelay (delay), as you will answer the contrary at your utmost peril." Dated Nov. 16, 1690, addressed "To Major Thomas Chambers and the rest of the Military Officers under his Direction in the County of Ulster."

Here follows an order "to Capt. Barent Lewis, Mr. Schemerhorne and their assistants," to press 20 men with arms and 300 skepples peas and 250 skepples Indian corne within the County of Ulster for the expedition of Albany.

The French expeditions having failed, the English projected two or three retaliatory invasions of Canada. In 1691, twenty-seven men were detached from the Ulster militia for the defence of Albany. They were:

Alb't Jance V. Steenwyck,
Arent Fynhout,
Arien Van Netten,
Jan Helmerse,
Isaac Kermer,
Thierebce Galone,
David Sunderland,
Jan Krispell,
Joshua Stare,
John Conner,
John Colledge,
Calem Meguiddech,
John McKlowed,
John Fortune,
Wm. Carmes,
Dirk Duytcher,
Claus Melgertse,
Pr. Quackebos,
——— Melgertse,
Jacob Hendrickse,
Adam Simpson,
Edward Blake,
Dirk Dirkse Vand'r Karr,
Cornelius Schemerhoorn,
Isaac Vredenburgh,
Ephraim Carpenter,
Joseph Burgess,
Thomas Matthew.

Turning to the militia rolls, we have in that of 1700—with the exception of the full list of field officers—apparently the first organized "regiment of militia in the counties of Ulster and Duchess," the latter county being then included with Ulster. The officers were:

"Jacon Rutsen, Lieutenant Colonel.

"Of a foot Company in ye said countys: Matthias Mattyson, Captain; Evert Bogardus, Lieut.; Teunis Tappen, Ensigne.

"Of another foot Company in ye s'd countys: Abso: Hasbrooke, Captain; Moses Quantaine, Lieut.; Lewis Bayea, Ensigne.

"Of another foot Company in ye said county: George Middah, Capt.; Gysbert Krom, Lieut.; Alex. Rosecrans, Ensigne.

"Of another foot Company in ye said counties: Aria Rose, Captain; John Rose, Lieut.; Aria Gerruntes, Ensigne.

"Of another foot Company in ye said countys: Jocham Schoonmaker, Captain; John Van Camp, Lieut.; Jacob Decker, Ensigne.

"Of another foot Company in ye said countys: Coenrad Elmendorf, Captain; Mattyse Sleight, Lieut.; Garret Wyncoop, Ensigne.

"Of another foot Company in ye said countys: Baltus Van Cleet, Captain; Hendrick Kipp, Lieut.; John Ter Bus, Ensigne. (This Company was in Dutchess County.)

"Of ye troop of Horse in ye said Regiment: Egbert Schoonmaker, Captain; Corn Decker, Lieut.; Abra. Gasbert, Cornet; Mattyse Jansen, Quartermaster.

"This regiment consists of three hundred five and twenty men."

Following the succession of Anne to the throne of England in 1702, the war known in Europe as the "War of the Spanish Succession," and in America as "Queen Anne's War," continued until April 11, 1713. New York scarce knew of its existence, although the province was put in condition for defense and offence. Among the records of that period is the following:

"County of Ulster, July, 1711. List of the Company under the command of Captain Wessel Ten Broeck; Lieutenant John Pawling and Ensigne Elyas Van Bunschoten, to March upon ye expedition to Canada, viz:

Sergjt. Jan Decker,	Volunteer,	Jacob Van Dermarke,	Volunteer,
Corporal, Christoffel Van Leuven,	"	Lammert Dolderbrink,	"
Drummer, Jan Mackleen,	"	William Sluyter,	"
Isaac Hasbrouck,	"	Willem Rosa,	"
Lammert Koal,	"	Gysbert Rosa,	"
Jacob Vernoy,	"	Mattys Van Rosendall,	"
Lowies Barree, Junior,	Hyred,	Arent Van Ostrande,	Detached,
Tobias Van Buren,	"	William Ringfold,	"
Dirck Janse,	"	Evert Terwillige,	Volunteer,
Rub Van Woerde,	Volunteer,	Maurits Klaarwater,	"
Jacobus Bos,	"	Jan Lefaber,	"
David de Duyster,	"	Ephraim Bogardus,	Hyred,
Jacob Koal,	"	Wilhelmus Beekman,	"
John Wood, Junior,	"	Albartus Provoost,	Volunteer,
Nathanyel Davinpoort,	"	Johannes Hornbeeck,	"
Willem Burhans,	"	Johannes Kuykendall,	"
Pieter Van Garde,	Detached,	Jacobiiet Soor,	"

Arie Van NiewKierck,	Volunteer,	Willem Koal,	Volunteer,
Mattys Slegt, Junior,	"	Jan Gerritse Decker,	"
Hasuel Mattysen,	"	Roelof de Duytser,	"
Thomas Armist,	"	Andries Brusie,	"
Marten Bogart,	Hyred,	Hilbrant Lootman,	"
Thomas Quick,	Detached,	Frans de Lange,	"
Matthew Beckwith,	Volunteer,	Hartman Rynderse,	"

The expedition was unfruitful. The Ulster contingent, with its associates reached the point of rendezvous, but the fleet with the naval forces was caught in a heavy fog and lost four or five transports with eight hundred men on board. The survivors made haste to get back to pleasant waters, and the colonial contingent, hearing of the disaster, made equal haste in reaching their rural homes. It is a little curious that no invading force of English colonists ever succeeded in accomplishing much in their expeditions against the French in Canada.

Turning over the leaves of the record we have, in 1715, a very complete enrollment of the regiments in the words and figures following:

A List of the Troop Under the Command of Cap'n. John Rutsen (Ulster County)

Cap'n John Rutsen,
Cornet Philip Hoogtieling,
Quarte Master John Baptist Dimond.

Arent van Woagene	Corp'll Gerret Newkerk
Corp'll Willem Shepmoes	Egbert Brink
Philip Viele	Gerret Newkerk Jun'r
Hendrick Haremans	Anthony Creppell
albert Kierstade	Nicolas Roosa
Christoffle Tappun	Loiwis Dubois Jun'r
Jacobus Cleverdorfe Jun'r	Corp'll Albert Palling
Johannes Lamater	Hendrick Krom
Salomon van Bunschoote	Jacob van dir marcken
Cornelia Lameter	Johannes Kooll
Peber Cantyn	Thomas Janse
Johannes Decker	Jacob Rutsen Jun'r
Arie Hendrickse	Corp'll Dirck Roosekrans
Johannes ten Broek	Tyerck De witt
Hendrick Janse	Samuel Schoonmaker
Corp'll Cornelis Vernoy, Jun'r	Frederick Schoonmaker
Peter Osterhout	Moses De Puy Jun'r
James Whittaker	Corp'll Louis Du Bois
Barent Burhans	Salomon Haesbrock
Thomas Mattyse Junn'r	Johannes West broeck
Hendrick Schoonmaker, Jun'r	Cornelis De Puy
wessell ten broeck, Jun'r	Daniell Haesbroek
Gerret Eleverdorp	Daniell Du booyi
Jacob Ten broeck	Phillip Du Bois
Symon Van Wagonen	Jacob Haesbroek

The Role of the Companie of Cap'n Wittaker in the Regiment of Collo Jacob Rutsen in Ulster County.

Commiss Officers
Cap'n Edward Wittaker
Lieft Hendrick Schoonmaker
Sergt Thomas Van Steenbergen
Sergt Matteys Van Steenbergen
Sergt Peter Tappen
Corp'll Cryn oosterhout
Corp'll Arie Van Vliet
Drum'r Ephraim Bogardus

Jan Post
Tierck Matteyson
Anthony Crespell
goose Van Wagne
John Devenport
Teunis Swart Jun'r
Jacob Louis Louw
Barent Newkerk
Jan Oosterhout
Johannes Burhans
Abraham Burhans
Samuell Burhans
Nathaniel Davenport
Wallerand Dumont
Wallerand Dumont Jun'r
Peter Ploegh
Jan Ploegh
Gysbert Peele
Lowrens Swart
Johnannes Trap hagen
Abraham Louis —— Louw
Barent Burhans
Charles Barwa
William Haris
Teunis Swart
William Wyt
Peter Oosterhout, Jun'r
Willem Ploegh
Jacobus Du Bois
David Burhans
Edward Wood
Aaris Van Steenbergen
Jury Beem
Willem Burhans
Christoffill Moull
Peter Winne
Jacob Cool
Thomas Persson
Johannes Masten
Pieter Peele
Jan Oosterhout Jun'r
Hendrick Oosterhout
Hendrick Brink
Isaac Burhans
Phillip Feller
Gerret Decker
Abraham Van Steenbergen
Johannes Swart
Johannes Van Steenbergen
Wilhelmus Hoogteyling
Abraham Ploegh
John Legg
Dirck Wynkoop
Tierck Shoemaker
Jacob Ploegh
Jan Peterse Oosterhout
Johannes Crespel

A List of a Ffoot Company of Mallitia for the Town of Under the Command of Cap'n Johannes Vernooy in the Regiment of Ulster County Jacob Rutsen Coll

Cap'n Johannes Vernooy
Lieut David Dubois
Insign Loderyck Horenback
Sergt Hendrick Rosekrans
Sergt Albertus Van Garde
Sergt Frederick Van Vliet
Corp'll Johannes Quick
Corp'll Cornelius Vancken

John Van Kampe
Samuell bevier
Willem Koole
Tobyas Horenbeek

Cornelis De Duyser
Jan Bevier
Peter Louw
Jan Van Vliet
Johannes Wasbroek, Jun'r
Anthony Wasbroek
Jan van Ette
Jacob Van Ette
Wouter West vael
Jurie West vael
Willem Decker
Johannes Horenbeck
Tyrck De Witt
Manis Koole
Matthys Louw
Jan after houdt
Thomas Quick
Jan Decker
Gerrit Decker
Jurie Quick
Cornelis Kortright
Peter Cort reght
Jacobus Wyn Koop
Jacobus Schoonmaker
Johannis Du puy
Dirck Krom
Manis Decker
Jan Kortright
Peter Van Garde
Hendrick Van Garde
Harme van garde
Barent Koole
Carnelis Koole
Cornelis Schoonmaker
Peter Dolderbrink
Hendrick Dolderbrink
Thomes Swartwout
Jacobus Swartwout
Harme Van Nim wegen
Peter De Maer
Jacob Koddeback

A List of a Ffoot Company of Mallitia for the Towne of Horley Under the Command of Capt'n Johannes Shepmoes in the Regiment of Ulster County Jacob Rutsen Collo-

Cap'n Johannes Shepmoes
Lieut Jacob Du Bois
Insign Jan Newkerk
Sergt Albert Roosa
Sergt William Van Vreedenburgh
Corp'll Gerret Constapel
Drom Johannes Van Ette

Corneelis Wynkoop
Petter Van Ette
Jacobus Van Ette
Huybert Suylant
Egbert Konstapel
Jan Crispele
Aarent Oostrande
Albert Janse Roosa
John Roosa Jun'r
Arie Roosa
Charles Wyle
Lambert Brink
Lowrens Kortreyt
Jacob Ten Eyck
Cornelius Newkerk
Jan Van Duese
Dirck De duyster
Abraham Ten Eyck
Jacob Brink
Jan Evertse ter Wilge
Hendrick Kon Stapel
Matthias ter Wilge

A List of the Ffoot Company of Mallitia of Marbletown Under the Command of Cap'n Wm Nottingham in the Regiment of Ulster County Under the Command of Collo Jacob Rutsen

Cap'n William Nottingham
Lieut Thomas Cock
Inse Matthias Blanchan
Sergt Cornelis Tack
Sergt Nicholas Keator

Sergt Jeremy Keettell
Corp'll Marte Bogart
Corp'll William Cock
Corp'll Lambert Dolderbrink
Drum John Van Luven
Clerk Charles Leatty

Henry Pawling
Cornelis Ettinge
Andries Van Vliet
Daniell Brodhead
Charles Brodhead Jun'r
James Robinson
Samuell Cock
Nicholas Blanchan
Robert Beatty
William Beatty
Nicholas Schoonhoven
Ariaen Van der Mark
Jacob Van Wagenin
Benjamin Van Wagenin
Abraham Van Wagenin
Jacob Dewitt Jun'r
Egbert Dewitt
Roderick Van der Mark
Cornelis Keyser
Jacob Keyser
Augustinus Van der Mark
Jacobus Boss
Roeloff Doldirbrink
Thomas Doldderbrink
Dirck Kerner
Teunis Koole
Jacobus Tack
John Tack
Abraham Tack
Gysbert Roosa
John Roosa, Jun'r
Simon Van Wagenin
Teunis Keyser
Nicolas Sluyter
Nicolas Dupuis
Gerret Van Campen
Jacob Van Campen
Abraham Van Kampen
John Biggs
Jurin Best
Peter Van Aken
Manuell Consales
Manuell Consales Jun'r
Peter Van Bommelen
Marius Van Bommelen
Christoffel Van Bommelen
Nicolas Schoonhoven
Mosis De Graef
Abraham De Graef
Jan Clyn
Johannes Willem
Harmanus Hommel
Teunis Turpenninck
Jan Syanners
Nicolas Rouw
Rehan Henneman
Felter Pinner
Hendrick Beem
Willem Swart
Johannes Schoonmaker
Symen Helen
Jacobus Van Etten
Johannes Swart
Richard Wels
Cornelis Lange Dyck
Johannes Crispel

Captain Hoffman, Ulster County, 1716.

Seryant Aberam Deyow
Korperal Hendark Van Wye
Korperal Hage Serenyunen
Jakop Klarwatr
Capt Schgryes Hofman
Levtt Andries Lowerre
Insyne Lewis Lowies Jun

Aberam De Boys
Aberam Schut
Tuns Klarwater
Att Klarwater
aberam ferer
yakop ferer
henderk de yoou
elyas yu
toms Spenek
Benjemen du boois
yan terpenega
henderik Dekar
hogo Stins
joswea Smedes
hender Schonmakr
felp meler

Court House.

huge Serem
kresbyan de yaw
yakop gertsedeker
Lendert Kol
anderis borin
ysack lefever
yan lafever
piter daow
Evert terwelge
Hyge Aberamse fere
ysak ferer
Symen ferer
Sems Spenek
hans meler
beniman hasberok
yoel de bois
wel soderlen
pitr makrigr
verek mynders
korporeal Andris Valk
hans serin
yakop werr
sandr garik
Melkert Schryn
Sy Sun heri
En sun tames

The reader must decipher some of the orthographies. Near the end of the list we may spell out the names of some of the Palatine immigrants, who located in what is now Newburgh, in 1709. Wel Soderlen stands for William Sutherland, and Pitr Makrigr stands for Peter or Patrick MacGregor, the latter the occupant at the mouth of Murderer's Creek, and the former in an adjoining patent. Verek Mynders stands for Burger Meynders who later owned what is now Washington's Headquarters. Korporeal Andries Valk stands for Andries Valck who held lot No. 9 of the German Patent (Newburgh). Melkert Schryn stands for Melgert de Schrynewerker whose land was near the present south line of Ulster. En sun looks like Ensign Thames or Thomas.

As one of the leading objects of this work is to put within easy reach records which are the foundation of local genealogical research, no apology is needed for a continuation of the military list of this era. To become established of record as a descendant from stock who wielded a sword or carried a gun in the Colonial wars is an honor of which any one may be justly proud. Passing on we have a complete return of the Ulster regiment in 1738, as follows:

ULSTER COUNTY MILITIA, 1738.

Collo A. Gaasbeek Chambers.
Le't Collo Wessel Ten Broeck.
Major Coenradt Elmendorp.
Quarter Master Cornelis Elmendorp.

ULSTER SS. A LIST OF THE TROOPERS UNDER THE COMMAND OF CAPT JOHANNIS TEN BROECK.

Capt Johannis Ten Broeck
Lieut't Wessel Ten Broeck Jun'r
Corn't Tho's Gaasbeek Chambers
1st Qr. Mas. Hendrickus Krom
2nd Qr. M. Johannis De Lamatre
Trump'r Abraham Constapell

1st Corpor'l Richard Wells
2nd Corpor'l Gerrit Elmendorph
3rd Corpor'l Arie Van Vliet
4th Corpor'l Martie Lamatre
5 Corpor'l Ffrederick Schoonmaker
6 Corpor'l Solomon Haasbrock

Solomon Van Bunschoten
Jacob Haasbrock
Cornelius Depue
Arent Ploegh
Samuel Schoonmaker
Tjerck Schoonmaker
Samuel Bovie
Benjamin Depue
Egbert Brinck
Jan Ffreer
Cornelis Ten Broeck
Johannis Wynkoop Jun'r
Daniel De Bois
Danill Haasbrock
Jacobus Schoonmaker
Thomas Nottingham
Abraham Van Wagenen
Cornelis De Witt
Cornelis New Kerck
Petrus Ten Broeck
Abraham de Lamatre
Wilhelmus Van Hooghtyling J'r
Joghem Schoonmaker Jun'r
Wessel Jacobs Ten Broeck
Jan Tuenis Oosterhout
Martie Middagh
Johannis Dubois
Arie Oosterhout
Wessel Broadhead
Simon Jacobs Van Wagenen
Simon Van Wagenen
Jacob Van Wagenen
Egbert De Witt
David Burhance
Edward Whittaker Jun'r
Petrus Tappen
Coenraedt Elmendorph Jun'r
Abraham Hardenbergh
Gysbert Hend'k Krom
Leonard Hardenbergh
Cornelis New Kerck
Jacob Rutsen Jun'r
Harma Rosekrans
Philip Dumon
Lucius Elmendorph
Abraham Kiersted
James Scott
William Krom Jun'r Totil 60.

A LIST OF THE FOOT COMPANY OF MILITIA OF THE CORPORATION OF KINGSTON UNDER THE COMMAND OF CAPT JOHN PERSEN

Capt John Persen
Lievte. Peter Oosterhout
Ensign Edward Whittaker
Sarja Aarey Newkerk
Sarja Ned Davenport
Sarja Jacobus Van Dyck
Corpo Samuel Nights
Corpo Nathan Dubois
Corpo Solomon Freer
Dromer Andries Van Leven

Samuel Wood
Jacobus Roosa
Coenradt Elmendorp
Jacobus Persen
Phillip Hoof
Hendricus Oosterhout
Daniel Whittaker
Samuel Davenport
Cornelis Persen
William Myre
Christian Myre
William Legg
Humphy Davenport
Mosas Youman
Brure Decker
John Decker
Tobias Winekoop
Jacobus Debois Jn'r
Samuel Debois
William Whittaker
Jacobus Whittaker
John Davenport Jn'r
Johanes Schram
Corne Longing Dyck

Peter Van Leven
Nemiah Debois
Ricard Davenport
Andris Hoof
Abra Harcenberge
Anthony Sleght
John Legg Jn'r
Johannes Humble
Godfrey Woolf Jn'r
Frederick Row
Michel Planck
Jurian Tappen
Robert Bever

Totall 47.

A LIST OF THE FOOT COMPANY OF MILITIA OF THE CORPORATION OF KINGSTON UNDER THE COMMAND OF CAPT. TJRCK VAN KEUREN.

Capt Tjrck Van Keuren
Lievten't Abraham Low
Ensign Dirck Winekoop
Serg't William Swart
Serg't Tobias Van Bueren
Corp'l Petrus Smedes
Corp'l Ephraim Dubois
Corp'l Marynis Van Aken
Drom'r Corn'l Jansen

Willem Eltinge
Peter Van Aken
Thomas Beekman
Evert Bogardus
Cornelis Van Kueren
Cornelis Sleght
David De Lamatter
Frans Hendrick
Nicholas Bogardus
Jan Heermans
Tuenis Van Steenbergh
Abra Van Steenbergh
Hendrikus Slegh
Johannis Dubois
Abra De Lamatter
Johans Ba: De Witt
Hiskiah Dubois
Evert Winekoop Jn'r
Tobias Van Steenbergh
Jan Van Aken
Johannis Chonsalisduck
Jan Perse Jn'r
Petrus Low
Isaac Van Wagenen
Abra Van Kueren
Gerett Freer
Corn'l Perse
Robert Beever
Mooses Jorck
Giedeon Van Aken
Joseph Chonsalisduck
Thimoteos Van Steenbergh
Jacobus De Ioo
Dirck Teerpen
Maas Bloemendal
Jacob Turck
Jacobus Eltinge
Jan Lome
Johannis Felter
Jame Letsin
Peter Vanderline
Petrus Eltinge
Cornl De Lametter Jn'r
Abra Lome Jn'r
Jacobus Van Kueren
Willen Krom
Petrus Van Aken
William Deen
Dirck Van Vleet Jn'r
Benjamin Van Vleet
Johannis Van Vleet

Totil 60.

A LIST OF THE FOOT COMPANY OF MILITIA OF THE CORPORATION OF KINGSTON UNDER THE COMMAND OF

Capt Tjrck Dewitt
Left Petrus Bogardus
Insi Igenas Dumont
Serj't Jury Snyder
Serj't William Wells
Serj't Petrus Viele

Corpo Lukas Dewitt
Corpo Peter Dumont
Corpo Wilhelmus Houghteling

Clark Jarman Pick
Phillip Viele Ju'r
Sam'll Wells
Corne Viele
Corne Marston
John Masten
Gerritt Viele
Jacobus Dumond
Benja Marten
John Maclene
Antony Hoffman
Hendr Vankuren
Tuenis Ploegh
Dirck Shepmoes
Johanes Wiele
Geritt Van Steenbergh
Corne Van Kuren, Ju'r
Johanis Masten
John Waters
Henry Ellis
Jacob Mauris
Isaac Wheeler
Humph Davenport
Peter Burgar
Isaac Dubois
Johans Shepmoes
Zacryas Hoffman, Ju'r
Petrus Edmundus Elmendorp
Lenard Herdenbergh
Jacob Hardenbergh
Peter Leehonte
Jacobus Deyoe
Johans Degrave
Corne Vankuren
Jacobus Vanetten
Mattys Merkell
Hendrick Vreligh
Coenrad Rechtmire
Heskia Winekoop
Gerrett Davenport
Art Masten
Coenra Vanburen
Albert Beein
Dirck Teepening
Christian Derick
Frederick Row
Tobias Winekoop
William Bell
Arie Delonga
Corne Vandenbergh
Johans Hoghteling
Jacob Dubois Ju'r Totll 61.

A List of the Foot Company of Militia of the Corporation of Kingston Under the Command of

Capt Hendrick H. Schoonmaker
Leut: John Sleght
Insjn Lawrens Van Gaasbeck
Sarj. Edward Wood
Sarj. Dirck Van Vleet
Sarj. Jacobus De Lametter
Corpo Teunis Swart
Corpo Johannes Snyder
Corpo William Oosterhout

Clark Benjamin Sleght
John Ploegh
Peter Winne
Heskiah Schoonmaker
Teunis A. Swart
Aarent Ploegh
John Wittaker
Abra Burhans
Cryn Oosterhout
Jan Peterse Oosterhout
Marta Snyder
Zachary Backer
Lawrence Salisbury
Aares Van Steenbergh
Abra Post
Abra Oosterhout
Jan Woolf
Johannis Burhans
Hendricus Ploegh Jn'r
Hendr Krynse Oosterhout
Petrus Krynse Oosterhout
Johannis Burhans Jn'r
Poules Pelen
Bowdewine Vanderlip
Teunis Van Bunschote
Wilhelmus Demyer
Jacobus Van Steenbergh
Hendricus Ploegh

Teunis Oosterhout
Jan Krinse Oosterhout
Hendrick Brinck
Jacob Brinck
Lawrens Swart
Abra Davenport
Petrus Oosterhout
Cornr Swart
Grieg Magriegere

Totll 46.

A List of the Foot Company of Militia of Marbletown Under the Command of Capt. Daniel Brodhead.

Capt Daniel Brodhead
Lievt John Dewitt
Ensign John Brodhead
Serjeant Martin Bogart
Serjeant Jacobus Bush
Serjeant Thomas Keator
Corporal Cornelius Van Kampen
Corporal Christopher Davis
Corporal Jacob Keator
Drummer Peter Vandenbergh
Clerke Ric'd Pick

Lambert Brinck
Johannes Van Luven
Andreas Van Luven
Jacob Keyser
Valentine Smith
Tuenis Klarwater
Frederick Davis
Gysbt Roosa
Jan Roosa
James Algar
Hartman Hine
Arien Vandermarke
Jacob Vandermarke
Jacob Middagh
Jacobus Tack
Isaac Tack
Johannes Jansen
Dirck Bush
Melgart Ketor
Thos Vandermarke
Augustinus Ketor
Hendr Vandermarke
Dirck Keyser
Samuel Davis
Samuel Cock
Benja Davis
Alexander Ennis
Andrew Kernith
Isaac Van Kampen
Samuel Mourits
Johans Thomas
Johannes Bush
James Robinson
Mathew Algar
Corne Tack Jn'r
Hendr Bush
John Price
Lambert Bush
Moses Depuy
Johans Vandermarke
Thoms Vandermarke
Nicholas Vandermarke
Thoms More
John Krom
Henry Krom Jn'r
Robert Maginnis
Lewis Bevier
Johanas Kool
Andreas Conterman
Henry Conterman
Adam Hoffman
Hendricus Van Steenburgh
Abra Constaple
Moses Cantien
Nicholas Keyser
William Hine
John Wood
Johannes Elting
Anthony Gerrits
Jacob Sleyter
Nicholas Sleyter
Nicha Sloyter Jn'r
Johannes Depuy
Richard Lonsberry
William Ennis
Augus Vandemarke
Ephaim Chambers
Dirck Keyser Jn'r
Jacob Keyser Jn'r
Fredr Schoomker

Henry Jansen
Thos Bush
Fredr Keator
Power Easel
Edward Robason
John Smith
Totll 80.

A LIST OF THE COMPANY OF MILITIA OF THE WALL A KILL UNDER THE COMMAND OF CAPT. JOHN BYARD.

Capt John Byard
Lievt William Borland
Ensign William Keils
Serj't John Newkerk
Corpo John Miller

Lendert Coll
Cornelius Coll
Barnat Coll
John Robeson
John McNeill
Andraw borland
John borland
John McNeill Ju'r
James Glispy
Thomas Glispy
John Willkine
William Wilkins
Andraw Graham
George Olloms
John North
John North Ju'r
Samuel North
James Young
Robert Young
Mathew Young
John Andraws
James McNeill
James Craford
John Craford
Alexander Milligan
Nathaneill Hill
Alixd kid
Archabald Hunter
James Hunter
John Wharrey
Benja Hins (Haines)
John McNeill Senior
Mathew Prea
William Craford
Robert hunter
James Munall
Gors Monull
John Munall
William Monall
Thomas Neils
Robert Neils
John Neils
Mathew Neils
Celab knep
Robert McCord
William fallkne
Ezrail Rodgr
Jeremiah Rodgr
Robert Buchanan
James Egar
Sojornars Her
Thomas McCollom
John Haves
M kam Clein
Jury burger
Hugh flenign
Benja benot
Patrick Mc peick
John Eldoris
Patrick Galasby
John Lowry
Samuel mith
Jopth Teall
James Craford
Joseph Sutter
David Cree
Edward Andrews
Samuel Crayford
Endrew Doell
Phillip Milsbugh
Cronamas Mingus
Stuffel Moll
James Rodgr
James Whit
John Manly
francius walls
Robert Hughby
Hendrick Crist
Hunas Crist
Lowrance Crist
Mattys Milsbigh
and his son
John Mings
Stevanis Crist
Jacob bush
Hannas Crane

David Gill, Jr.

Nathaniell jojter
John Neily ju'r
Joseph butteltown
Thomas Colman
Joseph Shaw
pathrick broodrick
William Soutter
John butfield
John Mc ye
John Jones
Joseph knap
Isakiah Gaill
John Yong
Hendrick Newkerk
Frederick Sanzabus
Cornelius walls
Cronamas falter
Richard Gatehouse
John boyls
Richard boyls
John Jameson
John McDonall
James Davis

totll 114.

A List of the Foot Company of Militia of Hurly Under the Command of Capt. Cornelis Wine Coop.

Capt Cornelis Wine Coop
Left Antonie Crispel
Insin Abraham Ten Eyck
Serje Hendrick Konstaple
Corp'l Solomon fer Willege
Corp'l Jacob Vanwagene
Drom'r Marynis Chambers
Jan Van Duese Clarke

Nicolas Blansjan
Lambert Brinck
Tuenis Oostrander
Jan Roosa
Hendrick Oostrander
Gerret Konstaple
Johannis Crospel
Johannis Suylandt
Arie Van Etten
Gerret Jeo Freer
Harmanus Oostrander
Robert Wieler
Wouter Sluyter
Evert Sluyter
Willem Smit
Gerret Van Wagenen
Johans Van Wagenen
Aert Van Wagenen
Matys Blansyan Ju'r
Simon Helm
Adam Sjeever
Jefta De Lange
Crisstoffel Brosie
Antonie Crispel Ju'r
Johan's Konstaple
Andries Van Vliet
Heyman Roosa
Jan A Roosa
Gysbert Roosa Ju'r
Jan Crispel Ju'r
Drick Roosa
Ned Wieler
Edvart Chammers
Daniel potter
Jan Ja: Roosa
Abra Roosa
Nicolas Roosa
Benja Clearwater
Jan ter Willege Ju'r
Jan Van Deuse Ju'r
Jan Brinck
Johannis Oostrander Ju
Willem Sluyter Ju'r
Hendrick Ja: Freer
Jan Waters
Albert Ja: Roosa
Mattheus Nienkerck
Benja Nieukerck
Petrus Crispel
Willem Burhans
Jacop Clyn
Jacop Oostrander

Totll 60.

A List of the Foot Company of Militia of Rocester (Rochester)

Under the Command of Capt. Cornelius Hoornbeck.

Capt Cornelius Hoornbeck
Lieut phillip Dubois
Ensign Cornelius B: Low
Serja Johannis Hoornbeck
Serja John Wesbroeck
Serja Harmanis Rosekrans
Corpo Samuel Swarthout
Corpo Tuenis Middagh
Corpo Manuel Gonsalis

Arien Van Vliet
John Schoonmaker
John Hillmen
Frans Kelder
Jacob Kelder
William Kelder
Felter Kelder
Benja van wagenen
John Robeson
Jacob Dewitt Ju'r
John Dewitt
Cornelius Winekoop
Jacobus Terwillige
John Terwillige
Jacobus Quick
Jacobus Depue
Joha Hendreickson
Joha Krom
Hendrick Krom
Daniel Schoonmaker
Jocham Fra: Schoonmaker
Johannis Miller
Josaphat Dubois
Jacob Vernoy
Tuenis Oosterhout Ju'r
Kryn Oosterhout
Nicholas Ketor
Petrus Oosterhout
Hende Oosterhout
Jonathan Westbroeck
Johannis Westbroeck
Matheus Terwillige
Nicklas Low
Abra Low
Cornelius Low
Jacobus Low
Johannis Oosterhout

Jeremia Van Derkerke
Benja Hoornbeck
Dirck Hoornbeck
Peter Westbroeck
Tobias Hoornbeck
Jacobus Hoornbeck
Lowrence Cortreght
Mathew Cortreght
Peter Cortreght
Hendrick Cortreght
Johannis Ketor
Isaac Van Aken
Charles Danneson
Richard Kittle
Benja Roggers
Wessel Vernoy
Coenradt Vernoy
Michel Helm
Petrus Low
Lawies Bovier Ju'r
Cornelius Bovier
Samuel Bovier Ju'r
Jacob Bovier
Manuel Gonsalis Ju'r
Jacob Middagh
Abra Middagh
Isaac Middagh
Johannis Middagh
Janies Simson
Jacob Vandermarke
Geradus Van Inwegen
Benja Coddebeck
William Coddebeck
Abra Coddebeck
Peter Jemare

Totll 81.

A List of the Foot Company of Militia of the Pals (Paltz) Under the Command of Capt. Zacharias Hoffman.

Capt Zacharias Hoffman
Lievt Benjamin Smedes Ju'r
Ensign Zacharias Hoffman Ju'r
Serj's John Teer penning
Serj's John Freer
Serj's Evert Terwillege
Corpo Christian Dujo
Corpo Hendrick Deyo
Corpo Isaac Lefever

Isaac freer
Tuenis Terpening
Jan Une
Jonas freer
James Agmodi
Simon Lefever
Petrus Low
Johannis Low
Josia Elting
Abra Dujo
Cornelius Dubois
Jonathan Dubois
Josua Smedes
Gerett Ja: Decker
Stevanis Swart
John Robertse
Hendr Dubois
Mosis Dujo
Auguste Van Deermerke
Jacob Ge: Decker
James Pinnick
Daniel Winfiel
Manewel ter Willige
Johannes Terwillige
Hendrick Decker
Petrus Terwillige
Thoms Janson Ju'r
William Rosekrans
Corns Schoonmaker Ju'r
Corns Cool
Johannis Cool
Lewis Pontenere
Andrew Grames
Robert Greams
John Blake
James Jonston
Salamon Isrel
Samuel Sampson
Roger Blamles
Richard Davis
Lawrence Eldorp
Tomas Maccoun
John Andrew

Arie Terwillige
William Schoot
Cornelius bruyn
William Ja: Decker
Jacob Ja: Decker
Abra Ja: Decker
Isaac Ja: Decker
Benja Ja: Decker
Jacob He: Decker
Abra He: Decker
Abra Terwillige
Isaac Terwillige
Evert Terwillige Ju'r
Robert Cain
John Gream
William Weller
Hendrick Weller
Isaac Haasbroeck
Jacob Haasbroeck Ju'r
Benja Haasbroeck Ju'r
Zacharias Klarwater
Abra Bovier
Mathues Bovier
Jacobus Bovier
Isaac Bovier
Abra Lefever
Nathael Lefever
Benja Haasbroeck
Symon Dubois
Isaac Lefever Ju'r
Peter De: jo
Huge Freer Ju'r
Hendrick Van Wijak
Abra Vandermerke
Lewis Sa: Bovier
William Armstrong
Robert Jong
Mathew Jong
John Jemeson
Robert Hanne
John Magdonel
Johannes Masseker

Totll 94.

A List of the Foot Company of Militia of the Presenk of tee Highland Under the Command of Capt. Thos. Ellison.

Capt Thomas Ellison
Lievt George Harrison
Ensign John Young
Serjent David Davis
Serjent Patrick McCloghry
Serjent Mosas Garitson
Corpo Jacobus Bruyn Jur
Corpo James Stringham
Corpo Jonathan Hazard
Clark Charles Clinton

John Umphrey
James Gamble
John Gamble
Cornelius McClean
John Umphry Ju'r
James Umphry
Peter Mulinder
Robert Burnet
Archibald Beaty
Arthur Beaty
David Olliver
Mathew Davis
Alexander Falls
Alexander Denniston
James Young
David Bedford
William Coleman
Joseph Sweezer
Thomas Coleman
John McVey
John Jones
Patrick Broderick
Joseph Shaw
Calab Curtis
William Sutten
Jeremiah Foster
Charles Beaty
Amas Foster
John Clark
Lodewick Miller
James Nealy
Robert Feef
Joseph Butterton
Samuell Lukey
John Markham
John Read
Joseph McMikhill
David Umphrey
Johannis George
Jeremiah Tomkins
Isaac Tomkins
William Watts
Josiah Elsworth
James Elsworth
Anthony Preslaer
Jonathan Tomkins
John Nicoll Ju'r
Alexander McKey
Robert Sparks
Jevriah Quick
Thomas Quick
Jacob Gillis
Joseph Simson
James Clark
Peter Miller
George Waygant
William Ward
William Ward Ju'r
John Mattys Kimbergh
William Smith Ju'r
James Edmeston
Tobias Waygate
Jerry Mause
Thomas Johnston
Casparis Stymas
John Monger
James Luckey
Thomas Williams
Robert Banker
Thomas Fear
Frederick Painter
Mosas Elsworth
John Marie
Jonathan Owens
Andrew McDowell
Daniel Coleman

Tot. 86

CHAPTER VII

THE FRENCH AND INDIAN WAR.

TO recount the connection of the people of Ulster County, through their representatives, with the great events of the world's history, is one of the duties of the local historian. Unfortunately it is a field of inquiry in which those of the present generation are not as a rule well informed, and unfortunately, the pages of a local history are too limited for a general review of the politics and the wars of Europe which affected the American Colonies. Substantially the first of the series of events which culminated, in 1760, in the final overthrow of the occupation of Canada by the French and practically of the domination of France on the North American continent, was what is known as the War of 1744, which involved England, France, and Spain; the capture of Havana and the West India Islands by England, the devastations by the French and of the Indians along the northern frontiers of New England, and the threatened invasion of the province of New York. True it is, as Bancroft wrote, "the little conflicts in America are lost in the universal conflagration of Europe."

It was not until 1746 that the province of New York began to make preparations for engaging in the pending conflict; its territory had not been invaded, thanks to the English alliance with the Six Nations, who, under their treaty of peace with the Abenaqui and the tribes in its alliance, held those nations to the line of the Housatonic, east of which the invaders might slay and burn without their interfering with treaty obligations, while on the west side farmers ploughed their fields in sight of the blazing dwellings of their neighbors. By the indiscreet act of passing the boundary line and capturing and burning Fort Massachusetts on the border of New York, the warriors of the Six Nations were released from their obligations and were ready for the fray—their territory had been invaded. The success which had attended the colonial troops of Massachusetts and Rhode Island in the capture of Louisburg, aroused the King of England to further aggressive action. "His most gracious Majesty having been pleased to set on foot an expedition for the reduction of Canada," reads the act of the Colonial Assembly of July 5, 1746, authorizing the expenditure of Forty Thousand Pounds "for carrying on an expedition against Canada," and asking the enlistment of volunteers to whom a bounty of six pounds each (about $14.40) was offered. Some enlistments appear to have been made in New York prior to the passage of the act, and some may have been made in Ulster. Of record only is the roll in 1746, without date of day or month:

"MUSTER ROOL OF CAPT. JOHN HASBROUCK'S COMPANY OF MILITIA, LIEUT. COL. JOHANNES HARDENBERG'S REGIMENT, IN GENERAL SCOTT'S BRIGADE, AT OR NEAR THE WHITE PLAINS:

Capt. John Hasbrouck, Present fit for duty.
Lieut. John Hunter,
Lieut. Jacobus Rosekrans, on command, with Col. Lasher.
Serg't James Hugg, Present fit for duty.
Serg't David Etkins " " " "
Serg't Joseph Chambers " " " "
Corp'l Samuel Lewis " " " "
Corp'l Jonathan Westbrouck " " " "
Corp'l Johannis Rosa " " " "
Private Stephen Nottingham " " " "
Petrus Oosterhoudt " " " "
James Robinson " " " "
Isaac Newkirk, Discharged.
Pieter Mowris, Present fit for duty.
Daniel Johnson, " " " "
William Conner, " " " "
Cornelius D. De Witt, " " " "
Peter Hendrickson, on command with Col. Lasher.
Henry Harp, sick, present,
Henry Oosterhout, Present fit for duty.
Thomas Crispell " " " "
Abraham Middaugh, Discharged,
John ——, Present fit for duty.
John Depuy " " " "
Johannes Keyser, " " " "
Jacob Shaw Craft, " " " "
Henry Kittle, " " " "
Cornelius Sluyter, sick, present,
Pieter Thompson, present fit for duty,
Jacob Harley " " " "
Thomas Shurley, Discharged,
Cornelius Coneway, "
William Benson, Present fit for duty,
Ghysbert Vab Demerke, Discharged.
Thyrn Oosterhoudt, Present fit for duty.
James Termon, " " " "

Hewitt Boice.

John Sluyter, on command with Col. Lasher,
William Sluyter, Present fit for duty,
James Phoenix, " " " "
Frederick Hymes, " " " "
Cornelius Krom, " " " "
Loderick Selie, " " " "
Gideon Dean, on command with Col. Lasher,
Pieter Frere, Discharged,
Benjamin Stanton, Present fit for duty,
Pieter Degarimo, sick, present,
Pieter Van Vlerke, Discharged,
William Wheeler, Unfit for duty
Hendrick Wessmiller, Unfit for duty,
James Malony, Present fit for duty,
Hendrick Krom, Absent with leave,
Hugy Lacy, Lister in the train of artillery,
John Jeffers, " " " " " "
David Burns, " " " " " "
John Crisby, " " " " " "
Dirick Sluyter, Deceased,
John Hyneson.

It should not be inferred that this company included all the enlistments from Ulster; it is simply the only return on file. This explanation will also apply to lists at later periods.

Nothing more than a petty warfare followed the arrangements for the reduction of Canada. Pending formidable aggressive movement in that direction, the war was closed by the Treaty of Aix la Chapelle in 1748, and the disbandment of the provincial forces followed in September of that year.

But peace was of short continuance; the opposing interests of France and England were inimical to peaceful relations; another factor was the Indians. Briefly summarizing the situation: By the treaty of Aix la Chapelle the "subjects of France, inhabitants of Canada," were not to "disturb or molest in any manner whatever" the Five Indian Nations which were the "subjects of Great Britain," nor the "other American allies" of the government; the boundaries between the English and French possessions, along the rivers St. Lawrence and Mississippi, were left entirely undetermined, and no provision was made for the removal of the fort, which the French had erected at Crown Point, on Lake Champlain, and at Niagara. Securing from the Onondagas, Senecas, Cayugas, and Oneidas the declaration that they were "independent tribes" and not the "subjects of Great Britain," the French resumed the policy of connecting the St. Lawrence with the Gulf of Mexico by a chain of forts along that river to Detroit and down the Ohio to the Mississippi. This policy was inimical to the interests of England; self-interest as well as self-defence demanded that the construction of the forts should be anticipated if possible—if not, that their occupation by the French should be resisted. Virginia organized what was known as the Ohio Company, for the ostensible purpose of securing the Ohio Valley, and gave patent to Christopher Gist to make treaties with the Indians and select locations. The Senecas, the Lenapes and the Shawanoes, whose territory was thus invaded by the opposing civilizations, did not regard these movements with favor. Looking over the situation the ruling Senaca chief remonstrated: "Where," he asked, "lie the lands of the Indians? The French claim all on one side of the river, and the English all on the other." He retired dissatisfied. The French went on with their forts; Virginia demanded that they give reason "for invading the British possessions"; the French commander knew no law but the orders of his general; the casus belli which Virginia sought was supplied; war followed, and the campaign and defeat of Braddock followed, but the end was not reached.

Meanwhile the Lenape, or Delawares, had some grievances to settle. They had been defrauded of their lands by the famous "walking purchase," and by the purchasers of the Minisink lands who had made them drunk and refused to pay them when they became sober. The Esopus chiefs joined in the complaint as parties in interest; the borders of New Jersey and New York, as well as the wildernesses of Pennsylvania, were filled with the protestations of disfranchised proprietors; the Five Nations gave them encouragement. No sooner had the frost reddened the maple leaves and hardened the yellow corn in the husk, than, with their allies, painted black for war, in bands of two or four, they moved eastward and the line of the Delaware and the Susquehanna became the scene of the carnival which they held with torch and tomahawk during many coming months; the French and Indian War of 1754 was inaugurated, not to cease so long as the flag of France waved in Canada; not to cease until it was determined whether America should be Catholic or Protestant—whether Catholic France or Protestant England should rule—the avant courier of the American Revolution, the abolition of sectarian rule, the enthronement of a nation that should know "no King but God." It practically terminated in 1760, September 5th, with the surrender of Montreal to the English. On that day French power in Canada ceased, although the formal treaty of peace and the cession of Canada to England was not concluded until the signing of the Treaty of Paris, February 16th, 1763.

In local history the general history of the war has only incidental place—its local events and the men who participated in them, principally its militia, are properly the field of review. The French forces came not upon the borders of the county—the invaders were the Lenape and their allies who carried fire and tomahawk and made its southwestern frontiers a weary burden. A paper endorsed "Observations on the State of Ulster and Orange counties, sent to the General Assembly in March, 1756," presumed to have been written by Colonel Thomas Ellison, recites: "The southern part of Ulster County, is in general a settled country, and the settlements and improvements generally made by poor people. * * By the frequent and repeated incursions of the Indians on that part of Pennsylvania adjoining to these counties, and afterwards on some parts of these counties, the people have been kept in frequent and almost perpetual alarm whereby the inhabitants have been in continued military duty so as to be rendered incapable of taking care of their private affairs for the support of their families, and the hardships attending these military duties in watching and ranging the woods has been so great that the people are distressed and almost worn out with fatigue. An extent of country on the west side of the Wallkill of 15 miles in length and 7 or 8 in breadth is now abandoned by the inhabitants." * * * For the protection of the exposed frontier, Gov. Hardy, in the summer of 1757, had block houses erected covering a distance of thirty miles, or from Mombaccus (Rochester) to Maghaghkamik, where they connected with the block houses of New Jersey extending along the border of that province. The block houses were garrisoned by detachments from the militia and specially enlisted companies of which there is of record only one under command of Capt. James Clinton.

The enrollment of the militia regiments, and of the companies of volunteers in the service of the Province during the war, is very imperfect. In 1757, the regiment which had existed for many years was divided, and two regiments constituted, the first under the command of Colonel Johannis Hardenbergh, whose associate field officers are not of record so far as ascertained, and the second under command of Colonel Thomas Ellison, who has been met on the rolls of 1738 as Captain of the most southerly company of the Ulster regiment of that period. Colonel Ellison's (second) regiment had for its field officers Charles Clinton, Lieutenant Colonel; Cadwallader Colden, Junr., Major, and Johannes Jansen, Adjutant, and was composed of thirteen companies, commanded respectively by Captains Johnathan Hasbrouck, Johannes Hardenbergh, Jr., Jacob Newkirk, William Ellison, James McClaughry, Thomas Jansen, Cadwallader C. Colden, Budewine Terpening, David Galatian, Moses Phillips, John Wollay, and John Crage. The territory which it covered has not been definitely ascertained, but from the names of officers of the regiment in 1772, it seems to have included the entire belt of country north of the original county line as far as the line of New Paltz and west from the Hudson to the Wallkill at Phillipsburgh. Colonel Hardenbergh's first regiment covered the remainder of the county. The headquarters of the first was at Kingston; the headquarters of the second was at New Windsor. It is doubtful if either regiment was at any time in the field *en masse*, the nearest approach to that field service being in 1755, when both regiments were ordered out to reinforce Colonel (Sir) William Johnson in his operations around Lake George and Fort William Henry, which will be noticed later. The principal field service was in detachments and companies of volunteers regularly organized, and of these the record is fragmentary and unsatisfactory, and that of the volunteer companies more or less mixed. The earliest in the field seems to have been a company commanded by Captain Cornelius Van Buren—Jacob Rutzen De Witt, Lieutenant; later Matthew Rea, Lieut. No list of this company appears of record. Captain Richard Rea had a company recruited from Duchess and Ulster, and Ebenezer Sealy, Jun'r, recruited one in southern Ulster, in 1758, of which James Clinton and Edward Erwin were Lieutenants. A company under Captain Stephen Nottingham of Shawangunk—Henry Jansen and Cornelius Wynkoop, Lieutenants—stand on the published roll: "Mustered the 15th of April, 1758, by Charles Clinton, Esq., Lieutenant Colonel of one of the Battalions of said Province." The roll is as follows:

A Roll of Capt. Stephen Nottingham's Company Voluntarily Enlisted in His Majesties Service in the Pay of the Province of New York & Mustered the 15th of April, 1758, by Charles Clinton Esqr. Lt. Colonel of One of the Batalions of Said Province, with the Time of Their Several Inlistments.

Captain.
Stephen Nottingham Esq'r.
Lieutenants.
Henry Jansen.
Cornelius Wyncoop.

Serjeants
Thom's Nottingham
Gerret Brodhead
Jacob Nottingham
John Johnson

Corporals
Jacob Vandermark
Petrus Schoonmaker

Barnet Mercle
Drum'r.
George Webster

PRIVATES.

Wilhelmus Mercle
Mortin Middagh Jun'r
John Dotey
John Keater
Dan'l McKinley
Petrus Clarewater
John Middagh
Mortin Krum
John Brodhead
Andries Davis
Luke Brodhead
Wm Ennist
Jacob Keater Jun'r
Gerardus Newkirk
Petrus Mercle
Isaac Roosa
Adam Huffman
Bruynus Vanderburgh
George Middagh Jun'r
Jacobus J. Bush
Abraham Keater
Nich's Slouyter
Benj'n Mercle
Dirck Chambers
Andries Kyser
Arie Keater
Japhtha Slouyter
Rich'd Lounsberry
Benj'n Eakerley
Jam's Alegar
Wm McConnell
Jacobus Turner
Johannis Ryder
Cornel's Hardenbergh
Koonrad Burger
Johannis Hornbeak
John Mullen
Benj'n Curtright
Nath'l Curtright
John Van Vleet
Wm Hyn
Chrisse Davids
Casper Ruyter
Johannis Turner
Jacob Clyn
Egbert De Witt Jun'r
George Mack
Andries Rudolf
Petrus Vernoy
Garton De Witt
Christopher Medler

Joseph Martin
Jacob Vanderlinde
Lucas De Witt
Johannis Stroup
Petrus And. Vanlieuven
Peter Luyick Junr
John Ebberhard Gochnat
John Cane
Joseph Griffen
Roger Blameless
Mortha Bayard
Philip Schoonmaker
Joost Koonst
Philip Swart
Solomon Osterander
Stephanus Weest
Jacob S. Freer
Aaron Rice
Nath'l Bryant
Baltus Kiefor
Hendricus Oosterhout
Benj'm Swart
Ezekiel De Witt
Petrus De Witt
Lucas Wyncoop
Johannis Sleight Jun'r
Jacobus Post
Hendricus Post
Hendricus Bedeker Jun'r
Barent Legg
Petrus Oosterhout
Coonrad Andries Tiel
Wm Shafe
Griffe Estel
Hendrick Beem
Peter Miller
Hermanus Dumont
Hugh Smith
Johannis Degraff
Wm Kiger
Jacobus Montanie
John Brede
Wilhelmus Chrispel
Garret Newkirk
Joseph Watkins
John Wheeler
Jacob Helm
Hendrick Clough
Petrus Schoonmaker
Jacob Sloughter
Martin Griffin

Albertus Anthony
Philip Miller
William Mercle
John Beneway
Sam'l Wells Jun'r
John Herman
Wm Snyder
John De Witt Jun'r
Cornel's Hendrikse
Petrus Post
John Vanderspagle
Rich's Brodhead
N. B.
John Johnson Serjt
John Dotey
Hendrick Beem
Johannis Degraff
Petrus Post &
Richard Brodhead

These were enlisted & sworn but not mustered.

A List of the Men's Names Inlisted by Stephen Nottingham Out of the First Regiment in Ulster County, (1758).

Garton DeWitt
Andreas Rudolf
Egbert Dewitt Jun'r
Petrus Vanoy
George Mack
George Webster Drumer
Wilhelmus Marker
Martha Midagh
Jacon Vandermark
John Keter
Barant Markle
Daniel McKinley
Petrus Clarewater
John Middagh
Jacob Notingham Serjeant
Martin Crum
John Broadhead
Andreas Davis
Luke Broadhead
William Ennis Jun'r
Jacob Keter Jun'r
Adam Hoffman
Bruyness Vanderbergh
George Middagh Jun'r
Jacobus Hanneste Boss
Richard Loonsberry Jun'r
Abraham Keter Jun'r
Nicholas Slouter Jun'r
Benjamin Markle
Dirck Chambers
Thomas Notingham Serjeant
Andreus Kyser
Jesta Slouter
Benjamin Swart
John Vanfleet
Jacob Klyne
Christopher Davis
Petrus Andreas Van leven
Peter Luiks Jun'r
Christopher Midler
Benjamin Ekly
Jacobus Turner
Johannes Kidder
Petrus Schoonmaker
Cornelius Hardenbergh
Cunerate Burger
Johannes Hornbeek
John Mullen
Benjamin Kortraght
Gerardus Newkirk
Petrus Markle
Isaac Roose
Casper Ryter
Johannes Turner
William Heyne
Nathanael Courtraight
William McConner Clarke
Phillip Scoonmaker
Joest Konnet
Phillip Swart
Solomon Ostrander
Stephanus Wist
Jacob Freer
Aaron Rice
Peter Vanlooven Jun'r
Nathanael Bryan
James Alliger
Cunerate Andreas Steel
William Sheaff
Petrus Ostrout
Griffith Asstith
Belta Kisser
Henrikus Osterout
Petrus Dewitt
Lukeas Wynkoop
Jacobus Post
Henricus Post
Henricus Rediker
Barant Legg
Johannes Strope

Albertus Antony
Phillip Miller
William Markle
John Beneway
Samuel Wells Jun'r
John Harman
William Snyder
John Dewitt Jun'r
Cornelius Hendrickse
Joseph Martin
Jacob Vandelinder
Lukeas Dewitt
John Eberhard Gohnat
Peter Miller
Hermanus Dumont
Hugh Smith
William Keyger
John Kain
Joseph Griffin
Ezekiel Dewitt

Johannes Wheller
Jacob Holm
Henrick Plugh
Petrus Johannes Schoonmaker
Jacob Slouter
Roger Blameless
Martha Byard
Johannis Sleight Jun'r
Jacobus Montany
John Brady
Wilhelmus Crespel
Gerret Newkirk
Joseph Atkins
John Vanderspegle
Abraham Post
Martynas Griffin
Arw Terwilliger
Aari Keter

P. CHAR. CLINTON.

John Doughty lying in the Small pox
John Johnson did not attend
Henrick Beam) did not appear.
Johannes De Graff)
These men are not mustered.*

This Company with that recruited by Captain Sealy and James Clinton, is presumed to have been in Lieutenant Charles Clinton's Brigade under General Bradstreet for the reduction of Fort Frontenac on the St. Lawrence. The expedition, it may be noted here, was successful. The fort was one of the strongest fortresses in America. It was taken by surprise, and with it came to the Provincial forces nine armed vessels, forty pieces of cannon and a large quantity of provisions and stores. George Clinton, son of Lieut. Col. Charles Clinton, accompanied his father on the expedition, and in 1777, became the first Governor of the State under the Constitution.

In 1760 James Clinton raised a company in southern Ulster, of which George Clinton and Isaiah Purdy were Lieutenants. In 1761 he recruited another company, of which William Stewart and Hendrick Johannes Sleght were Lieutenants. In 1762, he recruited another — Lieutenants William Stewart, Alexander Denniston, Mathew Smedes and John McNeal. The endorsement on the roll of this company reads: "For guarding the western frontier of Ulster and Orange Counties," in which service Clinton's previously recruited companies were engaged. The muster rolls are very complete in descriptive lists—where born, age, height, color of

* The last five.

hair and eyes, and give the reader a pretty correct idea of "what manner of men" composed the militia. The enlistments were in each case for one year. The men were clearly from Colonel Ellison's second Ulster regiment. They cannot be eliminated from the history of Ulster County by the new county line of 1798 without perpetrating a gross injustice. *Ulster, the mother county, borrows nothing from her sons; she takes that which belongs to her history.* In 1774 Colonel Ellison divided his regiment in two battalions, the first of which was placed under the command of James Clinton, whose next appearance will be in the forces raised in his native county for the war for National Independence.

Turning back to 1755, when the Ulster regiments were called out to re-inforce Colonel (later Sir) William Johnson at Lake George, a statement written by Colonel Ellison shows that the first regiment had transportation by sloop from Kingston, and the second by sloop from New Windsor to Albany. From Albany to Fort Edward the men marched on the west side of the Hudson, carried their equipments and provisions, waded through creeks "crotch deep," and camped "opposite Fort Edward," *i. e.* on the west side of the Hudson, were ordered "to go voluntarily" to the attack of a force of the enemy lying between Fort Edward and Fort William Henry. In less than an hour the whole force "waded through Hudson's River to Fort Edward." "The last of the militia had not got well through the river before the attempt was thought too hazardous, whereupon we were ordered immediately back to our camp," wrote Colonel Ellison in his narrative. After remaining in camp five days, and learning that the French "were destroying Fort William Henry," the regiments returned to their homes, and were criticised for so doing. Except in the alacrity with which they had hastened to the field of duty, it was not a "glorious campaign." The "retreat," if so it may be called, was justified on the ground of the necessity for protecting their own homes.

Leaving the local events of the war to the historians of the towns in which those events occurred, and referring to the report of the State Historian, 1896, Colonial Series, for such muster rolls of the Ulster militia as are in the archives of the State, we throw the view forward to the threshold of the war for Independence in the annexed list of officers, and of two companies of privates in the Second Ulster Regiment in 1773, compiled from original manuscripts found among Colonel Ellison's papers, now in Washington's Headquarters, *never before printed or published.* The list is as follows:

TO SIR WILLIAM JOHNSON, BAR'T MAJ'R GENERAL OF THE MILITIA OF THE NORTHERN DEPARTMENT OF THE PROVINCE OF NEW YORK:

"In obedience to your General Order of ye 16th of July, 1773, you have here underneath the return of the Second Regiment of the Militia of the County of Ulster, whereof

Thomas Ellison, Coll.
Charles Clinton, Lieut. Coll.
Cadwallader Colden, Junior, Major.
Johannes Jansen, Adjutant.

1. Jonathan Hasbrouck, Capt.; Samuel Sands, 1st Lieut.; Wolver Actor, 2nd Lieut.; Cornelius Hasbrouck, Ensign—4 Sergts., 4 Corporals, 1 Drummer, 141 men.

2. Johannes Hardenbergh, Junr., Captain; Jacobus Rose, 1st Lieut.; Corn'ls Maston, 2d Lieut.; Jonathan Hardenbergh, Ensign—4 Sergts., 3 Corp's, 1 Drummer, 101 men.

3. Jacob Newkerck, Captain; Matthew Fetter, 1st Lieut.; Hendrick Smith 2d Lieut.; Johannes Newkirk, Ensign—4 Sergt's, 4 Corporals, 1 Drummer, 69 men.

4. William Ellison, Captain; Judah Harlow, 1st Lieut.; John Nicolls, 2d Lieut.; Francis Mandeville, Ensign—4 Sergt's, 4 Corpl's, 1 Drummer, 70 men.

5. Thomas Bull, Captain; Samuel Watkens, 1st Lieut.; William Booth, 2d Lieut.; Stephen Harlow, Ensign—4 Sergt's, 4 Corpl's, 1 Drummer—63 men.

6. James McClaughry, Captain; James Humphrey, 1st Lieut.; Joseph Belknap, 2d Lieut.; James Burnet, Ensign—4 Sergt's, 4 Corporals, 1 Drummer, 160 men.

7. Thomas Jansen, Captain; Matthew Jansen, 1st Lieut.; Abraham Smedes, Sen., 2d Lieut.; Severyn F. Bruyn, Ensign—4 Sergt's, 4 Corporals, 1 Drummer, 73 men.

8. Cadwallader C. Colden, Capt.; Thomas Colden, 1st Lieut.; James Milliken, 2d Lieut.; Mathew Hunter, Ensign—4 Sergt's, 4 Corpl's, 1 Drummer, 100 men.

9. Budewine Terpening, Captain; Elisha Freir, 1st Lieut.; Jonathan Ostrander, 2d Lieut.; John Everitt, Ensign—4 Sergt's, 4 Corporals, 1 Drummer, 59 men.

10. David Galatian, Captain; Curdrow Graham, 1st Lieut.; Peter Hill, 2d Lieut.; Jacob Bodine, Ensign—4 Sergt's, 4 Corpl's, 1 Drummer, 67 men.

11. Moses Phillips, Captain; William Dirr (?), 1st Lieut.; Elijah Beaver, 2d Lieut.; David Mores, Ensign—4 Sergt's, 4 Corpl's, 1 Drummer, 70 men.

12. John Wollay, Captain; Latting Carpenter, 1st Lieut.; Humphrey Merrit, 2d Lieut.; Joseph Murry, Ensign—4 Sergt's, 4 Corpl's, 1 Drummer, 107 men.

13. Joseph Crage, Captain; William Sinnall (?), 1st Lieut.; John Graham, 2d Lieut.; John T. Graham, Ensign—4 Sergt's, 1 Drummer, 102 men.

The total strength of companies is given in uncertain figures in some instances. The total strength of the regiment is placed at 1350 men, 64 Sergeants, 53 Corporals, and 15 Drummers. John Wollay's company was surely a Marlborough organization. Thomas Bull's company was surely Captain William Faulkner's company in 1772, of which Thomas Bull was then 1st Lieutenant. Captain Faulkner returned 243 men. It was surely in the old Precinct of Wallkill on the west side, with western and northern limits undefined.

"A List of All the Rank and File Men Within the Precinct of Shawangunk, on the East Side of the Wallkill, Belonging to the Company of Militia Whereof Johannes Hardenberg, Jun'r, is Captain, Within the Second Regiment of the County of Ulster, as Follows:

Jacobus Roos, 1st Sergt.
Corns. Masten, 2d Sergt.
Teunus Terpening, 3d Sergt.
Corns. Rant, 1st Corp.
John Slaughter, 2d Corp.
Jonathan Dowel,
Will'm Dowel,
Alex'r Dowel,
Jonathan Hardenbergh,
Andries Dubois,
Justus Banks,
James Oliver,
Zacharias Terwilliger,
Alex'd Colter,
Jacob Ostrander,
Helmus Ostrander
Corns. Vernoy
Petrus Terwilliger,
Benj'n Terwilliger, Jun'r,
Petrus Terwilliger, Jun'r,
Jacobus Terwilliger,
Abraham Bevier,
Jonathan Campble,
Moses Bull,
Samuel Hegger,
James Harding,
Paulus Butten,
John Varliman,
John Stienbergh,
Mathewis Stienbergh,
Abrah'm Stienbergh,
John A. Roos,
Isaac Hannion, Jun'r,
Joel Cample,
Solomon Terwilliger,
Teunis Terwilliger,
Isaac Slaughter,
John Slaughter, Jun'r,
Jacob Terwilliger, Jun'r,
Benj'm Van Keuren,
Corn's S. Terwilliger,
Arry Terwilliger,
Will'm Erwin,
George Erwin,
John Erwin,
Samuel Erwin, Jun'r,
Simon Alsdorph,
Ezekiel Masten,
Art Masten,
Zachari Vandemarke,
Helmus Vandemarke,
Joh's Willer,
Dunkan McMollin,
John McMillin,
Embros Jones,
John Carnaran,
Joh's Alsdorph,
Jonathan Bevier,
Mathewis Masten,
Jon's Rank,
Phillip Rank,
Lowrance Rank,
Jeremiah Johnston,
Ebenezer Brown,
Hendricus Terpening,
Petrus A. Roos,
Daniel Hogain,
Will'm Lewis,
John Lewis,
Myndert Newkerk,—70.

Whereas my two Lieutenants, at our last meeting nave both resigned their commissions, I would beg leave to have the following gents returned as Officers in their room to serve as Lieut's, and also an Ensign in the room of Erwin, who is absent—as follows: Jacob Roos, Ju'r, 1st Lieut., in the room of Lieut. Van Keuren; Cornelius Masten, 2d Lieut., in the room of Lieut. Kain; Jonathan Hardenbergh, Ensign, in the room of Edward Erwin.

All from your Humble Serv't,

Joh's Hardenbergh, Ju'r.

177, August 24th.

To Col. Tho's Ellison.

"A List of a Company of Foot Militia Commanded by Cap'n William Faulkner, Taken the 13th Day of July, 1772.

Capt. William Faulkner,
Thomas Bull, } Lieuts.
Daniel Butterfield }
James Crawford, Ensign,
David Crawford, }
John Faulkner, } Sergts.
David Moore, }
Moses Phillips }
George McNish, Ju'r,
Clarke McNish,
David Corwin,
David Corwin, Jr.
Samuel Wybrant,
John Brown,
Archibald Brown,
Isaiah Veal,
Obadiah Veal,
Thos. McWhorter,
John Cox,
Jeremiah Cox,
Jacob Myers,
John Hill,
Waight Carpenter,
Mathew Smith,
Stephen Smith,
Henry Smith,
Israel Smith,
Daniel Smith,
Nathaniel Owen,
Jonathan Owen,
Casper Ritter,
John Green,
John Green, Jr.,
Ebenezer Green,
Thomas Denn,
Daniel Denn,
John Conkling, Jr.,
Jacob Harrison,
George Murry,
Wright Peterson,
Assa Cobb,
Joseph Cobb,
William Cooley,
Elijah Reeve,
Elijah Reeve, Jr.,
Elijah Seely,
Abraham Taylor,
William Gilbert,
Solomon Wheat,
Simeon Mash,
Thomas Mash, Jr.,
Timothy Coleman,
Robert Osburn,
Wm. Couples,
John Butters,
John Mingos,
Jonathan Jourdan,
Robert Dougherty,
Hugh Dougherty,
Phillam Muckelvaney,
Daniel Teers,
Johanas Crance,
John McHenry,
Daniel McHenery,
Samuel Willsson,
Pearce Mansfield,
John Gilcreest,
Wm. Quiggey,
Benjamin Bennett,
James Finch,
Joseph Finch,
Henry Mapes,
Jinks Corey,
Timothy Skinner,
John Gillett,
John Yeomans,
Samuel Davis,
Luke Carter,
Zeporon Cobb,
Eliakim Brown,
Nathan Howell,
Jonathan Corey,
Archibald McCurdy, Jr.,
Thomas Ager,
Joseph Sayre,
James Rogers, Jr.,
Edward Campbell,
Peter Cavanaugh,
Daniel McVey,
Samuel Dunning,
James Morrison,
Daniel McNeal
Thos. Johnston,
George Embler,
Samuel Marvain,
Daniel Wood,
Art. Yerks,
Neal McLaughlin
John McGowan,
Phillip Crist,
Thos. Neely, Jr.,
Wm. Bodle,
Moses Strain,
Archibald Scott,

David Smith, Jr.,
Joseph Smith,
John Daily, Jun'r,
Robert Burnett,
Wm. Rippe,
Stacey Beeks,
Phillip Ketcham,
Assa Brown,
Assa Brown, Jr.,
Thomas Lake,
John Connor,
Abel Wells,
Daniel Decker,
Isaac Decker,
Nathaniel Wells,
Reeves Cox,
Israel Wickam,
Mathew Wickam,
Isaac Smith,
Wm. Stubs,
David Stubs,
Samuel Stubs,
John Ludlum,
Archibald McEntire
William Wickam,
Tilton Eastman,
Benjamin Doughty,
Ephraim Everett,
Michael Rood,
Daniel Wollen,
Elihu Carey,
George Smith,
James Springsted,
Jonathan Webb,
Jonathan Webb, Jr.
Benjamin Veal,
Abraham Stanton,
Rufus Stanton,
Amos Parke,
Ebenezer Parke,
Abner Skinner,
Abiel Worden,
David Sprague,
Richard Johnston,
Andrew McCord,
John Willkins,
Wm. Willkin, Jr.,
John Faulkner,
Wm. Faulkner,
Robert Faulkner,
William Bull,
William Faulkner (Mason),
William Faulkner,
Samuel Faulkner,
John Patterson,
Henry Patterson,
Patrick Bodle,
Jacob Crance,
John Booth,
Thos. Carscaddan,
Jas. Carscaddan,
John Tuthill,
John Murry,
Alex. McVey,
Ephraim Watkins,
Hezekiah Watkins,
Samuel Watkins,
John McNeal,
Saml. Rogers,
Solomon Rogers,
John Booth, Jur.,
Stephen Harlow,
John McGarrah,
Pelethia Pierce,
Benjamin Booth,
Wm. Booth,
Wm. Forsythe,
Francis Burns,
Charles Finley,
David Moore,
Absalom Bull,
Ephraim McCoy,
Jas. Colwell,
Robt. Simerill,
Phillip Shay,
John Monnell, Jur.,
Anderson Deane,
Wm. Wire,
Thos. Curtice,
Benejah Curtice,
Edward Hopper,
Solomon Thompson,
David Booth,
Moses Clarke,
Israel Rogers, Jr.,
Robert Rogers,
James Wilkins,
Samuel Oliver,
James McCord,
John McCord,
David Daily,
Benjamin Daily,
Alexander Pray,
Wm. Morrison,
Wm. Smith,
Samuel Stubs,
Samuel Umphry,
Mathew Dillon,
James McVey,
Andrew Embler,
James Monell,
Samuel Wetherlow,

Lake Mohonk.

James McClure,
James Rogers,
John Jourdon,
Henry Marshall,
Henry Savage,
Adam Hoslander,
John Sweet,
John Moore,
John Thompson,
Samuel ——?
Ephraim ——?
Samuel Dowe,
John Zates,
Jonathan Jourdan,
Thomas Peck,—243.

The enlistments in the regular English regiments, of which there were many, is a field of inquiry that cannot be entered upon.

CHAPTER VIII.

MEN OF ULSTER IN THE REVOLUTION.

THE history of the men of Ulster "and what they did" in the war for National Independence is eminently a history of toils, privations and exposures to the contingencies of savage warfare and contentions with domestic and foreign enemies. In no portion of the State, except in the Mohawk Valley, did the burden of the war press more heavily, and in no portion was it borne with more unflinching determination. In our general histories — in the histories which form the text books in our schools in which our children are made familiar to some extent with Revolutionary events — full justice has never been paid to the people of the valley of Hudson's River, the view is invariably from the Boston standpoint of events, as though the "Sons of Liberty" of New York and Philadelphia, and Virginia were not as earnestly engaged in the contention of taxation without representation as were the people of Massachusetts. While we may remember that the first gun fired between the Provincials and the forces of the British Ministry was heard at Lexington, and Concord, and gave to our national history the stories of Bunker's Hill and the Boston Tea Party, it should not be forgotten that opposition to the taxation of the Colonies was as pronounced in New York as it was in Boston. Tea was not thrown overboard in New York Harbor, but ships cargoed with it were sent back; the statue of George III. was overthrown, and Governor Colden burned in effigy. The locally interesting fact may be added to the popular narrative that the most fearless leader of the Boston "Mohawks" — the man who shouted in Faneuil Hall, "Overboard with the tea!" was a son of Ulster County — Dr. Thomas Young — the playmate of James and George Clinton, who drew his inspiration with them from the same fountain, and subscribed with them the great principle, "Eternal hostility against every form of tyranny over the mind of man."

The war of the Revolution was the outgrowth directly of the French and Indian war which closed in 1763. The Ministry — "the Mother

Country" about which we hear so much in commendation in anti-Republican circles—demanded that the people of the Colonies should be taxed to defray, in part at least, the expenses of that war. To this end they imposed a tariff tax on teas imported by the Colonists, and failing in that followed with a tax payable by stamps on all legal papers, denied to the Colonists the privilege of manufacturing the goods which they might require, and quartered on the people large bodies of men to enforce their edicts. The Colonists remonstrated, and demanded that there should be no tax levied without representation. When the collisions with the Government occurred in Massachusetts, the sentiment of the people was voiced by Henry in the Virginia House of Burgesses, "Our chains are being forged; their clanking may be heard in the streets of Boston. I know not what others may do, but for myself give me liberty or give me death!" The effect was electric. "To arms! to arms!" rang through the colonies. Had not this spirit been aroused the collisions in Massachusetts would probably have passed into history as incidents of a heated discussion of public affairs. The people of New York, however, were eminently conservative and hopeful of a peaceful solution of the pending controversy, though not the less earnest in their convictions. The "Sons of Liberty" of New York City formed and sent out to the towns "Articles of Association" advising the appointment of "Committees of Safety and Observation." The towns responded with great promptness. The committees were formed, and the "Articles of Association" signed with great unanimity. The New York Association then invited a meeting of delegates from the counties of the Province to serve in Provincial Convention to assemble in New York April 20, 1775. The local committees of Safety forming a County Committee, met at New Paltz April 7th, and appointed Charles De Witt, George Clinton, and Levi Pawling as delegates from Ulster. This Provincial organization of the State Government of New York—the "rebel" Provincial government—held the reins of State, in successive assemblings, until the adoption of the State Constitution in 1777, a document that came from its hands. At the meeting of the convention in New York delegates were appointed to represent the Province of New York in a "General Congress," substantially the first Continental Congress, at Philadelphia, May 10th, 1775. The delegates were John Alsop, Simon Boerum, George Clinton, James Duane, William Floyd, John Jay, Francis Lewis, Philip

Livingston, Robert R. Livingston, Col. Lewis Morris, Col. Philip Schuyler, and Henry Wisner, a majority of those present at any session of the Congress being empowered to cast "the vote of the State" on any question under such "instructions" as should be given to them by the Provincial Convention of New York. To these "instructions" is due the fact that the vote of New York was not cast for the Declaration of Independence until July 9th, 1776, and the "immortal document" signed by only four of the representatives of New York. The steps to the formation of "a government of the people by the people, and for the people," were thus participated in by the people of Ulster at every stage of their progress—the Associations, the Committees of Safety, the Provincial, and the Continental Congresses.

The immediate subject for notice in connection with the facts which have thus been briefly summarized is the signers to the "Articles of Association" — the "Revolutionary Pledge," as it is sometimes called. While accepted to-day as *prima facia* evidence of the standing of the men who wrought in the ranks of "the Men of the Revolution" and while in most cases they were entitled to that rank in their subsequent action, the "Pledge" had no reference to an appeal to arms and separation from the English government. Leading up to that result they probably did, but their primary purpose was to bring the people up to the point of associated effort to secure a redress of the grievances of which they complained, and which were so powerfully given by Jefferson in the Declaration of Independence. The "Pledge" itself reads: "Until a reconciliation between Great Britain and America can be obtained," and in point is the fact that in the first meeting of the Ulster committees at New Paltz the Deputies appointed to the Provincial Convention were instructed to "move" in that body the appointment of a day "for public Fasting and Prayer to implore Divine aid in restoring a happy reconciliation between the Mother Country and her American Colonies." When the line came to be drawn "for" and "against" an effort for National Independence, many good men who had stood up for redress fell back — society was more or less divided, families were divided, churches were divided—men who stood high in the respect of the communities in which they lived, but who from personal attachments or official or religious connections were opposed to separation from the "Mother Country," became "Loyal Americans" in the field, while many of their followers became marauders and murderers. To the memory of those of the signers who stood firmly together in the struggle, as shown by their action in council and in camp, we bow our heads in reverence.

The signers to the "Articles of Association" were:

KINGSTON.

John Allen
David Achmudy
Pierre Ancton
James Allen
John Addison

Petrus Bogardus
Nicholas Bogardus
Richard Burhans
Cornelius Burhans
Barent Burhans
John J. Burhans
Samuel Burhans
Jacob Burhans
Jacobus Besimer
Adam Bear
Tjerck Beekman
Cornelis Beekman
Jacob Backer
Petrus Backker
John Brinck Jr.
Cornelis J. Brink
Jacob Brink
Francis Bedan
Abner Brush
Nicholas Britt
Peter Britt
Captain Evert Bogardus
Petrus Bogardus, Jr.
Isaac Burhans
John Burhans
Samuel Burhans
Edward Burhans
Jan Burhans
Petrus Burhans
Johannis Besemer
Juren Bear
Jacobus S. Bruyn
John Beekman
Johannis Backer
Hendrick Backer
John Brink
Petrus Brinck
Cornelis C. Brink
Petrus C. Brink
Johan Michel Berger
Johannis Beyman
Hendrick Britt

Moses Cantine Jr.
Cornelis Conway Jr.
Joseph Chip
Elisha Clark
David Cox
Wendell Crimer
Johannis Carter
George Calle
Moses Cantine
William Coleman
Michael Connolly
John Chipp
John Carman
William Austin Cox
Seth Curtis
Jacob Conyers

Jeremiah Dubois
Samuel Dubois
Hezekiah Dubois
Johannis N. Dubois
Johannis Dubois
David Dubois
Lucas Dewitt
Tjerck C. Dewitt
Andries Dewitt Jr.
Petrus Dewitt
Arie Dewitt
Joshua Dubois
Jacobus Dubois
William Dubois
Hezekiah Dubois Jr.
Jacobus Dubois
Johannis J. Dubois
Charles Doyl
Jan Dewitt
Johannis Dewitt Jr.
Jans Dewitt
Carnelis D. Dewitt

KINGSTON.—*Continued.*

John Davenport
William Davenport
Sampson Davis
Abraham Davenport
Peter Dumond
Cornelis Dumond
John Dumond
Peter Dumond Jr.
Jacobus Dumond
John Dumond Jr.
John P. Dumond
Philip Dumond
Hendricus Degraef
Egbert Dumond
Jurrie W. Dederick
Johannis Degraef
William Dederick Jr.
Jacobus Dederick
Johannis Dederick
Matthew Dederick
Abraham Dederick
Myndert Dederick
John Delamater
Gysbert Dederick
Abraham Delametter Jr.
Abraham J. Delametter
David Delametter
Benjamin Delametter
John Durnare
Abraham C's. Delametter
Jeremiah Demyer
Benjamin Demeyer
Christiaen Dull

Petrus Elsworth
William Elsworth
Frederick Eygenaer
William Eygenaer
Jacob Eygenaer
Johannis Eygenaer
Petrus Eygenaer
Cornelius Eygenaer
Peter Eyganaer
William Evens
John Elmendorph
Coenradt C. Elmendorph
Petrus Elmendorph
Cornelis Elmendorph
Benjamin Elmendorph
Jan Elmendorph
Abraham Elmendorph
Jacobus Elmendorph
Petrus Elmendorph
Coenradt Jan Elmendorph
Cornelis Elmendorph Jr.
Jacobus Elmendorph
Gerritt Elmendorph
Coenraedt G. Elmendorph
Ariegiertsie Elmendorf
Gerrett Coenraedt Elmendorph
Coenraedt Cornelis Elmendorph
Coenraedt Jacobus Elmendorph
Jonathan Elmendorph
Wilhelmus Emerigh
Johannis Emerigh
William Eltinge
William Eltinge Jr
Thomas Eltinge
Hendricus Eltinge
Jacobus Eltinge
Solomon Eckert Jr.
Michel Eenhart
John Ellis

Christian Fiero
Christian Fiero Jr.
Stephanus Fiero
Hendrick Fiero
Hendrick P. Freligh
Peter Freligh
Samuel Freligh
John Freligh
Johannis Freer
Abraham Freer
Solomon Freer
Solomon Freer Jr.
John Freer
Jacob Freer
Gerrett Freer
Anthony Freer
Samuel Freer
Jan Freer
Peter Felton
Johannis Felton
Jacob Felton
Benjamin Felton
Petrus Felton
Johannis Felton Jr.
John Fender
James Foran
Jacob Frans
Jacob Frans Jr.

Col. Jacobus Severyn Bruyn.

KINGSTON.—*Continued.*

Jacob Marius Groen
Jeronymus Gerrensy
Charles Gyles
Daniel Graham
Silvester Marius Groen
Elias Hasbrouck
Solomon Hasbrouck
Abraham Hasbrouck Jr.
Jerrie Hummell Jr.
Peter Hummell
Jacob Hendrickse
Johannis Hendrickse
Abraham Hoffman
Anthony A. Hoffman
Wilhelmus T. Hoghteling
Tunis Hoghteling
Wilhelmus W. Hoghteling
Jacob Heermanse
Abraham Hermanse
Michel Hoof
Jacob L. Hornbeck
Jacob Marius Groen Jr.
James Gregg
Joseph Gasherie
William Marius Groen
Peter Marius Groen
Abraham A. Hasbrouck
Colonel Abraham Hasbrouck
Martyanus Hummell
Hermans Hummell
Johannis J. Hummell
Jacob Hendrickse, son of Frans,
Phillip Hendrickse
Anthony Hoffman
John Hoghteling
Thomas Hoghteling
Wilhelmus Hoghteling
Jeremiah Hoghteling
John Hermans
Peter Hodler
Michel Human

James Jones
Matthias Jansen
Johannis Jansen
Henry Jansen
Johannis J. Jansen
Cornelis Jansen Jr.
Ephraim Jansen

Jeremiah Klaarwater
Martha Krook
Baltus Kiever
Johannis Kroce
Luke Kierstaede
Christoffel Kierstaede
Jacob Kline
Coenradt Krook
Lawrence Kiever
William Kiever
Wilhelmus Kierstaede
Nicholas Kierstaede
John Kallon

Daniel Lucas
Peter Low
Abraham C. Low
Abraham E. Low
Abraham Low
Cornelis Langendijct
William Legg
George Lassing
John L. Low
Benjamin Low
John Low
Jacobus Low
Abraham Low Jr.
Luyker Langendijct
Samuel Legg
William Litts

Dederick Materstock
Jacob Materstock
Johannis Materstock
Benjamin Masten
Johannis C. Masten
Cornelius B. Masten
Johannis Masten
Abraham Masten
Abraham Masten Jr.
Cornelis Masten
Jesaias Meyer
Adam Materstock
William Materstock
Jacobus Montanie
Ezekel Masten
Johannes B. Masten
Samuel Masten
Cornelis Masten
Benjamin Masten Jr.
Henry Masten
Andrew McFarland
Benjamin Meyer

KINGSTON.—*Continued.*

Benjamin Meyer Jr.
Christian Meyer
Petrus Meyer
Petrus Meyer Jr.
Samuel Meyer
William J. Meyer
Tobias Meyer
Stephanus Meyer
Jacob Mowers
Petrus Mowers
Nicholas Mowers
Nicholas Miller
John Monk
Myndert Mynderse
John McKarty
Robert Montgomery
Hendricus Meyer
William Meyer
Johannis Meyer Jr.
Petrus Low Meyer
Tobias Meyer
Johannis Meyer Jr.
Tunis Meyer
Peter J. Meyer
Johannis Mowers Jr.
Leonard Mowers
Johannis Miller
Christophel Miller
Harmon Minkelaer
John McKinney
John McLean

Arie Newkirk
Charles Newkirk
Jacobus Newkirk
Cornelis A. Newkirk

Jan L. Osterhoudt
John C. Osterhoudt
Hendrickus Osterhoudt
William Osterhoudt
James Osterhoudt
Petrus L. Osterhoudt
James P. Osterhoudt
Abraham Osterhoudt
Petrus P. Osterhoudt Jr.
Samuel Osterhoudt
Hendrickus Osterhoudt Jr.
Benjamin Osterhoudt
Joseph Osterhoudt
Petrus Osterhoudt

Cornelis Persen
Jacobus Persen
Matthew Persen
James Pickken
Abraham Post
Cornelis Post
Jacobus Post
Isaak Post
William Phoenix
Johannis Persen
John J. Persen
Adam Persen
Jacob Pulver
Jacobus Post
Martynus Post
Jan Post
Hendrick Post
Jeremiah Parcell

Peter Roggen
Jurrie W. Richtmeyer
Lodewick Roessell
Frantz P. Roggen
John Row Sr.

Hendrick Snyder
Benjamin Snyder
Isaac Snyder
Martijnus Snyder Jr.
Petrus Snyder
Egbert Schoonmaker
Egbert Schoonmaker
Edward Schoonmaker
Hendricus Schoonmaker son of Tjerck
Edward Schoonmaker
David Schoonmaker
Hezekiah Schoonmaker
Cornelis Swart
Martha Snyder
Abraham Snyder
Jeremiah Snyder
Johannis M. Snyder
Johannis Snyder
Peter Schoonmaker
Samuel Schoonmaker
Hezekiah Dubois Schoonmaker
Hendrick Schoonmaker
Tjerck Schoonmaker
Tjerck Schoonmaker Jr.
John E. Schoonmaker
Cornelius L. Swart

KINGSTON.—*Continued.*

Benjamin Swart
Samuel Swart
Petrus Swart
Tobias Swart
Lawrence Saulisbury
Augustinus Shoe
William Sawyer
Solomon Skutt Jr.
William Schepmoes
Oke Sudam
John Sparling
Alabartus Schryven
Stephanus Schryven
John Smedes
Petrus Smedes Jr.
Benjamin Sleght
Hendricus Slecht
Petrus Slecht

Adam Swart
Wilhelmus Swart
Phillip Swart
Hendrick Staats
Gilbert Saxon
Jerijmias Shoe
Solomon Skutt
John Schepmoes
Adam Short
George Sparling
Petrus Sax
Martynus Schryven
Johannis Schryven
Petrus Smedes
Teunis Sleght
Hendricus B. Slecht
Johannis Slecht
Hendricus J. Slecht

Hendrick Turk
Jacob Turk
Jacob Trimper
Wessel Ten Brock
Cornelis Ten Brock
Coenradt Ten Brock
John Trompour
William Teerpenning
Christoffel Tappan

Benjamin Turk
Abraham Turk
William Thompson
Wessel Ten Brock Jr.
Benjamin Ten Brock
Jacob Ten Brock
Matthew Edward Trompour
Jurryann Tappan

Cornelis Van Keuren Jr.
Abraham Van Keuren
Matthias Van Keuren
Cornelius M. Van Keuren
Phillip Van Keuren
Hezekiah Van Keuren
Peter Van Aken
Gideon Van Aken
Elephaz Van Aken
Jan Van Aken
Abraham G. Van Aken
Tobias Van Buren
Matthew Van Buren
Phillipus Viele
Christian Valkenburgh
Isaac Van Wagonen Jr
John Van Leuven Jr.
William Van Cleef
Thomas Van Gaasbeek
Abraham Van Gaasbeek
Lawrence Van Gaasbeek
Johannis Volck Jr.
Aaronhoudt Valck
Jacob Van Beenschoten
John Van Steenbergh
Abraham T. Van Steenbergh

Gerritt Van Keuren
Abraham Van Keuren Jr.
Matthew Van Keuren Jr.
Johannis J Van Keuren
Johnannis Van Keuren
Isaac Van Aken
Benjamin Van Aken
Petrus Van Aken
Mayorius Van Aken
Abraham Van Aken
Nicholas Vanderlyn
Philip Van Buren
Cornelis Viele
John Valkenburgh
Isaac Van Wagonen
Peter Van Leuven
Andries Van Leuven
Jacobus Van Gaasbeek
Abraham W. Van Gaasbeek
John Van Gaasbeek
William Van Gaasbeek
Wilhelm Valck
Solomon Van Beenschoten
Johannis Van Beenschoten
Petrus Van Steenbergh
Abraham Van Steenbergh

KINGSTON.—*Continued.*

Tobias Van Steenbergh Jr.
Benjamin Van Steenbergh
Jacobus Van Etten
Arie Van Etten
Johannis Van Vliet
Tjerck Van Vliet
Anthony L. Van Schaayck
Matthew Van Steenbergh
Hendricus Van Steenbergh
Johannis Van Etten
Abraham Van Vliet
Jan Van Vliet
Wilhelm Vollandt

Joseph West
Samuel Whittaker
Jacobus Whittaker
Barent Whittaker
William Whittaker Jr.
John Whittaker Jr.
John Whittaker
Edward Whittaker
Johannis Wolfin
Samuel Wolfin
Hendrick Wolfin
Jacobus Wolfin
John Wolfin
Peter A Winne
Benjamin Winne
Petrus Weist
Hendricus Wells
Johannis Weaver
Evert Wynkoop
Hezekiah Wynkoop
Cornelius E. Wynkoop
Dirck Wynkoop Jr.
James Welch
Peter West
Peter Whittaker
Benjamin Whittaker
James J Whittaker
Abraham Whittaker
Philip Whittaker
William Whittaker
James Whittaker Jr.
Johannis Wolfin Jr.
Godfrey Wolfin
Jeremiah Wolfin
Wilhelmus Wolfin
Laurence Winne
Arent Winne
Johannis Weist
Jan Wells
Cornelius Wells
John Walker
Peter Winkoop
Tobias Wynkoop
William Wynkoop
Johannis Wynkoop

John Young
Jurryann Young
Jeremiah Young

Signers in the troop of horse in Ulster County, dated in Kingston June 9, 1775 Philip Hoghteling, Captain; Sylvester Salisbury First Lieutenant; Peter Menderse Second Lieutenant; C. C. Newkirk, Cornet; Cornelius J. Dubois, First Quartermaster; James Roe, Second Quartermaster; Abner Houghteling, Clerk; Petrus Bruick Benjamin Bruyn, Abraham Burhans Daniel Broadhead Tobias Du Bois, Anthony Dumond, Cornelius J. Depue, Benjamin Depue Jr. Petrus Du Bois, William De Witt John J Du Bois, Isaac C. Davis Jacobus F. Davis, Jacob Elmendorph Jr. Gerrit Elmendorph Jr. Jonathan Elmendorph Jr. Johannis Ealigh, Jury Folland, James Hamilton, Martinus Hummel Jr. John Hasbrouck, Wilhelmus Houghteling Jr. Benjamin Krom, Petrus J. Keator, Tjerck Low, John Mynderse, Johannis Merkel, Phillip Newkirk, Arie Newkirk, Petrus Ed. Osterhout, Johannis H. Osterhout, Edward Osterhout, Petrus P. Osterhout, Moses Patterson, Petrus Smith, Felten Smith, Benjamin B. Schoonmaker, Johannis Turck Abraham Ten Broeck, Jacobus Van Waggenen, Abraham Van Waggenen, Jr. Frederick Vandermerken Jr. Adam Wolfin.

KINGSTON, June 9, 1775.

A list of the persons who have refused to sign the general association:

Jan Laurence Bogh
Johannis Burhans
John Cox Jr.
Benjamin Delameter Jr.
Jacob Dewitt
Stephanus Eckert
Andries Ealigh
Abraham Hommel
John Luecks
Johannis Plank
Johannis Row,
Albartus Sluyter
Johannis Smith
Jacob Trompour
Johannis Trompour,
Mattheus York,
William Burhans
Adam Bartolomews
Benjamin Dewitt
Richard Davenport
Owen Daily
William Ealigh
William Fiero
Peter Luecks
Josias Minklaer,
Johannis Plank Jr.
Frederick Row Jr.
Johan Samuel Schoonmaker,
Petrus Schoonmaker Jr.
Paul Trompour,
Nicholas Trompour,
John York.

HURLEY.

Johan Hardenbergh
Dirk Wynkoop
Abrm. Van Wagenen
Cornelius Newkerk
Johannes Dubois
Heugo Freer
Heyman Rossa
Gerredt Van Wagener
J Van Wagener Jr
Johan De Lametter
Hendrick Konstapel
Petrus Crispell Jr
Zacharias Sluyter
Jacob Winfiel
Jacob Freer Jr
Francis Delavigne, of Beilviel
Cornelis Crispell
Johannes Blanshan
Sam'l Schoonmaker
Petrus P Crispell
Jacob DuBois Jr
Petrus Roosa
Egbert Roosa
John Winfiel
John Clyn
Hendrick Smith
Jacob H Roosa
Johannes Suylant
Jacob Blanshan
Benjamin Crispell
John Van Deusen
J J. Van Wagenen
Jonetan Huchin
Zacharias Roosa
Huybert Ostrander
Coen'dt Elmendorph
Jacob Sluyter
David De Lamater
Ger. Hardenbergh Jr
Lucas Elmendorph
Matthewis Ten Eyck
A Wynkoop
Petrus Crispell
J H. Van Wagenen
Johannes Van Wagenen
Jacob Berger,
Johannes Wieler
Anthony Crispell
Simon Lafever
Petrus Wynkoop
Jacob Lafever
Abraham Crispell
C W Elmendorph
Abraham Sluyter
Heugo J. Freer
Jeremiah Freer
Daniel York
Cornelis Krom
Jeremiah Freer
John Borrow
Coenradt Lafaver
Elias Teerpenning
Hendricus Oosterhoudt
Petrus York

HURLEY.—*Continued.*

Petrus Van Wagenen
Samuel Lafever
Cornelis Cool Jr
Benjamin Sluyter
Benj. J. Van Wagenen
Benjamin H Freer
Robert Masten
Jacob Krom
Benjamin Winfiel
Mat Blanshan Jr
Jacob Kyser
John Davis
Samuel Burhans Jr
Gerret Konstapel
Ephraim Kyser
Abram Kyser
Benjamin Newkerk
Cornelius Cool
Johannes Ostrander
Jacobus Hardenbergh
Edward Bruin
Hue Borrow
Jan Van Leuven
Cornel. D Wynkoop
Charles DeWitt
Matthys Blanjan
Coenradt Newkerk
Abraham Krom
Jacobus Conway

A. WYNKOOP, Chairman

"Being *all* of the inhabitants of the town of Hurley."

MARBLETOWN.

Solomon Terwilger
Johannes Keator
Johannes Bogart
John Connor
Samuel Frame
Frederick Davis
Hen Pawling
James Murdruch
Nathan Smedes
William Krom
Gysbert Krom
Isaac Davis
Abraham Cantine
Jacob DeLametter
Edward Lunsberry
Johannes F Keator
Michael Lines
James Phenix
Petrus Oosterhoudt
Garton Nottingham
Daniel Mowris
Stephen Nottingham, Junr.
William Cantine
Mathew Keator
Samuel Mowris Jr
George Middagh
Samuel Keator
Benjamin Keator
Coenradt DuBois
Abraham Johnson
Hendrick G Krom
Philip Hardenbergh
William McGinnis
Abraham Hardenbergh
John Jack
J Van Wagenen Jr
Sol Van Wagenen
Th's Schoonmaker
Jeronomus Rappleyee
Casper Basemer
Richard Akerly
Benoni Moulks
John Batty
Dirck Slaughter
Frederick Schoonmaker
Thomas Klaurwater
John Van Leuven
Abraham Klaurwater
Hendrick Rosa
Abraham Constable
Samuel Gibson
Samuel Mowris
John Shaw
William Teets Jr
William Johnson
Henry Daorin
Petrus Van Leuven
Frederick Keaton
Jacob Keaton Jr
Melgert Keator
Benjamin Louw
Jacobus Reosekraus
John C DeWitt
Cornelius Keator
Jacob Snyder
Nicholas Keyser
Cornelius Brink
Andries Roosa
John G. Krom
Petrus Krom

Henry R. Brigham.

MARBLETOWN—*Continued.*

John Cushnicham
Arie Jack
Sil Vandermerken
Wilhelmus Roosa
William Orr
William Benson
Gysbert Van Leuven
Johannes Smith
James Peresanias
Dirck Schepmoes
Isaac Robison
Jacob S Freer
Jurias Roosa
John Constable
Abraham Constable Jr
Thomas Sammons
Cornelius Sammons
Abraham Helm
John Ernest
Hendrick Brink
Jacob DeWitt
Jacob S Louns
Abraham Roosa
Albert Smedes
Abraham Keaton
George Middagh jr
Joseph Hasbrouck jr
Jesse Smith
Benjamin Keator
J Vandermerke
Samuel Mowris
John Stokes
Johannes G Rosa
Dirck Bush
Frederick Wood
Thomas Wood
Johannes Middagh
Thomas Carver
Cornelius Bogart
Hendrick P. Osterout
James Robinson
Leonard Hardenbergh
Jacobus B Hasbrouck
Michael Pattison
Johannes Keator jr
John Van Vliet
James Van Wagenen
Edward Denoul
Frederick Kontraman
Mat. Kontraman
Andries Kontraman
Elias Kontraman
Jan Krom
Jacob Roosa
Samuel Davies Jr
John J Crispell
Henry Mowris
Garret Newkerk
Samuel Dodge
William Pattison
John Conway
Peter Misner
Jacobus H Bush
Frederick Merkle
David Vandermerke
Jacob Chambers
Thomas Chambers
Joseph Chambers
Wlihelmus Keator
Johannes H Krom
William H. Krom
Samuel Brodhead
James Stilwell
Richard Oliver
Samuel North
Levi Pawling
Jacob Hasbrouck
William Peck
Benjamin Peters
Cornel E Wynkoop
Andries J DeWitt
Thomas Schoonmaker
Cornelius Sluyter
Peter Sammons
Abraham Cantine
Alexander Munro
Andrew Oliver
John Cantine
Jacob D Lametter
David Bevier
F Schoonmaker jr
Chas W Brodhead
Edward Lounsberry
Jacob J Hasbrouck
Ephriam Chambers
Isaac Hasbrouck Jr
Cornelius Brink
John Brodhead
Roelof Eltinge
Cornelius Stillwell
Moses M Cantine
Philip D. B. Bevier
James McKemson
Nathaniel Cantine
Gerard Hardenbergh
Mathew Cantine
Adam Hoffman
Alexander McGinnis

MARBLETOWN—*Continued.*

Benjamin Davies
Jacobus Morris
Jacob J. Keaton
Egbert Brink
David Alkins
John J Krom
Wilhemus Bush
William Ernest
Johannes Roosa
Daniel Johnson
Robert Brink
Isaac C Daviss
Cornelius Krom
Jacob J Hasbrouck
John Davies
John DeWitt
Hendrick Bush Jr
Peter Johnson
William Nottingham
Moses Diamond
Peter Mowris
Martin Bogard
Benjamin Keator
Simon Van Wagenen
Gideon Keator
John Keator
Thomas Keaton
William Keator
John Keator jr
Petrus Keator
Nicholas Keator
Hendrick B Krom
Hendrick W Krom
Daniel Brodhead
Christopher Snyder
Michael Teets
Petrus Davies
Johannes Sluyter
Hendrick Kyser
Joseph Kyser
William Berry
Cornelis Keyser
William Sluyter
Richard Stokes
Cornelius Keyser
Dirck Krom
John Roosa
Art. Van Wagenen
Stephen Nottingham
Jessias Robbison
Cornelius Tack jr
Frederick Bush
Frederick Klaarwater
Corn. Vandermerken
Simon Van Wagener
Johan Bartlewalk
Severyn Hasbrouck
Peter McDowall
Leus Brodhead
Martinus Oosterhoudt
Joseph Klaawater
Andries Frier
Benjamin Krom
Thomas Vandemerken jr
Peter Van Wagenen
Hermanus Oosterhoudt
John Hasbrouck
Sol Vandemerke
John Vandemerke
Mart Middagh
Andries Davies
Jacob Rapelye
Isaac Charter
Casper Charter
Frederick Charter
Derrick Chambers
Jacobus Conner
Robert Betties
John Betties
William Dulap
Nathaniel Web,
John Slouter
Peter Smith
Peter Smith Jr
Cornelis Ernest
Thomas Darcy
Casparrus Marcius
Charles Adams
Edward Talbott
Jacobus Rosa
John Rapelye
Matthew Newkerk
Abraham Middagh
Gysbert Rosa
Johan Van Wagenen
Jacob Seely
Jacob Klaarwater
Daniel Klaarwater
Hendricus Crispell
John Smith
William Hardy
Johannes Van Leuven
Daniel Van Luven
Isaac Klaarwater
Jacob Kyser
Thomas Johnson

LEVI PAWLING, CHAIRMAN.

Only one person refused to sign, viz: William Wood.

NEW PALTZ.

Abraham Doyau
Nathaniel DuBois
Garret Freer jr
Thomas Tomkins
Jacob Hasbrouck jr
Jedediah Doan
Zophar Perkins
Oliver Grey
Leonard Lewis
John Stevens
Daniel Fowler
Daniel Woolsey
Alexander Lane
Jacharias Hasbrouck
Petrus Freer
Abram Doyau jr
Petrus Hasbrouck
Simon Freer
Louis F. DuBois
Abraham Vandermerken
Michael Devoe
Richard Tomkins
William Keech
Isaac Lefever
Andries Lefever jr
Abraham Elting
Johannes Low
Simon Deyo jr
Petrus Van Wagenen
Cornelius Elting
John A Hardenburgh
Joseph Hasbrouck
Peleg Ransom
Ebenezer Perkins
Johannes Eckert
Daniel Freer jr
Roelof J Elting
Samuel Bevier
Andries Lefever
Hugo Freer jr
Benjamin Hasbrouck jr
Nathaniel Potter
Daniel Diver
Samuel Johnson
John McDaniel
Ralph Trowbridge
Cornelius DuBois
Daniel DuBois
Johannes W. Smith
Jacob T Freer
Philip Doyeu
Isaac DuBois
Joseph Terwilger
Paulus Freer
Benjamin Elsworth
Isaac Thomkins jr
William Lane
Joshua Drew
Jonathan Johnson
Elijah Drew
John Decker
William Weaver
A Yelverton jr
John Presler
Richard Lewis
Peter Drew
William Tilson
Michael Leroy
Jacob Whitney
Thomas Sasson
Simeon Crandall
Solomon Elting.
Jehu Louw
Simon Doyau
George Nies
Isaac Freer
Jacob Bevier
Solomon Louw.
Benjamin Freer
Isaac Monyon
Christofel Dugain,
John Terwilger
Israel Cole,
John Neely
Petrus J. Schoonmaker
Abraham Hass
Josaphat Hasbrouck
Isaac Harris
Johannis M Louw
Jonathan Lefever
Henry Herald
Jacob DuBois
Lewis Puntenear
Hendricus DuBois
William Hood
Abraham Ein
Abraham Lefever
Elias Hardenbergh
Daniel Lefever
Jonathan Presler
H Wessemuller
Joseph Griffin
John Griffin jr
Jacob Louw
Simeon Louw
Mathew Lefever
John York
Solomon Bevier

NEW PALTZ.—*Continued.*

Jonas Freer
Jesaias Hasbrouck
Jonathan Doran
George Wirts
Jonas Freer jr
Teunis Van Vliet
Cornelius DuBois jr
Wilhelmus Schoonmaker
Isaac Louw
Henry Green
Robert Phenix
Jonathan Terwilger
Jacob Weaver
Joseph Elsworth jr
Thomas Lemunyun
Thomas Cole
Josiah Drake
John Way
William Elsworth jr
Samuel Lewis
Joseph Brooks
Moses Quimby
Hugh Cole
James Daeker
Isaac Seaman
Jacob Degarmo
Seth Hubble
Henry Deyo jr
Jeremiah Tomkins
Joseph Ransom
James Done
Wouter Slyter
Mortinus Griffin
Daniel Doyan
Johannes Walron
Henry Lits
Stephen Bedford
Jonas Bedford
Cornelius Bedford
Ebeneezer Gilbert
Nathaniel Wyatt
Justus Hubble
David Whitney
John Woolsey
Eleazer Cole
Samuel Dubois
Dirck D Winkoop
Jacob Carring
John Lemyon
Michael Palmeteer
Jacobus Hasbrouck
David Hasbrouck
Abraham Donaldson
John B Deyo
Daniel Freer
Zacharias Sickles
Frederick Hymes
Solomon Lefever
Thomas Shirky
Thomas Dunn jr
Samuel Teerpenningh
Thomas Dunn
Nathaniel Lefever
James Dunn
Joseph Freer
Johannes Freer
Simeon Campbell
Jedediah Thomson
Peter Viely
Hendricus DuBois jr
Petrus Vandermerken
Methuselem DuBois
Johannes Deyo jr
Henry Puntenear,
Petrus Lefever
Valentine Perkins
Abraham Concklin
Henry Hannes
Anthony Yelverton
Michael Weaver
Gideon Dean
Isaac Tomkins
John Riker
Petrus Bevier
Peter Doyo
Benjamin Dubois
Christeyan Doyo
Benjamin Doyo
William Allison
Abraham Dubois
Andrew Dubois jr
Daniel Dubois jr
Reuben Campbell
David Louw
John Lefever
William Donaldson,
James Auchmoutie
Abraham Devoe
William Elsworth sr.
Joseph Coddington
Daniel Turner
Casper Maybey
William Mozer
Peter Palmeteer
George Nies, jr
Laurence Nies

NEW PALTZ.—*Continued.*

John Lefever
Christofel Deyo
John Nies
John Lester

NATHANIEL DUBOIS, Chairman.
JOSEPH CODDINGTON, Committee Clerk.

Persons who refused or neglected to sign:

Nathaniel DuBois, Chn.
Joseph Coddington, Com. Clk.
Samuel Townsend,
Jacobus Auchmoutie
Matthew McKeely,
Richard Carmon,
Noah Elting, Esq.,
Nathaniel Waters.

NEW MARLBOROUGH.

Benjamin Carpenter
Lewis Dubois
Joseph Mory
Jurian Mackay
Gilbond Cotton
Jacob Wood
John Woolsey
Bordewin Terepanny
Eleazer Frazer
Michael Wygant
Solomon Warring
Richard Carpenter
Elija Farris
Elija Lewis
Henry TerBoss
Silas Purdy
John Duffield
Wright Carpenter
Peter Barrian
Abraham Quick
Abija Perkins M. D.
Benj Ely M. D.
Seth Perkins M. D.
Benj J Frazer
Lawrence Bokker
Abraham Cooper
Stephen Case
Ichabod Williams
John Montgomery
Jacob DeGroot
John Mulliner
Ananias Valentine
Zadock Lewis
Flavius Waterman
James Pride
Jacob Daton
Joseph Caverly
Nathaniel Mills
Ebeneezer St John
William Martin
Durneo Relyee
Christ. Ostrander
Henry Lockwood
John Polhemus
Stephen Purdy,
Noah St John
John Polhemus
George Landy
Jacob Kent
William Bloomer
Isaac Cropsie
Uriah Drake
John Bishop
Nath'l Goodspeed
Micajah Lewis
John Davis
Benjamine Huett
George Williams
John Schurdt
James Filkins
George Hallett
Thomas Quick jr
William Caverly
William Quick
Henry Decker
Terrett Lester
James Merritt
William Purdy
Henry Hide
William Pembroke
Eliza Gardner
John Bond
John Knowlton
John Scott
John Mackey
Mathew Wygant
Samuel Abbe
Andrew Ares

NEW MARLBOROUGH.—*Continued.*

Samuel Mackay
Andrew Young
David Mackey
Abraham Deane
Gilbert Bloomer
Joseph Bloomer
William Stanton
Bartholomew Baker
George Williams
David Martin
Abraham Lane
George Lane
Henry Ferris
Allen Lester
John Ares
Nathaniel Harcourt
John Wygant
James Wheeler
John Quick
Thomas Quick
Israel Tuthill
Jeriah Rhods
Jesse Wheeler
Oliver Wheeler
Job St John
Jonathan Woolsey
George Stanton
Daniel Bloomer
Job Wood
John Furman
Nowell Furman
Isaac Morele
Daniel Knowlton
Peter Caverty
James Hunter
Nathaniel Mills
Josiah Lockrad
Benjamin Dusenbury
Isaac Dyo
Daniel McQuinn
Janter Willidge
John Truilliger jr
William Relyee
Marcus Ostrander
Joshua Lockwood
Jacob Terepanny
John Terepanny
Joseph Gee
Simon Relyee jr
Stephen Seymour
Josiah Baker
John Baker
Moses Cary
Bartholomew Bacon
Alexander Cropsie
Thomas Silkworth
Joseph Carpenter
Pharaoh Latting
Samuel Hannah
David McMin
Andrew Cropsie
John Lester
David Brush
John Wilson
William Woolsey
William Hollister
Philip Aires
Henry Jones
Joseph Welles
John Wygant jr
Benj Stead
Henry Simpson
Adam Cropsie
George Woolsey
Eneas Quimby
Samuel St John
Abraham Mabee
Richard Woolsey
Wm Van Blaricon
Adam St John
James Jackson
Abel Barnum
William Ostrander
Adam Caser
Simon Relyee jr
Jonathan Tuttle
James Owen
Peter Looze
Abraham Mabee
Benjamine Comfort
Israel Tompkins
Hugo Scutt
Abraham Scutt
William Scutt
Robert Everitt
Metevis Fevin
John Smith
Alex. Mackey jr
Philip Caverty
Daniel Geldersleeve
Matthew St John
Isaac Van Benschoten
Petrus Ostrander
Nathaniel Kumph
Alex Mackey sr
Zephaniah Woolsey
Josiah St John
Jesse Farechild

Alonzo Rose.

NEW MARLBOROUGH.—*Continued.*

Nathaniel Hull
John Noll
Charles Mackey
Chas. Mackey jr
Nathaniel Quimby
Benjamin Woolsey
Samuel Hull jr
Nathaniel Hull jr
John Huitt
Thomas Pembroke
John Lester
Gideon Ostrander
Henrick Deyo jr
Daniel Ostrander
Garrett Benschoten
George Platt
Herman Chase
Abraham Lossom
Hendrick Huse
Durnee S Relyee
Francis Gaine
James Waring
Daniel Robertson
Nehemiah Smith
Henry Scott
James Van Blaricom
Walter Comfort
Joseph Bloomer
Jonathan Lily
Caleb Merritt
Thomas Merritt
Gabriel Merritt
Jacob Cannaff
Levi Quimby
James Quimby
Thomas Wygant
William Dusenbury
Jonathan Terepaning
David Ostrander
Thomas Mackey
Henry Deyo sr
Daniel Cook jr
William Wygant
Josiah Merrett
Daniel Merritt.

BENJ CARPENTER, Chairman
AZARIAH PERKINS, Clerk

Those who objected to signing the association were:

Isaac Garrison,
Letting Carpenter,
Moses Grigory,
James Grigory,
Nathel Hughson,
Samuel Merritt,
Elisha Purdy,
John Caverly,
John Young,
Edward Hallock,
Edward Hallock, Jr.
Solomon Fowler,
John Gero,
William Gero,
Nathaniel Gee,
Andrew Gee,
Henry Cronk,
Frederick Cronk
Frederick Gee,
George Harden,
Jonathan Lane,
Nathaniel Horton,
Isaac Horton,
David Horton,
Joseph Lane,
Samuel Devine,
Joseph Devine,
Durnee Relyee, jun.
Benj'n Relyee
William Place,
Obadiah Palmer
Samuel Hallock,
Daniel Cookseur
Isaac Cannaff
Jeremiah Cannaff
William Warren,
Jacob Rossell,
Humphrey Merritt.

NOTE—A number of these men were Quakers.

ROCHESTER.

A. DeWitt
Benjamin Hoornbeck
Johannes Bevier Junr.
Ephriam Dupuy
D Romeyn
Benjamin Kurtwright
Benjamin Bevier
Andrew Bevier
L. Schoonmaker
Petrus Schoonmaker
Sylvester Derby
Simon Dupuy
Elesa Roosakrauce
Cornelis Schoonmaker
Joel Hoornbeck
Moses Dupue jr
Cornelis Oosterhout
Peter Bruyn
Peterus Scott
Peter Inderly
Frederick Westbrook
Isaac Hoornbeck
Zacharias Rosekrans
Teunis Oosterhout
Peterus DeWitt
Hendricus Oosterhout
Cornelius Hardenberg
C Van Wagenen
Cornelius Hardenberg
John Sammons
James Burck
Petrus Hendrickson
Joachim D. Schoonmaker
Johanis Schoonmaker
Joachim Schoonmaker jr
Hendricus Hoornbeck
Jacob Van Wagenen
Conelis Dupuy
John Dupue
Johannis G. Hardenbergh Esq.
John Sleght
Minna Fisher
Philip Hoornbeck
Andrew White
Jacobus Oosterhout
Hendrick Roosakrance
Frederick Vandermerk
Jacobus Wynkoop
Jacob D Hoornbeck
Wm. A DeWitt
Hendericus Kittle
Mattheius Cr. Janson
Teunis Janson
Cornelius C Janson
Jacobus Schoonmaker
Patt Conolly
John Krom
Hartman Heyn
Frederick Rosekrans
Jonathan Westbrook
Henry Hoornbeck jr
Tojachem Depuy
Lodewyck Hoornbeck
Ephrain Depuy jr
Jacob Barley
Benj. Van Wagenen
Petru Ennis
John Scott
John McBryde
Coenradt Sealy
Jacobus J Quick
Benjamin Allegar
James Hill
Jarvis Jansen
John Low, jr
Daniel Wood
Jacob D. W. Schoonmaker
Marinis Chambers
Moses Depuy
Abraham Depuy
Matthew Newkerk jr
Benj C Newkerk
Benjamin Gonsalus
Isaac Newkerk
Reuben DeWitt
Warren Hoornbeck
Andries Vernaey
Manuel Gonsalus jr
Richard Brodhead
Simeon DeWitt
John Schoonmaker
Jacob Turner
Daniel Schoonmaker
John Evans
Corns. Hoornbeck
Art. Van Wagenen
Jacob Oosterhout
Andries Roodolf
Jacobus Divens
Samuel Gonsalus
Egbert DeWitt jr
Nicholas Simmerman
Jacobus Bruyn jr
Benjamin Merkel
Jacobus Kortreght
Petrus Burger
Abraham Kortreght
Arthur Morris

ROCHESTER.—*Continued.*

Benjamin Janson
John Low
Zacharias Low
John Brodhead
John Janson
J. Van Dermerkin
Simon Bevier
Henry Brodhead,
Abraham Bevier
Abraham Janson
Daniel McKindly
Mighel Sax
Peter Cantine
Josua Thompson
Wm DeWitt
Peter Cole jr
Henry Harp
Chester Benjamine
Dirck Westbrook
Samuel Hoornbeck
Michael Inderly
Kryn Oosterhout
John Kittle
Jacob Barker
Lodewyck Souly
Eliza Hoornbeck
Jacobus Chambers
Cornelis Chambers
Andries A DeWitt
Jacob Bevier
John DeWitt
Johannes Mack
Johannes Hoornbeck
Benj'in Oosterhoudt
Coenradt Burger
Johannes Oostenhoudt jr
Egbert DeWitt
Dick Hoornbeck
Nicholaes Burger
John Mullen
Mattheus Kortreght
Gideon Hoornbeck
Martin Burgher
Benjamin Depuy
Hartman Eennis
Corn. Oosterhoudt
Peter Harp
Edward Wood
William Wood
Edward Wood jr
Peter Wood
Cornelius Jansen
Thomas Mackkee
Jacobus Depuy
P E Oosterhoudt
Free Vandermerken
Samuel Oosterhoudt
Jacobus Quick jr
John Harp
Ezekiel Oosterhoudt
Jonathan Burly
Elias Merkel
James O'Bryan
J Hoornbeck Esq.
William McDonnell
Elija Benjamine
Jacob Van Dermerken
Arie Van Dermerken
Aldert Oosterhoudt
Jacobus Van Etten
Jacob Smit
Henderick Quick
Richard Davis
Philip Quick
Cornelius Quick
Elias Hendrickson
Jacobus Seneck
Jacobus Bos jr
Ephraim Baker
Gysbert Krom
Coenradt A Tiel
Barent Merkel
Jacobus Hendrickson
Cornelius Hoornbeck
Isaac Roosa
Johannes Keyser
Joseph Belder
John Hays jr
George Schaefer
Jacob DeWitt
John Belder
Solomon Krom jr
Alexander Katter
Coenradt Bevier
Benjamin Stanton
Henry Simmerman
Abraham Kadegal
Peter Helm
Cornelis Newkerk.
Wessel Vernooy
Jerry Mack
Jacobus Tornaer
Harmanns Rosekrans
Joseph Krom
Cornelius Vernooy
Johannes Kerson
Solomon Bevier
Henry Harp jr

ROCHESTER.—*Continued.*

Benjamin Bruyn
Abraham Heermans
Joseph Depuy
F Van Dermerken jr
Jacob DeWitt
Glondy Middagh
Jeremiah Kittle
Arie Oosterhoudt
Johannes Ousterhout, Junr.
Samuel Kerson
Philip Heyn
John A DeWitt
John Van Wagener
Abraham Klaerwater
John McNeal
James Buyrns
Jacobus Hendrickson
William Belder
Wessel Vernooy
Thomas DeWitt
Peter Sax
William Brodhead
Jerck DeWitt
John Wood
Nathan Vernooy
Johannes Vernooy
Josiah Bevier
Cornelius Cole jr
Benjamin Roosa
Daniel Schoonmaker
Martinus Klaerwater
Gerrit C Newkerk
Henry DeWitt
Jonathan Vernooy
Peterus Vernooy
Mighel Besemer
Stephen DeWitt
John Badly
William Davis
Jesse Bevier
Jacob Newkerk
William DeWitt jr
Jacobus Kortreght
Benjamin Van Wagenen
Solomon Krom
Andries Swiger
Timothy Hatch
Isaac Bevier
Lawrence Hoornbeck
Jonas Hasbrouck
Thomas Porter
Jothem Schoonmaker
Andrics A DeWitt

MAMAKATING.

John Youngs,
Philip Swartwout, Esq.
Benjamin Depue, Esq.
Capt. John Crage,
William Harlow,
John McKinstry,
Benjamin Cuttaback, Jun.
Robert Cook,
Haramones Van Inwagin,
Tereck V. K. Westbrook,
William Rose,
Capt. Jacob Rutson Dewitt,
Ely Strickland
Stephen Carney,
Joel Addams,
George Gillaspay,
James Curren,
Jacob Rosa,
Abraham Cuddeback, Jun.
Samuel King,
Abner Skinner,
Frederick Bender,
Valentine Wheeler,
Johannes Shuffelbam,
Johannes Shuffelbam, Jun'r
James Blizard,
Thomas Combs,
James McCivers,
Joseph Hubbard,
John Thompson,
Samuel Dealey,
William Smith,
John Harding,
Neathan Cook,
Jepthia Fuller,
David Gillaspy,
John Hay,
Joseph Shaw,
James Gillaspay,
Abraham Rosa,
Henry Newkerk
Efrim Thomas,
Hendrey Elsworth,
Joseph Thomas,
Abraham McQuinn,
John Sybolt,

MAMAKATING.—*Continued.*

Thomas Kyte,
Johanathan Brooks,
John Wallis,
Joseph Drake,
Ebenezer Parks,
Jacobus Swartwout,
Philip Swartwout, Jun.
Geredus Swatwot,
Isaac Van Tuile,
Joseph Westfork
Petrus Gumore,
Ezkiel Gumore,
Jacob Dewitt Gumore,
Daniel Van Flees, (Fleet)
Jacob Van Inaway,
Cornealis Van Inaway,
Moses Depue, Jun.
Jacobus Cuddaback,
Petrus Cuddaback,
Elias Gumore,
John Brooks,
Elisha Barbar,
Jonathan Derus,
Samuel Depue,
William Johnston,
James Williams,
Charles Gilletts,
Peter Simpson
Jonathan Miller,
Moses Roberts,
John Duglass,
Elias Miller,
Abraham Smith,
Asa Kimbal,
Lenord Henery,
John Gillaspy,
Tho. Lake,
Robert Comfert,
Gershom Sampson,
Johannis Wash,
Jacob Comfert,
Jonathan Strickland,
Samuel Patterson,
Joseph Skinner,
Joseph Arthur,
David Wheeler,
John Travis,
John Travis, Jun.
Daniel Decker,
Nathaniel Travis,
Ezekiel Travis,
Joseph Travis,
Jeremiah Shaver,
Joseph Ogden,
David Daley,
Daniel Walling,
Daniel Walling, Jun.
Rufus Stanton,
Ruben Babbet,
Matthew Terwilliger,
Jonathan Wheeler,
John Williams,
Ebenezer Holcomb,
Geradus Vaniwegen,
William Cuddeback,
Abraham Cuddeback,
Eliphet Stevens,
Elisha Travis,
Aldert Rosa,
Adam Rivenburgh,
Stephen Holcomb,
Daniel Woodworth,
Daniel Roberts,
Moses Miller,
Isaac Rosa,
George J. Deneston,
Josiah Parks,
Robert Milliken,
Matthew Neely,
Jonathan Barber,
David Dayly,
Joseph Rendal,
Ephraim Forgison,
Jacob Stanton,
Zepheniah Holcombe
Abraham Smedes.

The signers of the pledge in the Precincts of Hanover, Wallkill and Shawangunk are not of record. The New Windsor list is not of record, but is preserved in Washington's Headquarters at Newburgh. The Newburgh list is of record and with the New Windsor list may be found in "History of Orange County," edition of 1885. The Precincts referred to were nearly unanimous. Shawangunk and Hanover were among the first to burn (January, 1775) in public conflagration, the insidious pamphlet of the period, "Free Thoughts on the Resolves of Congress."

The Committees of Safety.

The Committees of Safety and Observation which were brought into the field of action in conjunction with the local associations, were, as has been already stated, very important bodies of men; they were the local *de facto* government during the first years of the rebellion. Unfortunately a full list of names of the Precinct or Town Committees, who also formed the county committees, cannot now be gathered from the fragmentary records which have been handed down. From the roll of attendants on the several meetings of the County Committee the following have been compiled:

Kingston—Joseph Gasherie, Capt. Johannis Snyder, Abraham Van Keuren, Egbert Dumont, Oke Suydam, Jacobus Van Gaasbeek, Col. Andries De Witt, Junr., Johannis Minderse, Johannis Sleght, Johannis Beekman, Tobias Van Buren. Joseph Gasherie, chairman.

New Paltz—Johannis Hardenbergh, Jacob Hasbrouck, Junr., Joseph Hasbrouck, Andries Le Fever, Daniel Le Fevre, Abraham Donaldson, Elias Hardenbergh, Peleg Ransom, Nathaniel DuBois, Ebenezer Perkins. Nathaniel DuBois, chairman.

Hanover—Doct. Charles Clinton, Arthur Parks, Alexander Trimble, James Latta, Capt. Jacob Newkirk, William Jackson, Henry Smith, Philip Mole, John Wilkin, James McBride, James Milliken, Samuel Barkley, James Rea, David Jagger. Alex. Trimble, chairman.

Newburgh—Col. Jonathan Hasbrouck, Thomas Palmer, Woolvert Acker, John Belknap, Abel Belknap, John Robinson, Benjamin Birdsall, Joseph Coleman, Doct. Moses Higby, Samuel Sands, Stephen Case, Isaac Belknap. Thomas Palmer, chairman.

Hurley—Col. Johannis Hardenbergh, Matthew TenEyck, Hubert Ostrander, Adriaen Wynkoop, Capt. John VanDeursen, Charles DeWitt. Adriaen Wynkoop, chairman.

Marbletown—Levi Pawling, Jacob LeLamater, Matthew Cantine, John Cantine, David Bevier, Cornelius E. Wynkoop. Levi Pawling, chairman.

Wallkill—Abimael Young, James Wilkin, Francis Byrns, Hezekiah Gale, Moses Phillips, Henry Wisner, Jr., John Wood, George Thompson. Henry Wisner, Jr., chairman.

New Windsor—Col. James Clinton, Capt. James McClaughrey, John Nicoll, John Nicholson, Nathan Smith, Robert Boyd, Jr., Samuel Brewster, Samuel Sly. After 1776, Clinton and Nicholson being in the field, Samuel Brewster, Robert Boyd, Jr., Nathan Smith, Hugh Humphrey, George Denniston, John Nicoll, Col. James McClaughrey and Samuel Arthur. Saml. Brewster, chairman.

Marlborough—Benjamin Carpenter, Lewis DuBois, Joseph Morey, Abijah Perkins, Silas Purdy, Henry TerBoss, Richard Carpenter, John Woolsey, Nick. Wygant, John Smith, Elijah Lewis, Henry DuBois. Benj. Carpenter, chairman.

Joseph Jagger

Rochester—Andries De Witt, Jacob Hornbeek, Johannis Schoonmaker, Joakim Schoonmaker, Peter Schoonmaker, Jacobus Van Wagnen, Johannis Bevier, Johannis F. Hardenbergh. Andries De Witt, chairman.

Shawangunk—Jacobus Bruin, Johannis Jansen, Matthew Rea, Benjamin Smedes, Capt. Thomas Jansen, Jr., Major Johannis Hardenbergh, Dirck Roosa. Jacobus Bruin, chairman.

Mamakating—Philip Swartwout, Isaac Van Zile (Tile), William Roos, John Young. List incomplete. John Young, chairman.

The County Committee held its meetings in New Paltz, generally at the house of Mrs. Ann DuBois.

CHAPTER IX.

REORGANIZATION OF THE MILITIA.

THE reorganization of the local militia was begun by the town or precinct committees of Safety and Observation as early as April, 1775, the committees probably acting by suggestion of the general committee. It was not, however, until the 22nd of August, 1775, that the Provincial Congress of New York, otherwise known as the Provincial Convention, passed an act under which the militia of the Revolution was formally constituted. This act provided that counties, cities and precincts should be divided by their respective committees, so that in each district a company should be formed "ordinarily to consist of about eighty-three able bodied and effective men, officers included, between sixteen and fifty years of age"; the officers to consist of one captain, two lieutenants, one ensign, four sergeants, four corporals, one clerk, one drummer, and one fifer. The several companies so formed were directed to be "joined into regiments, each regiment to consist of not less than five or more than ten companies," which should be commanded by "one colonel, one lieutenant colonel, two majors, an adjutant and a quartermaster." The regiments were to be classed in six brigades under "a brigadier-general and a major of brigade," and to be under the command of one major-general.

When the organization was completed the militia stood in four regiments, and, with the regiments of Orange County, five in number, formed the fourth brigade under Brigadier-General George Clinton.* The Ulster Regiments were the "First or Northern Regiment" including the companies raised in Kingston and Hurley, and north to the county line; the "Second or South End Regiment" including the companies raised in the southern tier of precincts, New Windsor, Hanover and Wallkill, and the settlements known as Paenpacht, and Mamakating, the latter now in Sullivan and the former in Orange; the "Third, or Western Regiment"

* This brigade should not be confused with the special brigade which was organized under General Clinton in August, 1776, composed of "all levies raised and to be raised in the counties of Westchester, Duchess, Orange and Ulster."

including the companies organized in New Paltz, Marbletown and Rochester, extending south to Wawarsing; the "Fourth, or Middle Regiment," including the companies raised in Newburgh, Marlborough, the present Plattekill and the ancient Shawangunk.

The lists of Field, Staff and Line officers of the several regiments given in this chapter are from original manuscripts as printed in the official "Calendar of New York Manuscripts," and compared with the lists printed in "Archives of the Revolution." They are unquestionably correct. The lists printed in the later volume, "New York in the Revolution," *are not correct,* especially in the assignments of line officers to regiments, in the Fourth regiment, for example, no less than thirty-four line officers being given to it that properly belong to other regiments. The lists of privates given as supplemental to the lists as printed in the "Archives of the Revolution," are presumably mixed also, as they would naturally follow the assignments of the line officers. Without the original returns the local historian can do nothing in the way of recollating the lists of the privates. "Sons" and "Daughters" of the Revolution have no higher duty to pay to the memory "of the Men of the Revolution, and what they did" than to secure an intelligible and reasonably correct recollation and reprinting of both of the volumes which have been referred to.

THE FIRST OR NORTHERN REGIMENT.

The Field and Staff of the "First, or Northern Regiment" as commissioned October 25th, 1775, were:

Colo.; Johannes Hardenbergh.
Lieut. Colo.: Abraham Hasbrouck.
Major; Johannes Snyder.
Major; Jonathan Elemendorf.
Adjutant; Petrus Elmendorf.
Qr. Master; Abraham A. Hasbrouck.

The appointment of Johannes Hardenbergh as Colonel was not satisfactory, and the following Field Officers were substituted, Feb. 13, 1776, viz:

Colonel, Abraham Hasbrouck,
Lieut. Col., J. Johannes Snyder,
First Major, Jonathan Elmendorf,
Second Major, Philipus Hoogtaling,
Adjutant, Abraham A. Hasbrouck,
Qr. Master, John Van Duersen, Jr.

Abraham Hasbrouck resigned the command early in 1776, and the Field and Staff was reconstructed:

Colonel, Johannis Snyder,
Lieut. Col., Jonathan Elmendorf,
1st Major, Adriaen Wynkoop,
2d Major, Phillipus Hooghtaling,
Adjutant, Abraham Hasbrouck,
Qr. Master, John Van Deursen.

By later promotion and appointments Phillipus Hooghtaling became Lieutenant Colonel; John Van Deursen became Qr. Master and later succeeded Abraham A. Hasbrouck as Adjutant; John Low became Qr. Master, and Peter Van der Lyn, Surgeon.

The companies included in the regiment and the officers of which were commissioned on same date with the first Field and Staff, were six from Kingston and one from Hurley, as follows:

1st Co. Capt., Everet Bogardus; First Lieut., Dan'l Graham; Second Lieut., Anthony Frere; Ensign, Johannes Persen.

2d Co. Capt., Moses Cantine; First Lieut., Phillipp Swart; Second Lieut., Abraham G. Vanaker; Ensign, Hendrik Tarpenning.

3d Co. Capt., Matthew Dedrick; First Lieut., Everet Wynkoop, Jun.; Second Lieut., Petrus Eyganaer; Ensign, Hendrick Myer (not in the Co. May 1, 1776).

4th Co. Capt., John L. Dewitt; First Lieut., Petrus Oosterhout; Second Lieut., Tobias Myer; Ensign, Petrus Brink.

5th Co. Capt., Lucas De Witt; First Lieut., Jeremiah Snyder; Second Lieut., Petrus Backer; Ensign, Petrus West.

6th Co. Capt., Hendrick Schoonmaker; First Lieut., Edward Schoonmaker; Second Lieut., Edward Whittaker; Ensign, Isaac Burhans.

7th Co. (Hurley). Capt., Gerardus Hardenbergh; First Lieut., Simon Lefever; Second Lieut., Saml. Schoonmaker; Ensign, Aart Joh'n Van Wagenen; Sergeants—Johannis Blanchan, Zacharias Sluyter, Jacob Le Fevre; Corporals—Jacob Crom, Matthews Blanchan, Elias Terpenning, Benjamin H. Freer; Drummer—Abraham K. Sluyter; Fifer—Willhelmus Sluyter.

Attached to the Regiment was a Kingston company of cavalry:

Capt., Phillipp Houghteling; First Lieut., Silvester Salisbury; Second Lieut., Petrus Myndertse; Cornet, Corns C. Newkerk; Quartermaster, Corns J. DuBois; Second Quartermaster, James Roe.

Names of the privates of this company will be found in connection with list of signers of the Association in Kingston, given on a previous page.

Many changes occurred in the officers of the several companies. In later notes appears:

Tobias Van Buren, Capt. Granadier Co.; Jacobus Van Gaasbeek, First Lieut.; Cornelius Beekman, Second Lieut.; Benj'n Elmendorf, Third Lieut.

Colonel C. B. Shafer.

Also a company described as "comprehending the settlements of Woodstock and Little and Great Shandaken":

Isaac S. Davis, Capt.; Philip Miller, First Lieut.; John's Van Etting, Second Lieut.

In the Hurley Company, Oct. 23d, 1779, the changes were:

Simon Lefever, Captain, vice Gerardus Hardenbergh, resigned; Samuel Schoonmaker, First Lieut.; Joh's Blanchan, Second Lieut.; Petrus Wynkoop, Ens'g, vice Van Wagener, resigned.

In the "Light Horse Company," June 16, 1778, Hooghteling, Captain, was succeeded by Silvester Salisbury, and was in turn succeeded by Cornelius C. Newkirk. James Roe became First Lieut.; Abr'm Van Gaasbeck, Jun'r, Second Lieut., and Abr'm Hoffman, Cornet. Moses Cantine resigned the captaincy of the Second Company, and Philip Swart succeeded him, with Abr'm Van Acken as First Lieut.; Hendrickus Teerpening, Second Lieut., Theophilus Elsworth, Ensign. In the Fifth Company Jeremiah Snyder succeeded Lucas E. DeWitt, with Petrus Backer, First Lieut.; Martynus Humble, Second Lieut.; Tobias Wynkoop, Junr., Ensign. In Bogardus's First Company, Anthony Freer was promoted First Lieut.; Joh's Persin, Second Lieut., and Solomon Hasbrouck, Ensign. In Schoonmaker's Sixth Company, Isaac Burhans succeeded Edw. Schoonmaker as First Lieut.; Ed'w Schoonmaker, Jr., succeeded Whittaker as Second Lieut.; and Andries Van Louven became Ensign, vice Isaac Burhans. Presumably other changes were made, but they are not of record.*

ENROLLED MEN.

Acker, Jacob
Ackert, Jacob
Ackert, Martin
Amorick, Peter
Artly, Jacob.
Auker, Henry
Acker, Solomon
Ackert, Jeremiah
Ackert, Stephen
Amrick, Johannis
Arshly, Jacob
Auchmoudey, David
Auker, Mar.

Badford Andrew
Badford, Simeon
Bauschten, Salomon
Bargher, Wilhelmis
Badford, John
Baer, Adam
Barger, Jacob
Barnes, Hans Jury

* The strength of the several companies at that date is reported:
1st Co. Everet Bogardus, Captain; 2 Lieuts., 1 Ensign, 8 Non-com., 68 Privates.
2d Co. Jan L. DeWitt, Captain; 2 Lieuts., 1 Ensign, 8 Non-com., 50 Privates.
3d Co. Hendrick Schoonmaker, Captain; 2 Lieuts, 1 Ensign, 8 Non-com., 50 Privates.
4th Co. Mattys Dederick, Captain; 1 Lieut., No Ensign, 8 Non-com., 48 Privates.
5th Co. Lucas De Witt, Captain; 2 Lieuts., 1 Ensign, 8 Non-com., 59 Privates.
6th Co. Moses Cantyn, Captain; 2 Lieuts., 1 Ensign, 8 Non-com., 60 Privates.
7th Co. Gerardus Hardenbergh, Captain; 2 Lieuts., 1 Ensign, 8 Non-com., 50 Privates.
Totals—Seven Captains, thirteen Lieuts., six Ensigns, fifty-six non-commissioned officers and 385 privates—in all 460.

ENROLLED MEN.—*Continued.*

Barnhart, Jeremiah
Barringer, Jacob
Barrow, Danell
Bear, Coffee
Bear, Henry
Bear John
Bear, Jurrie
Beaver, John
Beaver Peter
Bekman Hendrick
Bedford Andrew
Bedford Simon
Beekman Benjamin
Beekman Hendrick
Beekman John jr
Beekman John J.
Beekman Thomas
Burger Jacob
Burger Wilhelmus
Burner Hans Jurry
Bernhart Jeremiah
Besmer Johannis
Bever John
Bever Peter
Biar Adam
Biar John
Black John
Bogardus Nicholas
Bogardus Peter
Bogardus Petrus
Borrow Daniel
Biar Coffey
Biar Henry
Biar Jury
Breadsted Andrew
Breasted ——
Brett Peter
Briett William
Brinck Cornelius C.
Brinck Hendrick
Brinck Cornelius
Brinck Jacob
Brinck Jacob jr
Brinck John
Brinck John C.
Brinck John J.
Brinck Peter C.
Brink Henry
Brink John jr
Brink John A
Brink John C.
Brink John G.
Brink John T.
Brink Peter
Bristead Andrew
Britt Frederick
Britt Willem
Bruyer James
Buckman Benjamin
Buckman Hendrick
Buckman John J.
Buckman Thomas
Burhans Abraham
Burhans Barent.
Burhans Benjamin
Burhans Cornelius

Burhans Cornelius,
Burhans Edward
Burhans John
Burhans John sr
Burhans John jr
Burhans John W
Burhans Jonathan
Burhans Richard
Burhans Samuel
Burhans Thark
Burhans Tjurck
Buyer James

Callor John
Carareych Heronemus
Carnright Aronamis
Carrel Jury
Carrell George —
Caruyster Silvaster
Castell William —
Castle William
Cater Abraham —
Cator John
Crispel John T
Chrispell Abraham
Clearwater Jeremiah
Cole John
Colgrove Francis
Corns Causin
Conjes Jacob
Constaple William
Conns Jacobs
Cool Peter
Coolgrove Francis
Corns Causin
Corrie Gorg
Cramer Wandal
Crammer Wendell
Crispell Abraham
Crispell Jacob
Crispell Peterus T.

ENROLLED MEN.—*Continued.*

Crispell Petrus J.
Crispell John J.
Crook Martin
Croose Lenord
Crum Henry W.
Cruyslaar Silvester
Crisple Benjamin
Critsinger John
Croos John
Cross John
Crum Jacob

Davis John B
Davis Sampson
Davis William
DeBois Jacobus
Debois William
Decker Isaak
Dederick Cato
Dederick John
Dedrick Harmanus
Degraaf John
DeGrave John
DeGrave Henry
Delamater Abraham A.
Delamater Cornelius
Delameter Benjamin
De Lameter John
DeLimature Cor's J.
Delamater Cornelius
Devenport John
DeWitt Abraham
DeWitt Jacob
DeWitt Johannis
DeWitt John J.
DeWitt Tjerck C.
Dobois James jr
Dubois David
Dubois James jr
Dubois Johannes
Dubois John I.
Dubois John T.
Dubois Robert
Dull Christian
Dumond Cornelius
Dumond Egbert
Dumond Isaac
Dumond John jr
Dumond Peter jr
Dumont Peter jr
Davenport John
Davis Joseph
Davis Samuel
Davits John B
Debois James
Decker Ephraim
Decker Petrus
Dederick Gilbert
Dederick Jonathan
Dedrick Jacobus
Degraaf William
DeGrave William
Delafever Coenradt
Delamatter Abraham C.
Delameter Cornelis C.
Delameter David
De Lafever Jonathan
De Lemeter Abraham
Deronde Matthew
DeWett John T.
Dewitt Cornelis
Dewitt Jacob J.
Dewitt John
Dewitt Tjerck
Diederick Harmanus
Doyle Charles
Dubois James
Dubois Jeremiah
Dubois John
Dubois John J.
Dubois Matthew
Dubois William
Dumon John jr
Dumond Cornelius jr
Dumond Igenas
Dumond John
Dumond Peter
Dumont Peter

Eccor Jeremiah
Eccor Solomon jr
Eckert Henry
Eckert Jeremiah
Eckert Solomon
Eigener Jacob
Eigener Joh's
Eigener Peter P.
Eigeniar Cor's
Eccor Martin
Eckerd Stephan
Eckert Jacob
Eckert Marthinus
Eigeneer Frederick
Eigener John
Eigener Peter jr
Eigener William
Eigenor Jacobus

ENROLLED MEN.—*Continued.*

Eignuir Peter D.
Eligh Johannis
Elling William
Elmendorph Abraham
Elmendorph Coeuradt C.
Elmendorph Lucas
Elmendorph Peter jr
Eltinge Hendrick
Eltinge Peter
Eltinge William
Emert Matthew,
Emrich Johannis
Emrich Wilhelmus
Emrigh Wilhelmus jr
Enveigh Wilhelmus
Ersh Jacob
Ettings Hendricus
Eygenaar Frederick
Eygenaar John
Eygenaar Willem
Eygener Petrus jr
Eligh Jacob
Elling Hendrick
Elmendorf Coenradt Edward
Elmendorph Benjamin
Elmendorph Coenradt W.
Elmendorph Lucas jr
Elmendorph Petrus
Eltinge John
Eltinge Peter jr
Elyrah Jacob
Emighery Joh's
Emrich Peter
Emrich Wilhelmus jr
Emrugh John
Ernest Matthew
Etting Peter jr
Eygenaar Cornelis
Eygenaar Jacobus
Eygenaar Peter
Eygener Peter P.

Falk Johannis
Falkenbargh Abraham
Fanaka Abraham
Fellor Joh's
Felten Benjamin
Felten Johannis jr
Felten Philip
Felter Johannes jr
Felter Petrus
Felton John
Felton, John jr
Fernoo Christian, jr
Feroo Peter
Ferro Stephen
Freres Coenradt
Fiero Christian
Fiero Han Christian
Fiero Peter
Fietsel Johannis
Finis Counradt
Fernes Counradt
Folk Johannis
Follant Jacob
Follent Jury
Fowler James
France Cornelis
France Jacob jr
France Wilhelmus
Frans Wilhelmus
Frar Gerrit
Freer Benjamin
Freer Hugo
Freer Jeremyas
Falk Wilhelmes
Falkenbargh Joh's
Felie Johannis
Felrs Joh's
Felten Jacob
Felten Peter
Felter Jacob
Felter John
Felter Philip
Felton Peterus
Feroo John C.
Ferous Counradt
Ferro William
Fiero ———
Fiero Christian jr
Fiero John C.
Fiero William
Filton John
Firero Counradt
Foland George
Falkenburgh Abraham
Follen Jury
Fosburgh Abr'm
France Adam
France Jacob
France Johannis
Frans Joh's
Frans William
Freer Abraham
Freer Garret
Freer Jeremiah
Freer Johannis
Freer Peter

ENROLLED MEN.—*Continued.*

Freer Jonathan
Freer Samuel
Freland George
Freligh Hendrick jr
Freligh John
Frees Johannis
Freligh Hendrick
Freligh Samuel
Frier Benjamin
Frier Samuel

Gee Joseph
Gilbert Justin
Groen Jacob Marius jr
Groen Sylvester Marous
Groone Peter Morris
Groone Silvaster M
Gilbert Ephriam
Groen Jacob Marius
Groen Peter Marius
Groen William Marius
Groohe Saberster Mars
Groone William Monis

Haasbrouck Jacobus
Hanpaugh Peter
Hardenberg Peter
Hasbrouck Jacobus jr
Hasbrouck Jonathan
Heermanse Abraham
Hermanse Edward
Hendricks Jacob
Hendricks Philip
Hendrix Jacob
Hendrixson Jacob
Hendrixson Philip
Hinmans Abr'm
Hommel Abraham
Hommel Jurrie
Hommel Petrus
Hoogtaling Wilhelmus jr
Houghtaling John
Houghtaling Wilhelmus T.
Houghtaling William F.
Hudson Jonathan
Hummel Abraham
Hummel Harman
Hummel Jurry
Humstead Elias
Hance Willem
Hardenbergh Lewis
Hasbrouck Daniel
Hasbrouck John
Hasbrouck Solomon
Hermanse John
Hendricks John
Hendrickson Johannis
Hendrix Joh's
Hendrixson John
Herrington Moses
Hodler Solomon
Hommel Hermanus
Hommel Jurrie jr
Hooghtalin William jr
Houghtaling Jeremiah
Houghtaling Thomas
Houghtaling William T.
Huddlor Salomon
Huffman Abr'm
Hummel George jr
Hummel Harman jr
Hummel Peter
Hymback Peter
Hynpals Peter

Japh Jacob
Joung Jeremiah
Japle Jacob
Jurrie Hans

Karley George
Keater Abraham
Keeler John
Keffer Lourance
Keffer William jr
Kerlach Nicholas
Kersteed Wilhelmis
Kieffar William jr
Kieffer Lowrence
Kiffer William
Kierstead Wilhelmus
Krom Benjamin
Krom Henry B.
Kros Johannes
Krum Hendrick B.
Kaltor Abraham
Kaeter John
Keffer Ballije
Keffer William
Kellenburgh Isaac jr
Kersteed John
Kiefer Baltis
Kieffer William
Kierstead John
Kodler Solomon
Krom Jacob
Kroom Hendrick
Krous Leonard
Krum Hendric W.

ENROLLED MEN.—*Continued.*

Lafever Jonathan
Lamendyck Cor's
Lamendyck John
Langendyck John
Langendyke Cornelis
Langyan William
Langyare Christian
Lanjaar Christopher
Lanjaar Willem
Larway Peter
Lefever Conrad
Legg John jr
Legg Samuel
Lits Willem
Lomgendyck Cor's
Lousk Peter jr
Louw Abraham
Louw Cornelius
Loux Cor's
Loux Peter W.
Low Abr'm
Low Abr'm A.
Low Abraham C.
Low Abraham E.
Low Cor's
Low Frederick
Low Jacobus
Low Johannis
Low John C.
Low Peter
Low Tjerck
Luyks Cornelis
Luyks Peter jr
Luyks Peter W.

McCay John
McClean John
McCleen John
McFarling Andrew
McGroone Peter
McKenney Alexander
McKiney Alexander
Maderstock Adam
Magee Peter
Magee Peter jr
Magee Samuel
Maris Robert
Markul Johannis
Mars Robert
Marsial John
Marten Joseph
Martin Cor's B.
Martin Joh's B.
Martin Joseph
Masten Abraham
Masten Abraham jr
Masten Abraham A.
Masten Cornelius B.
Masten Cornelius C.
Masten Daniel
Masten Hendrick
Masten Johannes B.
Masten Johannes C.
Masten Johannes E.
Masters Joseph
Mastin Dainel
Materslock Johannis
Materstock Jacob
Materstock Johannis
Materstock Peter
Matterslock Adam
Matterstock John
Mauer Jacob
Menkelar Cor's
Menkial Johannes
Merkel Johannis
Meyer Christiaen
Meyer Peter L.
Mickel John
Minkalar Cornelius
Minkelar Harmanus
Mire Stephen
Morris Robert
Mosten Joseph
Mouries Jacob
Muories Johannis jr
Mousier Jacob
Myer Abraham
Myer Benjamin
Myer Benjamin jr
Myer Christian
Myer Cornelis
Myer Counright
Myer Ephraim
Myer Hendericus
Myer Henry
Myer Johannis jr
Myer Peter
Myer Peter jr
Myer Peter B.
Myer Peter L.
Myer Peter T.
Myer Stephan
Myer Thunis
Myer William jr
Myer Stephen jr

ENROLLED MEN.—*Continued.*

Neukeuk Charles

Oosterhaude Hendrick
Oosterhoudt Jacob
Oosterhoudt James
Oosterhoudt Peter
Oosterhoudt Petrus
Oosterhoudt Samuel
Oosterhoudt Willem
Osterhoudt Abraham
Osterhoudt Edward
Osterhout Abraham
Osterhout William
Ostrander Henry
Ostrander Samuel

Parsel Jeremiah
Percal Cornelis
Perse Cornelius
Persen Cornelius
Persen John J.
Persey Cor's
Phenix Abraham
Plough Hendrick
Plough Tunis
Post Abraham
Post Cor's
Post Isaac
Post Jacobus
Post John jr
Post Marteynus
Post Martin jr
Poust Cornelius

Rechtmeyer Hermanus
Rechtmyer George
Rechtmyer Johannis
Rechtmyer Peter
Richley Andrew
Rickle Andrew
Raase John jr
Rossell Lodewick
Rouce Benjamin
Russell Ludwigh

Salisbury Silvester
Schapmis William
Schepmoes William
Schoemaker Nicolas
Schoomaker Samuel
Schoonmaker David
Schoonmaker Edward E.
Schoonmaker Egbert C.
Schoonmaker Johannis
Schoonmaker John E.
Schoonmaker Thark

Newkerk Benjamin.

Oosterhoudt Benjamin
Oosterhoudt Jacobus
Oosterhoudt John
Oosterhoudt Peter jr
Oosterhoudt Petrus L.
Oosterhoudt Teunis
Oosterhout Joseph
Osterhoudt Benjamin
Osterhoudt Peter
Osterhout Samuel
Osterhoutt Elias
Ostrander James

Patterson Moses
Periall Cor's
Persell Jeremiah
Persen John
Persen Matthew
Perslow Henry
Ploegh Teunis
Plough Henry
Polhamus Daniel
Post Abraham A.
Post Henry jr
Post Isaac jr
Post John
Post Marte jr
Post Martin
Post Samuel

Rechtmyer Coenrad
Rechtmyer George jr
Rechtmyer Jurry W.
Richley Jacob
Richtmyer Johannis
Riehley Jacob
Roosa John jr
Root Henry
Rouw Benjamin

Sax Peter
Schepmoes John
Schitt Solomon
Schoemaker Petrus
Schoonmaiker Neh's
Schoonmaker Edward
Schoonmaker Egbert jr
Schoonmaker Hisakia
Schoonmaker Johannis jr
Schoonmaker Nicholas
Schoonmaker Thark jr

ENROLLED MEN.—*Continued.*

Schoonmaker Tjurk
Schryber Albertus
Schryber Stephan
Schut Solomon
Scryer Stephen
Scyriver John
Shears Andrew
Short Hendrick
Short Petrus
Sleght Hendricus B.
Sleght Petrus
Sleght Teunis
Snyder Abraham
Snyder Benjamin
Snyder Hendricus
Snyder Johannes
Snyder John
Snyder Martinas
Snyder Solomon
Sperling John
Stattas Henry
Steenbergh Thomas
Stoughtenburgh Isaac jr
Suyland Johannis
Swart Cornelius
Swart Cornelius L.
Swart Teunis
Swart Tobias
Schriver Johannes
Schryber Martinus
Schut Christian
Scryer Albertus
Scryver Marten
Share Andries
Shoe Augustus
Short Henry
Shue Augusteane
Sleght Salomon
Smedes Peter B.
Snyder Abraham jr
Snyder Christian
Snyder Henry
Snyder Johannes M.
Snyder John jr
Snyder Martyn
Sperling George
Staats Hendrick
Steenbargh Thomas G.
Steinbergh John
Sulant John
Swart Benjamin
Swart Cornelius jr
Swart Petrus
Swart Thomas
Swart William

Tappan Peter
Teerpening Gerrit
Teerpening Simon
Teerpenning Jacobus
Teerpenning Willem;
Ten Eyck Dirck
Terpenney Hendrick
Thompson Mathew jr
Thompson William
Thomson Matthew jr
Trimper Wilhelmus
Trompor Joh's.
Trompour Valentine
Trumpour Jacob
Turck Johannes
Turk John
Tarpenning Willem
Teerpening Petrus
Teerpenning Abraham
Teerpenning Jacobus jr
Tenbroeck John
Ten Eyck Richard
Thompson Jonathan
Thompson Matthew Edward
Thomson Jonathan
Tremper, Jacob
Trompor Johannis jr
Trumbonner John
Turck Hendrick,
Turck Johannes jr
Tutsell Joh's.

Ulmstead Elias.

Valck Johannes
Valkenburgh Abraham
Van Aken Benjamin
Van Aken Eliphas
Van Aken Isaac
Van Aken Peter G.
Van Beuren Philip
Valk Wilhelmus
Valkenbourgh John
Van Aken Cato
Van Aken Gideon
Van Aken Peter
Van Aken John
Van Beuschoten Solomon

ENROLLED MEN.—*Continued.*

Van Bunscholin Solomon
Van Burin Tobias
Van Gaasbeck, Abraham W.
Van Gaasbeek, John jr
Van Gasbuck, Peter
Van Hunbargh, John
Van Keuran, Cornelius M.
Van Keuren, Abraham
Van Keuren, Matthew
Van Keuren, Tjerck
Van Kunn, Mathias
Van Leuven, John
Van Leuwen, Zacheriah
Van Steenbargh, John jr
Van Steenbargh, Peterus
Van Steenbargh, Tobias, jr.
Van Steenbergh Benjamin
Van Steenbergh Henry
Van Steenbergh Matthew
Van Steenbergh Pontis
Van Steenbergh Thomas
Van Steenberghn Tobyes
Van Vleit Arie
Van Vliet John
Van Vliet Tjerck
Van Wagenen Abraham W.
Van Wagenen Henry
Van Wagenen Johannis J.
Van Waggoner ——
Van Waggoner Benjamin
Van Waggoner Jacob jr
Viele John
Vollant Jurrie
Van Buren Philip
Van Etten John
Van Gaasbeek John
Van Gasbeck Abr'm jr
Van Gesbuck John jr
Van Keuran Cornelius
Van Keuran Matthew jr
Van Keuren Gerrit
Van Keuren Philip
Van Kunn Abraham
Van Leuven Andries
Van Leuven John jr
Van Schayck Anthony
Van Steenbargh Paulus
Van Steenbargh Tobias
Van Steenbergh Abraham
Van Steenbergh Dirick
Van Steenbergh John
Van Steenbergh Peter
Van Steenberg Poulis
Van Steenbergh Thomas jr
Van Steenberghn Tobyes jr
Van Vliet George
Van Vliet Jurry
Van Wagenen Abraham B.
Van Wagenen Benjamin
Van Wagenen Jacob jr.
Van Wagenen Ysack Y.
Van Waggoner Abr'm W.
Van Waggoner Henry
Van Waggoner Joh's I.
Vollant George
Vosburgh Abraham.

Weaver John
Wells Cornelis
Wells Jacobus
Wels Peter
Whitaker Edward
Whitaker James
Whiteaker Abraham
Whiteaker Benjamin
Whiteaker Petrus
Whitteker John
Wiest Peterus
Will Christian
Windfield Benjamin
Winfield David
Winna John
Winne Peter A.
Winnen Arent
Winnen Cornelis
Winnen James
Winnen Peter
Winnen Peter J.
Wells Christian
Wells Henry
Wells James
Wenne Peter A.
Whitaker Edward jr
Whitaker Philip
Whiteaker Abraham jr
Whiteaker Jacobus
Whittaker James W.
Wiest Peter
Wiliker Petrus
Williams John
Winfield Daniel
Winfield Simon
Winne Benjamin
Winne Peter J.
Winnen Arent jr
Winnen Jacobus
Winnen John
Winnen Peter jr
Winnia Arant

ENROLLED MEN.—*Continued.*

Winnia Benjamin
Winnia Jacobus
Winnia Peter
Winnia Peter A.
Winns William
Witiker James I.
Witteker John
Wolf Adam
Wolfent Jeremiah
Wolfent John
Wolff John
Wolven Johannis jr
Wolvin Adam
Wolvin Johanis H.
Wolvin John H.
Wynkoop Hezekiah
Wynkoop Peter

Yaple Hanniele
Yeoman Moses
Yepeel Jacob
York Daniel
Young Jeremiah

Winnia Cor's
Winnia James
Winnia Peter jr
Winnia Peter L.
Witecker Jacob
Witteker Abraham
Woester George
Wolfen John
Wolfent Joh's
Wolfet John
Wolven Jeremiah
Wolven John
Wolvin Jeremiah
Wolvin Johannis jr
Wynkoop Evert
Wynkoop John jr
Wynkoop Willem

Yaple Jacob
Yeomens Moses
Yeuple Hanele
Young Abraham
Yourk Moses.

James H. Everett.

CHAPTER X.

THE SECOND OR SOUTH END REGIMENT.

THE Second or South End Regiment, extending over the territory west from the Hudson along the original south county line from the mouth of Murderers' Creek to the Delaware, was the south territorial part of the previous colonial second regiment of which Thomas Ellison was colonel prior to the opening of the Revolution. It was eminently the home regiment of the Clintons, James, George, and Dr. Charles, who had grown up with the sons of a large colony of Scotch-Irish immigrants whose fathers had accompanied Colonel Charles Clinton thither in 1729. Strong in their personality and in their social relations, James and George became still stronger by their marriages, the first with a daughter of Egbert De Witt of Paenpacht on the Delaware, and the second with a sister of Christopher Tappen of Kingston, of Dutch forbears. Under these conditions there was "fight" in the regiment from the beginning to the close of the Revolution. In no other regimental district was the militia more active, and in none were the enlistments in the Continental Army so large. The Field and Staff of the regiment was commissioned October 25th, 1775:

James Clinton, Colonel,
James McClaughrey, Lieut. Colonel.
Jacob Newkirk, Major (1st.)
Moses Phillips, Major (2d)
George Denniston, Adjutant,
Alexander Trimble, Qr. Master.

Colonel Clinton having been appointed Brigadier-General in the Continental Line, the Field and Staff of the regiment was reconstructed March 23d, 1778, by the appointment of

James McClaughrey, Colonel,
Jacob Newkirk, Lieut. Colonel.
Moses Phillips, Major,
George Denniston, Adjutant.
Peter Crance, 1st Qr. Master.
Evins Wharry, 2d Quarter Master.

Colonel McClaughrey, who was in command of the regiment as Lieutenant Colonel under Clinton, was taken prisoner in the fierce battle at

Fort Montgomery, Oct. 6th, 1777, and remained in captivity until about the close of the war, during which time the command devolved upon Lieut. Colonel Newkirk, from which fact the designation, "Newkirk's Regiment" is frequently met in records. As primarily enrolled the companies composing the regiment were:

1st Co. East side Willkill—Captain Samuel Watkins; Daniel Crawford, First Lieut.; Stephen Harlow, Second Lieutenant; Henry Smith, Ensign. (Daniel Crawford should read David Crawford.)

2d Co. New Windsor (Moodna)—John Nicoll, Captain; Francis Mandeville, First Lieut.; Leonard D. Nicoll, Ensign.

3d Co. Hanover Precinct—William Jackson, Captain; Henry Van Keuren, First Lieut.; Henry Munnel, Second Lieut.; Andrew Neely, Ensign (the latter so entered on Precinct minutes).

4th Co. Hanover Precinct—Mathias Felter (Felton), Captain; Henry Smith, First Lieut.; Johannis Newkirk, Second Lieut.; William Crist, Ensign.

5th Co. Wallkill Precinct (between the Willkill and Shawangunk Kill)—William Faulkner, Captain; Edward McNeal, First Lieut.; John Wilkin, Second Lieut.; John Faulkner, Ensign.

6th Co. Mamakating Precinct (Paenpacht)—Jacob Rutzen De Witt, Captain; Abraham Cuddeback, Jr., First Lieut.; Robert Cooke, Second Lieut.; Samuel King, Ensign.

7th Co. Hanover Precinct—Cadwallader C. Colden, Captain; James Milliken, First Lieut.; John Hunter, Second Lieut.; Matthew Hunter, Ensign. (Colden declined, and company reorganized—James Milliken, Captain; John Hunter, First Lieutenant; Matthew Hunter, Second Lieutenant; Robert Burns, Ensign.)

8th Co. New Windsor Precinct—John Belknap, Captain; Silas Wood, First Lieut.; Edward Falls, Second Lieut.; James Stickney, Ensign. (Belknap entered Continental Line. Co. reconstructed—James Umphrey, Captain; Silas Wood, First Lieut.; James Kernaghan, Second Lieut.; Richard Wood, Ensign.

9th Co. New Windsor Precinct (Little Britain)—William Telford, Captain; James Faulkner, First Lieut.; Alex'r Beaty, Second Lieut.; John Burnett, Ensign.

10th Co. Mamakating Precinct—John Crage, Captain; Manuel Gonsales, First Lieut.; William Rose, Second Lieut.; Isaac Roosa, Ensign.

11th Co. Wallkill Precinct—Wm. Denniston, Captain; Benj. Veal, First Lieut.; Joseph Jillet, Second Lieut.; David Corwin, Junr., Ensign. (Northwest of Little Shawangunk Kill.)

12th Co. Wallkill Precinct (between Wallkill and Little Shawangunk Kill)—Isaiah Veal, Captain; Israel Wickham, First Lieut.; John Dunning, Second Lieut.; Jonathan Owen, Ensign.

13th Co. Coshecton Company—Bazaliel Tyler, Junr.,* Captain; Nathaniel Reevs, First Lieut.; Moses Thomas, Second Lieut.; Nathan Mitchell, Ensign.

* Capt. Bazaliel Tyler was the first man killed in the battle of Minisink, July 22d, 1779. He was in the advanced guard. He is usually credited to the Goshen regiment, to which he never belonged, nor did his company.

On the 16th of March, 1776, Lieut. Col. McClaughrey reported the strength of the regiment as follows:

First Company—Capt. Watkins.

Commitioned Officers,	4
Non-Commitioned Officers,	8
Clark & Drummer,	2
Privits,	49
Minute Men,	19
	82

Second Company—Capt. Nicklos, Esq.

Commitioned Officers,	4
Non-Commitioned Officers,	8
Clark, Drum & Fife,	3
Privits,	60
Minute Men,	17
	92

Third Company—Capt. William Jackson.

Commitioned Officers,	3
Non-Commitioned Officers,	7
Clark & Drummer,	2
Privits,	68
The Above has been in the Minute Servis And now Returns themselves as such.	
Commitioned Officer,	1
Non-Commitioned Officer,	1
Privits,	32
	114

Forth Company—Capt. Mathew Felter.

Commitioned Officers,	3
Non-Commitioned Officers,	8
Clark, Drum & Fife,	3
Privits,	48
Minute Men,	0
Commitioned,	1
Privits,	13
	76

Fifth Company—William Falkner, Capt.

Commitioned Officers,	4
Non-Commitioned Officers,	8
Clark, Drum & Fife	3
Privits,	45
Minute Men,	28
	88

Sixth Company—Jacob Dewitt, Capt.

Commitioned Officers,	4
Non-Commitioned Officers,	8
Clark, Drummer & Fife,	3
Privits,	51
Torys,	2
Minute Men,	0
	68

Seventh Company—Ja Milegen, Capt.	
Commitioned Officers,	4
Non-Commitioned Officers,	8
Clark, Drum & Fife,	3
Privits,	55
Minute Men,	15
	85
Eighth Company—John Belknap, Capt.	
Commitioned Officers,	4
Non-Commitioned Officers,	8
Clark, Drum & Fife,	3
Privits,	46
Minute Men,	6
Listed in the provincials,	14
	81
Ninth Company—William Telford, Capt.	
Commitioned Officers,	4
Non-Commitioned Officers,	7
Clark, Drum & Fife,	3
Privits,	54
The Above has turned out Minute Men the 1st of This Inst.	
Listed in the provincial,	7
Militia,	21
	96
Tenth Company—John Crage, Capt.	
Commitioned Officers,	4
Non-Commitioned Officers,	8
Clark & Drummer,	2
Rank and File,	46
Minute Men,	0
	60
Eleventh Company—William Denniston, Capt.	
Commitioned Officers,	4
Non-Commitioned Officers,	8
Clark, Drum & Fife,	3
Rank and File,	35
Minute Men,	00
	50
Twelfth Company—Isaiah Veail, Capt.	
Commitioned Officers,	4
Non-Commitioned Officers,	8
Clark & Drum,	2
Rank and File,	51
Minute Men,	6
	71

Total,	963
Minute Men,	253
Militia,	710

Addison E. Dederick.

The following list of the enrolled men of the regiment is taken from "New York in the Revolution." It is presumed to be correct "as far as it goes." In making searches for particular names reference should also be made to the "Archives of the Revolution" as well as to the lists of other regiments.

ENROLLED MEN.

Abrahams, John
Adams Chester
Adcock, William
Atherston Joel

Bodle, William
Baily John
Barber, John
Barber Timothy
Barkley, Thomas
Barton Elijah
Bayard, James
Baylis Nehemiah
Bealy, John
Beatty Archibald
Beatty, James
Beatty Thomas
Beatty, William
Beaty Alexander
Baty, Arthur
Beaty John
Beaty, Robert
Belknap, Benjamin
Belknap, David
Belknap Isaac
Belknap, Isaac, Jr.
Belknap Jeduthan
Belknap, Jonathan
Belknap Jonathan Jr.
Belknap, Thomas, Jr.
Bell Mathew
Bennet Benjamin
Bennet John
Biram Asa
Black James
Black John
Blizzard Oliver
Bodine Lewiss
Bodle Samuel
Bodle William
Boides Robart Jr.
Bookstaver Frederick
Bookstaver Jacob Sr.
Bookstaver Jacob Jr.
Booth John
Booth Thomas
Boreland Charles
Boreland Thomas
Boyd James
Boyd Robert
Boyd Samuel
Brannen Ruben
Brewster John
Brewster Samuel
Britnow Henry
Brockway Jesse
Brooke Jeremiah
Brooks Jeremiah
Brooks John
Brooks William
Brown Archabald
Brown Duncan
Brown Gilbert
Brown James H.
Brown John
Brown Neal
Brundage William
Brurdish Gilbert
Buchanan Robert
Buchanan Alexander
Buchanan James
Buchanan John
Buchanan Robert
Buice James
Bull Moses
Bunet Jenjamin
Burnet John
Burnet Patrick
Burnet Robert
Burnet Thomas
Burns Francis
Burns Robert
Burns William
Buts Jacob

Caldwell James
Calwell William
Camble John
Campbell Levi
Campble Edward
Campble Ezekiel

ENROLLED MEN.—*Continued.*

Canfield John
Carman Yoest
Carney Stephen
Carskaden Thomas
Case Benjamin
Chandler Enos
Clark Jeremiah
Clark James
Clark Phineas
Clemons Daniel
Cobb Asa
Coddinton William
Coleman David
Congo David
Conkling John
Content Moses
Cook Thomas
Corethers John
Corwin David
Corwin Eli
Cox Jeremy
Cox Reeves
Cox William Jr.
Crawford Alexander
Crawford John
Crist Abraham
Crist David
Crist Henry Jr.
Crist Philip
Crodethers John
Cross John
Cuddeback, Abraham Sr.
Cuddeback, Abraham A.
Cuddeback, James
Cuddeback, William
Curtenius, Peter, Jr.
Curtice, Noah
Curwin, Barnabas

Cantine Moses
Carney Barnabas
Carpenter William
Carter Luke
Caulkin Oliver
Clark Henry
Clark John
Clark Joseph
Clawater Tice
Clark Henry
Coddinton Benjamin
Coddinton Joseph
Coleman John
Conkling Ananias
Content Benjamin
Cook John
Cook William
Cortwright Silvester
Corwin Eli
Cox Benjamin
Cox John
Cox William
Crane Benjamin
Crawford James
Crawford Samuel
Crist Daniel
Crist Henry Sr.
Crist Matinis
Crist Stophonis
Crons Adam
Cross Robert
Cuddeback Abraham Jr.
Cuddeback Benjamin
Cuddeback Peter
Currenton Richard
Curtice Benejah
Curtice Thomas

Daily, Samuel Jr.
Daly, David
Darkeas John
Davidson John
Davis Pathick
Davis William
Dealls William
Decay Jacob
Decker Evert
Decker Martinas
Den Christopher
Denn William
Denniston Alexander
Denniston William
Denniston John
Denton Joseph

Daily Samuel
Dales John
Daly John
David Henry
Davis John
Davis Thomas
Dealls John
Dearkis John
Decker David
Decker Isaac
Defrees James
Denman Isaac
Denna Hinnery
Denniston Charles
Denniston James
Denton Isaac

ENROLLED MEN.—*Continued.*

Depuy Benjamin
Depuy John
Devans James
Dickarson Benjamin
Dill David
Docksey James
Douglass James
Douty Benjamin
Drake Joseph
Dunen Samuel
Dunn George
Durham Andrew

Denton Samuel
Depuy Benjamin Jr.
Depuy Moses
Dick Thomas
Dickson Androw
Dill John
Donavan Daniel
Douglass William
Doxey James
Duffy John
Dunlap James
Dunn William
Duryee Jacob K.

Eager John
Easten Jeremiah
Edmondstin James
Elder Joseph
Ellison David
Elsworth Henry
Everit Nehemiah

Eager William
Eastman Tilten
Edmondston William
Elis James
Ellott John
English William
Evret John

Falls William
Finch James
Fitzjerrild Jeremiah
Frashor William
Fulton Thomas

Falkner William
Finley John
Fowler Stephen
Fuller Jepotha

Gage William
Gale Moses
Galloway John
Giles Charles
Gillispy David
Godfry David
Goldsmith Cabeb
Galow Christopher
Galow Joseph
Green Daniel
Green John
Gumaer Elias
Gumaer Peter 2d.
Gunsalis Daniel
Gunsalis Samuel

Gale Richard
Gale Samuel
Garisson Nathaniel
Gillispie Mathew
Gillispy John
Godfry David Jr.
Goldsmith Stephen
Galow John
Green Ebenezer
Green Israel
Green John Jr.
Gumaer Jacob
Gumar Ezeckiel
Gunsalis Manuel

Haines Charles
Hains David
Hains John B.
Halsey Jabas
Hanesey James
Hanyon Garret
Harlow William
Harris John
Hart Andrew
Hays James
Hegerman Thomas
Helms Vincent

Hains Benjamin
Hains John
Halabut John
Halstead Gershom
Hanmer John
Harden John
Harris George
Harskal Jonathan
Hasbrook Cornelius
Headin James
Helms Daniel
Hinneris Aron

ENROLLED MEN.—*Continued.*

Holsey Zephaniah
Homan Benjamin
Homan John
Homan Pheneas
Hopkins Garner
Hortin Jacob
Horton David
Horton John
Horton Joseph
Horton Silas
Howell Stephen
Hubart Joseph
Hubbard Joseph
Hulse John
Humphrey David
Humphrey George
Humphrey William
Humphry Charles
Humphry Oliver
Huse John
Hutson Richard

Inglis John
Inglis William

Jackson Silas
Jagger David
Jaques David
Jillett John
Johnson David
Johnson George
Johnson Robert
Johnson David
Jones Augustus
Jones Philip

Keen Jacob
Kelso Henry
Kernaghan Alexander
Kernaghan Charles
Ketcham James
Ketcham Joseph
Ketcham Philip
Kidd James
Kidd Robert
Kilburn James
King Clement
King Nicholas
King Stephen
Kingham Thomas
Knapp Zephaniah
Knox George

Lee Jepthah
Lee Jonathan
Lee Solomen
Leonard Henry
Lewers Williams
Liscomb John
Low James
Low Peter
Lowdy John
Lusk Francis

McArter John
Mc.Arthur Neal
McCallon Thomas
McCalough Alaugh
McClaughry John
McClean John
McClotham Joseph
McCollam Matt
McConnely John
McCord Andrew
McCord James
McCreary Alexander
McCurdy Archibald
McDawell William
McDonal Alexander
McDowel Thomas
Mc.Dowell James
Mc.Enty Michael
Mc.Ever Daniel
Mc.Garagh John
McGown John
McKee Thomas
McKessock Thomas
McLoy William
McMaster James
McMichel John
McMillian Mathew
Mc.Munn John
McNeas Clark
Mc.Neas George
McNeely David
Mc.Nes Daniel
Mc.Nish Clark
Mc.Swaney Daniel
Mains Francis
Mandevil Cornelius
Mandevil David
Mandevil John
Mapes Henry
Mapes Samuel
Mapes Smith
Mapes William

ENROLLED MEN.—*Continued.*

Marshall David
Martin John
Mathers James
Meloy James
Miller Elias
Milliken Alexander
Milliken James
Mills Daniel
Mills Jonathan
Milspaugh Adam
Milspaugh Jacob
Milspaugh Philip
Milspaugh Tice
Moffatt William
Monnel James
Moore James
Moore William
More John
More Nathan Jr.
Morrison Daniel
Morrison John

Martin Charles
Mathers Ebenezer
Matthews Amasa
Miller Edward
Miller John
Milliken Hugh
Millor Ezrah
Mills Jacob
Mills John
Milspaugh Benjamin
Milspaugh Jonathan
Milspaugh Philip Jr.
Moffat Samuel
Moncrief Charles
Moor William
Moore Robert
More David
More Nathan
More William
Morrison James
Mould Christopher

Neal Mal'h
Neely John
Neely Thomas
Newkirk Hendrick
Newston Robbart
Nicholson Daniel
Nickoll William Sr.
Nobel Jabes

Neely, Edward
Neely, John, Jr.
Newkirk, Adam
Newman Scuder
Nichols, William
Nicholson, Thomas
Nikols, Nathan

Obrien John
Oliver Thomas
Overton James
Owen David
Owen Jonathan Jr.
Owen Nathaniel
Owen Solomon
Owens Eleazer

Oliver, David
Outerman, Stephen
Owen Amasa
Owen, Eleazer
Owen, Joshua
Owen Oliver
Owens Amasa
Owin John

Palmer Henry
Parks Amos
Parshall John
Patterson James
Patton James
Perry David
Polley William
Post Zebulon
Price John

Park William
Pars Jonathan
Parshall Jonathan
Patterson Samuel
Pelton Gideon
Perry John
Porter Thomas
Potter Aaron
Puff John

Reed John
Reeder Charles
Reeve Nathaniel Jr
Rickey Andrew
Rittenbergh Aron
Roberts Daniel

Reed Moses
Reeve Ely Jr.
Rhoads Thomas
Ritenbergh Addam
Robert Danel
Robertson Benjamin

ENROLLED MEN.—*Continued.*

Robinson William
Rockefella Christian
Rockefella John
Roe Samuel
Rogers Robert
Rogers William
Roose Aldert
Rosa Evert
Rose Jacob

Rocefeller J—ndr.
Rockefella Henry
Rockwell Samuel
Rogers Moses
Rogers Solomon
Roosa Cornelius
Roose Jacob
Rosa Jacob
Rose Samuel

Sanders John
Sayer Stephen
Scates Bartholomy
Scott Archibald
Scott William
Seely Elijah
Seely Samuel
Seybolt John
Shaw William
Shea George
Shilp Johonis
Siah, Indian
Siears, Benjamin (Sears?)
Siers, Elethan
Simeril Robert
Simpson, Peter
Sinsabok, William
Slott, Cornelius
Slott, John Sr.
Slott, Jonas
Sly, Samuel
Smedes, Moses
Smith, Bastian
Smith, David Jr.
Smith, Jacob
Smith, Jeremiah
Smith, Jonathan
Smith, Joseph
Smith, Nathan
Smith, Simon
Smith, William
Sprague, Andrew
Springsteen, Henery
Stag, John
Steel, Alexander
Stewart, Robert
Stinson William
Strickland Eli
Stubs William
Swarthout Gerad
Swarthout Philip

Satan Jonathan
Sayres Stephen
Scavon Mills
Scott James
Seely Bezaleel Jr.
Seely Israel
Sergeant Nathan
Seybolt John Sr.
Shay John
Sheerman Henry
Shutter Robert
Sickels Zachariah
Siears John
Siers, Samuel
Simmonds Jacob
Sinsabok Henry Sr.
Skinner Abner
Slott John
Slott John Jr.
Sly John
Sly William
Smiley James
Smith David
Smith George
Smith James
Smith John
Smith Jonathan Jr.
Smith Mathew
Smith Samuel
Smith Stephen
Southerland, James
Springsted James
Squirrel Jacob
Stanton Rufus
Stewart, Alexander
Stickney James
Stout David
Strong John
Swarthout Cornelius
Swarthout James
Swartwoud Jacobus

Clarence P. Hendricks.

ENROLLED MEN.—*Continued.*

Taylor Abraham
Taylor James
Thomas Ephraim
Thomas John
Thomson John
Thorn Obadiah
Thorn Samuel
Tillford Alexander
Totton James
Totten Thomas
Travis Ezekial
Tremper George
Trewilliger Isaac
Trewilliger John
Trewilliger Math
Trimble John
Trumpoor Nicholas
Trumpore Peter
Tucker James
Turner Hugh
Turner John
Tuttle Borzila

Vail Alsop
Vail Josiah
Vail Obediah
Vanburah Court
Vanfleet Daniel
Vaninwagen Cornelius
Vaninwagen Jacob
Van Inwegen David
Van Inwegen Herman
Van Nosdall John
Van Vara Cort
Vanwey Henry

Wair William
Wallace William
Wallice John
Wastbrook Abraham
Wastval Joseph
Watkins Ephraim
Watkins Thomas
Webb Janathan
Welch John
Welch Thomas
Weller Lod'k
Wesbrook Abraham
Westbrook Terrie V.
Westlake Samuel
Westlick Benjamin
Westlick George
Whary James
Whaet Amos
Wheat Solomon
Wheelar David
Wheler Gilbert
Whit Geames
White James
White Silas
Wickham William
Wilkins Daniel
Williams Isaac
Williams Jonas
Willing Frederick
Willoughby John
Wilson Andrew
Wilson William
Winter Ezra
Wood Alexander
Wood Benjamin
Wood Daniel
Wood John
Wood Robert
Wood Samuel
Wood Silas
Wood William
Woodruff John
Woods Benjamin
Woodward Hezekiah
Woodward Hezekiah Jr.
Wool Ellis
Wooley Charles
Wright David
Wright Williams

Young Benjamin
Young Charles

CHAPTER XI.

THE THIRD OR WESTERN REGIMENT.

THE Third or Western Regiment was organized as were the other regiments of the county, Oct. 25th, 1775. As then constituted its Field and Staff were:

Levi Pawling, Colonel.
Jacob Hoornbeck, Lieut. Colonel.
Johannis Cantine, 1st Major.
Joseph Hasbrouck, 2d Major.
David Bevier, Adjutant.
Jacobus Bruyn, Junr., Qr. Master.
Surgeon, John Crieger.

On the 21st of February, 1778, in consequence of the resignation of Colonel Pawling, who had been appointed First Judge of the Court of Common Pleas of the county, promotions were made:

Johannis Cantine, Colonel,
Joseph Hasbrouck, Lieut. Colonel, vice Hoornbeck, deceased.
Jacob Hasbrouck, 2d Major, vice Joseph Hasbrouck, promoted.

The primary companies were:

1st Co. Marbletown, S. E. District—Cornelius E. Wynkoop, Captain; Chas. W. Brodhead, First Lieut.; Moses M. Cantine, Second Lieut.; Jacob Chambers, Ensign.

2nd Co. Marbletown, N. E. District—Frederick Schoonmaker, Jr., Captain; Benjamin Louw, First Lieut.; Jacobus Rosekrans, Second Lieut.; John C. De Witt, Ensign.

3d Co. Rochester—Petrus Schoonmaker, Captain; Philip Hoornbeck, First Lieut.; Cornelius Hardenbergh, Second Lieut.; Dirck Westbrooke, Ensign.

4th Co. Rochester—Andries Bevier, Captain; Richard Brodhead, First Lieut.; Reuben De Witt, Second Lieut.; Johannis C. De Witt, Ensign. Southwesternmost Dist.

5th Co. Rochester—Jochem Schoonmaker, Jr., Captain; John Depuy, First Lieut.; Cornelius Van Wagenen, Second Lieut.; Zacharias Rosekrans, Ensign.

6th Co. Rochester—Benj. Kortright, Captain; Dirick Westbrook, First Lieut.; Fred'k Westbrook, Second Lieut.; Jacob Hoornbeck, Ensign.

7th Co., New Paltz—Lewis J. Du Bois, Captain; John A. Hardenbergh, First Lieut.; Matthew Le Fever, Second Lieut.; Mathusalim Du Bois, Ensign. Called the Southern District Co.

8th Co. New Paltz—Jacob Hasbrouck, Jr., Captain; Abraham Deyo, Jr., First Lieut.; Petrus Hasbrouck, Second Lieut.; Samuel Bevier, Ensign. Called the Northern District Co.

9th Co. New Paltz—Peleg Ransom, Captain; Nathaniel Potter, First Lieut.; Hugh Cole, Second Lieut.; William Danielson, Ensign. Called the East District Company.

The southeast Marbletown Company, on the appointment of its Captain, Cornelius E. Wynkoop, as Major of the Ulster Regiment of Minute Men, was reconstructed by the promotion of Charles W. Brodhead, Captain; Jacob De Lamater, First Lieut.; Moses M. Cantine, Second Lieut.; Jacob Chambers, Ensign. In asking for the promotion of Brodhead, the company also asked that the company should be designated as Grenadiers. The petition bears the endorsement of the Committee of Safety (March 20th, 1776): "Petition of the Marbletownians. They are grown to the stature of Grenadiers. Let them be commanded as such by Charles W. Brodhead. Amen." Originally Grenadiers were soldiers who carried and threw hand grenades; later, they were companies which had place on the right of the line and wore a peculiar uniform. Presumably the company had thereafter place at the right of the regimental line, but had no grenades to throw or special uniforms to wear.

The names of the line officers of the regiment having been given in connection with the companies to which they were attached, require no repetition. The list given in "New York in the Revolution" is not complete and is not correct; it omits the early regimental roster, and it includes certainly five captains who never belonged to the regiment. As the names of enrolled men usually follow the returns made by captains, it is reasonable to presume the list of the enrolled men of the regiment is also more or less mixed. In examinations, it may be repeated, reference should always be made to the compilations in "Archives of the Revolution." Lest the names of some of the men should not be met in other connections, the list in "New York in the Revolution" is copied as follows:

ENROLLED MEN.

Achmodey, Jacobus
Airs, William
Aldridge, Daniel
Aldridge, Robert
Aller, John
Annist, Corn.
Arnet, John
Atkins, David
Acker, Johannis
Aker, John
Aldridge, Gilbert
Allen, Isaac
Anderson, William
Annist, Peter
Aston, Jeremiah

ENROLLED MEN.—*Continued.*

Baker, Bartholomew
Barber, William
Barley, Jonathan
Barrett, John
Bartholamoo, John
Beasmer, Michel
Beaty, Robert
Bell, William
Benjamin, Darius
Benjamin, Uriah
Berry, Peter
Bevier, Abraham
Bevier Benjamin
Bevier, Cornelius
Bevier, Matthew
Bevier, Petrus
Bishop, John
Black, John
Blows, John
Bodel, Samuel
Bogardus, Petrus
Braden, Thomas
Bay, William
Bride, James
Brink, Robert
Brodhead, Henry
Brodhead, William
Brown, George
Brown, Joseph
Brown Peter
Bunsehoten Jacob
Burge Thomas
Burger Petrus
Burhans Abraham
Burpans Edward
Buswell Zachariah

Cambell Robert
Camble Rubin
Campbell John
Can, Abraham
Cantine John jr
Carflow Henry
Carson Johanis
Cater Wilhalmes
Celder Hendrick
Chambers Jacob
Chambers Joseph
Chenix William
Clarwater Thomas
Clee Hugh
Clouse Henry
Clyn Johannis
Cole John
Colman Israel

Barager, William Helmus
Barger, Wouler
Barlow, Nathan
Barten, Isaac
Beaker, Ephraim
Beatty, John
Beck, Nathaniel
Benjamin, Chester
Benjamin, Devyno
Berrit, John
Besemer Jacobus
Bevier, Abraham jr
Bevier, Coenradt
Bevier, Jacob
Bevier, Nathaniel
Bevinns, David
Bishop, James
Black, Robert
Bodeley, John
Bodley, John
Bogart, Cornelius
Bradley, Daniel
Brian, James
Brink, John
Brodhead, Daniel
Brodhead, Samual
Brooks, Joseph
Brown, John
Brown, Josiah
Buch Jacobus jr
Buoy William
Burger Nicholas
Burges Thomas
Burnet Isaac
Bush Jacobus
Buyker Ziles

Camble I. Reuben
Camble Simeon
Campbell Joshua
Cantine John
Cantine William
Carner Andrew
Carson Samuel
Cavere Miles
Chambers Cornelius
Chambers John
Chambers Thomas
Clark John
Claurwater Joseph
Cley Hugh
Clyn Jacob
Coddington Jacob
Cole Simon
Colter John

ENROLLED MEN.—*Continued.*

Comfort Richard
Coningham William
Conklin Seven
Connely Patrick
Conner Jacobus
Conner John
Connor Daniel
Conaway John
Constable John
Content Moses
Conway Cornelius
Cook John
Cope William
Cortraght Henry
Cortreght Jacobus
Cottenton Jonah
Cottenton Josiah
Coudegal Abraham
Cowen Thomas
Cox John
Crane James
Crans Peter
Crawford Robert
Crispell Abraham
Crist David
Crist Martines
Crom John
Croover Aaron
Croover George
Cross Noah
Crum Hendrick jr
Crum William jr
Cruppell Benjamin
Currenton Richard

Daily Robert
Dan John
Danaldson Abraham
Davis Andrew
Davis Benjamin
Davis Frederick
Davis Isaac
Davis Jacobus
Davis John
Davis Peter
Davis Richard
Davis William
Deake Josiah
Dealy David
Dean Gidon
Dean Isaac
Dean Jedediah
Decker Benjamin
Decker Frederick
Decker Jacobus
Decker Noah
Decker Ruben
Degair Elias
Delametter David
De Lametter John
De Lemetter Benjamin jr
Denniston James
Deny Nicolas
Deo Hendrick
Deo John
De Pew Jachim
De Pew Jacob
De Pew Moses I.
Depue Benjamin
Depue John jr
Depuy Cornelius
Depuy Cornelius jr
Depuy Ephraim
Depuy Ephraim jr
Depuy Joachim
Depuy Joseph
Depuy Moses
Depuy Simon
Devenpart Gerritt jr
Devenport Jacobus
Devoe Abraham
Dewitt Andries A.
Dewitt Cornelious
De Witt Egbert jr
Dewitt Jacob J.
De Witt Jacob T.
De Witt Jacobus
De Witt John
Dewitt John I.
Dewitt Jone
Dewitt Peterus
De Witt Stephen
Dewitt Tjerck
Dewitt William
Deyeo Henry
Deyeo John
Deyes Abraham jr.
Deyes Ezekial
Deyo Danial
Deyo Isaac
Deyo John
Deyo Simon
Deyow Ezikeal
Deyoy Abraham B.
Dick Thomas
Dickason Joseph
Dickerson Benjamin
Dickson Andrew
Diel Thomas

ENROLLED MEN.—*Continued.*

Dimon Moses
Dodge Samuel
Dolson Theunis
Dongarmo Elias
Douglass John
Doyoo Levi
Drake William
Drew Josiah
Dubois Andrew
Dubois Conradth
Dubois Daniel jr
Dubois Henry
Dubois Jacob
Dubois John
Du Bois Nathaniel
Duboys Jacob
Dugin Christopher
Dumond John D.
Dumond Peter
Dunbar Charles
Dunn Jeremiah
Dunn Thomas jr
Dupuy Brisk
Diver Daniel
Dolson John
Donadson Abraham jr
Donoven Daniel
Doyoo Daniel
Drake Josiah
Drew Joshua
Drew Oliver
Du Bois Aseph
Dubois Danial
Dubois Hendricus
Dubois Isaac
Dubois Jacobus
Dubois Matthewsen
Dubois Wessel
Duffield John
Dumond Johannis jr
Dumond John P.
Dumont Cornelius
Dunlap William
Dunn John
Dunn William

Ecker Solomon
Elder Joseph
Elmendorph Abraham
Elmendorph Coenradt C.
Elmendorph Garret C.
Elmendorph Petrus.
Elsworth Benjamin
Elsworth John
Elsworth William
Elting Abr'm
Ennerly Petrus
Ennest Hartman
Ennest William
Een Abraham
Ellen Jesse
Elmendorph Benjamin
Elmendorph Coenradt W.
Elmendorph Jonathan jr
Elsworth Henry
Elsworth Joseph
Elsworth William W.
Enderle Peter
Ennest Cornelious
Ennest Peter
Every Henry

Feer Stephenes
Filips Ebeneezer
Frair Isaac
Fraklen Bejenen
Frame Johannis
Frare Jacob jr
Freer Jacob S.
Freer Paulis
Friar Joseph
Friar Solomon jr
Fiffer William
Fitch Samuel
Frair Thomas
Frame Jacob
Franklair Benjamin
Freer Jacob J.
Freer John I.
Freer Peter
Friar Powles
Fulton William

Geggy John
Giddes Hugh
Gilaspy George
Gildersleeves Daniel
Givens James
Graham Daniel
Gellaspy Matthew
Gilaspy David
Gilbert Ebeneezer
Ginggy John
Goodspead Nathaniel
Graham Jacobus

Albert Mauterstock.

ENROLLED MEN.—*Continued.*

Graham John
Graham Phasso
Graham Robert
Graham Silvanus
Grahams James
Grahams Jacobus
Grahams Thomas
Gray Abraham
Greatreaks Silvanus
Green Henry
Green Jacob Marius
Green Peter Maurius
Green Sylvester Marius
Greenwalt Daniel
Griffen Benjamin
Griffin John
Griffin Joseph
Griffin Matthew
Guiggy George
Gunsallus Benjamin

Haasbrouck Jonas
Hadley Moses
Haip Hom'y jr
Halsted Josiah
Hamilton William
Hance Henry
Handricks Johannis
Handricks Lawrence
Haner Robert
Hanie Henry
Hannes Henry
Hausbrouck John
Happy George
Hardenbergh Elias
Hardenbergh Jacob jr
Hardenbergh Johannis
Hardenbergh John
Hardenbergh John C.
Harp Henry
Harp John
Harp Peter
Harret Thomas
Harris George
Harris Henry
Harris James
Hasbrock Jonas
Hasbrook Solomon
Hasbrouck Benjamin
Hasbrouck John jr
Hasbrouck Severyn
Hass Nicholas
Hatman Danial
Headley Moses
Hedger Evert
Hedger Samuel
Heermause Edward
Hellister William
Helm Daniel
Helm Simon
Helms Daniel
Hendricks Lawrence
Hendrickse Peter
Hendrickson Jacobus
Hendrickson Petrus
Hennis James
Hermanse Abraham
Hermanse Jacob
Herrington Alexander
Hess Nicholas
Hess Robert
Hewit Benjamin
Heyer Hartman
Himes Fradrick
Hoghteeling Thomas
Hoghteeling William
Hollister William
Holsted Joseph
Holsted Josiah
Homan John
Hood William
Hooghteling John
Hoornbeck Gideon
Hoornbeeck Cornelious
Hoornbeeck Petrus
Hoornbeek Benjamin jr
Hoornbeek Isaac
Hoornbeek Jacob, jr.
Hoornbeek Jacob D.
Hoornbeek Joel
Hoornbeek Johannes
Hoornbeek Lowerens
Hoornbeek Philip
Hoornbeek Samuel
Hoornbeek Warner
Hoornbeck Henry
Hornbeek Cornelius jr
Hornbeek Samuel
Huey James
Hull Nathaniel
Hull Samuel
Humphrey James
Hutchin George

Impson Benjamin
Ireland Thomas
Irwin Jerred
Irwin John
Ivery Henry
Ivory Helmus

ENROLLED MEN.—*Continued.*

Jansen Tunis
Jarman James
Johnson Abraham
Johnson David
Johnson Isaac
Johnson John
Johnson Jonathan
Johnson Peter
Johnston Elexandrie
Johnston William
Jones Ebinezar

Karner Andrew
Kater Jacob jr
Keator Cornelius
Keator Cornelius jr
Keator John P.
Keator Petrus I.
Keator Samuel
Keator William jr
Keatter William N.
Keel Samuel
Keifer Laurence
Kelder Hendrickes
Kelder Joseph
Keley John
Kelley John
Kelsey John
Kerk Gerrit N.
Keter Jacob
Keter Jacob F.
Keter Petrus
Keter Samuel
Kiersted Wilhelmus
Kilsey Thomas
King Jeremiah
Kirkpatrick Samuel
Kittle Henry
Knox Thomas
Kole Petrus
Kortreght Louwerens jr
Kortrecht Lowranse
Krinn Benjamin G.
Krinn Hendrick B.
Krom Jacob
Krom Jacob D.
Krom John
Krom Reuben
Krom William
Kroom Jacob
Kroom William
Kroum Johannis jr
Krum John G.
Krum Simon

Lafaver Johannis
Lafaver John A.
Lafaver Philip
Lalmatier Abraham
Lamb Samuel
Lane Benjamin
Lapowl Johan's
Laroy Francis
Laroy Simion
Laroy Trop.
Lefavour Andries
Lefavour Noah
Lefever Jonathan
Lefever Solomon
Lefevor Matthew
Lefevre John
Lemunyan John jr
Lent Eenus
Leroy Francis
Leroy Rop.
Leroy Simon
Litts John
Lockwood Isaiah
Lofovor John
Lofovor Matthew
Louw John C.
Low Abraham C.
Low Cornelius
Low Jehue
Low Johanius
Low John
Low John J.
Low Samuel
Lyons Thomas

McBride Francis
McCay Alexander
McClougen James
McClughen Robert
McCollum Samuel
McConnel John
McCord John
McCreary John
McCreary Robert
McCue James
McDonnel William
McDougall Alexander
McDougle Hugh
McDowl Daniel
McElvannon Barney
McEwen Duncan
McGinnes William
McGlaughlin John

ENROLLED MEN.—*Continued.*

McHenry John
McKee Thomas
Macky John
McMullen William
McMunn John
McNeal John
Makaive Matthew
Markell Benjamin
Marshall Jeremiah
Marth Peet
Master Cornelius B.
Masten Johannes B.
Masten Joseph
Matt Ezekiel
Megrorty Patrick
Meloy William
Merkell Benjamin
Mickle Frederick jr
Middagh Claudea
Middagh Joh's
Mildun Daniel
Miller Philip
Milliken John
Millspaugh John
Milspaugh Mathias
Mourief Charles
Morris Arthur
Mouris Petrus
Muir William
Murdough Lecky
Myer Peter L.
Myer William jr

Mack Johannis
Mckinsey John
McMaster James
McMunn James
McNay James
McSweeny Daniel
Marcle Samuel
Marshall Henry
Marshall John
Masten Abraham jr
Masten Cornelius C.
Masten John C.
Masten Robert
Mawris Samuel
Meldown Daneal
Merkel Elias
Merkle Frederick
Middagh Abraham
Middagh George
Middagh Martin jr
Miller Johannes
Miller William
Mills David
Milspaugh Abraham
Milton John
More Nathan
Mowris Daniel
Mours Samuel jr
Mulks Benony
Myer James
Myer Samuel
Myers Michael

Neass Jerry
Neely Abraham
Newkerk Aron
Newkerk Isaac
Nicholson Charles
Nuble Justis

Neef Jurry
Newkerck Matthew jr
Newkerk Henry
Newton George
Nottingham Thomas

O'Brien John
O'Farrel Michal
Oosterhoudt Henriccus P.
Oosterhoudt Samuel
Oosterhout Benjamin
Oosterhout Cornelius jr
Oosterhout Hendrickes
Osterhout Henry

Odle Jonathan
Oin Abraham
Oosterhoudt Martines
Oosterhoudt Teunis
Oosterhout Cornelius
Oosterhout Ezekiel
Oosterhout Hendrick
Ostrander William

Palmater Michal
Palmiteer Henrey
Patterson Samuel
Pattison William
Perkins Ebenezer
Perkins Jordan

Palmeter Abraham
Patterson Michel
Patterson William
Pemuel Michal
Perkins Goddam
Perry David

ENROLLED MEN—*Continued.*

Perslow Henry
Petibone Daniel
Palaniteer Peter
Pressler John
Preston John

Quick Hendricous

Rabye Dene
Ramson Jacobus
Redigher Hendrick
Reider Johannes
Remsen Herre
Richards Nathaniel
Roads Cornelius
Roberts Gilbert
Robinson Josiah
Roesa Jacob
Rogers Samuel
Roose Abraham
Rosecrane Jacobus
Rossa Teunis
Ruger John
Ryder Benjamin

St John Noah
Samenons Johains
Sammous John
Sanmaker Frederick
Sasson Thomas
Sax John
Sayre Joshua
Schepmoes John
Schoonmaker Benjamin
Schoonmaker Daniel
Schoonmaker Jacob
Schoonmaker Jochem D.
Schoonmaker John E.
Schoonmaker Martin
Schoonmaker Petrus
Schoonmaker Wilhelmus
Sears Nathan
Semple Robert
Sergeant Robert
Shear Abraham
Shorter John
Simon O. O.
Sleght Henry B
Sloat David
Sluyter Abraham
Sluyter Jacob
SluyterJohn
Slyter I. Benjamin
Smedis Jacob
Smith Henry

Peterson Alexander
Pettigo Daniel
Pontimer Henry
Pressler Jonathan
Pride James

Quick Jacobus

Radman Michal
Rank John
Reed John
Reighter John
Richard Daniel
Rider Benjamin
Roberts Daniel
Roberts John
Roe David
Rogers James
Roosa Egbert
Rosacran Hendricus
Rosecrans John
Row David
Russel Alexander
Rylya Denie

Samanins Joseph
Sammon Johannis
Sanders John
Sarjent Wite
Satchwell William
Sax Peter
Scapmus Derick
Schepmaes William
Schoonmaker Cornelius
Schoonmaker Isaac
Schoonmaker Jacob Dewitt
Schoonmaker Johanis
Schoonmaker Lodewyck
Schoonmaker Martinus
Schoonmaker Thomas
Scofield James
Seile Coeuraet
Senough Jacob
Shaw Thomas
Shorter Chrispares
Shucraft Jacob
Simons Joseph
Sleght Teunis
Slowter Walter
Slyter Cornelius
Sluyter James
Sluyter William
Smedis Benjamin B.
Smith Abraham
Smith Jacob

ENROLLED MEN.—*Continued.*

Smith James
Smith John
Smith Peter jr
Smith Valentine
Snyder Christopher
Stanton Benjamin
Stilway Cornelius
Stumble Abraham
Swart Isaac
Swartout James R
Smith Johannis
Smith Jonas jr
Smith Thomas
Smith William
Sparks Jacob
Stephenson John
Stinson William
Swart Cornelius
Swart Tobias

Tarwillen Simon
Terwiliger Tunis
Terwilleger Joseph
Terwilliger Joshua
Theator Gideon
Thomas John
Thompson Archibald
Thounsend Ben
Thuttle Barzile
Tolten James
Tomkins Jeremiah
Tompson Joshua
Tornuer Jacob
Travis Gabril
Turner Jacobus jr
Tutle Israel.
Terwiligar Arry
Terwilleger Hans jr
Terwilliger Evert
Thaxter Benj F
Thlarwater Joseph
Thompson Aaron
Thompson William
Thrum John
Tirwilleger Johannis
Tomkins Isaac
Tomkins Jonathan
Tompkins Thomas
Toursen Samuel sr
Trowbridge Ralph
Turner William

Van Beuren Philip
Vanburen Christopher
Vandamarck Orry
Vandemark Cornelius
Vandemerke John
Vandemerke Lodewyck
Vandemerken John
Van Demerker Frederick
Vandermarke Arie
Van Dermarke Jacob
Van der merk Ghysbert
Vandermerkon Frederick,
Van Gasbeck Thomas
Vanheran Christopher
Van Keuren Abraham
Van Keuren Matthew
Vanlauvan Petrus
Van Luvan Christopher
Van Steenbergh Abraham
Van Steenbergh John
Van Stienbergh Dirck
Vanvlack Cornelius
Van Vlerkum James
Van Wagenen Dainel
Van Wagenen Jacob
Van Wagenen Peter
Varner Philip
Ver Rooy Nathen
Van Blascom James
Van Curen Ruben
Vandamark Ezekiel
Vandemark Solomon
Vandemerke Joseph
Vandemerken George
Van De Merken Joseph
Vanderhoff Cornelius
Vandermarke Fradrick
Vandermarke Joseph
Van dermerk Solomon
Van Gaasbeek Abraham
Vanheng Abram
Van Ining Abraham
Van Keuren Mattheus
Van Keuren Tcherick
Vanlauven John
Vanluven Andria
Vansteenbergh Benjamin
Van Steenbergh Matthew
Van Stienbergh Tobias
Vanvliet Teunis
Van Wagenen Benjamin
Van Wagenen John
Vanwagenen Levi
Van Wagenen Simon
Vernooy Johannis
Viely John

ENROLLED MEN.—*Continued.*

Wackman Daniel
Walker Justus
Wallas William jr
Waters Nathaniel
Weekman Daniel
Weeler William
Wells Jacobus
Wells Peter
Wherry David
White Silas
Whitney David jr
Wilder Daniel
Williams John
Wilmiller Henry
Winfield Simon
Winne Peter I.
Witney David
Wolsey Henry
Wood Theophelus
Woolsey Daniel jr
Wynkoop Cornalius
Wynkoop Tobies

Waismiller Henry
Wallace John
Wasbrouck Jonathan
Waugh Robert
Weeks Abraham
Weller Frederick
Wells James
Wesmiller Jeremiah
Whitaker John
Whitney David
Whitney Jacob
Williams Abraham
Willson Thomas
Winfield David
Winn John
Wismiller Jeremiah
Wolsey Daniel
Wood Job
Woods Silas
Wright William
Wynkoop Dirck D
Wynkoop William

Yaple Adam
Yelverton Anthony
York Johannis
York Petrus
Young John

Yates Thomas
Yelverton Anthony jr
York John
Young Alexander

Peter C. Black.

CHAPTER XII.

THE FOURTH OR MIDDLE REGIMENT.

THE Fourth or Middle Regiment covering parts of the present counties of Ulster and Orange, but then entirely in the country of Ulster, was formally organized October 25th, 1775, by commissions issued to the following Field and Staff:

Colonel, Jonathan Hasbrouck.
Lieut. Col., Johannis Hardenbergh, Jr.
Major (1st), Johannis Jansen, Jr.
Major (2d), Lewis Du Bois.
Adjutant, Abraham Schoonmaker.
Qr. Master, Isaac Belknap.

Through a clerical error Belknap was not commissioned, and Lewis Du Bois was then enlisting a company for Colonel James Clinton's "Third New York Continental Regiment" for the campaign of 1775, against Canada. Their places were supplied, but by whom is not on record. In consequence of failing health (he died in 1780) Colonel Hasbrouck resigned in 1778, and on February 27th, 1779, the Field and Staff was reorganized:

Johannis Hardenbergh, Jr., Colonel.
Johannis Jansen, Jr., Lieut. Colonel.
Samuel Clark, Major (1st).
Jonathan Hardenbergh, Qr. Master.
Adjutant, Abraham Schoonmaker.

Later — John Gillaspy was promoted Major, and Henry Van Wyan (?) succeeded Jonathan Hardenbergh as Qr. Master. The roster of the Field and Staff as given in "New York in the Revolution" is not correct. Jonathan Elmendorf was never Lieutenant Colonel of the regiment, and some of the other names are very doubtfully placed. The names given above are correct. It is not clear that Colonel Hardenbergh resigned, and was succeeded by Lieut. Colonel Jansen; it is only clear that the regiment is on the rolls as "Hasbrouck's," "Hardenbergh's" and "Jansen's," the latter frequently printed "Johnson's," through the ignorance, probably, of the compiler, but not the less annoying to investigators.

To add to the annoyance the list of the line officers given in the volume referred to contains no less than thirty-six who were never on the rolls of the regiment.

The companies composing the regiment, and necessarily the line officers of the regiment, as given in "Calendar of Historical Manuscripts" and in "Archives of the Revolution," were, as far as of record:

1st Co. Newburgh, North District—Auther Smith, Captain; Isaac Fowler, First Lieut.; John Foster, Second Lieut.; Daniel Clark, Ensign. And the company remained so officered in 1779. In 1778 Reuben Tucker, Ensign, vice Daniel Clark, deceased.

2nd Co. Newburgh Southeast District—Samuel Clark, Captain; Benj. Smith, First Lieut.; James Denton, Sen., Second Lieut.; Martin Wygant, Ensign. Benj. Smith was succeeded by James Denton, Sen., as First Lieut.; Martin Wygant, succeeded Denton as Second Lieut.; and Monson Ward succeeeded Wygant as Ensign. On the promotion of Captain Clark to Major, James Denton succeeded to the Captaincy; William Palmer became First Lieut.; Isaac Hasbrouck, Junr., Second Lieut., and Ebenezer Gidney, Ensign.

3d Co. Newburgh Western District—Jacob Conkling, Captain; Jacob Lawrence, First Lieut; David Guion, Second Lieut.; Roger Barton, Ensign. The latter went over to the enemy, and was succeeded by John Crowell, Ensign. William Irwin, Junr., succeeded the latter in 1783.

4th Co. Southeast Marlborough—Lewis Du Bois, Captain; Caleb Merritt, First Lieut.; Dr. Abijah Perkins, Second Lieut.; Matthew Wygant, Ensign. Du Bois entered Continental service, and was succeeded as Captain by Caleb Merritt; Abijah Perkins, First Lieut.; Stephen Case, Second Lieut.; Matthew Wygant, Ensign. In 1780 the roll stood: Stephen Case, Captain; Matthew Wygant, First Lieut.; John Banta, Second Lieut.; Nathl. Du Bois, Ensign, vice Alex. Cropsey, displaced.

5th Co. Northeast Marlborough—Jacob Wood, Captain; Juryan Mackey, First Lieut.; Nathaniel Goodspeed, Second Lieut.; John Knowlton, Ensign. Annan Smith, First Lieut., vice Macked, resigned; Nathl. Kilsey, Second Lieut.; Nathl. Harker, Ensign, vice Knowlton, removed.

6th Co. Northwest Marlborough—Bordawine Tearpenning, Captain; William Martin, First Lieut.; Uriah Drake, Second Lieut.; James Lyons, Ensign. In 1779, David Ostrander, Captain; James Lyons, First Lieut.; Jacob Terwilliger, Second Lieut.; Hugo Sheet, (?) Ensign.

7th Co. Northwest side of Shawangunk River—Thomas Jansen, Jr., Captain; Matthew Jansen, First Lieut.; Alvin Snider, Second Lieut.; Peter Decker, Ensign. Later—Matthew Jansen, Captain, vice Thomas Jansen, Jr.; Peter Decker, First Lieut.; Nicholas Hardenbergh, Second Lieut., vice Smedes, displaced; Jacob Rosekrans, Ensign.

8th Co. Between Shawangunk and Paltz Rivers—Matthew Rea, Captain; 'siah Robinson, First Lieut.; Petrus Roosa, Second Lieut.; James Hunter, Jr., Ensign. 1778, Oct. 4, 'siah (Isaiah) Robinson, Captain, vice Rea; James Hunter, First Lieut., vice Robinson; James Kain, 2d Lieut.; Eert Hoffman, Ensign. 1783, Dirck Roosa, Jr., Ensign, vice Hoffman, moved out of beat.

9th Co. Southwest side of Paltz River—Jacobus Roosa, Captain; Cornelius Masten, First Lieut.; Wilh's Van Demark, Second Lieut.; Isaac Hardenbergh, Ensign. Later—Cornelius Masten, Captain; vice Roosa (Rose); Isaac Hardenberg, Second

Lieut.; Wilhelmus Ostrander, Ensign. W. Ostrander, Second Lieut. Hardenbergh removed out of beat; Michael Pelleyer, Ensign, vice Ostrander, promoted.

10th Co. Galatian's—Shawangunk—John Galaspie, Captain; Jason Wilkins, First Lieut.; Robert Hunter, Jr., Second Lieut.; Saml. Galaspie, Ensign. 1780, Saml. Galaspie, Second Lieut., vice Hunter left the regiment; Jason Wilkins, Captain, vice Gillaspie promoted Major; Johannis Robinson, Ensign, vice Saml. Gilaspie promoted.

11th Co. Shawangunk—Wm. Cross, Captain, vice John Graham, displaced; John Graham, First Lieut., vice Barkley, displaced; Robert Thompson, Second Lieut., vice Thompson promoted; Robert Mould, Ensign, vice McCurdy, displaced.*

On the 20th of March, 1776, Colonel Hasbrouck reported that the regiment comprised eleven companies and a total of six hundred and eight men, officers included; "likewise four hundred and fifty firelocks, two hundred and ninety-three swords, one hundred and eighty-eight cartridge boxes, thirty-two pounds of powder, one hundred and twenty-eight pounds of lead." The limited supply of arms and powder is noted in all the regiments. Looking back over the field we see many unarmed men, strong only in their belief in the justice of the cause in which they had embarked.

From the disconnected compilation of the regimental returns given in "New York in the Revolution" is taken, without guaranty of completeness, the following list of

ENROLLED MEN.

Admins, Samuel
Albertson, Joseph
Albertson, Stephen
Albertson, William
Aldrich, Gilburth
Alekenbrgh, Peter
Allen, John
Alsdarf, Lawrence
Alsdarf, Philip
Alsdorph, Jacobus
Alsdorph, Johannis
Alsdorph, Philip
Alsdurf, Jacobes
Anderson, William
Anthony, Alard
Anthony, John
Anthony, John jr
Arslen, Daniel.

Bach, Joh's Lenz
Bading Isaac
Baily Thomas
Bain David
Baker Bartholomew
Ball Thomas
Bancker Solomon
Bang Samuel
Banks, Justus
Bardine William
Bark, George
Barker Isaac
Barkly, James
Barman Peter
Barns, Stephen
Barrik George
Barthy, James
Bartley James
Barwill, James
Bealy John
Bedford, Jones
Beleger Frederick

* There were certainly five companies in Shawangunk. See N. Y. Historical MSS. i, 444. Governor Clinton wrote in 1777 that there was a "Park of artillery" there. The original organization of the company has not been found of record.

ENROLLED MEN.—*Continued.*

Bell Thorne
Bell, William
Bevier Abraham
Bevier Daniel
Bevier Nathaniel
Billiger Michael
Blenstram, Matthew I.
Bloomer, William
Bodine, Isaac
Bodine, William
Boons, Daniel
Borwell, James
Bout, John
Brannen, Addam
Brinck, Sollom
Brink, John
Brink, John jr
Brook Abraham W.
Brown Edward
Brown Jonathan
Brown William
Brusie Andries
Bruyn Cornelius
Bruyn Johannis
Bruyn Zacheriah
Bump Cornelius
Burdin William
Burhans Samuel

Bell Thomas
Beroon Anthony
Bevier Cornelius
Bevier Jonas
Beymer Joh's
Binson Peter
Blensham Matthew J.
Bodine Francis
Bodine John
Bonker John
Borton Isaac
Bouen Daniel
Bowings Daniel
Breaden Thomas
Brink Cornelius
Brink Peter
Brink Solomon
Brown Ebeneezer
Brown Isaack
Brown Jonathan jr
Brush Eliakim
Bruyn Abraham
Bruyn Ebenazer
Bruyn Safryn
Bull Daniel
Burdin Francis
Burdine John
Burns Charles

Cahill Daniel
Camble John
Carman John
Carpenter Wright
Case Joseph
Cerley Israel
Christice Johan
Clark James
Clarwater Joseph
Cline Jacob
Coldwell John
Cole Johannis
Coleman Duncken
Colter John
Combs Solomon
Comfort John jr
Conkling William
Cool Maritie
Cornes Solomon
Coulter John jr
Cox William
Cramer Wendle
Crank Frederick
Crans Ezekiel
Crans Philip
Crawford Jonathan

Caldwell James
Camp Eldard
Carny Stephen
Case John
Caviler John
Chisem Hendrick
Claarwater Jeremiah
Clarwater Jacob
Cline Jonas
Cole Cornelius
Cole William D.
Coleman Joseph
Colwell Jacob
Comfort Benjamin
Comfort Samuel
Cool Cornelius
Cool William
Coulter John
Cowen Martin
Crage Francis
Cranses Henry
Crans Cristuphel
Crans Henry
Crawford David
Crawford Nathan
Crawford Samuel

ENROLLED MEN.—*Continued.*

Crawford Robert
Credit Benjamin
Criswell John
Crousk Fradrick
Crous Ezekiel
Crook Conrad
Cropsey Henry
Crosby Thomas
Crover Aron
Crover John
Cruger Arnest
Cunbergh Matthew
Crestise John
Crofferd Samuel
Cronee Ezekiel
Crooger Barnest
Croover John
Cropsey Matthew
Cross Leonard
Crover George
Crowford Nathan
Crumm Jacob

Dacker Elezar
Dalls William
Days Handrick
Deane Solomon
Decker Abraham jr
Decker Benjamin
Decker Benjamin J.
Decker Elisha
Decker Evert
Decker Jurry
Decker Noah
Decker Peter
Decker Uriah
Decker William
De Lefever Coenrad
Denniston John
Devenport Robert
Dill David
Divenu Jacobus
Dobins James
Dolson John
Drake William
Dubois Hezekiah
Dubois Nathaniel
Duboys Aadris
Du Mott Isaac
Du Witt Jacob
Dailey Robert
Davis John
Dealls William
Decker Abraham
Decker Ambrick
Decker Benjamin jr
Decker Benjamin T.
Decker Elias
Decker Elizar
Decker John G
Decker Manasse
Decker Peter jr
Decker Wilhelmes
Dederick Lucas
Demott James
Derlin David
Devins Jacobus
Dinager George
Divins Jacobus
Docherty Cornelius
Douglass James
Dubois Andries
Dubois Jonathan
Dubois William
Duffield John
Dunlap John

Eaker Steven
Edmons Samuel
Empson John
Ennis James
Eckert Stephanus
Empson Benjamin
English John
Erwen Robert

Farris James
Forbes William
Forcits William
Forsght William
Frayer Jeremiah
Freer John
Frons Philip
Ferguson Samuel
Forbes William G
Forgeson Samuel
France Youst
Freeman Samuel
Frint Jacob

ENROLLED MEN.—*Continued.*

Galation James
Gee Anders
Gee John
Gillaspy David
Gillespy James
Gillespy John
Graham James
Graham Thomas
Grahams James
Gray Benj.
Green William
Gunsalis Samuel
Gutches Hendricus

Garrison Isaac
Gee Jeremiah
Gee Nathaniel
Gillespy George
Gillespy James jr
Goetschus Henrocus
Graham Robert
Graham Wilyham
Gray Andrew
Green John
Griffise Barne
Gunsalus Danel

Hadger John
Hains Henry
Hallett George
Hannah Samuel
Harcourt Nathaniel
Harris Alpheus
Hathy Fredrick
Hauter Isaac
Heady Marcus
Hedger Wilhelmus
Heemanse Edward
Herr David
Hide Henry
Hill William
Holester Isaac
Hollet William
Hollister Isaac
Holmes Asa
Hoole John
Hosbrock Benjamin
Hufmen John
Hughes William
Hull Samuel

Hadly Fredick
Halett Moses
Hallett William
Harcourt John
Harding James
Harris Jonathan
Hatley Frederick
Hawkins James
Hedger John
Hedgner John
Hendrickson Jacob
Herrinton Moses
Hill George
Hofman John
Holl John
Hollett Moses
Hollister William
Homes Reubin
Hornbeek Ephriam
Huffman Nicholas
Hughes Evert
Hull Nathaniel
Hunter Archebel

Imson Benjamin
Irvine William

Innis James
Irwin Robert.

Jacklin Daniel
Jansen Nicholas
Johnson Abraham
Johnston Ritchard

Jansen Jacobus
Johnsen Richard
Johnston Arthur
Jonson John

Kain, James
Kanter, Isaac
Kunbarrack, Matthew
King, Clayman
Kirkpatrick, Samuel
Kline, Jacob
Knifin, John
Knox, Thomas
Kyrk, William

Kane Cornelius
Keyser Ephraim
Kimbary Mathew
King Nicholas
Kitchen Richard
Kline Jonas
Knolton Daniel
Kraus Henry

Grove Webster.

ENROLLED MEN.—*Continued.*

Lair Adam
Lane George
Lane William
Lattimore Roger
Laughlin James
Lawrence John
Lawrence William
Laybolt Jacob
Lenderman Cornelius
Lester Allen
Lewis Cornelius
Lewis John
Lewis Ritchard
Lewis Samuel
Lilley John
Linn George
Lister Allon
Litch Rulif
Lits Evart
Lits Rulif
Loomis Timothy
Lotts Conrad
Lovell Alexander
Lovell Jost Minard
Low Jacob
Luts Henry
Lutts John
Luwes Corneles

McBorney William
McCay Alexander jr
McCleen John
McClouchan Robert
McClughan Robert
McColhem Robert
McCullom William
McColm Robert
McColough John
McCord John
McCoughan Robert
McCreery John
McCreery Robert
McCue James
McCurdy John
McDermont Lawrence
McDowal Daniel
McDowell Jonathan
MacDugal Duncan
McElvin David
McIlvean David
McIlwain David
McKay John
McKenny Matthew
Mackey Alexander
Mackey Alexander jr
McLackler John
McLaughlin John
McMullen John
Macord John
Malford David
Mance John
Marshall Jeremiah
Marten John
Masten Abraham
Masten Art
Masten Ezekiel
Masten Jonathan
Masten Matthew
Masters Daniel
Maston John
Matterstock Joh's
Mentz John
Merritt George
Milbourn Andrew
Miller Abraham
Miller Hans
Miller Jacobus
Miller James
Miller John
Miller John jr
Millin Alexander
Mills David
Millspaugh Abraham
Milspaugh Fredrick
Milspaugh Isaac
Milspaugh Mathias
Milspaugh Matthew
Milspough Mattichia
Minthorn John
Mirrit Thomas
Mole Philip
Moor Jacob
Moor Martin
Morse Benjamin
Moss Benjamin
Moule Philip
Mullen Michel
Mullen Michal
Mumford James
Murdogh Lackey

Nainy Samuel
Nicols William
Nox Thomas.

ENROLLED MEN.—*Continued.*

O'Bradly Dainel
Odle Jonathan
Oproght George
Osterhoudt Henry
Ostrander Christophel
Ostrander William
Owns Benjamin
O'Cain Edward
Opright Malaicah
Osborn Daniel
Osterhoudt Peter
Ostrander Jacob
Owen John

Palmer William
Parsel Jeremiah
Penny James
Penny Stephen
Perveer James
Pifer Hendrick
Pixley William
Plumsted Joseph
Potman John
Purdy William
Putnam John.
Palmiteer William
Pembrook William
Penny John
Pensil Peter
Phelps Shadrick
Pixley Jona
Place William
Post Abram, jr
Potter Edward
Putnam Henry

Radicker Henry
Rainey David
Raljay Denye
Rank Cornelius
Rea Matthew jr
Read Stephen
Reany David
Rekman Harmanes
Relyea Dene T.
Richard Nathaniel
Ricknen Harmanus
Ronk John
Roos Avart
Roos Peter A
Roosa Aldert
Roose Evert
Rose Evert jr
Rosekrans Hendrick
Rosekrans John
Rosekrans William
Ross Finley
Rossell Ludwigh
Rump Henry
Rain James jr
Rainey Samuel
Raljay Simon
Rank Philip
Rea Stephen
Realya Simon
Reighter John
Relyea Dene
Relyea John
Richman Harramanis
Roe John
Roof John
Roos Evert jr
Roos John
Roosa Derrick
Rose John
Rosekrans Hendrick W.
Rosekrans Wilhelmes
Rosman Hendrick
Ross William
Rump Christian
Russell William

Sageman Jacob
St John Adam
St John Samuel
Sammons Jacob
Sammons Matthew jr
Scarscadden Robert
Schoonmaker Isaac
Schoonmaker Wilhelmus
Schutt Abraham
Scott James
Sears Lawrence
Sager Malachy
St John Noah
Sammons Cornelius
Sammons Matthew
Sammons Tunis
Schoonmaker Abraham
Schoonmaker Jacob
Schriver Martin
Schutt H
Scott William
Segor Malacchia

ENROLLED MEN.—*Continued.*

Seneebanch Henery
Seoos John
Shammons Jacob
Shaw Thomas
Shoecraft Jacob
Sidman Jacob
Silkworth William
Simmons Sylvanus
Sincebaugh Henry
Sinkler John
Skit Hugh
Slauter John
Slot William
Smedes Benjamin B.
Smith George
Smith Ladlaw
Smith Ludlow
Snider Daniel jr
Snyder Henry
Snyder John
Sparks Abraham
Sparks Robert
Springsteel Joseph
Starks Robert
Stevenson Hugh
Stitt John
Stowell John
Strickland Jacob
Summons Tunis
Swart Benjamin
Swart Isaac
Swingel Harromus
Sension Adam
Shafer George
Shaver Daniel
Shear Salvinus
Shorter John
Sifertis Manasa
Simmons Jacob
Simmons Tunis
Sinclair John
Sinsepough Henry
Slaughter Isaac
Sloot William
Smedes Benjamin
Smith Francis
Smith John Meribray
Smith Leege
Smith William
Snyder Daniel
Snyder Jacob
Sommons Matthew
Sparks Jacob,
Sprage Amasa
Stalker Seth
Steenbargh John
Stitt James
Storm Jacob
Strickland Abraham
Striker Abraham
Swart Abraham
Swart Daniel
Swart John
Swingle Cronimus

Taerpanning, Lavi
Tarepening, Richard
Tarepenning, Lawrence
Tarpenney, Elias
Taylsor, John
Teero Lowrence
Terpening Abraham
Terwelgen, Petrus Vas
Terwiliger, Hezekiah
Terwillager, Joseph
Terwilleger, Daniel
Terwilleger, James F. jr
Terwilleger, Matthew
Terwilleger, Wilhelmus
Terwilligar, Jacobus
Terwilligar, Peter N.
Terwilliger Abraham jr
Terwilliger, Arra
Terwilliger, Cornelius jr
Terwilliger, Hendrick
Terwilliger, Isaac
Terwilliger, James
Tampson Archibald
Tarepining Samuel
Tarpening Derrick
Tarpenny Abraham
Teerpenning Teunis
Terbos Henry
Terpening John
Terwilagar Philip
Terwiliger John
Terwilleger Arie V.
Terwilleger Isaac jr
Terwilleger Jonathan
Terwilleger Simon H.
Terwilleg Zacharias
Terwilligar Josiah
Terwilliger Abraham
Terwilliger Aroon
Terwilliger Benjamin
Terwilliger Evert
Terwilleger Isaac
Terwilliger Jacob
Terwilliger James F.

ENROLLED MEN.—*Continued.*

Terwilliger, Jonas
Terwilliger, Petrus
Terwilliger, Simon
Terwilliger Tunis
Terwilliger William
Thompson Andrew
Thompson Richard
Tirwillegar Henry
Traith John
Trapp James
Tucker Ruben
Terwilliger Peter P.
Terwilliger Petrus Vas.
Terwilliger Solomon
Terwilliger Tunis C.
Thompson Alexander
Thompson Archabald
Tice Henry
Tooker Reuben
Trape James
Trumpurt Jacob
Tuttle Israel.

Upright George
Upright Nathan
Upright Malichia

Vanamburgh Hanry
Vancuran Benjamin
Van Delyne Peter
Vandemarken Ezekiel
Vandenmark Jacob
Vandermerke Wilhelmis
Vangorden James
VanKeuren ——
VanKeuren Charick
VanKeuren Hazael
VanKeuren Jacobus jr
Van Keuren Ruben
Van Steenbergh John
Van Wagenen Benjamin I.
Vawn Richard
Vanamburgh Jeremiah
Vancuren Levi
Vandemark Ezekial
Vandemarken Jacob
Vandenmerk Jacob
Vangarden Jacobus
Vangorden James
VanKeuren Benjamin
VanKeuren Cornelius
VanKeuren Jacobus
VanKeuren Levi
Vankuren Benjamin
Van Steenburgh Abraham
Van Wegan Henry
Viburgs Peter

Wackman Henry
Waderwan William.
Wakman Henry
Walles William jr.
Wallis William
Ward Richard
Warkman Henry
Washburn John
Watts Nicholas
Welsh Ephriam
Weller John
Whany John
Whorrey John
Wigens Michal
Wiggons Annon
Williams John
Williams William
Winfield Elias
Wintfield Peter
Wood Abraham
Wood Stephen
Woodward Daniel
Wygant Martin
Wackman Marcus
Wagenor Johannis
Waller John
Wallis Hugh
Ward David
Ward William
Warrey John
Wath Nicholas
Weed Samuell
Weller Frederick
Westbrook Abraham
Wharing James
Wigant John
Wiggan Michael
Williams Adam
Williams Richard
Wilsey William
Winfield Peter
Wintworth John
Wood Job
Wood Timaty
Workman Henry

Yorks Aron
Young Johan Christ.
Young Christian

CHAPTER XIII.

SERVICES OF THE MILITIA.

IN the preceding compilation from official records has been given the territorial locations of the militia regiments of the Revolution, the town or precinct locations of the several companies, the Field Staff and Line officers, and the names of the enrolled men, *a compilation which has never been printed in any publication, local or state*. Comparing the names of the rank and file with the names by towns of the signers of the "Articles of Association" will show in most cases, the residences of the militiamen, aid materially in identifying them, and take the history of the events in which they were actors into the very neighborhoods where they resided, and where for many years later their long muskets and powder horns hung on hooks over their mantel pieces.

It is proper to remark in passing, that the militia were not "enlisted men," as classed in "New York in the Revolution," but the body of male residents constituted by nature and by law as competent and available for military service, enrolled in distinct districts under regularly appointed officers, liable to be called into service at any time to suppress insurrections and repel invasions and at all times liable to draft to reenforce regularly constituted armies and for special duty. It is in the field of detachments and levies for special service in special organizations, and in enlistments in the regular or continental army of the Revolution that the militia of Ulster will be most frequently met in these notes.

There was another class of the militia, as there is now, called "exempts," that is men who were exempt from field service by reason of age or infirmities, previous service, professional occupation, etc., but who, nevertheless, during the Revolution, were regularly enrolled, made liable to service, in emergencies, and subject to a special tax for the purchase of arms and to supply men in the active force. It is to be regretted that in the returns which have been preserved the exempts are only limitedly represented. To the honors of service in the Revolution they are as fully entitled as were the men who were on the active roll. Returns of men enrolled as Exempts in three companies in Colonel Hasbrouck's Regiment are available. In "Archives of the Revolution" may be found lists of officers of companies of exempts in New Windsor, Kingston, Marbletown, Marlborough, Rochester, Wallkill, Hanover and Shawangunk. It is presumed that the law was complied with in all the company districts. The companies were continued during the war.

The changing by the British Ministry of the seat of war from Boston to New York in 1776, the constitution of the Hudson as the strategic centre, the sending of Burgoyne and a strong army of Quebec in 1777 to cut his way through to the Hudson and hold possession in conjunction with the British forces in New York City and by separating the eastern colonies from the western and southern make the suppression of the rebellion less difficult, and the securing through the Johnsons of an alliance with four of the six nations of Indians under Brant, gave to the counties of Ulster and Orange two especially exposed frontiers, the southern and the western, and contingent exposures on the north. In no part of the nation was so heavy a burden placed on the militia as on Ulster, especially in the early years of the war. So it comes that we read of detachments of the Ulster militia under General Morin Scott, in the battle of Long Island in August, 1776; of detachments of Ulster militia under General George Clinton at Harlem in the lower Westchester in the same year; detachments sent out to guard the passes in the Highlands; detachments on guard on the northern and western frontiers, and detachments to aid Generals Schulyer and Gates in resisting the advance of Burgoyne. In addition to those fields of service the Provincial Convention, early in 1776, resolved to establish forts in the Highlands and obstruct the navigation of the river by a chain, *chevaux-de-frise,* fire rafts and a navy.

The works were constructed mainly by the militia of Ulster, Orange and Duchess, and by the same bodies in varying detachments they were mainly garrisoned. The entire militia contiguous to the forts were required to hasten to them on signal given by flags and the discharge of cannon by day, and by beacon fires on the hills at night; no matter what the exposure the militia must go.

The first of the special organizations of the militia were those known as Minute Men, whe were required to meet and drill and hold themselves in constant readiness for the field. They came in under the militia law of 1775, which provided that after the regular companies had been

ALBERT K SMILEY.

organized, "every fourth man of each company" should "be selected" for that particular service who, when in service, should be subject to the orders of officers of the continental army. The plan, while reading very well on paper, did not prove satisfactory in operation, and it was abolished in June, 1776. Meanwhile its provisions had been generally complied with. A regiment of Minute Men was organized in Southern Ulster; Thomas Palmer, Colonel; Thomas Jansen, Jr., Lieut. Colonel; Arthur Parks, 1st Major; Saml. Logan, 2d Major; Severyn Bruyn, Adjutant; Isaac Belknap, Qr. Master. In northern Ulster was also formed a regiment of which Charles De Witt was Colonel; Andries De Witt, Lieut. Colonel; Christopher Tappen, 1st Major; Corn's E. Wynkoop, 2d Major; Oake Suydam, Adjutant; Corn's Elmendorf, Qr. Master. The officers of the companies in the regiments are of limited record, but there are no lists of men aside from those enrolled in the regular companies. Except that Colonel Palmer's Regiment was on duty in the Highlands in the winter of 1775, and in McClaughrey's Second Ulster, there is no record of field service, although there was service obviously.

Kindred special organizations came in under a law of the Provincial Convention, July 22, 1776, authorizing the formation of companies of Rangers "for the protection of the inhabitants of the northern and western frontier of the province." These companies were to hold themselves in constant readiness for service, with a view especially to prevent the incursions and depredations of Indians and Tories, the latter a despicable element in the contest, of less honor than their Indian alliants. Making their abode in the mountains on the north and west where they were in touch with their dusky allies, they became spies, informers and pilots and shared in the spoils of bandit warfare. Their forays upon the scattered dwellings on the frontiers were frequent. Some of the members of the bands were caught and hung, and more of them richly deserved the same fate. The Rangers were to be confined to the territory of the county in which the companies were recruited, unless by the unanimous consent of the committees of Safety and Observation of adjoining counties, or unless otherwise directed by the Provincial Convention by its Committee of Safety. Three companies were raised in Ulster commanded respectively by Captains Isaac Belknap of New Windsor, Jacob R. De Witt of Paenpacht, and Elias Hasbrouck. The latter two were in service on the frontiers, but Belknap was directed to report with his command to the Provincial Convention, which had then retreated from White Plains, Westchester County, to Fishkill Village above the Highlands. As Belknap's was the only company that was under the orders of the Convention, and was actually at Fishkill, Belknap was obviously the Capt. Townsend of Cooper's story "The Spy." The names of the officers and privates of the company have been preserved; in other companies we have the names of officers only.

The entire militia force of the county could not have numbered over two thousand men. The largest number from any one regiment on duty at any time was 500 men from Colonel Hasbrouck's Fourth, July, 1777, and 460 in October at the burning of Esopus. It seems to have been the strongest of the four regiments. Governor Clinton had no little confidence in it, and particularly in that portion of it known as the "Shawangunk Militia." As a rule circumstances would not admit of the calling out of any full company from its "beat"; some portion must necessarily remain at home. Portions of regiments were in almost constant motion, some going out and others returning. The only illustrative report of their movements is of record from Colonel Hasbrouck's regiment for sixteen months:

Dec. 12, 1776—	At Ramapo	300 men,	27 days.
Jan. 7, 1776—	" "	100 "	14 "
Jan. 28, 1777—	" "	200 "	40 "
Jan. 1777—	" Fort Montgomery	150 "	12 "
Mch. 7, 1777—	" " "	130 "	90 "
Mch. 1777—	" Peekskill	250 "	40 "
July 1777—	" Fort Montgomery	460 "	8 "
Aug. 1777—	" " "	500 "	8 "
Oct. 1777—	" " Constitution	200 "	10 "
Oct. 1777—	" Burning of Esopus	460 "	30 "
Nov. 1777—	" New Windsor	120 "	45 "
April 1778—	" West Point	420 "	8 "

No doubt similar reports were sent in by the commanders of other regiments — they were called for at least, and we know that Snyder's, Pawling's and McClaughrey's regiments were out in detachments, as has been stated. The entire force was seriously handicapped by the scarcity of arms and ammunition. Guns and powder "cannot be had for love or money," wrote Lieut. Colonel McClaughrey of the Second Regiment; of 293 men exclusive of officers of the First Regiment, July 17, 1777, ten were in want of arms, and 282 in want of ammunition, wrote

Lieut. Colonel Elmendorf, and Captain Jeremiah Snyder, of the First regiment, who had been sent out with his company to garrison a block house on the western frontier at Shandaken, wrote, August 15, 1778: "My company consists of forty-one men besides sergeants, and corporals, and these I cannot supply with three cartridges apiece. From this you may judge what defence we can make." And the wonder is that they made any. The Provincials Convention, to supply the place of guns, had 3000 spontoons (short spears) made and distributed. They were good for close action, but were next to nothing against Tories and Indians armed with guns. There was plenty of patriotism in stock, and that was about all.

It so happened that on the capture of the forts in the Highlands by the British (Oct. 6th, 1777), only two of the Ulster Regiments, McClaughrey's (Second) and Hasbrouck's (Fourth) were on duty there, but it only happened so because it was their "turn." The detachment of 200 men from Hasbrouck's regiment, however, were not in the action; it was stationed in Fort Constitution on the east side of the river, with a company of Lamb's artillery under Captain Ebenezer Mott, and with that company were idle spectators of the desperate struggle on the west side of the river where the defense of the forts fell upon McClaughry's detachment, detachments from Allison's and Woodhull's Orange County regiments, two companies of Lamb's artillery, and six companies of Du Bois's Fifth Continentals. Fort Montgomery, the largest and best equipped, was on the north side of Poplopen Creek, and Fort Clinton was on the south side of the same stream. Allison's and Woodhull's detachments were in the latter, and McClaughrey's in the former. Both suffered heavily in killed, wounded and prisoners, the latter including both of the commanders named and several of their subordinate officers.

FALL OF THE HIGHLAND FORTS.

The forts were defended with spirit and bravery. The enemy were held in check from three in the afternoon until dusk when, in the final bayonet charge of the assailants the defenders were overwhelmed by numbers — they did not surrender! Governor Clinton and his brother General James escaped over the parapets, the latter to the bed of the creek, the former to the Hudson where a boat conveyed him to General

Putnam's Headquarters at Peekskill. Colonel Du Bois was wounded, but escaped over the parapets, as did many of his men. Governor Clinton and Putnam were fairly outgeneralled by Sir Henry Clinton who commanded the British forces. Feigning an attack on Putnam, Sir Henry threw a column of three thousand men on the west side of the river and came upon the forts in the rear where there were no parapets and where there were no cannon in place to defend. The forts could hardly be classed as forts; they were more strictly batteries for the defense of the chain which had been stretched across the Hudson from Fort Montgomery. The batteries taken the chain amounted to nothing; it was quickly swept away. The *chevaux-de-frise* from Nicoll's Point was more formidable, but it was only a matter of a few days that intervened before the navigation of the Hudson was opened for the raid of the British fleet with Kingston as the immediate objective point and the forming of a junction with Burgoyne the principal purpose. The Provincials lost everything — forts, guns, powder, provisions, and clothing. The blow was severe, but it inspired desperation. "Every man between sixteen and fifty to the front!" rang out the order of Governor Clinton; "Burgoyne must be defeated or all is lost."

BURNING OF KINGSTON.

Governor Clinton did not sleep. In his interview with Putnam plans were formed for doing what could be done with the forces at their command to protect the settlements along the river, and possibly prevent a junction of the British forces with Burgoyne. Putnam was to move up on the east side of the river, and Governor Clinton on the west, and to strengthen the latter Putnam gave to him Webb's Connecticut Continentals. On the morning of the 7th Clinton established headquarters at the Falls House in upper New Windsor; fugitives from the forts came in; the militia came in and preparations were made to move to the defense of Kingston as soon as the enemy passed the *chevaux-de-frise*. While Governor Clinton was busy getting together his shattered forces, his namesake, Sir Henry Clinton, was busy in destroying the forts and in opening a clear passage in the *chevaux-de-frise*. This was completed on the 12th,* and an armed schooner, two row galleys and a small brig passed through and went up the river; on their return the British fleet composed of the Friendship, 22 guns, the Molloy, the Dilligent, the Dependence, the Spitfire, the Crane, the Raven and twenty galleys and flat boats, sailed through on the morning of the 13th. Governor Clinton's forces were off too. Their route was on the west side of the Wallkill to Marbletown where they arrived two hours too late, Kingston was in flames! Many of the First and Third militia regiments were away with Gates or on the frontier. Governor Clinton had ordered the remainder to Kingston and had directed them to throw up breastworks at the landing and do everything that they could to check the advance of the enemy. The militia responded by turning out one hundred and fifty men who made the best defense they could, but were quickly dispersed. Sir John Vaughan, who was in command of the British expedition, no doubt wrote correctly the general facts of the attack and the defence of the town in his report to Sir Henry Clinton, dated October 17th:

"I have the honor to inform you that on the evening of the 15th instant I arrived off Esopus; finding that the rebels had thrown up works and had made every disposition to annoy us and cut off our communication, I judged it necessary to attack them, the wind at that time being so much against us that we could make no way. I accordingly landed the troops, attacked the batteries, drove them from their works, spiked and destroyed their guns. *Esopus being a nursery for almost every villain in the country,* I judged it necessary to proceed to that town. On our approach they (the militia) were drawn up with cannon, which we took and drove them out of the place. On entering the town they fired from their houses, which induced me to reduce the place to ashes, which I accordingly did, not leaving a house. We found a considerable quantity of stores which shared the same fate. Our loss is so inconsiderable that it is not at present worth while to mention it."

Sir James Wallace, who commanded the fleet wrote under the same date:

"We arrived at Esopus Creek where we found two batteries, one of two guns and one of three, and an armed galley at the mouth of the creek, who endeavored to prevent our passing by their cannonade. General Vaughan was of opinion such a force should not be left behind. It was determined to land and destroy them, and immediately executed *without reducing our proceeding up the river.* The General marched to the Town and fired it."

* The *chevaux-de-frise* was not what Webster describes as "a piece of timber on an iron barrel traversed with pointed spikes or spears," but timbers about thirty feet long pointed with iron and held on angle in cribs filled with stone sunk on the bottom of the river. It required time to remove them; the boats of the British fleet were employed for many hours in removing them. Governor Clinton thought they would not have succeeded had not the carriage of the 24 lb. cannon on Nicoll's Point been broken. Something unfortunate seems to have been happening all the time.

An armed galley and some small vessels lying in the creek were burned. Rivington's Gazette added to the official report that "the rebels deserted their guns and made no defence after the British forces landed. The 13th, the date given by Lossing as that on which the burning occurred, is not correct. Vaughan and Clinton wrote 16th. The Provincial Convention, and in its recess the Committee of Safety of that body, had been holding sessions in Kingston since March 6th. The first Constitution of the State had been adopted there and George Clinton elected Governor under it. On the fall of the forts in the Highlands the archives of the State and County were hurriedly taken to the Town of Rochester, and also such army stores as could be removed. Most of the inhabitants had also made retreat to the country with such possessions as could be taken, and those who had not removed fled on the approach of the British forces. Substantially the town was in the keeping of a limited number of militiamen who, as shown by Vaughan's report, made the best defence they could. The dwellings were mostly low stone structures in which the woodwork burned rapidly leaving blackened walls.* In Rivington's Gazette of November 3d, it is said: "326 houses with a barn to most every one of them" were burned, but the precise number is not certain. The excuse which Vaughan gave for burning the town was probably coined for the occasion; he was sent out to destroy the place, he intended to destroy it, and he did destroy it because it was the headquarters of the rebels in the then Province of New York. True, he called it "A nursery of villains!" but he could not have paid to the people of the town a higher compliment. He went but little further north, burning some buildings on Livingston Manor on the opposite side of the river, and then turned back to New York, his last ship disappearing below West Point on the 25th. Why did he return? He found that the destruction of the forts and the obstructions in the Highlands had so detained him that he was too late to help Burgoyne, who, when he heard of the occurrences on the river below him, had already signed the agreement of capitulation. The six days that had been especially lost in removing the *chevaux-de-frise* at Nicoll's Point in order to give free passage to the fleet, were important days. "As soon as I see that the enemy is likely to pass the *chevaux-de-frise*" wrote Governor Clinton, and that

* Some of the dwellings were reroofed, the woodwork restored and remained in occupation for years. The principal one now standing is "The Senate House," a mecca to which the feet of many of the Sons and Daughters of Ulster are turned with reverence.

Jacob H Kemper

evidence he did not have until the morning of the 13th. In other words, the detention of the English fleet by the *chevaux-de-frise, which had been constructed by detachments from the militia* was an important factor in the surrender of Burgoyne. Had it not been in the river the fleet would not have been delayed, and if the fleet had not been delayed Burgoyne would not in all probability have been compelled to surrender, the Province would have been dismembered and the contest for national independence almost certainly lost.

A contributing cause leading to Burgoyne's surrender was the delay in receiving information from Sir Henry Clinton. The latter had dispatched a messenger to him, Daniel Taylor, on the 8th, but it so happened that his steps led him into Governor Clinton's camp at New Windsor. Fairly caught he endeavored to conceal his mission by swallowing the silver bullet in which it was encased. It was taken from him by an emetic, and its contents read. Then Taylor was tried by court-martial and condemned as a spy, which he certainly was not. As a prisoner he was taken with Clinton on the march to Kingston, and when Hurley was reached and Kingston in flames came in view the soul of Daniel Taylor was sent to its giver from the limb of an apple tree. A second messenger sent by Sir Henry Clinton to Burgoyne did not reach him until the 14th. The silver bullet and its message have been preserved, as has also a single spear-head from the *chevaux-de-frise,* the factors which contributed so largely to save the infant Republic. They seem to have been the master-keys of an Overruling Power.

The re-building the Highland forts at West Point during the succeeding winter and the placing of the historic chain across the river at that point, pressed heavily upon the Ulster militia. The building of the walls of Fort Putnam, and the redoubts known as Fort Wylis and Fort Webb required men; the Stirling Iron Works required one hundred and eighty-two men to aid in making the chain, wood cutters, carters, men for making steel, men for making iron, welders, etc. Although Washington brought his Continental Army into the Highlands within supporting distance of the forts, it was not until the signing of the preliminary articles of peace in April, 1782, that the militia of Ulster was relieved from duty.

CHAPTER XIV.

THE CONTINENTAL LINE.

WHILE the service of the Ulster Militia in local fields was, in detachments and continuous during the entire war, its contributions to the Continental Line* was not less pronounced. Acting in concert with New England legislators who regarded the invasion of Canada as the most promising strategic movement, the Provincial authorities of New York, in the summer of 1775, authorized the organization of four regiments to serve for six months, commanded respectively by Alexander McDougall, Goose Van Schaick, James Clinton and James Holmes. The first was recruited in New York, the second in Albany, the third in Ulster, and the fourth in Duchess, the last three, however, were more or less mixed. They were fine bodies of young men, well armed and handsomely uniformed. The first had blue broadcloth dress-coats with crimson cuffs and facings; the second had light brown coats with blue cuffs and facings; the third (Ulster) had gray coats with green facings and cuffs; the fourth had dark brown coats with scarlet cuffs and facings. Their breeches and waist-coats were of Russia drilling; the former were short (to the knee) and the latter were long (to the hips). Their stockings were long (to the knee) of "coarse woolen homespun," low shoes, linen cravats and low crowned broad brimmed felt hats. Drums and fifes they had, and on parade were "very pleasant to the eye"; in the field their dress was quite less showy.

The officers of the Third Regiment (Ulster) were:

James Clinton, Colonel; Edward Fleming Lieut. Colonel; Cornelius D. Wynkoop, Major; George Slosser, Adjutant; James Hamilton, Qr. Master; Samuel Cooke, Surgeon.

Captains—Daniel Griffin, John Nicholson, Jacobus Bruyn, Andrew Billings, Lewis

* The Continental Line was composed of organizations under pay of the Continental Congress, and in service as the regular army and liable to duty in any part of the country, while the militia as such could not be taken outside of the states in which they resided. Washington learned very early in the war that the militia could not be a force which could be relied upon—that there must be a regularly constituted army. It was the militia, however, who won the battle of Bennington, and compelled the surrender of Burgoyne. For the making of an army no better material was ever found than the men drawn from the militia of Ulster.

Du Bois, John Hulbert, Elias Hasbrouck, John Grinnell, Daniel Denton, Robert Johnson.

First Lieutenants—Benj. Marvin, Isaac Belknap, Thomas DeWitt, Ezekiel Cooper, Elias Van Benschoten, John Davis, Cornelius T. Jansen, Wm. Phillips, Jr., Balthazar De Hart, Martin Goetchius.

Second Lieutenants—Nathaniel Norton, David Du Bois, James Greeg, John Langdon, Cornelius Adriance, Wm. Havens, Albert Pawling, Philip Conkling, Jonas Bellows, Philip Du Bois, Brevier.

The regiments were brigaded under General Richard Montgomery, and marched away to Canada. The severity of the weather and the fatigues of the march had reduced the four regiments to 900 effective men on the first of December. Three weeks later Montgomery led them "into the jaws of death" in the narrowest point under Cape Diamond. A storm of grape-shot from an English battery swept him and both of his aids from among the living and with them several privates. But the story of the Canada campaign may be read elsewhere — we have not room to repeat it here.

The term of service of the New York regiments (six months) soon expired. Some of their members were willing to remain for another six months, others had broken down, others had aspirations in other directions. The outcome was that from those who were willing to remain a new regiment was formed, which may be called the fifth of the first series of the New York Line. Captain John Nicholson, of Hanover Precinct, who had gone out with Clinton in the Third New York, and had been therein promoted to Lieutenant Colonel, was appointed Colonel of the new organization, and several of the officers from Ulster in the old Third remained with him. The further prosecution of the invasion of Canada having been abandoned, the regiment was sent to the northwestern frontier, headquarters at what is now Johnstown, Fulton County, and there completed its term of enlistment. Colonel Nicholson retired from service with impaired health and closed his life on his farm. Ensign Charles F. Weisenfels went into the new Third New York and attained the rank of Lieutenant Colonel, and Gershom Mott became Captain in Lamb's Artillery. In brief, nearly all the officers who had served in the Canada regiments of 1775, continued in subsequent organizations.

On the 8th of January, 1776, the Continental Congress issued its first formal call for troops to reinforce the army in Canada under which a single battalion was furnished by New York. The second call was issued on the 19th of the same month and required four battalions from New

York. These battalions were assigned to Colonels Alexander McDougal, James Clinton, Rudolphus Ritzema and Philip Van Cortlandt. To Colonel Clinton's (second) battalion Ulster County sent three companies — Capt. John Belknap's of New Windsor; Capt. William Jackson's of Hanover, and Capt. Cornelius Hardenberg's of Hurley. They were all short term regiments. The 1st, 2d, and 3d regiments were assigned to the defence of New York City, and were brigaded under Brigadier Generals Alex. McDougal and James Clinton, who had been promoted to that rank. The second (Ulster) was sent to Saybrook, Conn., under Lieut. Col. Henry B. Livingston. The 1st and 3d were in the battle at White Plains and in the sharp fight at Chatterton's Hill. Ritzema's (third) regiment, then under Lieut. Col. Weisenfall, suffered the greatest loss. In the retreat through New Jersey the 1st and 2d formed part of Lee's division, which subsequently joined Washington, and were in the surprise and capture of the Hessians at Trenton, December 25th, 1776, the anniversary of the first grapple with the enemy at Quebec. Immediately after they were ordered home, their terms of enlistment having expired.

The third call for men was issued by the Continental Congress on the 16th of September, 1776, for four regiments "to serve during the war" — the grand old New York regiments of the Continental Army, which were organized under the commands respectively of Colonels Goosé Van Schaick, Philip Van Cortlandt, Peter Gansevort and Henry B. Livingston. To Gansevort's regiment (3d) Ulster sent three companies, viz: Cornelius T. Jansen's, Thomas R. De Witt's, and James Gregg's. With other companies of Gansevort's regiment they were shut up in Fort Schuyler (old Fort Stanwix) in August, 1777, and defended that post against the forces under St. Leger. Capt. Gregg was later caught in the woods by the Indians and scalped. His little dog licked his wounds and when the Captain recovered consciousness, was sent to the fort for assistance. He was brought in and ultimately recovered. The story of Fort Schuyler is an interesting chapter in the history of Burgoyne's expedition.

To the number of regiments recruited under the call was added a fifth recruited under Colonel Lewis Du Bois of Marlborough, who has been met in Colonel Hasbrouck's regiment of militia, and in Colonel James Clinton's Canada regiment. His regiment (the Fifth) was eminently

Noah Wolven.

the Ulster County regiment of the New York Continental Line. Its Field and Staff at organization were:

Lewis Du Bois, Colonel; Jacobus S. Bruyn, Lieut. Colonel; Samuel Logan, Major; Henry Du Bois, Adjutant; Albert Pawling, Aid-Major; Nehemiah Carpenter, Qr. Master; Saml. Townsend, Paymaster; John Gano, Chaplain; Samuel Cooke, Surgeon; Ebenezer Hutchinson, Surgeon's Mate.

Captains—1. Jacobus Rosekrans; 2. James Stewart; 3. Amos Hutchins; 4. Philip Du Bois Bevier; 5. Thomas Lee; 6. Henry Goodwin; 7. John F. Hamtrack; 8. John Johnson.

First Lieutenants—1. Henry Dodge; 2. Alexander McArthur; 3. Patton Jackson; 4. Michael Connelly; 5. Henry Pawling; 6. Solomon Pendelton; 7. Francis Hanmer; 8. Henry W. Van der berg. Henry Pawling was transferred to the regiment from Gansevort's.

Second Lieutenants—1. Samuel Dodge; 2. John Burnett; 3. John Furman; 4. ——— ———; 5. Samuel English; 6. Ebenezer Mott; 7. ——— ———; 8. James Betts.

Ensigns—1. Henry Swartwout; 2. John McClaughrey; 3. ——— ———; 4. ——— ———; 5. James Johnson; 6. Abraham Leggett; 7. ——— ———; 8. Henry J. Vanderbergh.

The figures refer to the companies in which the officers served. The list is not the same in all respects as that given in 1777. (N. Y. Historical Manuscript, P. 50); the changes subsequently made may be omitted here.

The regiment was stationed in the spring of 1777, on garrison duty at Forts Montgomery, Clinton and Constitution, in the Highlands, and was there on the 6th of October of that year when the forts were captured by the British forces under Sir Henry Clinton. In this action — the first baptism of fire which the regiment had sustained — the losses of the regiment were heavy. Lieutenant Colonel Bruyn, Major Logan and Qr. Master Carpenter, Captain Goodman, Lieutenants McArthur, Jackson, Pawling, Pendleton, Samuel Dodge, Furman and Mott; Ensigns Swartwout, McClaughrey and Legg, and Sergeant Henry Schoonmaker, were taken prisoners,* and "missing in action" was written on the roll-call on the 7th against the names of ninety-six privates, some of whom, however, had escaped from the forts in the final rush and reported for duty later. Over one-third of the regiment in action were among the

* Several of these officers were not exchanged until the war was practically over. Militia officers were not recognized as exchangeable. Line officers were exchanged for those of equivalent rank, or for an equivalent number of privates, the exchange running from two privates for an ensign to seventy-two privates for a colonel. The officers who were prisoners were carried on the rolls and given half pay for life. Lieutenants Henry Schoonmaker and Henry Pawling returned in 1780, and also Major Logan; Solomon Pendleton in 1781. Lieut. Colonel Jacobus Severyn Bruyn was held on parole on Staten Island until near the close of the war. On the organization of the "Society of Cincinnati" at Temple Hill, in New Windsor, May, 1783, twenty-four Ulster County officers of the Line signed the roll as members.

killed, wounded and prisoners. The men lost all their clothing except that which they had on them, and most of them their arms also. Demoralized and broken as the regiment was, however, Colonel Du Bois rallied its survivors around Governor Clinton at his headquarters in New Windsor, and marched to the defence of Kingston. In the winter following the regiment was in barracks at Fishkill and in a deplorable condition from the loss of clothing. General Putnam wrote in January, '78: "De Bois's regiment is unfit to be ordered on duty, there being not one blanket in the regiment, very few have either a shoe or a shirt, and most of them have neither stockings, breeches or overalls." Chastellux wrote that many of them were absolutely naked, "being covered only by straw suspended about the waist." Of course this condition did not last long after Governor Clinton heard of it. In July, 1778, the regiment was at White Plains, Westchester County; in 1779, it was, with Colonel Du Bois in command, under Brigadier-General James Clinton in the Sullivan campaign against the Six Nations of Indians, and on the return of that expedition was stationed at Fort Stanwix in the Mohawk Valley. Here Colonel Du Bois resigned (Dec. 31, 1779);* and the regiment was placed under Lieut. Colonel Marius Willett, formerly of the Third and was in service under him in the events at Fort Stanwix in 1780. Colonel Du Bois was also there in command of a regiment of "Levies of the State to reinforce the Army of the United States," and did most excellent work in the battle of Klock's Field, now in Montgomery County, on the 19th of October of that year. Later, what remained of the Fifth seems to have been consolidated with the Fourth, and the latter with the Third, and in that connection was under General James Clinton in the Siege of Yorktown, October, 1781, From that last great battle of the war the three remaining New York regiments came (Nov. 1782) to the last encampment of the army of the Revolution at Temple Hill in New Windsor, the home of the Second Ulster militia, and from thence, on the dissolution of the army by furlough (June, 1783), passed "out of mortal sight,

* The roster of officers of the regiment in the Sullivan campaign included Lewis Du Bois, Colonel; Henry Du Bois, Adjutant and Captain Lieutenant; Henry Dodge, Captain and Lieutenant; Michael Connoly, Pay-master and Second Lieutenant; James Johnston, Quarter-master and Ensign; Samuel Cooke, Surgeon; Ebenezer Hutchins, Surgeon's Mate; Captains—James Rosenkrans, John F. Hamtrack, John Johnston, Philip Du Bois Bevier, James Stewart; Henry W. Vanderburgh, Lieutenant; Daniel Birdsall and James Betts, Second Lieutenants; Bartholf Vanderburgh Francis Hammer, and Henry Vanderburgh, Ensigns. Lieutenant Colonel Bruin, Major Samuel Logan and other officers who were taken prisoners at Fort Montgomery in October, 1777, were still in captivity, and their places on the active roll could not be filled. This condition of affairs led to the resignation of Colonel Du Bois and to the consolidation of the regiment with other regiments of the New York line.

but into immortal history." Perhaps in the future a son of Ulster will compile the personal record of every man who stood in the ranks in the fray that "won a rescued world." Meanwhile their names on the rolls is their monument.

CHAPTER XV.

KINGSTON

1652-1777.

By HOWARD HENDRICKS.

THE ancient history of this old town, covering its first century-and-a-quarter, is so fully treated on the preceding pages by Mr. Ruttenber, that it seems unnecessary to repeat or elaborate the details in this chapter. The events and doings during that primitive period of the settlement's existence being in fact the history of Ulster County, it was proper to treat the subject at length in the general article referred to.

Geographically the present city is on the west bank of the Hudson River, about midway between the northern and southern limits of Ulster County. The Rondout Creek forms its southern boundary and affords a fine stretch of navigable water-front with ample and advantageous wharfage. The Esopus Creek flows along the northern boundary, making a sweeping curve to the Hudson twelve miles north. On the east is the broad and majestic Hudson and the new town of Ulster, and on the north and west are the towns of Ulster and the remnant of the original town of Kingston, which still retains that name. Between the Rondout and the Esopus is a comparatively level plain, high, with precipitous banks, rising to bluffs along the river. On the west and north are the low, alluvial lands of the Esopus valley, which rise gradually to hills and mountains beyond. The river bluffs are often interspersed by pleasant slopes, producing a great variety of scenic effect, much of which is strangely rugged, and all wondrously picturesque.

Among the aboriginal names of places in this section are "Waronawanka," at (or on) a cove or bay; "Sepuus," a brook, by corruption, "Esopus," and "Atkarkarton," as generally written, and according to the version of Marius Schoonmaker, the Kingston historian, but lately written, "Atharhacton," by Dr. Corwin and others. The meaning of either of these appellations is uncertain, though claimed to have been

Howard Hendricks.

the name of the "Groot Plat" (Great Flat) on the north and west of the town.

The ancient Dutch name "Wildwijk," now "Wiltwyck," is still retained in the latter form in some connections, and often locally applied to the central section of the present city, for some occult reason. The old Dutch "Rondhout" is now "Rondout," and the Dutch "Punthockje," the point of a small cone or bay, has given place to "Ponckhockie."

The "Columbus Point" of ancient days is now known as "Kingston Point." The "two little Indian houses" that once stood on its southerly side, have given way to the commerce and traffic of a large section of country and the busy traverse of trolleys and steam cars.

It would indeed be interesting to trace the orthographical metamorphosis of these ancient Dutch and Indian names which adorn the old records, if the limits of space allowed.

THE CRADLE OF NEW YORK STATE.

KINGSTON, 1777-1907.

Kingston was the cradle of New York State, and the infant commonwealth began its career amid scenes of turmoil and the smoke of battle. The enemy were encamped on every side, and Governor Clinton scarcely dared to leave his post in the army long enough to assume the affairs of State. But victory was in the air and every man of the patriot band in the field was inspired with new courage. The triumph of liberty was about to dawn.

Among the first to congratulate Governor Clinton was Dominie Doll, pastor of the old Dutch church in Kingston, which had borne so conspicuous a part in the long struggle against oppression. In this he wrote, "All have pledged their lives and fortunes to support and defend you in this exalted station, and the Consistory of Kingston cheerfully unite in the implicit stipulation, and promise you their prayers."

The Legislature of the new State had been called to meet at Kingston, August 1st. But the condition of the country was such it was considered unsafe to convene that body until the twentieth, when it was again prorogued until September 1, for the same reason. The assembly finally met and organized on that day, but the Senate was not in session until nine days later, for lack of a quorum. Thus, on the tenth of September, 1777.

the Legislature of the new State became fully organized and the wheels of government were started. The three departments, the legislative, the executive, and the judicial, were thus launched together in Kingston. Being unable to occupy the Court House, because of the session of the Supreme Court, the Assembly organized at the hotel of Evert Bogardus, corner of Maiden Lane and Fair streets.

This was the first Court under the first Constitution of the new State, and it was opened by Chief Justice Jay on the ninth of September, 1777. The Grand Jury was composed of 22 of the best men in the county. On that day Chief Justice Jay delivered the first charge to a Grand Jury of which there is any record. It was a memorable judicial address of great importance, and will stand as a model for all time. A single sentence only is quoted here. "The Americans are the first people whom Heaven has favored with an opportunity of deliberating upon and choosing the forms of government under which they should live; all other constitutions have derived their existence from violence or accidental circumstances."

OLD SENATE HOUSE.

The Senate organized at the house of Abraham Van Gaasbeek, corner of Clinton Avenue (then East Front Street) and North Front Street. This ancient stone structure, now known as the "Old Senate House," was built in 1676 by Col. Wessel Ten Broeck. It was owned by Van Gaasbeek during the Revolution, and afterward passed successively to Sarah, wife of Peter Van Gaasbeek, F. E. Westbrook, and Mrs. Marius Schoonmaker, who sold it to the State in 1887. It was then thoroughly repaired, preserving the ancient features as far as possible, and has since been kept as a sacred relic and memento of the historic past, where the antiquarian and curious may find a large collection of articles pertaining to bygone years. It is visited by thousands from every land, and the number increases every year. It is built of native limestone except the rear wall, which is of large brick imported from Holland. The mortar used in these massive walls over 200 years ago, is to-day solid as adamant.

The regular sessions of the Legislature were held in this house until the meetings were broken up by the near approach of the British forces after the capture of Fort Montgomery in the Highlands of the Hudson, Oct. 4, 1777. On receipt of this news in Kingston, Oct. 7, the Legislature dispersed, the members rushing to join the patriot army, and in defense of their families. Governor Clinton, who had been inaugurated in Kingston three months before, having remained in command at the Fort, was there overwhelmed by the enemy, he himself having slid down a precipice toward the river and escaped in a boat. With the destruction of these forts there was nothing to hinder the advance of the British up the river under Sir Henry Clinton, and the defenseless homes of Kingston were thus endangered.

Governor Clinton wrote the Council of Safety, in session here, that he was trying to rally his scattered forces, persuade the Militia to join him and make a forced march to the defense of Kingston. But he found the soldiers too solicitous about the safety of their families to remain on duty. Meanwhile the Legislature at Kingston, realizing the importance of immediate action, formed a "joint Convention for the State to provide for the Public Safety." Pierre Van Cortlandt, president of the Senate, was chosen president of this Convention. A new Council of Safety was appointed, with William Floyd as president. This Council met Oct. 8 and ordered all persons then in jail here, transferred to Hartford, Conn., in the expectation of the enemy's attack. Two days later all male inhabitants of the district capable of service were ordered to secure arms and ammunition, and hold themselves in readiness to meet the foe. All money in the State treasury at Kingston, public records, and other State property, were packed in boxes and removed to Rochester, by Gerard Bancker, the vice State treasurer; £1,000 were, however, kept for immediate use, subject to the order of the Council.

On Oct. 11, Governor Clinton was advised by the Council that the local Militia had been ordered to rendezvous at Kingston and Shawangunk. On the same day the British commander, Clinton, sent a reconnoitering expedition toward Poughkeepsie. Finding the way comparatively clear, the marauding expedition of Gen. Vaughan was easily organized. This consisted of 7 naval vessels and some 20 galleys and flatboats, with 1,600 men. The start was made from Peekskill Oct. 14, and the fleet anchored off Esopus Island next day. They were discovered by Governor Clinton's men early in the morning, and he at once expressed a letter to the Council of Safety at Kingston, warning of the enemy's approach. His reinforcements had not arrived, but he sent all his available troops on to Kingston in great haste, feeling sure the new State capital, and at that time the capital of the nation, would be the object of attack.

Meanwhile the Council of Safety was in session in Kingston at the tavern of Conrad Elmendorf, on the southeast corner of Maiden Lane and Fair streets, which is still standing. The last session of this famous Council was indeed a memorable meeting.

BURGOYNE'S SURRENDER.

It was on the afternoon of Oct. 15, 1777, and the members present were Pierre Van Cortlandt, president, Messrs. Yates, Dunscomb, Floyd, Van Zandt, Parks, Scott, Webster, Rowan, Harper, Pawling and Morris. It was at this meeting the news of Burgoyne's surrender was received. One Bernardus Hallenbeek was the bearer of the letter, and he was promptly voted a reward of £50.

For this news the people of Kingston had waited long. The final overthrow of foreign oppression and misrule was now assured, and the banner of Liberty was in the sky. But there was little time for rejoicing. The redcoats were rapidly approaching from the south, and the town was practically defenseless. The patriot forces under Governor Clinton could not reach Kingston in time to repel the invaders. Even at that moment, the alarm guns were booming, and the enemy was about to land at Kingston Point, at the mouth of Rondout Creek, then known as "Columbus Point." About five o'clock that afternoon, the Council sent word to Governor Clinton, who was then on his way to Kingston, of the enemy's approach, also the Burgoyne dispatch. But the messenger proved dilatory and stopped for the night at a wayside farmhouse.

Having pushed on ahead of the army, Clinton arrived with his staff about 9 o'clock that night. He found great commotion, and the most intense excitement prevailed. The defenseless people were packing their goods and valuables and fleeing out of reach of the vandal hordes as fast as possible. They went to Hurley, Marbletown, Rochester and Wawarsing. Finding it impossible for his troops to reach Kingston in time, he sent word that they should proceed no further and repaired to Marbletown himself on the morning of Oct. 16.

Meanwhile Vaughan's forces had already anchored at the mouth of the creek and opened a heavy fire upon the galley Lady Washington which lay in the stream, and upon the batteries and earthworks, which had been hastily thrown up on the Ponckhockie heights, where five light cannon were in position. This fire was returned for some time, but there was

Old Senate House—1777.

little damage on either side. Soon after noon Vaughan's soldiers began to land in two divisions, one at the Old Cantine dock on the creek, and the other in the cove north of the Point. The breastworks were stormed and carried at the point of the bayonet, there being only 150 men under Cols. Pawling and Snyder, who had already spiked the guns. The only three houses on the creek were burned, and a negro was seized and compelled to guide the invaders to Kingston.

The news of Burgoyne's capture was conveyed to Vaughan by Jacobus Lefferts, a New York city Tory who was then living in Kingston with his family. But Vaughan knew there was ample time to carry out his despicable purpose here and that he would meet with little or no resistance.

The veracious and careful historian, Marius Schoonmaker, says that old residents of Kingston who were in the Militia on that memorable occasion told him, there was an armed body of patriots, 100 strong, concealed in the woods near where the City Hall now stands, and that some of these men begged permission to fire and pick off some of the officers of this invading force as they passed on their way to Kingston, but the commander forbade it. The fact seems to be, nearly everybody had fled from their homes and the enemy met no resistance on reaching the village, in spite of the apologetic language of Gen. Vaughan in his official report, in which he sought to show that the people fired upon his troops from their houses and for that reason he was "induced to reduce the place to ashes, which I accordingly did, not leaving a house."

BURNING OF KINGSTON.

The troops scattered into small parties and fired all the buildings on every street as rapidly as possible, gathering what plunder they could, and returning to their ships in three hours. They knew Clinton's army was on the way, and they fled to the Point in great confusion, expecting any moment to meet the advance of the patriots. The Governor's order to halt, if ever received at all, must have been countermanded, because the advance division of Clinton's forces arrived an the Kuykuyt Hill, now called Golden Hill, or Keykout, in time to see the whole village in flames and the red-coated vandals fleeing to their ships.

The *New York Gazette*, a Royalist paper, of November 3, 1777, in its account of this expedition, says, that 326 houses, with a barn to almost every one of them, filled with flour, grain, crops of all kinds, furniture and effects, were destroyed. 12,000 barrels of flour, 14 cannon, and 1,150 stands of arms were burned or blown up.

Immediately after this overpowering calamity Governor Clinton concentrated his forces at Hurley, having sent the sad news to Gen. Gates at Albany. Thereupon Gates, on October 19, sent the following stinging letter to Gen. Vaughan who led this marauding gang.

"With unexampled cruelty, you have reduced the fine village of Kingston to ashes, and most of the wretched inhabitants to ruin. I am also informed, you continue to ravage and burn all before you on both sides of the river. Is it thus your King's generals think to make converts to the Royal cause? It is no less surprising than true, that the measures they adopt to serve their master, must have quite the contrary effect. Their cruelty establishes the glorious act of Independence, upon the broad basis of the general resentment of the People.

"Other Generals, and much older officers than you can pretend to be, are now by the fortune of war in my hands; their fortune may one day be yours, when, sir, it may not be in the power of anything human to save you from the just vengeance of an injured People.

HORATIO GATES."

The full force of this staggering blow to Kingston and its people cannot be described. All they had in the world was destroyed. Even their winter stores were gone. They had neither shelter nor food. But the fire of patriotism had been kindled anew in every bosom, and it burned brighter than ever. The women who had been driven from their homes were inspired with righteous vengeance, and the gratifying news of British defeat, over which they had not even been permitted to rejoice, now gave them new courage.

The only building that escaped this fire was the Van Steenburgh House, which is still standing on the westerly side of Wall St., foot of Franklin St. A suitable tablet was placed in the wall a few years since by the Wiltwyck Chapter, Daughters of the American Revolution. The house of the Tory, Lefferts, which stood on the present site of John Forsythe's residence, back from Albany Ave., was also saved, but this was outside of the stockade.

An old document giving a list of sufferers from this fire, contains 113 names, and states that there were 115 dwellings, 103 barns, 146 barracks,

17 storehouses, including a market and a brewhouse, a church, an Academy, 2 Schoolhouses and a Court House destroyed.

This wanton act aroused a thrill of sympathy which quickly spread over the land, and there was a cry of indignation and shame on all sides. Though the people were impoverished by war and oppression, donations and offers of assistance were received from various parts of the country. From the sister State of South Carolina, came a check from Abraham Livingston in behalf of her citizens, for £3711.10. Robert R. Livingston gave 5000 acres of land, which was subsequently divided into fifty-acre lots arranged into ten classes of ten lots each, and then allotted to the Kingston sufferers. As the winter was approaching, they did what they could to provide shelter. Most of the houses being of stone, many of the walls were still standing. Roofs were put on and lean-tos added. But their barns and crops were gone and some sort of shelter was needed for the stock. It was indeed a crucial period for these sturdy patriots. But they had been reared in the bitter school of adversity and they were undaunted now. They resolved to surmount every obstacle. Materials and labor were high, and building was only possible with a few men of means. Governor Clinton was appealed to for assistance and reminded of the faithful loyalty and persevering assistance of the Kingston people. He gave prompt response and did what he could for their relief.

Christopher Tappen was then the Deputy County Clerk and clerk of the corporation of Kingston. It is said his family devoted their entire energies toward the preservation of the public records at the expense of losing all his chattels and private papers in the fire.

There are many incidents connected with this burning of Kingston which have been related with considerable detail by veracious writers. Some of these would be of interest to the general reader even now. But unless presented with some detail much of the interest would be lost; and there is so much of the actual historic record pertaining to this important town, the writer feels scarcely justified in using the space with such minor incidents. The following Dutch doggerel, characteristic of the flight to Hurley, having now become a local classic, will, however, be quoted. "Loop, jongens, loop, de Rooje Komme. Span de wagon Voor de paerde, en vy na Hurley toe." The English version would be "Run, boys, run, the red-coats are coming. Harness the horses before the wagon, and to Hurley ride."

The stores and effects so hastily removed to Hurley were carefully guarded by the Militia. On Oct. 21, Governor Clinton wrote Gen. Gates, fully explaining the situation, and giving the reason for his inability to prevent the attack upon Kingston. He showed how Gen. Putnam had sent him less than 400 troops, when he asked for 3000, how other reinforcements had been refused him, and how, if the enemy landed in force, he must either retreat and leave the entire section to be ravaged and destroyed, or sacrifice his few men and the valuable artillery, for lack of troops. He said: "Kingston hath been destroyed merely because I have been so deceived in my expectations of assistance, that it was impossible to take measures for its security."

If Vaughan had intended to proceed to Albany, the plan was abandoned after Burgoyne's surrender. He rejoined the British forces in the Highlands Oct. 24. The Council of Safety reconvened in Marbletown and recommended a distribution of the distressed persons and families of Kingston, with their cattle, through the counties of Ulster, Dutchess, Orange and Westchester, where they might be furnished with shelter and subsistence at a moderate price. The Council continued there for a time, and afterward met at Hurley until Dec. 17, when it adjourned to Poughkeepsie and continued there until Jan. 7, 1778.

Governor Clinton was again appealed to for relief on Feb. 9, by a Kingston committee, which reminded him of the enemy's bitter resentment, which had been incurred by the conspicuous service and loyalty of the people, and which had led to the destruction of all their property. This brought such relief as lay in his power. The Court House was ordered rebuilt at public expense; those engaged in rebuilding the town were exempted from military duty, and other measures were adopted. In this way some of the houses were partially restored.

The first election for trustees and other corporation officers after the fire, was held the first Tuesday in March, 1778, at the Van Steenburgh House on Wall St. The British forces under Sir Henry Clinton, had then returned to New York, but their Indian allies and the Tory bloodhounds were still menacing the people of this section. The cruelty of the Tories far exceeded that of the red-coats. In some cases they covered themselves with war-paint in imitation of the savage warriors and seemed destitute of every vestige of humanity, being inspired with hatred of their country and their liberty loving countrymen. A single instance, showing

The Du Flon House.

the difference between the Tory and the Indian nature, will illustrate this fact. Entering a house where a child was sweetly sleeping in its cradle, the Indian withheld his tomahawk because of the infant's smile. But the Tory stepped quickly forward and cleaved the skull of the innocent babe with a single blow, rebuking the savage for his tenderness. Some of these Tories served as spies for the Indians, and no man was safe in the border settlement, who openly avowed the cause of liberty. Savage raids by Indian bands, with Tory allies for purposes of robbery, and to procure scalps for redemption by the British, were frequent.

After the fire these Kingston patriots took their full share of the trials and suffering incident to the conflict. They were in constant dread of the bloody attacks of the Tories and Indians, who were instigated by British emissaries still infesting the region.

The town was fortified with timber stockades, and guards were kept at various points of approach. Although the hostile armies were now in other parts of the country, Kingston, throughout the whole period, and until the last shot was fired, furnished its full quota of men and materials for the support and defense of the country. No section endured more hardships or rendered more patriotic and effective service to the cause of Independence, than this colonial town.

The recognition of Independence by France in Feb., 1778, and her alliance with the cause, dispelled every doubt as to the ultimate success of the war, and the contest was soon ended.

WASHINGTON VISITS KINGSTON.

Kingston was honored by a visit from Gen. Washington in November, 1782. On his arrival in the town with his staff, he was met by the trustees and a large body of citizens. Henry J. Sleght, president of the Board, made the address of welcome to which Washington responded in these words: "Your polite and friendly reception of me proves your sincerity. While I view with indignation the marks of a wanton and cruel enemy, I perceive with the highest satisfaction, that the heavy calamity which befell this flourishing settlement, seems but to have added to the patriotic spirit of its inhabitants; and that a new town is fast rising out of the ashes of the old. That you and your worthy constituents may long enjoy that freedom for which you have so nobly contended, is the sincere wish of your most obedient humble servant, George Washington."

The Consistory of the old Dutch Church united heartily in this greeting of the hero, and also presented him with an appropriate address, the response to which was in his own writing, and is now a cherished memento occupying a niche in the vestibule wall of the present church structure. On that occasion Washington stopped at the Bogardus Tavern before alluded to. After dining with his staff, at the house of Dirck Wynkoop in Green St., he attended a ball that evening given in his honor, at the Bogardus Tavern, where the ladies were introduced to him. He resumed his journey to West Point early next morning.

Two weeks later a preliminary Treaty of Peace was signed, and the war was ended; although the final Treaty, acknowledging the Independence of the United States was not signed until Sept. 3, 1783.

As the people of Kingston had been among the foremost and firmest in this battle for liberty, enduring the most tremendous sacrifices with undaunted courage, never doubting the final result, they were now most exuberant in their rejoicing over the glorious termination of the conflict.

KINGSTON AT THE CLOSE OF THE REVOLUTION.

During the war a large part of Kingston was an open Common, wholly without buildings. These "Plains," as they were called, embraced all the territory east of a line drawn from Pearl to St. James Streets, at about Fair St. This was then laid out in building lots and every purchaser was bound to build and improve his lot within two years, or forfeit £60 and his lot. Many failed to build and much trouble resulted. Finally in Feb., 1790, it was decided that if these delinquents would reconvey their lots to the trustees, their forfeits would be returned. These Plains included the present Academy site, which was a sporting ground and skating-pond for the boys, known as the "Water-ploss." Beyond the junction of Maiden Lane and Albany Ave. were the "Second Plains," which were used as a military parade ground.

In 1783, when Congress was looking for a site for the Capital of the new Republic, these Dutch burghers tried to impress upon that body the peculiar appropriateness of these Kingston "Plains." They took prompt action in the matter too, and were heartily seconded by the Legislature. They offered a square-mile of land within the town limits, which offer was conveyed to the Congress at Philadelphia in March, 1783, by Governor Clinton himself. The matter was deferred until the first Monday in Oct. in connection with similar offers from Annapolis, Md., and other points. In September the grant of land was increased to two-miles square. But no action was taken at the time, and the choice of the National Capital was finally bestowed elsewhere.

Meanwhile the old Court House was rebuilt, with the jail and dungeon in the south end. There was a whipping-post in the front yard, and a regular town-whipper was appointed. There were also stocks for the punishment of minor offenses.

In 1797 the Legislature authorized the organization of a Fire Department, to be made up of men living within half-a-mile of the Court House. A fire-engine was purchased in place of the one burned, and Conradt Ed. Elmendorf was made Captain, and thus became the first Fire Chief of Kingston. This company was disbanded in 1802 and a new one formed, with Nicholas Vanderlyn, Jr., at the head.

The town poor had been under the care of the trustees since the incorporation, both by charter and legislative enactment. Poor people could not be brought into the town unless some responsible freeholder became security for their care. The matter of building an almshouse was frequently discussed, even until 1799, but nothing was done.

EARLY FINANCIAL CONDITION OF KINGSTON.

It is interesting to note the financial status of Kingston at the opening of the nineteenth century. On the thirtieth of June, 1800, the committee thus reported: Interest due on bonds and notes, £345-6-6. Rent in arrear 3171 bush. of wheat @ 8/, £1268-8, 733 fowls, £36-13. Total liability, £1650-7-6. Annual income: 720 bush. wheat for rent @ 8/ £288, £3600 out at interest, whereof about £600 are bad debts, £180, About $200 annual excise, £80, Rent payable in money, £16-17. Total income £564-17. In April, 1803, the sale and conveyance of lands known as the "Commons," was finally authorized. Heads of families, natives of the town, having an estate of £200 received a 45-acre lot on payment of $16.50. Those having £100 got a 30-acre lot for $30. Those who came in town after 1777 had to pay $40. for their lot.

ANCIENT POLITICS OF KINGSTON.

Soon after the formation of the new Republic, politics began to assert itself, and early in the new century the strife between the factions then known as the "Federalists and Republicans," became bitter. Thus after a sharp contest in the spring of 1804, the old Federalist Board of Trustees was routed at the polls and replaced by Republicans. The sale of lands had left a handsome fund in the treasury after the payment of debts and the support of the poor. The records do not show any important service of this new Board until the near approach of the March election. Then a radical political measure worthy of a later period, was decided upon under the guise of religious fervor. Various sums of money were voted to the three Dutch churches, the parent church in Kingston, and the churches at Brabant and Klyne Esopus. But, as so often happens in these modern times, the trustees were defeated, and the new Board found a depleted treasury.

KINGSTON VILLAGE.

Kingston was duly incorporated as a village April 6, 1805. John Van Steenbergh, James S. Bruyn, Tobias Van Buren, Philip Van Keuren, and Barent Gardinier, were chosen Directors, and Tobias Van Buren became the first president of the village. Matters were amicably adjusted between the new village and the old corporation trustees. A new fire-engine was purchased, and many additional precautions against fire were adopted and enforced; as the place had been visited with a most disastrous fire in that year. On or about that time there was an outbreak of malarial fever with typhoid features, in the new village, and it prevailed for some years afterward. The trouble was finally attributed to the old Bogardus Mill-pond west of Green St. This was condemned and drained in 1806. Mr. Bogardus demanded damages because the pond had supplied the mill with power for over 100 years and he received $500 in settlement.

In 1811 the town of Kingston was divided by setting off the present town of Saugerties on the north, and Esopus on the south. The trustees of the old corporation however rebelled and refused to make the proper transfer on the ground that the act was unconstitutional. They were indicted by the Grand Jury and brought to trial, and the case went to the higher court. The people stood by the trustees and reëlected them annu-

The De Wall Tavern.

ally until 1815. But they finally lost, and were supplanted by a new Board in March, 1816, and the old corporate existence of 130 years was permanently dissolved. Concerning these old trustees it was said they were always chosen from the leading citizens of the town, and always labored for the triumph of right and justice. The same careful writer adds: "Such an incorporation as that would be out of place now." A new Court House and a fire-proof County Clerk's office was built in 1818, the lines of the old structure being preserved as far as possible.

The capture of Washington in 1814 caused great alarm throughout the land, and every citizen of Kingston liable to military duty, went forth in defense of his country. But all returned unharmed three months later, and on the seventeenth of the following February, the old village was publicly illuminated in token of the joy over the return of the blessings of peace.

With the return of business prosperity the Kingston people began to build new and better houses and to improve the old ones. Instead of a bridge across the Esopus creek, as now, there was only a fording-place previous to 1790. The second bridge there was carried away by a freshet in March, 1818.

FIRST ROAD-BUILDING.

The business people of the town soon saw the need of a roadway or thoroughfare, to reach the trade of the interior toward Delaware county, the west and north. This led to the building of the Ulster & Delaware Plank Road which was originally designed to extend into Chenango county, 104 miles distant. Much of this road was finally built at an average cost of $1,000 per mile. But the company became overwhelmed in debt from which it never emerged. The income from the tollgates was totally inadequate, and the road was sold and divided into districts. But the interior trade was secured. Meanwhile several other road projects had been started with little success. Among these was the "Neversink Turnpike Road," leading from Kingston to the Delaware river at Cochecton. Lucas Elmendorf, a prominent and wealthy citizen, was the controlling spirit in this enterprise, and he pushed the road to partial completion. Hence the name given to Lucas Avenue. He is said to have spent $40,000 in the enterprise and lost it all. It therefore appears that the matter of road-building received some attention in this old town nearly a hundred years ago, crude and faulty as these early efforts and methods would be regarded now.

In addition to the old King's Highway, leading from Albany to New York on the east side of the Hudson, there was communication with these cities by water in sloops in those early days, and later in steamboats.

SPEED OF OLD AND MODERN STEAMBOATS COMPARED.

Passengers were regularly carried in sailing vessels even down to 1820, and later. But the trip from Kingston to New York was a voyage of several days at best, depending upon wind and tide, and was not wholly unattended with danger at times. While the principal part of the sloop was devoted to freight, there was always a cabin fitted with ten or more berths for the accommodation of passengers, the crew using the forecastle for cooking and lodging. The custom was to arrange congenial parties for this New York trip, because of the time required. During adverse winds when no progress could be made, the vessel would anchor, and the passengers went ashore and had a good time. They could either bring their own provisions, or board with the Captain. Each had a big chest which was usually stocked with cooked food, and there was always an apartment at one end with well filled flasks of Holland Gin, a favorite beverage those days. As the commercial intercourse of Kingston increased, this sloop traffic finally grew into a weekly service by a regular packet line to New York. Soon after that, rival lines entered the field; one owned by Abraham Hasbrouck, the other by William Swart.

The first steamboat to enter the Rondout creek seems to have been the "New London," in 1826; and she came towing the hull of a vessel built for steam, to an anchorage. There had then been regular steamboat traffic on the river for some fifteen years or more. This competition between rival lines brought the fare down, lessened the time to New York, and at length displaced the sloop passenger traffic entirely.

The opening of the Delaware and Hudson Canal in 1829 brought a new era in this river traffic. More sloops were added to the four already plying to New York from Kingston. The steamer "Congress" began to carry passengers and freight between Twaalfskill (Wilbur) and New York in 1829, and she was doubtless the first passenger steamboat on this route. The next was the "Hudson," in 1831, and soon after that came the famous old "Norwich," which has been kept afloat ever since, and is to-day known as the "Ice King" of the Hudson, belonging to the Cornell Towing Line. The writer well recalls his first trip to New York on this historic boat, while she was serving as the "Palatial Passenger Steamer" between Kingston and New York. His uncle was the captain, and the lad was in charge of his grandfather. The "Norwich" was built in 1836, for passenger service between New York and Norwich, Conn. Being too small for the Sound service, she was sent here, where she has been nearly ever since, enjoying the distinction of being the oldest steamboat in the world now in service.

The normal speed of those steamers at that time was less than 8 miles an hour, and the schedule time between Kingston and New York was 12 hours. But this time was usually exceeded. There were few or no staterooms, and there was always a grand scramble for the best berths or bunks. Little was heard then of the grand scenic beauties of the Hudson, and its glorious Highlands. The old Dutch settlers were too much absorbed in the practical affairs of life to indulge in sentiment. These river trips were, therefore, made by night, and it was not until some years later that the day line was started.

FIRST KINGSTON DAY LINE.

In 1854 the "Alida," which had been running as an independent line three times a week from Wilbur, since November 4, 1853, began daily trips between Kingston and New York, April 18, 1854, leaving here at 6:15 A. M. and returning from New York at 4 P. M. "Through in Five Hours," was the slogan, and she continued these trips until the following October. Her first daily run was a great event for the people of Kingston, who could then leave home in the morning, transact their New York business, and get back at night. Strange to say this boat seems to have made nearly as good time on this route then as the famous "Mary Powell" makes now, with her improved model and modern machinery. But the project proved a failure financially, as it was ahead of time and not warranted by the traffic. The boat had been purchased from Abram Van Santvoord, who was then operating a day-line of steamers between Albany and New York. Marius Schoonmaker, William Masten and Nicholas Elmendorf, the owners, lost heavily in the venture. One reason given now by an old resident familiar with the project is, "there were too many captains." In July, 1860, the "Alida" ran from New York to Pokeepsie in 3 hours and 27 minutes, making five landings.

This Kingston daily service was resumed a few years later by the "Thomas Powell," which was replaced in 1862 by the "Mary Powell," the favorite Kingston day-boat ever since. She is to-day one of the most famous river steamboats in the world. Her lucky model made her without a rival for speed for many years, and her supremacy on the Hudson is rarely questioned. Her record time, New York to Rondout, including 8 landings, is 4 hours and 12 minutes. Almost during her entire career the "Powell" has been in command of a Captain Anderson. First it was Captain A. L. Anderson, son of Nathan Anderson, an old resident boatman, and afterward Captain A. E. Anderson, son of the former, who is still in command. She has traveled over a million miles, and carried about six million passengers.

Among other steamers running from this port at different times were the "Emerald," "Santa Claus," "Splendid," "Mohegan," "North America," "Rip Van Winkle," "Thomas Cornell," "City of Kingston," "James W. Baldwin" (now "Central Hudson"), and "William F. Romer."

In the olden time Columbus Point, now Kingston Point, was the river landing for Kingston and the surrounding country. Stage lines were run from the village to the Point; and for a time there was fierce opposition between rival lines, with dangerous racing and reckless forcing of machinery, which finally resulted in the burning of the "Henry Clay," July 28, 1852, with large loss of life, off Tarrytown, and other accidents. In the early days of steamboating, landings were made by small boats attached to long tow-lines, there being few docks. This took much time, was laborious and often dangerous.

SPEED OF OLD STEAMBOATS.

It is a remarkable fact that during the last fifty years so little progress should have been made toward increasing the speed of river steamboats. In view of the marvelous advance in nearly every other branch of mechanism, and especially in motor appliances upon land, including railways and motor cars of every description, little or no improvement has been made in the propulsion of vessels through the water. In 1841 the old "South America" ran from Albany to New York in 7 hours and 28 minutes, making 7 landings. In 1849 the "Alida" made 12 landings and covered

The Hasbrouck House.

the distance in 7 hours 45 minutes. In 1852 the "Francis Skiddy" made it in 7 hours 24 minutes with 6 landings. And in 1864 the "Daniel Drew" did the trick, with 9 landings in 6 hours 51 minutes. To-day the schedule time of the largest river steamboat in the world the "Hendrick Hudson" fresh from the modern marine ways, is 9 hours and 30 minutes, with 9 landings.

Of course, the enormous increase of traffic, which takes much more time at the landings, must be considered; also the unfairness of a comparison between record runs and schedule time. But allowing for all this, there is still a wide margin for the old-timers. Captain A. L. Anderson said nearly 25 years ago, "My experience teaches me, steamboats will not go much, if any faster, than they do as long as they are so heavily weighted with top-hamper. It is difficult to see how marine engines can be built better than they are now. If we increase the power, we must increase the weight of the engine; and to do that is to load the boat more heavily." Does it not seem that the famous old boatman was prophetic?

THE DELAWARE AND HUDSON CANAL.

A most important factor in the prosperity of Kingston was the construction of the Delaware and Hudson Canal, from Rondout to Honesdale, Pa. This project was begun in July, 1825, and the Canal was opened for use in October, 1828. Kingston at once became an important tide-water coal terminal, being a direct outlet for Pennsylvania coal. The distance was 107 miles, and there were 107 locks, the summit being 585 feet above tide. The Company was incorporated in 1823 with a capital of $1,500,000 and the right to use $50,000 in bank until 1844. The total cost of the canal was $2,037,117. The State loaned the company $800,000 in the beginning, which was repaid with interest. The capital was afterward increased and the canal enlarged.

A large increase in trade from the interior resulted, and the growth and commercial importance of Kingston were greatly enhanced; especially the lower end of the town, afterward known as Rondout. In fact, this part of the town on the creek owed its development almost entirely to the opening of the Canal and the rapidly increasing river traffic. James S. McEntee, a well-known resident for many years, and the father of Jervis McEntee, the artist, was the leading engineer in the construction of this Canal and the terminal docks at Rondout, and he became one of the most prominent and influential citizens. For many years the Canal was operated by John and Maurice Wurts. Enormous quantities of coal were brought here and reshipped to market.

In the construction of this Canal large deposits of natural cement rock were uncovered in the town of Rosendale, and when these quarries were opened, and the manufacture of cement began, there was a new traffic, for this end of the canal, and thus another impetus was imparted to the prosperity of Rondout and Kingston. Seven thousand tons of coal were brought to tidewater the first season, and six years later the amount had increased to 500,000 tons. The first boats used were small and carried only about 28 tons. One horse did the towing, and the round trip took ten days.

A lithographic sketch of Rondout in 1840 shows 9 storehouses, 42 dwellings and 24 vessels of different kinds in the creek. After 70 years of successful operation, this Canal was sold and abandoned. It had outlived its usefulness and been superseded by railways, which carried the coal cheaper. This abandonment of the Canal, however, was a sad blow to Kingston. But the large shipping interest was not wholly dependent upon this Canal traffic, and the harbor still bristled with masts and belching smokestacks. The freight and passenger traffic had begun soon after the opening of the nineteenth century, and increased steadily for over fifty years. It was then far in excess of any other intermediate point on the river, and perhaps greater than all other points combined. In addition to this vast freight business, there had grown up one of the most extensive steam-towing lines in the United States, known as the Cornell Steamboat Company. This was originally established by Thomas Cornell, a citizen of wealth and prominence, and since his death has been controlled and conducted by Samuel D. Coykendall, who is the President and owner. He is now widely credited with owning more steamboats than any other person in the United States, having in recent years purchased other lines on the Hudson. Over 60 steamers are operated and 400 men employed.

DEVELOPMENT OF KINGSTON AS A RAILWAY CENTER.

In 1865 and 1866 the railway fever struck Kingston. In the latter year it broke out on two sides of the town, and local capitalists were induced to start the projects. Both proved costly for the people of Kingston and the various towns through which the roads ran. But in the end all have been benefited beyond estimate.

The Rondout and Oswego, was the original title of the company, now known as the Ulster and Delaware Railroad. The purpose then was to build to Lake Ontario. It was afterward changed, on the reorganization of the company, to the New York, Kingston and Syracuse, and finally to the present title, in June, 1875, when the road came into the ownership of Thomas Cornell, and it is now in full operation from Kingston Point to Oneonta, 108 miles, and from Phoenicia to Hunter and Kaaterskill, 22 miles. The track is steel, standard gauge, and the equipment is of the most approved modern character. It has proved the great developing factor of the Catskills as a summer resort, and of incalculable value and importance to the people of Kingston, bringing a vast amount of trade and produce from the interior mountain region of Ulster and other counties. It has also added materially to the population of the town, and has of late become an important outlet for coal. The extensive railway shops in the lower part of the city are operated by electricity, and furnish employment to hundreds of men. Samuel D. Coykendall is president of this railway system, and the road is owned almost entirely by him. It carried nearly 500,000 passengers last year.

In 1866, the Wallkill Valley Railway was projected from Montgomery, Orange County to Kingston; first terminating at New Paltz, next at Rosendale, and finally reaching Kingston. It passed into the hands of Messrs. Cornell and Coykendall in June, 1877, and afterward became the property of the New York Central Railway Company, by whom the line is still operated.

ADVENT OF THE WEST SHORE RAILWAY.

The next railway line to enter the town was the West Shore Trunk Line. And the completion of this double track road to this city was an event of the highest importance to Kingston. The first passenger train left here for New York on the morning of June 25, 1883; and during that day the incoming trains were met by bands of music and the ringing of bells. A few weeks later the road was opened to Albany and Syracuse.

But there was still another railway project ripening for Kingston. The fertile valley of the Rondout Creek to Ellenville had only a feeble stage line, and the old Canal for its transportation facilities. Even before the abandonment of the Canal, many railway projects were proposed and discussed from time to time. Finally in 1902 the Ellenville and Kingston branch of the Ontario and Western Railway was built and opened for traffic. The first train left Kingston December 22, 1902.

STAGES AND STREET RAILWAYS.

Early in the last century a stage-line between Albany and New York on the west bank of the Hudson, and through Kingston, was established. Three trips a week were made during the winter season, continuing thus until December 20, 1814, after which four horses were attached to each stage and daily trips were made either way, except on Mondays. The changes were made at Goshen, New Paltz and Catskill. This method continued until 1820, prior to which the Kingston people had no daily stage for the Metropolis on the west side of the river, and during the close of navigation they had to get their mail by way of Rhinebeck.

In 1866 a horse railway was built from Rondout to Kingston, terminating near the Kingston bridge over the Esopus. Previous to that, stages were run at frequent intervals between the two ends of the town, and to Kingston Point, to meet the river steamers. The fare for this two-mile trip was 12½ cents, and there was a tollgate midway; there being a so-called plank-road from which the company sought profit.

STREET HORSE-CARS.

The advent of the horse-car was regarded as an improvement, although the track, rolling-stock and motive power were crude and inadequate, and the management seemed to deteriorate as time went on. The enterprise was unprofitable from start to finish, and everybody connected with it lost money. The first car was run in August, 1866. It was drawn by four horses and preceded by a band of music. The fare was ten cents. Even in 1879 when the road was felicitously known as "Winne's Rapid Transit Line," it took the best part of an hour to make the trip under the best conditions. The old cars seemed to have little affinity for the small rails, and they left the track several times most every trip. But, of course, there were few trains to catch then, and one could always get out and walk, when the mules gave out.

THE ELECTRIC TROLLEY SYSTEM.

After some 27 years of this method, a new track was built and the mules gave way to the electric trolley, introduced by the new owner, who,

The Hoffman House.

Southwest bastian of the old fortifications.

however, encountered much opposition from residents along the line, who feared the noise. Soon after that an opposition line was built on a somewhat different route, and this resulted in a maze of legal complications. Finally the first electric car was run July 31, 1893, and the fare was reduced to five cents. One line was known as the Kingston City and the other the Colonial. They were consolidated in January, 1902, and for the year ending June 30, 1906, 2,686,244 passengers were carried. Meanwhile, soon after electric power was adopted, Kingston Point was purchased by the new owner, Mr. Coykendall, who at once converted the property into a public park at large expense, erecting many buildings with modern park amusement features, fashioning lagoons and bridges, planting a variety of shrubbery, etc. Then the electric cars were taken there, and the place has now become one of the most attractive public parks on the Hudson, as well as a favorite summer resort for Kingston people. It is visited by nearly a million persons annually.

CIVIC DIVISIONS AND CHANGES.

After its incorporation as a village in 1805 and subsequent to 1816, Kingston continued to grow in progress and importance, keeping pace with other settlements in the State. In April, 1818, small change becoming scarce, nearly three thousand dollars in scrip was issued by which the village made $690, by unredeemed paper. The care of the old village clock caused some controversy between the trustees and the directors. It cost $20 a year, and a new eight-day clock was finally purchased in 1823 for $440. In 1819 the village bakers were required to make their loaves weigh 47 ounces each and sell them at 12½ cents. In May, 1830, grocery licenses were granted at $6 each to Sharpe & Voorhees, Jacob Burhans, Joseph S. Smith, Jacob K. Trumpbour, Eliphas Van Aken, Austin DuBois, Lewis Mason, Conrad Crook, Charles DuBois, John Hume, Hiram Radcliff, William Kerr, Peter Tappen, Jr., J. & J. Russell, O'Neil & O'Neil, and a few others. Tavern licenses were issued to John H. Rutzer, Hannah Radcliff, and what is now the Kingston Hotel.

The extension of Fair street was agitated in the fall of that year, but the plan was not carried out until some years later.

The opening of the Delaware and Hudson Canal in the previous year served to develop that end of the town rapidly, and there soon arose a spirit of rivalry between these people and the citizens of the village. This feeling increased as the years went by, and finally led to sectional factions that were difficult to harmonize. The general progress and development of the town was obstructed to some extent by this lack of unanimity. This at length culminated in another village on the creek, which had always been known as "The Strand."

INCORPORATION OF RONDOUT.

This was incorporated in May, 1849, under the name of Rondout, after the old "Ronduit" or "Redoubt," a fort, established there more than a century before, although its precise location cannot be determined now. At the first meeting of the Trustees on May 3, George F. Von Beck was chosen president, the other directors being Edmund Suydam, Terrence O'Reiley, William H. Bridger, and Michael Dougherty. Only 287 votes were cast at the first village election, but this increased to 1,365 at the last corporate election May 3, 1871. The following Presidents succeeded Von Beck: Hiram Roosa, 1850; Edmund Suydam, 1851; James G. Lindsley, 1852; George Thompson, 1853; Thomas Keys, 1854-55; Geo. F. Von Beck, 1856-58; Nathan Anderson, 1859-63; Lorenzo A. Sykes, 1864-66; James G. Lindsley, 1867-69; John Derrenbacher, 1870-71.

THE CITY OF KINGSTON.

In May, 1872, the villages of Kingston and Rondout were united and incorporated into the City of Kingston, the charter being dated May 29, 1872. The hamlet of Wilbur, formerly Twaalfskill, which had long been a bluestone shipping point, was now included. The first joint election took place April 16, 1872; 3,271 votes being cast for mayor. James G. Lindsley was the first citizen to be thus honored, and he was chosen from Rondout.

The city was divided into nine wards, each ward being represented in the Council by two Aldermen. This arrangement continued until the present year, 1906. The first ward, in the northern part of the city, embraced the old Wiltwyck or Stockade of Kingston in Colonial times. This includes all the County buildings and most of the old stone houses, and is the historic part of the town.

At that time the large shipping interests and the big cement manufacturing plant had built up Rondout until it had some ten thousand inhabitants, while Kingston contained somewhat less. Thus it was the Rondout people had already sought a city charter from the Legislature the previous year, and they wanted to call the city "Rondout." But this fired the more conservative descendants of the ancient burghers in Kingston with indignation and ardent zeal. They would not listen to any proposition that would wipe out the historic name of Kingston, and finally the better counsels prevailed.

The formation of the city left all the old territory of the town of Kingston outside of the villages, into a town by itself which still retained the old name. This remnant of the old town nearly encircled the new city, except on the southeast. Resolving not to be obscured by the importance of the city, it began to make history of its own in vigorous fashion at once. While yet with the two villages, the old town began to dominate the politics of the county, and controlled most of the offices; and some of the methods employed were of the most corrupt nature, belonging to the period of political graft when office holding first became a profession. Unprincipled bosses were in full control of the civic machinery of the county. A political ring had the taxpayers by the throat. The town elections were a farce and often attended by tragic features. When the city was organized, most of this ring-rule was transferred to the town, and there, under the fostering care of the old leaders, it flourished and grew more powerful and corrupt than ever, arousing the attention of the press all over the State, in denunciation and rebuke. The better citizens went to the polls and voted against the ring, almost in peril of their lives at times. But few of their votes were counted, and the returns were canvassed by ringleaders in a certain city livery-stable for a time. Matters finally culminated at the spring election of 1879, which was held just over the Kingston bridge in the classic precinct known as "Mutton Hollow." There was a riot, and many were assaulted, one man being nearly killed. This was the end, however. There was a prompt investigation by the Legislature, and the active leaders were brought to justice by a fearless District Attorney.

THE TOWN OF ULSTER.

Then in December 1879 the town remnant was again divided, a small part on the northwest being annexed to the town of Woodstock, and the larger portion, north of the Esopus creek, and between this stream and the Hudson, together with another small area on the southwest, being carved into a new town called "Ulster." This left the old town of Kingston with little beside the name. It was rough, rocky and unproductive, although having large deposits of bluestone. Its few remaining taxpayers were now too poor to interest politicians.

The new municipality began its career under better auspices than had prevailed in the old town. A spirit of economy and thrift succeeded, although the construction of the City Hall was soon projected, and the authorities insisted that it should be a structure of which the city might be proud for many years to come. There was much opposition to the erection of so large a building in advance of its need, because of the heavy cost. But the imposing structure was completed substantially as it now appears in 1875, upon a most commanding site in the center of the city, and there are to-day few who regret the outlay. All the various municipal offices are centered there and various public bodies hold frequent meetings in the building. It cost about $75,000, and some $20,000 more were spent in repairs and improvements upon it in 1896. For the first few years rooms were occupied by the Supreme Court there, in which the noted legal contest between the New York Elevated Railway Companies, in their early history, was heard by Justice T. R. Westbrook, in the fall of 1881.

A large city almshouse was erected in 1874, at a cost of $31,500. This is managed by a Board of Commissioners, seven in number, appointed by the Mayor. The last report shows that it cost $22,530.44 to maintain the city poor there in 1905.

In 1879 the State was induced to build a large Armory on Broadway, which was completed in the fall of 1880 at a cost of over $25,000. This has just been remodeled and improved this year at a large additional cost, and is now occupied by Company M, 1st Regiment, N. Y. N. G.

The telegraph was first brought to Kingston about 1852, and the first operator here was Jacob DuBois. The principal business for this new method of communication being at that time in Rondout. The people there made an effort to get another office more convenient for them, and for a time a loop was run there, as the line came down from Albany. But this company soon failed, and then some time afterward another company established an office with Winter Brothers in Rondout, who managed telegraphic affairs there for some years before coming to Kingston with an office.

The telephone was introduced in 1880, although a small local private

The Houghtaling House.

line had been in operation for some months before. There are now two companies, the Hudson River, and the Citizens' Standard, in full operation in the city, connecting with all distant points, having some 2,600 separate telephones. Many of these wires have been placed in modern underground conduits this year, and both companies have just completed large and costly exchange buildings fitted with every latest appliance.

THE KINGSTON WATER SUPPLY.

The water supply of Kingston is gathered and stored among the Catskills, near the base of Overlook Mountain, and is of the purest quality. It is led to the city by gravitation in a double line of main pipe about seventeen miles long, one being 18 and the other 20 inches in diameter.

For the first twelve years the city had no public water supply. Wells and cisterns were relied upon, as had been the case for over a century. There were a few fire-cisterns in the streets. The water-works system was introduced by a local company in 1884, and this plant was acquired by the city in March, 1896. It was then greatly enlarged and improved in every way, the city being bonded for $750,000 altogether. The new plant was completed in September, 1900. There are now forty-seven and one-half miles of street mains, and there is a storage supply of 305,000,000 gallons in three reservoirs. The mechanical filtration plant has a capacity of over 6,000,000 gallons daily, and the present average daily consumption of water is 5,000,000 gallons. It is delivered at a pressure of from 100 to 120 pounds to the square inch. The total cost of the water plant to date is not far from a million dollars.

Gas was first introduced in Kingston in 1854 by a local company, at Rondout. It is now supplied by the Kingston Gas and Electric Company, which has thirty-seven and one-half miles of street mains and about 200 miles of conducting wire. The average daily consumption of gas for lighting and fuel is about 160,000 cubic feet, and the electric energy supplied per month aggregates 63,215 kilowatt hours, or about 84,739 horse-power. Of this amount 22,677 kilowatt hours are used for commercial lighting, 33,040 kilowatt hours for public lamps, and 7,498 kilowatt hours for power purposes.

The city Police Department was established in May, 1891, and the original force, consisting of nineteen, two from each ward and the chief, has not been increased, although a Board of Police Commissioners of five members, with the Mayor as president, has been created. Stephen D. Hood has been the Chief of Police from the first.

Various amendments to the original city charter have been made from time to time, the most important of which was that passed by the last Legislature, providing for a redivision into thirteen wards, under which the municipality is now operating.

The Street Department is under the nominal control of the Street Superintendent, who is appointed by the Mayor. In 1873, $17,220 were spent upon the streets and roads of the city, $6,080 of this amount being for permanent improvements. During the past nine years this department cost $288,133.13. The year ending Nov. 30, 1905, the cost was $46,635.82. There are about seventy-two miles of streets, twenty-eight of which are macadam roadways, and about one mile of brick and asphalt pavement. The main thoroughfare, now known as Broadway, was formerly "Union Avenue."

The Health Department was organized in 1883, and consists of six commissioners presided over by the Mayor, with a Health Officer and a Sanitary Inspector. During the administration of Mayor Block, two women commissioners were appointed, but they have been succeeded by men.

The Fire Department is still a volunteer force, with fourteen hose, hook and ladder and truck companies, the present Chief being Rodney A. Chipp. There is also an electric fire alarm system, and the fire-fighting force and appliances are prompt and efficient.

There is a Plumbing Board with four members; four local Civil Service Commissioners, and six social clubs. The leading men's clubs being known as the Kingston and Rondout Clubs. Each of these have well equipped and finely furnished suites of rooms and large memberships. The Kingston Opera House and the Rondout Opera House are the only amusement halls of note, and these are supplied with dramatic entertainments most of the time during the season. There are some fourteen smaller assembly halls of various kinds.

Various musical societies have been organized, but most of them went down after a short career. The most important of these was the "Kingston Philharmonic Society," which had a most successful and artistic career lasting several years. It was organized in 1888 with Samuel D. Coykendall as president and financial sponsor. It was mainly devoted to the study of choral music of the better class, and some of the best conductors in the country were engaged. The active membership embraced all the leading vocal talent of the city, and the associate list included most of the prominent families. Some of the most celebrated vocalists and instrumentalists of the land, and large orchestras, were engaged for the concerts at large expense, and these concerts were notable affairs both in musical and society circles. But in 1895 the society suspended for lack of support. To-day the only musical society in the city is the Rondout Mannerchor, a German social and singing club of many years standing, save the Mendelssohn Club, a double male quartet, and the Kingston Band, under Geo. Muller.

There is a large Public Library, nearly opposite the City Hall, built in 1904, at a cost of $30,000, which was donated by Andrew Carnegie on condition that the city obligate itself to raise ten per cent. of this amount annually for the support of the library. This has been done, and there are now 4,930 volumes upon the shelves. These books are in active demand by all classes, and the library is much appreciated. The building is a fine structure of the most solid and substantial character, of which the city is justly proud. The Library Association was formed in June, 1899, and until the completion of the new building, a room in the City Hall was used.

One of the finest modern jails in the country was erected by Ulster County, in the rear of the Court House, in 1902, at a cost of over $75,000. The walls are of huge native limestone blocks, rock-finished; and the interior is of chilled steel, fitted with every modern sanitary appliance and convenience.

A large addition to the Court House, in the rear, was also built a few years previous. In this are the court room, supervisors' rooms and various public offices, which are handsomely fitted.

There are twenty-nine different fraternal society organizations in the city, representing some fifty-six branches or divisions, which hold regular meetings. Some of these lodge rooms, including the Masonic Lodges of Kingston and Rondout, and the Pythian Hall, are large and handsomely fitted.

KINGSTON BOARD OF TRADE.

This association of business men was established in 1886, Reuben Bernard being its first president. The organization has directed its attention more especially to the introduction of new manufacturing industries in the city, and in that way to build up the general business prosperity of the place and increase the population. These efforts brought some good results. In 1902 the board published an illustrated brochure which gave the first comprehensive summary of the attractions and advantages of Kingston ever issued. Complete statistics of all the manufacturing industries were presented for the first time. From this it appears that over $3,500,000 were then invested in the city industries, which produced an annual output valued at over $5,000,000. Four thousand eight hundred and seventy persons of both sexes were employed in this work, earning a weekly wage of over $37,000. Over thirty separate industries were enumerated, and some fifty different plants. The largest was the American Cigar Company, which started here in 1886. It is one of the largest cigar factories in the United States, employing some 1,800 persons, and turning out an annual product valued at nearly two million dollars, making 250,000 cigars a day. The Peckham Manufacturing Co., with a capital of $500,000 and a force of 250 men, made car-trucks and steam snow plows valued at over half a million dollars in 1901. This plant has now passed into other hands and is devoted to other interests. Over $250,000 is invested in the manufacture of builders' woodwork, with an annual output of over $300,000. Engines, boilers and machinery are made in a complete modern electric plant, to the value of $125,000 a year, employing nearly 300 men. One hundred thousand dollars worth of shirts are made by some 300 operators. Tinfoil and bottle caps, $125,000; ribbed underwear, $100,000; household furniture, $100,000; lager beer, $200,000; brushes, $100,000. And there are many smaller industries which cannot well be enumerated in detail here.

The United States Lace Curtain Mills operates a most extensive and interesting plant near the center of the city, which was started in 1903 by a New York company. The building cost nearly $100,000, and the machinery not far from $200,000. There are nine Jacquard looms, and some four tons of cotton thread are used weekly in about 35,000 yards ot lace. Only lace curtains are made, and some 125 persons are employed. The power is wholly electric.

Ship building is carried on in different boat yards along the creek, especially the building of large brick barges, small steam crafts, and general repairing, to an amount of nearly $100,000 annually, some fifty men being thus engaged.

The Old Academy.

THE CEMENT INDUSTRY.

The making of Rosendale cement began in Kingston in 1851, by the Newark Lime and Cement Company, with a large plant at Rondout. although the native rock had been quarried there for seven years before, and shipped to the company's mills in Newark, N. J. This brand of cement was afterwards used extensively in all important masonry, including the Croton aqueduct and all important government work. Some 1,200 barrels a day were turned out at these mills for several years, and a large force was employed. This factory was an important factor in the early development of Rondout. James G. Lindsley was in charge of the works here, and being a man of great force of character, he became influential in public affairs. This extensive plant has lain idle, however, for the past two years because of the decline in the use of natural cement, which has been largely supplanted by Portland cement, an artificial product. This company made over 245,584 barrels of this cement in 1886, when the total output in Ulster County was over 2,000,000 barrels. In 1887 this county product swelled to 2,300,000 barrels; and between 1856 and 1892 this annual county product increased from 510,000 to 2,833,107 barrels. The demand began to fall off in 1900, and now, with the rapid increase of concrete, the price has again risen.

The manufacture and shipping of bluestone is also an important Kingston industry, which, however, is treated at length on other pages of this work.

THE BRICK INDUSTRY.

Brick-making is a large and important industry on the city river front, in which nearly 1,000 men and boys are engaged at good wages during the season of navigation. Over $500,000 are invested in this business within the city limits, and the value of the annual output from these yards doubtless exceeds this amount; the price of brick for the past two years having been unusually high and the demand large. The clay of this section is found to be of the best quality for the production of a standard article. The sand is brought from other points along the river. These various yards in the city produced over fifty million bricks in 1895, and the present output is nearly seventy-five millions. This is about one-thirteenth of the total product in the United States in 1889.

The labor industry in the city has four trade organizations and some twenty-seven labor unions, which hold meetings at stated periods.

There are eight public cemeteries, Wiltwyck, Montrepose and St. Mary's being the largest. The former was established near the center of the city in July, 1850, and has been greatly enlarged and improved from time to time. Montrepose is in the Rondout section, and this has also been made most attractive in recent years.

POSTAL FACILITIES OF KINGSTON.

The history and development of postal affairs in any town is perhaps a fair general record of its progress. The marvelous growth and increase of the business of the Kingston post-office is shown by the comparative summary here presented. The office must have been established prior to the Revolution, but there is no authentic record of local postal affairs until some time after the formation of the Republic. On August 17, 1793, the following official postal notice appeared in the *Farmers' Register,* a Kingston newspaper of that period: "Those gentlemen who wish to have their letters forwarded by Post, are requested to send them to the Post Office at Kingston on Wednesday evening." Even as late as 1815, the list of uncalled for letters in the Kingston office included names of residents in the different towns in the county, indicating that it was then the only post-office in the county.

Postal facilities were of course crude and meager in those days. A newspaper known as the *Ulster Plebeian,* published in 1815, had great difficulty in delivering the paper to its subscribers in the outlying districts. For a time a special post-rider was employed, and it cost the publishers over a dollar a year for each subscriber, which was more than half the price of the subscription. Finally in 1817, a post route was established between Kingston and Milford, Pa., and on the 13th of November the first United States mail carrier left Kingston on horseback, making one trip a week. If comparison could be made of the receipts of the old Kingston post-office in those days with those of the present, it would be interesting; but unfortunately that old data has not been preserved, and the reader must be left to form his own estimate. In 1902 the receipts aggregated about $45,000, and nearly $200,000 in money orders, with 41,000 pieces of registered mail were handled. For the year 1905 this aggregate was increased to $50,560, and the money order business amounted to $280,878.43; 10,600 special delivery letters were handled; $14,850 in salaries were paid to the postmaster and his clerks; and the letter carriers and other free delivery incidentals, cost $14,567. The railway postal clerks and weighers upon the roads terminating here were paid $8,258. The rent of offices cost $1,600 and the surplus, of nearly $9,000, was turned in to the Government. Free city delivery began May 1, 1895, with eleven carriers, which has been increased to sixteen. Kingston became a first-class post-office July 1, 1901. The main office has been located in the Kingston Opera House building since 1869.

An appropriation of $110,000 has been made by Congress for a Public Building. Plans have been drawn for a new post-office, a site secured and the foundation completed at the junction of Prince street, Pine Grove avenue and Broadway, $25,000 having been thus expended. It is now said that the contracts for the superstructure will be given out early in 1907.

The Rondout post-office was established some time prior to 1830 and continued there until 1895, since which time it has been maintained as a station of the Kingston office. The Wilbur post-office, established about 1856, was also abolished in 1895. The following is a list of the Kingston postmasters and their terms of office, beginning with the existing records: Conradt Elmendorf, early in the century, succeeded after some years by William Cockburn, Jacob K. Trumpbour, 1829-39; Benjamin M. Hasbrouck, 1839-41; William Culley, 1841-45; Isaac Van Buren, 1845-48; Daniel Young, 1848-49; William H. Romeyn, 1849-53; William Kerr, 1853-61; Caleb S. Clay, 1861-69; Joseph S. Smith, 1869-73; Daniel Bradbury, 1873-82; William M. Hayes, 1882-86; W. S. Gillespie, 1886-90; Noah Wolven, 1890-94; H. G. Crouch, 1894-98; Geo. M. Brink, 1898-1902; Walter C. Dolson, 1902 to the present time.

The list of Rondout postmasters is as follows: Edmund Suydam, William Sims, John Hudler, John H. Stratton, Rensselaer Acley, William Winter, 1871-77; Andrew N. Barnes, 1877-84; Richard Mooney, 1884-98; David Gill, 1888-92; Henry Beck, 1892-95.

Wilbur postmasters: Thomas Booth, Henry H. Pitts, Michael A. Rush, Daniel Zoller.

The Young Men's Christian Association was organized in September, 1876, with thirty charter members. Andrew E. Schepmoes was the first president. A fine new building was erected at a cost of $46,000 in 1896. It includes a large public hall, a well fitted gymnasium, reading-room, parlors and other convenient rooms, and there is now a total membership of 500.

The Industrial Home, corner of Chester street and Highland avenue, for orphan and indigent children, was organized in 1876. It has been successfully managed by charitable ladies of the city. Over 700 needy children have been placed in good homes, and many others temporarily cared for. The present new building was built in 1903, at a cost of $17,000. Mrs. Mary I. Forsyth is now the president.

The Kingston City Hospital is a commodious and useful structure located near the City Hall. The association was formed in the spring of 1890, with John E. Kraft as president. Three years later the new building was erected by subscriptions, donations, and various public charitable entertainments; and to-day the hospital is one of the most beneficent and useful institutions in the city. The original cost of the building, site and fixtures, which are most complete in surgical appliances, was about $15,000. About five years ago Mr. Samuel D. Coykendall spent about $10,000 in repairs and improvements, and he is now building a new nurse's hall, which will cost some $10,000 more, making the present value of the plant about $35,000. The association, of which Rev. Dr. R. L. Burtsel is president, has now the following endowments: John Wesley Shaw, $5,000; Ira Davenport, $5,000; Katharine S. Davenport, $500; Rev. John B. Gleason, $500; Henrietta Wynkoop, $400; Margaret E. Hess, $500. The hospital receives an annual appropriation from the city of $4,500, and $2,000 from the county.

There are two sanitariums in the city. The Sahler Sanitarium was established about seven years ago on lower Wall street and was greatly enlarged this year. The total cost of the building to this date is not far from $50,000. The Benedictine Sanitarium, which partakes more of the character of a public hospital, is a most imposing brick structure standing upon a sightly bluff overlooking the city, west of Broadway, opposite the City Hall. It was erected a few years ago and cost about $50,000. Both these institutions are doing good work.

The Wiltwyck Chapter of the Daughters of the American Revolution was organized here in October, 1892, with fourteen charter members. Mrs. De Witt Roosa is the present Regent, and there are 150 members.

RANDOM NOTES.

The first doctor in Kingston, then known as Wiltwyck, was Gysbert Van Imborch, whom Governor Stuyvesant induced to settle here in 1662. Prior to that time the people trusted to the skill of the Reader, comforter

The Tappen House.

of the sick, and Chorister, Van der Sluys, the Indian medicine men, and to Mrs. Slecht, a midwife.

The first Government Light House at the mouth of Rondout Creek was built in 1837 by James S. McEntee. This structure was carried away by a freshet two years later and rebuilt. Mrs. Murdock has kept this light for nearly fifty years, since 1858.

At the opening of the eighteenth century, Kingston had less than 100 houses. Until 1822 there was only one piano in the place. Then another was brought in by a French lady. At that time the post-office was located on the corner of North Front and Fair streets. In 1798 the post-office seems to have been in an upper room on Green street.

The first brickyard was operated near the present site of the Kingston Bridge, where brick were made for home use.

The Eagle Hotel was built in the spring of 1835 by Thomas Clark. The house was burned in 1876, and rebuilt by B. J. Winne in 1877, who ran the hotel for some years, since which it has remained under the present Winne management. The old Ulster County House was among the earlier hotels in Kingston, and stood on Wall street, opposite the old Dutch Church. Solomon Brown, a famous hotel man of that period, kept this house from 1835 to 1847, and bought the present Kingston Hotel in 1853. The Schryver Hotel, at the head of Main street on Clinton avenue, was a prominent house long known as the "Temperance House."

The Mansion House in Rondout was opened in 1832 by James S. McEntee, and was the only hotel there for many years. The Kingston Hotel is probably the oldest in the city; part of the present structure went through the fire in 1777, as the charred beams show.

The first school house in Rondout was built upon a ledge of rocks at the foot of Wurts street in 1832, at a cost of $500.

A story is told of one of Molly Elmendorf's colored female servants who fled with her mistress to Hurley on the approach of the British. When told of the destruction of the Elmendorf mansion in the great fire, the old negress stoutly contradicted it, insisting that it could not be so, because she had the key of the house in her pocket.

In 1822 Fair street was known as "The Doverstraucha," and it extended only from North Front to John street. Wall street then ended at John street from the south, and did not extend to North Front as now.

James S. McEntee built what is known as the "Island Dock" in the upper creek, in 1846. He also built the old plank-road between Rondout, Wilbur and Kingston, which was found so difficult to get rid of after the city charter was obtained.

The name "Wiltwyck," which is now applied to a small region of Kingston east of Broadway, near the center of the city, was of course the old name for the stockaded part of Kingston in 1663. "Higginsville" was formerly applied to the lower end of North Front street near the Bogardus Mill of 1800, the Bridge, and the original Kingston Depot of the Ulster & Delaware Railway. The old tannery there, and the many stone teams from the Flagstone quarries made it a busy spot in former years.

Ponckhockie, an Indian name, was an early appellation applied to the northern part of Rondout, toward Kingston Point. It was somewhere in this section that the old Dutch fort is believed to have been built although the exact site of that historic redoubt cannot now be determined.

Rondout was visited by the cholera epidemic in 1832, and again in 1849. The first did not prove serious, but the last was fearful in loss of life, and was followed by great depression of business. The White Storehouse on the dock was turned into a hospital. It came again in 1852, but this visit had a beneficial effect on the health and cleanliness of the community. The streets and yards were cleaned up as never before. The yellow fever also broke out there in 1844, having been brought from the West Indies in a cargo of pineapples.

The Kingston and Rhinebeck ferry across the Hudson is operating under a very old franchise granted by Queen Anne. Originally the boat was run from Columbus Point, on this side, and was propelled by horse-power for a long series of years. About 1815, or thereabouts, steam power was introduced into the "Rhine," which is thought to have been the name of the ferryboat at that time. Then in 1852, after the opening of the railway, the ferry was brought into the Creek, where it has since remained. The old "Rhine" was succeeded by the "Lark," which in turn was followed by the "Transport," still in use.

The first local baggage express in Kingston was started by Winter Brothers in 1866, and has been operated by them ever since, although there are now many rival companies in the business.

No effort seems to have been made toward grading or regulating the Rondout streets until 1859. A stream of water was constantly pouring down Division street hill (now Broadway) from a spring at about the

The Wynkoop House.

present junction of Spring street. During the heavy rains this water would carry tons of sand down the steep hill to the Creek, often leaving thick deposits upon the store floors near Ferry street. About that time, however, this enthusiastic spring was taken in hand by a new board of trustees, and the water was deflected elsewhere. Then the grading of streets began, Ferry street receiving the first attack, closely followed by Hunter, Wurts, Hasbrouck avenue, Meadow and Abruyn streets. And all this was done without any expense for engineers.

The Twaalfskill Club has a fine golf course on Andrews street, near the center of the city, where a handsome and convenient club house has been erected. The membership includes many of the more prominent citizens of Kingston. Judge A. T. Clearwater is now the president.

A curfew law was adopted in Kingston in April, 1906, requiring all persons under sixteen years of age to be off the streets after 9 P. M. in summer, and 8 in the fall and winter. But so far there is no record of any attempt to enforce the ordinance, which would probably be somewhat difficult in view of its vague provisions.

FIRST STATE CENTENNIAL OBSERVATION AT KINGSTON.

The one hundredth anniversary of the inauguration of the State government at Kingston, was most appropriately commemorated July 30, 1877. It was a memorable event worthy of the occasion. The city was most elaborately decorated in every part, scarcely a house being omitted. The day fell on Monday, and it was very hot and threatening. But the town had been filling up with people all day Saturday and Sunday from all parts of the State. Guns boomed and bells were rung at midnight, both up and down town. Early in the morning the city became packed with people. At noon the great military procession, under Major General James W. Husted, the Grand Marshal, and his staff, formed on the Strand and moved up Union avenue toward Kingston, branching off toward the westerly side opposite the City Hall to the place prepared as the "Centennial Grounds," where the public exercises were held. Justice T. R. Westbrook delivered the address of welcome, and was followed by other formal addresses by Chauncey M. Depew, Gen. George H. Sharpe and others. These may be found in full in the "Centennial Volume," issued by the State in 1879. There were brilliant fireworks in the evening.

KINGSTON IN THE REBELLION.

While it is somewhat difficult to separate the town of Kingston from the balance of the county, in speaking of the services of her citizens in the Southern Rebellion, something should be said concerning the attitude of the people here during that conflict, and what they did.

It must be admitted that even in the face of the glorious record of patriotic valor which had been achieved by many of their ancestors in past centuries, these people now were not all in favor of this civil war to preserve the Union. Some were not even sure it was worth saving. Even some of the most prominent citizens, lawyers, politicians and business men were openly opposed to the plan of coercion adopted by the administration, and they labored against it. But happily, they were in the minority. It would be unkind to mention any of these names now in this connection. The term "copperhead," by which they were known, sounds harsh and uncharitable now. Many were doubtless sincere and honest in their opinions at that time, although it is safe to say nearly all of them lived long enough to see their mistake.

However, some of the best fighting regiments in the war went out from Kingston, and they made a record in the service of their country second to none in the entire Union army. The first rebel gun that belched forth on Fort Sumter brought a big mass meeting in the old Court House, at which John B. Steele presided. Patriotic speeches were made and measures were adopted to enlist men for the war. At the first call of President Lincoln for volunteers the old 20th Regiment, State Militia, the "Ulster Guards," under Col. Pratt, promptly responded, leaving Rondout April 28, 1861, 815 strong, for three months. Company B, Captain George H. Sharpe; Company C, Captain Tappen; Company F, Captain Flynn; Company G, Captain Hendricks, and Company H. Captain Derrenbacher, were composed mainly of Kingston men. The boys re-enlisted for three years, "or the war," and returned to the front for business of the most serious importance, Oct. 25, with 987 men. They were kept in the thickest of the fight and lost very heavily.

The 120th Regiment of Volunteers was then quickly organized by General George H. Sharpe, who was its Colonel, and mustered in Aug. 22, 1862. This included some of the best men of Kingston. The regiment was promptly ordered to the front, with little chance for drill, and after participating in many other important battles, finally covered itself with

The Van Steenburgh House.

glory at Gettysburg, losing 218 officers and men. The fine monument in the old Dutch Churchyard was erected by Gen. Sharpe some years ago, "to the undying renown of the rank and file" of that famous regiment, which has since been known as one of the "300 fighting regiments of the war."

The 156th Regiment of Volunteers was also organized in Kingston by Col. Erastus E. Cooke, and mustered in the service Nov. 17, 1862, doing valiant service on many a bloody field at great sacrifice of life.

General Sharpe became a member of Gen. Grant's staff, and had the honor of signing the paroles of Lee's shattered army at Appomattox; and other military officers from Kingston won much distinction.

THE HONORABLE CITIZENSHIP OF OLD KINGSTON.

The following graceful tribute to the memory of the ancient dwellers of Kingston, paid by General Sharpe in a most interesting and comprehensive address on the old homesteads of Kingston, delivered Dec. 20, 1875, seems a fitting paragraph with which to close this paper.

He said in his opening: "The old citizens inhabiting all these homesteads, were a prudent, economical, and frugal people, of strong religious principles, simple and unostentatious in their lives. They were farmers to a greater of less degree, each man having a portion of the lowlands, or the fields on the Arm Bouwery. By the side of every residence was a barn directly upon the street, and, as every householder kept cows, these were seen issuing forth in large numbers to the meadows in the morning, and their returning bells made the evening hour melodious. Beside the smaller shops or stores, many citizens were engaged in trade, purchasing cereals and other large products from the surrounding country and forwarding them in bulk to New York with the yield of their own broad acres."

CHAPTER XVI.

TOWN OF DENNING.

By Charles E. Foote.

THE town of Denning was formed from Shandaken by a division of the territory of the latter on March 6, 1849. Ten years afterward, the town of Hardenbergh was taken off, which left the boundaries about as follows: On the northeast by the town of Shandaken, on the southeast by the towns of Olive and Rochester, on the southwest by the town of Wawarsing and Sullivan County, and on the northeast by the town of Hardenbergh. It contains 64,050 acres of land.

What has been called a spur of the Catskill mountain range extends across the town from northeast to southwest, to an elevation of from 1,500 to 2,000 feet. Other authorities consider that it is no part of the true mountain range, but is more properly the "foothill" region, such as is found adjacent to the lower elevations of nearly every mountain system. Whichever it be, it is remarkably picturesque, with narrow valleys extending between high and steep hills in every conceivable direction, hills so steep at times as to be inaccessible, and in other rare instances sloping upward in gradually elevating contour until the verdure-clad top is reached.

Within the town of Denning is found the true watershed between the waters of the Hudson and those of the Delaware rivers. The Rondout Creek is in the eastern part, with its east and west branches, and the Neversink in the western portion with similar branches, and numerous brooks and rivulets almost interlacing, form in most absolute perfection the ideal watershed of two great systems. The Rondout Creek, its branches joining just inside the county line, flows southwesterly some miles into Sullivan County, as though bound to reach the Delaware. Suddenly turning to the southeast it flows across the town of Wawarsing until it reaches the foothills of the Shawangunk mountains, then with another abrupt turn to the left it flows northeasterly to the Hudson at Kingston; the Neversink, only a short distance to the west, joins its branches just outside the county, and, taking a southerly course, reaches the Delaware at Port Jervis.

In the northern part of the town, between the two branches of the Neversink, is the State Deer Park, a large tract of land the title to which has been reassumed by the State. It abounds in trout streams, which unlike other sections of the town, can be fished by all. Where the heads of the Neversink and Rondout Creeks are in the closest proximity, in the north part of the town, are the Hanover mountain, Lone mountain, Table mountain, 3,865 feet, and Mt. Peak o'Moose, 3,875 feet above tide, which are among the highest peaks in the town.

In the earlier years there were vast forests of hemlock on the sides and summits of the hills, which gave rise to the extensive saw-mill and tanning industries. With the exhaustion of the bark the tanneries have mostly closed or moved elsewhere, while the few saw-mills (five of them) still in operation, are using up the odds and ends of timber, or are getting out some special cuts from the second growth hardwood which abounds profusely.

In the summer the town of Denning is a paradise for those who love the wilds of Nature. There is plenty of small game in the hills and plenty of fish in the streams. There is not a railroad within the town limits; but there are numerous places where the world-weary pilgrim can get accommodations and live, during the heated season, close to nature, with all the really necessary accompaniments of civilization; or he may pitch his tent in a gully between the hills, and make himself as comfortable or uncomfortable as his tastes and means will permit.

There are many clubs of various kinds who own many miles of trout streams, which are held for the exclusive use of their members. These usually have a rustic club-house where their families and themselves may find shelter in bad weather. None of them, so far as the information at hand has demonstrated, are given to elaboration, though some very wealthy men are said to be among the members.

The town was named in honor of William H. Denning, who formerly owned a large portion of the land in the town. The earliest settlement, so far as known, was at Dewittville, about 1827, when a saw-mill was built there by Dewitt & Reynolds. It has been found that the settlements were usually made on the nearest arable land to the mills and tanneries, that the products of the soil should be grown on the spot. With the removal of the industries the farmers found other markets, and Denning, in its moderate way, remained prosperous and hardy.

Of the 64,000 and odd acres of land in the town, it is doubtful if more than ten per cent. is cultivated. It is possible, of course, that the steep side-hills may be put to use and made profitable, but it would hardly be in the raising of general farm products or in dairying. Goats or certain breeds of sheep might be grown to advantage, and there is a theory that for grape culture those side-hills cannot be excelled.

The settlements are all along the creek valleys. Anthony Schwab is said to have been the first settler. He located on Read Hill in 1841. John W. Smith, who had previously built a saw-mill, erected a tannery in 1849. Other early settlers were:

Hiram Depew,
Conrad Bevier,
Cornelius Drew,
Harvey W. Hoyt,
Michael Schwab,
John Scott,
Ezra S. Bliss,
Bradford D. Donaldson,
Abram Van Buskirk,
Herman Depew,
John DeWitt,
Abraham DeWitt,
James Johnson,
Albert Van Dover,
Nathan Kogone,
Joseph B. Anderson,
Charles Rhodes,
Jacob Rosekraus,
John W. Smith,
Cornelius Bevier,
Peter T. Bush,
Nathan Sheely,
Henry J. Whipple,
James Evans,
Baily Beers.

There are two churches in the town, one is a Methodist Episcopal, located in the Sundown valley, along the Rondout Creek. Services were begun there in 1856, and a church building costing $2,000 was erected in 1868. The first pastor was Rev. F. N. Andrews. The society was formally incorporated in 1878.

There being no railroad in the town, its sources of communication are by way of Claryville, just over the line in Sullivan County, at the junction of the two branches of the Neversink Creek; also by way of Big Indian, an Ulster & Delaware railway station in the town of Shandaken, a few miles to the north, and through the towns of Rochester and Wawarsing to what was formerly the Delaware and Hudson canal, now the Ellenville & Kingston Railway.

The productions of the town are ample for the support of the population. There is considerable poultry raised, and the making of maple sugar and syrup is given much attention in the early spring.

There were seventy-four men enlisted for the service in the Civil War from the town of Denning. They were in different regiments, but prob-

Conrad Hiltebrant.

ably a larger number were members of Co. E of the 120th, than of any other single organization.

There are ten schools in the town, located at the most accessible points along the valleys. Three of these are on the east branch of the Neversink Creek, one just inside the town line above Claryville, another just above Dewittville, and the third a short distance below the little hamlet of Denning near the center of the town. Another is in the Sundown valley and another at Red Hill. The others are scattered.

The civil organization of Denning was established at a town meeting held at the Red Hill school house, April 6, 1849, at which were elected the following officers for the newly created town:

Supervisor—Abraham DeWitt.

Town Clerk—John DeWitt.

Justices of the Peace—Herman Depew, Abrm. Vanbuskirk, Bradford D. Donaldson, Ezra S. Bliss.

Assessors—Jacobus Rosekraus, Harvey W. Hoyt, Cornelius Bevier.

Commissioner of Highways—Peter T. Bush, Nathan Sheely, Henry I. Whipple.

Overseers of the Poor—Abrm. Vanbuskirk, Stephen Peck.

Denning is the central village and post-office, and John W. Smith was the first postmaster.

Dewittville is in the valley below on the east branch of the Neversink, near Sullivan County. On the west branch is the most thickly settled region, known as the Satterlee section, and at the junction of the east branch and the Rondout Creek is the poetic locality known as "Sundown Valley."

Lumbering is the leading industry, although even in this roughest town in the county the farmer has managed to grow a few crops.

CHAPTER XVII.

TOWN OF ESOPUS.

By CHARLES E. FOOTE.

THE town of Esopus is located on the Hudson, immediately south of the city of Kingston. It presents peculiar physical features, having a high, mountainous ridge or backbone extending north and south through its center, which reaches a height of 1,000 to 1,600 feet in places. From this ridge eastward toward the Hudson the ground is rolling and undulating; toward the west it is broken and hilly, sloping and terracing down to the valley of the Wallkill and Rondout.

The boundaries are: On the north, the city of Kingston; on the east, the Hudson river; on the south, the towns of Lloyd and New Paltz; and on the west, the towns of Rosendale and Ulster, from both of which it is separated by the Wallkill and Rondout. It has an area of 19,898 acres.

The titles to the Esopus lands seem to descend from three old patents: the Kingston patent to trustees for the benefit of freeholders and inhabitants and superseding the Dutch grant, dated May 19, 1664; the New Paltz patent, made to Louis DuBois, and eleven others, dated May 28, 1677, and the Hurley grant, made by Governor Stuyvesant under the original Dutch regime, and later confirmed by the English authorities.

There are many records which give the names of most of the original settlers of what was known as the Kleine Esopus, or Little Esopus, in contradistinction from the larger tract to the north and west to which the name of Esopus seemed generic.

On February 13, 1688, the Trustees of Kingston granted to Claes Westphaelen and Abel Westphaelen a tract of land "lying and being upon Hudson's river to the northward of Kalikoon Hook, and so along said river to the bounds of Capt. John Sprague."

This description shows that Capt. John Sprague was already there.

Among the land papers on file at Albany, and dated June 12, 1685, is the "Description of a Survey of 2960 acres of land, lying upon Hudson's River, betwixt the Rondout Kill and the Kleine Esopus and known by the name of Hussey's Hill, including the Kleine Esopus ffly and sunken ffly at the mouth of Rondout Kill, with the two lakes, laid out for Ffrederick Hussey and others by Phillip Welles, Surveyor."

That portion of the original town of Hurley which was on the east side of the Wallkill, and the east side of the Rondout below the mouth of the Wallkill, is in the present town of Esopus. The road list for this section, dated March 28, 1781, gives the following names, which were probably all the male adults living there at that time:

Johannis Hardenbergh,	10 days	Ephraim Keyser,	1 days
Timothy Telsey,	3 "	Daniel York,	2 "
John Winfield,	6 "	Johannis York,	2 "
Benjamin Winfield,	2 "	Jonathan Hardenbergh,	2 "
Hendrick Smith,	7 "	Isaac Hardenbergh,	2 "
Jonathan Hutchinson,	3 "	David Turner,	2 "
Joseph Gee,	3 "	Jeronemus Burger,	1 "
Dirck Keyser,	1 "	Zacharias Sluyter,	6 "

In 1724 (March 25) Arien Gerretse acquired title to several tracts of land in this region. One was "on the southeast side of the Rondout Creek and both sides of the Paltz Creek (Wallkill), beginning on the south side of a certain creek commonly called Swarte-Kill, where the falls on the Paltz Creek, being the bounds of Coll. Jacob Rutsen; then along his line and said Swarte-Kill to the northernmost part thereof; and from thence east to the line of Kingston; then along said line of Kingston to the patented lands of the heirs of Jacob Aerste; then along said land to the patented lands of Mattys and Nicolas Blasyan, so as to run to the land of said Rutsen, and along the same to the first station; being bounded easterly, to the land of Kingston, southerly by said Coll. Jacob Rutsen, northwesterly by the lands of the said Mattys and Nicholas Blasyan, and the heirs of said Jacob Aertse."

There was also a deed to four acres on the south side of Swarte-Kill by the two falls, and privileges to build two dams there.

It is difficult to determine, except by reference to the other towns, and a comparison of the names with those of the residents after the town of Esopus was created, who the early families were, with some exceptions; even by this comparison the neighborhoods were in sufficiently close proximity so that the date of individual settlement in what is now Esopus cannot be determined. Certain family names of early settlers may be depended on as early settlers in this region.

Some old election returns are found, showing that Esopus cast votes in 1811: For Lieutenant Governor, Nicholas Fish, 109; DeWitt Clinton,

19; for State Senator, Elisha Williams, 109; Erastus Root, 20; William Saber, 20.

The Pound was near the house of William I. Houghtaling. It was established about 1812. At about the same period the town offered a bounty of $12.50 "for each wolf killed within the town of Esopus," and required that "the person killing the same must bring the head with the ears on, and make oath to the fact."

At the first town meeting in 1811 there were 155 votes cast. It was held at the house of William Ellsworth, and John J. Lefevre was elected Supervisor.

The house of William Ellsworth, where the first and some other town meetings were held, was a notable tavern of those days, and for many years before and afterward. It was located about two miles south of Port Ewen, and Widow Gitty Ellsworth secured a tavern license there as late as 1830.

The assessment roll of 1816 shows assessable property amounting to $87,200. Of these, twenty-six persons were rated $1,000 or over, amounting in total to $39,450. Three of the twenty-six went above the $2,000 mark—Jeremiah Houghtaling & Sons, $3,600; Elapahs Van Aken, $2,600, and Garret I. Freer, $2,200.

For a number of years the town meetings were held at the house of Tjerck F. Terpenning, which was a tavern south of Ulster Park, near the Reformed Church. The first meeting held there was in 1813—and that continued to be the place of election, probably without break, until 1833. In 1834 it was held at the tavern of Thomas M. Holt at Ulster Park. It was held there occasionally until 1840, after which it was the regular meeting place for many years and under the management of a variety of proprietors.

The Reformed Protestant Dutch Church of Kleine Esopus was organized in 1791. The Classis accepted the petition of ninety-three inhabitants, and the church was instituted by the Rev. Stephen Goetchius and a committee of the elders of the church of New Paltz. Two years later the body was incorporated. Until 1799 the church seems to have had no settled pastor, but was supplied by Rev. S. Goetchius of New Paltz, Rev. Mr. Doll, Rev. Mr. Van Horn and others. In 1799 Rev. T. G. Smith was called, and the church has had a regular pastor since that time. Rev. Mr. Smith continued to officiate for about ten years, and was

Charles C. Lang.

succeeded by Rev. J. R. H. Hasbrouck. The first church building was erected in 1792, and remained in use until 1827, when a fine church was erected which has attracted much attention on account of the beauty of its architecture.

The District school system provided for by the State legislature in 1812 was adopted by the town of Esopus at its town meeting in 1813. Previous to this time the records of educational affairs are extremely meagre, and there is practically nothing to show by what methods the youth of the previous century-and-a-half had received their education. But there must have been schools, as the inhabitants were educated people.

As Esopus did not exist as a town organization previous to 1811, it has no separate records of Revolutionary times. Those who fought in that war, and those who subscribed to the Articles of 1775, who were residents of the territory now comprising Esopus, will be found among the lists from Kingston, New Paltz and Hurley. Most of them may be traced by the names and location of the property as given in the records on file.

In the War of 1812 the following persons enlisted from Esopus:

Abraham Degraff,
John Deyo,
Tobias P. DuBois,
Isaac Houghtaling,
Samuel Ostrander,
Stephen Terwilliger,
John B. Van Aken,
Thomas Wells,
William Wise,
Henry Ellsworth,
Henry Degraff,
Purdy Dickinson,
Theophilus Ellsworth,
Henry Freer,
Samuel Lefevre,
John L. Plough,
Mahlon Thorp,
Charles B. Van Wagner,
John Winfield, Jr.

In the Civil War, Esopus furnished about four hundred and twenty-five volunteers, distributed through the various regiments, which were raised either partially or entirely in Ulster, though some were in other organizations. There were twenty-one enlistments in the Navy. The death list from Esopus was heavy and the examples of distinguished bravery numerous. Among the most distinguished of Esopus soldiers was Colonel Daniel Butterfield, who enlisted May 9, 1861, in the 9th regiment, was promoted to Brigadier-General, September 7, 1861, and to Major-General, November 29, 1862.

Other Reformed churches in the town are, one at Dashville Falls, incorporated in 1833, church built that year and remodeled in 1859; one at Port Ewen, incorporated in 1851, church built the following year;

another at St. Remy, organized in 1857, as a branch of the first Esopus Church. Among the Episcopal churches are the Ascension church, incorporated in 1842, and Grace church, in 1845. Among the Methodist churches are one in Port Ewen, organized in 1870, another, in another part of the town, organized in 1845. There is also a Catholic church, organized in 1875.

There are several pretty lakes in the town, one known as Esopus Lake, another as Mirror Lake, which furnish good fishing.

There were many old taverns or road houses, and among the older bonifaces there were Peter L. Hardenbergh, John Burger, Martinus Schryver, Caleb Merritt, Jacob Weist, William Wise, Gitty Ellsworth and Thomas M. Holt. Among the old merchants were Jonathan J. Lefevre, Israel Hammond, John H. Schryver, Cheney Ames and John P. Sleight. The first physicians were Dr. William Clarke, Dr. Hasbrouck, Dr. Thomas M. Holt and Dr. Morris Wurts. The early lawyers were William H. Irving, John F. Slater, John B. Livingston, Peter R. Decker, Jonathan Sluyter, Benjamin Neice and Marinus V. Wheeler.

Port Ewen, near the mouth of the Rondout, was founded in 1851 by the Pennsylvania Coal Company, which had a coal depot there until 1865 when they removed to Newburg, where they received their coal by the Erie Railway instead of the Delaware & Hudson Canal, as at Port Ewen. This is still a thriving village, with a charming location on the bank of the Hudson, 180 feet above the river. The view is fine, and there are many fine houses, a post-office, stores and shops, with churches and schools. The name was bestowed in honor of President John Ewen, of the Coal Company. South Rondout, further up the creek, is another lively hamlet with a brewery, boat yard, malt-house, ice-house, stores, etc. Sleightsberg is also a hamlet near the mouth of the creek with a boat building plant, stores, coal yard, ferry to Kingston, etc. Rifton Glen is a pretty manufacturing settlement on the Wallkill in the southwestern part of the town. It was formerly known as "Arnoldton," because of the cotton mill of B. J. Arnold & Co., built there in 1828. At present, and for many years past, the principal industry has been the extensive carpet factory and woolen mills of J. W. Dimmick & Co., which afford employment to many skilled operators. Ellmore's Corners is another old center of the town with a hotel and other buildings.

Ulster Park, formerly known as Amesville, has a post-office, hotel, stores and shops and a railway station near at hand. This is the center of the fertile fruit section where small and orchard fruits of all kinds are successfully and extensively grown for market. Peaches, raspberries, strawberries, grapes, cherries and pears are the leading fruits raised, and many large farms are devoted to them. The fruit industry is also successful in other parts of the Esopus township. The great Pell farm, on the bank of the river, just below, was a place of much note some years ago, which attracted many visitors. This place showed the peculiar adaptation of the Esopus soil and location for fruit-growing. Robert L. Pell was the owner and, being a man of wealth, intelligence and energy, he brought these 600 acres to a high state of cultivation, spending many thousands of dollars in the construction of artificial lakes, islands, underdrains and bridges, and planting large orchards. It was on this farm that the celebrated Newtown Pippin apple was raised to its greatest perfection, and marketed most sucessfully, both here and abroad. He had an orchard of many thousand trees which was cultivated with the greatest skill and care. He was the first man to market American apples in Europe for which he received fancy prices. In fact, it might be said that Mr. Pell created a market for American apples in foreign countries. But unfortunately his methods of careful selection and honest packing have not been faithfully followed in all cases since then, which has weakened the demand in those countries, lowered the prices for American fruit, and led to much distrust. The English people went wild over Pell's Newtown Pippin apples, and they have never got over the supreme quality of this fruit since then. The current prices for these Esopus apples in New York was then $8 a barrel and the choicest specimens were carefully packed, 100 in a box, and sold for $8 a box. All imperfect fruit was converted into cider. Mr. Pell also had a large vineyard of Isabella grapes, which he grew successfully. Since his death this farm has been neglected, although his fine mansion is still standing, and the large stone warehouse on the Pelham dock where his fruit was stored previous to shipment.

Just below this place is "Rosemount," the summer home of Alton B. Parker, which, with its owner, achieved so much prominence during the presidential campaign of 1904, when he became the Democratic candidate for President of the United States. The town of Esopus leaped into public notice that year with a single bound, and the place was visited by men of prominence and various public bodies from different parts of the country. A fine new railway station was built on the West Shore road at Esopus, and most of the fast trains were stopped there that summer. But the defeat of the Esopus farmer and ex-Judge, who had resigned the office of Chief Judge of the New York Court of Appeals to accept this hope of reaching the White House, left the old town in its customary placid condition.

The population of Esopus in 1905 was 4,786, 4,516 being citizens. Its area, as given last year was 22,247 acres, and the assessed valuation of taxable property amounted to $1,818,820.

James E. Phinney.

CHAPTER XVIII.

TOWN OF GARDINER.

By Charles E. Foote.

THE town of Gardiner is one of the interior towns of Ulster, south of the center of the county. It was created by taking that portion of the original Rochester patent which lies east of the Shawangunk territory, and was organized in 1853. It is bounded on the north by the towns of Rochester and New Paltz, on the east by the town of Plattekill, on the south by the town of Shawangunk, and on the west by the towns of Wawarsing and Rochester. It is hilly in the west along the foothills and slopes of the Shawangunk Mountains, and rolling in the central and eastern portions through which the Wallkill flows. The soil is productive and much attention is given to market gardening for city markets. Strawberries, especially, are produced in large quantities and of most excellent flavor. Much attention is also given to dairying.

The settlement of Gardiner took place previous to its formation and is treated in the historical sketches of the towns from which it was created. It was within this town that the Huguenots, who settled at New Paltz, and the Dutch of the town of Rochester, were brought into most intimate relations. It seems to have been this contact, and the intermarriages between the two races at an early day, which gradually caused the French language of the Wallkill valley to be supplanted by the Dutch. A large proportion of the present population count members of both nationalities among their ancestors, and the names of both are among the leading ones in the town.

Among the earlier settlers of this tract were G. Burnett, S. DuBois, H. L. DuBois, Lewis DuBois, M. Schoonmaker, J. Rutsen, Jacobus Bruyn, and T. Lord. Some of the land was held by speculators for a series of years. John Hoornbeck was an early settler, as were Benjamin and James Hoornbeck. All had families, most of whom intermarried with other families of the neighborhood.

Adjutant Abraham Schoonmaker, of Revolutionary fame (Fourth Regiment Ulster County Militia), was another of the early settlers. His father, Hendricus, owned a tract of about 2,000 acres in the southern portion of the town, all of which passed on the father's death to Isaac, the oldest son. He, however, at once transferred nine hundred acres to Abraham, who married Sarah Van Wyck, and raised eight sons. At his death the land was divided between them, and all except Albert remained permanent residents of the community.

Another of the first settlers was Matthew Sammons, who owned seven hundred acres, extending from Tuthill to Mark Kill, in which the present site of Tuthill was included. Gustavus, his oldest son, married Maria Terwilliger, and had three daughters and four sons, who married into the Schoonmaker, Hollister, Deyo, and other families, and left numerous descendants.

Sophrine Bruyn owned about two thousand acres and settled at an early date. He had three sons, Jacobus and Sophrine being two of them. Some authorities state that the name was "deBruyn," but a patent issued November 26, 1719, for two lots in Shawangunk, does not justify this claim. The State Index to land papers, records, under date of November 16, 1719, a "Petition of Jacobus Bruyn, praying for a patent for two certain parcels of land laid out for him in the woods upon and near the Shawangunk Creek, being a part of the land formerly granted to Capt. John Evans, since resumed to the Crown," etc.

On this tract Jacobus built a house in 1724, which was located on the west bank of the creek, and for many years was a famous landmark. It was destroyed by fire a few years ago. This property is now owned by U. S. Strait, and the balance of the original tract is in the hands of others, the Bruyn family being represented in the town by descendants of daughters who have intermarried here.

John J. Evans settled early in the vicinity of what is now Rutsenville. He had nineteen children, some of whom settled in Shawangunk, and some emigrated to the newly opened territory westward.

At and near Libertyville, there were located at an early date, the Merritt family, Charles, Jonas and Lewis DuBois. These families held tracts of land in the vicinity, much of which is still owned by their descendants.

In the neighborhood known as Kittleburgh, the LeFevres were the first settlers, and owned a large tract of land, which is still owned by their descendants, who form a large proportion of the residents of the locality.

Among others who settled in the immediate vicinity was one of the Deyo families, which is still there.

The Sammons family has been referred to as owning the original site of Tuthill. In addition, however, there were the Van Keuren family, who lived on the other side of the Wallkill, and Selah Tuthill, for whom the place was named, who bought a portion of Sammons's land.

A tract of seven or eight hundred acres was owned by General Joseph Hasbrouck, who lived in the central portion of the town, and Zachariah Hoffman's land extended from Hasbrouck's to the Shawangunk Kill.

The McKinstry family has been a prominent one in the town for many years, and still has numerous representatives there.

There was a log school-house at a very early day near Unionville, but there is only tradition as to its exact location or its preceptors. A man named Berry is said to have taught the grandfathers and great-grandfathers of the present generation, about the time of the war of 1812. There was a school at Tuthill at a later period. Isaac Schoonmaker was the first superintendent of common schools. He was appointed in 1843. Among the early teachers in the town appear the names of C. H. LeFever, Benjamin DeWitt, Isaac Scudder and James Johnston.

The oldest of the few villages or settlements in the town is Tuthill, at which was probably located the first post-office. Among those who held the office of postmaster seems to have been Mr. McCullough, Joseph O. Hasbrouck, James S. DuBois and Mathew LeFever. This post-office was discontinued a generation ago.

Gardiner is one of the newer villages and is located on the Wallkill in the northeast part of the town. Abraham Deyo was the first postmaster.

The Reformed Dutch Church was organized in 1833 with twenty-three members, who were previously members of the churches of Rochester, Shawangunk and New Paltz. The Roman Catholic Church has a congregation at Ireland Corners, a handsome edifice, sufficiently large for the needs of the community, which was erected a few years ago, together with a substantial rectory. The parish, under the present charge of Rev. William J. Stewart, appears to be in a flourishing condition.

The names of those serving in the war of the Revolution, who lived in the territory now covered by the town, cannot now be determined except in isolated cases. Among those known are Abraham Schoonmaker and

Peter Decker. Among those who served in the war of 1812 were the following, but there were probably many others:

Philip DuBois,	Robert Jordan.
Samuel Fowler,	Jacob Jansen,
Peter I. Crispell,	Aaron Halwick,

In the Civil War there were one hundred and thirty-six persons from the town of Gardiner, probably a majority of them belonging to the 156th Regiment, although the other Ulster County regiments had a fair representation, and several enlistments were made outside the county. There were a number of line and field officers among them.

In the early years there were a number of industrial enterprises in the various parts of the town. Among these were a grist mill and saw mill on the Wallkill at Libertyville, built by Charles DuBois at a very early date, and operated by various persons. The saw mill is now destroyed and the old grist mill is used by the Kays Brothers as a knife factory. A grist mill, saw mill and carding mill were built on the Shawangunk Creek by Selah Tuthill. These mills were operated by different parties, including a Mr. Harlow, Jacob I. Schoonmaker, Joseph O. Hasbrouck and Benjamin I. Freer. At present only the grist mill is left, which is operated by Ludwig Brandt. A tannery, established by Daniel McKinstry, an important industry in the hands of that family for many years, and the grist mill and saw mill of Joseph Stephens in the western part of the town, have been long out of business. The tannery was destroyed by fire. The mills at Galesville have also passed away. George Slaughter operates a creamery at Gardiner. There is also located at that point a factory for making Italian cheese, which is owned and operated by people of that nationality.

Among the early merchants in Gardiner were Selah Tuttle, Daniel S. Tuttle, Selah T. Jordan, Jacob S. Schoonmaker, John B. DuBois, Isaac Schoonmaker, James Jenkins, Luther LeFever, Erastus Mack and Mathew Sammons. John Young and Mr. McCullough were among the older tavern keepers. The earlier physicians were Dr. Daniel Deyo, Dr. Joseph Hasbrouck and Dr. Samuel J. Sears.

The Wallkill Valley Railway has stations at Gardiner and Forest Glen. The construction of this railway was a most important event of great advantage to the farmers and others of that region.

The first town meeting for the election of officers was held at the house

Anthony H. Lawatsch.

of Stephen Traphagen, May 17, 1853. Abner Hasbrouck was then chosen the first supervisor. Albert Decker is the present representative in the Board.

Abraham D. Bevier served in the State Assembly from Ulster County in 1843.

The leading industry has always been agriculture, and the soil responds well to good cultivation. Fruit is grown to a considerable extent and successfully.

The population of Gardiner in 1905 was 1,437, of which 1,414 were citizens. Three hundred and sixty-one persons voted at the general election last year.

The total acreage of the town as now estimated is 26,588. The value of taxable property in the town last year was placed at $668,951.

CHAPTER XIX.

TOWN OF HARDENBURGH.

By Howard Hendricks.

THIS interior town of Ulster presents some of the most rugged and austere natural features to be found in the county. None but the most experienced mountain farmer would be inclined to locate in Hardenburgh. There are more rock and stone than soil, and there is little reason to believe that Nature ever designed it for an agricultural paradise. Nor has it ever been among the suspected sites of the Garden of Eden. And yet the general topographical features are invested with peculiar charm. The towering mountain crags and scattered bits of valley, the wildwood and forests primeval, are dimpled over with beautiful lakes and thickly threaded with purling streams, which abound with trout. And there are wild and picturesque glens where the true artist may revel in his work without recourse to his imagination. There is grandeur in these vast mountain forests, and there is placid beauty in the lovely lakes. Rarely indeed is the contrasting landscape so happily posed as we find it in this wild mountain town.

The present area is placed at 53,647 acres. In 1905 these acres were valued at $90,104, or an average of $1.68 per acre. These people were assessed for only $600 personal property last year.

The town is bounded on the north by Delaware county and the town of Shandaken, on the east by Shandaken and Denning, on the south by Shandaken and Sullivan county, and on the west by Delaware county. It was formed from Denning and Shandaken in 1859, and named after Johannes Hardenburgh, who was the original patentee of a vast mountain tract which covered large parts of this and adjoining counties. The average elevation of the town is about 1,800 feet, and there are three lofty mountain peaks within its limits. These are Graham Mountain, 3,886 feet, Balsam Mountain, 3,601, and Eagle Mountain, 3,566 feet above tide. The principal streams flowing south and southwest, to the Delaware Valley, are the Beaverkill, Mill Brook and Dry Brook. All these afford excellent trout-fishing. Expert anglers are attracted here in large numbers and they are rewarded with fine sport. But large parts of the best streams are controlled by private fishing clubs.

The town was settled at the beginning of the nineteenth century, and even before this it is believed there were a few sturdy pioneers of the white race who were courageous enough to locate in these remote valleys. Samuel Merwin of Connecticut, was one of these early settlers, and he located in Dry Brook valley on the place afterward known as the Dyer-Todd farm. Derrick Haynes soon followed him there, and Hiram Seager came in about the same time, between 1800 and 1810. Next came Samuel Todd and his sons Lyman and Burr Todd, and other members of that family, which soon intermarried with the Seager family. Among other Dry Brook settlers in 1820 were Alfred Ackley, Oren Baker, Peter Hayes, Hezekiah Platt, Barney Rider, Harmon Utter, Robert Utter, Edward O'Neill and Thomas O'Kelly. The first settlers in Mill Brook valley included David Delemater, Samuel Gavitt and Blasel Gavitt. There was an old Quaker who located near Balsam Lake, on the upper Beaverkill, soon after the Revolution. The Messrs. John, Harry and Joseph Banks also located there a few years later, also Nicholas and John Barnhart.

Small specimens of coal and lead have been found near the sources of the Dry Brook and Mill Brook, and it is said the Indians used to carry out lead there during their occupancy of the region. But diligent search has thus far failed to reveal any deposit of either of these valuable minerals.

The first town meeting was held May 31, 1859, at the house of James Close, and Samuel M. Seager was then elected the first Supervisor. He served the town in that capacity also in 1860-68-72-79-81. Marcus A. Marks served in 1861-62 and 1880. Philo Flint, 1863-64; Hiram D. Cook, 1865-66-82-85-86; Amos Wamsley, 1867-69-71-73-74-77; James Murdock, 1878-83-84-87; Revilo H. Molyneaux, 1888; Robert S. Jones, 1889-93-96-99; Hiram D. Haynes, 1894-95; George F. Marks, 1900-01; Robert J. Hoag, 1902-3; Stratton D. Todd, 1904-05-06.

There are no incorporated villages in the town, but several small hamlets where post-offices have been established, as follows: Belleayre, Hardenburgh, Dry Brook, Seager and Turnwood. Dry Brook is the oldest of these, and it was formerly known as West Shandaken. There was a post-office there over sixty years ago, and the mail comes in by way of Arkville on the Ulster & Delaware Railway, which has long been the best point of egress to this mountain town. Previous to the construction of this railway the region was indeed much more remote and difficult to reach. This Dry Brook hamlet contains a Methodist church, a schoolhouse, blacksmith shop, store, and several dwellings. It is the site of the pioneer schoolhouse established probably 75 years ago. There are eight other school districts in the town, one in the upper Dry Brook region, another in Mill Brook valley, also at Turnwood, and on the upper Beaverkill, and one at Shin Creek.

Previous to the erection of the Dry Brook Methodist church in 1868, religious meetings were held in the schoolhouse by the Methodist people. Among the early preachers there were Daniel Morrison, Daniel Bullock, and John Beagle. They were assisted in the active Christian work by Burr Todd, Eber Merwin, Hiram Seager and Derrick Haynes. The first cost of this little Dry Brook church was $2,600, and there were fifteen members. Religious meetings were also held in some of the schoolhouses. After 1870 the Rev. James Beecher, brother of the noted Henry Ward Beecher, took up his residence on what was afterward known as Beecher's Pond, living at first in a tent. He afterwards built a neat and comfortable cottage there. Of this he said: "I have done all the work myself and there are associations connected with every clapboard and shingle even, that is laid." He seemed fascinated with the rare scenic charms of the place and said he could live there on $300 a year more comfortably and enjoyably than he could in New York on $3,000. Rev. Thomas Beecher, his brother, often spent the summer with him, and he was also visited by his distinguished sister, Harriet Beecher Stowe, and his brother Henry Ward Beecher. He usually preached in the old Shin Creek schoolhouse every Sunday, and the people traveled miles to hear him.

The principal pursuit in the town is lumbering, and there are many mills on the different streams. The Seager mill on Dry Brook was built about fifty years ago by Hiram Seager, and rebuilt in 1880. Further down this stream Hiram D. Cook built a sawmill in 1860. Soon after that the Todd mill was started further down. Then on the Beaverkill are other mills, including those of Jones, Wamsley, Jackson and Murdock.

The record shows that 36 of the Hardenburgh citizens served in the Union army in the Civil War, in which nearly one-third of this number lost their lives.

Daniel B. Stow.

Much might be said of the beautiful lakes in Hardenburgh. Furlough Lake, near the center of the town, is a circular sheet of mountain spring water that is much admired. It was formerly owned by Thomas Cornell of Kingston, who sold it to George J. Gould some years ago. Mr. Gould has built an elaborate summer home there, and he always spends a part of every summer there with his family. His property covers 3,258 mountain acres, only fifty of which have been cleared. Most of this primeval forest has been fenced in for an elk and deer park, and the enclosure contains one of the finest herds of these beautiful animals to be found in the country. Various other highly bred animals, such as rabbits, pheasants, ducks, geese, peacocks and other poultry are raised by experts there. He has also a fine stable of blooded horses, Jersey cattle, sheep and swine, and an extensive dovecote for pigeons. Mr. Gould's dog kennels contain some of the most valuable specimens of the canine species in the country, especially of the Russian wolf-hound. The Lodge building and residence is quaintly designed and partly rustic, with bark logs below and shingles on the upper story; with broad piazza all around. The inside finish and fittings are, however, quite elaborate. The barns and other buildings are also extensive and most elaborately fitted. The lake and stream for several miles, are well stocked with brook trout, but the fish are carefully guarded from poachers. This fine lake is an eight-mile drive from the railway station at Arkville.

Balsam Lake is another choice bit of mountain water some four or five miles south of Furlough Lake. But this is also practically private property, being controlled by a club of New York gentlemen for its fishing privilege. They have a commodious clubhouse, and their lease covers several miles of the Beaverkill stream.

The "Salmo Fontinalis" is another old club on the Beaverkill, composed of elderly New York bankers and business men of wealth and prominence. Their clubhouse is also quaint and attractive. The Beecher Pond, before alluded to, is a small secluded lake near the western town line, made famous by the Beecher family occupancy.

Alder Lake is a beautiful sheet of water near the Beecher Pond, and one of the largest in the county. Samuel D. Coykendall, of Kingston, is now the owner of this charming lake, which is most picturesquely surrounded by lofty mountain peaks.

CHAPTER XX.

TOWN OF HURLEY.

By Charles E. Foote.

THE title to the territory of the present town of Hurley is derived from the original treaty of the Dutch with the Indians, and the grants given to the settlers which were later confirmed by the English government, and a number of other grants made. Among the early grantees are the following:

1667—Philip Pieters Schuyler,
Matthew Blanchar, (probably Blansham),
Cornelius Wynkoop,
Roeloff Swartwout,
Jan Thommassen,
Peter Stuyvesant,
——— Crespel,
Louis DuBois,
Jan Valckert,
Goosen Gerritse,
Thomas Hall,
Nicholas Varlett & Co.,
Heynear Albertse Roose.
1685—Waldron Dumont.
1686—Henry Pawling,
John Jost.
1687—J. Cornelisen.
1693—Anthony Crispell.
1685—Wyrtje Allards Heymaus and her children.
1708—Cornelis Cool, Adrian Gerritse, Matthias Ten Eyck, Jacobus DuBois, Johannes Schepmoes, Roelof Swartwout, Cornelius Lamestre, Pieter Pisterre, Lawrence Osterhout, Jannittie Newkirk.

The original grants by the Dutch government were made in 1660-1664, so the earlier grants among those noted above seem to be simply a confirmation of title to the settlers and original grantees; the 1708 grant, to Cornelis Cool and others, appears to have been that large tract which was given to trustees for the benefit of the inhabitants, and which was divided and distributed one hundred years afterward.

Hurley is bounded on the north by Woodstock, on the east by Woodstock, Kingston and Ulster, on the southeast by Rosendale, on the southwest by Marbletown, and on the west by Olive. It is irregular in shape,

James Millard.

and has an area of approximately 18,175 acres. It is upland, ranging from undulating to moderately hilly. It is supposed to have been named in honor of the Barons Hurley of Ireland, of which family Governor Lovelace was a member.

The waters of the town are the Esopus, which crosses the southeastern part of the town on its northward course, and several small streams which enter it. In the northwest is the Beaver-Kill, formed by a number of small streams which flow through the town of Olive and into the Esopus on its southerly course. The Beaver-Kill is the outlet of Temple Pond, a beautiful sheet of water in the northwestern portion.

In its early settlement the region was known as Niew Dorp. It was made by the spreading out of the people from Kingston after the treaty of Peace with the Indians following the first Esopus war, to take advantage of the fine lands further to the west, and to secure larger areas for cultivation. The village thus formed, about 1661 or 1662, was about three miles west of Kingston. On June 7, 1663, while most of the men were at work in the fields, the village was attacked by the Indians and burned, only an unfurnished barn remaining. Members of every family are said to have been killed or taken prisoners. The list is as follows:

Killed:—Martin Harmensen, found dead and stripped, near his wagon.
Jocques Tysson, found dead near ruin of Barent's house.
Derrick Ariaensen, shot from his horse.
Prisoners:—Jan Gerritsen.
Wife and three children of Louis DuBois.
Two children of Matthew Blanshan.
A woman and two children from the family of Anthony Crispell.
A woman and two children from the family of Lambert Huybertoon.
A woman and four children from the family of Marten Harmenson.
A woman and two children from the family of Jan Joosten.
A woman and one child from the family of Barent Harmensen.
A woman and three children from the family of Grietie Westercamp.
A woman and one child from the family of Jan Barents.
Two children from the family of Michael Frere (probably Freer).
One child from the family of Hendrick Jochems.
One child from the family of Hendrick Martensen.
One child from the family of Albert Heymans.

Nearly all of the prisoners were finally recovered, though some of them were for several months in the hands of the Indians, and endured many hardships. It does not appear, however, that they were treated with cruelty, further than the nomadic habits of their captors made necessary. They were generally taken to camps and placed in the hands of squaws for safe keeping.

The people of Hurley resumed possession of their farms soon after this, and after the recapture of the prisoners, and the re-uniting of the families, the work of rebuilding the houses proceeded, and the crops were harvested. The large force of soldiers sent into the territory made work safe, and it is presumed that those settlers who were not with the militia, were pushing the work of restoration.

The early records of Hurley exist only in fragmentary form, and are not sufficiently complete to make a connected story. According to some of the old State documents, the population in 1703 was one hundred and seventy-four. From an old record it appears that the first trustees of the town or public lands, granted in 1708, were not appointed until 1719. The following appears:

"Whereas Colle Peter Schuyler, late president of the council of New York, by the letter pattents or a confirmation under the great seal of said province of New York, bearing date the 3d day of September 1719, did appoint Cornelis Kool, Arien Gerritse, Jacob DuBois, Barnardus Swartwout, Jacob Rutse, Nicholas Roosa and Charles Wyle to be the first trustees of Hurley and to continue to the first Tuesday of April, 1722."

The above record was evidently made as an explanation for the election of a trustee in 1720, which meeting is the first for the election of municipal officers of which there is any record. It is known, however, that as early as 1674 Louis DuBois was a magistrate in Hurley, but at that time the administration of Hurley may have been included in that of Kingston.

The Elmendorph or Van Elmendorph family was one of the early ones in Hurley. The original members of this family seem to have been Heermanse, Pieter and Jacobus, the first two came with their wives, and settled in Kingston about 1664, Jacobus married Griete Aertsen in 1677, and some of his children intermarried with the families of Hurley, and his son Conraed, settled there. The Koenraedt, Jr., named in the conveyance was a grandson of Jacobus Van Elmendorph and a son of the Hurley settler. He married Sarah DuBois, granddaughter of Louis DuBois, in 1736 and raised a large family, many of whom are still residents of the town.

There were ninety-four persons in Hurley to affix their signatures to the Articles of Association in 1775, previous to the opening of the War of the Revolution. Eight of those were said to belong to other towns, and were on duty in the town with the militia company to which they belonged. It has been stated that there was not a dissenter in the town.

When Kingston was burned in 1777 the State records were removed to Hurley and for a time it was the headquarters of the executive officers of the State. The Committee of Safety met there, and the Governor made it his headquarters, when not in the field. It was practically the capital of the State until they adjourned to Poughkeepsie, December 17, where the Legislature was called in session January 7, 1778. The spy, Taylor, who had convicted himself by demanding to be taken before "General Clinton," and finding him not the General Clinton he expected, was hanged at Hurley, October 18, two days after the burning of Kingston. The troops, who had so narrowly missed being able to protect Kingston, were present at the execution. The village was crowded to its utmost to accommodate the refugees from Kingston. The people rose to the occasion, however, and the very unusual sight was presented of a town of five or six hundred people sheltering and feeding the people of a destroyed town of seven times its size, besides providing for a State government.

An interesting communication, evidently a report, is found:

Hurleytown, Oct. 20, 1777.
Headquarters.

"A morning report of the officers of the day, who visited the guards and pickets.

"Col. Webb's pickets, Col. DuBois and Col. Sutherland all sufficient.

"Col. Hasbrouck's and Ellison's deficient in Arms and Ammunition.

"By report of officer of the main guard, countersign "New York." The sentinels being frequently visited, found alert on their posts, and the guard consisting of"—(Here follows a tabulated statement of guards.)

"The number of prisoners confined in the main guard, 27 with the crimes given, and nine without crimes.

"Given under my hand

"John Hardenberg,
"Col."

"P.S.—The guard at Kingston deficient in Light Horse and guides."

So far as can be learned, Louis DuBois was the first merchant of Hurley, having been among the original settlers who pushed forward after the first Esopus War with the Indians. It was from here that he organized the New Paltz theory into a practical result, being said to have based the idea on a knowledge of the region of the Wallkill valley, gained while with the soldiers looking for and finally recapturing the prisoners of the second war, among them were his wife and children. At his death he left considerable property in Hurley, and many of his descendants still reside there. There seem to be about twenty or thirty of the early families whose names have followed through the entire history of the town from its earliest settlement to the present, and a glance at the old church records of Kingston and Hurley shows that they are so perplexingly intermarried, that only the professional genealogist can untangle the snarled threads of relationship. It is asserted that fully fifty per cent. of the modern population of the town of Hurley are related to each other in varying degrees of consanguinity—practically one large family.

A careful comparison of this list of seventy-five families, with all the names of residents obtainable, indicate that practically every family of any considerable standing held slaves at that period. Sometimes they were sold and purchased as is indicated by the following:

"The bearer, Sym, his wife, a young healthy wench, and a negro boy of about two years old, are for sale. The negro man has Permission to look a master for himself and his wife and child." The Terms of the Payment will be made easy to the Purchaser. Whoever is inclined to purchase is desired to apply to

"Coenradt Elmendorph.

"Hurley, March 12, 1785."

In this particular case the negroes were not sold, as is shown by some old papers given to his son Jonathan some years afterward for love and affection.

On the fourth of April, 1806, the General Assembly enacted a law providing for the distribution of the lands belonging to Hurley in common. The basis of the distribution was that every freeholder having an estate valued at three hundred dollars, and being resident of the town at the time of the enactment, should have one certain tract or lot of land and every resident freeholder with an estate valued at less than $300 was to have a proportionate share of one such tract. The lands were surveyed into 168 lots, or tracts, and the book of description and bounds is carefully preserved, as is also a map of the survey.

November 13, 1806, the commissioners who were to make the distribution, met at the house of Peter Elmendorf to make the necessary arrangements. It was finally decided to make the distribution by drawing. The commissioners were John S. Dewitt, Levi Jansen and Andrew Snyder. Levi Jansen was appointed to make the drawing, which was done the next day at the tavern of Gerret H. Newkirk, at Bloomingdale.

No record is found of the persons from Hurley who were in the War of 1812. There are various legends, and probably many of them are true, but the verification is lacking.

In the Civil War there were about one hundred and seventy-five volunteers from the town, according to the best available figures. They were distributed throughout the various regiments and took part in the heavy work of the Army of the Potomac. The record shows a number of promotions, and several instances of serious suffering and fatal results from imprisonment in southern military prisons.

In Hurley, as in other towns in Ulster County, the records of early schools seem to be missing, and the legendary information vague. In 1812 the district system was put into effect and the list of commissioners and inspectors to 1844 furnish the names of the same families as those previously given, as does also the list of town superintendents from that time to 1856. It is beyond question, however, that there must have been good schools from a very early day, as there are a sufficient number of ancient autographic documents extant to show that practically the whole population were educated. Probably many attended school at Kingston.

The population of the town in 1905, according to the State census report of that year, was 1,677. This was a decrease of 844 since 1880, and 1,337 since 1875. If this count was accurately made, it seems difficult to account for this loss during the last thirty years; although the decline in the bluestone industry in the northern part of the town, known as West Hurley, during that period will account for some of it.

This ancient historic hamlet, known in modern times as "Old Hurley," which in the early history of the State was for at least one month virtually the Capital of the State, has changed little in outward appearance since that time. Most of the quaint old stone houses, some of which were built in the last half of the seventeenth century, are there today in a good state of preservation and with little change in their form or size. Many visitors are attracted by these sentinels of the past.

CHAPTER XXI.

TOWN OF LLOYD.

By John H. Coe.

THE town of Lloyd, as a separate municipality, dates from 1845, when the Legislature took territory from New Paltz and formed the new town. Previous to that the records of New Paltz covers its history.

The surface of the town is principally hilly upland, sloping to a bluff, which averages about two hundred feet in height, along the Hudson River. It is bounded on the north by the town of Esopus, on the east by the Hudson, on the south by Marlborough and Plattekill, and on the west by New Paltz. It has an area of 18,573 acres, exclusive of the public properties, highways, churches, school lands and grave-yards. West of the town flows the Swartekill, northward through the town of Esopus, emptying into the Wallkill a short distance above the junction of that stream with the Rondout.

Early school records are vague and scarce. It is stated that the early preachers on the Methodist circuit, which was established shortly after the close of the Revolution, taught the rudiments of education to the rising generation for four or five days of each month. Another statement is that Rev. James I. Ostrom, who organized the Presbyterian Church at Highland, came to that place as a teacher, after concluding his theological studies, and finally succeeded in establishing the church in 1808. These are not supported—neither are they denied—by any known records. It seems probable there were schools, and good ones, from the very earliest settlement. The intervening period, from the earliest occupation, to the maturity of those who studied under the public school system in later years, shows no great ignorance. There are practically no documents signed with "his mark." The development was along lines of educated intelligence, and there is every indication that the children of those days were taught in some way, whether at home, by their parents, or by regular masters, who could wield the rod.

The first record of value is dated in 1813. There seems to have been a

Harcourt J. Pratt.

school conducted by Quakers in the vicinity of Clintondale, but in which town as at present organized is not known. That year the town voted one hundred dollars to assist in supporting the school, which was attended by pupils from all the country around. There were also district schools at Highland and Riverside, the next district north of Highland.

Among the largest land owners in the town of Lloyd were the Hasbroucks and Eltings. Zachariah Hasbrouck (son of Daniel, grandson of Abraham of the patent) was born in 1749, and according to the division of the Paltz grant in 1774, was given one one-hundred-and-twentieth of the tract as his share. As the members of this family always had "good heads for business," it seems probable that this amount had been augmented by the purchase. He and his family lived in the southwestern part of the town and were classed among the wealthiest men of the region.

Noah Elting was a very early resident and a large land owner, rating, according to the best information, next to Zachariah Hasbrouck, among the largest holders of real property in this section. He owned most of the land where Highland village now stands. Abraham, his son, while a large property holder, gave most of his attention to matters of transportation, organizing freight lines into the interior settlements, of which New Paltz was the center, to carry in supplies and bring out the farm products intended for the market. The necessities of his own business forced him to establish a ferry between Highland and Poughkeepsie, which was operated first by oars and then by sail, afterward by horse-power and finally by steam. It was not long after the establishment of the ferry for his personal uses that the demand was sufficient to open it to general traffic for hire. The ferry at Poughkeepsie was known for many years, from one end of the river to the other, as a famous property, and its proprietor as one of those men whom it was a pleasure to know.

The Deyo family was among the most prominent. Henry Deyo, grandson of the New Paltz patentee, is supposed to have settled in Lloyd somewhere between 1755 and 1765. He had formerly lived in Shawangunk, where his eldest son, Hendricus, was baptized in 1754, while another son, Joseph, was baptized in Kingston in 1765. The elder Henry, or Hendricus, died December 12, 1804, aged seventy-four years, and is buried in the old Presbyterian cemetery, which is the oldest burial place in this section.

The son Hendricus married Phoebe Woolsey, and it is from them that the Deyo family of Lloyd descend. He long carried on a milling business at the Shadagee, but his residence was a stone house about two miles south of Highland, which is now owned by Nathan Williams. He left six sons and two daughters, all of whom left families, many of which left descendants who still reside here.

James Howell was here before the Revolution. He came from Long Island and is said to have lived in Marlborough and Plattekill before settling in Lloyd. Of his five sons and two daughters, two sons, John and James, remained in the town. The former was a ship carpenter, but subsequently abandoned it and settled on a farm. Hester Howell is the only representative of the family left in the town. The Halstead family settled at Centerville, as did Daniel Ostrom. At an early day the latter had a woolen mill just north of the hamlet. The VanWagoners and Saxtons were also prominent in that section.

Among the different families connected with the earliest history of the town, living on what is known as the Post Road, was David Woolsey, who owned the property now belonging to William Strothaff. Reuben H. Hinds lived on the same road. He was prominent in local affairs, later moved to New York. This property is now owned by the Irving Deyo estate. He was Supervisor from 1884 to 1889. William Coe, John H. Coe, and Abram Coe lived on farms bought by their father, Daniel Coe, who moved here from Rockland County in 1787, and settled on the bank of the Hudson. Wells Lake was prominent in local and State affairs. He was a Representative in Congress for three years, and State Senator four years, between 1820 and 1830, before Lloyd was set off from New Paltz. He was also Supervisor of the town for some time. William C. Perkins now resides on the farm. Philip Elting at one time owned nearly all the land on which Highland village is located.

Reuben Deyo, son of Sheriff Joseph Deyo, kept the tavern about a mile south of Highland, on the old Post Road from New York to Albany. For many years he kept the stage house, where horses were changed and refreshments served, continuing until the Hudson River Railroad was built. The old stone tavern still stands, and is in good condition.

In 1903 the old school house, in which our fathers and grandfathers were educated, was sold, a new site was bought on the New Paltz Turnpike, and a new brick edifice, costing fifteen thousand dollars, was erected, which is a credit to the town.

In the year 1891 the business part of the town of Highland was

Albert Reed, M.D.

destroyed by fire. It was a severe loss to the merchants and others, but the great energy of the people resulted in rehabilitating the burned district with larger, better, and more modern buildings, with improvements not thought of a generation or two ago. The people of Highland never fail to express their profound thankfulness and gratitude for the courtesies and substantial benefits which they received from the neighboring cities and villages at that time.

Dr. Barnabas Benton was an early physician. Dr. Hasbrouck began practice about 1825 and continued many years. Joseph Deyo was Sheriff of the county in 1821-1822; as was Silas Saxton in 1873.

Among the earlier members of the State Assembly from Ulster County were the following from the town of Lloyd: Wells Lake, 1820-22; Reuben H. Hine, 1844; Job G. Elmore, 1847; John B. Howell, 1853; A. E. Hasbrouck, 1867-68-69.

The County Clerks from Lloyd have been Silas Saxton, in 1858, and Nathan Williams in 1864.

The first merchants of Highland and vicinity were Abram Elting, Solomon Ferris, and John B. Caverly. Their stores were at the landing where all the business of the village was carried on. Others later were John Howell, Thomas Deyo, Absalom Barrett, George Rose, C. B. Harrison, DuBois & Bond, DuBois Brothers, etc. W. W. Mackey and Charles Letts have hotels at Lloyd.

About six years ago the First National Bank of Highland was organized with a capital stock of $25,000, most of the stock being taken by the people of the town. It seems to be doing a safe and profitable business under an efficient corps of officers. George W. Pratt is now the president. The first president, George W. Rose, died in 1903.

The trolley road from Highland Landing to New Paltz was built in 1897, along the line of the Highland and New Paltz turnpike. It has a heavy freight and passenger traffic, and has been the means of building up a large summer boarding business through that wondrously attractive region.

The milling business of Highland is done by Philip Schantz, with his brothers, Martin and Joseph, as assistants; L. Traphagen has what is known as the Blue Mill, in connection with his cider mill. Mr. Uhle also manufactures cider, and Abram Relyea, of Lloyd, buys large quantities of apples for the same purpose. Amos Weed is running what was formerly the Saxton grist and saw mill in Lloyd.

The berry and grape-crate manufacturing industry is large and important, and employs more help than any other industry in the town. The combined work of the four factories, Marenns Prester, James Wescott, George Pratt & Son, of Highland, and Abram Relyea, of Lloyd, resulted in the production and sale, in 1905, of the following goods:

12,542,000 pint and quart cups,
1,750,000 grape tills,
224,000 berry and grape crates,
50,000 peach baskets,
10,000 apple boxes and grape trays,
5,000 apple barrels.

The postmaster at Highland is Frank Simpson. There are four rural deliveries from this office, with daily service, each covering a distance of about twenty-two miles. The revenues of the office aggregated about $4,500 during the fiscal year ending June 30, 1906.

The shipping from Highland is heavy and represents the industry of the community. During the year 1905 there were shipments, by rail and water, aggregating 250,434 packages. It is estimated that the average bulk of the packages would be about a bushel each.

One of the most interesting cemeteries to be found anywhere, is the Old Lloyd burying-ground, or as it is perhaps better known, the old Methodist burial ground. There are a number of old stones with inscriptions which may be deciphered. Among them are the following:

"Samuel Duncombe, Esq., born August 26, 1779, died Feb. 5, 1827."
"Joseph Quick, died Dec. 11, 1868, aged 74 years, 4 months, 26 days."
"Henry A. Elting, died June 1, 1810, æ 48 years and 3 months."
"Rev. Stephen Jacob, died April 24, 1819."
"Michael Le Roy, February—1815, in his 70th year."
"Henry Deyo, died Dec. 12, 1805, Æ 74."
"Andrew Du Bois, died May 9, 1716, aged 62 years."
"Joseph Deyo, died Feb. 10, 1834, aged 59 years, 1 month and 10 days."
"Noah Elting, died April 6, 1813, Æ 49 years, 5 months and 4 days."
"John Le Fever, Sept. 10, 1836, aged 60 years."

On a monument in the new Highland cemetery are the names of thirty soldiers from the town who lost their lives during the Civil War. The monument is handsome and was erected by the Ladies' Monument Association of Highland. Lieutenant C. W. Ransom is also buried here. Lloyd furnished about one hundred and thirty men to that memorable struggle.

After the enactment of the law creating the town of Lloyd, a town meeting was held at the residence of Lyman Halsted on May 6, 1845, and the following officers were elected:

Supervisor, Reuben Deyo.

Town Clerk, Hasbrouck Le Fevre.

Superintendent of Schools, Aaron Tuthill.

Justices of the Peace: Silas Saxton, John B. Howell, John S. Deyo.

Assessors: John H. Coe, David S. Degarius, William J. Relyea.

Commissioners of Highways: Robert Woolsey, Alexander Hasbrouck, Robert E. Rose.

The present Supervisor of Lloyd is Philip Schantz, who also served in that capacity in 1898-1901-02-03. He was also elected Sheriff of Ulster County in 1894.

Previous to the construction of the West Shore Railway along the fine river front of this town, there were many handsome residences with attractive grounds on the bank of the river, owned and maintained in fine style by wealthy men of New York and other cities. But as the railway line begins to descend to the river shore soon after entering the town from the north, these fine country seats were broken up and destroyed by the grading and excavations for the tracks, and the operation of trains makes it undesirable for residence. Thus many of these large estates have been divided and sold for other purposes. Among other things, one or two large religious schools or convents have been built there. There are two railway stations on the West Shore in the town, one at Highland, another at West Park. One of the finest railway bridges in the world spans the Hudson from Highland to Poughkeepsie. This bridge was built several years ago and it is now being greatly strengthened at a very heavy cost, in anticipation of largely increased traffic in the immediate future.

An important annual event at this point in the river is the college boat races, which take place in the Hudson over a four-mile course every summer in June, and attract vast multitudes of people from all parts of the country. This is considered the finest rowing course in the land, and the races are keenly contested. The most favorable point to view the contest is from the Highland side of the Hudson.

The soil of this town is most favorable for fruit growing. It is well tilled and yields excellent crops of small fruits, peaches, etc. In 1875 the number of apple trees growing was placed at 18,1556; and these orchards then produced 46,116 barrels of apples and 495 barrels of cider. The grape yield was estimated at 295,315 pounds.

The population of the town in 1905 was 2,722, of which 2,606 were citizens. Last year the total assessments of taxable property in the town were $876,952. There were 638 citizens who voted at the election in 1905.

Clarence T. Frame.

CHAPTER XXII.

TOWN OF MARBLETOWN.

By C. T. Frame.

MARBLETOWN is in the central part of Ulster County. Bounded on the northeast by Hurley, southeast by Rosendale and New Paltz, southwest by Rochester, and northwest by Olive. The area of the town is 31,696 acres. Of this, 20,538 acres were improved and 9,262 acres unimproved or woodland in 1875.

The title is derived from the patent given by Queen Anne, Jan. 25, 1703. The town trustees under this patent adopted a seal, bearing the name "Marbletown" at the top, and at the sides the motto: "Be just to trust." The upper part of the central shield is occupied by two deer and the lower part by three sheaves of wheat, signifying the hunting grounds of the upland forests and the fertility of the lowlands. This seal is still in the Town Clerk's office. In an agreement between the Trustees of Rochester and Marbletown, dated 1768, January 3, in regard to the boundary lines, we find a statement of the original bounds as given to the following Town Trustees: "Granting unto Col. Henry Beekman, Capt. Thomas Garton and Capt. Charles Brodhead, their heirs and assigns forever, all that tract or parcel of land lying and being in the town of Ulster aforesaid and beginning at the bounds established and laid out by the Commissioners appointed by Col. Lovelace, Late Governor of the said

Province of New York, in the year of our Lord Christ 1669, between the said town of Marbletown and the town of Hurley, thence running southeast to the northwest bounds of the New Paltz, thence along the northwest bounds of the New Paltz to Capt. John Evans, his land, till opposite the southwest side of John Van Kamp's land; thence with a northwest line of the Great Mountain, commonly called the Blue Hills; thence northeast, something northerly, along the said hills as far as to run a southeast line to the place where first began, and then by said southeast line to the place where first began." A portion was taken from the above to form a part of the town of Olive in 1823, and another portion in 1844 to form part of Rosendale. Previous to those dates the records are found in the record of Marbletown.

Marbletown was settled in 1669, according to the following report: "The Commissioner, who had named the new village "Hurley," reported that he had assisted in forming another settlement beyond, which was Marbletown," which is now called North Marbletown, and was so named from the ridge of marble or lime-stone which extends across the town for a distance of eight miles.

The surface consists of the foothills of the Catskills and western slopes of the Shawangunk Mountains, broken by the valleys of the Rondout and Coxingkill at the base of the Shawangunk Mountains, and the valley of the Esopus coming down from the Catskills, which turns at a right angle near Stone Ridge and extends northeast toward Kingston. Standing on Sky Top, the highest point of land in the town, 1,500 feet above sea level, the eye scans the entire township spread out like a fan to the base of the Catskills, or "Great Blue Hills," as they were called in the earliest records. Here and there you see the silver sheen of the Rondout as it flows through a fertile valley dotted with many well-kept farms. Looking toward the northeast we see the cone-shaped Joppen Bergh, which was formerly a corner of Marbletown but now is in Rosendale; and in the distance a glimpse of the Hudson; while toward the north the ravine of the Esopus is seen, and toward the west rises High Point at an elevation of 3,098 feet.

The ridge between the Rondout and the Esopus forms a watershed upon which is located the village of Stone Ridge and the old King's Highway from Kingston to Ellenville, which was formerly an Indian trail to the Neversink valley.

The population, as given in State Documents for the year 1703, was 227, at which date, June 25, 1703, the patent was obtained from Queen Anne. Those who had already settled within the limits of Marbletown, as well as those afterward coming here, received from the town Trustees deeds. These are on record in the Town Clerk's office, except one volume, Book D, which is lost. The proceedings of the Town Trustees are also recorded, and the annual election of officers in an unbroken series for two hundred and three years in the most authentic and concise form. The following extracts taken from the first volume of town records are given. "Att a meeting of Trustees of Marbletown at said town this 23rd day of Sept., 1703, present Coll. Henry Beekman, Capt. Thomas Garton, Capt. Charles Brodhead, Trustees, and John Cock Sen. Esq. Richard Brodhead Assistants, and the major part of the freeholders and inhabitants of said town, it is ordered and established that no land be given out, but wood and stone shall be reserved free for the use of the town and freeholders and inhabitants thereof of any part of said land that shall not be fenced in, also sufficient ways over any of the said lands to be reserved, and if any take up land are to pay for lowland 12 pence, and upland six pence per acre." While the settlers were thus making rules to appropriate the lands, we find an Indian Chief of whom the Dutch purchased land lying in Marbletown, as the original deed now owned by Charles Hardenbergh shows, viz: The first deed recorded is to Gysbert Roosa for 73 acres in town parcels the greatest by a small run of water under the northeast side of a mountain called Jobsenbright (Joppenbergh) lying on the northwest side of Rosendale the smaller near Capt. Henry Pawling called Cocksink, Deed dated 1704.

The above Capt. Pawling was the first Sheriff of Ulster County, whose son, Capt. Levi Pawling, commanded the troops at the defense of Kingston, Oct. 16, 1776. Their names appear as residents of the town of Marbletown. Capt. Levi Pawling was an officer in the Old Marbletown Church, as was also Major Albert Pawling. Among the earlier settlers, according to researches made by the late Historian, J. W. Hasbrouck, were Christopher Bersford, Jan Joosten, Richard Cage, Jan Briggs, William Ashfordby, Frederick Hussey, Teunis Claes, Anthony Addison and George Hall.

For several years after settlement the growth of the town was slow, owing probably to the nearness of the Indians. We have no record of any fights between the Indians and settlers in this town, but the reason was perhaps that the Dutch secured deeds from the Indians. The settlers confined their attention to the lowlands along the Esopus and the sloping hills, toward what is now Stone Ridge, known at that time as the "Butterfields." These settlers were largely engaged in dairying, as the uplands furnished rich pasturage for their cattle, which roamed over the commons free. The Mormel, butter and cheese were exported.

At this time the settlers, who had planned their homes near one another found it more convenient to secure lands outside the village (Marbletown). We find that Anthony Addison and John Garton obtained permission to leave the village and settle on the other side of the Esopus at what is now called Lomontville, and that John Beatty moved to Stone Ridge and erected the first white man's dwelling-house.

About the same period Hendrick Cornelius Bogart purchased on the old creek near the mill of William Eltinge, just constructed at the picturesque falls, owned in later years by Cornelius Bogart, and known as Bogart's Glen. William Nottingham purchased near the mill of Charles Hardenbergh, a descendant in direct line. The grant of lands in Butterfield to Beatty and Ashfordy was followed by grants for portions of the same tract to George Hall, and Thomas and John Kerton.

The Documentary History for the year 1755 shows that, while the settlers were exporting butter, cheeese and wheat, they were importing slaves to do their work, whose descendants still live in the town.

The Marbletown Roll of Honor. The names of the signers of the Articles of Association. On Saturday, the 29th day of April, 1775, ten days after the battle of Lexington, "The Freemen, Freeholders and Inhabitants of the City and County of New York" adopted the bold and manly "Articles of Association" which was sent to all the Counties in the State for subscribers. When it reached Ulster County, many openly declared it treason, but a large number immediately signed it and offered their lives and fortunes in the defense of Liberty, though every town had its Tories and spies ever ready to help the enemy. Though a century has rolled by since those days, those Tories are despised to this day.

Levi Pawling, a resident of Marbletown, was County Judge of Ulster, elected Jan. 15, 1778. James Oliver, of Marbletown, was elected County Judge March 9, 1779. As early as Nov. 4. 1674, George Hall was appointed Sheriff of Ulster County, William Ashfordley, Oct. 1683, and Henry Pawling, October, 1685.

The patent for the territory of Marbletown was granted June 25, 1703. Trustees were at first appointed to have charge of the lands. They had authority to regulate public matters to the extent of protecting the settlers in the enjoyment of the titles granted to them for their land.

The commons land was disposed of by Act of Legislature passed in 1802. The commissioners in charge of the sale were John A. Dewitt and Jacob Chambers. William Nottingham was the first town clerk, and he was employed by Marbletown and Rochester. It is said he came from England with Col. Nicolls at the time of the surrender of New Netherlands to the British crown in 1664. The forms and wordings of the entries show that he had a great deal of ability, with an education far in advance of the other settlers.

A letter of Charles Dewitt, dated Hurley, August, 1763, is important:

DEAR SIR:

* * * * * * * * *

We have the greatest crops of wheat here that we have had for many years past and the most fruitful year that I can remember. * * * We manage in general as usual, only we have taken a particular turn this year to build schoolhouses; which at present are more plenty with us than schoolmasters. The upper end of Marbletown at Daniel Cantine's they have built one after the old fashion, viz., a large heap of white oak, black oak and perhaps other sorts of timber piled up to convenient height and two or three holes cut in for the children and light to pass. This building is not so magnificent as another built near Father Dewitt's, of stone, a shingle roof, two floors, but they tell me the upper floor is not planed very smooth, the joists ugly, etc.; however, two large sashes are made therein, besides another place where the master and his children pass and repass. * * *

MARBLETOWN THE CAPITAL OF THE STATE.

The organization of the State government had been commenced at Kingston by the inauguration of George Clinton as Governor, July 30, 1777. The first Legislature, with Col. Levi Pawling, of Marbletown, as one of the Senators, had met at Kingston, Sept. 9th, and remained in session until Oct. 7th, when they appointed a new Council of Safety and adjourned; the British having been successful at Fort Montgomery, and an invasion of Kingston being deemed probable. The Council of Safety were thus, *ad interim*, the real executive authority of the State, Governor Clinton being in the field with the Continental forces.

At the burning of Kingston the Council of Safety fled to Marbletown; and on the 19th of October, three days after the invasion, they commenced their sessions at the home of Andrew Oliver. They remained for one month, issuing orders and providing for all the exigencies of public affairs. On November 18th they removed to Hurley and met at the house of Captain Jan Van Deusen until December 17th, when it is reported that on account of cold and uncomfortable quarters they adjourned to Poughkeepsie. Marbletown was a village of forty-three houses at this time. Andrew Oliver came from Ireland and settled in Marbletown about 1740. His homestead is the present place of John Oliver a great-great grandson, and the house in which the Committee of Safety met stood between the present dwelling and the barns belonging to the farm. The house of Andrew Oliver was taken down some time after 1800, and the present spacious mansion erected, in which Dr. James Oliver had a medical school for a time.

On a map of the Oliver farm, drawn in 1795, in possession of John Oliver, there is a rough drawing of the old house where the Committee met. It was a large two-story stone building. In the front there were six upper and five lower windows with the door making an equal number; while beyond is the Old Dutch Reformed Church erected in 1774, and across the road is pictured the Davis tavern, of historic interest, as the place where the public business of the Marbletown patent was transacted, and the annual meetings of the inhabitants held for many years before the Revolution. The records show these meetings to have been "at the house of Janitze Davis," "the Widow Davis" and "at the house of Frederick Davis." These different references refer to the same house. It is still standing and evidently of great age. Its low doorways and general appearance point back to the days of the early settlement, as this was the center of the Marbletown of early colonial days.

In the old burial-place close by we find numerous head-stones bearing date 1692, 1693 and 1699, which indicates a large settlement. Beyond the town-gate, which was located at the junction of Ashokan and Neversink trails, the village was located in 1669.

The following is a list of a company under Capt. Daniel Brodhead. Compared with the list that went into the army during the Revolution and the Civil War, it will be seen that the same family name often occurs, showing that the heroic blood of their ancestors flows in the veins of the children, who are prepared at any time to defend with their lives the heritage their fathers gave them.

Muster-roll of a company of Militia of the town of Marbletown in the year 1738:

Capt. Daniel Brodhead, Lieut. John Dewitt, Ensign John Brodhead, Sergts. Martin Bogart, Jacobus Bush, Thomas Keator, Corporals Cornelius Van Campen, Christopher Davis, Jacob Keator, Peter Vanderbergh; Clerk, Richard Pick, Lambert Brink, Johannes Van Leuven, Andries Van Leuven, Frederick Davis, Gysbert Roosa, Jan Roosa, Jacob Keyser, Balentine Smith, Teunis Clearwater, Johannes Bush, James Robinson, Matthew Algar, James Algar, Hartman Hine, Arien Van Demark, Jacob Van Demark, Jacob Middagh, Jacobus Tack, Isaac Tack, Johannes Jansen, Dirck Bush, Melgart Keator, Henderick Roosa, Thomas Van Demark, Augustinus Keator, Hendrick Van Demark, Dirck Keyser, Samuel Davis, Samuel Cock, Benjamin Davis, Alexander Ennis, Andrew Kernitts, Isaac Van Kampen, Samuel Moorits, Johan Thomas, Moses Cantine, Nicholas Keyser, William Hine, John Wood, Johannes Eltinge, Anthony Gerrits, Cornelius Tack, Jr., Henry Jansen, Thomas Bush, Frederick Keator, Hendrick Bush, John Pierce, Lambert Bush, Moses Depuy, Johannes Van Demark, Thomas Van Demark, Jr., Nicholas Van Demark, Arie Keator, Thomas More.

Under the act of the Council of Safety, passed Nov. 11, 1777, at the house of Andrew Oliver, the export of flour, meal and grain to any part of the country in possession of the enemy was strictly forbidden. A license to make a single sale was necessary. David Bevier was a commissioner for this section, and several oaths on procuring such licenses are among the papers of his grandson, Louis Bevier. Leonard Hardenbergh had a license (Feb. 10, 1778), to export not more than four barrels of flour, on condition that he brought into this country an equal value of salt, either for the use of his family, or to retail to others. Others licensed were Johannes Roosa, Jacobus Morris, Daniel Johnson, Christopher Snyder, Roeloff Eltinge and Abraham Terpening.

At this date the inhabitants had increased in prosperity and wealth, also in deep religious beliefs. The total amount of tax collected in 1811 was $409.72. For the same area, nearly a century later, in 1907, it is $17,812.90.

The Marbletown Reformed Church is among the most ancient religious associations in the county, being probably second to the parent Dutch Church in Kingston, with which its early history seems closely interwoven. While the precise date of the organization is not definitely known, though stated in the "Manual" as 1737, the records show that as early as Sept. 27, 1677, a petition signed by the consistory of Kingston, Hurley and Marbletown, was sent to Lord Andross, Gov. General under James, Duke of York, reading as follows: "Inasmuch as we, in the three villages, are at present without a Pastor, and cannot be served by our neighbors, being so far from each other, we have by voluntary promises, secured 600 bushels of wheat, for which we would gladly call a Pastor, and in which may your Honor be pleased to be favorable to us in the calling of the same." This request was signed by Wessel TenBroeck, Jan Mattyssen, Dirck Schepmoes, Jan Hendrickse, Allardt, Heymanse Roosa, Roelof Hendrickse, Jan Jorsten and Wm. Jansen. It was promptly approved, and Dominie Laurentius Van Gaasbeck was sent over from Holland. While at Kingston he seems to have served the Marbletown people, and in 1679 he reported 20 mefbers there. There seem to have been meeting-houses in Hurley, Marbletown and other places in 1730, but all were appendages of the Kingston church at that time. A unity of feeling and general thirst for the gospel not easily understood in these days, is shown to have existed then, by the fact that three and four different congregations would call a single pastor and dwell together in harmony.

The first church building, 44 x 54, capable of seating 250, was completed in 1746 at a cost of £225. The pews were sold to cover this outlay, with the reservation of certain free pews for the Justices, Dominie's family, and the consistory. This list of original pewholders contains 132 names. In 1750 the churches of Marbletown, Rochester and Wawarsing combined, and continued thus unitl 1795. But they were unsuccessful in securing a permanent pastor for a time, owing perhaps to a somewhat unique system of mathematics which seems to have prevailed in the minds of the consistory which made out the calls. For it is said that a copy of one of these ancient documents now in possession of Mr. Louis Bevier, of this town, states that "Marbletown was to receive three-sixths of the pastor's services, Rochester three-sixths, and Wawarsing "one-seventh." A new church was erected on the present site in 1851.

The North Marbletown Reformed Church, an offshoot from the old church, now at Stone Ridge, was built in 1852, near the site of the original church in the burial-ground, about half way between Kingston and Rochester. The following is the early succession of pastors of the old church: Hendricus Frelinghuysen, 1754; Dirck Romeyn, 1764; J. R. Hardenbergh, 1781; Abr. Van Horne, 1789; Stephen Goetschius, 1796; John H. Carle, 1814; Christian E. Paulinson, 1826; Cornelius L. Van Dyke, 1829; J. L. McNair, 1854; William A. Shaw, 1859; J. L. McNair, 1860; Wm. W. Brush, 1868; Victor M. Hulbert, 1872; Bastion Smits, 1884; Wm. W. Schomp, 1885.

There are several other churches in the town, including Methodist churches at Stone Ridge, High Falls and Kripplebush, and an Episcopal church at Stone Ridge.

The fertile soil of Marbletown is especially adapted to farm cultivation, and it has often been called "the garden spot of Ulster County."

The first Supervisor of Marbletown was Moses Cantine, Jr., who served from 1808 to 1810. Louis Bevier, who is still living, served for eight years, beginning in 1874, and Dr. Herman Craft served nine years. The present Supervisor is Lemuel Bogart.

The rare scenic beauty spot of this old town is Lake Mohonk, a small part of which nestles in the triangular point on the southern border near the Rochester line. This of late years has become one of the most famous and favored summer resorts in the country. For romantic beauty and wild wood rocks it has no equal east of the Rocky Mountains. The place is also unique and notable because of the fact that it is one of the very few popular resorts in the land which has been operated strictly upon the temperance plan with high moral standards from the very start, and has proved a continued success in every way. The following paragraphs from a recent descriptive writer as to its scenic charms will be of interest:

To a lover of nature in its wildest, most romantic and picturesque phases, there are few localities on the American continent offering more attractions than Lake Mohonk and its immediate surroundings. In certain of its aspects the region has much to remind one of Switzerland, with its cliff-encircled glens, its high mountain reaches and wide-spreading vistas of hills and valleys. Situated on a plateau of the Shawangunk Mountains, thirteen hundred feet above the Hudson, the Lake Mohonk estate comprises an area about six miles in length by nearly a mile wide. Near one end lies the little lake from which the place takes its name, a body of water which the Indians called Moggunk (Sky Top), changed in later days to the more euphonious Mohonk. This lake, which is more like an enormous bowl of clear, cold water, carved out of the solid cliffs which rise sheer from its edge on every side save one, has a depth of from forty to eighty feet and a circumference of something over a mile. Towering above the lake on its eastern side, and three hundred feet above its surface, is Sky Top, the highest peak of the Shawangunk range. From this elevated point, which has been made accessible by a winding footpath up the cliff, and also by an easy carriage road, a panorama rolls out which is scarcely paralleled for magnificence in the world. Within the

REFORMED CHURCH OF MARBLETOWN.

(Built 1744-1746.)

vision are portions of six States—the hills of New Jersey and northern Pennsylvania, the Berkshire Hills of western Massachusetts and Connecticut, the Green Mountains of Vermont, and, in the foreground on the east, the Highlands skirting the Hudson River valley, and on the west and north the Catskills. In the nearer foreground on the east, and immediately below, at the foot of the mountain, lies the broad and fertile valley of the Wallkill with its orchards, cornfields, and wide-rolling meadows, and in the midst of these, the thrifty old town of New Paltz. Immediately below the mountain-crest on the west, stretches away the Rondout valley in an entrancing vision of rich farm lands, pretty villages and winding streams, with the classic country of Rip Van Winkle on the distant horizon. Truly, one must have less than the eye of an artist or the soul of a poet to look out over this encircling landscape of mountains, valleys and uplands, when mantled in the fresh greenery of early June, or when decked out in the glories of October, and not feel a thrill at the heart and the coming of thoughts too deep for words.

Stretching along the cliffs west of the lake opposite Sky Top, is the great hostelry with its battlements and towers, suggestive of some old castle on the Rhine, within whose spacious walls have been held for these twenty years and more the two conferences which have given the place world-wide fame.

While the utmost care has been taken to preserve and develop all the natural beauty of the Mohonk estate, the finest landscape art and a vast amount of money have been drawn upon to enhance its loveliness and make it accessible with ease and comfort to guests and tourists. To this end some fifty miles of macadamized roads have been constructed under the cliffs and around the mountains, while half as many miles of winding paths, carefully guarded at dangerous points, lead to the glens, the caves, the peaks, the ledges above the lake, and other places of interest. At frequent intervals along these roads and paths pretty little summer houses thatched with straw after the Swiss pattern, have been erected and provided with restful seats. Running out from the lake and the hotel at their northern extremity is an open space of fifteen acres converted from a rock-strewn forest plot into spacious lawns and gardens, wherein is a profusion of the rarest vines, shrubs and flowers.

The first humanitarian work to which Mohonk opened its doors was in behalf of the Indians. The first conference in their interest was held at the Lake in October, 1883, and has been held annually in that month ever since. Mr. Albert K. Smiley was prompted to this step by the fact that he had been a member of the Board of Indian Commissioners for some years previous and had become deeply concerned in the welfare of the aborigines. In 1904 this conference broadened its scope by taking under its consideration the native peoples of Porto Rico, Hawaii and the Philippines.

The establishment of the second conference, that in the interests of international arbitration, was in 1895. These conferences are usually held about the first of June, while the Indian conferences are held in October. To each of these conferences Mr. Smiley invites and entertains as his personal guests some three hundred men and women, carefully selected from among those who have special knowledge of the subjects to be considered, and the interest and influence to make their knowledge felt by the public at large and in places of power.

C. Meech Woolsey.

CHAPTER XXIII.

TOWN OF MARLBOROUGH.

By Hon. C. M. Woolsey.

IN this brief history no attempt is made to give all the events that have transpired in the town from its first settlement, but merely to record the earlier events, the trials and struggles, the habits and customs, of the sturdy, industrious people who settled here, and carved a home and name among these stony hills and valleys. They are worthy of all praise for what they accomplished, because several colonies at different times had previously examined and inspected these shores, and discouraged at their ruggedness and barren soil, settled in other places. These settlers had hardly completed comfortable houses and buildings, and cleared a small part of the land, when they were called upon to face a long and bitter war with a foreign nation, and many of their neighbors took sides in opposition. They had to endure great suffering and privation. But the earlier papers and records have disappeared, and little has been left to us. In this paper, family history is omitted. My great-great grand parents, Richard Woolsey and Sarah Fowler, were among the first settlers. They had twelve children, all of whom left families, and I cannot even give all the descendants correctly. It appears impossible to trace the bounds and locations of the various patents of land correctly except the Bond Patent, so they are simply referred to.

Some new information has been gathered, mostly documentary. I have personally examined the records and originals and consider them correct.

There was no civil organization of the lands now embraced in the Town of Marlborough, until the colony called the Palatines, settled where Newburgh now is, in 1709, when the Precinct of Highlands was formed and attached to New Paltz, all within the County of Ulster as it then existed.

Prior to 1697 "Dennis Relje," or, as he was afterward called, "Old Dennis" and "The Old Man," came here. He was the first settler and was probably put into possession by Capt. John Evans (of the Royal Navy), who had an immense tract of land along the river from Cornwall north, about eighteen miles, and extending back into the woods a long distance. This patent, granted to Evans in 1694, vacated and set aside in 1699, required that there should be an actual settlement within three years after the grant, and Relje was put on it for that purpose and settled on the Kill where Marlborough now is.

It was claimed by the people who petitioned to have the Evans patent annulled, that there was but one house upon the tract and that was where Cornwall now is. But Evans claimed that he had several settlers on the tract and had expended considerable sums of money on improvements. It appears by the petition of Egbert and Hendrick Schoonmaker that they asked for about 600 acres "on both sides the Oudtman's Kill or Creek." This petition was dated 1697, and the Kill was so named at that time, being the Kill running from Lattintown to Marlborough and the river.

This Kill was named after "Old Dennis," and has ever since gone by the name of "Old Man's Kill," or Creek.

The organization of the territory remained the same until 1743, when by Act of Assembly three full precincts were formed, having all the officers of towns and exercising all their duties. These were Wallkill, Shawangunk, and Highland. Highland embraced what is now Marlborough, Plattekill, Newburgh and New Windsor, covering the patents along Hudson River, from Murderer's Creek (Moodney Creek) to the line of New Paltz. It was bounded on the east by Hudson's river, on the south by the line dividing the counties of Ulster and Orange; on the west by the precincts of Wallkill and Shawangunk and the neighborhoods annexed to the New Paltz; and on the north by the bounds or line of New Paltz Town. "The precinct meetings were to be held at the house of John Humphrey, Jr., on the first Tuesday of April, annually," for the election of officers. This house was at Little Britain.

In 1743, by an Act of Assembly for the better clearing and further laying of public roads, Capt. Thomas Ellison, Capt. Alexander Coldon, and Zacharias Hoffman, Jr., were appointed Commissioners. The roads were to be four rods wide except through meadow and improved lands. Each Commissioner received a sum not to exceed six shillings a day for his care and trouble.

The Highlands precinct remained in existence until 1762, when it was divided into Newburgh and New Windsor "by a line beginning at the mouth of Quassaick Creek and running thence along the south bounds of a tract commonly called the "German patent," to another tract granted to Alexander Baird, and then along the southerly bounds of this tract to the Wallkill precinct; all the lands in Highland, lying southward of the dividing line to be called by the name of New Windsor, and all the lands within the said Highland precinct, lying to the northward to be called Newburgh.

The Act dividing Highland into Newburgh and New Windsor directed that the first precinct meeting for Newburgh should be held at the house of Capt. Jonathan Hasbrouck. This house is the present Washington Headquarters at Newburgh. At this time the population was about equally divided between the Newburgh precinct and the other two precincts. It all remained Ulster County until the Act of Assembly, April 5, 1798, when Newburgh and other towns were taken off.

These precincts did not take the names of towns until 1788. And in 1800 the Town of Plattekill was set off and Marlborough was left as it is to-day. When the Law of 1813 was enacted, dividing the counties into towns, the boundaries of Marlborough were stated as follows:—

"That part of the County of Ulster bounded easterly by the middle of Hudson's river, southerly by Orange County, westerly by a line beginning on the line of the said County of Orange, two chains and seventy-five links east of the north corner of a tract of land called the five patentees from thence on a straight line northward to the most easterly bounds of Robert Teft's land where it joins the Town of New Paltz, and northerly by a tract of land granted to Louis DuBois and his partners, called the New Paltz patent, shall be and continue a town by the name of Marlborough." The area is 14,300 acres.

EARLY PATENTS AND LAND GRANTS.

What is known as the Evans' tract, mentioned elsewhere, formerly embraced the whole territory of this town and much more. This was an immense tract, granted by Governor Fletcher, of this Colony, to Capt. John Evans.

There was a controversy during 1691, 1692, 1693, as to the right to make a grant so large. On the accession of the Earl of Bellomont to the governorship, he annulled the transaction, but his act was not approved by William III. The English government took up the matter in 1698, and the grant was annulled on May 12, 1699, the land reverting to the crown. After that date it became the policy of the government to make grants of land only to actual settlers, so far as possible.

Few of the old applicants for patents lived in Marlborough. Among them Capt. Bond was probably the first. He came with his daughter, Sukie or Susanna, and built a cabin in the vicinity of the Hicksite meeting house. He was Deputy Surveyor in 1717, and the legend is that he and his daughter were both buried near the site of the cabin. He had many slaves, and kept up style for those times. There were seven taxpayers in Marlborough in 1714 and 1715.

Francis Harrison was a resident in 1623. Part of the Harrison patent, 500 acres lying south of Marlborough, was purchased by Samuel and Isaac Fowler, in 1647. Francis Harrison paid taxes in 1726. The Bond patent near the center of the town is now a great fruit district.

Capt. William Bond was the first settler of that part of the town, now known as Milton, of whom there is any authentic record. He appears on the tax roll of 1714-15 as Capt. Bond, and on the succeeding tax rolls. His patent appears to have covered the present site of the railroad depot, the Milton dock property and the south part, if not all, of Milton Village

TOWN OF MARLBOROUGH IN THE REVOLUTION.

ELECTION OF DELEGATES TO THE PROVINCIAL CONVENTION.

At a meeting of the Committees of the several Towns and Precincts, in the County of Ulster, to appoint Deputies, to serve in the Provincial Convention, at the City of New York, on the 20th day of April, or at such other Time and Place as may be agreed on, held at New Paltz in the County aforesaid, the 7th day of April 1774. Col. Johannes Hardenburgh was chosen President, and Charles DeWitt, George Clinton and Levy Paulding, Esquires, were elected Deputies to serve in the Provincial Convention, for the purpose of choosing delegates, to represent this Colony in General Congress, to meet at the City of Philadelphia, on the 10th of May next; with full power to declare the sense of this county relative to the grievances under which His Majesty's American Subjects labor, and of the measures pursuing and to be pursued for obtaining Redress, and to Join with the Deputies for the other Counties and Cities, in this Colony at such Provincial Convention, in instruction to the delegates so as by them to be appointed, if they shall deem it necessary.

Ordered that the same be signed by the President.

JOHANNES HARDENBURGH.

ELECTION OF DEPUTIES TO THE PROVINCIAL CONGRESS FROM ULSTER COUNTY.

At a meeting of the Committee of the Several Towns and Precincts in the County of Ulster, held at New Paltz, at the house of Mrs. Ann DuBois in the County aforesaid, the 11th day of May 1775.

The following appeared for the different towns and precincts:

For New Marlborough.

Lewis DuBois

Benjamin Carpenter, Esq.

Joseph Morey.

Charles D. Witt, Esq., was chosen chairman. Col. Johannes Hardenburgh, Col. James Clinton, Egbert Dumond, Dr. Charles Clinton, Christopher Tappen, John Nicholson and Jacob Hornbeck, Esquires, were chosen Deputies for the said County, to serve in Provincial Convention at the City of New York, on the 22nd day of May.

On the 29th of May, the Provincial Congress directed the Committee holding the pledge to return the same before the 15th day of July, 1775, with the names of the signers and those who refused to sign, which was done. All who signed were avowed friends of the American Cause, whose efforts and influence the Patriot leaders could depend upon, while those who refused to sign were equally well known by all as the supporters of the king and ministry. In 1775 there were 270 in the male population of the town of sixteen years and upwards.

Lewis DuBois, born September 14, 1728, Captain 3rd N. Y., 28th of June, 1775; Major, 25th of November, 1775; Colonel, 21st of June, 1776; Colonel, 5th N. Y., 25th of November, 1776; to rank from 25th of June, 1776. Resigned 22nd of December, 1779. He served also as Colonel on N. Y. levies. He died December 29, 1802. Some years after, when his son's house was burned, all his commissions and valuable papers were lost.

It appears that Lewis DuBois, of the Precinct of New Marlborough, was a Captain and William Martin a Lieutenant in the 4th Regiment of the line in 1775, upon the Invasion of Canada.

On the 8th of January, 1776, the Continental Congress issued its first formal call for troops, for the purpose of reinforcing the Army in Canada. Under this call Ulster County furnished one Company, of which William Martin, of New Marlborough, was Captain.

Capt. Lewis DuBois was promoted to Major in Canada, and on February 28, 1776, James Clinton was Colonel and Lewis DuBois, Major of the 4th Regiment of the line while at the siege of Quebec.

Major or Colonel Lewis DuBois, who was a man of means and prominence here, had many recruits from the precinct, and some were killed in Canada, and at Forts Clinton and Montgomery. In October, 1777, the brunt of the battle here fell upon DuBois and his regiment, and many were killed.

By the town records of 1778, it appears that the precinct meeting "voted that the donations collected in this Precinct be applied to such poor, whose husbands or parents were either killed or taken prisoners at Fort Montgomery, etc."

A part of Colonel Cantine's Regiment, the 3rd of the line, were from this part of the country, but their names cannot be traced; and others from the town served in other regiments. William Woolsey was an Ensign in 1778 in Roswell Hopkin's Regiment of Dutchess County.

It appears that Col. Lewis DuBois and Capt. William Martin were the most prominent soldiers in the service from this town. They were both with the army upon the invasion of Canada and the siege of Quebec, and at other places where they took active part.

TORIES.

Josiah Lockwood was arrested for being unfriendly to the cause of Liberty and gave a bond for 300 pounds, dated March 7th, 1777, Uriah Drake as surety, to appear before a General Court Martial for trial.

There were several who opposed the colonies, some of whom returned after the war, and were left unmolested, though their names were long after used with contempt, and the rest took up their residence in Canada.

Samuel Devine, from the western part of the precinct, was very reckless in his conduct and conversation, and was arrested and tried twice for being a Tory. He was released on the first charge, but on the second he was court-martialed and sentenced to be hung, but was pardoned under the gallows by Governor Clinton.

A few Tories joined the English Army, and, after the war, settled in Canada, a bond was given by one who was suspected.

No part of the town was ever invaded by the enemy. When Brant and his Indians massacred the soldiers, who went out from Goshen to meet him at Minisink on the Delaware, there was another scare, but it soon subsided as Brant got no further. But our ancestors had their troubles; there was war and rumors of war all the time. They were taxed to the limit; their property pressed in the service; many of their men were in the service of the country, and much of their lands uncultivated. But they were true and loyal and their rejoicing was great, at the favorable termination of the war.

There appears to have been no large tribe of Indians about here, and no forts or camping places can be determined. The Esopus Indians, the

Charles Young.

Wappingers, the Mohawks and other tribes, sometimes passed through in small squads and camped about, as Indian clubs and arrow heads are often found. A gentleman at Milton has quite a collection of stone-clubs or pestels, which he has picked up on his farm; also a flint tomahawk and several arrow heads. They undoubtedly at one time had a small camp there, where they hunted and fished. But there is no tradition about the Indians here, except that there was a small trail through this town, from the back country to the river.

They must have been peaceable, at least, as there is no record they ever injured any person or destroyed any property.

In 1776 there were seventeen persons licensed to keep taverns in the town of Marlborough. The record for that year is given as follows:—

Peter Mackoon
Robert Gilmore
Cerstophel Deyo
Samuel Drake
Wright Carpenter
Isaac Bloomer
David Merritt
Benjamin Carpenter
John Benson
Thomas Mott
Edmund Turner, Jr.
Carlvian Lieger
Henry T. Bush, Jr.
Wheeler Case
Jacob Powell
Isaac Hill
Robert Simonds

An enumeration of the people of the town in 1782 gave the following results, not counting slaves or free persons of color:—

White Males under sixteen	491
" Males over sixteen and under sixty	335
" Males sixty and upwards	24
" Females under sixteen	402
" Females above sixteen	366
Total	1618

The water power of the various streams was utilized at an early date, while it cannot be known definitely, it is thought that the site of the Old DuBois Mill, near the Village of Marlborough, was one of the first, and probably the first to be erected. Sawmills and gristmills were erected by James Hallock, Foster Hallock, Auning Smith and others.

A carding-mill was erected in 1810-1811, and another shortly afterward. Most of the mills were on Jew's Creek, Old Man's Creek and Hallock's Creek, and the sawmills remained until the region tributary was practically denuded of timber. During the first half of the nineteenth century there were numerous manufacturing establishments built.

Most of the old settlers came from Long Island and Westchester County. They were people who were established in those places, having their farms and property there. Some came up in sloops, and others crossed in scows from the opposite side of the river. They brought their families, their cattle and horses, and their worldly goods with them, and when they arrived, they were all ready to erect their log or stone houses and commence clearing the land, and after the first arrivals their friends, who were already here, helped them. Perhaps no community started with better or more favorable prospects. They did not come destitute as a large body of foreigners have done, for in a short time they could change their original abode and start life anew, with all their household goods, properties, comforts and conveniences, that they had enjoyed in their previous homes.

Old letters, papers and records show this. In fact, the same names can be traced in the records and papers of Westchester and Long Island, and spelled the same as our people then spelled their names. These people visited together and kept up their relationship and friendship for a generation or more; and many of our people can trace their ancestors to these places. A few settlers drifted in until 1740, or thereabouts, when they commenced to arrive more frequently.

From that time on the population rapidly increased. In one year, twenty or more families arrived. In 1782, the population was 1482. In 1790, the enumeration of inhabitants, including Plattekill, colored people and slaves, was 2,241; Newburgh having only 2,365. And this population was supported by ordinary farm crops on stony land, which first had to be cleared. There was no fruit to sell them. The families were large, having from six to fifteen children. Edward Hallock, who landed his sloop and his family at what is known as Grandfather's Rock, at the river south of the Bond Patent, had ten girls and two boys.

These were an honest, industrious people, law abiding and God-fearing. No great crimes were committed. Churches and schools were plain but plenty; almost as many schools were supported then as now. A chattel mortgage was almost unknown. A person never borrowed money, except under necessity, and then paid it as soon as possible. Notes scarcely ever were taken. The borrower considered he was under a sacred obligation, and he often went without necessaries to make his payment.

Very few judgments were entered, but the execution went against the body and the debtor was put in jail, if he did not pay. But people were very lenient, and there was not much oppression. There were very few real estate mortgages on record before 1800. The debts must have been fixed up in some other way. Until the Constitution of 1777, the choice of candidates at the Precinct meetings was determined by viva voce vote.

The entire patent of land, formerly granted to Augustine Graham and Alexander Griggs, covers the railroad depot and docks, at the river and the entire village of Marlborough, and all the valuable farms and lands surrounding it; and this extensive and now valuable property, worth in the neighborhood of $2,000,000, was obtained by Lewis DuBois without the payment of a dollar. It seems that he was in possession, and living upon these lands, at the time that the deed was given in 1763, and the presumption is he had been there several years. He had undoubtedly obtained the Ida Hoffman or the Jury Quick title, for that one undivided one-half, and was living on the place under that title for years before he got the above mentioned deed; for at the time he was interested in various projects about the place and had agreed to give to the Marlborough Society two acres of land. On April 8th of the next year, he executed a deed for the land to John Woolsey and Stephen Case, first Trustees. He was the largest subscriber, giving 15 pounds on the first and 8 pounds on the last subscription list, so he must have been a man of means. He had previously, though the year cannot be fixed, erected a large house, substantially the same as it now stands, which was an expensive house then, and which is now owned by John Rusk. It was all forest at the time. The trees were cut down and hewn into timber, where the house stands. It was one of the first frame houses in the country. Its size and general appearance made quite a sensation, and people came long distances to see it.

Richard Woolsey, born in Westchester County, 1697, came here when a young man, married Sarah Fowler, and had twelve children.

Among the other families, who settled early in Marlborough, were the Purdys, Wygants, Anning Smiths, Youngs, Merritts, Quimbys, Clarks, Cropseys, Bloomers, Pembrakes, Conklins, and many others.

The town records give, in the road list of 1788, a practically complete list of the male inhabitants over twenty-one years.

Another of the very early families was that of Joseph Carpenter, who was born on Long Island about 1704 or 1705. He settled at Lattintown at a very early date, and raised a large family of children, said to have numbered eighteen sons and daughters. Their descendants are still numerous in the country. Edward Hallock came to Marlborough from Long Island in 1760, and engaged in farming and milling. His brother Samuel came soon afterward, purchased 1,000 acres of land, near the Village of Milton, and erected a house, which still stands. He left six children and Edward left twelve. Many of their descendants still live here. Leonard Smith, with five sons and two daughters, were Long Island people, and settled here in 1762.

At a special Town meeting, held at the house of Robert Gilmore, in the Town of Marlborough, the 8th day of March, 1800, the following notes were by a majority entered into, viz.:

Voted that the Town of Marlborough be divided as follows (provided the assent of the Legislature can be obtained for that purpose): beginning on the line between the Town of Newburgh and the Town of Marlborough, two chains and seventy-five links east of the northwest corner of the five patentees, from thence northward on a straight line, to the northeastern line of Robert Tifft's land, where it joins the Town of New Paltz. Voted also that the new town on the west side of the mountain be called the Town of "Patteekiln"; and the first town meeting to be held at the house of Robert Gilmore. And the remainder of the town, on the east side of the mountains, retain the present name of Marlborough, and the first town meeting be held at the house of David Merritt, in Lating Town. Voted that Joseph Morey, Esq., and Cornelius Drake be appointed to carry a petition, and the proceedings of this meeting to the Legislature, and to have twenty-four dollars for their services, to be paid by the town.

THE WAR OF 1812 AND THE MEXICAN WAR.

Both of these wars were very unpopular with the people of Marlborough. There were a few attempts to get up enthusiasm, but they were dismal failures. Most of our people thought they were uncalled for, and that they should have been avoided. A few may have drifted off and enlisted, but no record can be found thereof. Certainly no one of any prominence from here took part in either war.

Slavery existed in those days.

Slaves were bought and sold; the following is a specimen of a bill of sale:

KNOW all men by these presents, that I Joseph Sherwood, of the Town of Newburgh, County of Ulster and State of New York, for and in consideration of the sum of twenty pounds of Current Lawfull money, to me in hand, paid by Josiah

Merritt, of the Town of Marlborough, County and State aforesaid, HAVE granted, bargained and sold by these Presents, DO grant bargain and sell unto the said Josiah Merritt, one Negro Girl, named Syl, aged seventeen years, To have and to hold the said Negro, unto the said Josiah Merritt and his Executors, Administrators and Assigns, for and during the Natural life of Her, the said Girl. And I the said Joseph Sherwood, for myself, my Executors and Administrators and Assigns against me, the said Joseph Sherwood, my Executors, Administrators and Assigns, shall and will Warrant and Defend, by these Presents; In witness whereof, I have hereunto set my Hand and Seal, this twenty-eighth day of March, one thousand seven hundred and ninety-three.

JOSEPH SHERWOOD, (L. S.)

The slaves generally took the name of their masters and were usually kindly treated, but it appeared hard to punish anyone for killing his slave. A man living at Lattintown, who owned a negro man slave, coming home one day was met by his wife in great excitement and she said to him, "Jim, that d— nigger has run away. Bring him back dead or alive." So Jim put a double-barreled shotgun in his wagon, and started on the back road, toward Newburgh—the route his wife indicated the slave had gone. He overtook the slave just below the limits of the town, near a small graveyard, in the Cosman neighborhood. Jim called to the slave to stop, but he ran across the graveyard, and Jim shot him. He put him in his wagon, and took him back dead to his wife, thus obeying her better than most men do their wives.

He was arrested and taken for examination before a Justice of the Peace, living where Washburn Baxter recently died. During the examination, he escaped and remained away some time, and that was the last of it. The man's name was James ————. He owned the place afterward owned by Sheriff Harcourt.

A slave-holder complained of being very poor. He said that his "niggers" raised a big crop of corn every year, but the corn was fed to the hogs, and the niggers ate all the hogs, and he had nothing left.

With some of the slave holders, the slaves were thought much of and treated almost as members of the families. An old man with a large tract of land had among his slaves one called "Harry." He was large and a fine looking fellow, and dressed well, the leader of a company of colored men, who formed a militia company and drilled as such. His old master was proud of him, he always rode his owner's big black stallion on such occasions, and his master used to help him to get started. He was holding his horse on one occasion, and he handed his master a shilling, and some one observed, "What did you do that for, Harry?" Harry replied,

"Ain't that the way the white people do?" Afterward his master manumitted him.

A company of cavalry was organized in 1804, under the command of William Acker. It was composed of Marlborough and Newburgh men. Nathaniel DuBois served several years as Captain. The last Captain was Robert D. Mapes, of Marlborough. It was disbanded about 1838. David W. Woolsey, of Marlborough, was commissioned as Captain, 1823, by Joseph C. Yates, Governor, in the 14th Regiment of Infantry.

William Martin was a Captain of a company; and some other companies, or parts of companies, were organized in the town at different times. In November, 1867, C. M. Woolsey was commissioned, and served as Commissary, (1st Lieut.) of the 20th Regiment of N. Y. State Militia, until the regiment was disbanded.

Horatio Gates Safford, LL.D., in a Gazetteer of the State, published in 1824, describes Marlborough as follows:

"Marlborough, a small Township in the southeast corner of Ulster County, on the west shore of the Hudson opposite Barnegat, 23 miles south of Kingston, bd, N. by New Paltz, E. by Hudson, S. by Newburgh and County of Orange, W. by Plattekill. Its medial extent N. & S. is about six miles and it may be three wide, its area about eighteen sq. miles. The land is under general cultivation and it produces of all the common agricultural products of the region. The inhabitants consist of a larger proportion of English families than in most of the Towns of this County.

The road of the Farmer's Turnpike and Bridge Company terminates in this town. There are a good many "Friends" in this Town, who have a Meeting House, and there is also one for the Presbyterians.

There is a small Hamlet called Milton, a neighborhood called Lattintown, besides some river landings and places of business. The lands are held by right of sale. Population, 2,248. Taxable property, $108,172. Electors, 364. Acres of improved land, 9,436. 1,665 cattle. 424 horses. 2,092 sheep, 10,887 yds. of cloth, made in families, 7 grist-mills, 5 saw-mills, 2 fulling mills, 3 carding machines, 1 cotton and woolen factory and 1 distillery. One of the stated places of monthly meeting.

N. H. DuBois

TOWN OF MARLBOROUGH IN THE CIVIL WAR.

The following is a list of those who enlisted in the Army and Navy:

ARMY.

James Anderson
Sidney Barnhart
Jacob Berrian
Reuben R. Bloomer
Oscar B. Bloomer
James Bailey
Walter M. Bailey
Chas. A. Bailey
Thomas Brown
Patrick Conley
Jas. D. Cassidy
Henry Cassidy
David C. Crossbary
Geo. W. Detmar
Daniel Davis
Ferris G. Davis
Benjamin C. V. DeWitt
Peter E. DeWtt
Geo. J. Fowler
Luther P. Hait
John Harding
John Kenney
Edward H. Ketcham
John T. Ketcham
John McVay
Wm. Miller
Geo. H. Miller
John McCarty
John H. Mackey
Charles Lee Mackey
David F. Mackey
Nehemiah Mann
Morris Lee
Wm. J. Purdy
Peter V. L. Purdy
Alonzo S. Petit
Stephen J. Poyer
Geo. W. Quimby
John D. Quimby
Thos. Elliot
Chas. H. Free
Geo. Palmateer
Stephen Rhodes
Geo. Ryer
Reuben H. Rose
Aaron Rhodes
Theodore Rhodes
Walter Rhodes
David M. Weed
James N. Whims
James B. Williams
John Wordin
Isaac Fletcher Williams
Charles C. Wygant
John S. Wood
Chas. L. Woolsey
C. M. Woolsey
William York
John H. Dingee
Wm. H. Duncan
James C. Brewster
James M. Benson
R. F. Coutant
Cevonia Lounsbery
John Hendrickson
Lewis Hornbeck
Isaac N. Hornbeck
Daniel B. Martin
Hezekiah Martin
John Margison
Elmore Terwilliger
Wm. L. Dougherty
Jesse E. Knapp
Oliver Lawson
Geo. Duncan
Wm. Duncan
Isaac Sims

NAVY.

Cornelius Atherton
David Johnson
Horace B. Sands
John W. Williams
Martin Fisher
Geo. W. Smith
Henry Scott
Isaac Lewis
Phineas H. Smith
Isaac Theals
Peter Terwilliger
Jeremiah Terwilliger
James Terwilliger
Matthew Terwilliger
Danel Tuthill
Samuel Valentine
John H. Valentine

The following were the Commissioned Officers: Nehemiah Mann, Captain in the 4th N. Y. Cavalry. Killed at Cedarville, Virginia, August

18, 1864. John Ketcham, 2nd Lieut., 4th N. Y. Cavalry. Died in Libbey Prison, October 8th, 1863. Edward Ketcham, 2nd Lieut., 120th N. Y. Infantry. Killed at Gettysburg, July 2, 1863. William J. Purdy, 2nd Lieut., in the 156th N. Y. Infantry. C. M. Woolsey, 2nd and 1st Lieut. and Brevetted Captain, in the 2nd N. Y. Cavalry, and 2nd Lieut., 1st Regiment U. S. C. Troops. Oliver Lawson, 2nd Lieut., 1st Mounted Rifles. There has been a post, called Ketcham Post, 495, G. A. R., Department of N. Y., in the town for many years, organized August, 1884. C. M. Woolsey was first Commander; P. V. L. Purdy and H. B. Crowell have also been Commanders. C. M. Woolsey is the present Commander. Out of the whole number, who enlisted as above named, not more than twenty are alive and in the town.

Among the men of special prominence, which Marlborough produced, or who were identified with the interests of the town, were:

Ebenezer Foot,	Member	of	Assembly,	1792, 1794, 1796, 1797.
Selah Tuthill,	"	"	"	1804.
Nehemiah L. Smith,	"	"	"	1811.
David Staples,	"	"	"	1814, 1818.
Abram D. Soper,	"	"	"	1829. Also County Judge from 1828 to 1836.
William Soper,	"	"	"	1843.
L. Harrson Smith,	"	"	"	1853.
Jeremiah Clark,	"	"	"	1860.
C. M. Woolsey,	"	"	"	1871, 1872, and Justice of Session, 1866, 1867.
E. F. Patten,	"	"	"	1881.
Sands, Haviland,	"	"	"	1901.
Benjamin Harcourt, Sheriff, 1832.				

On April 5th, 1764, Lewis DuBois conveyed to John Woolsey and Stephen Case, two acres of land, but the Society, thinking that one and one-half acres was sufficient, reconveyed half an acre to the donor. In the old burying ground attached to the church, are buried many of the first settlers.

Marlborough now has many factories and stores, four churches, a large graded school, and three taverns. It has recently been incorporated and Frank L. Snyder is its President. It has a system of waterworks and electric lights. Population about 800. It is a flourishing village and a desirable place of residence.

	Postmasters.	Date of Appointment.
Marlborough.	Daniel G. Russell	July 13, 1824.
"	Miles J. Fletcher	April 14, 1826.
"	Robert B. Mapes	Aug. 12, 1841.

Postmasters.—*Continued.*

"	Miles J. Fletcher	June	7, 1843.
"	James S. Knapp	April	10, 1856.
"	Charles D. Jackson	April	8, 1861.
"	Dallas DuBois	Aug.	20, 1866.
"	John H. Baxter	Aug.	4, 1869.
"	John C. Merritt	April	1, 1875.
"	Martin V. B. Morgan	Aug.	5, 1885.
"	H. Scott Corwin (not commissioned)	Feb.	28, 1889.
"	Charles H. Kniffen	May	3, 1889.
"	Willam S. Wright	Aug.	3, 1893.
"	Charles H. Kniffen	Feb.	15, 1899.
"	Charles I. Purdy	Feb.	26, 1903.
"	James A. Johnston	Apr.	19, 1904.

Milton was so named previous to the Revolution. The name is found in an old record of the earlier Methodist Society. "In October, 1788, Rev. Ezekiel Cooper held the first Methodist meeting in the County, at the house of John Woolsey." Milton had good water-power, and saw and grist-mills were soon built. There has been a steady growth of population. It was very flourishing from 1820 to 1850. A turnpike was built about 1820, and a large tract of country to the west had its outlet here

David Sands carried on a large ship yard. There was a pin factory, soap factory and two hat factories at one time, and a paper called the *National Pioneer*, was printed here in 1829, edited by Daniel S. Tuthill, or as he was generally called, Selah Tuthill, a son of Selah Tuthill, the Member of Congress. The *Pioneer* was issued every Wednesday, at $2.00 per annum, "payable quarterly, or $2.50 at the end of the year." This price was for village subscribers, and those who got their paper through the post rider. There were four pages of six columns each.

From the advertising columns of the *Pioneer*, more is to be learned about Milton than from the reading matter. Advertisements appear from David Brower, tailor, in Milton Village; Anson St. John, manufacturer of cabinet ware and fancy chairs, also painter; C. S. Roe, general store-keeper, agent for threshing machines, real estate agent, dealer in rye, oats and corn, and owner of a tow boat; Mrs. M. B. Taylor, milliner, of Marlborough; Chas. Field, hat manufacturer; Longbottom & Co., announcing the retirement of James Kinworthy; and many others of more or less interest. From one of these, we learn that the proprietor of the paper, D. S. Tuthill, also kept a store at New Paltz landing, (Highland). Here he sold goods "at reduced prices," just as the modern merchants do.

Daniel S. Tuthill, or Selah Tuthill, as he was commonly called, was a man of considerable ability and business enterprise.

From the files of the *Pioneer,* we learn that Cornelius Polhemus kept a public house in Marlborough in 1830.

Cornwall S. Roe was one of the most prominent men in Milton, in 1830, if his advertisements in the *Pioneer* prove anything. In one copy of the paper he had no less than sixteen advertisements of various kinds. He kept a general store, where he sold dry goods, groceries, crockery, hardware, lumber, tar, plaster, salt, fish, pork, etc. He bought grain and flaxseed at "highest cash prices," and purchased patent rights for agricultural machinery. He also speculated in land. In one place he advertises, that the ladies of Ulster County can be supplied with Navarino Hats, either in the flat or made up, in the newest manner at short notice. In another place behold: "The Tow boat Atlanta, Capt. C. S. Roe, now performs her passage with all regular speed; and to meet the economical views of all, passengers are taken at the low rate of four shillings, who find themselves:—Six shillings and found. She arrives both ways before daylight." C. S. Roe. Milton, April 7, 1830.

There was a ferry at Milton called Lattimer's Ferry from the old stone house across the river. This was in operation during the Revolution and for many years afterward; it was said that during the war, regular communication was kept up between the Patriots of Boston and the forces in the Highlands and New Jersey. Money to pay the troops and valuables were carried by this ferry. The old stone house was a short distance south of where the railroad depot now is, and it was torn down when the railroad was built.

Jacob Powell and his son kept store there, and ran a line of sloops to New York about the year 1800. In 1795, they took out license for a tavern. Farmers took their produce there for shipment, and bought their goods. The same business was carried on there for many years after. At the road running down to it, at Northrop's corner, there was a blacksmith's shop, a store, a church and a house. Jacob Wood and Philip Caverly had a shipyard at the foot of Dog's street (lane), and built sloops and vessels. David Sands had a yard at Sand's Dock, and built vessels and kept store there. About 1850, Geo. Hallock had a brick yard. The clay was taken from his pond. From that time and for many years, Jacob Handley ran a horse-boat across the river.

There are five churches, several factories and mills, and stores at Milton. Population, about 800. It has always been a favorite landing place for steamboats and has enjoyed greater benefits and conveniences from them than any of the adjoining villages.

The first Town meeting was held here, in 1840, at the house of Robert S. Lockwood.

Lattintown, formerly "Latting Town," the oldest neighborhood or hamlet, is so called in the early records of the War of Independence, and prior to that time, just about 1740 or soon afterward, there being several families of Latting living there at that time. The first Town meeting, 1772, was held at the house of Henry Deyo, and the next, 1773, at the house of Richard Carpenter, both of whom are supposed to have lived at Latting Town. From that time up to and including 1779, the meetings were held at Silas Purdy's, which was the Henry E. Geade place.

	Postmasters.	Date of Appointment.
Milton.	Abraham D. Soper	Aug. 20, 1822.
"	Willam Soper	Apr. 2, 1836.
"	Nancy Soper	Jan. 19, 1849.
"	Calvin F. Bulkley	Dec. 4, 1849.
"	David Sands, Jr.	July 20, 1853.
"	Peter M. Carpenter	May 26, 1854.
"	Theodore Quick	Apr. 8, 1861.
"	Ethan Parrott	Jan. 12, 1866.
"	Roswell H. Stone	Feb. 15, 1869.
"	Jacob Rowley	Nov. 12, 1869.
"	Ethan Parrott	Nov. 22, 1869.
"	Edward W. Carhart	Feb. 23, 1882.
"	Edward W. Pitcher	Mar. 25, 1884.
"	Frederick H. Smith	June 12, 1886.
"	William H. Townsend, Jr.	May 24, 1889.
"	Frederick H. Smith	Aug. 23, 1893.
"	C. Meech Woolsey	Aug. 28, 1897.
"	Frederick W. Woolsey	Aug. 8, 1902.

Purdy had a mill there and kept a tavern. He also kept the stocks, in which persons were put to be punished, and kept the pound where stray cattle were kept. Purdy was an officer in the War, and one of the Committee of Safety and Defence. His place was virtually a part of the Lattintown valley.

In 1780, and for the next fifty-eight years up to and including 1838, meetings were held at Lattintown except the year 1801, when the Town meeting was held at Nathaniel Harcourt's, which was the place owned by Jesse Lyons on the post road. And in 1841, 1849, 1852, the meetings were held at Lattintown, which were the last. For twenty years the meetings were at David Merritt's house, seven years at John Hait's, ten years at Thomas Warren's and other houses in Lattintown. It was a great place for racing horses on Town meeting day. The Militia had their trainings there, Courts were held, and there much of the town business was transacted in those times. It was the center of population for many years. The smooth country and fertility of the lands, which were well watered, invited the early settlers. Large tracts of land were cleared and well cultivated, while the more stony and rugged lands between that and the river were mostly forests. The oldest graveyard in the Town was there, in which the first settlers were buried. This was situated on what is now the Odell place, on the grounds now occupied by his barn and orchard. At Lattingtown there was also a school, church, stores, wagon and blacksmith shops, a tannery and distillery in early times. There were also a shoemaker, tailor and undertaker. All of these except the school have ceased to exist.

THE PEOPLE, LANDS, AND CONDITIONS OF THE TOWN.

We have seen that most of the original families had previously settled in this Country. They were descended mostly from English and Holland families who had lived in England some time before they came to America, but the tide of foreign emigration did not set in until about 1850. Some had come in from time to time, but since 1850 the emigration has been rapid, mostly from Ireland, though many German families have settled here. They have generally been an agriculturist class, being small farmers in their own country. They were good people—honest and industrious. They accumulated means, bought farms, raised large families, and were honored and respected. Many of our best and more enterprising people have descended from these emigrants.

The Irish people have erected and supported two large and flourishing Catholic churches, with parsonages, separate priests, and a large and fine cemetery. Most of the emigration is now from Italy. Many families arrive each year and buy the smaller and cheaper places. They are frugal and industrious, and consider a debt a sacred obligation and pay promptly.

The water courses of the town are confined to a few small streams emptying into the Hudson; in former times they had a larger flow of water, and afforded power for many mills and factories, and they also had many trout. There are several small attractive lakes and ponds. The surface is broken and hilly, rising from the bluff at the river to the Marlborough Mountains, a rocky ridge along the west bounds, an elevation of about a thousand feet above tide.

The soil is a dark rich loam or clay and admirably adapted to general agriculture and grazing. In fact, before the advent of fruit, a large population was supported prosperously on the farm crops they raised. But during the past forty or fifty years the lands to a great extent have been given up to the raising of fruits which grow in great abundance and are generally profitable. There are many large vineyards, and strawberries, raspberries, blackberries and currants have shown enormous yields. Large quantities of peaches are also raised. The farms have been cut up in small tracts of five acres and upwards, upon which families live and prosper. The soil stands dry weather well. With proper cultivation, fertilizing and attention the yield is very large. From 100 to 200 bushels of berries to the acre are generally raised.

The great hotels of New York City, Philadelphia, Boston and Montreal are furnished with peaches and other fruit direct from here. In fact, no better peaches are raised in the world, and the price for first-class fruit is always high. The gross receipts of some of the fruit growers here are from $10,000 to $20,000 a year. Large sums are paid out for working and picking the crop, and any man, woman or child can find ready employment at good wages. There are 1,000 extra people who come here to help during the packing season. Though none of our people grow rich, yet many keep town and city places, and spend their winters in Europe or in the south. Over half a million dollars worth of fruit is shipped or sold from here every year.

Lands are now selling readily, and advancing in price. The yield of most varieties of fruits has been large this year and the prices good, especially grapes, which have not been so high for years. They raised in value from the commencement of the picking, and the last of the crop sold as high as $65 a ton.

The increase in population has been remarkable. The population in 1865 was 2,733; in 1900 it was 3,978, showing a larger percentage of increase than the city of Kingston or any of the towns, except Rosendale, and this while most of the towns have stood still or lost in population.

CHAPTER XXIV.

TOWN OF NEW PALTZ.

By Hon. John N. Vanderlyn.

ONE of the most interesting of the original settlements in Ulster County, or elsewhere, is the Huguenot Settlement of New Paltz. The land on which these Frenchmen and their families settled was not patented to them as trustees, for the benefit of the whole, but to a copartnership of the twelve individuals for their personal use. either as a body corporate or subject to division, presumably in twelve equal shares.

The settlement was one of the earliest after that of Kingston and Hurley, but it is generally supposed that some of the patentees had settled there some years previous to the date of the patent. The following documents, which are still extant, show the purchase from the Indians, and the subsequent confirmation by the patent. (The manuscript is in Dutch.) :—

"By approbation of his Excellency, Governor Edmund Andross, dated April 28, 1677, an agreement is made on this date, the 26th of May, of the year 1677, for the purchase of certain lands between the parties named herein and the undersigned Esopus Indians.

"Matsayay, Nekahakaway, Magakahas, Assimerakan, Wawawanis, acknowledge to have sold to Lowies du Booys and his partners the land described as follows:—

"Beginning from the high hills at a place called Moggonck, from thence southeast toward the river to a point named Juffrous Hoock, lying in the long reach, named by the Indians Magaatramis, then north up along the river to the Island called by the Indians Raphoes, then west toward the high hills to a place called Waratahaes and Tawentagui, along the high hills southwest to Moggonck, being described by the four corners with everything included within these boundaries, hills, dales, waters, etc., and a right of way to the Rouduyt Kill as directly as it can be found, and also that the Indians shall have the same right to hunt and fish as the Christians, for which land the Indians have agreed to accept the articles here specified:—

"40 kettles, 10 large and 30 small; 40 axes; 40 shirts; 400 fathoms of white net-work; 300 fathoms of black net-work; 60 pairs of stockings, half small sizes; 100 bars of lead; 1 keg of gunpowder; 100 knives; 4 kegs of wine; 40 oars; 40 pieces of "duffel" (heavy woolen cloth); 60 blankets; 100 needles; 100 awls; 1 measure of tobacco; 2 horses—one stallion and one mare.

"Parties on both sides acknowledge to be fully satisfied herewith, and have affixed their own signature *ad ut Supra*.

"Matsaya X (his mark)	"Andrie Lefeber
"Waehtonck X (his mark)	"Jan Broecq
"Seneraken X (his mark)	"Piere Doyo
"Magakahoos X (his mark)	"Anthony Crespel

John N. Vanderlyn.

"Wawateanis X (his mark))
"Lowies Du Booys
"Christian de Yoo X (his mark)
"Abraham Haesbroecq
"Abraham Du Booys
"Hugo Freer
"Isaack D. Boojs
"Symon Lefeber

"Witnesses:
"Jan Eltinge,
"Jacomeyritje Sleght,
"Jan Mattyse,

"Agrees with the original,
"W. La. Montague, Secry.

"I do allow of the within Bargaine and shall grant patents for Same when payments made accordingly before me or Magistrates of Esopus.

"Andross.

"We, the undersigned persons, former owners of the land sold to Lowies Du Booys and his partners, acknowledge to have been fully satisfied by them according to agreement, we therefore transfer the designated land with a free right of way for them and their heirs, and relinguishing forever our right of way and title, will protect them against further claims, in token whereof we have affixed our signatures in the presence of the Justice, Sheriff, Magistrates, and Bystanders, on the 15th of September, 1677, at Hurley, Esopus Sackmakers.

"Witnesses:
"Sewakuny X (his mark)
"Hamerwack X (his mark)
"Manvest X (his mark)
"Papoehkies X (his mark)
"Haroman X (his mark)
"Pagotamin X (his mark)
"Mahente,
"Pochguget X (his mark)
"Pagotamin X (his mark)
"Harommi X (his mark)
"Wingatiek X (his mark)
"Wissinahkau X (his mark)
"Mattawessick X (his mark)
"Matsayay X (his mark)
"Asserwvaka X (his mark)
"Umtronok X (his mark)
"Wamanies X sister in his absence called Warawenhtow
"Magakhoos X (her mark)
"Wewajask X (his mark)
"Nawas X (his mark)
"Tomaehkapray X (his mark)
"Sagarowauto X (his mark)
"Machkamoeke X (his mark)

Witnesses:
"Jan Eltinge;
"Roelof Henderycks;
"John Ward;
"Gars X Harris;
"Albert Jansen;

"Testis:
"Thomas Chambers, Hall, Sherriffe;
"Wessel Ten Broeck,
"Dirk Schepmoes,
"Hendrick Jochensen,
"Joost de Yaduo,
"Garit X Coonelise,
"Lambert X Hybertse,

"Mattay has publicly proclaimed and acknowledged in the presence of all the Indian bystanders that the land has been fully paid for, in which all concurred."

"Testis: W. Montague, Secr."

The grant by Governor Andross, dated the 29th of September, 1677, is given in the fuller and perhaps more legal verbiage and covers the same ground; in naming the partners, however, the name Laurens Bevier is added, making the twelve patentees. When the purchasers applied to Governor Andross for liberty to settle on their land, he coupled his permission with the provision that they must "build a Redoute there first for a place of Retreat and a Safeguard upon occasion."

There are different views concerning the beginning of the settlement. By some it is stated that one or more of the patentees had squatted on portions of the land some years previously, and becoming nervous through practical isolation, the syndicate was formed to purchase the ground, amounting approximately to 36,000 acres, and erect a settlement; by others it is alleged that there were no habitations on the tract, and that the patentees and their families, with the exception of Crespel, journeyed up the Wallkill from Kingston in three carts, till they decided upon the place of location. As there seems to be no documentary support to either suggestion, both being founded on the legends in which the neighborhood richly abounds, the reader must take his choice.

It is a matter of record that more land was desired later. On February 13, 1683, the Special Session Court, held at Kingston, granted permission to buy land of the Indians westward to New Fort. For some reason the purchase was never completed. Three of the patentees, Louis, Abraham and Isaac DuBois, were the father and two sons; the younger, Isaac, being but eighteen years old; the two Deyos or Doys were father and son; the two Lefevers were brothers, as were also the Hasbrocs, though Jan or Jean had left off the first syllable of his name, calling himself Broec. Abraham DuBois, the two Hasbrouck brothers and Simon Lefever had married the four handsome daughters of Christian Deyo, so that the whole company were united either by ties of blood or marriage, with the exception of Hugo Freer. Anthony Crespel did not settle in New Paltz, but sold his share in 1699 to Louis Bevier. It is proper to reproduce this conveyance in full, as it is the first recorded sale of land in the patented tract, and while there seems to have been a division of the land there is no record of the fact. Such were the conditions that a century later, after the War of the Revolution, a special act of the New York legislature was required to clear the ancient titles and confirm the legality of the acts of the patentees and their descendants. The deed translated is as follows:—

"Personally appeared Anthony Crespel, a laborer living at Hurley, County of Ulster, who declares and confesses to have sold, ceded, released, conveyed, and by these presents sells, releases and conveys to Louis Bevier, a laborer living at New Palle, a certain piece of land in a thicket adjoining the said Village of Palle making one of the twelve parts according to the partition by the proprietors of said Palle. This said part is bounded by the pasture of Abraham DuBois and by Louis Bevier on one side, on the south it bounds on the Washmaker's land and on the other side at the north on the heirs of Simon Lefebre. And I, the said Crespel, promise to have the said Bevier enjoy and hold thereof without trouble or hinderance; and the said sale has been made upon payment of 140 schepels of wheat which I the said Crespel have received to my satisfaction, and absolve thereof the said Bevier and all others.

"In testimony whereof I have signed this.

"Done at Quinstown this 10th day of April 1699.

"Antoine Crespel"

"Jean Cottin
"Jaque DuBoois
Witnesses."

The first transfer of land of which any record is known, was a deed of gift of a cottage and lot to Jean Cottin, a schoolmaster of New Paltz. This deed, in addition to conveying the real estate, gives Cottin the right to cut wood for building and gives pasturage for two cows and calves, a mare and a colt; it reserves the right to discharge him as schoolmaster when they think "proper and fit," and requests him not to sell the property to anyone not of good life and manners. This record has a dual valuation, showing that at that early date the cause of education was of paramount importance, and hardly less so that of so controlling the property as to prevent the influx of undesirable neighbors.

There are a large number of documents concerning the early history of New Paltz in various collections held by some of the descendants of the original settlers. It is shown that for about forty years the prevailing language was French, then for nearly seventy years the Dutch language, or the Dutch and French together, were used; so that it was not until the War of the Revolution that the English language became in general use. It had been taught in the schools, however, for some time previous.

The original dwellings were built of logs, some of them large and comfortable for large families, others of smaller size. They gave way, gradually, after twenty or thirty years, to stone structures of some pretension, several of which are still standing, and occupied by descendants of the original Syndicate of Patentees.

The antecedent history of the Huguenots has been written in extenso. The persecutions which they suffered on account of their apostasy from the Roman Church, have been written in the blood of thousands and the expatriation of hundreds of thousands. The particular company which came to New Netherland—later New York—seems to have been composed of those who, for some years had been refugees in the Palatinate on the Rhine. One work on this subject associates DuBois with the Lefevers, Hasbroucks, Crespels, etc., at Manheim.

Anthony Crespel and Louis DuBois were sons-in-law of Matthew

Blanchan. Crespel came to America in 1660, Blanchan and DuBois the year following. They settled in Hurley, and at the burning of that town in 1663 by the Indians the wife and two children of Louis DuBois, the wife and one child of Anthony Crespel, and the two children of Matthew Blanchan, Jr., were carried into captivity, where they remained for three months, until rescued by the military force under Captain Kregier.

The LeFever brothers came to Kingston in 1665. Jean Hasbrouck, with his wife and two unmarried daughters, came in 1673. The wife was the daughter of Christian Deyo. Abraham Hasbrouck came in 1675. Louis Bevier, who later purchased Crespel's share in the New Paltz, came in 1673, with his wife and sons, Hugo, Abraham and Isaac. Bevier was a cousin of the Hasbrouck brothers. Later came Christian Deyo, with his three daughters who afterward married Abraham Hasbrouck, Simon LeFever and Abraham DuBois. Also came Pierre Deyo, son of Christian, with his wife and child. Abraham Hasbrouck is said to have served with Governor Andross in the English army, and his influence in getting the patent is mentioned.

Ralph LeFever, in his history of New Paltz (1903) comments on the delay of four months between the date of the original agreement with the Indians, May 26, 1677, and the issuance of the patent, September 29, 1677, but the translations of documents in the same volume shows that there could have been no such delay, from such cause. Governor Andross had endorsed the contract of purchase with his approval, and directed a patent to issue on payment of the terms before him or the Magistrates of Esopus. By the date of this document this was not done until September 15, 1677, and the patent was issued two weeks afterward. It is, of course, possible that payment had been previously made, but the acknowledgement of the same before the Esopus Court was a necessary provision.

The dates of the death of some of the patentees of New Paltz are known, but of others no record is known to exist. Isaac DuBois died at the age of 31, in 1690. Louis DuBois, who had moved to Kingston in 1686, became one of the Judges of the County and died there in 1696. The only grave of the original pioneers marked by a stone in the New Paltz churchyard bears this inscription:—

"1731, A. D. Bois, surviver of 12 patentees."

Jean Cottin, the first teacher of the New Paltz school, was succeeded about 1696 by Jean Tebenin, who remained four years and received a recommendation in 1700. Cottin went into business in Kingston, and later married the widow of Louis Du Bois. Neither Cotton nor Tebenin left descendants. Cottin willed his property to the church at Kingston, and Tebenin bequeathed his belongings to the church at New Paltz. The church at New Paltz was organized in 1683. According to the old French record which is still preserved, "Mr. Peter Daillie, Minister of the Word of God, arrived at New Paltz and preached twice the Sunday following, and proposed to the heads of the families to choose by a majority of the votes of the fathers of the families an Elder and a Deacon, which they did, and chose Louis Du Bois for Elder and Hugh Frere for Deacon to aid the minister in the management of the church, meeting at Paltz, who were then confirmed to the charge of Elder and Deacon. The present minute has been made to put in order the things which appertain to the church.

The extract is dated January 22, 1683.

The record extends to 1702 and several different handwritings are found. It is mostly a record of marriages and baptisms. The last mention of Rev. Mr. Daillie appears in 1692, and the first mention of Reverend Mr. Bourepos in May, 1696.

Gradually as the years passed, the French and the Dutch began to blend. None of the Patentees had Dutch wives; of their children there were several. Solomon Du Bois, son of Louis, married Tryntje Gerriteen some time about 1690. In the latter part of the same decade Mary Deyo married Jacob Clearwater. Abraham Deyo married Elsie Clearwater in 1702. In 1703 Sarah DuBois married Roelif Eltinge. Jacob Freer married Altie Van Weyen in 1705; Hendricus Deyo married Margaret Van Bummell, in 1715. In 1706 Joseph Hasbrouck married Elsie Schoonmaker and in 1721 Solomon Hasbrouck married Sarah Van Wagenen. Some others who lived outside the Paltz also married into Dutch families.

In the third generation the young people seemed inclined to marry more diversely. Johannes Hardenbergh, Jr., a German, married into the LeFever family as did also Jacob Hoffman, a Swede. Elias Ean or Un, whose nationality is not disclosed, married Elizabeth Crespell, the daughter of Anthony Crespell, and settled four miles north of the village on a farm. The farm is still in the possession of their descendants.

When the split came in the church in 1766, the dividing line between the races seems to be shown in the names of those adhering to the beliefs of the two parties. The seceding faction built a new church, but when the matter was settled all came together again in harmony.

There were other elements of intermixture among the surrounding families. The Brodheads were English; the Hardenberghs came from Germany, and the Terpenings and Ronks from Flanders; the Auchmoodys were Scotch; the Bruynes Norwegian, and the Wurts and Goetcheons families were of Swiss descent. All this tended to a change in the language, first to the Dutch, which was predominant outside the settlement itself, and then, gradually to English, which was the official language, and which it was necessary to teach in the schools.

There were several grants of land outside the original patent, secured by the patentees and the descendants, and consideration of the original grant has been separated for the erection or enlargement of other towns. Thousands of the descendants of the original families went into other counties and States, but it is probably a fact that nowhere else in the United States does the population consist so largely of the direct descendants of the original settlers, who occupy and cultivate the same land as did their ancestors two and a quarter centuries ago.

In 1728, fifty years after the original settlement, the list of freeholders shows but few changes of names from those of the original twelve.

In 1738, the foot company of militia gives a fair indication of the strength of the settlement, as every able-bodied man between the ages of sixteen and sixty were supposed to be enrolled, and the age limits were elastic in cases of able-bodied persons over or under age.

Following is the militia company:

Captain Zacharias Hoffman
Lieutenant Benjamin Smedes, Jr.
Ensign Zacharias Hoffman, Jr.
Sergeants: John Teerpenning
John Freer
Evert Terwillige
Corporals: Christian Duio
Hendrick Duio
Isaac Lefever.

PRIVATES.

Isaac Freer
Jan Une
James Agmodi
Petrus Low
Josia Elling
Cornelius Dubois
Hendr. Dubois
Agustus Van Dermerke
Abra. Bovier
Isaac Bovier
Mathues Bovier
Benj. Hasbroeck
Isaac Lefever, Jr.
Huge Freer, Jr.
Abrm. Vandermerke
William Armstrong

Frank J. LeFevre.

PRIVATES.—*Continued.*

James Dimmick
Manewel ter Willige
Hendrick Decker
Thomas Janson, Jr.
Tuenis Terpening
Jonas Freer
Simon Lefever
Johannis Low
Abm. Duio
Jacob Ge Decker
Daniel Winfiel
Johannes Terwillige
Petrus Terwillige
William Rosekraus
Josua Smedes
Stevanis Swart
Andrew Grames
John Blake
Solomon Isrel
Roger Blamles
Lawrence Eldorp
John Andrew
William Short
Jacob Ja Decker
William Ja Decker
Benj. Ja Decker
Abr. Terwillige
Evert Terwillige, Jr.
Corns. Cool
Louis Pontenere
William Weller
Isaac Hasbroeck
Benj. Hasbroeck, Jr.
Mathew Jong
Robert Hanne
John Jemson
Gerrett Ja. Decker
John Robertse
Rober Guames
James Jonston
Samuel Sampson
Richard Davis
Tomas Macconn
Arie Terwillige
Cornelius Bruyn
Abr. Ja. Decker
Isaac Ja. Decker
Abr. He. Decker
Isaac Terwillige
Cornu. Schoonmaker, Jr.
Johannis Cool
John Gream
Hendrick Weller
Jacob Hasbroeck, Jr.
Zacharias Klarwater
Abr. Lefever
Jacobus Bovier
Nathaniel Lefever
Symon Dubois
Peter Duio
Hendrick Van Wiiak
Lewis Sa. Bovier
Robert Jong
Robert Cain
John Magdonel
Johannes Wasseker

The New Paltz Government was the most simple on earth. All there was to it, was for the heads of the families to get together and make regulations and decisions. These do not seem to have been numerous or important, as there are no records of them left. There are reasons for supposing that originally the lands were worked in common, then for a time in severalty, by selection and agreement, and later by a division.

What are known as the Huguenot Papers, which were preserved for a century or more in the Huguenot Bank, and since removed to the Town Clerk's office, give much information along these lines. Among these is a document called "New Paltz Orders," which are recorded by W. Nottingham, Clerk. The orders pertain to the building of line fences, character of fences, times when animals may run free, and when they must be enclosed, fines for violations, and many other matters. The meeting at which these orders were made was held February 23, 1712.

In 1728 the "Dusine" or "Twelve Men" was organized. These were to be chosen annually, and they exercised absolute legislative, judicial and executive powers. Twice during the existence of the "Twelve Men" there were divisions of property, made necessary by the increase in population, but there is no record of an appeal from their decision to the Colonial Courts. This organization continued until after the War of the Revolution, an act incorporating New Paltz being passed in 1785.

The document establishing the "Twelve Men" is among the papers preserved, and it bears the signature of the twenty-four owners of property within the Paltz patent, with the recording acknowledgment of Ulster County, signed by D. Wynkoop, Jr., who was apparently County Clerk or Recorder at the time.

Town officers were elected by popular vote at town meeting.

Among the papers are the names of those who signed an agreement of similar import on May 23, 1744. The names indicate that they are members of the same families as the freeholders of 1728, but some of them were evidently a younger generation who had come of age and inherited property. The agreement was a pact to mutually contribute whatever money might be necessary to protect the patent, according to his or her share in the whole. This was to continue for fifteen years.

The agreement of April 30, 1774, bears signatures and seals of the following persons with their shares in the patent duly agreed to:—

Daniel LeFevre 1/64
Jacob Loun 1/468
Andres LeFevre, Jr. 1/43
Abraham Donaldson 11/360
David Auchmoudy 1/300
Josaphat Hasbrouck 1/120
Margrietye Bovier 1/229
Jonas Freer 5/234
Benjamin DuBois 31/720
Benjamin Hasbrouck 1/120
Isaac Hasbrouck 1/120
Simeon Loun 1/468
Zacharias Hasbrouck 1/120
Johannis Bevier, Jr. 1/210
Benjamin DuBois 1/210
Benjamin Doyo 1/80
Nathaniel LeFevre 11/240
Cornelius L. Brink 1/270
David Bevier 1/120
Anthony Yolverton 1/32
Mickel Devoe 1/216
Andr. Bevier 1/105
Jonas Hasbrouck 1/420
Benjamin Freer 1/100
Jacobus Hasbrouck 1/80
Petrus Hasbrouck 1/40
Huge Freer 1/65
Isaac LeFevre 1/64
Johannis Bevier 1/270
Peter Bevier 1/270
Johannis Freer, Jr., 1/94
Gerrit Freer, Jr., 1/174
Abraham Ein 1/36
Mathieu LeFevre 1/37
Petres LeFevre 1/50
Jacob Hasbrouck, Jr., 3/40
Christeyan Dooyo 1/400
Solomon Bovier 1/540
Samuel Bevier 1/810
Elias Bevier 1/810
Abraham LeFevre 1/270
John Terwillige 1/234
Sophia Eltinge 11/180
Noah Eltinge 1/17
Abraham Dorau 67/720
Simon DuBois 81/720
Philip D. Bevier 1/120
Margaret Rosekrause 11/360

There have been several changes in the boundaries of the town. The tract was enlarged in 1775. A part of Hurley was annexed in 1809. In 1842 Esopus took a part of New Paltz; in 1844 Rosendale got a portion; the new town of Lloyd was taken wholly out in 1845, and Gardiner got a slice in 1853.

The "Dusine" or "Twelve Men" who were in office at the time the town was incorporated under the State government in 1785, consisted of the following persons:

Simon Dubois	Jacobus Hasbrouck
Johannes Freer	Jacobus Hasbrouck, Jr.
Abraham Donaldson	Abraham Eltinge
Petrus Hasbrouck	Samuel Bevier
Benjamin Deyo	Isaac Lefever
Matthew Lefever	Abraham Ein

The French church at New Paltz, when originally organized, and while under the pastorate of Revs. Daillie and Bourepos, had no connection with any classis, or other ecclesiastical body. After the departure of the last-named gentleman, several years elapsed without the services of a regular clergyman, and many of the marriages and baptisms are recorded as having taken place in Kingston. One authority alleges that there was no settled minister until 1730, at which time the Dutch was the prevailing language. In the meantime the factional split had occurred and the new church was built in 1720.

The consistory of New Paltz united with those of Rochester, Marbletown and Shawangunk in 1741, and called Rev. Casparus Fryenmoet as their pastor. He was to receive one hundred pounds per year, of which New Paltz and Shawangunk together paid 31 pounds.

Rev. Johannes Mauritius Goetschius assumed the pastorate of the churches of New Paltz and Shawangunk in 1760. Each congregation was to pay him 40 pounds in gold, the Shawangunk church, with farm and buildings, and New Paltz to lodge himself and horse while there.

A new stone church was erected in 1773. This was replaced in 1839 by another, which after several enlargements still stands.

The union between the New Paltz church and the Reformed Dutch church was made in 1772. The use of the English language in the services and records began in 1799, when Rev. John H. Meyer became pastor. Previous to this time Rev. J. H. Goetschius, a nephew of Rev. Johannes Maurilius Goetschius officiated from 1775 to 1796. After Mr. Meyer's departure in 1803, the church was without a pastor until 1807. From that time they were as follows:

Rev. Peter D. Froeligh, 1807 to 1816.
Rev. William R. Bogardus, 1817 to 1831.
Rev. Douw Van O'Luida, 1832 to 1844.
Rev. John C. Vandervoort, 1844 to 1847.
Rev. Charles H. Still, 1848 to 1865.
Rev. Peter Peltz, 1865 to 1881.
Rev. Ame Vennema, February 17, 1882, to February 13, 1886.
Rev. Abel H. Huizina, P. H. D., April 12, 1886, to July 6, 1894.
Rev. Abel H. Huizina, Ph.D., April 12, 1886, to July 6, 1894.
Rev. John G. Fagg, November 3, 1894, to December 9, 1895.
Rev. E. C. Oggel, D.D., the present pastor, was called February 3, 1896.

and installed by the Classes of Kingston, April 8, 1896. Doctor Oggel is a man of ability and energy and highly esteemed by his people.

The Methodist Episcopal Church was organized over the territory of this region as an adjunct to the Philadelphia Conference in 1786. Services were held at the houses of Hendrick Deyo and Henry DuBois, in New Paltz. In 1804 the New York Conference annexed the Albany district, in which Ulster County was located, and the name of the New Paltz charge was given this circuit in 1824. The Church in New Paltz was built in 1840. That at Plattekill had been erected in 1825 and 1826. The Church at Centerville was dedicated in 1852, at Cold Spring in 1861.

About the year 1894 the St. Joseph's Roman Catholic Church was erected at New Paltz, the same having been completed during the pastorate of Rev. John B. McGrath, who was an able man and energetic worker, and he succeeded in canceling the church debt. He was succeeded by Rev. John J. Morris, who took charge of the parish comprising the churches of Gardiner and New Paltz, on July 1st, 1899. Important repairs were made to the church building in the summer of 1900, and other repairs have since been made. The church edifice is a neat and substantial building located in the southern portion of the village. The present pastor is Rev. Wm. J. Stuart, who was appointed April 11, 1905. The parish is at present in a prosperous condition, and the pastor is zealous in all that tends to the material and spiritual welfare of the people.

New Paltz took its proper place in the War of the Revolution, as one of the leading communities of Ulster County. Most of those who fought during that war were members of the Fourth Regiment, otherwise known as the Hardenberghs, and a considerable number of the officers were New Paltz men. Their names will be found in another portion of this work as will also the names of the subscribers to the Articles of Association of 1775.

During the war one of the most difficult duties of the people of New Paltz was guarding the frontier against the Tories and Indians. Many of the savages, led by the Tories, committed fearful outrages, murder and arson among them. One whole family was slaughtered. By extraordinary care a considerable number of Tories were captured while trying to reach the English lines, and several of them were subsequently executed at Kingston.

At the beginning of the nineteenth century there were about eighty slaves belonging to the families of New Paltz. They were manumitted gradually.

In the Civil War, the town of New Paltz was well represented, about one hundred men enlisting in the Union Army and nearly half that number in the Navy. Most of those in the Army served in the 156th Regiment, though there were a large number in other organizations. On a monument in the New Paltz Cemetery are the names of those who laid down their lives for their country as follows:

Lieut. George P. Lord, U. S. N.,
Captain Johannes Lefever,
Sergeant David H. Hay,

Richard Ellsworth,
Abraham Hunt,
Charles Booth,
Luther Freer,
Ananias Johnson,
John Harp,
Silas Booth,
Joseph R. Wood,
Henry Osterhout,
Benjamin Smith,
Thomas Close,
Simon Freer,
George Brundage,

Andrew Yaple,
William Ackert,
Richard Oliver,
John S. Humstone,
Jahn Van Tekel,
John Beck,
Charles Ketcham,
Ezekiel Freer,
James L. Hess,
John Anson,
Conard Bowviece,
William Eckert.

NEW PALTZ VILLAGE.

This is located on the east bank of the Wallkill near the center of the town. It is the largest and most important village in the town, and is one of the most interesting points in the county. It contains four churches: The Reformed Protestant, Methodist Episcopal, St. Joseph's Roman Catholic and African Methodist. There are two newspapers: *The New Paltz Times* and *The New Paltz Independent*. The Huguenot

National Bank, a flourishing and successful institution, is situated on Main street, at its junction with Plattekill avenue. The New Paltz Savings Bank has a large deposit, and is located in the lower part of the village on Main street.

There are five hotels: The Tamney House, Brodhead House, Steen's Hotel, The Riverside Cottage and The Schoonmaker House; also a number of large and substantial store buildings, many of brick, in which are conducted progressive and up-to-date business with the large surrounding country.

The village is furnished with a supply of mountain water by the New Paltz Water Works Company, which was organized in the year 1892, and is well lighted by the Electric Light Company of New Paltz.

The village was incorporated in December, 1887, and the first president was Jacob M. Hasbrouck.

The board of trustees at present has the following members:

Jacob M. Hasbrouck, President.

Lewis H. Woolsey.

John C. Kaiser.

Elting Harp.

Henry Hasbrouck.

John Schmid has been the village clerk since its incorporation.

BANKS.

The Huguenot National Bank was organized February 10th, 1853, with a capital of $125,000. The first board of directors consisted of Edmund Elting, Abram P. LeFevre, Mathusalem Elting, John Howell, Garret LeFevre, Jacob G. DuBois, Roelif Elting, Alfred Deyo, Oscar Hasbrouck, Timothy Seymour, Capt. Abram Elting, Moses P. LeFevre, Abram V. N. Elting. Edmund Elting was the first president, A. G. Ruggles, the first cashier. During the financial crisis of 1857 the bank passed into the hands of a receiver. It was later reorganized and Roelif Elting was elected president; Nathan LeFevre cashier, and Edmund Elting, assistant cashier. In 1875 an entire new organization took place; Hon. Jacob LeFevre was chosen president, and Mathusalem DuBois cashier. The change from a State to a National bank was effected in 1865. In 1875 the capital was reduced to $100,000.

The New Paltz Savings Bank was organized in May, 1871, in accordance with an act of the Legislature passed in March of that year. The original trustees were Jacob LeFevre, Daniel L. Heaton, Zachariah Bruyn, Thaddeus Hait, Edmund Bruyn, Derrick W. DuBois, Elijah Woolsey, Oscar Hasbrouck, Peter LeFevre, Solomon Deyo, Calvin T. Hazen, Huram Hasbrouck, Jesse Lyons, Floyd S. McKinstry, Nathan Williams, Abner Hasbrouck, Charles W. Deyo, John B. Deyo, Edmund Elting and Jonathan Deyo.

NEW PALTZ FIRE DEPARTMENT.

The fire department here is considered not only the best for a village of this size, but takes its place on inspection day with many long established city companies of high standing. The first fire department of New Paltz consisted of Huguenot Fire Engine No. 1, organized September 16, 1861. This company was equipped with a hand engine, purchased at Poughkeepsie. After the disbanding of this company the village was without fire protection until July, 1889, when Ulster Hook and Ladder Company No. 1 was organized. This company served as a bucket company until the completion of the waterworks system in New Paltz, in 1892, when the Star Hose Company was also organized. These companies are both in a flourishing condition at this time. Ulster Hook and Ladder now has about sixty-five members and Star Hose Company about forty-five. William Bleeker is the Fire Chief.

Eltinge Post Number 212, Department of N. Y. G. A. R., was chartered December 14th, 1883, with the following veterans of the Union Army in the Civil War as charter members: Charles J. Ackert, Charles H. Bleeker, Alexander Ferguson, Joseph Uhrviller, Charles Smith, John I. Rosencrans, George W. Van Voorhis, John W. Ackert, Zachariah Berryan, Stephen J. Yeaple, Samuel D. W. Morey, Benjamin F. DuBois, Thomas Johnson, Jacob Wynkoop. All are still living except Charles J. Ackert and Samuel D. W. Morey. Charles J. Ackert was the first commander of the Post. Since his death William H. D. Blake has been the commander. Since its organization there have been ninety-four honorably discharged soldiers and sailors mustered in as members. At the last semi-annual muster there were thirty-eight members in good standing.

There is in this village, Mohonk Lodge No. 565, Independent Order of Odd Fellows, which was instituted a number of years ago. The present

Noble Grand is Irving D. Sutton. The lodge is in a flourishing and prosperous condition. There is also the Wallkill Lodge Knights of Pythias, and the organization has erected a handsome building on Chestnut street on the second floor of which are their lodge rooms. The present C. C. is Luther Hasbrouck.

BURIAL PLACES.

The old burial place in the village, nearly opposite the Memorial House, is in good condition. The remains of many of the old settlers, were here interred. The oldest stone records the death, on October 7th, 1831, of Abram DuBois, the last "survivor of the twelve patentees." And there are a number of other old inscriptions, among which are the following:

"In memory of Roelif Elting, who died the 21st Feb'y, 1792, aged 59 years, 6 months & 9 days."

"Here Lyeth the Body of Joseph Hasbrouck, Esqr, aged 40 years, 3 months and 18 days. Died January 28th, 1792."

"Here Lies Interred the Body of Elsie Hasbrouck, Widow of Joseph Hasbrouck, Esqr. Dec'd ye 27 Day of July, 1764, Aged 73 Years, 8 Months And 3 Days."

"In memory of Noah Elting, Esqr, who departed this Life Sept. 27th, 1778, aged 57 years, and Jacomintje, his spouse, who departed this Life August 27th, 1790, aged 75."

The New Paltz Rural Cemetery was incorporated February 18th, 1861. The grounds are located about a mile south of the village, and comprise about twenty acres. It contains many substantial and handsome monuments, including one of Quincy granite, erected to the memory of the soldiers who died battling for the Union. It is inscribed with the names of the patriotic dead from this town who gave their lives, that government "of the people, for the people and by the people should not perish from the earth."

PROMINENT MEN OF THE TOWN.

The town has been the residence of many men of ability and reputation. A large number of these have preferred the quiet life of private citizens, and have made their homes in this historic spot and passed their days in the pursuit of agricultural, mercantile or other vocations, content in the respect and esteem of their immediate neighbors, and the devotion and love of the home circle. There are some, however, who have attained positions of trust and responsibility in the public service and many have achieved eminence.

Among these was the Hon. Jacob LeFevre, who was born in the town of New Paltz, and resided here until his decease in 1905. Mr. LeFevre was born in April, 1830, and lived here during his whole life, except when occupying official positions at the State or National capital. His home was on the farm of his ancestors, and came to him in direct line of descent from Jean, son of Simon LeFevre, the patentee. He was a public spirited man and of remarkable energy and activity, always willing to give not only of his time but means to assist any worthy project in which he became interested. He was Supervisor of the town in 1861-62, member of the Assembly in 1863-64-65-67, delegate to the national convention in 1888, and representative in Congress 1892-96. He was one of the directors of the Wallkill Valley Railroad Company during its construction. He was for thirty years president of The Huguenot National Bank, and also a director of the Hanover National Bank, New York City; vice-president of the New Paltz Savings Bank; vice-president and director of the Dutchess Insurance Company; a director of the New Paltz Huguenot Memorial Society; member of the Holland Society; member of the local board of the New Paltz Normal School; Trustee of the New Paltz Academy; member Mohonk Lodge 565 I. O. O. F., New Paltz, N. Y.; member of K. of P., Wallkill Lodge 162, New Paltz, N. Y.; member of Ardonia Lodge No. 718 F. A. M., Highland, N. Y.; member of the Masonic organization, and affiliated with Kingston Lodge, No. 10. Mr. LeFevre married Ann Amelia Woolsey, daughter of Elijah Woolsey, who survives him, together with four children, George LeFevre, Frank J. LeFevre, Albert LeFevre, and Mrs. Catharine Poucher, wife of J. W. Poucher, M. D., of Poughkeepsie, N. Y.

One of the most respected and honored citizens of Ulster County is Hon. Frank J. LeFevre. He was born in the town of New Paltz in 1874, and has always retained this as his place of residence. His ancestors resided in this town since its settlement by the Huguenots in 1668. For a time he engaged in the banking business in New Paltz, and in 1902 he was elected to the State Senate from the twenty-fifth senatorial district, consisting of the counties of Ulster and Greene. He was superintendent of the New York State Building at St. Louis during the Louisiana Purchase Exposition. While there he was nominated for Congress from the twenty-fourth district, comprising the counties of Delaware, Otsego, Schoharie and Ulster, and was elected to the Fifty-ninth Congress with little opposition. Mr. LeFevre succeeded his father, Hon. Jacob LeFevre, as president of The Huguenot National Bank, and has since occupied that position. He is also a director of the Poughkeepsie Trust Company; a director of the Dutchess Fire Insurance Company, and a trustee of the Old Senate House of Kingston, N. Y.

Hon. John N. Vanderlyn has been a resident of the town of New Paltz and practicing attorney there for the past thirty years, and during that time has won the respect and esteem not only of his own townsmen but of many people throughout the county with whom he has been brought in contact in the performance of professional or official duties. He is a native of Orange County, and first read law in the office of that veteran of the bar, Hon. J. M. Wilkin. After one year of preparatory study, Mr. Vanderlyn attended the Albany Law School, from which so many eminent practitioners have graduated.

After graduation from this school he entered the law office of Newkirk & Chase, of Hudson, N. Y., Judge Newkirk, the senior member of this firm, being an uncle of Mr. Vanderlyn. After several years' practice at Hudson he removed to New Paltz, and has since made this his home. On January 31, 1878, Mr. Vanderlyn married Miss Magdalena L. Hasbrouck, of New Paltz, N. Y., a daughter of Joseph Hasbrouck and Sarah (LeFevre) Hasbrouck. They had one child, Joseph H. Vanderlyn, now a practicing attorney at New Paltz. In 1886 Mr. Vanderlyn was elected District Attorney of Ulster County by a large majority, succeeding Hon. A. T. Clearwater in that position. He was again elected in November, 1889, and completed the full term of six years as prosecuting officer of the county. During his incumbency of the office many important criminal cases were tried, and Mr. Vanderlyn established the reputation of an efficient and capable official.

It was during his second term that the defaulting treasurer and assistant treasurer of the Ulster County Savings Institution were indicted and tried for having appropriated about $600,000 of the depositor's money; and the diligence, vigor and ability shown in this trial reflected credit upon the prosecuting officer; both of the defaulters being convicted and imprisoned at Dannemora State Prison.

In 1897 Mr. Vanderlyn's name was brought before the Republican County Convention for County Judge, but he failed to secure the nomination. During his many years of practice he has been engaged in many cases of importance and has a large clientage in the southern portion of the county. He has a reputation for ability and integrity.

Beside New Paltz, a number of smaller villages and hamlets are located in the town, perhaps the most important of these is

OHIOVILLE.—Situated along the direct line of the trolley road from New Paltz to Highland, about two miles from the former. It is a beautiful little place, having a good hotel, a general store and post-office kept by J. E. Vanderlyn; blacksmith shop, and a number of fine summer cottages. Having good connections with both New Paltz and Poughkeepsie, it makes almost an ideal summer home.

PUT CORNERS is a hamlet about a mile or so east of New Paltz, along the trolley line, and was named in honor of Napoleon Purdy, who came from Putnam County, N. Y., and located there.

SPRINGTOWN is a growing summer resort located in the northwestern part of the town, between the Wallkill River and the Shawangunk Mountains, along the line of the Wallkill Valley Railroad. A large number of city people pass the summer months at this place.

BUTTERVILLE.—About two miles west of New Paltz, is near the base of the mountain and in the midst of a prosperous farming country.

CHAPTER XXV.

TOWN OF OLIVE.

By DeWitt C. Davis.

THE town of Olive was formed from Marbletown, Shandaken and Hurley, April 15, 1823. A part was annexed to Woodstock and a part of Woodstock annexed to Olive in 1853.

Olive is situated near the center of the county, with the Catskill Mountains rising on the northern and northwestern borders, and the Esopus, the principal stream in the town, flowing southeastward a little north of the center. The smaller streams, tributary to the Esopus, flow southeasterly and southwesterly.

The first on the west is a small stream flowing through Tongore, near the late residence of Gordon C. Davis, northerly into Tongore brook. Tongore brook rises in Kromville and flows easterly through the farms of Walter North, Ward Cornish, Willis Davis and others, and empties into the Esopus just above Winchell's Falls. On this stream were formerly two saw-mills, one built in an early day which later was owned and operated by William H. Krom, of Kromville; the other was on the premises of Ward Cornish. Both are gone.

The next stream rises in the Deer Park and flows through the farm of Jacob and Henry Winchell, which was once owned by Aaron Winchell and his father. Another stream rises in the vicinity of Little Point, unites with the former, and flows easterly to the Esopus, just above Bishop's Falls. On this stream Henry Winchell, grandfather of the present owners had a saw and grist-mill, and on the other branch was a saw-mill owned by Josiah Turner. Lower down the stream was a large tannery, once operated by James R. Goodwin, then by Gideon M. Sprague, and afterward by Lewis Hollister. Nothing but the foundations can now be seen of any of these. The name of the stream is Clay Kyle Fountain Kill. The next stream is small, running through Olive city and discharging into the Esopus near the old Turner place, now owned by Willis Barton.

The Bukkabom or Bookabome rises at the foot of High Point, and empties into the Esopus at Brodhead's bridge. There were, at one time,

DeWitt C. Davis.

four saw-mills on this stream, but none are in operation now. One was owned by the Brodheads at Brodhead's bridge; up the stream was one owned by Joseph Bell and John B. Davis. A stave mill, in which in May, 1858, the owner accidentally amputated the fingers of his right hand, belonged to D. C. Davis; up the stream at Bridal Veil Falls was a mill built by David Abbey and afterward owned by Abram Blom. It is now obliterated. Up near the mountains Stephan Winchell had a saw-mill, but only the foundations can be seen.

There is a small spring brook which rises on the farm of William B. Ennist and flows into the Bakeman; next is the Jackey Brook, named after old Jack Crispell, a negro, formerly owned by the Crispell family. This is joined by a large spring brook rising on the farm of Thomas Eckerts and flowing through the maple-sap grove of Martin H. Crispell, and near West Shokan, empties into the Bakeman below the mill of Z. P. Boice. The Bakeman, flowing through West Shokan at Boice's saw-mill, is formed by spring brooks within a mile above the station and empties into the Esopus near the residences of Frank Boice and Osten Rider. This stream is noted for trout.

The Bushkill is the most noted stream in the town for trout. It rises in Waldron Hollow, and is made up by the Gulf Hollow stream, the Canape Brook, the Mine Hollow stream, the South Hollow stream, the Wittenberg stream and the Dry Brook. It empties into the Esopus about half a mile above the Shokan bridge. On this stream there have been five saw-mills, two or three stave mills and a large tannery. All are now gone. The tannery was owned by Nathan W. Watson who was supervisor for several years, and in 1857 a member of Assembly from this district. The Traver Hollow stream rises back of Sam's point, at the foot of Cross mountain, and empties into the Esopus half a mile below Boiceville. There have been two saw-mills on this stream, one owned by Millard H. Davis, still in running order.

On the east side of the Esopus, the first stream is the Beaverkill, which flows through the Beaverkill swamp. It is fed by several small streams from the hills and mountains, and discharges into the Esopus half a mile above Winchell's Falls. One saw-mill owned by Marshall Winn and Benjamin Van Steenberg, is now in operation. A small stream crosses the State road near the house of Edward Davis, and supplies Peter R. Elmendorf's saw-mill and empties into the Beaverkill.

Butternut Brook, originally known as Olymute Brook, is formed by two streams; one comes from the Coons' neighborhood, the other from above the farm of Ephraim Weeks, and they unite below the bridge near the house of John DuBois, three-quarters of a mile from its mouth. It empties into the Esopus near the Mayer's tannery. Lemuel Boice and John P. Boice formerly had saw-mills and Andrew Hill a grist-mill on this stream. Another small stream rises in the hills near Joseph Whittle's place and reaches the Esopus just below Boiceville. A legend is that Abram D. Ladew, who once lived on the Swarthout place, was bitten by a rattlesnake while looking for his cows up this stream, and used remedies which cured him. It has been suggested by the whimsically inclined, that there was a snake remedy factory in this region but there is no authority for the statement.

Further along is the Beaver Creek, which forms the line between the towns of Olive and Shandaken, and reaches the Esopus at Cold Brook.

The mountains of Olive are romantic and picturesque. Near Little Point is the Gap, called since ancient times the "Wagon Road," though there is no road there. The Gap is about 100 feet wide, with sheer rock sides, as though by some convulsion of nature the mountains had been broken apart.

Round Mountain is a ridge extending from the Gap to High Point, and is 3,100 feet high. From High Point the City of Kingston and the Hudson may be seen in clear weather, and the view to the south, east and west has been called the finest in the Catskills. On High Point and Round Mountain, huckleberries abound. The Point is level on top and all about are great flat rocks where names have been cut by visitors, some of the inscriptions being very ancient. To the north and northwest is a succession of mountains as far as vision extends.

Next is South Mountain,, also famous for huckleberries. Crossing South Hollow there is another mountain, extending to the Canape, and from High Point to Watson Hollow; across the Canape is the Mombaccus Mountain, noted for huckleberries and bears. The writer has seen the bear traps there. The Mombaccus Mountain extends to the Shandaken line at Gulf Hollow. The Shandaken line crosses Breath Hill, the Hanover Mountains, the Blackberry Mountains, Sam's Point and Quarry Mountains.

On the east side of the Esopus is Toran's Hook, where it is said the

Indians had a sort of a carousal. There is what is known as the Indian dancing floor, described as a "place of flat rocks," which has been much visited. Near this is the Tice Ten Eyck, so named for a member of that well-known family. It was supposed that there was a mine on this mountain the location of which was known to the Indians, but no white man has ever been able to discover it, though repeated attempts have been made.

The first settlement was made at Olive City. At this point was located the first Old School Baptist Church. The building is still standing though a new one has been built near Hog's Back, which is occupied by the congregation. A short distance west was a tannery owned by James R. Goodwin. The Post Office at Olive Bridge is at the store of John H. Looke, who is also town clerk. Bishop's Falls is a short distance below; there is a very old grist-mill here, which still grinds. It was once owned by a very remarkable character, named Jacob Bishop, who was blind. It is said that he never made mistakes in his grist nor in the bags of his customers. The mill is now owned and operated by Jesse B. Boice. Across the falls is an old mill formerly owned by Henry DeWitt, long out of use. Here are also three boarding houses, owned by William Haver, John Beesmer and Alex Van Kleek.

About a mile above Olive City, half or three-quarters of a century ago, was a hotel owned by William J. Davis, where the elections were held and town business transacted. Darius W. Hover now owns it and maintains a boarding house. Near this the first bridge across the Esopus was built in 1825, which was washed away many years ago.

The first Methodist Episcopal Church was built at Tongore, in 1822 or 1823, and the congregation embraced all the families of that faith in the town. Among the earliest members were Jacob Van Steenberg and Benjamin North, both local preachers of note. District No. 2 schoolhouse is located here.

A store was kept where Alonzo G. Davis resided before his death, and where Gordon Craig afterwards lived, and conducted a small store. Craig was the first supervisor of the town after its organization in 1823, and in 1832 was member of Assembly for Ulster County. Other members of Assembly from Olive have been, Conrad Brodhead in 1840, John D. La Montague in 1846, Martin Schutt in 1856, Nathan W. Watson in

1857, Benjamin Turner in 1860, Thomas Hill in 1863, and Charles H. Weidner in 1887.

KROMVILLE is three miles south of Tongore, in the extreme south-western part of the town, and is a farming region. It has a Reformed Church, a school-house, a store and post-office. Samsonville, in the western part of the town, has a Methodist Church, which belongs to the Tongore Circuit, a school-house, a store and a post-office. A tannery owned by Pratt and Samson once made much business here. It burned down, and there is now a saw-mill and grist-mill.

BRODHEAD'S BRIDGE is a station on the Ulster and Delaware Railroad. A stone "dock" once owned by Hewitt Boice, and now by S. D. Coykendall, does a large business. It is in charge of John J. Boyce. The store and post-office is kept by Ira Elmendorf. Mrs. Bessie James conducts a large boarding house, which will accommodate 150 guests.

Two miles above is WEST SHOKAN, a railroad station called Shokan. Matthews & North are large merchants here, requiring the services of four clerks. The trade is large, much of it coming from the town of Denning. Z. P. Boice, now Sheriff of Ulster County, has a saw-mill which employs fifteen men and four teams. Logs are drawn six to eight miles. The product is chiefly heading, shingles and boat timber. A hotel owned by Satterlee & Hamilton will accommodate fifty guests. George Siemon and William Dibbell have blacksmith and wagon shops. Herbert Bell is in the livery and harness making business, and John Van Kleek and Abner D. Winne are also in the livery business. During the summer season there is great activity by reason of summer boarders. There is a meat market, barber-shop and post-office. The shoemaker, Allen F. Eckert, has been in business here for more than fifty years. Here is also a school employing two teachers, and a physician, Dr. J. D. W. Dumond. The Baptist Church is located about half a mile above the village. There is also a variety store and jewelry repairing shop, conducted by Oranzo Giles. The oldest house in the village is owned by Mrs. Jemima Elmendorf; it was originally the property of Hendricus Crispell, who owned it during the war of the Revolution.

On the east side of the Esopus is SHOKAN, originally called Ashokjan. There are two churches here, the Reformed Church and the Methodist Episcopal. The Reformed Church was organized in 1799. There is a general store, owned by Azarias Winchell & Son. Charles H. Davis deals in groceries and boots and shoes, and runs the post-office as deputy postmaster; Mayer's tannery occupies the ground on which Hoyt Brothers had theirs forty or fifty years ago; John J. DuBois does wagon-making and blacksmithing. The district school has two divisions. A. E. Schoonmaker is the undertaker near the Shokan bridge. There are also a millinery establishment, conducted by Mrs. Elwyn Winchell, two dressmakers, Mrs. William Dibbell and Mrs. James Diamond, and a number of boarding houses which cater to the summer trade. Dr. B. B. Bloom, a physician, resides here.

BOICEVILLE is a hamlet located on the Ulster and Delaware Railroad. The store of John C. Hornbeck and the post-office, which is kept there, are in charge of Benjamin Church. An excelsior factory, owned by John C. Hornbeek, employs about twenty men and there are several summer boarding houses. The school-house is on the west side of the creek.

COLD BROOK, a railroad station, is a large shipping point for quarry-stone, which comes from the mountains in abundant quantities. The Esopus is bridged at this point for the convenience of the people from Woodstock and Wittenberg who patronize the railway.

OLIVE, the village which bears the name of the town, is about two miles from the Olive Branch station on the railroad, in the southwestern part of the town. It was formerly a business point of some importance. It is surrounded by a farming region, has one store and a blacksmith shop. The post-office is kept by Isaac Delemater at his residence.

BROWN'S STATION was formerly known as Brook's Crossing, and is the first station on the U. & D. railroad after it reaches the town. Levi Elmendorf is a merchant and postmaster, and there is a school-house nicely located. There is a Reformed Church and a blacksmith shop. The church has no pastor at present. The Hudson River Wood and Pulp Mill at Winchell's Falls does a large business. The falls were once the property of Lemuel Winchell, who had a store and foundry there about one hundred years ago. Gideon Perry had a carding and fulling mill about the same time. It was from here that the Bush boys, Isaac, Stephen and Cornelius, were kidnapped by the Indians during the war of the Revolution. It was years afterward when they returned. Two of them, Stephen and Cornelius settled here; Isaac settled somewhere in the western part of the State. There are two large boarding houses, conducted by Albert Brown and Egbert Dederick.

ACORN HILL is the center of a good farming region. There are also a number of fine stone-quarries, and the Wesleyan Methodists have a small church here.

WINCHELLS is the site of a school-house located about half way between Olive Bridge and Samsonville. Near it is Little Point and Bear Spring, which tradition says was formerly used by the bears as a summer resort for bathing purposes. It is an excellent spring of clear cold water.

WATSON HOLLOW was formerly the center of active business. Nathan W. Watson had a large tannery, and there were two saw-mills and a stave mill. The tannery was burned and many of the houses have been torn down and moved away. Mr. Watson was supervisor of the town in 1850, 1857, 1864, 1865, 1866, and was a member of the Assembly in 1858.

HOG'S BACK is so called on account of the shape of the hill; Coons' neighborhood lies between Tice Ten Eyck and Toran's Hook; there are several good farms there, among them those of Henry Coons, John J. Weeks and Willis Everett. Huckleberry Hill is near the foot of High Point. Charles Hamilton and Richard O. Constable had farms near. The Constable place remained in the family for three generations. It is now owned by Michael Dwyer.

The first hotel was at Olive City and was kept by Conrad DuBois. Lemuel Winchell opened the first store at Winchell's Falls.

There are twelve school districts in the town and fourteen teachers are employed, Shokan and West Shokan each having two.

The northern and western part of the town is from the Hardenberg patent, while the southern and eastern portion comes from the Marbletown Commons. The Hurley Patentees' settlements began about the middle of the eighteenth century. George Middagh settled near Olive Bridge in 1740, where he was joined in 1742 by Samuel Cox, and in 1745 by William Nottingham. John Crispell located just east of Shokan in 1747 and Hendrick Crispell at Shokan in 1760, on the place now owned by Zadoc P. Boice and others. West Shokan is built principally on this farm. John Coons settled early near Brown's Station, and many others whose names appear in the early histories of the towns from which its territory was taken were the early builders of the town of Olive.

The house owned by William D. Every at Shokan, was for many years the only one there. It was not until after the construction of the Kingston and Middletown Turnpike in 1832 that other settlers located at that point.

The first bridge across the Esopus in the town was built about 1825, near the boarding house of the heirs of Darius W. Hover. This was the only one in the town for many years. It was carried away by high water, and in 1852 the bridge was built at Shokan.

The first post-office in the town was at Tongore. It was called Olive P. O., and the mails were carried from Marbletown to Shandaken weekly. The Olive post-office was afterward moved to Beaverkill, and kept by John J. Tappen.

A considerable portion of the town was owned by landlords until about 1842 and 1843, when the tenants refused to pay rent because of unsatisfactory conditions of tenure of the leases. The landlords generally sold the property to the settlers, and when the war was over landlordism was abolished.

The early industry of the town was lumbering, and the utilization of the bark in tanning. After the timber was cut and the saw-mills and tanneries had passed away, the energies of the people found an outlet in quarrying bluestone from the hills where it abounds in inexhaustible quantities.

The average elevation of the lowlands of the town is about 800 feet. A curious fact worthy of note is that the towns of Olive, Rochester and Denning corner on a mountain 2,700 feet above tide.

The earliest physicians in Olive were Doctors Connelly, Quinlin and McClellan. The area of the town is 37,370 acres.

The present population of the town, by the State census of 1905 is 2,347, having decreased from 3,083 in 1870.

CHAPTER XXVI.

TOWN OF PLATTEKILL.

By DeWitt W. Ostrander.

THIS is one of the southern tier towns. It is bounded on the north by the south line of the New Paltz Patent; on the east by the town of Marlborough; on the south by the northerly line of the County of Orange, and on the west by the towns of Shawangunk, Gardiner and Lloyd. Its area is about 20,890 acres.

The town was originally formed from the town of Marlborough by act of the Legislature passed March 21, 1800. A part of Shawangunk was annexed April 3, 1846, but was restored March 28, 1848. Although formed in 1800, yet for many years previous, and for a long time preceding the Revolution, it was a large factor in the old town of Marlborough.

The surface is generally a rolling upland, the easterly border is traversed by a range of hills known as the Marlborough Mountains, along the summit of which is the dividing line between Plattekill and Marlborough.

The town is well watered with small streams, the largest of which is the Quassaick Creek, which rises in the easterly part and flows southerly into Orange County. The Black Creek rises in the central part of the town near Ardonia and flows northerly through Clintondale and empties in the Hudson north of Elmore's Corners in the town of Esopus, and the Plattekill Creek rises near the center of the western border of the town, flows northwesterly and empties in the Wallkill.

The soil is a fine quality of sandy loam, fertile and productive. Large quantities of hay and grain are raised in the southerly and westerly part of the town, while the central and northerly part ranks high as a fruit producing section.

This town is included in the bounds of the extravagant patent, known as the "Errus Patent," which was cancelled in 1689, and afterward divided into smaller parcels. Among the early grants within the town are found the following patents of land granted by King George, the Second:

Dewitt W. Ostrander.

Patent granted to William Bond, dated July 7, 1720, conveys a tract of 500 acres in the southeasterly part of the town. Patent granted to William Bradford, dated Sept. 1, 1727, conveys 2,000 acres in the southeasterly part of the town. Patent granted to Andries Marschalk and John Spratt (known as the Spratt and Marshall Patent), dated April, 1828, conveys 1,000 acres in the northwesterly part of the town.

The Richard Durham Patent is dated October 13, 1752, and conveys 2,000 acres in the northeasterly portion of the town. The Bradley and Jovan Patent, granted to Richard Bradley, Attorney-General of the Province of New York, and Millan Jovan, is dated June 4, 1726, and consists of one parcel containing 400 acres, and another of 4,000 acres, situated in the southwesterly part of the town. The Patent known as the "Richard Bradley Children," was granted to "Ann Bradley, Sarah Bradley, Catharine Bradley, George Bradley and Elizabeth Bradley, "the daughters and younger son of our Attorney-General of our Province of New York," dated March 26, 1739, and consists of two parcels, one containing 817 acres, and another of 1,783 acres.

Other patents were granted during our Colonial existence, and after independence the State conveyed such lands as were found to be vacant and not covered by Colonial grants. These Colonial grants, made before the Revolution, were declared valid by the State, and the patentees either settled on their grants or sold to others.

Plattekill is a town of homesteads; nearly all the farms and houses are owned by their occupants and have been built from the cultivation of the soil. It is mostly the middle class that populates the town; the steady, moral, thinking class; industrious and prosperous, unsoiled by wealth and not unnerved by poverty. With prosperity comes culture and morality, a condition always found where neither "riches nor poverty abound."

The first market vineyard in the Hudson River valley north of Cornwall was planted in this town by William T. Cornell in 1845. This vineyard occupies land in Clintondale. From that small beginning, fruit culture has spread in the towns of Marlborough, Lloyd, Esopus, and a part of Orange County, and thousands of tons of the finest grapes in the world are shipped to the great cities, especially New York, Boston and Philadelphia. Among the vineyardists was William Kniffin, a stone-mason, who had a few acres of land. Mr. Kniffin was a man of clear perception and accurate judgment, who observed and experimented until he perfected a system of grape-pruning known as the "Kniffin System," which is the "drooping" system, and is most largely practiced by vineyardists throughout the United States. Plattekill therefore stands forth as the mother of the Hudson River vineyard industry and as the most peerless instructor of the nation in grape-pruning.

It may also be noted here that the "Isabella" was the pioneer grape, which has long since been discarded, and that the now famous standard variety, the "Concord," was introduced in the Hudson River valley by Andrew J. Caywood, who formerly lived near Ardonia.

The first town meeting was held April 1, 1800, pursuant to an act of the Legislature passed March 21, 1800, by which the town was formed from Marlborough.

The following officers were elected: Supervisor, David Ostrander; Town Clerk, Daniel Everett; Commissioners of Highways, Samuel Baldwin, William Drake and Jabez Close; Assessors, Peter Esterly, James Rose and Thaddeus Hait; Overseers of the Poor, Jonathan Bailey, Peter Esterly; Constables, Robert Gilmore, Cornelius Polhamus; Collector, Robert Gilmore. One of the post-roads laid out and used as a highway was from Modena to connect with a highway in Orange County leading to Newburgh. The turnpike leading from Milton to Tuttletown in the present town of Gardiner and known as the Farmer's Turnpike, was laid out in 1809 by three commissioners, who completed the whole distance of about twelve miles in three days. The turnpike to Modena was opened in 1866-7. The roads are generally in good condition and well cared for.

Prior to 1802 there were no stores in the town, so far as can be learned. Before any were opened the inhabitants patronized the river towns, but most of the trading, especially from the westerly portion of the town, was at the general store of Gen. Joseph Hasbrouck, situated just south of the Guilford Church in the present town of Gardiner.

CLINTONDALE.

This village is located in the extreme northeast of the town, and partly within the southwesterly tongue of the town of Lloyd. Situated on the westerly slope of a range of hills, surrounded by vineyards, orchards and fertile fields, with no manufacturing establishments, it is clearly seen that the chief resource of the place is from the soil.

There are three churches, Methodist Episcopal, Friends and Pentecostal; one school-house, a large, beautiful building, erected at a cost of about $2,500, and known as District No. 11, of Plattekill, although partly in the town of Lloyd. There are two general stores, a stove and tin store, meat market, drug store, two blacksmith shops, a wagon shop, two temperance hotels and one public hall. There is one physician, one lawyer and one dentist. The railroad station, named after the village, is situated about one and a half miles northwest of the village proper, on the line of the Central New England.

The early settlement began about 1750, mostly from the southerly part of the town, and was known as "Quaker Street," until the post-office was established in 1849, when it received its present name. The first general store was kept in the house now owned by Anthony Sutton in 1810. John Underhill kept a store in 1820. Harry Palmer kept another from 1836 to 1844. From 1832 to 1834 James Stewart kept a grocery and sold whiskey near the Quaker meeting house. Among the other early merchants were Benjamin Roberts, Jeremiah Relyea, D. L. Horton, W. B. Roberts, E. S. Andrews, D. F. Geralds and John Lowell.

William Cornell invented and patented a waterproof overshoe in 1830, which was the forerunner of the present "arctic" overshoe. These shoes were manufactured by William Cornell and John Thorn for thirteen years in various parts of the village.

During the time, or shortly after the Revolution, Zachariah Hasbrouck erected a grist-mill near the "Stone Bridge," which he continued to run until 1830. James Turner built a grist-mill and saw-mill on another stream in 1834, which was run for a number of years, when the flour machinery was removed and a saw and planing plant was substituted.

Among the early ministers who preached in the Clintondale Meeting House were Dr. Adna Heaton, Nathaniel Silleck, Nathaniel Thorn, Stephen Wardell, Sarah Roberts and Esther Weeks, who became noted throughout the United States.

In 1904, the Friends' Society purchased a house and lot in the village, which has since been used as a pastoral residence.

PLATTEKILL

Is located in the southerly part of the town along the Quassaick Creek and is surrounded by fertile and productive land. It was known as "Pleasant Valley," or "The Valley," until the post-office was established February 24, 1819. It is the oldest hamlet in the town. General stores, hotels and blacksmith shops have been there for more than one hundred and fifty years. There is now a creamery, general store, temperance hotel, blacksmith shop and a physician. There is a Methodist church and parsonage, and the district school house. In this region, and near Modena, is where the early settlers located.

The first store in the town was operated in 1802 by John Warner and Daniel Sands; then followed others kept by Daniel Alsdorf, Solomon Ostrander and Simon Alsdorf in 1805; in 1806, John R. Drake; 1809, Robinson Penny, and 1819, Robert R. Underhill. Among other old merchants were William Welch, James Bloomer, Jasper Crapsey, Daniel Hunt, Charles Drake, Daniel Martin, DeWitt Garrison, John L. Gerow, Moses Everett, Elias Heaton, W. H. Fowler and James Dayton.

MODENA

Was first known as "Clark's Corner," the name being changed to "Modena" in 1829. It is in the northwesterly part of the town, on the line of the old Milton Turnpike, and has always been an important and influential location, where the early physicians and lawyers settled and most of the first town officials lived. Much of the wealth centered here in the early days, and the most important stores were located here. Among the early traders were John C. and Richard Brodhead, Abram A. Deyo, Abram DuBois, Robert T. Everett, Martin Esterly, William P. Storms, Christopher Constable, Philip Dusenberre, Joseph A. Deyo, Amos DuBois, Russel Lock and Paul Smith.

ARDONIA

Is about two miles southwest of Clintondale, and about the same distance east of Modena, on the old Milton Turnpike, formerly known as "Charles Palmer's Corner." A post-office was established here July 27, 1882, and a general store was opened about the same time by George T. Seymour, which was afterward operated successively by Ennis F. Seymour and Anson Armstrong. In 1863 a society known as the "Modena Literary Society" was organized and a public hall erected, which was a credit to the enterprise of the society and an ornament to the town. Many noted speakers lectured in this hall, among them being Horace Greeley and Theodore Tilton.

UNIONVILLE

Is a small settlement situated about two miles east of Plattekill, near the foot of the Marlborough Mountains, on the highway leading from Plattekill to Marlborough, known as the "Huckleberry Turnpike." There is a collection of dwellings, a place for public worship called the "Chapel," and a school.

TUCKERS CORNERS

Is another small settlement on the easterly border of the town at the road crossing and just west of the Marlborough Mountains, on the old Milton Turnpike. There has been a small grocery kept there at intervals for many years, and at one time there was a blacksmith shop. A school house is located just south of the cross-roads, known as District No. 3.

THE METHODIST CHURCH.

Concerning the history of the Methodist Church in Plattekill, we quote the following from a sermon of the Rev. J. H. Lane:—

"Plattekill was, from the first, the garden of Methodism in southern Ulster. Here a class was formed and regular preaching service held as early as 1788, at the home of Aunt Huldah Hait. The Plattekill Church was built in 1829. Daniel Ostrander, the first class leader, was afterward licensed to preach and became prominent in the church. He was elected eight times a delegate from the New York Annual Conference to the General Conference. He died in 1843 after fifty years in the ministry. Rev. Phineas Rice was another man of note in Methodism. Another society was organized in the western part of the town at Modena; the preaching place being for some years at the old stone school house on the Modena and Highland Turnpike. The first church was built in 1826 on the main road one half a mile from the present village, and was removed to the present site under the pastorate of Rev. Charles Isham. Another society was organized in the southeast part of the town at an early date and a church built in 1840, under the pastorate of Rev. Z. N. Lewis, and called the Rossville Church. The church at Clintondale was removed from Lattintown in 1871 and rebuilt under the pastorate of Rev. G. S. Keyser."

Methodism was introduced here at an early date. In 1786, Rev. Ezekiel Cooper and Rev. John McClaskey were appointed to East Jersey by a Philadelphia Conference, which was a circuit embracing a large portion of Sussex County, N. J. To this were added the counties of Orange and Ulster, N. Y., forming what was known as a six weeks' circuit. In Ulster County the first preaching was at the house of John Woolsey at Milton, and Hendrick Deyo and Henry DuBois in the town of New Paltz. At a Conference in Philadelphia, in 1788, the charge was called the "Flander's Circuit." At this Conference Rev. Jesse Lee and Rev. Aaron Hutchinson were appointed to "Flanders," and during the time they were in charge of the circuit the churches at Modena and east Plattekill (Hait's Hill) were organized. It is not known where the first preaching was held.

The first M. E. Church in the town was built about half a mile south of Modena near the school house in 1825, and it was called the "Plattekill Church." In 1802, the charge was called "Ulster" in the New Jersey District, Philadelphia Conference, and in 1803 it was included in the Albany District, and Gideon R. Knowlton and John Crawford were appointed to the Circuit. In 1804 the Albany District was changed to the New York Conference and Ulster then became an appointment of that Conference. Another change in the district was made in 1811, when Ulster came in the Hudson River District, with William Jewett and E. Hibbard as Circuit preachers. In 1824 the charge was called New Paltz, and Nicholas White was appointed to the Circuit. In 1825-26 Bradley Selleck was the preacher in charge, and during his term in 1826, the Plattekill Church was erected, as above stated.

In 1829, during the pastorate of Rev. Eben Smith, the East Plattekill Church was built. In 1795, Daniel Ostrander was licensed to preach. At the age of 19, Dr. Phineas Rice was one of the preachers of the Circuit. In 1830-31 Benjamin Griffin and Valentine Buck served the Circuit, and in 1832 the Newburgh District was formed and H. Wing was appointed to the charge; in 1833 and 1834 E. Washburn, J. D. McFarland and D. Webster; in 1835, J. W. Lefever, J. Shaw and Mr. Ferguson; in 1836, C. Stillman and J. Shaw; in 1837, Valentine Buck and E. Crawford; in 1838, J. C. Green and Eben Smith. In 1840 the name of the appointment was changed to Plattekill and New Paltz, Ira Ferris and R. K. Reynolds, preachers. In 1841, Ira Ferris and M. D. C. Crawford were the preachers.

In 1842, Ira Ferris reported preaching places at Plattekill, East Plattekill, New Paltz Landing, Krom Elbow and Dayton Hollow. Conference then appointed Edward Aldrin and Eli Westbrook to the Circuit; 1843, Edward Aldrin and J. W. Lindsay; 1844, Thomas Newman and J. W. Lindsay; 1845, Thomas Newman and John Davy; 1846, C. W. Carpenter and J. Reynolds; 1847, C. W. Carpenter and J. K. Still; 1848-9, A. S. Larkin and J. C. Washburn. In 1850 the Circuit was divided; three more appointments had been added during the pastorate of Thomas Newman, viz.: Tuthill, Clintondale and Old Paltz. By this division the Plattekill Church, East Plattekill and Clintondale were set off by themselves and established into a charge called Plattekill.

In 1854 J. C. Brodhead donated a lot for a new church at Modena Corners. The new church was built in 1855 at a cost of $4,528.18, and dedicated by Rev. L. W. Vincent, Presiding Elder of the Newburgh District, free from debt. In 1856-7, Uriah Messiter was pastor; 1858-9, William Ostrander; 1860-1, William Stevens; 1862, William Blake; 1863-4, Mr. VanDeusen; 1865-6, J. C. Hoyt; 1867-9, M. M. Curtis; 1870, Angelo Ostrander; 1871-2, J. H. Lane. In 1871-2, the East Plattekill Church was repaired, enlarged and a bell put in the steeple. The Society of Clintondale purchased the old M. E. Church at Latintown for $600, and placed it on the site donated by J. J. Hull and John Turner for $1,100 more, making a total of $1,700. The church was then removed and erected in 1872, and dedicated by Rev. G. H. Covey. Pastors: in 1872-4, S. G. Keyser; 1874-5, J. G. Slater; 1875-6, D. H. Hanaburgh; 1876-9, W. W. Shaw; 1879-81, J. O. Kern; 1881-4, R. H. Travis; 1884-6, M. R. Lent; 1886-8, E. H. Hofficker; 1888-90, J. H. Michell; 1890-1, S. J. McCutcheon; 1891-5, G. C. Francis.

In 1894 the church building at Clintondale was sold to John H. Hull for $100, and the present elegant house of worship was erected the same year. The new church was dedicated June 20, 1894, and paid for on the day of dedication. The cost was a little over $5,000. Pastors: in 1895-8, W. R. Hunt; 1898-9, W. W. Wilcox; 1899-02, F. B. Crispell; 1902-6, Emmet Shew; 1906-7, R. J. Trevorrow. The Plattekill Valley Church organization was incorporated three times, viz.: December 7, 1846, January 29, 1860, and July 6, 1875. The other three churches in the town have always been presided over by a single pastor, but this church has been a separate charge. The first church was erected in 1840, and has been modified and repaired at different times, and is, at present one of the most elegant and substantial church structures in the town, with a large and flourishing congregation.

THE REFORMED CHURCH AT NEW HURLEY.

On November 8, 1770, the Consistory of the Church of Shawangunk met the communicants of New Marlborough at the house of Andrew DuBois. Rev. D. Romeyn, from Marlborough, presided over the meeting. Permission was asked to form a church near the east bank of the Wallkill, assigning among other reasons that "our Communicants and neighbors are withdrawn from us on all sides, the one part to the Baptists (in the valley), and the other part to the Episcopalians (at St. Andrew's). We fear that without provision is made for us we shall all be scattered and brought to nothing." The first petition remained unanswered. A second petition was presented to the Classis and that body appointed a committee, which visited the locality of New Hurley on October 17 and 18, 1770, and inquired into all the circumstances, and finally reported that the petitioners "be permitted to accomplish their desire to be constituted into a church with this condition, viz.: That they locate their church edifice on the high ground where the land is sufficiently flat in New Hurley and not along the Wallkill. A site for the church was selected, consisting of one acre, and purchased, and the first house of worship was erected in 1774. This was succeeded by the present church in 1835. The first church was a building 30x40 feet. Foot-stoves were used for many years, and when these stoves were introduced they were placed on a foundation erected on the backs of seats.

The society was duly incorporated December 6, 1790, by Stephen Goetschins, minister; Christoffel Ostrander, William Graham, Simeon Alsdorf, Wilhelmus Ostrander, Johannes Alsdorf, Ebenezer Brown, Arthur Masten, Arthur Terwilliger, Elders and Deacons.

THE PENTECOST CHURCH.

An Episcopal Church was erected at Clintondale in 1879, under the direction of Rev. Mr. Johnson, rector at Highland, N. Y., but it never developed any denominational strength and was seldom used for services. The building and grounds were finally sold to the Pentecostal denomination, which considerably improved the property by erecting sheds and grading the grounds, and regular services have been held in the church since that time.

POST-OFFICES.

There are now four post offices in the town: Ardonia, established July 27, 1882; Clintondale, May 15, 1849; Modena, formerly "Clark's

Corner," June 1, 1826, changed to Modena, June 15, 1829, and Plattekill, established February 24, 1819. The New Hurley post-office was established January 23, 1834, and discontinued July 31, 1905.

PHYSICIANS.

Dr. Jonathan Bailey was among the first to practice medicine in Plattekill. He came in 1800. Dr. John Hunt followed in 1814. Among other doctors in that section were Dr. Charles Drake, Dr. Uriah Drake, Dr. Carmon, Dr. Joshua Garrison, Dr. Hiram Howland, Dr. Elijah Osterhoudt and Dr. Becker, who is now located at Plattekill.

At Clintondale, Dr. Adna Heaton was the first physician. He came from New Paltz, was a member of the Friend's Society, and a preacher in that Church. Among other physicians who located here were Dr. David Carpenter, Dr. Eben H. Heston, Dr. John Mann, Dr. Joseph E. Freston and Dr. William G. Birdsall. Dr. Heston is still in active practice here. At Modena, Dr. William Dusenberre, who came from Rockland County, was perhaps the first physician to locate. Other physicians were Dr. Brodhead, Dr. Daniel L. Everett, Dr. Stephen Ostrander, Dr. Charles Hait, Dr. Everett Hasbrouck, Dr. Maurice Wurts, Dr. Stephen Gerow, Dr. Theo. Milspaugh, Dr. Hiram Terry and Dr. Henry P. Chase. There has been no physician at Modena since Heston left in 1880.

LAWYERS.

The legal profession has had a small representation in this town. John Cole, the first lawyer, commenced the practice of his profession at Milton, and moved to Modena in 1818, where he opened an office and continued to practice until his death in December, 1854. Oscar Theodore Noyes graduated from Yale College, studied law at Kingston, was admitted to the bar in 1846, and practiced here until his death in 1854. Amos P. Cotlaw was a lawyer at Modena in 1820, and there has been no lawyer located here since 1854.

Solomon G. Young was admitted to the bar May, 1854, and began practice at Clintondale, where he remained for six years, when he moved to Highland, where he continued until his death in 1884. Solomon G. Carpenter opened an office in Clintondale in 1880, and remained about six months, when he moved to New York City. In 1884 he moved from New York to Highland, where he has since continued to practice. DeWitt W. Ostrander came to Clintondale in 1870, was admitted to the bar in

November, 1880, and began the practice of his profession at Clintondale in 1881, where he has continued.

The following citizens of the town have served in public office: John C. Brodhead, Representative in Congress 1831, 1833, 1837, 1839. Sheriffs of Ulster County: John C. Brodhead, 1825; Derrick DuBois, 1828; John Everett, 1834; Charles Brodhead, 1846; Maurice Wurts, 1855; Abram A. Deyo, Jr., 1858.

Abram A. Deyo was State Senator from 1843 to 1846, and the following persons served as Members of Assembly: Derrick Westbrook, 1816; John C. Brodhead, 1822; Albert Carpenter, 1837, 1839; David L. Bernard, 1840; Solomon P. Thorn, 1898, 1900, 1902.

THE MILITARY HISTORY.

During the Revolution, this town formed a part of Marlborough, and its early war history is therefore included in the history of that town. But this sparsely settled section contributed its full share of men in that struggle. The military forces of the Colony and State during the Revolution were divided into three classes: The Line, The Levies and The Military. The soldiers from this section belonged to the latter class. Sometimes a regiment would be called out several times a year, and again it might not be needed for an entire year. At one call they were in one regiment or company, and at another in some other. For that reason it is difficult to trace the men.

The following is a list of Revolutionary soldiers who served from that part of the town of Marlborough which was set off in 1800 and named Plattekill: Capt. David Ostrander, Lieut. Wilhelmus Ostrander, Christophel Ostrander, Simeon Ostrander, Isaac Garrison, John Dusenberre, John Snyder, Samuel Dusenberre.

Prior to the war of 1812, the town had been set apart from Marlborough, and it contributed men to the national army. But this roll of honor cannot be definitely made up now.

Again in the Civil War of 1861, the town of Plattekill gave patriotic support, furnishing over 150 men for the Army and Navy of the Union. Ten of these belonged to the Negro race. Some thirty or more died in the service of their country.

CHAPTER XXVII.

TOWN OF ROCHESTER.

By Charles E. Foote.

ON June 25, 1703, the English Crown issued letters patent for a tract of land known as the Rochester Patent, and described as follows:

"All the tract or parcel of land lying and being in the county of Ulster aforesaid, and beginning at the south bounds of the land of Jan Van Camp, now in his possession; from thence running in a south-east line, to the land of Capt. John Evans, and so along the northwest bounds of the said Capt. John Evans, his land, till you come over against the said hills; from thence in a northwest line to the great mountains, commonly called the Blue Hills; thence northeast something northerly along the said hills to the bounds of Marbletown; and thence along the bounds of Marbletown to the place where first begun."

The tract thus enclosed included not only the present town of Rochester, but the town of Wawarsing and a portion of Sullivan County. The town as at present organized, is bounded on the northeast by Olive and Marbletown; on the southeast by Marbletown, New Paltz and Gardiner; on the southwest by Wawarsing, and on the northwest by Wawarsing and Denning. Its area is 43,982 acres, of which more than half is in a high state of cultivation.

The southeastern and northwestern edges of the town are bordered by high ranges of mountains. On the southeast is the Shawangunk mountain range, which divides the Rondout from the Wallkill valleys; on the northwest, a continuation of the Catskills, with their tops rising high in the air.

The patent was issued in the names of Captain Joachim Schoonmaker, Moses DePuy, and Colonel Henry Beekman, as trustees for settlers, and in the possession of the town clerk are the original records of their action in the distribution of lands. This venerable volume, now more than 200 years old, is in an excellent state of preservation, and the writing is perfectly legible, though both the paper and ink are becoming faded. The covers of the record book seem to be made from sheets of old copy-books pasted together, while the back is of the old time bookbinder's "pigskin."

Previous to the issue of the patent in 1703, there were a number of settlers in the town. The Anna Beck patent was dated in 1686, and the Joachim Staats patent in 1688, and the Rochester patent alludes to a "saw-mill" and a "corn-mill" as being already built. There is evidence showing that a church existed as early as 1700, and perhaps before that time. The Documentary History of the State gives the population as 334 persons at the date of the issue of the patent, but other contemporary facts do not bear out so great a number. There were probably fifty or sixty persons, belonging to the following families:

Jan Gerritse Decker,
Seendert Kool, Sr.,
William De La Montaigne,
Jan Cartwright,
Andries Davies,
Lodewyck Hornbeck,
Anthony Hornbeck,
Teunis Osterhoudt,
Gysbert Van Garde,
David DuBois.

The records in the town clerk's office are full and complete. There are maps of old surveys and descriptions that hold good to the present day. The trustees began business at once.

A poll list, evidently used as a tally sheet at the election of trustees in the year 1740, contains a list of voters, but it cannot be told at this time whether it was a complete list of those entitled to vote, or only those whose votes were cast. It was probably the latter. It forms, however, an excellent guide as to the settlers at that period. The list is as follows:

Teunis Osterhoudt,
Cryn Osterhoudt,
Petrus Osterhoudt,
Ceaxmon Coddebock,
John Schoonmaker,
Moses Depuy, Jr.,
Jacobus Quick,
Johanis Hendrickson,
Wallen Cool,
Abraham Bevier,
Peter Kortright,
Jan Osterhoudt,
Charles Denniston,
James Simpson,
Jacobus Depuy,
Daniel Schoonmaker,
Johannis Hoornbeck,
Jacob Rutsen,
Jacobus Hoornbeck,
Laurens Kortright,
Cornelius Wynkoop,
Philip DuBois,
Jacobus Swartout,
Mathis Louw,
Egbert Dewitt,
Peter Westbrook,
Jacob Vandermark,
Jan Westbrook,
Jacob Dewitt,
Cornelius Ver Nooy,
Cornelius Louw,
Rotsert Kettel,
Neckelas Keator,
Benjamin Schoonmaker,
Joggum Schoonmaker,
Jacob Hardenbergh,
Jacobus Schoonmaker,
Teunis Meddah,
Efrom Cambers.

The first record of a religious organization begins with the Dutch Reformed in 1701, but outside the fact that there was a church organization, and that it was presided over at times by Rev. Petrus Vas, and others, little seems to be known. In 1732 the members of the church in Rochester subscribed to the support of Rev. G. W. Mancius at Kingston, with the provision that they should be allowed to withdraw whenever other arrangements were made. Rev. Mancius visited Rochester frequently and preached as late as 1749. A student named Jacobus Frelinghuysen was sent to Holland in 1751 by the churches of Rochester, Wawarsing and Marbletown. He completed his studies at Utrecht and was ordained by the Classis at Amsterdam, but died on the passage home. Rev. Theodorus Frelinghuysen of Albany officiated occasionally, as did Rev. J. Schuneman of Catskill. Henricus Frelinghuysen, brother of the deceased Jacobus Frelinghuysen, was the subject of considerable correspondence between the church at Rochester and the Classis at Amsterdam, the church desiring that he be ordained in this country on account of the expense and loss by the death of the brother. He was finally licensed, and, tradition says, ordained, but there seems no record of the ordination. Two weeks after his induction into the ministry he was taken with smallpox and died. His remains were buried under the pulpit at the old Marbletown church. After this there was no regular pastor until 1766, when Dirick Romeyn was ordained and officiated at Rochester, Marbletown and Wawarsing for nine years. Then for several years Rev. Reyner Van Nest, of Shawangunk, made monthly visits; in 1781 Rev. Jacob Rutsen Hardenbergh took charge of the three churches, but the Princeton College, giving him the title of Doctor of Divinity, he was called in 1785 to become the president of Queens, later Rutger's College, at New Brunswick, New Jersey.

There were several pastors who occupied the charge for a few years each, Rev. Abram Van Horne, Rev. Garret Mandeville, Rev. Ralph Westervelt, and some stated supplies, until 1814, when Rochester, Wawarsing and the Clove called Rev. James Murphy.

There is no record of schools in Rochester until after the Revolution, when the State educational system was established. But there is every indication in the town records that there were good schools. The names and work of many of the second and third, and sometimes the fourth, generation of the original settlers appear in these old records, and the chirography, as well as the language, denote that the writers were educated men, as education at that day was considered.

Rochester seems to have suffered comparatively little from the Indians from the time of its settlement to the beginning of the Revolution. On October 14, 1757, there was an attack on the house of Peter Jan, in which his daughter and two soldiers stationed there were killed, and the house set on fire. Another ranger, according to the report of Col. Hasbrouck to Lieutenant Governor Delancey, made a good defense, used all the arms in the house which were charged, beat the enemy off and brought off Jan's wife and two daughters to Captain Brodhead's, a mile away. Jan and his two sons were in the field. Next night the regiment marched but discovered nothing.

The fort at that time was at Pine Bush, in the corner of the road at the top of Deyo's hill. This old fort stood for many years, but was burned in 1868. In early times a garrison was maintained there, which accounts, in a large degree, for the general immunity of the people from the violence of the natives. The property where the fort stood is now owned by Andrew B. Van Wagonen.

On August 5, 1857, J. H. Van Wagonen, of Kyserike, while repairing his house, which was the old homestead of the family, found behind a window casing, the following document, written just one hundred years before:

"To Benjamin Van Wagonen, Jr., Greeting:

"I do hereby command you in his Majesty's name for to warn all the men whose names are wrote on the back side hereof, to be and appear in Kingson, at the house of Coll. Josiah Hasbrouck this twelfth day of September, to march from there with me directly to Albany and hereoff fail nott.

"Given under my hand this 5th day of August 1757.

"JACOB HORNBECK."

On the back were the names of

Cornelius Van Wagonen,	Ephraim Depuy.
Thomas Graham,	Petere Harp,
Edward Wood, Jr.,	Daniel Wood,
Henry Harp,	Johin Louis,
Aurdt Van Wagen,	

The town is bordered by ranges of mountains on its northwestern and southeastern sides, and a rolling upland fills the space between. The Rondout Creek flows across the town in a northeasterly direction and has as tributaries from the south, Stony Creek, Sanders Kill and Peters Kill. Coxing Kill also passes through the southeast portion and empties into the

Rondout in Rosendale. The principal tributary to the Rondout from the north is the Mettacahonts Creek, which rises in the hills in the extreme northern point of the town. Into this many streams flow, including the Mombaccus Creek, or Mill Brook, as it is sometimes called, which rises in nearly the same neighborhood as the Mettacahonts but takes a more southerly course and adds the Fantine Kill to its waters before discharging into the stream a short distance above the village of Accord. There are also the Fountain Kill, the Beaver Dam Creek, and many smaller streams, which swell the parent stream. In the western end of the town is Vernooy Creek, which rises in the same neighborhood as the Mettacahonts and the Mombaccus, and taking a course almost due south passes into the town of Wawarsing, where it empties into the Rondout near Port Benjamin.

The soil of the valleys is a sandy loam, and that of the upland and hills between the water courses principally gravelly loam. Both are very productive.

Lake Mohonk is an attractive feature of the town. It has long been regarded among the most desirable summer lake regions in the United States by the better class of tourists because of its charming location, picturesque wildness and its careful and progressive management. Among its patrons are some of the best people in the country, and even the large hotel accommodations have usually been inadequate. The first summer boarding house there was established by John F. Stokes nearly fifty years ago, when the place was locally known as "Paltz Point." The property was purchased by Albert K. Smiley in 1879, and he at once began to build and develop it in the most energetic and practical manner, spending thousands of dollars every year upon the mountain roads, walks and various picturesque structures, with singular intelligence, good taste and judgment. Being a great lover of nature, and most enthusiastic in his admiration of this marvelous region, he knew just what to do to make these rare native attractions available and enjoyable without disturbing Nature's handiwork. He has thus labored there for thirty-seven years, and to-day this mountain estate embraces 5,000 acres, upon which over fifty miles of excellent roadways have been constructed, with numerous mountain paths, attractive rustic summer houses, seats, arbors, bridges and various other picturesque structures, at a cost of hundreds of thousands of dollars.

The lake is a charming bit of placid mountain water, which is held in a basin of solid rock 1,245 feet above tide. Three hundred feet above the water is "Sky-Top" mountain, and all around is a wall of tumbled rock piled in sublime confusion, with a labyrinth of wild variety and beauty which challenges the admiration and wonder of every beholder, and surpasses anything of its kind east of the Rocky Mountains. The large hotel at the north end of the lake accommodates about 450 guests. Two important public conferences are held here every year, the International Arbitration Conference in the early summer, and the Indian Conference late in autumn. This hotel is in the town of Marbletown, as the boundary line crosses the lake west of the house.

When it is stated that Mohonk has been conducted strictly on the temperance plan from its inception, with a code of Quaker blue-laws rigidly enforced at all times, the great success of the enterprise seems the more marvelous.

The Minnewaska Lake resorts, some miles south of Mohonk, known as the Cliff House, and the Wildmere, are alike charming in scenic beauty. The lake is larger than Mohonk, the cliffs higher. It was owned by a brother of Mr. Smiley until his death, and is now run by his sons. It is included in another vast mountain estate, which reaches west to another beautiful Shawangunk lake shown as "Awosting," which, however, is in the town of Wawarsing. All these names are of Indian origin.

During the Revolutionary period Rochester was intensely loyal, some two hundred and seventy men signing the Articles of Association at the beginning, and the names of the families in the town being well represented in the different regiments of militia. In the First Regiment it would seem that the two Captains Schoonmaker, Hendrick and Edward, Major Adrian Wynkoop, Lieutenant Abraham Van Aken and several others, must have been Rochester people. Adjutant Denniston of the Second, bears a name well known to the records of Rochester; in the Third Regiment, Colonel John Cantine, Lieut. Col. Jacob Hoornbeck, Quartermaster Philip Hoornbeck, Captains Cantine, Hardenbergh, Kortright, Frederick and Joachim Schoonmaker, Lieutenants Brodhead and Van Wagonen, and several others, present an array of Rochester names, while the Fourth Regiment, with an adjutant and a Captain Schoonmaker, Captains Hoornbeek, Cantine and Swart, Lieutenants Cantine, Hardenbergh, Depuy and Osterhoudt, all indicate that Rochester held a high place in supplying officers as well as men for that great conflict.

During the war there was much trouble from the Tories and Indians. In 1777 or 1778 the Indians, presumably led by Tories, attacked the houses of Shurker, Miller and Baker at Pine Bush. The two former were killed and the latter was probably carried away and subsequently killed, as his remains were not found. Captain Benjamin Kortright got a band together and attacked the Indians, driving them away. It was found that the women and children had not been harmed. Captain Kortright pursued the Indians as far as his supplies would permit and returned.

At that time, according to a pamphlet published in 1846, and assumed to be reliable, there were 200 to 300 troops at the fort on Honkhill. An expedition was fitted out, which was placed in charge of Lieutenant John Graims, or Grahams, who volunteered for the service. He only took eighteen men, one sergeant and a corporal. They planned to intercept the Indians by getting ahead of them, and did so, but the Indians in great number took them by surprise and shot them down. Three men escaped, one of them Abraham Van Campen, having been detailed to hunt game for the expedition, not being present at the massacre. A large body of troops set out at once, but their only duty was to bury the dead; the Indians had gone into the wilds.

In 1778 a petition was presented to Governor Clinton by the people of Rochester asking for greater protection against the Tories and Indians. As no reference is made to the Pine Bush and Grahamsville massacres, it is probable that the petition was made previous to the attack. The document was signed by Captain Benjamin Kortright, Captain Joachim Schoonmaker, Lieutenants Dirick and Frederic Westbrook and Jacobus Bruyn, Jr., Ensign Jacob Hoornbeck, Jacobus Wynkoop, Moses Depuy, John Sleight and many others.

In the civil organization the trustees provided for in the patent were the dominant factors of government. They seem to have been the only government until 1709, when a supervisor, two assessors and a constable and collector were elected. The first supervisor was Capt. Joachim Schoonmaker; the assessors were Moses Depuy and Lodewick Hoornbeck, while Jan Cortrecht was constable and collector. In 1710 a surveyor of roads was elected, Hermanus Decker being chosen.

From 1713 to 1729 there is no record of town officers except Trustees, except for the single year of 1717, when the officials are named as follows: Supervisor, David DuBois; Constable and Collector, Cornelius Cole; Assessors, Moses Depuy, Sr., and Johannis Ver Nooy; Surveyors of Highways, Derrick Rosekraus and John Van Camp, Jr. There is every indication, however, that the organization was practically continuous after 1709. The records give a list of the trustees for one hundred years, elected annually, after the Revolutionary War, and the changes brought about by the State government, the final settlement of the land titles under the constitution, their duties became perfunctory, and their election of no moment.

After the adoption of a State Constitution, and its permanent establishment by the arbitrament of war, long, bloody and costly in men and money, Rochester, as did other towns in Ulster County and elsewhere, turned its energy and productive capacity again to the establishment of material prosperity. The school system was organized, new church organizations gradually came into existence, new industries were opened up; greater area of land was planted; more saw-mills, grist-mills and tanneries were constructed. The denudation of the forest lands served the double purpose of supplying the mills and adding to the arable area. Thus passed more than two generations of progressive civilization, prolific in its production of American men and women, brainy and energetic in its accumulation of material advantages, and sending off from the body of its population, into other parts of this, and other States, the brains and broad ideas, the bone and sinew, as well as the means, which has broadened and enriched the development of the country from the Atlantic to the Pacific.

There is a record of the appointment of Abraham T. E. Dewitt, Andrew Bevier, Jacobus Bruyn, Richard Brodhead, Jacobus Wynkoop and Richard Davis as school commissioners of Rochester in 1796, and Philip D. Bevier, Benjamin Kortright and Jacobus Bruyn in 1797, 1798, 1799, and 1800. There is no further action recorded until 1813, when the modern school system was organized under the law of 1812. From that time until the change in the law in 1814, school commissioners and inspectors were elected annually. Practically all of them came from the early families of the town. In 1813 the first school-tax of record is noted.

In the Newtown district, Simeon J. Van Wagonen taught one year, from January 9, 1798, to January 30, 1799, for twenty-eight pounds and board. Barbazon Nugent followed him for three months, beginning February 4, for ten shillings a week and "to find himself." Jacobus Shenich and Cornelius Hoornbeck were the trustees.

Isaac Frinch taught the Mombaccus school for the year ending February 12, 1795, for twenty-seven pounds, ten shillings "and to be boarded," and was employed the next year at forty pounds and "to be boarded." He was still teaching at the same salary in 1799, according to the report of Jacob Coddington, Henry Dewitt, Jr., and Cornelius Hoornbeck, trustees, so it must be assumed that he was a good teacher and gave general satisfaction.

The Kyserike school was presided over by Henry J. Hoornbeck, from May 14, 1798, to March 18, 1799, at a salary of seventy-five dollars a year. The Pleasant Ridge school, near the Coxing Clove, was taught by Benjamin Louw.

The Luren Kill school was taught, December 7, 1795, to March 7, 1796, by Levi Bradley. The trustees were Richard Brodhead and Conradt Bevier. Elizah Devoe taught the school at Fantine Kill from April 9, 1795, to March 1, 1796. Andries Bevier and Simon Bevier were the trustees.

A work of vast importance to the town of Rochester was the construction of the Delaware and Hudson canal in the valley of the Rondout. This enterprise was incorporated April 23, 1823, and the full employment of labor, and the home market for supplies, created by the large force of workmen during the five years of the work, gave a mighty impetus to agricultural development. Many fine residences were built during that period, some of which are still standing. The opening of the canal in 1828 gave an opportunity to place agricultural products in the large markets cheaply; it also made an outlet which permitted the fuller operation of the bluestone quarries and the easier shipments of the Esopus millstones. The canal was enlarged at great expense in 1842 and again in 1851.

The churches in the town, except the Dutch church, the early history of which has been mentioned, are as follows: The Reformed Church at Cherrytown, which was organized in 1858. The Methodist Episcopal at Port Jackson in 1847; that at Alligerville in 1857, and that at Cherrytown in 1867.

The territory of the town of Rochester has been changed materially since the original patent in 1703. The formal incorporation under the State laws was in 1788. In 1789 a portion of the territory was annexed to Delaware County and is included in the present town of Middletown; in 1798 the town of Neversink, Sullivan County, was separated from it; in 1806 Wawarsing was created from a part of Rochester, but some of the territory was returned in 1823. The town of Gardiner was taken off in 1853, leaving Rochester as it stands at present.

The canal was abandoned in 1899, and the railroad, which had been talked off "for forty years, more or less," and surveyed several times, was opened in 1902.

For the Civil War Rochester furnished one hundred and sixty-two soldiers, according to the most reliable information. These were scattered through the various regiments and parts of regiments raised in Ulster County, with a fair sprinkling of representation in regiments from other localities. Several officers of prominence were among them.

Among the historic places of interest in the town of Rochester are the following residences which date back to ante-Revolutionary times:

The old stone house formerly known as the Depuy homestead, now owned by Lucas E. Schoonmaker. The stone house owned and occupied by Cyrus Schoonmaker, which was built by his ancestors in 1756. The old Hoornbeck homestead in Whitfield, now owned by Lincoln Dunn. The Philip Hoornbeck homestead, now owned by Morris Myers. The old Davis Sahler homestead, now owned by the New Paltz savings bank.

Of the grist-mills which were once plentifully distributed along the creeks, only two now remain. One of these is located at Pataukun, and is known as the Wilkinson mill. It stands on the site originally granted by the trustees of the township to Anthony and Joost Hoornbeck in 1709; the other is located at Mill Hook, and owned at present by Friend Wilklow. It stands on the site granted to Capt. Joachim Schoonmaker in 1703, where his saw-mill then stood.

The Schoonmaker family of Rochester presents a very interesting history, not only by reason of its numerous members, but also on account of the influence which it has always maintained in civil affairs, and in the military history of the town, county and State. There has never been a war in which the State was engaged, that one or more members of the family were not engaged in it, nor has there been a period, except possibly a year or two, since the time of the original settlement of the town, when there was not a Schoonmaker in public office. The family as a whole, is well-to-do; and so numerous have been the intermarriages during the various generations, that a large proportion of the population possess Schoonmaker blood, more or less remote. Mr. John J. Schoonmaker, the present Town Clerk, is the eighth generation from the original settlers, whose son was trustee under the patent.

Among the old Rochester merchants were Joshua Dumond, William N. McDonald, James Gillespie, and Joachim Schoonmaker. Among the early tavern-keepers were Caty Depuy, Henry T. Oosterhout, Andries Dewitt, Elizabeth Dewitt, Elisha Hoornbeck, Cornelius P. Low, Benjamin Coddington, Peter Aldrich, and many others. Dr. Dewitt was an early physician in the seventeenth century, and Dr. Louis D. Bevier some years later.

Only 744 votes were cast in the town at the general election last year when the taxable property was assessed at $795,101. The present town area is placed at 51,575 acres.

CHAPTER XXVIII.

TOWN OF ROSENDALE.

By Charles E. Foote.

THE town of Rosendale is located immediately west of the town of Esopus, from which it is separated by the Wallkill and Rondout. Further to the north a small portion of its eastern boundary is made by the town of Ulster. It is bounded on the south by the town of New Paltz, on the west by the town of Marbletown, and on the northwest by the town of Hurley, the northernmost portion being the apex of an acute angle. It has an area of 11,413 acres.

The town was erected by act of General Assembly, April 26, 1844, parts of Hurley, New Paltz and Marbletown being taken in its formation. A stiff fight was maintained for some years by the people of the section for separation, on the ground of convenience in official business, and the untiring energy and persistence was tardily, but finally rewarded by the act named. The law thus enacted gives the boundaries as follows:

"All the territory hereinafter described, agreeable to a map made by Jacob A. Snyder, being part of the towns of Hurley, Marbletown and New Paltz, in the county of Ulster, shall be and hereby is set off into a new town by the name of Rosendale, commencing at the Wallkill on the bounds of the farm of Jonathan Deyo, late of New Paltz, deceased, and the farm now in possession of Abraham Relyea; thence running along said bounds north eighty-four and a fourth degrees west, eighty-seven chains to the bounds of Marbletown, on the farm of John J. Stokes; thence north ten degrees west, one hundred and seventy-five chains to the towing-paths of Delaware and Hudson canal, northeasterly as it winds and turns about, thirty chains, to the cement quarry of William P. Cole; thence north twenty-seven degrees west, one hundred and one chains sixty-four links to a white-oak tree standing at the south side of the road leading to a stone ridge on the farm of John D. Gillespie; thence north thirty-five degrees east, two hundred and thirty-three chains twenty links, to a stake and stones on the farm of James Hardenburgh, now in the possession of Mr. Weeks; thence north seventy-four degrees east, one hundred and seventy chains to the bounds of Kingston at a chestnut tree on the farm of Mrs. Pink; thence along the said bounds of Kingston south one hundred and fifty-seven chains to the Rondout Creek; thence up along the same southerly as it winds and turns, one hundred and twenty-five chains to where the Wallkill intersects said Rondout; thence up alongside Wallkill to the place of beginning."

The Rondout flows northeasterly through the center of the town, and there are a number of small streams tributary to it and to the Wallkill.

which forms the southern portion of its eastern boundary. One of the noticeable physical features is a chain of lakes called the "Binnewaters," and named by the numerals one to five inclusive. The first is on the line between Rosendale and Hurley, and is of considerable size; the second and third are almost due south, within a short distance to the southwest.

The surface is a rolling and hilly upland, much broken in places, with deep gorges and ravines, presenting some remarkably attractive scenery. There are plains in the eastern part along the valley, which originally gave rise to the name of the locality, which is found in old records as far back as 1700, nearly a century and a half before the region received the name by law.

In its early settlement the record of Rosendale is found in that of the three towns from which parts were taken for its creation. The names of a majority of its people can be recognized as being those families, who, in the early days, settled Hurley, Marbletown and New Paltz. The natural, and, in fact, the only logical inference, is, that the families whose names were originally recorded in those towns, and in later years appeared in Rosendale, had settled in those portions of the older organizations which were taken to form the new town of Rosendale. Reference is made to those towns for the earlier records.

Among the land papers at Albany is a description of 963 acres of land in "a place called Roasindale, on the south side of the Rondout River," surveyed by Philip Wells, surveyor for Jacob Rutsen. This is dated May 28, 1685. Another survey and description of similar kind must have been located where the Wallkill enters the Rondout, as it is described being "672 acres of land lying upon both sides of Rondout Kill or river, including part of the Paules river," surveyed for William Fisher, dated two days before Rutsen's, May 26, 1685.

October 21, 1723, Jacob Rutsen received a deed from the town of Hurley for 600 acres of land, located apparently to the south and east of his previous tract.

In the assessment roll of Marbletown for 1811, the following names seem to constitute a practically complete list of those families in the part of that town which was subsequently detached in the creation of Rosendale. In that list is embraced the following:

Abraham Auchmoody,
Charles Burr,
John Churchwell,
Jacob Coutant,
Abraham Coutant,
Oswall Dewall,

Andrew I. DuBois,
Cornelius A. Delemeter,
Christian Deits,
Frederick I. Elmendorf,
Cornelius Keyser,
Moses Keator,
Jacobus and other Keators,
John Sluyter,
Henry Snyder,
Jacob Snyder,
John Sammons,
Cornelius D. Sluyter,
Heber Williams,
Abraham Deits,
Philip Dewall,
Jacobus Elmendorf, Jr.,
Joel Hine,
Benjamin A. Krum,
George Patterson,
Abraham Sluyter,
Cornelius Sammons,
Christopher Snyder,
Jacob A. Snyder,
Abraham Sammons,
John M. Williams,

Probably others might be disclosed by a complete and exhaustive examination of the Assessment roll, and a comparison of the result with the property holders of record.

Cornelius Lefevre was from New Paltz and had a large family, most of whom settled in the neighborhood. His four daughters married John Ostrander, Caleb M. Roosa, James E. Schoonmaker, and one of the Snyders. Other settlers in the upper part of the town were Peter Van Wagener, Johannis and Jacob Van Wagenen.

Charles Dewitt settled early on the Green Kill and built the Dewitt Mills. He was a member of the Provincial Congress when it met at Kingston. The old family residence is marked with the date 1736.

The schools of Rosendale were under the control of the original towns during the entire period of the original district system, Rosendale being created a separate municipality the same year that the law was enacted placing the schools in charge of town superintendents. Of the earlier teachers, the names of Abram Hasbrouck, Tammerlane Hine, Dr. Andrew Snyder, and John James Snyder are mentioned, and there were probably many others whose names do not appear. The superintendents during the dozen years during which the law was enforced were as follows:

1844—Jacob A. Snyder.
1845-1846—James H. Bogardus.
1847—Jacob A. Snyder.
1848—James H. Bogardus.
1849—E. W. Buddington.
1850-1853—Simon Schoonmaker.
1854—Isaiah Snyder.
1856—Simeon Schoonmaker.

The beginning of the religious worship in what is now Rosendale began at Bloomingdale along in 1796 or 1797. Previous to that much difficulty had been experienced by the devout inhabitants in attending divine worship, on account of the great distance, and the movement to establish a church began by the appointment of a committee to consult with the consistory of the Kingston Church, of which Andries Snyder, Simon Lefevre and John C. Dewitt were the members. When their report was made, a committee, consisting of Petrus Smedes, Simon Lefevre, and Samuel Schoonmaker, was appointed to petition the Classis for permission to organize, which was soon accomplished, the official organizers being Rev. Stephen Goetchius and Moses Freligh.

In 1800 the Church joined with the Kleine Esopus Church in calling the Rev. Thomas G. Smith to the joint pastorate, a position he held for some years. It was joined with the Esopus Church until 1835, and was incorporated December 6, 1797. On the same day Abraham Van Wagenen deeded to the trustees a piece of land nearly an acre in extent, for church purposes, and on July 7, 1798, the trustees of the town of Hurley made a grant of thirteen acres. The first church edifice was erected in 1797 and stood until 1846, when it was destroyed by fire. It was at once decided to rebuild, and George W. Lefevre and Abram Van Wagenen had charge of the work. The new building was erected some distance north of the old one, and a handsome parsonage is near by.

The Friends, or Quakers, established meetings about the year 1800, in what is now the town of Rosendale, and meetings have been held, with occasional interruptions, since that time. The organization here is a branch of the Marlborough Monthly Meeting.

CEMENT.

The production of Hydraulic Cement, now generally known as natural, or native rock cement, has long been one of the most important industries of Rosendale. For nearly three-quarters of a century the mining and manufacture of this cement was so extensively carried on in this town that the article itself became generally known as "Rosendale Cement," to distinguish it from the Portland, or artificial product, with little regard to the place of manufacture. And to-day this term is largely used by engineers and builders in making this distinction. The quality of the Rosendale rock was found superior to that of any other locality, and the product has always been regarded of the highest grade. For a long series of years previous to the present active demand for Portland cement, all important masonry contracts specified that "Rosendale Cement" must be used. It thus became a trade-mark of great value and the name was often fraudulently applied to inferior grades made elsewhere. This resulted in some damage to the reputation of the genuine article.

This immense deposit of cement rock in the town of Rosendale was discovered in the summer of 1825 by the engineers who were constructing the Delaware & Hudson Canal. The first specimens were burned in a blacksmith's forge at High Falls, and then reduced to powder by pounding. A test revealed its excellent quality, and it was decided that no more cement need be brought for the canal from Chittenango, Madison County, N. Y., where it was then made. Mr. Canvass White first discovered this rock and its properties, in this country, while working on the Erie Canal, in 1818. For this valuable find he was voted $20,000 by the State in that year.

The quarrying, burning and grinding of cement was begun in this region in the spring of 1826; one John Littlejohn having the contract to furnish all that was needed in the construction of the canal. On its completion the cement business ceased for a short time. But it was revived soon afterward by Judge Lucas Elmendorf of Kingston. He began operations at the present village of Lawrenceville, which was named after Watson E. Lawrence, who soon succeeded Elmendorf in the business. This burned stone was first ground in the old Snyder Mill. The Hoffman works soon followed, and also the extensive factory at Whiteport, by Hugh White, for whom that place was named. Much of the cement used in the Croton Aqueduct was made at these mills.

Mr. White was succeeded by the Newark and Rosendale Lime and Cement Co., in 1847, which greatly increased the plant, having three mills at Whiteport and Hickory Bush. They increased the daily output from 450 to 1,000 barrels per day, having spent over $120,000 upon the improvements. This company continued for over fifty years. Among other companies in the town were the Rosendale Works of F. O. Norton, the Bruceville Works of James H. Vandermark, the New York Company at Rock Lock, and the New York and Rosendale Works erected in 1873. When the industry was at its height there were a dozen or more different plants in operation in the town, and over 5,000 men were engaged in the work.

The Rosendale plant alone, in 1898, ground about 4,000 barrels of cement a day. The price had then fallen from $1.80 per barrel in 1883 to $0.75 in 1898. Beginning with a total annual output in Ulster County, in

1856, of 510,000 barrels, it increased to 2,833,107 barrels in 1892. At the present time the industry has greatly declined because of the extensive manufacture of American Portland cement, which has lowered the price of that grade and brought it in direct competition with the rock cement.

A few years ago most of these Rosendale companies were bought by a New York syndicate and merged into one known as the Consolidated Cement Company. This large plant is now being operated, and 6,000 barrels of cement are now turned out daily with some 300 men employed. There are only two other plants now in operation, one being that of the A. J. Snyder Company, and the other the Miller Company, producing about 1,000 barrels a day each, and employing about 150 men.

Most of these Rosendale quarries are deep, and tunnels are run to reach the deeper strata, which are usually considered the best quality. Many of these are far below the bed of the Hudson, and the mines are well worth visiting. They have proved of inestimable value to the town, and yielded many fortunes to the operators, while thousands of laboring men have been benefited.

It is a curious fact that the raw cement rock crushed and ground will not produce any hydraulic property in the cement whatever. It must first be roasted or calcined, which is done in huge kilns of brick. This reduces the weight about one half. But the precise change which takes place in the stone by this roasting process, though presumably chemical, has never been satisfactorily explained.

Rosendale furnished about ninety-five soldiers to the War of the Rebellion, distributed in the various regiments, though there were probably more in the old Twentieth than in any other.

The State census of 1905 places the population of the town at 4,670. Of this number, 4,436 were native born.

There is a fine railway bridge over the Rondout Creek in Rosendale village, which carries the track of the Wallkill Valley Railway. It is 900 feet long and about 160 feet above the creek. This bridge was rebuilt recently in a much more substantial manner required for the heavier trains and rolling stock of the road now in use on that line.

CHAPTER XXIX.

TOWN OF SAUGERTIES.

By Charles E. Foote.

THE town of Saugerties is the northeastern town of Ulster County. It was incorporated April 5, 1811, from the territory which had previously been included in the town of Kingston. Evidently an error had been made in the boundary line, as a correcting act was passed by the General Assembly the next year, and an addition was made to the area of the town in 1832, by taking more of Kingston.

Saugerties is bounded on the north by Green County; on the east by the Hudson river; on the south by the towns of Ulster and Kingston, and on the west by the town of Woodstock and the county of Greene. Its area is 37,603 acres.

The surface of the eastern portion, along the Hudson river, is undulating, with occasional rocky bluffs and breaks, of no considerable elevation, but abrupt in their character; to the west and northwest there is a natural gradient, somewhat hilly and broken across the foot-hills and to the Catskill mountains proper. The scenery is most picturesque, the high mountains to the northwest being in plain sight on clear days from the eastern and southern border limits.

The Esopus Creek, which enters the town from the south at a point about two miles from the Hudson, flows due north about half the length of the town, then turns east, and after a series of curves, breaks through, falls over the bluffs, and enters the Hudson, creating a most excellent though narrow harbor at its mouth. It has numerous tributaries, of which the Plattekill, rising in the mountains in the extreme northwest, flows southward by a few degrees easterly and reaches the Esopus near the south line of the town. In the northeastern part of the town, a mile or two from the Hudson, rises the Saw Kill, which flows southeasterly, and reaches that river just above the mouth of the Esopus. The Beaver Kill, evidently contrary minded, rises between the Esopus and the Plattekill in the southerly part of the town, and flows northward between the Plattekill on the west, and the Sawkill on the east, both flowing in oppo-

John Maxwell.

site directions, and empties in the Catskill Creek at the northern limits of the town.

There seems no method of establishing, at this time, the date of occupancy or the identity of the very earliest settlers. The land was a part of the Kingston patent and it is naturally supposed that as soon as it could consistently be accomplished, those families who subsequently became prominent in Saugerties, selected their locations in that territory and assumed possession at as early a date as possible, for the purpose of growing the crops, utilizing the water power, and constructing the buildings.

A grant of land was made in May, 1687, of a tract of about 442 acres at the mouth of the Esopus Creek, to George Meals and Richard Hays. A description of this property was filed early in 1686, together with several other tracts, surveyed by Ro. Fullertown "for George Meals and others." One of the other tracts was 252 acres, lying on the side of a run called the Beaver Kill, about three miles west of the mouth of the Esopus, also being a part of the tract called Sagiers; also 300 acres along the Hudson from the mouth of the Esopus, being part of the Sagiers tract; also a tract of 201 acres, about a mile northwest of the mouth of the Esopus and crossing the Sawkill, which was also a part of the Sagiers tract. Incidentally, Surveyor Fullertown laid out a tract of 797 acres for himself while surveying in this region, in the neighborhood of Wanton Island.

The reiteration of the name "Sagiers," as applied to this region, at that very early date, indicates the source of the evolution which has produced "Saugerties." But the logic, or the philosophy, of the evolution does not satisfactorily appear, nor does the origin or parentage of the word itself. Some suggestions have been made from time to time, as to a different source, but they are all so entirely impregnated with an acrostic taint, that they are valuable only as examples of ingenuity.

Whether or not Meals and Hays ever resided on the properties, or caused them to be settled, is not known. Several conveyances were made, evidently within the company or family, and in 1712 the tract at the mouth of the Esopus Creek was transferred to John Persen. He died in 1748, and left the property subject to the life interest of his widow, to his son Jacobus, and his daughter Vannitte, wife of Myndert Minderse. In the will is mentioned the original grist-mill of the section, though no statement is made of the time of its erection, or even whether it was on the ground when he purchased it in 1712. This does not appear likely, however, as the deed of transfer would probably have made some mention of it.

In the winter of 1710-1711, a large colony of immigrants, called Palatines, came up the Hudson and established camps on either side of the river, that on the west side being known as West Camp, that opposite as East Camp. Most of these were Huguenots, though some were Dutch, and all are said to have derived the cognomen of "Palatines" from the fact that all came from the Palatinate in the Netherlands. They seem to have spread out within the next few years, until the entire northern portion of the town was occupied by them. One of the earliest permanent settlements seems to have been at Katsbaan, as a church was organized there about 1730. There is an old gazetteer which states that the Lutheran church at West Camp, was organized in 1708, but inasmuch as there are no obtainable records, and the colony of Palatines did not reach West Camp until about Christmas, 1710, the statement must be an error, typographically or otherwise.

A list of the persons and families of the immigrants from the Palatinate who came about Christmas, 1710, and encamped at West Camp, was made the following June (June 24, 1711). They had separated themselves into three groups, known as Elizabeth Town, George Town, and New Town. The reports were as follows:

John Christopher Gerlach, listmaster of Elizabeth Town, reported the inhabitants to be forty-two families,—one hundred and forty-six persons;

Jacob Mauck, listmaster of George Town, reported forty families,—one hundred and twenty-eight persons;

Philip Peter Granberger, listmaster for New Town, reported one hundred and three families,—three hundred and sixty-five persons;

Making a total of 185 families—639 persons, who were among the very earliest real settlers of Saugerties and the Sawyer's Creek region.

There seems to have been some feeling over the settlement of the Palatines. The Board of Trade at Kingston, had proposed to give them, should they come, a tract of land on the west side of the Hudson, "twenty miles in breadth, and forty miles in length," and Governor Hunter reported, November 14, 1710, six weeks before their arrival, that he had "settled" them in two villages on the Sawyer's Creek. This seems to mean that he had selected sites for two villages for their settlement.

On the other hand there seems to have been no action taken to supply any such tract of land which would have amounted to something like a

Martin Cantine.

The Martin Cantine Company's Coated Paper Manufacturing Plant, Saugerties, N. Y.

half million acres. An order of the court, dated October 5, 1711, seems to indicate that there was some friction over settlements on lands. It reads as follows:

"At a meeting of Justices in Kingstown, this 5th October 1711, present Coll. Jacob Rutsen, Capt. Dirk Schepmoes, Mr. Evert Wynkoop, Mr. Cornelis Coal, Coll. Rutsen having received a letter from Mr. Secretary by his Excellency's order, setting forth that severall Pallatines leave their settlements and seek to settle themselves on particular men theire land, and ordered Ye Justices to send them to their own towns, ordered that each constable be served with a coppy of this order, that they cause all the pallatines to go to theire own settlements, and fore-warne all theire Districts that they do not harbour any Pallatines att theire perrill."

The oldest religious body in the town of Saugerties is the Lutheran church of West Camp. A gazetteer published by Hamilton Child in 1871, says that it was organized in 1708, by the Palatines, but as there seems to have been no Palatines there until 1712, and as there does not seem to have been any Lutherans among the Dutch, this is probably an error. The most reliable advices place the organization of the church at 1711, with Rev. Joshua Kocherthal as its organizer and first minister.

There seems also to have been members of the Dutch Reformed Church among the Palatines; both joined together and built a church where each held services. As nearly as can be determined, the erection of this church building was accomplished the first season of occupancy by the Palatines, in 1711.

The original bell was a present to the church from Queen Anne, but during the early years of the nineteenth century it was exchanged for a larger one. It is said to be one of the first, if not the first Lutheran churches established in America, and services have been held there almost continuously.

The following is a copy of a document which has much historic significance. It is preserved among the papers of the Russell family:

"*To all Protestant Christians of every persuasion:—*

"Whereas, in the year of 1710, many German Protestants of the Lutheran persuasion were invited from Europe to North America by the late Queen Ann of England, and at their arrival in the country a number of them settled at the West Camp, now in the county of Ulster, in the state of New York; not long after their settlement they formed themselves into a Congregation and built a Church or House of Worship, as well as their then circumstances would permit, but many of said Congregation having since, from year to year, removed to a great distance, whereby the present congregation is become very weak and their church in a rotten condition, and finding themselves unable to build a new one, therefore we the subscribers, Elders, have with the consent of the Congregation resolved on a collection, hoping that every well wishing Protestant will kindly assist us to perform so necessary a Task for the Honor of God according to their free will and inclination. We have, therefore, unanimously chosen our trusty friend, Ludwig Roessell, the bearer hereof, and his companion Johannes Eligh, to go forth and receive such free gifts as every Christian who may chance to be requested by them will be pleased to bestow. In gratitude whereof we shall, if an opportunity is offered to us, be ever ready to return the kindness with gladness. Given under our hands this 11th day of October 1791."

"PETRUS. EGNER.
"PETER MOWER."
"JOHANNIS MOWER."

"West Camp, county of Ulster."

"Ulster County, State of New York, ss:—

"I do certify that the Purport of the above Petition is founded on truth, and that I am well acquainted with the persons therein named, and that they are men of good character, as witness my hand in Kingston this 13th day of October, 1791.

"D. WYNKOOP.
"First Judge of the Court of Common Pleas for Ulster County.
"JOHN SNYDER.
"Assistant Judge of Said Court.

"The above Ludwig Roessell and Johannis Eligh are personally known to me, and bear the character of honest men.

"Given at Greenwich this 22nd October 1791. "GEO. CLINTON."

It is impossible to state at this time whether the improvements in 1791 were the remodeling and the repairing and enlarging the old one, or whether a new edifice was built. A new and commodious church was erected in 1871. It still maintains the Augsbury Confession, and was incorporated in 1854.

Saugerties is filled with historic matter the use of which the limits of this volume will not permit, except in their most salient features. The Snyders, the Russells, the Dedericks, the Posts, the DeWitts, the Newkirks, the Van Steenburghs, the Wolvins, the Wynkoops, the Ploeffs, the Ten Broecks, the Rightmeyers, the Wells, the Kiersteds, and a large number of other families are in possession of old documents and records which are of absorbing interest, as showing the conditions which prevailed from 100 to 200 years ago.

Andrew Brink was the captain of the "Clermont," Robert Fulton's first steamboat.

The following letter has been preserved, addressed to him:

"NEW YORK, Oct. 9, 1807.

"CAPTAIN BRINK—Sir:—Enclosed is the number of voyages which it is intended the boat should run this season; you may have them published in the Albany papers. As she is strongly manned, and every one except Jackson under your command, you must insist on each one doing his duty, or turn him on shore and put another in his place; everything must be kept in order, everything in its place, and all parts of the boat scowered and clean. It is not sufficient to tell men to do a thing, but stand over them and make them do it. One pair of quick and good eyes is worth six pair of hands in a commander. If the boat is dirty or out of order, the fault shall be yours,—let no man be idle when there is the least thing to do, and make them move quick.

Robt. A. Snyder

"Run no risques of any kind; when you meet or overtake vessels beating or crossing your way, always run under their stern, if there be the least doubt that you cannot clear their head by fifty yards or more; give in the amounts of receipts and expenses every week to the Chancellor.

"Your most obedient

ROBERT FULTON."

Mr. Brink was also the first town clerk of Saugerties.

In 1788 there were five road districts in that part of the town of Kingston which afterward became the town of Saugerties.

Saugerties was a part of the town of Kingston during the war of the Revolution, and, of course, had no independent military history. In the war of 1812 the town was represented by some 85 of her citizens.

About 1808 or 1810, one or more military companies was organized in the town. The trainings were mostly in one company and was known as the Rangers. Its officers were: Captain, J. Clark; Lieutenant, L. Kierstead; Ensign, A. Post; Orderly Sergeant, Peter P. Post. In 1813 this company joined with one from Kingston and another from Marbletown under the command of Captain Elmendorf and Lieutenant Peter P. Post. There was a draft of one-sixth of the militia in 1814, but the term of service was short.

Nearly a thousand men fought in the war of the Rebellion from the town of Saugerties, including the substitutes furnished when the drafts were made. The men from Saugerties were distributed through the various regiments organized wholly, or in part, in Ulster County, and many members of various other organizations.

CHAPTER XXX.

TOWN OF SHANDAKEN.

By Henry Griffeth.

SHANDAKEN is the northwest corner town of the County of Ulster and was formed from a part of the town of Woodstock, April 9th, 1804.

It is an Indian name signifying rapid waters, and was applied to the town, or to the territory out of which it was formed, on account of the numerous streams which flow down its steep gorges and mountain ravines. The name is appropriate and should not be changed for any other.

The settlements known as Woodstock, and Great and Little Shandaken, were, by act of the Legislature, passed April 11th, 1787, formed into a township under the name of Woodstock. The town as first formed embraced a large territory and took in the present towns of Woodstock, Shandaken, Denning, the most of Hardenburgh and a part of Olive.

At the Woodstock town meeting held the first Tuesday in April, 1796, it was unanimously voted that the town be divided, but no division was made till 1804, when the Act creating Shandaken was passed. The following year, on the first Tuesday in April, the first town meeting was held, and Benjamin Milk was chosen Supervisor, William B. Rogers, Town Clerk. Rogers had held the same office in the town of Woodstock since 1801. He was the father of the late Joseph H. Rogers who died in Shandaken some years ago at an advanced age. Supervisor Milk, at the time he was chosen, resided at the place now called Slide Mountain, near the head of Big Indian Valley, on the farm lately occupied by James W. Dutcher. He afterwards moved to Dry Brook, in what is now the town of Hardenburgh, and settled on the farm now, or lately, owned by William Todd. Milk continued to represent the town as its Supervisor until 1810, when Aaron Adams was chosen and re-elected till 1816; when he was succeeded by Henry W. Rogers.

Supervisor Adams resided at Pine Hill. He settled there and made the first clearing, before the year 1800. About 1810, he built a hotel on the

Henry Griffeth.

site now occupied by Billor's summer hotel, formerly known as "Glen Hall," and continued to reside there, keeping tavern, until about 1816, when he moved away and settled near Rochester, N. Y. Adams served one term in the Legislature while he lived at Pine Hill; he was a good fiddler and a man of energy. He was also the first postmaster of Pine Hill, but at that time there were only three post-offices in the town. Pine Hill, Aaron Adams postmaster, one at the O'Neil place now owned by Giles Whitney, between Shandaken and Phoenicia, Henry W. Rogers postmaster, and The Corners, Lazarus Sprague postmaster.

At the time Adams lived at Pine Hill there was little there except his tavern and a saw-mill set down in a small clearing. His tavern was a frame building, lathed and plastered, and was the first building of the kind built in the town. People came for miles around to see it; it was such a curiosity. All other houses in the town at that time were constructed of logs. The tavern at Pine Hill, after Adams left, was kept by John Higgins, father of the late Marical Higgins; then by Samuel Smith; then by Ezekial Griffin, father of the late Matthew Griffin; then by one Strattabus, a Frenchman, who rebuilt it. In after years it passed into the hands of the late Thomas and Floyd Smith, and finally to Mrs. Mahala Floyd, who in 1874 erected "Glen Hall," and the old Pine Tavern, to well and widely known for many years, passed away.

Henry W. Rogers was Supervisor from 1816 until 1825, having been elected nine times in succession, which gave him more years in office than any other Supervisor of the town. He also kept a tavern in connection with his post-office. But in those days a Shandaken tavern was a primitive affair, the same room frequently answering for a bar-room, dining-room and kitchen. He was succeeded in office by Herman Landon, who was Supervisor until 1827. He was succeeded in turn by James O'Neil, father of the late Thomas H. O'Neil. Herman Landon was a son of John Landon who settled on Pine Hill, coming from Columbia County about 1805. He made the first clearing, where the "Grampian" now stands.

Pine Hill, and almost the entire town, at that time was a dense wilderness, with here and there a clearing. Bears, wolves, deer and other wild animals held almost universal sway.

Milo Barber, Sr., kept a small store near Phoenicia on the road to Chichester as early as 1826, and about the same time Lazarus Sprague started one at The Corner. Very little, however, was done in the mercantile line until the building of tanneries later on.

The following is a sample of pioneer life in Shandaken. Old Peter Crispell, came to the town as a pioneer settler from Marbletown before 1800. He settled at Shandaken Center, as the village of Shandaken was formerly called, on the property now owned by Bernard Garrety, where he built a stone house, which is still standing. The country was then a wilderness, and he depended on Marbletown for his supply of provisions. A horse owned by him, named "Figure" and a boy living in the family, made frequent visits to Marbletown and brought back such supplies as were most needed. On one occasion, in the spring of the year, after they had planted potatoes, they found that their stock of provisions was nearly exhausted. The boy was placed on Figure's back and started for Marbletown, which he reached in safety, but before he was ready to return, a heavy fall of rain so flooded the streams that they could not be forded, hence the boy and Figure were detained in Marbletown until it was considered safe for them to return. In the meantime, the Crispell family were compelled to dig up the potatoes they had planted and use them for food. This was in the "good old times," but, really, were there ever any "good old times?" We think not. "Good old times" may do for sentiment, but has no foundation in fact.

Modern Shandaken, according to the census taken in 1905, has a population of 3,045, of which 2,988 are citizens and 57 aliens. It has a voting population of 925, and is divided into three election districts. Its town meetings for the election of town officers are held biennially in connection with the general elections. That portion of the town which has been brought under cultivation is mostly a long, winding, narrow valley, extending from the town of Olive to the Delaware County line on the top of Pine Hill, a distance of nineteen miles, with here and there a smaller valley branching from the main valley, studded on either side by grand and lofty mountains. The soil, especially in the valleys, is mostly a sandy loam, which, if well fertilized, brings a quick and generous crop. Both soil and climate are well adapted to fruit. All kinds do well, except peaches and grapes, although fine peaches have been grown. Apples do well.

The Esopus is the largest stream of water. It rises on the western slope of Slide Mountain, flows down Big Indian Valley, is joined by Birch Creek, near the village of Big Indian, and from thence moves down

Shandaken valley to the town of Olive. It is subject to great rise and fall, sometimes swelling to the dimensions of a flood, carrying away bridges and doing material damage. In times of extreme drouth it recedes to the proportions of a modest brook.

Its next tributary, after leaving Big Indian, is the Bushnellville Creek, which meets it at Shandaken, three miles further down the stream. This creek takes its rise in a genuine canyon called Deep Notch, about two miles from West Kill, Greene County. Traveling about one mile farther down the Esopus we come to the Peck Bushkill, which empties into the Esopus from the north, and the Fox Hollow stream, which reaches it from the south.

Its next tributary, called the Bradstreet Hollow stream, meets the Esopus from the north near Elm Shade two miles below Shandaken. About two miles further down the Woodland valley stream empties into the Esopus from the southwest. One mile below at Phoenicia the Barber Bushkill mingles its waters with the Esopus. The next and last tributary is the Little Shandaken Creek, which flows down the valley from West Woodstock, better known as Little Shandaken. All these streams are subject to sudden rise and fall. Melting snows and prolonged rains swell them far beyond their normal size, and protracted drouths reduce them to mere brooks; they are all well stocked with Brook, California and German Brown Trout.

There is a legend connected with Big Indian which is well worth relating. Tradition has it that in the time of the Revolution, there lived in Big Indian valley an Indian of enormous stature and strength who was an implacable enemy of the whites. He would suddenly emerge from his retreat and, after depredations, as suddenly retreat to his hiding place. The whites resolved that he must die, and when he was discovered prowling about near where Birch Creek empties into the Esopus, he was killed. They held him up against the body of a large pine tree, and, in a rude way, cut his profile upon it, which lasted until the tree was cut down, long after the Revolution, and worked up into shingles by a local Methodist preacher. Ever since, the valley has been called Big Indian. The railroad station and village post-office bear the same name. The Ulster and Delaware Railroad traverses the whole length of the town.

Before the woodman's axe began its destructive work there were thousands of acres of bark-lands in Shandaken, which attracted the attention of men who wished to embark in the tanning business. Large tracts of hemlock forest were bought up and tanneries were built. The first tannery built in the town was erected on Birch Creek, at Pine Hill, in 1831, by Augustus A. Guigou, a Frenchman, who came to this country in 1827, from Marseilles, France. He served nine years as a private and officer in the army of the first Napoleon, and had been a tanner and manufacturer of paper in his native country. He was succeeded in business by his son, the late Theodore Guigou, in 1846, and died about the year 1851. His was the Empire tannery, which was destroyed by fire in 1858, and never rebuilt.

Following Birch Creek two miles from Pine Hill, we come to Smithville. Here Smith and Ferman built a tannery in 1844.

Passing down Birch Creek, about half a mile further, we come to the Esopus. Here, not far from the junction of the two streams, Robert Humphrey built a tannery in 1835, which he operated till about 1845, when it passed to George W. Tuttle, and afterward to S. R. and T. C. Wey, who operated it till the supply of bark gave out.

The next tannery, down the Esopus, was built at Shandaken by Bushnell and Dewey, and was one of the first to be erected. They were succeeded by Isham & Co., who afterward took in Eliakim Sherrill as a partner. Sherrill came to the tannery from Greene County, where he had failed in business as a tanner and hired out as a teamster. He was a man of great shrewdness and perseverance, and after awhile Isham & Co. took him as a partner and finally sold out to him and Simeon Gallop; later on he bought out Gallop and became the sole owner. In 1856 he sold to Hiram Whitney and moved to Geneva, N. Y. When the Civil War broke out he raised a regiment, which he commanded, and was killed in the battle of Gettysburg. The next tannery, down the Esopus, was built near Phoenicia, six miles below Shandaken, by Moore and Ellis about 1836, and was known as the Phoenix tannery. Other parties afterward operated it. The late James A. Simpson operated it for forty years and was the last proprietor. Simpson was a man of much originality. The late Col. H. D. H. Snyder built a tannery in Woodland valley, two miles from Phoenicia, in 1851, and operated it till the bark was exhausted. The next was at The Corner, owned and operated for many years by the late H. A. Ladew. A tannery was built at Bushnellville at an early period by Capt. Aaron Bushnell, and conducted by him for many years. Not one of these old tanneries is now standing. They were for many years the scene of

James C. Cornish

much life and activity, but belong to the past. Their very existence is fast fading from memory. To keep these tanneries going, took a vast quantity of bark. No use was made of the trees after the bark was stripped, except to a limited extent. Millions of these choice trees were left to rot on the ground where they fell, or to be consumed by forest fires.

Slide Mountain, so called on account of a landslide which carried away a portion of it on the south side many years ago, is within the town and is the highest peak of the Catskills. It affords a view from its summit that must be seen to be appreciated. Its altitude is 4,220 feet, and it is reached by way of Big Indian valley. The Wittenburgh comes next, and is one of the grandest mountains of the Catskill range; it is reached by way of Woodland valley. Other mountains are Mt. Sheridan, Balsam Mountain, and Mt. Garfield. Monka Hill, modest and unassuming, is worthy of mention on its own merits. It is easy of ascent and is reached by a path leading from the Grand Hotel to its summit. The view is far-reaching and magnificent. There is a stretch of shelving rocks on the west, standing upon which one looks down hundreds of feet into the valley below upon the tops of giant trees that add sublimity to the view.

There are fifteen neat and substantial church edifices in the town, of which the Methodist Episcopal denomination has five. The Roman Catholics have three, one at Phoenicia, one at Elm Shade, and another at Pine Hill. The Episcopalians have three; the Dutch Reformed have one at The Corner, built in 1836, which gives it rank as the oldest church in the town. The Wesleyan Methodists have one at Chichester. The Baptists have one at Phoenicia, and the Free Methodists have one at Elm Shade.

The industries of the town are farming, lumbering, quarrying bluestone for flagging and building purposes, and entertaining city people through the summer, if that can be called an industry. There is one chair factory in the town, located at Shandaken. At Chichester, two miles from Phoenicia, there is a furniture manufactory, owned and operated by Wm. O. Schwarzwalder. Both of these factories are large. The Ulster and Delaware Bluestone Co., incorporated in 1894, is located at Allaben and has branch mills at West Hurley. This company deals in all kinds of bluestone and is under the management of Edmund Riseley. The Pine Hill Crystal Spring Water Company, incorporated in 1901, is located at Pine Hill, employs about twenty hands, and ships to New York from six to nine carloads of this water per week. E. C. Clifford is the general manager. Besides there are excelsior and heading mills in the town which do considerable business.

The residence of the late Davis Winne, is located along the State road about six miles below Phoenicia. Here it was that a fort was erected in May, 1779, by order of Governor George Clinton, as a protection against the incursion of the Tories and Indians. It was built of logs, and Major Adrian Wynkoop had charge of its construction. It was large enough for two hundred troops and stood a short distance beyond the barn of Mr. Winne towards the residence of H. B. Hudler. John Winne, grandfather of Davis Winne, came from Holland, and lived in the old fort while he was building his house.

There is an incident bearing upon this old fort which I will relate. Old Peter Crispell, to whom reference has been made, has a brother Abram who was a sergeant in the War of the Revolution, and stationed at the Shandaken fort. On an occasion before the close of the war Sergeant Crispell, with a party of men, started from the fort on an expedition to hunt Indians. They went westward as far as the Cockburn place near Margaretville, when they fell in with a party of Tories and Indians led by one Shaver. Each party supposing the other to be the stronger, fell back. But Crispell and Shaver knew each other, and both at the same time sprang behind trees to cover themselves. There they stood for some time, neither being willing to retreat or expose himself lest the other might get a shot at him. After waiting awhile, Shaver saw a small portion of Crispell's body exposed from behind the tree and fired at it and ran. Crispell was not hit and, springing from behind the tree that had covered him, fired at Shaver as he ran. The ball took effect and Shaver fell severely wounded, and was taken prisoner by the Crispell party. It being near night they took him to the house of one Van Wagenor on the Dimmick place at Arkville. He was placed on some deer skins for a bed, and the next day they carried him a prisoner to the fort in Shandaken. The wound was probed, the ball extracted, and Shaver recovered. Crispell kept Shaver's gun and gave it to Benjamin Crispell, and it remained in the Crispell family for many years. After the war Crispell and Shaver became good friends.

CHAPTER XXXI.

TOWN OF SHAWANGUNK.

By Charles E. Foote.

THE town of Shawangunk, as well as the mountains and creek bearing that name, were so called from the Indian appellation of the country lying between the Shawangunk Kill and mountains. It lies along the southern borders of the county and is bounded on the north by Gardiner and Plattekill, on the east by Plattekill and Orange County, on the south and southwest by Orange and Sullivan Counties, and on the northwest by the town of Wawarsing. It is a broken and hilly upland, with the high ridge of the Shawangunk mountains along the northwest border, and has an area of 33,851 acres.

The Wallkill crosses the eastern portion of the town from south to north, and has Dwaar's Kill as a tributary from the southwest. Shawangunk Creek or Kill, rising in Sullivan County, flows northeasterly along an irregular boundary of the town, crosses the town at its narrowest point, about midway between its eastern and western boundaries, and empties into the Wallkill in the town of Gardiner, some miles northeast. It is fed by Verkeerder Kill, Platte Kill, and Dwaar's Kill, all from the northwest; this Dwaar's Kill not being the same stream as that which empties into the Wallkill a few miles east.

The date of the earliest settlement has been lost in obscurity, but it must have been between 1670 and 1680. Jacob Bruyn and his wife, Gertruyd, were among the earliest settlers, and there is a record of the baptism of a son, Jan, in the Kingston church records of October 6, 1678. As they were not known to have lived in Kingston, it may be inferred that they had settled in Shawangunk. On March 2, 1682, Jacob Bruyn and Michael Modt petitioned the Court at Kingston for permission to purchase a tract of land "behind the Paltz," from the Indians. Whether this is the same tract afterward secured by his widow, for herself and children, and afterward known as the "Gertruyd Bruyn patent," cannot now be stated with certainty, though it seems the most probable deduction. The son Jan does not appear further in the records. There were two other children, Jacobus and Esther. Gertruyd Bruyn, after the death of her husband, Jacob, married Severyn Tenhout in 1694. He was a baker who formerly lived at Kingston, and had acquired the Lloyd tract. They had no children, and at his death Tenhout left his property to his wife's children. The Lloyd farm, left by Tenhout, was settled on by Jacobus Bruyn, who married Katrina Schoonmaker, and raised a large family of children, said to be fifteen in number.

Esther married Zachariah Hoffman, October 19, 1707, and lived on the east side of Shawangunk Kill. They had five children.

Among the earliest settlers, besides Jacob Bruyn (oldest documents spell it Bruin), were Cornelius Schoonmaker, Abraham Schutt, Zacharias Hoffman, Benjamin Smedes, Jacob Decker, John Terwilliger, Johannes C. Decker, Robert Kain, Robert Graham, David Davis, Daniel Winfield, Hendrick VanWegen, and James Pennock. On November 14, 1709, Jacob Bruyn and Benjamin Smedes jointly petitioned for and presented a survey of a tract of 400 acres in Shawangunk, "near a small hill." On the 28th of the same month Zacharias Hoffman presented a description of 330 acres of land laid out for him on the east side of the Shawangunk River, and on the same date John McClean did the same regarding a tract of 300 acres on the northwest side of the Paltz Kill, in Shawangunk; and Matthias Mott presented a petition that Sovereign Tenhout be compelled to divide up some of "the good land upon the said (Shawangunk) river," which he had previously secured. The records do not show that the desired relief was given.

One of the first stone houses in the town was erected by Cornelius Schoonmaker. The Bevier family settled first at "Muddy Kill." George Graham, a north-of-Ireland native, settled on land located near what is now Shawangunk village, and the family has since been prominent in the affairs of the county.

Thomas and Johannes Jansen were among the early settlers, and erected stone houses about two miles apart, in the northwestern portion of the town.

In 1728, the following persons comprised the list of Freeholders of Shawangunk, according to the list as returned July 7 of that year, by Sheriff VanDyke to the Court at Kingston:

Capt. Jacobus Bruyn,
Benjamin Smedes,
Jacob Decker,
Josua Smedes,
Evert ter Willige,
Mattys Slimmer,
Hendrick Kraus,
——— Gallatian,
Johannes Decker,
James Spennick,
Henry Wileman, (attorney)
George Andrew,
Jerommus Minigus,
Christophel Moul,
John Williams,
Caleb Knap, Jr.,
Coll Cortland.

Capt. Zacharias Hoffman,
Abraham Schutt,
Evert ter Willige,
Cornelius Schoonmaker,
Hendrick Decker,
Hendrick Newkirk,
Edward Gatehouse,
Jerommus Weller,
John Howard,
Cornelius Cool,
John North,
John Macknell,
Thomas Mackolm,
Samuel Neely,
Caleb Knap, Sr.,
Alaxander Neely.

There seems something about this list which needs an explanation which cannot be made after the lapse of years. From a comparison of records there seems to be omissions of importance. The Hardenbergh patent, issued in 1719, called for land on Verkeerder Kill, and another tract four miles from Shawangunk Kill; the Peter Barberie patent is dated March 24, 1709; the John Rutzen patent, June 16, 1712. Beside these were patents given in 1709 to Beckman, Van Dam, Phillipse, Deyo, Vernoye, Teunis Jacobsen Clearwater, Jacob Clearwater, and a number of others; the Stephen DuBois patent on Verkeeder's Kill was dated 1722, and the Sacket and Hazard patents in 1727. These names and others appear constantly in the records of that period, and it is apparent that many of them resided in the town with their families at the time the list was made.

The civic organization of Shawangunk was established in 1709. The boundaries, as stated in the Court order creating the precinct, read: "On the west by the foot of the Shawangunk mountains; on the south and west by the precinct of Wallkill; on the east by the line or bounds of three thousand five hundred acres, granted to Rip Van Dam and others, by the east bounds or line of two thousand acres of land granted to Barberie, and by the east bounds or line of two thousand acres granted to Huddleston; and on the north by the north bounds or line of the said two thousand acres granted to Huddleston, by the north bounds of the two thousand acres granted to Peter Mathews and others; on the south by a line crossing the said Wallkill river to the mouth of the Shawangunk; and running thence south westerly all along the northwest side of Shawangunk river to the southwest corner of the land granted to Col. Jacob Rutzen, and on the west by the westerly bounds or line of said land granted to Rutzen to a salt pond called "the Great Salt Pond," and from thence upon a west line to the foot of Shawangunk mountains aforesaid."

The first meeting for the election of a Supervisor and other local officials was held at the house of Benjamin Smedes, Jr. At the beginning the precinct was attached to New Paltz for administrative purposes. It was given an independent jurisdiction in December 27, 1743. Some changes were made in the boundaries in 1846, 1848 and 1853. At the latter change, a part of Gardiner was taken off. The other changes gave some land to Plattekill, and restored it to Shawangunk two years later.

The first record of a town meeting in the town for public purposes, is that following:

"Att an Election held for Chusing of Officers for the Precinct of Shawangunk, on the first Tuesday in April, Anno Domini 1746, at the house of Abraham Terwilleger, at Shawangunk, The following Persons were Chosen, Viz: Jacobus Bruyn, Supervisor and Clerk; Thomas Jansen, Isaac Hasbrouck, Assessors; Hendrick Van Wegen, Constable and Collector; William Deder, Overseer of the Shawangunk Road; George Graham, Overseer of the Wallkill Road; Benjamin Smedes, David Davis, Overseers of the Poor."

"Agreed that the Election for the Ensuing year be held at the house of Robert Kerr, at the Wallkill."

"J. Bruyn, Clerk."

The people of Shawangunk were well represented in the War of the Revolution. Johannes Jansen was Lieutenant Colonel of the Fourth, (Hardenbergh's) regiment of Militia. Among the line officers of the same regiment, were Captain Isaac Davis, Matthew Jansen, Cornelius and Matthew Masten, David Ostrander, Peter Roosa, Lieutenants Jacobus S. Bruyn, Peter Decker, William Ostrander and various others. The lists of privates in that regiment seems to embrace the names of nearly every family in the town, though there are some who belonged to other organizations.

The roads of the town were given much attention at a very early day. They were made and kept in repair by an assessment of as many days' work as the property of each freeholder or male inhabitant over twenty-one years of age should justify. In 1817 there were three divisions of road, one "West of the Kills," in which there were twenty-four road districts; "between the Kills," with fourteen districts, and "the New Hurley road," with twelve districts.

There is an entry in the old records which must appeal strongly to the modern politician, as an illustration of how "things in politics" were done "in the good old days" when every one, as seen through the reversed telescope of history, was supposed to have been sober, industrious, religious, and personally and politically pure; when votes were "counted as cast," etc. The extract is as follows:

"April, 1773." "A motion then being made by several persons to Remove the place of election for the Chusing of officers for this precinct for the Ensuing Year to the house of Henry Goetschius, The Clerk began to take the votes, and after he had Entered Down Nineteen Votes for Removing the place of Election and two votes against it, a great Disturbance and Confusion Arising, The Tables was taken away from the Clerk, and Night Comeng on, and Many of the people being Intoxicated with Liquor, they were not able to proceed any farther."

"Entered from the proceedings of the Election p. me.

"J. Bruyn, Clerk."

The town of Shawangunk is rich in the records of men who have attained special distinction. Several members of the Bruyn family have been in the legislature. Johannes Bruyn was a member of the Assembly in 1781, 1782, 1783, 1796-97, and in 1800. Severyn T. Bruyn occupied the office in 1789-90, 1792-93, and 1795, and Charles Bruyn in 1826.

Another family of special prominence was the Grahams. Dr. John G. Graham was a member of the Assembly in 1791, and of the State Senate from this district for the four year terms beginning in 1798, and in 1806. His son, George G. Graham, was a member of the Assembly in 1841, and a member of the Constitutional Convention in 1846. His son, James G. Graham, was member of Assembly from Ulster County in 1849 and in 1866, and he moved to Orange County later, which he represented in the same body in 1877 and 1878.

The Schoonmaker family has left its impress upon the historical affairs in Shawangunk as well as other sections of the county. Cornelius C. Schoonmaker was a member of the first Assembly, in 1777, and held that office throughout the Revolutionary War and until 1790, when he was elected a member of the House of Representatives of the Second Congress of the United States. He was again member of the State Assembly in 1795. He was born in Shawangunk, married Sarah Hoffman, and left a considerable family.

The old Indian fort, which was destroyed by Captain Kreiger and his men, while pursuing the Indians for the recapture of the prisoners taken at the Esopus and Hurley massacres in 1663, is supposed to have been on the Shawangunk Kill, on the property now owned by Mrs. Laura Varick, of Poughkeepsie.

The firm of James B. Crowell & Son was established by the senior member of the firm in 1872, and began the manufacture of hand sleighs, ox bows and baker peels, to which later they added brick moulds and bearers, and they now make nearly all kinds of brickmakers' supplies. The firm first started in an old saw mill, which was converted to their needs, which, with various additions that had been made, was destroyed by fire in 1896. A new plant was erected, and again burned in 1899. It was at once rebuilt, on a larger scale than before, and is doing a prosperous business. The plant includes the large shop, a saw mill, store houses, and lumber sheds, and employs some twenty-five men throughout the year. It is located about two miles west of the village of Wallkill.

The Ulster Hat Company has a large brick factory in the village of Wallkill, and employs about one hundred and twenty-five hands in the manufacture of soft felt hats. The building is on the site of an old paper mill, which was formerly operated there. The company was incorporated in 1900.

The G. B. Mentz Co., of Wallkill, have an inportant factory in the vicinity of the railroad, and manufacture brick moulds, wheelbarrows, trucks, and all kinds of brickmakers' supplies. The plant was established in 1886 by Charles J. Langer, who erected the present building. It was purchased by the present company in 1905. About twenty-five men are employed.

There is a large factory at Dwaarskill, located on the site of one of the old mills, where wagon rims are made. It is owned by Wilson Bruyn, and has been in operation many years.

There were many taverns in this town in the olden time. Among the first was that kept by John Graham, near the site of the Reformed Dutch Church. This remained in the possession of the Graham family for many years. During the Revolution George Smith kept a tavern at Bruynswick. Among other old bonifaces there were Cornelius Louw, William T. Schoonmaker, Eli Wilkinson, Andrew Schoonmaker, Simon Mullen, John Hart, W. E. Marnes, and Hugh O'Donnel. Among the oldest merchants were Robert Hoey, McEwan & Houselander, Cornelius DuBois Bruyn, Jonathan Vernooy, and Thomas Edwards. Among the first physicians was Dr. John Smedes. He was followed by Dr. James G. Graham and many others. John L. Lyon seems to have been the first practicing lawyer in 1830.

The name "Shawangunk," besides being difficult to pronounce, has given rise to controversy and speculation regarding its origin and signification. The commonly accepted pronunciation is "Shong-um." In Mather's "Geology of New York," the meaning of the word is given as "the place of white rocks." Others claim it to be "South Mountain," "South Water," "swift current, or strong stream," "Mink River," "the place of leeks," etc. The origin is unquestionably Indian.

In an old census report of 1782, the population of the town is placed at 1,343—males 717, females 626. In 1870 this total was increased to 2,823, and in 1880 to 2,910. Last year the State census made it 2,467, of which all except thirty-one were citizens. There were 555 persons who voted in the town last year. The total value of real and personal property last year was given as $866,899. The farms were valued at $1,574,970.

CHAPTER XXXII.

TOWN OF ULSTER

By Charles E. Foote.

THIS is the youngest town in Ulster County, and its birth was due to years of political misrule in the old town of Kingston, its civic parent. It is located on the Hudson river, beginning just north of the city of Kingston and extending to the south boundary line of the town of Saugerties. From the river it extends westward, embracing the lower portion of the Esopus Creek to the town of Kingston, with an extension between the city and town of Kingston which reaches the bounds of Hurley. Geographically, it is bounded on the north by the town of Saugerties; on the east by the Hudson river; on the south by the city of Kingston, and on the west by the towns of Hurley, Woodstock and Kingston. It was organized in 1880.

It is in many respects one of the most attractive towns in the county. Along the river front it has the high and sometimes precipitous bluffs usual along this section of the Hudson, with deep ravines, and noisy, chattering brooks breaking or cutting through at intervals, in a way to delight the artistic eye of the landscape gardener who is preparing the surface for the summer homes of those who can afford them, or arranging and beautifying the ancestral homes of those families whose forebears wrested the ground from the denizens of the forest.

To the westward, the surface is undulating, sometimes hilly and occasionally rocky. The Esopus Creek, which flows northward almost the extreme length of the town, presents many attractive historical aspects which are more properly treated in the town of Kingston, but the physical beauties belong to Ulster.

It would be difficult to find a more delightful section of country than the valley of the Esopus as it flows through the town of Ulster. The "alluvial flats" which are a part of the early colonization of the Esopus region, are here seen in their perfection, and their value as agricultural lands have maintained the promise which they held forth nearly three centuries ago. The only tributary to the Esopus in the town of any importance is the Sawkill, which comes in from the west about midway of the town, and adds variety to the aspect.

In the northern part is Lake Katrine, a handsome sheet of water, with private camps on the western side for those who desire relief during the season of heat, and farms and fruit gardens in the vicinity for the comfort and profit of the inhabitants.

The authorization for the erection of the town of Ulster was the enactment of the Board of Supervisors, the preamble of which reads as follows:

"An act to divide the town of Kingston, in the county of Ulster, and erect therefrom the town of Ulster and attach a part thereof to the town of Woodstock, in said county, passed by the Board of Supervisors at their annual meeting the 28th day of November in the year one thousand eight hundred and seventy-nine. Two thirds of all the members of said board voting in favor thereof under and in pursuance of Chapter 319, of the Laws of 1872."

This action of the supervisors was ratified at the session of the Legislature, the following winter, and the first town meeting was held on the first Tuesday in March, 1880. This was at George A. Stoddar's hotel, and the presiding officers were Tunis P. Osterhoudt, Gilbert S. Lockwood and Josiah Lefevre.

One section of the law creating the new town provided that the change should not abridge the terms of local officers who might find themselves in the town by reason of the change; consequently there were some officials on hand when the meeting was called.

James Myer, Jr., was the first Supervisor.

There are various commercial enterprises in the town. The farming, gardening and dairying industries are extensive and profitable.

But the most important and extensive industry in the town of Ulster at this time, and since its formation, is the manufacture of brick. The vast deposits of clay which are found along the entire river front, and the convenient shipping facilities, have made this part of the town very valuable. Most of the farms there have been sold at large prices, far beyond their agricultural value, and converted into immense brickyard plants. These have been fitted with every modern appliance for the most profitable operation, and the product ranks well in the market.

In this way many country homes with fine river-views, once so highly prized, have been given up to the merciless march of commercialism. The broad sweeping lawns that sloped so gracefully toward the river-bluff or beach are now yawning chasms of raw clay flanked with immense kiln-sheds and docks, and thickly strewn with various other rude structures required in the business.

Thus today there are twelve separate brickyard plants on this busy river front upon which nearly three thousand men are employed in the heart of the brick-moulding season, which covers over five months of the year. Beginning at the north end of the line, near the town of Saugerties, the following yards are now in operation:

The Burhans yard, the Ulster Brick Company, the Goldrick yard, the Rose Company, Smith Brothers, Lynch Brothers, the Dinan yard, Washburn Brothers, the Hendricks Brick Company, the Terry Yard, Brigham Brothers, and the Schultz yard. The largest of these are probably the Schultz and Brigham yards. The total output of these various yards for the season of 1906, as estimated by a practical and intelligent member of one of these firms, was about 140,000,000 bricks. Taking his low estimate of the average price for the whole season of $5.75 per thousand, the total value of this product would be $795,000. While many of these laborers reside in the town permanently a large number remain only during the brick-moulding season.

Another important industry on this river front is the gathering and housing of ice from the Hudson in the winter months and its shipment to market in summer. There are many huge storehouses which require thousands of men in the season of ice-cutting, gathering and storing, who earn good wages at a season when they would otherwise be idle.

Ulster lies so close to the city of Kingston, that for educational purposes, some of its territory was included in the District of Kingston. There are now, however, schools in what is known as the Dutch Settlement, at the north, one in Pine Bush neighborhood on the east side of the Esopus, and two in the extreme northeast corner of the town; one in the Flatbush neighborhood, along the Hudson, one in East Kingston, and one at Eddyville.

As to the early settlement of the territory covering the town, one has only to glance at the names of the present inhabitants and connect them with the families of the early settlers of more than two centuries ago.

There were among those strong characters of the earlier years the Osterhoudts, the Burhans, the Hendricks, the Delmaters, Whittakers, Livingstons, Wynkoops, Leggs, Van Akens, Shufeldts, Bruyns, Keators, Heermances, Fredenberghs, Hasbroucks, Schoonmakers, Kroms, and many others. Their descendants are here and form a fair proportion of the population of the town, and control a considerable portion of the acreage. Ulster as a town is an example of the permanency of hereditary attachment to the soil.

For their religious worship many of the people are affiliated with the various churches at Kingston or Saugerties. There is a Roman Catholic Church near the Dutch settlement, also one at East Kingston, and Methodist Churches at Eddyville and East Kingston. Eddyville Church was organized somewhere about 1825 or 1830 and incorporated August 25, 1836. For services it was connected far nearly twenty years with either Kingston or Rondout, but began to have a regular pastor about 1855. A church building and parsonage were erected in 1871 at an expense of about $18,000.

CHAPTER XXXIII.

TOWN OF WAWARSING.

By Hon. Thomas E. Benedict.

ABORIGINAL DAYS.

IN the year 1663, one hundred and twelve years before the battle of Bunker Hill was fought, an armed force of one hundred and twenty-seven soldiers, with eighty-three Indian allies, under the command of a gallant Dutch Captain and two Lieutenants, entered the territory now comprising the town of Wawarsing. They were well armed and equipped, and had with them two cannon. They took possession of a palisaded Indian fort which had been abandoned two days before by a force of Indian warriors, who had taken part in the burning and massacre of the inhabitants of Wiltwyck, (now Kingston), a short time previous. The Indians had brought a part of their prisoners, women and children, to this fort. There is no evidence that a white person had set foot in Wawarsing prior to the coming of Captain Martin Creiger and Lieutenants Stillwell and Courvenhover, who had been sent by Governor Peter Stuyvesant from Albany, (Fort Orange) to punish the Esopus Indians. While this military expedition was bloodless, it was no holiday undertaking, for the command was pursuing a victorious band of Indians through a pathless wilderness for over twenty miles and upon their own territory. Capt. Creiger, in his report of the expedition to the Indian fort, wrote thus of the locality:

"When about four English miles from the fort, Lieutenants Corvenhover and Stillwell, and Ensign Niesen, with one hundred and nineteen men, were ordered forward to effect the surprise, if possible" (while he followed with the cannon). "They executed their task with great celerity but found the fort abandoned." * * * * * When night came on they had only taken a squaw and three horses, the latter having been carried off at the time of the massacre. At the break of day (July 28, 1663), the officers held a council and determined to go in search of the Indians to the mountains, where Mrs. Van Insbroch, the guide, had been a prisoner. Accordingly one hundred and forty men ascended the rugged

Thomas E. Benedict.

mountain sides of the blue hills (Shawangunk Mountains), taking the squaws with them, but met with no success. They were then directed to a great high mountain, whither the Indians had fled, taking with them seven Christian prisoners. After experiencing vast difficulty, no Indians were found there. * * * * "As our forces were discovered on all sides, and the friendly Indians advised against any further pursuit, because the whole tribe was alarmed, the expedition returned to the fort, having failed to find the Indians." Capt. Creiger wrote further: "I went out of their fort with fifty men to a distance of half a mile, there cut down several plantations of maize, threw into the fire divers pits full of maize and beans." On July 31, Creiger at early dawn set fire to the Indian stronghold, and, while it with the council house were in full blaze, took up the return march to Wiltwyck, where he arrived the same evening.

Beside this mention of the Indian fort, it is recorded by Captain Crieger and confirmed by statements of Mrs. Insbroch and the squaws, that the fort was on a high hill near a stream as wide as the Esopus at Wiltwyck, within speaking distance of the blue hills, Creiger having parleyed with the Indians thereon from the fort. It is further described as near a stream with rifts and rapids in three or four places, with table lands around, and with great hills west and southwest. While it is idle to attempt to rescue from the two centuries and a half which have nearly elapsed since the location of this historic fort, it seems that the great majority of the facts brought down to us point to Indian Hill, at Wawarsing, east of the old cemetery, as the place indicated by the late Jonathan W. Hasbrouck in his history of the fort. The location of the fort at the head of the Kerhanksen creek, west of the village of Kerhonkson, in a rocky ravine near the boundary line between Rochester and Wawarsing, by Rev. Charles Scott, D.D., in a paper read before the Ulster County Historical Society, does not appear to be supported by the facts. Indian Hill, in 1663, was probably much higher than now, as the erosions of time on such a glacier moraine have greatly depressed its lines. At that period it must have stood nearly one hundred feet above the creek (Rondout), which then flowed at its east base, some hundreds of feet west of the present channel. An accurate estimate of the distance of Creiger's march to the fort must be based upon the time taken. Any distance more than twenty-six miles southwest direct from Wiltwyck would place the fort south of Napanoch amidst surroundings not supported by any three of the necessary physical facts required by its accurate location. There is no point which can successfully challenge the location at Indian Hill, except the promontory at Lost Corners, between Wawarsing and Napanoch, at the great bend in the stream which gave the name of Wawarsing to this locality. An authentic location of this ancient fort would render the spot a worthy object of interest among the historic colonial landmarks of New York.

E. M. Ruttenber, author of "The Indian Tribes of the Hudson Valley," writes me as follows regarding the old fort:

KAHANKSEN and -SON in treaty of 1665; KAHANSINCK in patent to Peter Lowe, 1708-22, etc. It takes interest from its connection with the location of what is known, historically, as the "Old Fort," as distinguished from the "New Fort," in the war of 1663, when both forts were destroyed by the Dutch. Its site is uncertain. It is spoken of without name in the treaty of peace of 1664, in connection with a *district of country admitted to have been "conquered by the sword,"* extending as far as *the "two captured forts."* In treaty of 1665, with Governor Nicolls, the district is described as "A certain parcel of land *lying and being to the west and southwest of a certain creek or river called by the name of Kahankson, and so up to the head thereof where the Old Fort stood, and so with a direct line from thence through the woods and crosse the meadows to the Great Hill lying to the west or southwest, which Great Hill is to be the true west or southwest bounds, and the said creek called Kahanksen the north and northwest bounds of the said lands."* In treaty deed with Governor Andross, April 27, 1677, the *boundary lines* of the tract, *"as they were to be thereafter,"* was described: "Beginning at the Ronduyt Kil, thence *to a kil called Kahakasnix,* thence *north along the hills to a kil called Magowasing-inck, thence to the Second Fall, easterly to Freudeyack-Komick on the Groote River, south to Ronduyt Kil."* The stream called Magowasing-inck seems to be *certainly identified* in patents to Henry Beekman and Ann Beake in 1685, as that now known as Wawarsing creek, and its identification, if correct, places the creek called Kahankson *south* of that stream. Its location is perhaps made specific in patent to Peter Lowe in 1722, the survey of which located its south line as *"Beginning by a Great Fall called Honeck,* thence up the creek northerly to ye *High Mountains,* including several small pieces of land, * * * *from ye bounds of Kahansinck to the bounds of the High Mountains, as the bounds were formerly settled by the articles of peace."* The record evidence seems to be conclusive that *the fort was in the vicinity of the stream now known as the Sandberg* or Napanock creek, the falls called Honeck, now called Honk, being at Napanock a short distance north of Ellenville. More specifically than this record location its site cannot be fixed. Two efforts have been made in that direction, evidently by parties who did not have the opportunity to examine the records, or who knew nothing concerning them. The first was by the late John W. Hasbrouck, who assigned it to Vernoy creek, opposite Wawarsing; and the second by the late Rev. Charles Scott, D.D., who, in a paper read before the Ulster County Historical Society in 1861, assigned it to the head of what is now called Kahanksen creek, some miles north of "the Great Fall called Honeck," "on the south side" of that stream "near the boundary line between the townships of Wawarsing and Rochester, just north of what is now called Shurter's hill, about two miles from the mouth of the stream and one mile from its head, in a rocky ravine and difficult of access." Aside from the record location quoted above, which cannot be disputed, there are several points in the Doctor's location that would require examination and comparison with Kregier's Journal, the Great Hill to the west and southwest especially, and his estimate of thirty miles from Wildwyck. Kregier wrote: "The road or course from Wildwyck to the fort of the Esopus Indians lies mostly to the southwest, about ten (Dutch) miles from our fort." Dutch miles were frequently counted as equal to four English miles. By standard measure the distance would be about thirty-six English miles. Kregier's miles were probably based on the time rule of one and one-quarter hour's walk to a Dutch mile, which was a fraction over three and one-half English. His time on his return trip over the road which he had made on going out, was about sixteen hours, probably more, as he set fire to the fort "at the dawn of day" and marched out, and arrived at Wildwyck at nine in the evening. Sixteen hours' walk would yield a fraction over forty-four English miles. The location of the fort seems to have been well known when the treaty deed of 1677 was negotiated. Dr. Scott's site may be about thirty miles from Kingston, but it was not Kregier's site according to his Dutch miles.

The fort was a palisaded village larger than that at Shawongunk. Around it were maize fields and pits filled with maize and beans, and "full half a mile" (Dutch, about two miles English) from it were several plantations of maize which were cut down by Kregier's soldiers, in all "about fifteen morgens," or about two hundred and fifteen acres. There were meadows beyond also, while on the "west or southwest," was "the Great Hill." There was no defence of the fort; its occupants had abandoned it "two days before" Kregier's troops entered it. A particular description of it has not been handed down. Under date of July 31, 1663, Kregier wrote: "In the morning at dawn of day, set fire to the fort and all the houses, and while they were burning marched out in good order." And so disappears forever the Indian stronghold, even its precise site unknown. Probably since Kregier left it in flames its site has never been trodden by an intelligent white man.

The several orthographies of the name of the creek, near the head of which the fort stood, may, apparently, be resolved into KAHANGH'SING, from Lenape Gahan, (with guttural aspirate gh), meaning "shallow, low water—next to being dried up"; es, 's, diminutive, "less than" at, and -ink, location, the combination reading, "Near a place of shallow water." In other words, the fort was near the head of a small stream of water, a spring or fountain.

E. M. RUTTENBER.

THE WAWARSING CLAN.

The Esopus Indians were the equals of other contemporary savages anywhere in the land. They were distinguished as agriculturists. Captain Creiger, in his report to the Governor of the Colony after the capture of the Indian fort in 1663, said the Indians raised enough corn and beans in Ulster to supply the whole colony of New York. The Wawarsing Indians were the peers of any others of their tribe. The capital village of the tribe, with the council house and their largest fort was located among them. They were the guardians of the pits filled with corn and beans for use in war or famine. They were located midway on the great trail from the Hudson to the Delaware. Within their territory converged from the West the trails which centered at the Rondout from the Neversink and Esopus rivers, and which led to the Delaware at Peenpack (Cuddebackville), up the Neversink to the Beaverkill, thence down the East Branch of the Delaware to the main stream and thence to a point further West. Until the advent of the white man, there was no doubt an inflow and outflow of rival parties over these trails, which did not stop when civilization set its foot in Wawarsing, as it was over these very trails that Brant and his Tory allies came to massacre and strike terror at Pine Bush, Fantinekill and Wawarsing over a century later. Across these trails General Sullivan led his army which in 1779 destroyed forever the war power of the Six Nations within this State.

Amidst these environments, the Wawarsing Clan kept well the charge given them. They celebrated here the sacred feasts of the seasons and of war, danced and performed the weird rites of their worship, and roused their fury for the war path. Their surrender of their fort and capital to Captain Creiger was dictated by the fact that they had not yet learned the use of firearms, and had no chance of success against the force of well-equipped and experienced soldiers with cannon. This clan afterward lived in peace with the whites to whom they sold their lands. It is probable that the settlers with whom they came in contact were more prudent in dealing with Indians than were those of Wiltwyck, where the selling of rum to the savages was the prime cause of the troubles that led to the Esopus wars. Indians held small tracts of land in Wawarsing up to 1787, as on May 2d of that year an Indian sold to Johannes G. Hardenbergh a tract of land south of Kerhonkson.*

WAWARSING AN INDIAN NAME.

The town was incorporated under the name of Wawarsink. In the treaty deed with the Esopus Indians, made by Governor Stuyvesant in 1667, it is written "Magowaassinghinck." The incorporate name was no doubt taken from the Indian deed given William Petersen Beake in 1680, and the survey of patent given to his widow, Anna Beake, in 1685, in which the name is spelled "Wawarsink." Old deeds and surveys of the colonial period spell the name Wawarsincke, Warsink, Wawasing and Wawesinck. There is no doubt as to the name being of Indian origin, as it has been applied to this section from its earliest history by the whites, who evidently adopted it from the Indians. Sylvester's History of Ulster County quotes Rev. N. M. Jones, of Samsonville, an authority on Indian names, as defining its meaning to be "Holy place of sacred feasts and dances." Mr. E. M. Ruttenber, author of the "Indian Tribes of the Hudson River," writes that "Mr. William R. Gerrard, an Algonquin student

* This deed I have in my possession. It conveys for the consideration of eighteen shillings current money of the province of New York a small parcel of land. It is signed by Awannamock, the Indian, and is witnessed by Jacob Hoornbeek, Dyrk Hoornbeek and Wishela, the Indian.—AUTHOR.

J. T. Scoresby Eastgate M.D.

of the highest authority, gives the reading of Wawarsink as from 'Wa-wa,' meaning winding around, turning in and out, twisting as an eddying current or repeated bends. The second word he reads as 'Naw'as-ink,' from Nawa's, a point of promontory, and 'ing,' location at (or in or near), where paths or boundaries come together." Mr. Ruttenber adds: "The place took its name from a topographical feature in the proximity. Nothing is more frequent in Indian names than the dropping of an initial syllable and the changing of initials arising from the speech of the Indian in throwing the voice forward to the penult. Another peculiarity is the dialectic exchange of l, n and r. There are many examples to be quoted in Ulster County." Another necessary result of the work of the early scribes was the effort to make an Indian word somewhat resemble the general sound, just as one would spell a German or Russian name "by ear." This reading of the word plainly indicates the locality which gave the name to Wawarsing. It is at the Lost Corner, north of the bend in the Rondout just below the Humiston house between Napanoch and Wawarsing. The promontory is there, with the high ridge leading to it (through which the highway is cut), thrust directly in the path of the Rondout, which for a distance, flows as straight as an arrow, directly striking the high promontory, some seventy-five feet in height, then turning to the right at a degree more than a right angle against a large rock, which juts into the stream from the left bank. The stream then flows for a short distance in shallow water to a point where it turns sharply to the left toward Wawarsing. Here in the stream is the "winding around," "the turning in and out," here are the "repeated bends," and here is the "eddying and twisting current," caused by the great rock, which juts nearly athwart the stream. Here was the ford which the Indians used to enter the mountain trail, which led up to the Topatcoke spring and across to the new fort on the east side of the Shawangunk. All these physical features were more pronounced two and a half centuries ago, when the Indians marked these topographical features of earth, rock and water, at a period when the water flowed throughout the year near flood-tide and the contiguous hills had not been denuded by the erosions of over two centuries. The map of the Anna Beake patent deed shows that the Rondout in 1685 bent sharply to the northeast at the east side of the Lost Corner promontory and flowed to the junction of the VerNooy Kill at a distance of several hundred feet west of its present channel, giving it then a long curve toward the hills on the west as it passed the present road to Wawarsing railroad station.

TOPOGRAPHY.

The topography of the town of Wawarsing is quite unlike that of any other town of the county. It is without mountain peaks, yet it has but little low lands, these being a narrow strip through the town along the Rondout and Sandburgh streams. The range of the Shawangunk Mountains occupies about one-fifth of the town's acreage. It lies on the east side, and the great section of the mountain is wholly within the town excepting its steep eastern incline. The range here rises to its greatest height. It is very unique as a mountain elevation, as its escarpment terminates abruptly in a broad plateau or tableland, one to three miles wide. This presents a rugged area of cliffs, rocky slopes, broad levels, high ridges, lakes, swamps, dark ravines and soilless face. In places, however, there is tillable land, while streams traverse it, with several waterfalls, one being sixty-four feet high. Sam's Point rises to a height of 2,200 feet, and this and other points give a widely extended view, covering the Hudson and Wallkill valleys and the Catskill mountain regions. The mountain lakes of Mohonk, Minnewaska, Awosting, Maratanza and the Mud Pond are all near, lying near the level of the mountain top, and all but Mohonk and Minnewaska are within the town. The Coxingkill, Peterskill, Sanderskill and Stonykill streams rise in this section, and flow northward beyond the boundaries of the town into the Rondout. Several small streams, rising near the eastern slope of the mountain, fall in beautiful cascades down the steep incline and enter the Shawangunkill. Natural ice caves are caused by the freezing of water and lodgment of snow in the deep crevices and ravines in the mountain top and near Sam's Point. From the west bank of the Rondout near Napanoch down the valley, and above that place along the Sandburgh, and at other points not characterized by intervening lowlands, start the foothills which rise among the highest peaks of the Catskill Mountains some twenty miles away. These ridges, often broken, rocky and serrated, enclosing intervening valleys traversed by streams, rise to a height of nearly two thousand feet within the town, on either side of the lower ridges of the VerNooy Kill and Lackawack neighborhoods. Amidst these elevations the sources of the Sandburgh, Greenfield, Good Beerkill, Fantinekill and VerNooy Kill streams have their origin, and all flow in nearly parallel lines with the Rondout, which enters the town from Sullivan county at the northwest border. Streams deemed worthy of mention by early surveyors, flowing into the Rondout and Sandburgh from the west slope of the Shawangunk Mountain, have ceased to exist except in seasons of high water. The town has an area of about 60,000 acres. It borders on Sullivan county on two sides, and touches the towns of Denning, Rochester, Gardiner and Shawangunk. Not over one-third of the acreage can be called improved land. Over one-half is wooded, mostly with small second growth. Most of the ridges are of rock formation, with high ledges, and the lower lands are made up mostly of hills, which are largely moraines and deposits of the glacial and drift periods. Flag stone abounds generally on the west slope of the town. From a period as early as 1730, lead has been known to exist in the mountains near Ellenville, and veins of lead and zinc have been worked at different periods for over sixty years at Ellenville, but without profit. Iron ore of an inferior quality is found in considerable veins in the ridge on the west side of the State road leading from Ellenville to Kerhonkson. The water of the town is excellent, and that flowing from the west slope of the Shawangunk is exceptionally pure, owing to the siliceous character of the rock preventing the solution of mineral substances. Many beautiful waterfalls and glens abound along the streams, and the whole township is rich in natural features of great beauty. The landscape is generally exceedingly picturesque, and the elevations afford wide views of unsurpassed variety and grandeur. In many respects, the town is unsurpassed in unique and charming natural scenery.

FIRST WHITE SETTLERS.

With the settlement of Hurley in 1662, it is probable that whites as hunters or prospectors, found their way up the valley of the Rondout. At that period, the table lands south of Hurley had been largely denuded of trees by the burning of the forests by Indians, and extensive corn fields and orchards had taken their place. The first recorded white persons to be at Wawarsing were the prisoners taken there after the burning of Wiltwyck in 1663, and later rescued by Capt. Creiger's command of Dutch soldiers. The glowing accounts of the country he had invaded, as given by this officer, on his return to Fort Orange (Albany), excited the speculative interest of several merchants, who soon afterward made considerable purchases of lands of the Indians in Mombaccus, Wawarsing and Mamakating. Among these purchases were Jocham Staets and William Petersen Beake, to whom deeds were given later by the Governor of the Colony. The deed of the Beake purchase was given to his widow in 1685. These two patents covered the central portion of Wawarsing, north of the Rondout at Napanoch and beyond Wawarsing village. These grants were soon followed by the Knightsfield patent and the DeGrootin transport patent. It does not appear that these original white landowners did anything toward the settlement of their purchases. They later sold to others, the new purchasers being residents of Ulster. On September 15, 1705, Louis Bevier, one of the New Paltz patentees, purchased of Col. Jacob Rutsen, of Marbletown, several hundred acres of land located at Napanoch, and about the same time Col. Rutsen conveyed to Cornelius Ver Nooy, a Hollander, a tract of land which had been patented to Anna Beake in 1685, which covered the site of the present village of Wawarsing. Cornelius VerNooy later occupied his purchase and erected on the VerNooy Kill the first grist mill within the present territory of the township. This mill was brought from Holland by the pioneer himself. Louis Bevier settled one or more of his sons at Napanoch in 1720. By his will, he conveyed to his five sons, share and share alike, all his lands, tenements, etc., at Napanoch. It appears that a considerable settlement must have grown up at this period, but the exact date of the arrival of the first resident of the town is not known. At the end of the first quarter of the eighteenth century the line of settlers had reached Leurenkill and Mamacotting, and the trail to Mahackamack (Port Jervis) had become the mine road known later in military operations of the Federal government.

Besides the Beviers and VerNooys, among the earliest names of the Wawarsing pioneers were those of Hoornbeek, DeWitt, Low, Hardenbergh, Kettle, Nottingham, Kortright, Helm, Van Vleit, Middagh, Benton, Heesel, Rogers, Simpson, Turner, Terwilliger, Denniston, Rutsen, Ten Broch, Bettle and Osterhoudt. Up to the period of the Revolution, the settlements were confined to the valley, with the exception of a few houses up the VerNooy-kill. As late as 1786, but eight settlers were on the Rondout above Napanoch, and these nearly all were in the district south of the stream above Honk Falls. In 1799, no road had been opened up the Good Beerkill or Greenfield streams, and the field notes of State

surveyors on file at Albany, at that period refer to but one settler along the Sandburg above the Homowack neighborhood.

The first settlers were mostly of Dutch and Huguenot extraction. They had not come to their new homes in a spirit of adventure nor as soldiers and traders, but as men seeking homes for high conscientious purposes and to escape tyrannical religious influences which they abhorred. They met at first in family worship, but later was erected at Wawarsing Corners, about 1745, the first church edifice in the town. Here the Dutch language was at first used in the service, but later, as the English-speaking settlers increased, the Dutch and English tongues were used alternately.

COLONIAL PERIOD.

For a period of forty years after Captain Creiger had made his victorious march to the heart of Magowasinghinck, the Indian remained in undisputed possession, kindled his council fires, and danced his corn dance in peace. During this period, land speculators, excited by Captain Creiger's glowing description of the valley of the Rondout, no doubt obtained by purchase from the Indians much of the land from the Kahansinck creek on the north to Mamacotting on the south, and from the blue hills in the east to the "great Hill" (probably the Peekamoose) in the west. These lands were later patented to persons who purchased rights of the speculators. From the first settlement at Wawarsing Corners, about 1706, up to the period of the Revolution, the sturdy, homespun pioneer forefather and foremother, on foot and on horseback, extended this line of settlement along the great trail from Esopus to Peenpack. Their log and stone houses were builded near and around the central palisaded house-fort, for safety and defense when needed. Within these rude homes the wide, open fireplace gave cheer, and the fertile lands and forest and stream afforded abundant grain and game for their use. The flax field and the home flock met the demand for household needs of wearing apparel, fashioned by domestic skill. Social life was free and unfettered in an atmosphere of equality and neighborly sympathy. The first grist mill being at Wawarsing Corners, it became for that reason the more important business center. Occasional loads of surplus grain, with furs, hides, etc., were sent to Wiltwyck, to barter for molasses, powder, rum, metals, and other necessities. The increased value of land gave increased property value, and the bringing of negro slaves added to the more thorough development of the farms, and increased production.* Certain men became leaders, by sheer force of ability, in each neighborhood. The settlers were largely farmers, and both men and women were prudent, economical and industrious, and beyond doubt happy in their unostentatious lives. They were as a community strongly religious. The early citizenship was stirred with the politics of change from Dutch to English rule, as the colonial government slipped from the hands of its original founders. These conditions remained much the same up to the throwing overboard of the cargo of tea in Boston harbor by the Massachusetts patriots.

THE REVOLUTIONARY PERIOD.

News of the battle of Lexington probably reached Rochester about May, 1775, having been received in New York April 25 of that year. Electrified by the intelligence, the patriotic burghers began the work of preparation for the inevitable conflict. They zealously followed the leadership of their distinguished fellow citizen, the patriotic George Clinton, and kept in close touch with the independent movement which centered at Kingston.

Two hundred and twenty-eight of the male inhabitants of the town of Rochester, which at the time included Wawarsing, signed in 1775, the articles of association adopted by "The Freemen, Freeholders and Inhabitants of the City and County of New York," which articles were sent to each county in the State. When these articles reached Ulster, its citizens were almost unanimous in endorsing them, and it is not recorded that a single male inhabitant of the town of Rochester refused to sign and so to pledge his life, fortune and honor in support of representative and independent government.

Andres DeWitt, Jacob Hoornbeek, Johannes Schoonmaker, Joachim Schoonmaker, Jacobus Van Wagenen and Andrew Bevier represented Rochester at the Revolutionary Convention held in New Paltz in May, 1775. Two of these patriots lived within the present territory of Wawarsing.

Officers and soldiers from the present Wawarsing territory took part in the battles of Saratoga, White Plains and the defense of Forts Clinton

* I have in my possession the original vendue list of sale of personal effects of Cornelius Bevier, dec., of Napanoch, held June 3, 1790, at which sale two negro slaves were sold, also inventory of estate of Tjatie Dubois, dec., naming as part of her personal property three negro slaves named Tone, Peit and Beaty. Also permits for slaves to visit for a day from their homes, and leases of slaves for hire.—AUTHOR.

and Montgomery at West Point. The territory west of the valley of the Rondout and Mamakating was termed in the military annals of the Revolution " the Western Border," and it received the especial care and supervision of General Washington, as commander-in-chief. He speedily discovered that an attempt would be made to assist the plan to effect a junction of the British forces of Clinton and Burgoyne on the Hudson, by an expedition of Tories and Indians, into the central Hudson Valley from the west, through Ulster county. The Indian raid at Pine Bush, below Kerhonkson, September 5, 1778, warned the people of the Rondout valley that war was at their very doors. The massacre of the ill-fated command of Lieutenant Graham, with nineteen men, at the Chestnut Woods (Grahamsville) immediately followed. At this time there was a military encampment above Honk Falls.* This was undoubtedly situated on the flats on the east side of the present power-plant lake. Here Colonels Van Cortland, Pawling and Cantine, in turn, commanded during the Revolution. The massacres at Fantinekill and Minnesink, in 1779, were due to the attempt of the British to frustrate the contemplated expedition of General Sullivan. Governor Clinton at once took steps to stop the Indian raids, and directed the erection of forts from the Esopus to the Delaware. One fort was to be erected at Leghweck (Lackawack). On May 22, 1779, Colonel Pawling wrote Governor Clinton that, "owing to the heavy rains, little has been done at Leghweck." This fort was to be a "block-house inclosed by a breastwork proof against musketry, with an abattis redoubt. The works are to be of such size and so constructed as to be defensible with one hundred and fifty men or two hundred men." On May 16, 1779, Governor Clinton wrote General George Clinton: "I have ordered the levies to rendezvous at Leghweck and Shandeacon," a small "part of them having already been at these places, and others are on the march." Colonel John Cantine wrote Governor Clinton under date of

"Rochester, May ye 15th, 1779.

"Dear Sir:

"I have met this day with the Inhabitants of this town in order to get carages and tools to Begin the Works at Lackawack, with which they have cheerfully furnished me."

Colonel Clinton also reported the troops at "Honk" at that time as 111, of which 27 had been assigned to Mamacitting (the block-house was at

* Original Indian name Hoonck. The Peter Low deed of 1708 says the bounds began at the fall called Hoonck. This word stands Haueck, "a rapid river," an adjectival prefix probably being lost—Keht-Haueck, a strong stream or great stream, descending rapid slopes.—Ruttenber.

the present location of Wurtsboro), twenty to guard the stores at Brown's, in Wawasinck, and the balance being available for the march to Lackawack. On May 29, 1779, Major Van Benschoten reported fifty men at Lackawack. There was maintained at this time a regular horse guard patrol between the Lackawack fort and those at Peenpack and Shandaken, through the woods over the Peekamoose trail and the Neversink trail, each being through forests without a settlement for a distance of over twenty miles. The center of all these operations was in Wawarsing, and the locality became of the same strategic importance in the revolutionary war that it had been in the councils of the Esopus Indians a century before.

In 1780 a small force of Indians came over the Neversink trail and committed depredations in the Lackawack and Wawarsing vicinity. The last raid was in 1781, at Wawarsing Corners, when several houses were burned and the old Dutch church injured.

When the British were attempting the conquest of the Hudson valley, Governor Clinton ordered the removal of the State papers from Kingston to Rochester. They were in part placed in the old store-house erected in 1762, now standing one-half mile south of Kerhonkson on the Rondout. It was occupied by that great patriot and leading citizen, Johannes F. Hardenbergh.

On December 17, 1777, the State Council of Safety, in session at Hurley, took this action:

"WHEREAS, The public records of this State are now placed at Napenagh (Napanoch), in Ulster County, under a guard subject to the direction of Hendrecus Hoornbeek and Johannes Hardenbergh and Comfort Sands, Esquires, in which situation they are for the present esteemed in a place of safety; and from the condition of the roads and uncertain state of the weather at this season of the year, it is unpractical to remove said records at present to any place of safety,

Resolved, That the said records of this State remain in their present situation under guard as aforesaid, etc."

During this period a body of British prisoners was quartered near Napanoch, removal from Kingston being made before the burning of that place.

During the winter of 1780-81, when Washington's army was suffering from lack of food and clothing at Valley Forge, the New York legisla-

Dwight Divine

ture passed an act authorizing the military authorities of the State to issue certificates in payment for supplies to be sent to the army at Valley Forge. These certificates were to be receivable at full value for taxes. Dirk Wyncoop, of Kingston, was appointed agent in Ulster county to receive supplies and issue the certificates. The people in Wawarsing valley contributed liberally to this purpose, supplies being received at Johannes G. Hardenbergh's, who distributed the certificates. Many of the receivers of the certificates never applied them for tax payments, but made their value a patriotic contribution to the continental cause.*

Circumstances warrant the belief that General Washington passed through Wawarsing valley one or more times to meet Governor Clinton, who was his strong right arm in the operations of the northern army. On his visit to Kingston, 1783, it is very probable that he took the Delaware-Mamakating-Rondout Valley route, as he passed the night before he reached Kingston at the Lounsbery mansion in Stone Ridge.

It must have been owing to the familiarity of the people of Wawarsing with the stirring military operations around them, as well as with the great revolutionary characters of the time, that they exercised so little care in preserving either traditions or permanent records regarding the sites of forts or defences of the revolutionary era, or erected physical marks for the benefit of posterity. They even neglected to hand down many of the high honors belonging to some of the active patriotic families of that day, and whose descendants still reside in the town.

BUSINESS HISTORY.

History does not record any especial business enterprise or effort on the part of the early settlers of the section of Wawarsing. Up to the Nineteenth Century, the scattered neighborhoods, so far inland, had but little encouragement for enterprise in trade, depending as it did on long and heavy transportation outlay. Surplus farm produce and furs were the chief articles of trade. The communities were practically self-sustaining. Enterprise and labor were directed to clearing new lands and promoting settlement. The local blacksmith and wagonmaker were at every center of population. The traveling cobbler made his annual visit to each family. At distant intervals a local tannery and cloth mill was

* I have in my possession Certificate No. 6,212, issued to Margaret Ver Nooy for wheat and corn to the value of £4 10s. and Certificates No. 6213-14, issued Cornelius Bevier, value £7 12s., neither of which were applied in tax payments.—AUTHOR.

established, to meet the neighborhood needs in the manufacture of leather and home grown wool. The house linen was spun and woven in nearly every family from home-grown flax. Wawarsing Corners was the business center for a period of over one hundred years. Here Cornelius Ver Nooy, the pioneer, erected the first grist mill, which he brought from Holland. Here also was built the first church, and the first roads projected into the western wilderness were here started up the VerNooy Kill and towards Lackawack. The supremacy of Wawarsing Corners as the center of business, social, religious and political activity, remained unchallenged for nearly one hundred years in the progress of the colonial and early State development of the territory comprising the present township of Wawarsing.

The formation of the town of Wawarsing from the town of Rochester, in 1806, and the inauguration of its own civil government, marked the beginning of a new era in settlement and development. New roads were at once built and needed bridges erected, opening the Greenfield and Drowned Land sections, with their wealth of hemlock and pine. Ellenville was settled at this period and began to grow rapidly, as it drew to it the trade of the then growing neighborhoods of the Good Beerkill and Greenfield streams, as also those of the Leurenkill and Mamacotting to the south.

At the period of town organization, Wawarsing's families comprised the following representative names: Allen, Akerly, Addison, Bruyn, Burger, Botsford, Bevier, Barber, Broadhead, Belew, Besley, Brown, Boggs, Black, Crossman, Cantine, Cristle, Chambers, De Witt, De Puy, Doll, Devens, Devoe, Douglass, Davis, Demarest, Divine, Evelin, Freer, Fairchild, Fair, Gere, Gilbert, Grey, Hardenbergh, Himrodt, Hawley, Hoornbeek, Helm, Holmes, Heermance, Hixon, Hook, Hassock, Johnson, Kortright, Kettle, Kimball, Knox, Kellock, Lemly, Le Fevre, McKnight, Mitchell, Mullen, Newkirk, Oostrander, Payne, Pride, Price, Schouten, Skidmore, Shaver, Sarles, Sheely, Turner, Tompkins, Tyrrell, Thompson, Van Wagener, Ver Nooy, Van Gorder, Wodin, Washburn, Woods and Wilson.

The first large Tannery was started in Greenfield in 1814, by Henry Southwick. It did not prove a success, owing to the long haul to market of its product. While settlements increased and much new land was brought under cultivation, the small needs of each family kept the com-

Benjamin F. Neal, M.D.

munity in a primitive condition, until the work of erecting the Delaware and Hudson canal commenced in 1824. This great internal improvement caused a business boom in the valley, which grew with the completion of the work in 1828. The low cost of canal transportation started industrial enterprise at once. At Napanoch, in 1829, the Southwick Bros. commenced making axes, and within a few years large tanneries were in course of erection or completion at Greenfield, Ellenville, Napanoch, Homowack, Lackawack, and Wawarsing. The saw mill followed the bark-peelers, and millions of feet of hemlock and pine from the forests of the Cape, Drowned Land and Greenfield section found ready market. Every canal port became a business center, with canal store-house and retail store. Ellenville grew rapidly, and Kerhonkson, Port Ben and Homowack were soon postoffices and centers of trade. Boat building developed into a profitable industry at several points along the canal. In 1836 the Ellenville Glass Works were established, and the enterprise and strength of its management at once placed Ellenville in the van as the growing trade center of the canal line between Rondout and Honesdale. Napanoch was its equal in business importance at this time. Here the enterprise of the Southwick Bros. in a large tannery and in axe making was carrying the name of the place into the business marts of the whole country. The virgin soil of the town, as it was denuded of the forests by the axes of the bark-peelers and lumbermen, was brought rapidly into improved lands by the sturdy German and Irish workmen, who found employment in the glass works, iron mills and tanneries of the locality.

In the early 50's the plank road era began. The citizens of Wawarsing united with those of Newburgh and Sullivan county, and constructed plank roads, leading from Ellenville to Newburgh and Woodburn, and from Napanoch to Grahamsville. In 1853 the Bange iron forge was erected at Napanoch, and a blast furnace was put in operation in 1859 to convert the iron ore found in that vicinity into pig iron. The axe industry was also greatly enlarged, and later, mills for rolling merchantable iron and making knives used in the manufacture of tobacco and the making of straw paper were added to Napanoch industries. All these enterprises were the product of local capital in the main, and all were conducted with varying success up to the 70's, when changed trade conditions determined it to be more profitable to do the work elsewhere. The Ellenville Glass Works contributed more to the town's prosperity and growth than any single industry. But all the industries mentioned, with the wealth of hemlock bark and lumber, and aided by the cheap canal transportation and cheap coal, added greatly to local prosperity and development up to the period of the Civil War. The first bank—the First National—was established in 1863 at Ellenville. Previously the banking business of the town had been transacted mostly at Kingston, Newburgh, Middletown and Rondout. The town's activity continued during the Civil War period and up into the 70's. In 1870 the first railroad reached the town of Ellenville. Funds for its construction were provided by town bonds issued to the amount of $259,000. This burden, added to the issue of Civil War bonds, then unpaid, had a blighting effect upon the town's property values and no doubt retarded for a period the town's growth materially, as the burden of taxation became heaviest at the period of trade transition which followed the decline of the tanning industry for want of bark, and the loss of the iron industry owing to the development of the great iron and coal regions of Pennsylvania and Michigan.

By 1880 the great industries which had made the town of Wawarsing a populous and growing community had gone out of existence within its borders, or retained but a fitful and unprofitable life and soon expired. With their decline the name and fame of Ellenville and Napanoch became almost lost for a period in the markets of the country and the world, and within the town many homes were abandoned to ruin and many acres of improved lands returned to the wilderness. Of the old industries there remains only the Russell Tobacco Knife Works at Napanoch.

WAWARSING AT PRESENT.

For a period of several years, up to the beginning of the Twentieth Century, Wawarsing lost in population, business and capital. Its enterprising citizens were not lacking either in spirit or effort to meet the new conditions surrounding them. Many efforts were made by individuals, and through co-operation, to start new industries. Among these, the making of pocket cutlery was undertaken at Ellenville in 1874, through a co-operative organization. The venture was not successful and the factory passed from one management to another until it became the property of Dwight Divine, who now conducts the works under the name of the Ulster Knife Company. It is now a large and prosperous concern, employing the largest number of employees of any single concern in the town. The Ulster Paint Works, at Ellenville, is also a large plant.

Napanoch, owing to its fine water power, is still in the lead as the largest center of heavy manufacturing. Here are three paper mills, a tobacco knife works, the Napanoch Knife Co., making pocket cutlery, and a mill making ground wood pulp for use in the making of explosives and linoleum. The Honk Falls Power Co., at Honk Falls, of 2,000 H. P. capacity, is one of the finest plants in the line of electrical construction in the country and noted for its efficiency and economy. It supplies electric current for lighting Ellenville and Kingston, as well as to several small villages and many homes within an area of thirty miles distant. Agriculture has attained a more important development in the town of late years, due in a measure to the successful management of the Ulster County Agricultural Society, the annual meetings of which have been held at Ellenville for many years. Several local dairies have a State reputation for the high class of stock and product. Fruit culture is also making headway as a profitable industry. The abandonment of the Delaware and Hudson Canal in 1902 was a serious blow to Wawarsing interests. The loss was met in a measure by the early construction and extension of the Ellenville branch of the Ontario and Western Railroad to Kingston, and the inauguration of a most liberal management and service by that corporation, which has greatly enhanced the summer hotel and boarding business of the town. The near proximity of the great and growing city of New York is now Wawarsing's greatest asset. This influence has of late advanced real estate values, built many summer homes and developed several most beautiful estates in the hands of new and wealthy residents.

A large Hebrew population has, since 1903, settled in Wawarsing, mostly in the Western part of the town, and this accession promises to be an important factor, in the future of the town's growth. They have purchased many farms and are conducting many large boarding houses for summer guests. The large summer hotels at Minnewaska, Mr. Meenaga and Lackawack have high reputations throughout the country as popular resorts. A large sanitarium for invalids is located on the west slope of the Shawangunk mountain, near Kerhonkson. The population of Wawarsing in 1905 was 7,215, showing a loss of nearly 1,000 in twenty-five years. Ellenville (incorporated) is the leading village, with 2,872 inhabitants, two banks, the First National and the Home National, the latter established in 1873, also the Ellenville Savings Bank, established in

1869. It has Reformed, Methodist, Episcopal, Lutheran, German and English Catholic churches. Its public schools have a State reputation for their excellence, and its fire department in efficiency and morale is equal to any in the State. Its water system, owned by the municipality, was erected in 1871. The water is most excellent, owing to its purity. The village is situated amid picturesque surroundings, with wide, well kept streets, lighted with electricity and finely shaded, with flagged sidewalks, and its local government is efficient and popular. The two local papers, the *Journal*, established in 1849, and the *Press*, established in 1870, are well conducted and are successful local news purveyors. Flourishing fraternal lodges of Masons, Odd Fellows, Red Men, and Knights of Pythias center at Ellenville, and lodges of the Junior Order of United American Mechanics are at Ellenville, Napanoch and Kerhonkson. Napanoch has a population of 683, with Methodist and Reformed churches. Wawarsing has 240, with a Free Chapel, and Kerhonkson has 546, with Reformed and Methodist churches. The post offices of the town are Cragsmore, Spring Glen, Ellenville, Greenfield, Dairyland, Ulster Heights, Montela, Lackawack, Wawarsing and Kerhonkson. During the summer a post office is maintained at Minnewaska. There is a Baptist church at Lackawack, Methodist churches at Montela and Ulster Heights, also a German Catholic church at the latter place. The New York City Catskill water supply project, which includes the valley of the Rondout river above Honk Falls, will obliterate the neighborhood above Honk Falls to Montela and destroy the water power at Napanoch when the work is completed. This work will have a disastrous effect upon the industries of the town. The influence which is adding growth and prosperity to Wawarsing to-day is its proximity to New York City, of which it will be merely a suburb when the Hudson river tunnels are completed and electric power is applied to railroad trains. Then Wawarsing, without a rival in its attractions within the area of its distance from that great city, will become a growing and prosperous community to a degree unknown in the past.

John C. Hoornbeek.

CHAPTER XXXIV.

TOWN OF WOODSTOCK

By Howard Hendricks.

THIS is one of the interior towns of Ulster County, and it is located on the northern boundary adjoining the county of Greene. The towns of Saugerties and Kingston are on the east, those of Hurley and Olive on the south, and the town of Shandaken on the west. It now covers an area of about 37,085 acres, of which nearly one-half is under some form of cultivation. The balance consists of mountainous woodland, forest slopes and quarries.

While the general aspect of the town is unfavorable to easy cultivation, there are many fertile valleys and some fine uplands where fine fruit and other farm crops are successfully grown. The soil and location seem well adapted to the growth of fine flavored apples which are produced to a profitable extent. The general altitude of the farming section is about 600 feet above the Hudson. But the northern part consists of high mountains rising abruptly from the base to the height of 3,150 feet above tide, as in the case of Overlook Mountain, one of the eastern sentinels of the Catskills. Not far below this summit is Echo Lake, or Shues Lake, as it is often called, and at a lower elevation near the center of the town is Cooper's Lake, which covers about eighty acres. The principal streams are the Beaverkill, Sawkill, and the Mink Hollow brook. These with their numerous tributaries furnish valuable water power and some fine trout-fishing.

The region was settled just previous to the Revolution. Philip Bonesteel, the first settler of record, came in 1770 and made his "clearing" about one mile below the present Woodstock village, on what is known as the old Hudler farm. He was followed six years later by Edward Short, who located in the region since known as "Yankeetown." Next came Peter Short, in 1784, and four years later, Jacob DuBois, Ephriam Van Keuren and Philip Shultis. Among other early settlers were Bement Lewis, Henry Shultis, John Hutchins, William Elting, Matthew Keip,

Peter Vandebogart, Johannes Kipp, Peter Van Benschoten, Peter Harder and Jeremiah Reynolds.

Jacob Montross seems to have built the first grist-mill of which there are now two or three others in the town. Among these are the old Disch Mill, near Woodstock village, and the Shufelt Mills at Zena. All these mills get their power from the Sawkill stream. There are also many steam saw-mills in the town, which are operated certain seasons of the year.

Tavern-keeping seems to have been a profitable occupation in the early history of Woodstock, judging from the large number of licenses granted. In fact, it was the pioneer industry, because Philip Bonesteel got his license in 1789, and the following persons were licensed in the same year; the fee then being 8 shillings. Stephen Kierce, George Ellwyn, Richard Peck, John Tuttle, Julius Edgar, Martinus Loriway, Gilbert Decker, Robert More, William Goss and John Van Loan. During the next decade there were a host of other tavern-keepers licensed. As to the other important industries of that period which contributed toward the support of these numerous hotels, the record is far less complete. Dr. Stephen L. Heath seems to have been among the earlier physicians of the town.

Nineteen days after the inauguration of George Washington as the first President of the United States, on April 11, 1787, Woodstock was incorporated as a town. The territory had previously been included in the old town of Hurley, and consisted of the settlements known as Great and Little Shandaken. The fact that the name Woodstock originally covered a wide territory is shown by the statement that ten years after its formation a part was taken off in the formation of the town of Middletown, Delaware County, and in 1798 another portion was annexed to Windham in Greene County, and in 1804 nearly all of the present town of Shandaken was taken from Woodstock. Then in 1853 the southern town lines were again changed, by which parts of Hurley and Olive were added, and another bit of Woodstock went over to Olive. And finally in 1879, a small part of the historic old town of Kingston, on the north, was annexed to Woodstock.

The first town election was held the first Tuesday in June, 1787, at the house of Elias Hasbrouck, who was then chosen the first Supervisor. He was succeeded by John Van Gaasbeck, Jr., 1792-98; Wilhelmus Rowe,

1799-1802; Benjamin Olmstead, 1803-05; Cornelius Dumond, 1806-07; John Wigram, 1808-09; Isaac Elting, 1810-22; Daniel Elliot, 1823-26; Henry P. Shultis, 1827-29; Samuel Culver, 1830-37; Andrew A. Newkirk, 1838-41; Henry P. Shultis, 1842-44; Herman Reynolds, 1845-47; Andrew A. Newkirk, 1848; John H. Lockwood, 1849; Peter Reynolds, 1850; William M. Cooper, 1851, 1865, 1867, 1870; Peter Reynolds, 1852, 1862-64; Joseph Miller, 1855; Cornelius, Risely, 1856-57; Herman Reynolds, 1858-59; William Johnson, 1860-61; Albert H. Vosburgh, 1866, 1867, 1881-85, Edward B. Harder, 1868; Orson Vandevoort, 1871; Edward B. Harder, 1872-73; Mark C. Risely, 1874; William H. Reynolds, 1875, 1878; Alex H. Elwin, 1876; William F. Cooper, 1877, 1886-88, 1890-92; Isaac W. Mosher, 1879; Lyman B. Smith, 1880; Alfred Reynolds, 1889; Vactor Shultis, 1893, 1894, 1904-06; Henry P. Vanderbogart, 1895-1899; Christian W. Winne, 1900, 01-02-03.

The only village of importance in the town is Woodstock, in the southeastern part, about twelve miles from Kingston. The location is invested with rare scenic charm; nestled there at the base of the gigantic Overlook Mountain crag which forms a towering background for the tall church spires, and the neatly painted stores, shops and dwellings. There is a good hotel, a post-office, telegraph office, two general stores and many shops and comfortable dwelling houses. In the summer season many of these houses entertain city boarders at moderate prices, and they are charmed with the rural environment and the healthful surroundings.

There are nine churches in the town, the oldest of which is the Reformed Church which was incorporated in 1805. The present church edifice was erected in 1842. There are two Lutheran churches, the older dating back to 1806, and the other 1878. The first Methodist church was incorporated in 1835, the society having been formed seven years earlier with twenty members. The first church was built in 1833. The second Baptist church is next in order of date, starting in 1844. Ten years later the first Wesleyan Methodist church began with 23 members, an offshoot from the parent Methodist church. Then in 1856 came the second Methodist church, and in 1870 still another Methodist church in the hamlet known as Bristol. Three years later the South Woodstock Methodist church was organized.

There are seven post-offices in the town known as Woodstock, Bearsville, Lake Hill, Zena, Willow, Shady and Wittenberg.

The hamlet known as Bristol was the site of the old glass factory which ceased operations about fifty years ago. From this factory at that time there was a turnpike-road built to the Hudson at Glasco which seems in some way to have derived its name from this mountain glass factory. Lake Hill is another hamlet with a Baptist church and a few dwellings. It was the site of the noted Cooper's Hotel.

Under the early school laws commissioners were chosen annually to manage the schools. William B. Rogers, John Van Gaasbeck, Jr. Stephen Simmons and Justice Squire being the first commissioners in 1797. In the early part of the last century the records do not show any important official action of the town authorities in respect to local educational affairs. Under the new school act in 1813, the management became vested in inspectors and commissioners who were elected annually. This continued until 1844 when the system of superintendents was begun. Then in 1856 the present plan of district commissioners was inaugurated, and the schools were no longer under town control.

The principal cemetery is at Woodstock village, and it is nicely kept. There are many ante-revolutionary monuments and an interesting mound known as the "Elm-Tree Grave." In connection with this there is an interesting tradition regarding a sad incident of domestic infelicity with tragic features, in which Dame Nature seems to have taken an important rôle in the final act, and left an indelible mark upon the scene. Many of the older Woodstock residents will give these details more fully than they could be presented here.

The records show that some ninety or more citizens of the town of Woodstock served in the Civil War, many of whom lost their lives on the battlefield, and others as a result of this service for their country.

The famous Overlook Mountain, before alluded to, is of course the great native attraction of this old town. The scenic beauties of this massive mountain crag overshadow and dominate every other feature of Woodstock. From this airy crest, 3,150 feet toward the sky, it must have been that "Leatherstocking" that most original and eloquent character in all fiction, whom Carlyle characterized as "the one melodious synopsis of man and nature," stood when he said he saw "all creation, and looked at the ways of men, and upon all that God had done or man can do." Parts of seven different States can be seen on a clear day from this summit, with some seventy miles of the Hudson which shimmers in the sunshine like a silver ribbon. This vast mountain crag is always a gigantic background of beauty to Woodstock, no matter from what point it is seen. For many years a large summer hotel near its summit, so plainly seen from the Hudson, known as the Overlook Mountain House, was a famous summer resort with tourists. The first hotel there was built in 1870, and opened by John E. Lasher in 1871. It was much larger than the present structure, and was run by Lasher until 1873 when, in the winter of that year, it burned down, and for three years the property stood vacant. At length it was purchased by the Kiersted brothers who built the present hotel in 1876-77. It was then managed by Col. Smith for four years, who was succeeded by C. K. Haskell and others, and finally closed a few years ago for lack of profitable patronage, because of the long stage ride to reach it, and the opening of other mountain hotels nearer the railway. During the past year the property has passed into new hands and the house was partly opened this season, with a promise of greater development next year. With improved means of access this Overlook Mountain resort is sure to become one of the most famous and popular in the Catskills.

George Mead was the pioneer landlord of this mountain. In June, 1863, he began to build his hotel half way up the slope, where it now stands. The place was then a dense wilderness and a woodsman had built a small rude shanty in the clearing. Mr. Mead bought up his claim and began to entertain a few visitors in the fall of 1863. Christopher Agar and H. B. Schoonmaker are the first names on his old register, which now contains a long list of names of eminent men and women of fame and importance. There was then only an old Indian trail from his hotel to the Overlook crest. In 1869 Mr. Mead raised money from some Kingston business men and built the first wagon road up that very steep slope. This road was afterward improved by the hotel company and was well kept for some years at considerable expense. The Mead hotel was the first mountain house built south of the Kaaterskill Clove. It has since been much enlarged and is now in charge of W. S. Mead, the son.

The Overlook House is about 500 feet higher than any other hotel in the State, and the air is always cooler than any other point in the Catskills.

The public roads of Woodstock have been materially improved during recent years. The main thoroughfare to Saugerties has been rebuilt with the assistance of the State, and the road to West Hurley has been greatly improved.

The great Woodstock watershed, which is now furnishing water for the city of Kingston, was first brought into requisition in 1883. The water is gathered into three large reservoirs and conveyed to the city by gravity in a double line of mains. It is of exceptional purity. The main streams are the Sawkill and the Mink Hollow. The former begins at Echo Lake not far below the Overlook summit on the northwesterly slope. This watershed covers an area of about 35 square miles, and there is a storage capacity in the three reservoirs in the town of 305,000,000 gallons. The mechanical filtering plant has a daily capacity of over 6,000,000 gallons.

The Bluestone industry is also carried on to a considerable extent in Woodstock, although the work here is confined to the quarrying, and carting the stone to market. There is an abundance of stone, and numerous quarries have been opened on the lower mountain slopes and hills. Some fine large platforms and other varieties of flag are secured. Most of this stone is drawn to the river at Glasco, Saugerties or Malden and sold to the Hudson River Bluestone Company, or to James Maxwell's Sons, who are now the only buyers and manufacturers in this vicinity. In fact, it may be said that the Hudson River Company practically controls the bluestone industry and output in Ulster County at the present time.

"Byrdcliffe" is the name applied to an important artist colony settlement on the mountain slope north of Woodstock village at an elevation of about 1,500 feet above tide. It was established by Mr. Whitehead, an English colonist, a few years ago, and it now contains some 25 or more cottages and buildings of different kinds upon which much money has been spent. The grading and construction of roads has also been done at large cost. The place has been made attractive to artists endowed with artistic tastes and inclinations, and the colony has many summer visitors. A summer class of from twenty to thirty students has worked there in what is known as the New York Art School, and much talent is being developed. It is said that over half a million dollars has been expended in the establishment of this colony and the subsequent improvements.

J. G. van Slyke

CHAPTER XXXV.

THE REFORMED PROTESTANT (DUTCH) CHURCH.

By Rev. John Garnsey Van Slyke, D.D.

THE Reformed Church in America," commonly known as "Dutch," like every other type of ecclesiastical life in our country, is an exotic. Its beginnings in Ulster County were due to seeds brought hither from the Netherland. In that ancient "Hollow-land," the doctrines of the Reformation early found a peculiarly congenial and nutritious soil. That same vigorous type of character which has been emblazoned in the annals of patriotism, found equal illustration in the religious life of our Dutch ancestors. The principles of an emancipated Gospel were incorporated in their bone and sinew, and found ardent and unequivocal assertion in their theological dogmas.

But while we glory in our Dutch ancestry, we are not unmindful of the multitudinous strains of that French Huguenot blood which were transfused into the veins of our progenitors. This blend of the characteristic qualities of the vivacious Gallic race with the more plodding Batavians, issued in a product which united the better elements of both. And in the fact that the Dutch provinces offered asylum from the persecutions of neighboring realms, where the benignant air of toleration encouraged the growths of a pure religion, there was imparted a liberal breadth and kindly sympathy which allowed the diversities of faith. A freedom from tolerance and narrowness has been a constant aspect of people of Dutch stock. While they have not been indifferent in maintaining a purity of creed, no bigotry nor zealotry have incited them to brandish the sword of persecution.

From a people incorporating such distinguishing elements, the Dutch Church of Ulster County traces its direct sources. From the time of its transplanting two and a half centuries ago, it has preserved the birthmarks which avouch its noble parentage.

The Dutchman under alien skies reproduced precisely the type of doctrine and modes of ecclesiastical government which had prevailed in

Holland. It is suggestive that it was not until the year 1800, that the Colonists or their children would consent to abandon the use of the Dutch language in public worship.

These facts predetermine the phases of our history as a denomination in this county. They imposed on our expansion some limitations which delayed our thorough Americanization, and were the occasion for the upspringing of diverse churches which declined to be assimilated with a body which so long remained essentially foreign. This foreign adhesion is illustrated in the case of the old mother-church in Kingston which refused to sunder its ecclesiastical relation with the Classis of Amsterdam until near the beginning of the nineteenth century. But notwithstanding this perpetuation of an old world type, it was the Dutch Church which, in a human way, created the spiritual climate and fructified the soil, which has enabled churches of different orders to spring and flourish about us. Their vitality is the transferred legacy and endowment of such Christian forces as have issued out of the loins of the church which we still fondly call "Dutch."

The moulding of the moral history of Ulster County is to be largely credited to influences and impulses which had their birth in the old Dutch Church of Kingston, and which incited the various ecclesiastical activities of our present time. The earliest crystallization of the religious instincts of our fathers culminating in the formation of a church in Kingston—then called Wiltwyck, and afterward Esopus, is overhung with a mist of obscurity. The earliest annals recite that on the 29th day of May, 1658, and the day following, being "Ascension Day," "the people having no church edifice, assembled at the house of Jacob Jansen Stoll, to keep the festival." They appear to have had at this time no minister in full orders, but were served by a schoolmaster, who was appointed as a "Voorleser," *i. e.,* whose office virtually corresponded with that of a Curate in the Church of England, whose duty it was to act as a lay reader, and catechise the children and instill the elements of Christian faith.

Tradition has named the first appointee to this office, one Andrus van der Sluys. The name of Andries Jacobus van Slyke, has also been named by one authority as this person. From exact similarity of meaning, *i. e.,* a sluice-way, the one name may have been substituted for the other. This Voorleser was appointed by the Colonial Governor Petrus Stuyvesant. That his appointment was justified is seen by the fact that a spirit was developed under his curacy which took shape in a definite church organization, according to the polity of the mother country, which was predominantly Presbyterian. In August, 1659, this newly-formed church invited Hermanus Blom from Holland, to become its pastor. They promised to provide Dominie Blom with a good farm or bowerie, house and barn, cows and oxen, and pay him 700 guilders, *i. e.*, $280, at beaver valuation, to commence from the 5th of September, in 1660. Entering on his ministerial duties, he made the first record, in the first volume of the books of the church, as follows:

"I, Hermanus Blom, the first preacher in the land of Esopus, preached my first sermon on the 12th day of September, 1660, having arrived there on the 5th day of the month in the Company's yacht."

The Reverend Blom was born in Amsterdam in 1628, and graduated from Leyden University in Theology in 1652. After seven years service in Esopus, he returned to Holland. His original commission reads, he was "ordained to preach on water and on the land and in all the neighborhood, but especially at Esopus." He appears to have been a man of superior parts, under whose pastorate the young Church rapidly developed. The Dominie being a virtual autocrat, largely shaped by his personal force as well as his official character, the opinions and life of the nascent community. It must have been an idyllic state of things when a true and faithful servant of God could thus dominate the entire population.

The first Church edifice was constructed of logs, in 1661, on ground now occupied by a barn of the late Augustus H. Bruyn. This first rude building was, two or three years later, replaced by a commodious stone structure on the southeast corner of the present Church-yard. This, later, became a point toward which the scattered inhabitants of outlying districts as far away as New Paltz, Stone Ridge, Woodstock, and Saugerties converged Sunday by Sunday. Space forbids a recital of the quiet growth which advanced until the Revolutionary period; for several generations the history of religious life in Ulster County coincided mainly with the history of the Church now commonly designated as "The First Dutch." The imposing Charter of this Church, written on a large sheet of parchment, was issued by the English Government, under whose care the young colony had passed, and bears the date of Nov 17, 1719.

The several Churches of the Reformed order which sprang up in the adjacent parts of the County, were all progeny of the mother in Kingston, and some were directly due to her incubating influence. The history of any particular Church in this contribution to the story of Ulster County, from the nature of the case, as well as the limitations of space, can consist of little more than superficial annals and statistics. Back of these are impalpable spiritual elements which distinguish a true Church of God from various human organizations, and which are beyond the compass of narration.

In chronological order, the first Church springing from the loins of the mother Church, was the Reformed Church of New Paltz. The Huguenot Refugees from France and the Palatinate who had found among the Dutch in Kingston, welcome and hospitality, withdrew in a body to the fertile and beautiful valley of the Wallkill, and directly organized a Church where they might worship in their native French tongue. Under the moulding hand of the Rev. Pierre Daillie, its formal life began in 1683, since which time its uninterrupted life has grown into noble proportions. For a number of years, it stood apart by itself without ecclesiastical relation to the Denomination in this country. In 1772, it became affiliated with the general body of the Reformed Church. Until this date, its people had refused to take sides in a schism which unhappily divided the entire Dutch Church, and which is known as the Coetus and Conferentiae controversy. The point at issue was the question whether the Church should find its ministry in our native soil, for which the Coetus party contended, or whether they should be drawn only from the schools of the Netherland, as the Conferentiae faction resolutely contended. The sharpness of the controversy laid an arresting blight on the expansion of the Church, nowhere more unhappily than in Ulster County, and neutralized to a material extent the advantages of prior occupancy, while it afforded opportunity to other ecclesiastical bodies to press in and possess the land. Moreover, the tenacity with which the Dutch congregations clung to the use of their original language, long after the English tongue prevailed as the vernacular in social and business life, operated as a limitation on expansion.

The Americanization of the Church has long since effaced almost the recollection of these phases of an earlier life. In no Church of the County have the surviving spirit and vigor found more conspicuous illustration than in the well-equipped and influential Church of New Paltz.

The next Church to crystallize in an organization in 1701, was that at Accord, in the town of Rochester—coinciding with the beginning of the life of the community itself. It shared for several years, the fostering care of the Revs. Petrus Vas and G. W. Mancius of Kingston. The certificate of incorporation of this Church was executed in 1788. After enjoying the intermittent services of occasional supplies of its pulpit by Theodorus Frelinghuysen, Schureman, and others, in 1766, the notable Dirick Romeyn was ordained, and as Pastor, took charge of the three Churches of Rochester, Marbletown and Wawarsing. He has been described as "unquestionably the first man in our Church in his day, and among the first in the entire American Church." This particular Church appears to have bred men of exceptional power, among whom may be named Martinus Schoonmaker, and Henricus, his brother, Cornelius D. Westbrook, John Hardenbergh and James B. Hardenbergh.

What is now known as the Reformed Church of Saugerties is, so far as the ecclesiastical organization is concerned, identical with the old Church of Katsbaan. The first house of worship was built in 1732 on the beautiful hill where the present Church of Katsbaan now stands. The early records of the Church yield little matter for history. The twin Church of Saugerties was separated from Katsbaan in 1839.

The life of the Church of Marbletown, now known as Stone Ridge, dates from the year 1737. North Marbletown was organized in 1851, and was an offshoot of Stone Ridge.

Another Church which dates from the Eighteenth century is that at the place described as Klein Esopus, organized in 1791, and incorporated in 1793. The picturesque old brick edifice crowning a hill at Ulster Park remains a center of hallowing influence.

The Reformed Church of North Esopus at Port Ewen, an offshoot from Klein Esopus, was organized in 1851, since which time it has steadily grown in membership and usefulness.

Another Reformed Church which also dates from the Eighteenth century is that of Bloomingdale, which took definite shape in 1796.

Very nearly coinciding in their antiquity are the Churches of Shokan, organized in 1791, and Woodstock, in 1799.

The first to decorate the beginning of the Nineteenth century was the Church of old Hurley, which began its independent existence in 1801.

The earlier half of the Nineteenth century was the fecund age of the Dutch Church in Ulster. A wave of fervor and zeal manifested itself at widely separated points. This was expressed at Roxbury in 1802, in the Church which has recently been reconstituted as the Jay Gould Memorial Church. Next following in 1807, the Church of Flatbush was started. The Reformed Church of the Clove (High Falls) also dates from 1807. Dashville Falls was originated in 1831. The Church of Guilford crystallized in an independent organization in 1833. Next in order of time were Plattekill in 1838 and the village Church of Saugerties in 1839. Blue Mountain emerged into history in 1851 in the same year, as stated above, with Port Ewen and North Marbletown. Shandaken Church took form in 1854. Next following the Churches named came the organization of the Church at Rosendale in 1843; its branch Church at the Plains assumed shape in 1897. West Hurley followed Rosendale in 1848.

The vital and prosperous Fair Street Reformed Church of Kingston, a swarm from the over-crowded hive of the First Dutch, was formed in 1849. Blue Mountain began simultaneously with the Churches of Port Ewen and Krumville and North Marbletown in 1851. In 1864, St. Remy was constituted an independent Church, though under the care of a neighboring Pastor.

The Church of the Comforter in Kingston, frequently called the Church of Wiltwyck, owes its origin, in 1863, to the generous enterprise of a single Christian family, whose large benificence has since been amply justified. In 1876, the Church of Lyonsville was born; in 1891, that of Gardiner; and in 1898, that at Brown's Station, whose expressive name is "Church of the Faithful." By the proposed reservoir of New York this last is destined to be effaced.

The Churches thus far enumerated are confederate in two groups, known as the Classis of Ulster and that of Kingston.

The Classis is the unit of ecclesiastical power in the Reformed Church, and has supreme control in the government and supervision of individual Churches and in the settlement and removal of ministers. It holds two regular sessions each year in the various Churches in rotation, at which reports of the individual Churches are rendered, as well as such special sessions as occasion may require. It is constituted by a Minister and one Elder from each Church.

Other Churches lying outside the jurisdiction of the two Classis of Ulster and Kingston, though within the bounds of Ulster County, are those of Shawangunk, whose organization is uncertainly placed by some as early as 1737; and that of New Prospect, constituted in 1815.

The Wallkill Valley Church was incorporated in 1869; New Hurley in 1770; Plattekill in 1839; Ellenville in 1840; Wawarsing, at Napanoch, in 1845. These Churches in their respective localities continue to yield gratifying evidence of abounding vitality while illustrating a wide-spread leavening influence.

The mere dates and annals to which this sketch confines us, while exhibiting the external chronicles of the Reformed Churches which have sprung up within the bounds of the County of Ulster, are manifestly incompetent to unfold all the lore of history of which they are the external exponents. They avouch a high measure of spiritual devotion and earnestness; and the usefulness and prosperity which have accompanied their growth attest the sanction and favor of Heaven. As qualified by human conditions, some of them, very few indeed, have suffered impoverishment and decline, from changes in secular fortune which have befallen them; but the greater number remain in abounding usefulness and expanding power, as citadels of the Kingdom of God in this County.

CHAPTER XXXVI.

THE ROMAN CATHOLIC CHURCH.

By Monsignor, the Very Reverend Richard Lalor Burtsell, D.D.

WHILE the Dutch were following up their discovery of the Hudson River by their settlement of Esopus and Fort Orange, the Jesuits were extending their labors among the Indians inhabiting the present State of New York. The first missionary who entered about 1642 within the borders of the State, Father Jogues accompanied by a party of Hurons, was taken captive by the Iroquois or Mohawks. Though beaten with clubs and stones, his finger nails pulled, the index finger of both hands gnawed, the thumb of his right hand cut off by an Algonquin woman—a Christian—at the command of her Iroquois master, yet as soon as he had the chance, he instructed such Indians as he found disposed, in the mysteries of the Christian faith, and baptized dying children. He afterwards made his escape by the assistance of Arendt Van Curler, who had previously made several attempts in his favor. The Dutch protected him even at the risk of war, and paid the Indians one hundred pieces of gold for his ransom. The minister of Fort Orange, John Megalopensis, took a great interest in him. Sailing down the Hudson, they certainly touched at Ronduit—the redoubt to protect Esopus or Wiltwyck. Governor Kieft and the inhabitants of New Amsterdam received him with great kindness; the Governor provided him with a passage to Holland. In New Amsterdam, Father Jogues found only two Catholics, a Portuguese woman and an Irishman. Governor Dongan was directed by the Duke of York, to detach the Five Nations from the French, who had gained great influence through the zealous labors of the missionaries. To counteract this a Jesuit mission was established in New York, and the purpose was to form at Saratoga a Catholic village of Iroquois Indians under English influence. Fathers Harvey, Harrison and Gage actually started in New York a college, of which Jacob Leisler, a later fanatical usurper of the government, wrote to the Governor of Boston in August, 1689:

R. L. Burtsell D.D.

"I have formerly urged to inform your Honr. that Coll. Dongan in this time did direct a Jesuit colledge upon collour to learn Latine to the judges West, Mr. Graham, Judge Palmer and John Indor did contribute their sones for some time but no boddy initating them, the colledge vanished."

We read in the Records and studies, U. S. Cath. Histor. Society, Jan. 1899, Vol. 1, p. 35, that from 1683 to 1690 "Fathers Harrison, Harvey and Gage, Jesuit ministers to the Catholics scattered through New York and New Jersey and traces of their ministrations are found from Esopus in Ulster County to Staten Island." Father A. E. Jones, S. J., in Griffin's Amer. Cath Historical Researches, Vol. XXI., Jan., 1904, tells of a Jesuit Father Francois Vaillant de Guesilis who on December 31st, 1682, was sent from Canada to plead for peace with Gov. Dongan, but was back in Montreal by the end of February following. Griffin in Amer. Cath. Hist. Researches, Jan., 1901, p. 12, says that this "Father Vaillant was at Cutaracony (Kingston, N. Y.) in the year 1688, escorted by two Indians who were sent by Gov. Dongan to prevent him from having any intercourse with the Mohawks, his former flock."

We have a curious item mentioned in Doc. Hist. N. Y., Vol. XI., p. 205: "Some articles of value which heretofore belonged to the Canadian Jesuit, Valiand of Canada" 12 little patrenoster chains (rosaries) 1 priest's white surplice. Leisler writing to Governor of Boston, 7th April, 1690, wrote: "In searching Livingstone's house we found a case belonging to a French Jesuit of Canada and some Indian Categisms and the lesson to learn to make their God before they ate him, with crucifix."

In 1673 the enactment of the last of the Dutch Governors, reviving the Stuyvesant system, directed the local magistrates "to take care that the Reformed Christian religion be maintained in conformity to the Synod of Dordrecht, without permitting any other sects attempting anything contrary thereto." The Catholic English Governor Col. Dongan in 1683, had passed in the first legislative Assembly in New York the Bill of Rights which declared that "No person or persons which profess faith in God by Jesus Christ shall at any time be anyways molested, punished, disquieted or called in question for any difference of opinion or matter of religious concernment, who do not actually disturb the civil peace of the province."

This was in accord with the instructions of James, Duke of York in 1679 to Governor Andros. Marius Schoonmaker, the historian of Kingston, goes out of his way to apologize for the revocation of this liberal spirit and the intolerance of Governor Bellmont under King William in 1700 when he sanctioned the law requiring Jesuits and Popish priests to leave the province by the 1st of November following under penalty of perpetual imprisonment. This Bellmont was the son of a Colonel Coote whose butcheries of Catholics in Ireland stand out horribly even on the records of that unhappy island. The preamble of the law is a tissue of lies: "Whereas divers Jesuits, Priests and Popish Missionaries have of late come and for some time have had their residence in the remote parts of this province and others of his Majesty's adjacent colonies, who by their wicked and subtle insinuations industriously labour to debauch, seduce and withdraw the Indians from their due obedience to His most sacred Majesty, and to excite them up to sedition, rebellion and open hostility to His Majesty's government."

The law enacted that every priest remaining in the province after the passage of the law, or coming in after November, 1700, should be "deemed and accounted an incendiary and disturber of the public peace and safety, and an enemy of the Christian religion, and shall be adjudged to suffer perpetual imprisonment. Any priest imprisoned under the act who escaped from his dungeon was liable to the penalty of death if retaken. Any one who harbored a Catholic priest was subject to a fine of two hundred and fifty pounds, and was to stand on the pillory for three days." The next year a law passed by which "Papists and Popish recusants were prohibited from voting for members of Assembly or any office whatever from thenceforth and forever. The usual oaths against Transubstantiation and of allegiance to the house of Hanover were taken by the members of the Council and other officials. An effect of these proscriptions was the hanging in New York of a Rev. John Ury in 1741 ostensibly on account of a pretended participation in the notorious negro plot, but in reality on account of his being supposed to be a priest. The few poor Catholics who lived there must have suffered many trials. A man did not dare avow himself a Catholic, says Watson: "It was odious."

It is pleasant to remember that Kingston is permanently connected with the memory of the Constitution of New York of 1777 which "guaranteed the free exercise and enjoyment of religious worship, not degenerating with license inconsistent with the public peace"—though against the wishes of some one who would exclude Catholics. John Jay's influence prompted the giving to the Legislature "discretion to pass an act to naturalize persons born out of the United States on condition of their abjuring all foreign authority ecclesiastical as well as civil"—the ecclesiastical abjuration being directed against Catholics. Congress, however, having reserved to itself the power of making laws of naturalization, this clause and the accompanying amendment became inoperative. By act of April, 1801, the clauses against transubstantiation and foreign ecclesiastical allegiance, were inserted in the official oath. Such Catholics as were in the city of New York in 1781-1782 heard mass in private houses. At the time of its evacuation by the British troops in 1783 they began, perhaps 200 in number, to assemble for the open celebration of the offices of religion. A Jesuit, Father Farmer, whose real name was Steenmeyer, was the first priest to officiate for them. He came on from Philadelphia occasionally for that purpose. The law of 1700 in regard "to Popish priests and Jesuits" was repealed by an express act of the Legislature of New York in 1804. The Catholics must have increased rapidly for to the petition got up by the Trustees of St. Peter's Church in 1806 for the abrogation of the obnoxious clauses of the official oath, there were 1,300 signatures, presumably of Catholics, as the wording of the petition would indicate. The petition was granted by the Legislature of 1806.

These facts explain sufficiently why not many Catholics had settled in New York during the century which elapsed from King William's reign and the triumph of American Independence. After this, however, there was an increase in the number of Catholics, not a few of whom scattered throughout the State. The needs of the greater number who remained in New York City retained, to a great extent, the services of the few priests whom they could obtain from abroad. Yet the priests would not omit going in search of those scattered, but began to look them up, lest they should be absolutely deprived of the ministrations of their faith; hence came the title of "roving priests" given to these early pioneers of the Catholic faith throughout New York.

The one first mentioned as likely to come in contact with Ulster County is a Father Arthur Langdill who was stationed in Newburgh by Bishop Connelly from 1817 to 1818. In Bishop Connelly's note book we find these notes: "Oct. 22, 1817. I addressed a letter to Rev. Arthur Langdill empowering him to celebrate mass, administer the sacraments and perform all priestly duties that do not require the Episcopal character throughout this diocese of New York (excepting the districts of New York and Albany, unless with the consent of Clergy serving those two districts) until further orders, or as long as I do not consider it necessary to recall said powers." "Jan. 29th, 1818 I answered the Rev. Arthur Langdill's three letters, and sent him said Indult (for the ensuing Lent), and addressed the letter to the care of Mr. M'Intire, New Burg." He afterward went to Paterson, New Jersey, while Father Philip Lariscy, who had said the first mass in that city, was commissioned to look after the missions on the Hudson in 1822. Father Lariscy was a priest of the Augustinian Order and a man of abundant energy, zealous and untiring, but somewhat rough and fierce. He talked Irish well and was in great demand. He traveled over all New England. He built St. Augustine's Church in Boston. Under his direction a chapel was started in New Bedford. He was a native of Cork, Ireland, and died at St. Augustine's, Philadelphia, in 1824, aged forty-two years.

A pleasing incident in connection with Ulster County may be recalled in the decision given by De Witt Clinton, identified with Kingston in a celebrated case, which was of much importance to the Catholic community. Restitution had been made to a man named James Keating through the Rev. Father Kohlman. Keating had complained against one Philips and his wife, as having received the goods thus stolen, and as Keating testified that the goods had been restored to him through the instrumentality of Father Kohlman, the priest was cited by the Magistrates to give evidence in regard to the person from whom he had received them. This he refused to do on the ground that no court could require a priest to give evidence in regard to matters known to him only under the seal of the confessional. De Witt Clinton thus summed up his decision: "We speak of this question not in a theological sense, but in its legal and constitutional bearings. Although we differ from the witness and his brethren in our religious creed, yet we have no reason to question the purity of their motives, or to impeach their good conduct as citizens. They are protected by the laws and constitution of this country, in the full and free exercise of their religion, and this court can never countenance or authorize the application of insult to their faith or of torture to their conscience." The principle of this decision was afterward embodied in a statute, through Clinton's influence. "No minister of the Gospel or priest of any denomination, shall be allowed to disclose any confessions made to him in his professional character, in the course of discipline enjoined by the rules or practice of such denomination." Passed as part of the Rev. Stat., December 10th, 1828, and signed by N. Pitcher, Lieut. Gov.: Governor Clinton having died in February of that year.

Saugerties was the first place in Ulster County where Catholics settled in sufficient number to warrant the erection of a church. They were mainly Irish enticed to the neighborhood by the expectation of employment in the iron works and paper mills and in the stone quarries which brought into existence the thriving village of Saugerties. The first Catholic priest who gave his services to them was the Rev. Philip O'Reilly of the Order of St. Dominic. The first two Bishops of New York from 1808 to 1825 were of the same order. Born in Scabia, County Cavan, Ireland, he was educated in Bologna, Italy. He probably came to New York about 1818. In 1829 he was stationed at Utica, and his active missionary spirit prompted him to go in search of the scattered Catholics of Otsego, Chenango and Schoharie Counties. In 1830 he was deputed by the Bishop of the Diocese of New York (the Rt. Rev. John DuBois), to form missions and build churches on the banks of the Hudson River as far as his zeal would urge him. The diocese embraced all New York and half of New Jersey. He first erected at Cold Spring, on the cliff overlooking the Hudson River, the site being given by Gouverneur Kemble, the romantic church of "Our Lady" which Weir the painter portrayed, dedicated by Bishop Dubois in September, 1834. Mr. Kemble had also given generous contributions of money, for which he was denounced in the newspapers "for abetting the idolatry of the mass." Father O'Reilly gave new proof of his energy by laying the corner-stone of a church at Saugerties as early as 1833. He had visited Saugerties in 1832 where he at once held religious services in various private dwellings, one Sunday of each month. The welcome given him by the Catholic families is proved by the fact that a church was speedily erected large enough for the number of people at the time. This, no less than the fame of the increasing prosperity of the industries, attracted many more Catholics to Saugerties until it was found necessary from time to time to make additions to the church, and in fact its formal dedication took place in 1843, though it was used in the preceding years for mass. The church has a commanding position overlooking the village of Saugerties and the valley of the Hudson, and the surrounding country for many miles. It is a handsome and spacious edifice. Around it have been buried several generations of Catholics in its beautiful cemetery.

The earnest zeal of Father O'Reilly is proved by his solicitude in behalf of the Catholic people that began to gather at Rondout then at the beginning of its development in consequence of the building of the Delaware and Hudson Canal. On the 22nd of September, 1835, the few Catholics of this hamlet held a meeting to express their anxiety to have a church; their first contribution was $32.02. It was not a very large sum, but their effort was followed by a visit of Father O'Reilly on November 30th, 1835, to sanction and encourage their laudable desire. Father O'Reilly had also under his charge Newburgh and Poughkeepsie. In 1837 Father O'Reilly was appointed Pastor of St. John's Church in Paterson, New Jersey, from whence he went in 1844 to Troy, New York, where he built the fine Gothic Church of St. Patrick. In 1851 he was at St. Peter and Paul's Church in Williamsburgh giving aid to the Rev. Sylvester Malone, from whence he went to St. Bridget's Church to aid the Rev. Thomas Martin, who like himself, was a member of the Order of St. Dominic. Worn out with nearly 40 years of hard missionary work in the States of New York and New Jersey, he died at St. Bridget's on December 7th, 1854. The Rev. S. Malone who died in December, 1899, pastor as he had been founder of the Church of St. Peter and Paul in Williamsburgh, was most enthusiastic in his praise of the Rev. Philip O'Reilly, for his cleverness and geniality and wit. Cardinal McCloskey used to relate that Father O'Reilly had a great liking for military matters and would recite from memory the whole history of Napier's Peninsular War. He was a large and powerfully built man of commanding presence, good family and brilliant social qualities. Before he came to this country he is said to have been Chaplain of the Duke of Norfolk. Father O'Reilly's successor in Saugerties was, in 1837, the Rev. Patrick Duffy, who had already built a church in Paterson, New Jersey, and became pastor of Cold Spring with his missionary field extended to Newburgh, Poughkeepsie and Saugerties. His first recorded administration of baptism in the Saugerties Registry was on May 14th, 1837, and the baptized were James McDade, Sarah Ann Fallon, Mary Ann Shields, William Walsh, Francis Reynolds, Margaret Shea and Peter Branigan. Toward the end of this year Newburgh was made the center of a separate mission, and the Rev. Patrick Duffy was appointed its pastor. In Poughkeepsie during his brief administration St. Peter's Church had been dedicated in November, 1837, by Bishop Dubois, assisted by Rev. Wm. Quarter and Rev. Patrick Duffy. In Newburgh Father Duffy did good work in the erection of a church and school and the establishment of the cemetery. He died there after seventeen years of pastorate in 1853, in the 59th year of his age; his name there is to this day held in benediction. On his appointment to Newburgh, Poughkeepsie was made a separate parish with Saugerties and Rondout as dependencies. The Rev. John McGinnis was in 1837 appointed by Bishop DuBois "because he could rely upon his prudence and zeal, pastor of Poughkeepsie, Saugerties and Rondout, with the instruction to distribute his services, if they concurred, to the best of their abilities for his support, so that each should be attended at least once a month." He was in charge till the end of 1838. Being known for exceptional zeal and ability, he was then called to New York City where the rapidly increasing number of Catholic immigrants demanded the establishment of more churches. There he built the church of St. John the Evangelist, and was made pastor of St. Andrew's, New York, and afterward of Jamaica, Long Island, where he had hard missionary work. The Rev. John N. Smith became pastor of Poughkeepsie, Saugerties and Rondout in 1839. Born in County Tyrone, Ireland, he came to the United States in early youth in 1818, and was ordained about 1828; from 1833 to 1837 he did service in Alexandria, District of Columbia; he was assistant at St. Peter's, New York, in 1838, to the Rev. Dr. Power, V. G. He was an energetic, brusque and charitable priest. Among other works he erected a small frame church at Rondout. He was thoroughly devoted to his calling and mention is made of his trips to Rosendale in search of stray Catholics. He was active at Saugerties till 1842, when he was called to St. James' Church, New York, where he remained as pastor till 1848 in February, when he died a martyr to charity, having contracted the ship fever at the dying bed of the learned Father Mark Murphy, then at the quarantine station of Staten Island, taking charge of the immigrants. His successor as pastor of Poughkeepsie, Saugerties and Rondout in 1842 was the Rev. Myles Maxwell. Born in Ireland, educated for the priesthood at Lafargeville and St. Joseph's Seminary, Fordham, ordained by Bishop Hughes on January 5th, 1841, Father Maxwell was for a short time assistant to the Rev. John Smith at St. James', New York, and was with him transferred to Poughkeepsie, succeeding him there as pastor.

Father Maxwell was noted for his zeal, learning and fidelity to duty, as well as for his candor and winning simplicity. In 1845 Saugerties and Rondout were made an independent parish. In May, 1847, the diocese of Albany was established under the Episcopal charge of the Rt. Rev. John McCloskey, and Saugerties became a part of this diocese, because the line of division was fixed at the 42d degree north latitude, which falls about midway between Saugerties and Kingston. At the division of the diocese Father Maxwell, who had become in 1845 pastor of Saugerties and Rondout, residing in Saugerties, remained attached to the diocese of New York, and the care of Saugerties and Shandaken was, for more than a year, assigned to the Rev. Michael Gilbride, pastor at Hudson, who already had charge of Hunter, Middletown and Scienceville. This plentiful work did not prevent him from giving due attention to Saugerties and other places connected with it. The Catholic laborers, principally quarrymen of Fish Creek, known also as Clove, were accustomed to go on Sundays to Saugerties for mass, and not a few inconveniences and sometimes disorders ensued, and Mr. Russell, the owner of the quarries, offered to Father Gilbride the ground for a church; he gladly accepted the offer, and erected St. John's Church. Father Gilbride's earlier missions had brought him to Ellenville, where he was the first priest to officiate, in 1844. He died as pastor of Waterloo, New York, in 1854. In 1849 the Bishop of Albany appointed as pastor of Saugerties the Rev. John Gilligan, who had charge till 1852. Under the Bishop of Albany the Rev. Lawrence Consadine had charge of Shandaken from 1849 to 1852, but had several other missions in different counties. In 1852 the care of Shandaken passed into the hands of Rev. Eugene Carroll, though his residence was in other counties. The Rev. Michael C. Power was in 1852 appointed by the Bishop of Albany, the Rt. Rev. John McCloskey, to be pastor of Saugerties. Father Power, born in Cork, Ireland, had been educated for the priesthood at the Irish college in Paris, and his abilities and theological knowledge were conspicuous. He wielded a strong influence and during his twenty-five years of pastorate from 1852 to 1878 his duties called him to every part of the town of Saugerties in consequence of the great increase of Catholics who were attracted by the prospects of work to the neighboring stone quarries. The Irish immigration was at its flood tide between 1846 and 1858, and the strong arms of the Irish laborers, forced from their country by the cruel famine, which desolated it, were brought into play in the building of railways, the quarrying of stone and the digging of canals. A customary sight on Sundays was the marching of hundreds of men under the leadership of their foreman to the churches eight and ten miles away to hear mass. As can be fancied, some broke loose from the self-imposed leadership, and at times disorders marked especially their return journey. The vast outpouring of a people into a strange land is always accompanied by the loosening of family ties, and by consequent freedom of restraint of their home environments. Hence the few priests who could be secured for the care of these streams of humanity, were overburdened and overwhelmed by the vastness of the task assigned them. Oftentimes when the men had come to this country with their families they were compelled by necessity to leave them in the larger cities, especially New York, until they had gone out to earn enough to provide a permanent home for them. This gathering of large bodies of men without immediate family ties easily gave rise to disorders, to remedy which the country local authorities were often glad to call the priests' influence, which never was exercised in vain with the most stubborn Irish laborer, in whom is innate a deep respect for religion and its ministers. Thus it was that the Rev. M. C. Power's influence springing from his kindly sympathetic nature and the indefatigable work for his people was recognized by the whole community. He built a fine church at Quarryville. In 1864 when the Rt. Rev. John McCloskey was appointed Archbishop of New York, it was also decided to have the division of the two dioceses follow the county-lines, and Saugerties was annexed to the diocese of New York, and its pastor Rev. M. C. Power was transferred with it. His work continued till 1878, when he retired quite advanced in years to Wappinger's Falls, aiding there his friend and classmate Father Sheehan and continuing there till his death, under his able successors Rev. M. C. O'Keefe and the Rev. Dr. C. V. O'Mahony. There he gave a large piece of ground for a park around the church, and he also left a fair fortune to be used for religious purposes by this last friend, whose hospitable care he had always received.

In 1878 the Rev. John F. Lynch attended to the spiritual wants of the Catholics of the township of Saugerties from February to October. On November 10th, 1878, the Rev. Denis Paul O'Flynn became pastor. He was a native of County Cork, Ireland, and had successfully made his studies for the priesthood at the famous University of Louvain, Belgium, where he obtained the degree of Licentiate in theology. His pastorate was earnest and vigorous, extending to the missions of Quarryville and Clove till they were erected on April 1st, 1886, into a separate mission and placed under the charge of Rev. Michael Haran. This enabled Father O'Flynn to direct his efforts to the building of a substantial church in Glasco, where there was a thriving industrious people first attracted by the Woodstock Glass Co. and later by the flourishing brickyards in the neighborhood. In 1889 on transfer of Dean Dougherty to New York, Father O'Flynn was appointed by Archbishop Corrigan at the synod in New York in November, Dean or Vicar-forane of the counties of Ulster and Sullivan. In 1892 the Church of St. Mary in Saugerties was seriously damaged by fire, and Father O'Flynn undertook its renovation and enlargement on an expensive scale, placing in it splendid marble altars, fine pews and other ornamental furniture. This was, however, done at a time of great financial depression when quite a large amount of the business of Saugerties was discontinued, and the burden of debt upon the church plant has hampered the efforts of succeeding pastors. Connected with the church he had built a fine rectory and a substantial brick schoolhouse where four sisters of charity have since then been engaged as teachers. The Rev. D. P. O'Flynn in 1893 was promoted to the permanent pastorate of the important church of St. Joseph on Sixth Avenue in New York, where he continued till his death in August, 1906, to display the energy for which he was distinguished at Saugerties. Here he was succeeded by the Rev. M. J. Murray, who, ordained at Mt. St. Mary's, Emmittsburgh, Maryland, had been assistant at St. Joseph's, New York, and pastor for several years at Rhinecliff. During Father Murray's administration a hall was erected near the church which became the center of many social and dramatic gatherings of Catholics and non-Catholics attracted by Father Murray's personality. Glasco had meanwhile become quite an Italian settlement, which necessitated the frequent ministrations of an Italian priest. It has had for several years the services of Rev. Henry Newey, whose education in Rome enabled him to deal with them very satisfactorily. He continues to do this even since the transfer of Father Murray to Riverdale, New York, under the pastorate of the Rev. John J. McCabe, who came to Saugerties in April, 1905. Strenuous efforts have been made to diminish the heavy load of debt.

The Rev. John J. McCabe had been for many years assistant at St. Stephen's, New York, since his ordination at the Troy Seminary on December 21st, 1889, and has therefore been able to call upon his friends in that congregation for aid in his arduous task.

The Rev. Michael Haran was transferred to West Hurley in 1903, and was succeeded by the energetic assistant at St. Thomas', New York, Rev. Thomas Halpin as pastor of Clove and Quarryville. Besides the two churches already built at Clove of St. John the Evangelist, and at Quarryville of St. Patrick, he has for the convenience of the congregation set apart a chapel under the invocation of St. Thomas, near the rectory, besides renovating and refurnishing the two other churches.

RONDOUT.

The first record connected with a Catholic church in Rondout is "an account of names of men who subscribed towards the building of a Roman Catholic Church in Rondout, and its vicinity by order of the Rev. Mr. P. O'Reilly" on September 22d, 1835. The contributors were Thomas Penny, James Diamond, John O'Reilly, Terence O'Reilly, Patrick Donnely, Patrick McCanna, James Melton, Larry Fallon, John McCarten, James Murray, Thomas Rigney, Roland Mulholland, Daniel Riordan, William Williams, Garrett Connolly, Michael Quin, Edward Moloy, Matthew Walsh, Edward Brown, Patrick Flanigan, Barney Daly, ODy O'Rorke. The amount of this first collection was $32.02. Another meeting was held on October 6th, when the amount contributed reached $72.99, one-quarter of which was deposited on October 21st, in the Ulster County Bank. By November 4th, the amount had been increased by eleven dollars, and the Rev. Philip O'Reilly came in person on November 30th, 1835, and he gave his sanction and encouragement to the effort made in these words: "As a clergyman deputed by the Bishop of the Diocese of New York to form missions and build churches on the banks of the Hudson River I do by these presents fully and entirely approve of the above manner of collecting money for the building of a church in this village of Rondout, as also of the manner used in depositing the sums collected in Ulster County Bank as mentioned above. In testimony of which, etc., Philip O'Reilly, Pastor of the Congregations on the Hudson River, Diocese of New York, Rondout, Nov. 30th, 1835." The moneys in bank were deposited by John Diamond, John O'Reilly, Thos. Rigney, Michael

Quin and John Kenney. Frequent meetings were held by the people to advance the collection of the necessary amount. The next recorded visit of the Rev. Philip O'Reilly was on May 30th, 1836, when he met in John O'Reilly's house about thirty-three Catholics. At the end of this meeting the amount collected had reached $156.95. On August 18th he again visited Rondout, and left the following record: "I have on this day, Thursday, the 18th of August, 1836, audited the accounts of James Diamond and John O'Reilly with the Catholic Church of this village up to the present day and find them to be substantially correct. The amount in hand at the present time is 193 dollars and 38 cents which is deposited in the office of the Hudson and Delaware Canal Co. in the name of the Bishop as Trustee for the congregation Philip O'Reilly, Pastor of the congregations on the Hudson River."

Rondout at this time was little more than a hamlet. While the other stations were attended with fair regularity once a month on Sunday, Rondout probably had the benefit of any fifth Sunday occurring in the month, but it had to rely mainly on the visits of Father O'Reilly at long intervals on week days. Mass was said in various private houses such as John O'Reilly's and Thomas Penny's. On the Sundays the larger apartment of a blind and sash factory in the corner of Mill St. and Division St. (later Union Avenue, now Broadway), was kindly placed at the disposal of the Catholics for mass. As the greater number of the Catholics were employed in connection with the Delaware and Hudson Canal and therefore lived along the Wilbur Road, in January, 1837, a lot was there purchased for the $200 gathered up to that time, on which a church was to be built. Meanwhile, however, Rondout was made dependent upon the pastor of Poughkeepsie, the Rev. John Smith, who in 1838 thought it desirable to have the church erected on its present site, which was purchased from Abraham Hasbrouck on which payment was made of $100 on November 4th, 1839. At this time 77 names of men appear on the records as contributing toward the purchase of this property, and at Poughkeepsie on the same November 4th, 1839, is recorded "An article of agreement between James Crowley and the Rev. John Smith on behalf of the Building Committee appointed by the said Rev. John Smith for the purpose of building a Catholic Church in Rondout, Ulster Co., State of New York. The said James Crowley binds himself to build a church 40 feet by 24 feet in width, 12 feet high of sound materials, frame of which must be set on posts 3 feet high for the sum of $400 dollars, $100 of which must be paid before the work commenced and the balance as may be collected from the subscribers or paid in by the Building Committee to the said James Crowley, who binds himself to cover in the building in one month from the above date."

This gave a great impetus to the collection and by January 1st, 1840, $416.00 had been contributed by 87 persons, with an additional aid of a collection from Bishop Hughes, Rev. Starrs and Rev. McGurry amounting to $160.00. In this contribution are found the names of the first two women contributors, Mary Giddy, Ann O'Reilly. The new position of the church was thought to suit the convenience of not a few Catholics who were living further inland, toward and in the mountains. In fact there were probably scattered in a large territory about one hundred families, but in those early days not a few of the Irish Catholics working along the canal route in Rosendale and others in Stony Hollow were known to walk every Sunday the eight or ten miles to hear mass in St. Mary's Church in Rondout. The Baptismal Record of St. Mary's Church, Rondout, was begun by the Rev. John Smith in January, 1841, and the first name recorded is that of John Flanigan, born December 27th, 1840. The first recorded burials in the cemetery attached to the church was of two children of Patrick Malia and James Burke in February, 1840. In July, 1841, a second payment of $100 was made to Abraham Hasbrouck for the land on which the church was to be erected.

When the Rev. John Smith was in 1842 transferred to New York, he was succeeded as pastor of Poughkeepsie by his assistant the Rev. Myles Maxwell, whose duty it was to attend Poughkeepsie on two Sundays of each month, and on one, Saugerties, and on the other Rondout. He had this very arduous task till 1845, when Saugerties and Rondout were formed into a separate mission of which Rev. Myles Maxwell was appointed pastor. His first recorded official act was on Sunday, July 24th, 1842, the administration of baptism to nine children.

The balance in hand of Treasurer was $65. The collection in the church on that day was $31. John Reilly was still collector and treasurer, and the amount collected to September 27th, of that same year, 1842, $210 more; in all $306, and of this amount $283.31 were spent before that date for the enlargement and painting of the church and for putting a fence around it. On November 28th, 1842, a memorandum is made of a payment made to Abraham Hasbrouck in his house of $100 for the land on which the church was situated. Thus we realize the rapid increase of the congregation when Father Maxwell so soon found need to enlarge the frame church barely completed in 1840.

In 1845, Saugerties and Rondout having been made into a separate mission, Father Maxwell took up his residence in Saugerties attending Rondout every second Sunday. Many drove, some even walked on the other Sundays to Saugerties to hear mass.

In 1847 Father Maxwell's zeal prompted him to visit Shandaken, but in May of this year took place the establishment of the diocese of Albany already mentioned in reference to Saugerties, which with Shandaken were incorporated into the new diocese, and the Rev. Myles Maxwell was left in charge of the mission of Rondout but as it embraced the territory now dotted with the separate churches of Port Ewen, Stony Hollow, Jockey Hill, Wilbur, Eddyville, Whiteport, Flatbush and Kingston, it is clear that there was ample space for his earnest zeal. When relieved of the care of Saugerties and neighboring places, he redoubled his energy in behalf of Rondout. He at once planned the erection of a large and splendid brick church. He engaged the services of the brilliant architect Keeley of Brooklyn and undertook, under his guidance, what for those early days was a wonderful and daring project, that of erecting the splendid building which is still recognized as an ornament of the town. The corner-stone was laid on May 21st, 1848. The frame building was left standing within the new edifice till a short time before the solemn blessing of the present building which took place on July 8th, 1849. Father Maxwell did not long survive the completion of the work to which he had bent all his strength. He died on August 31st, 1849. His remains were first interred in the adjoining cemetery and afterward placed within the precincts of the church which he had built.

It has been thought proper to go into somewhat minute details of the pioneer work of the founders of the first parishes of Ulster County, Saugerties and Rondout, to bring out the difficulties under which they labored, and to place on record the indomitable energies which laid the foundation of the prosperous spiritual and material conditions of the Catholic Church throughout the county. The great bulk of the Catholics was from the ranks of the hard-working Irish immigrants, wrenched from their home environment of lively faith and purity of morals, and cast into completely new surroundings, amidst a population hostile to their religion, and of traditional racial prejudices. Very many were bereft of family ties and of the many influences emanating from them, yet their strong faith, their wonderful supernatural love of their religion remained. Deprived as they necessarily were of frequent contact with the exercise of their religion, they were not free from disorders, some by intermarriages outside the church allowed their children to be lost to the church; but it is remarkable how quickly their own faith was rekindled when the priest appeared on the scene, and they once more had a chance to approach the practices of their religion.

Rev. Thomas Quinn and Rev. Wm. Quinn, afterward Vicar-general of New York, administered to the spiritual needs of Rondout till November, 1849, when a very energetic missionary of the order of St. Dominic, in whom Bishop Hughes reposed great confidence, the Rev. Thomas Martin, was appointed pastor. Born in Ireland about 1794, shortly after he reached the years of manhood he came to this country and entered the Order of St. Dominic in St. Rose's Convent in Kentucky; he was ordained in 1824. After twelve years of arduous tasks in Kentucky, and a visit to Rome on business of his order, he was persuaded to give his services to the diocese of New York. In 1840 he had charge of Newport and Schuyler, in 1845 of Utica, where he established a temperance society. He was in Troy, 1847, and at St. Peter's, New York, in 1849. He was a laborious disinterested priest who always asked the hardest place. When he had brought all to peace and harmony or had helped to build a church or get rid of a crushing debt, his only anxiety was to begin the same work elsewhere. The early demise of Father Maxwell, so soon after the completion of the church, had left it in a very difficult position to meet the large outlay required for this really serious undertaking. The people responded generously to Father Martin's appeals, and he was able at a cost of $1,500 to procure even a fine organ for the church. His zeal prompted him to erect a church in Rosendale in which mass was said for the first time in August, 1850. Before that the Catholics of Rosendale attended mass in Rondout, whence the priests had still to give their services till 1860. Father Martin's zealous pastorate continued in Rondout till January, 1852. Then a new emergency arising in St. Bridget's Church in New York from the illness of its founder Father Kein, required the exercise of Father Martin's zeal and winning ways. A similar need called him in 1855 to the Church of the Holy Cross. As Father Martin's short pastorate left a deep impress upon the Catholics of this neighborhood, we have thought well to recall the eulogy made by Bishop Hughes at his funeral in May, 1859, at St. James' of which he had recently been appointed pastor:

"From St. Bridget's he went to the then hardly formed congregation in 42d Street (Holy Cross) when, without haranguing, he began silently and noiselessly to work to show them their way through their difficulties, until the people began to understand themselves and to be a congregation —a numerous congregation." He was 69 years of age at the time of his death. He was succeeded in the pastorate of Rondout by his assistant the Rev. John Madden, who had come from Ireland with his brother Michael, who became an influential parishioner of St. Mary's.

During these years an old time schoolmaster Stephen Hardy, who also acted as church sexton and superintendent of the nearby cemetery, held despotic sway over the children. When he left the class, there was an uproar, and then the guilty and innocent alike were treated to dire punishment. The special one for the boys was to be tied by their thumbs to the door lintel.

In 1851 the lot running through from Division St. (now Broadway), to Adams St. had been purchased by Father Martin, and in 1852 the Rev. John Madden built thereon the rectory. Till then the priests had occupied a small frame house on the opposite side of the street. He also purchased in 1855 in Higginsville, Kingston, a large lot of ground on which he intended to build a church for the many Catholics in the neighborhood or in the nearby mountains at Jockey Hill and Stony Hollow. The lot, however, was afterward sold, though kept till 1870.

At the beginning of 1858, came the Rev. Francis McNeirny, afterward Bishop of Albany, whose pastorate ended in May, when he had as successor the Rev. D. G. Durning, who remained in charge for about 18 months. Then in the fall of 1859 the Rev. Felix H. Farrelly came from New York to be pastor of Rondout. A native of Ireland he had been ordained to the priesthood in 1854 at All Hallow's College, near Dublin, and on his coming in that year to the United States was assigned as assistant at the Church of the Nativity in New York and within two years appointed to the charge of the Church of the Annunciation in Manhattanville. His discharge of his duties here showed so much zeal for the good of souls and such ability that the now important parish of Rondout was entrusted to him. His services were of the greatest benefit to this parish, as he remained five years, effecting great good and infusing order and system into all parochial affairs. At this period of the Civil War his influence greatly calmed the violent protests aroused against the draft for soldiers. He encouraged many by his own spirit of patriotism. He did not hesitate to show his disgust for slavery. A trip which with other priests, the Revs. Thomas Farrell and Sylvester Malone, he had made to the south some time before the war, had impressed him particularly with the immoral results of slavery, involving as they did the whites, as much as the negroes. He introduced into the parish of Rondout the Sisters of Charity under whose charge he established St. Mary's Academy. He had for the boys as teacher a Mr. Shelter, a former Christian Brother, whose teaching was excellent, and his influence very great; his memory was long in benediction among the children. Father Farrelly also purchased the spacious cemetery on the Flatbush road, where the remains of the Catholics of Kingston, Port Ewen, West Hurley are still interred. Many are brought from distant places to be laid with the remains of their forefathers. The name of Farrelly Street at the eastern end of the cemetery records his connection with it. With his coöperation Stony Hollow was formed into a separate mission in charge of Rev. S. Mackin in 1865, with Jockey Hill as a station. Father Farrelly, however, was this year recalled to New York to take charge of an immense congregation attached to St. James' Church in New York. He died pastor of St. Joseph's in 1883. He was succeeded at Rondout in 1865 by the Rev. Edward Briody who had been ordained in 1849 by Bishop Hughes, and had established churches in Port Jervis and Ellenville. He made several improvements, the principal of which was the introduction of furnaces for the heating of the church. He was transferred to St. Patrick's, Newburgh, in 1867, and was followed in the pastorate of Rondout by the Rev. James Coyle whose earnestness and zeal are still spoken of by the parishioners of his day. He was a very strong advocate of total abstinence from all alcoholic beverages, and to his enthusiasm was due the formation of a very large and zealous society whose good influence has extended through time for the great improvement of the parish. To his zeal was due in 1868 the long planned formation in the village of Kingston of the parish of St. Joseph, to which was assigned as Pastor the newly ordained Rev. James

Dougherty, a native of Kingston and the first of Ulster County to be raised to the priesthood. Father Coyle also purchased in 1867 the ground on the corner of McEntee Street and Union Avenue (now Broadway) on which he erected a large parochial school which was soon crowded with children. When Father Mackin had occasion to go in 1867 to Ireland, Father Coyle did not hesitate to take charge of Stony Hollow and Jockey Hill, in both of which he built churches, and on Father Mackin's return in 1870 gave to him a full account of the moneys collected and the expenses. The spiritual welfare, however, of all the people committed to his care was Father Coyle's chief concern. At a mission during his pastorate over 5,000 persons approached the sacraments. He died suddenly in New York, and at his funeral in Rondout on July 4th, 1872, the preacher stated that since his ordination in 1852 he had built thirteen churches or chapels. His remains were buried under St. Mary's Church. Father Coyle's grasp of financial details was not strong and mechanics and contractors availed themselves of his indecision, forgetfulness or change of plans to involve the church property by heavy floating debts.

For ten months his successor was the scholarly Rev. M. J. O'Farrell, who had been educated at the celebrated Seminary of St. Sulpice in Paris, and as a member of the Order, had already done good work in Montreal, Canada. While here he was visited by the distinguished Dominican Father Burke, who made excellent use of Father O'Farrell's fine library in the preparation of his famous lectures to be delivered in the Academy of Music, New York, in refutation of Froude's one-sided views and misstatements of English and Irish history. Yet he showed himself very practical in financial matters. At a fair he raised $3,000 to meet the floating debts left by his predecessor. He gave proof of his earnest spiritual zeal by giving a two weeks' mission, preaching the usual four sermons a day alone, and hence within the time of his short pastorate 1,010 children and adults were confirmed by Bishop McNeirny. He was soon promoted to the pastorate of St. Peter's Church in New York, and in 1881 he was made first Bishop of Trenton, New Jersey. He died in 1894. His successor at Rondout was the Rev. Michael Carthage O'Farrell, who, full of energy, came there in June, 1873; he had been assistant at St. Peter's, New York. His first work was to enlarge the pastoral residence, then to establish an academy or college under the Franciscan Brothers, for which he erected a building alongside the church through a bequest of $10,000 of Thomas Murray, who died in April, 1873. Churches were established by him in Port Ewen, erected into a separate mission under Rev. Michael Phelan, and also in Flatbush now known as East Kingston. In July, 1876, he was appointed pastor of St. Teresa's Church, New York, and is now rector of the Church of the Holy Innocents, New York. In Rondout he was in August succeeded by the Rev. John J. Duffy, D.D., who remained pastor of St. Mary's till his death in April, 1888. During his pastorate the trustees of District No. 3 of Rondout finding that the school house of the district was unable to contain all the children of the district, made an arrangement with the Franciscan Brothers to act as teachers for boys in the building next to the church, which was hired as a branch school for the district. This arrangement continued till 1895, when the trustees of District No. 3 influenced by the clamor that a public school was thus placed under sectarian influence, enlarged the main building, and discontinued the employment of the Franciscan Brothers as teachers. These, therefore, withdrew to their mother-house in Brooklyn. Dr. Duffy had graduated in the classical and law departments of the University of New York, and then going to the American College in Rome, had attended the theological course at the Propaganda. He was ordained in Rome, and on his return home in 1872 was stationed at St. Joseph's Church, of which the pastor was the Rev. Thomas Farrell. Dr. Duffy gained fame as an eloquent speaker and at the inauguration of the monument of the sailors and soldiers of the War for the Union on the terrace in front of the Kingston City Hall, a patriotic discourse delivered by him made quite a lasting impression. In a mission given by the Jesuits in 1879, nearly 4,000 persons approached the sacraments. Dr. Duffy had been ambitious to clear off the whole of the church debt, but in his later years in consequence of failing health his energy fell off, and on his assistant the Rev. J. L. Hoey, devolved the more laborious work of the parish. Dr. Duffy died in April, 1888, and his successor, the Rev. Peter J. Prendergast, found an indebtedness of about $13,000 to which he was obliged to add to meet the expense of a needed thorough renovation of the rectory. Father Prendergast had come from Middletown; his pastorate in Rondout lasted two years, and he was then transferred to New York, on July 31st, 1890, to be made rector of the Church of the Epiphany in place of its founder the Rev. Dr. Burtsell. He died there after an incumbency of ten years.

Rev. R. L. Burtsell, D.D., came to Rondout on November 8th, 1890, in his 51st year. He had spent all the years of his ministry since 1862 in New York City, for five years as assistant at St. Ann's and for more than twenty-two years as pastor of the Epiphany parish, which he had established and in which he had built the splendid church, rectory and school, leaving behind him the comparatively small debt of $60,000, though the actual cost of the property belonging to the Church of the Epiphany had been over $328,000. Archbishop Corrigan had taken umbrage at Dr. Burtsell's advocacy of the right of Rev. Dr. McGlynn to teach the politico-economical theory of Henry George which the Archbishop thought to be in conflict with Catholic doctrine, and had thought it wise to remove Dr. Burtsell from the principal scene of the agitation, New York City.

Dr. Burtsell accepted without a murmur the decision, and gave himself with energy to the work assigned him in his new mission. In 1891 he undertook a complete renovation of the interior as well as exterior of St. Mary's Church, which had fallen into a state of decay. The church exterior was painted, and extensive decorations of the ceiling and walls brightened the appearance of the church. In the same year St. Colman's Church in Flatbush (now designated East Kingston) was considerably enlarged and in October Bishop Conroy dedicated it anew, the people being so in earnest as to meet all the expenses of $2,000 within the year.

Dr. Burtsell in December, 1892, had the consolation of obtaining from the Pope's Delegate, Mgr. Satolli, the complete reconciliation of his friend Rev. Dr. McGlynn, with the church authorities, and the declaration of the Delegate, after investigation by the professors of the Catholic University in Washington, D. C., that his politico-economical land theory was not in opposition to the teachings of the Church. The Pope, in May, 1893, received Rev. Dr. McGlynn, as a sanction of his Delegate's action. This question brought about in the fall of 1893 and in 1894 a stay of several months of Dr. Burtsell in Rome, which proved eminently satisfactory, and gave him ample opportunities to submit to the Pope many views of things that seemed useful for the direction of the Church in the United States, but Dr. Burtsell did not allow such matters to prevent his attention to the spiritual needs of the parish of Rondout. In fact he had called the Paulists to give a mission in the parish in 1893. In 1896 the Passionists, in 1899 and 1902 the Diocesan Band of Apostolic Missionaries and again in 1904 the Dominicans gave very successful missions, which were extended to East Kingston. A most agreeable feature of both visits of the Diocesan Band of Missionaries was the attendance in large numbers of distinguished non-Catholics at a series of special lectures which they gave on those doctrines and practices of which erroneous impressions have alienated from the Catholic Church many otherwise enlightened and truth loving souls. Catholics realize that the best way to bring about the Christian unity for which there is to-day such earnest desire, is the thorough explanation of the doctrines of the Church. Their consistency and reasonableness cannot but make a deep impression upon all upon whom the Holy Spirit is breathing his inspirations to truth and charity.

There has been no lagging in the material improvements in the parish. During 1895 the whole congregation took an active interest in the thorough renovation and beautifying of the church. The laying of a new flooring, handsome pews and artistic stained glass windows were a considerable part of the renovation. The crowning improvement was in 1896, the erection of the three marble altars of the church and the complete renewal of everything connected with the sanctuary. The response by the parishioners to every appeal was so generous as to meet all these expenses besides doing away with all the former indebtedness on the church property. The Church was thus placed in the condition fitting for its consecration. This conspicuous ceremony of the Consecration of the Church was performed by Archbishop Corrigan on the first Sunday of September, 1896. Bishop Shanley of Fargo, N. Dakota, preached at the solemn high mass, and Dr. James Loughlin of Philadelphia at Vespers on this occasion. Since then have been added the artistic oil paintings of the Way of the Cross, and a series of oil frescoes on the Sanctuary wall by the hand of Filippo Costaggini, who painted many of the historical subjects in the dome of the Capitol at Washington, D. C. In 1898 a thorough census was taken of the parish, and there were found in Rondout 712 families with 3,300 souls and in East Kingston 80 families and 370 souls.

In the year 1898 the parish of St. Mary's, Rondout, was declared by Archbishop Corrigan to be henceforth a permanent rectorship, and the present rector to be its first permanent rector. This honor confers upon the rector of the parish the irremovability from the rectorship except by special canonical process, and also a positive voice in the nomination of candidates for the archbishopric of New York. The commemoration of the fiftieth year of St. Mary's Church was solemnly held on the first Sunday of September, 1899, when Archbishop Corrigan celebrated pontifical mass, assisted by the Revs. Wm. L. Penny and Edward F. Slattery, natives of Rondout of the earliest generation. The preacher in the morning was the Rev. James Dougherty, pastor of St. Monica's in New York, a native of Kingston. Others officiating, as the Revs. J. J. Boyle, J. J. Keane and R. Burns, received their first impulses to the priesthood while serving around its sanctuary. Monsignor Joseph Mooney, Vicar-general, a native of Pennsylvania, but brought up in Rondout, preached at Vespers. Revs. J. L. Hoey, Patrick Morris and M. J. Fitzpatrick, who also took part, had been formerly attached to St. Mary's. The Revs. J. J. Hickey and John B. McHugh were the actual assistants of the rector.

Rondout has been recognized in the annals of the diocese of New York as giving more priests to the sanctuary and more members to the various sisterhoods than any place outside New York City. At the synod of November, 1901, Archbishop Corrigan appointed Dr. Burtsell Vicar-forane, or Dean of Ulster and Sullivan Counties. Dr. Burtsell interested himself not only in St. Mary's parish, but in public civil matters as well, gladly taking part in the plans of the Board of Trade, in the Association for good roads; he was instrumental in the establishment of the City Hospital and of the public library, and also in the introduction of the Sanitarium in charge of the Benedictine Sisters. That his work was appreciated by the citizens, non-Catholics as well as Catholics, was proven by the great spontaneous demonstration in the Church and the public Armory at the celebration of his 40th year of priesthood on August 10th and 11th, 1902. At the church Bishop (then Administrator, now Archbishop) Farley, presided; Monsignor Loughlin, of Philadelphia, preached; Bishop Chatard, of Indianapolis, and Monsignor Cannon, of Lockport, were prominent among 30 clergymen in the Sanctuary. In the Armory addresses were made by Chief Judge Parker, who presided, by Judge VanEtten, Alderman William Roach on behalf of the parishioners; Hon. John J. Linson, Mayor Block, in the presentation of Resolutions by the Common Council of the City; John W. Heany, in the presentation of a purse of $1,000 on the part of the parishioners; Michael J. Joyce, representative of a large delegation present from the Parish of the Epiphany, New York; Congressman George J. Smith and Judge A. T. Clearwater.

Attention is called to this, because it was a public recognition of the intertwining of the sympathies of all classes and religious denominations, a manifestation of the thorough disappearance in civil matters of all racial and religious prejudices which are easily overcome by the intermingling of all in works of common public good, and the consequent better knowledge of one another attained by citizens of all classes and races.

Rev. Dr. Burtsell paid another visit to Rome in 1904, to assist at the 50th anniversary of the Definition or Solemn Recognition by the Church that the Mother of Jesus had by His merits been freed from incurring the stain of original sin; he had been present at the Definition itself. He had the honor of presenting the addresses in the name of the Diocese of New York to Pope Pius X, and Archbishop Farley took occasion, through his auxiliary, Bishop Cusack, to send a petition to His Holiness to honor Dr. Burtsell by admitting him to the membership of the Pontifical household as one of his private chamberlains. On Dr. Burtsell's return from Rome another public demonstration was offered him of the affection of his people and of the citizens at large, by a procession through streets illuminated and bedecked with flags, amidst skyrockets and other fireworks, and ending in a grand reception at the Kingston Armory. It is a delightful thought to him that he has been an instrument to break down barriers of prejudice, and to unite the people of this city in common interests, and all through some slight efforts made by him for the common good of the whole city.

ROSENDALE.

The Rev. John N. Smith, pastor of Poughkeepsie, extended his solicitude as far as Rosendale in 1840, and in 1841, looking after the scattered Catholics. Father Myles Maxwell, succeeding him in Poughkeepsie, in 1842, celebrated mass in Petrie's cooper shop, afterward the dwelling-house of James Lee. Of course, he continued this care of Rosendale, when he was made pastor of Rondout, and it became a separate mission.

In 1849, in November, the Rev. Thomas Martin, O. S. D., then pastor at Rondout, celebrated mass in Rosendale at the house of Walter Delmar, and henceforth services continued to be held regularly and steps were taken to erect a church. A convenient building was opened in the summer of 1850, the first mass being said on the Feast of the Assumption of the Blessed Virgin Mary, August 15th. The priests of Rondout continued the good work by frequent regular visits to Rosendale, till 1855, when it was separated from Rondout, of which the assistant, Rev. Edward Lynch, was appointed the pastor.

However, in the next year he was called to the charge of a church in Yonkers, and Rosendale had to wait till the end of 1860 for the appointment of a permanent pastor, it being meanwhile looked after by the pastors of Rondout. In December, 1860, the Rev. Lawrence O'Toole, a learned priest, and a great advocate of total abstinence from intoxicants, became pastor, remaining there till November of 1864. He afterward was at Rhinecliff parish, where he established a college or academy. The Rev. Patrick Brady became pastor of Rosendale, having a fairly successful pastorate of ten years, till July, 1874, when he was transferred to Montgomery, Orange Co. His successor was the Rev. Martin O'Flaherty. He was ordained in St. Joseph's Seminary, Troy, on June 11th, 1870, and after four years at St. Cecelia's, in New York, came in July, 1874, in the full vigor of his zeal and strength, to Rosendale. Finding that the church was too small for the ever-increasing Catholic population, attracted by the cement quarries and by the demands of the Delaware & Hudson Canal, he erected, under the guidance of an able architect, Arthur Crooks, a spacious church on the beautiful plateau which overlooks the village of Rosendale and the Rondout valley.

It was completed in 1876, and mass was said in it for the first time on Christmas day. No finer situation could be had for the church edifice. Its picturesqueness is simply charming. The design of the church is excellent. The rectory, begun at the same time, is twenty feet away from the rear of the church. The two combined form a work of art. The cost was about $31,000. The Catholic population at the time was about 1,400. Father O'Flaherty died in 1881. He was immediately succeeded by the Rev. John J. Gleason, who added to the parish a fine school and a residence for the Sisters of Charity. He incurred a great expense by fitting up an elaborate heating apparatus for all these different

Rev. Edward J. McCue.

buildings. Too full of the spirit of material improvements, he overburdened the place with debt, which, owing to the decrease of the congregation consequent upon the precariousness of the work in the cement quarries, and the gradual falling off of work on the canal, became a great burden on the congregation and a source of such worry to the pastor that his health failed, and he was unfitted for his pastoral work for several years previous to his death, in 1894. Father Gleason left a legacy of $500 to the Kingston Hospital. Among those who aided him during his pastorate should be mentioned the Rev. Reuben Parsons, whose work in six volumes of "Studies in Church History," is a splendid monument by which he will be long remembered. Another worthy of mention is the Rev. Dr. Daniel Burke, for several months the administrator of the parish. A native of New York, who made his ecclesiastical studies at the Jesuit Colleges of Innsbruck and Rome, Professor of Philosophy at St. Joseph's Seminary of Troy, he had shown himself an indefatigable worker in the parishes of the Epiphany and St. Leo in New York, as also at Highland Falls. Archbishop Corrigan began to utilize him to take difficult places, such as this at Rosendale, and then again at Wilbur. Now after services at the Church of the Good Counsel and St. Charles Borromeo's, in New York, he has undertaken the erection of two churches for Italians, one completed in Bedford Park, the other just initiated in Belmont.

Archbishop Corrigan had in 1894 detached Whiteport from Rosendale, placing it in charge of the Rev. Wm. McGill, who, being a native of Rondout, had been able at a very moderate price to raise there a fine brick church. At Father Gleason's death Whiteport was again attached to Rosendale under the charge of the Rev. Wm. M. McGill, who, however, within a few months of his appointment, died suddenly on a visit to the Home of the Immaculate Virgin in New York.

The Rev. Thomas Cusack, ordained at St. Joseph's Seminary, Troy, on May 30th, 1885, was appointed in September, 1895, to the pastorate of Rosendale. By his energy he brought order out of financial chaos, funded and considerably reduced the debt. Archbishop Corrigan, however, asked him in 1897 to head the Apostolic Band of Missionaries to give missions, including lectures to non-Catholics, throughout the diocese, especially in small country parishes. The Rev. P. Maughan came in 1897 from Tivoli to take charge of Rosendale. He had been a soldier in the war for the Union, and had many friends in the Grand Army. He erected, supervising the entire structure, the large hall which has become the centre of all social and dramatic gatherings of the congregation as of the township. Father Maughan was called in 1903 to New York to undertake the erection of a new church in the upper western section of the city. His successor was the Rev. Francis C. Lenes, who also came from Tivoli, but he, as his predecessor, found himself hampered by the large debt, the burden being aggravated by the slackness of work at the cement quarries. He was transferred to Montgomery, Orange County, in 1905, to be succeeded at Rosendale by the present pastor, Rev. John J. Lennon.

WEST HURLEY.

Another offshoot of St. Mary's Rondout was the parish of Stony Hollow and Flag Quarries. The last mentioned was attended in 1853 by the Rev. Eugene McGuire and Thomas Joyce, from St. Mary's, and continued to be visited at intervals. Rev. Felix Farrelly and Richard Brennan said mass in the school-house at Jockey Hill in 1860 and 1861. Stony Hollow increased rapidly in population because, as its name indicates, it became the centre of the bluestone quarries, and received frequent attention as early as 1860. The work, however, soon increased in Rondout to the extent that Father Farrelly deemed it wise to have Stony Hollow and Jockey Hill placed under the separate charge of the Rev. Stephen Mackin in 1865. The workmen were very generous. However, Father Mackin was called away to Ireland, and the charge of the two places was taken up again by the pastor at Rondout, the Rev. James Coyle. His indefatigable zeal prompted him to erect a small frame church at Jockey Hill, which was soon superseded by a better structure in the nearby Sawkill. He also erected St. John's Church in Stony Hollow. Father Mackin returned in October, 1870, and Father Coyle gave him a full account of all the moneys collected meanwhile, as always a detailed account of the outlay for the building of the two churches. He continued in charge till 1875, and besides the two mentioned places, had to attend to the spiritual interests of the Catholics in Bruceville, Shandaken and Phoenicia. An interesting financial report rendered by him in January, 1874, for the two preceding years, shows receipts at Stony Hollow of $5,636, and at Sawkill of $2,311, with the indebtedness reduced from $9,204 to $8,103, and from $4,000 to $3,813, respectively. The ever-increasing population prompted the erection of a finer and larger church on a site known as Bristol Hill, midway between Stony Hollow and West Hurley. The Rev. Eugene McKenna, who had come from Ireland in 1871, and was attached to St. Andrew's Church in New York, was appointed pastor of West Hurley in 1875. He built, in 1877, a large frame church in Allaben, near Shandaken, under the title of Our Lady of Lourdes. Yet his report of January 1st, 1881, showed that he had reduced the debt of St. John's, at West Hurley, to $5,500, and in 1890 the whole indebtedness of the parish was on St. John's Church, West Hurley, $4,000, and $200 on the cemetery which he had provided in Phoenicia in the preceding year. When in 1877, he had extended his work along the Ulster and Delaware Railroad, it had been arranged that Sawkill should be cared for from St. Joseph's, Kingston. In 1890 the number of souls attached to St. John's, West Hurley, was about 700, and to the Church of Our Lady of Lourdes, at Allaben, about 200. In 1894 the Rev. Eugene McKenna was transferred to Tarrytown, and Rev. Michael Montgomery, coming from St. Columba's, New York, took his place at St. John's, West Hurley. In 1893 a small church was built at Shokan at the expense of a Mr. Wentworth, under the invocation of St. Augustine. This involved a division of the parish, and the Rev. Francis Fagan was appointed to take charge of Phoenicia, and that part of the mission extending to Pine Hill. Father Fagan ordained, in December, 1887, had been at St. Gabriel's, New York, and then at Dobb's Ferry, in control during the last illness of Father David O'Connor, the pastor. Father Fagan built a church in Pine Hill, though undergoing no little hardship at Phoenicia, having no suitable residence.

During Father Montgomery's incumbency St. John's Church, at Bristol Hill, was in 1896 burned to the ground, but was soon rebuilt and enlarged. In 1897, because of Father Fagan's transfer to Whiteport, the charge of Shokan, Allaben, Phoenicia and Pine Hill devolved upon Father Montgomery. He was succeeded for a few months by Father Kean, who had been an assistant at St. Joseph's New York, but whose health failed rapidly. He died in a sanitarium in New Jersey within a year. In 1899, Rev. Charles Reid came to West Hurley. Born in New York, he had been sent to his uncle, a Bishop in Ireland, for his education. After his ordination he had returned to New York and was assigned to St. Bridget's, as assistant. Within three years, by watchful assiduity, he paid off much of the indebtedness caused by the rebuilding of St. John's Church. His success prompted his promotion to the mission of Wappinger's Falls, in 1903, when he was succeeded by the present rector, Rev. Michael Haran. Coming from Ireland in 1873, he was ordained to the priesthood at St. Joseph's Seminary, Troy, in 1879. His first appointment was at Pawling, then at St. Joseph's, Kingston, whence he went as pastor to Quarryville in 1886, where he did good work for seventeen years. He has Shokan for a station, to be regularly attended, especially in summer.

Meanwhile in 1902, Phoenicia, with Allaben and Pine Hill, came under the jurisdiction of the La Salette Fathers, represented by Rev. M. J. Ginet, M. S. He has built in Phoenicia a splendid stone church, procured a fine rectory and beautiful cemetery. He continues to manifest his zeal in search of stray Catholics in distant hills, who had been overlooked, and had fallen away from the faith. A curious question was this year submitted to arbitration under the authority of the Archbishop of New York, and the Bishop of Albany, Rev. Dr. Burtsell, and Rev. James Curtin, of Troy, being the appointed arbiters. The Grand Hotel is situated on the line dividing Ulster County, in New York Diocese, and Delaware County, in Albany Diocese. Priests from either diocese had exercised their jurisdiction there without any hesitation, and the Rev. M. J. Ginet had even established, in 1904, a service for the help of the hotel. This brought out a counterclaim from the Rev. J. F. Slattery, of Stamford, Delaware County, to the exclusive control of the Grand Hotel from the ecclesiastical point of view, because the far greater part of the hotel was situated in Delaware County, and his predecessor in Stamford, Father Livingstone, as early as 1893, had prior positive possession. The arbiters, after the examination of the proper survey, maps and the hearing of statements of the former pastors of Stamford and West Hurley, recognized the claim of Albany Diocese.

ST. JOSEPH'S, KINGSTON.

St. Joseph's Parish, in Kingston, was the most important offshoot of St. Mary's, Rondout. As early as 1855 the Rev. John Madden had purchased a large lot of ground in Higginsville, the most westerly part of the village of Kingston, and the centre of quite a thriving business population, among whom there were many Catholics. The site was not only convenient for these, but being on the threshold of the city, by which

Catholics from Stony Hollow and Jockey Hill were accustomed to enter it, a church there would save them on Sundays the extra walk to the lower end of the city, where St. Mary's was situated. However, Stony Hollow and Jockey Hill, by 1865, had so increased in population that they received a pastor in the person of the Rev. Stephen Mackin. This probably hastened the establishment of a church in Kingston, though Father Coyle's first thought was probably to retain it as a dependency of Rondout. He came to the conclusion that the former site was not as desirable as at the time of the purchase. To satisfy the impatience of the people of Kingston he purchased for $2,600 the Young Men's Gymnasium, on the corner of Fair and Bowery Streets, which was at once turned into a church, and in which mass was said for the first time on Sunday, September 21st, 1868, by the Rev. James Dougherty, the Rev. Dr. Edward McGlynn, being the preacher. Father Dougherty was a native of Rondout, born in 1843, had gone to St. Mary's Parochial School, then to the Christian Brothers' College in Troy, and had graduated at St. John's College, under the Jesuits, at Fordham. He made his three years' theological course at St. Joseph's Seminary in Troy, and was ordained to the priesthood on December 21st, 1867. He was sent at once to St. Mary's, Rondout, to aid Father Coyle, and was at once utilized to devote special attention to the Kingston Catholics. The small chapel was so quickly overcrowded that a larger building was sought. The former Dutch Reformed Church on the corner of Wall and Main Streets had, after the building of the more imposing building opposite, been turned into a hall for lectures and amusements, and at the beginning of the Civil War into a drill room and armory. It came into the possession of General Gates and John C. Brodhead, who sold it to Father Coyle for $10,000, though it required a much greater outlay to be put into shape for a church. It is hard for us to-day to understand the excitement and agitation caused among the people of the staid old Dutch town at the prospect of having a Catholic Church in their very midst, especially so when it was known that a building once used for their own worship was to be occupied for the celebration of mass. However, the genial ways of Father Dougherty quickly dispersed the clouds of discord when it was found that the new church was a centre of earnest piety and good works.

He at first took up his residence in a small house on the corner of Wall and Pearl Streets, till about 1874, he secured the lot at the rear of the church, on which he built a convenient rectory. During the nigh twenty years of his pastorate, no one could be more welcome even among the non-Catholics than he. The new church was dedicated to the service of God by Archbishop McCloskey, on Sunday, July 26th, 1869. The frame building on the Bowery was turned into a school-house. When, about 1877, the pastor of Stony Hollow or West Hurley, extended care to the newly built church of Allaben, near Shandaken, an arrangement was made by which Jockey Hill, or Sawkill, was made dependent upon St. Joseph's Church. In 1884, Father Dougherty undertook the erection of a church in Wilbur, which was for several years attended from St. Joseph's, till it was erected into a separate mission in 1887. In 1886, the Rev. James Dougherty was appointed at the Diocesan Synod, as the representative of the parishes outside of New York, one of the six members of the first diocesan board of consultors which was established in accord with the decrees of the Third Plenary Council of Baltimore. Their duty is to assist by their advice the Archbishop in the administration of the diocese. He was also appointed by Archbishop Corrigan his vicar-forane, or dean, for the counties of Ulster and Sullivan, and also Chairman of the Board of School Examiners, selected at this same synod for these counties. In March, 1888, he was transferred to St. Monica's Church in New York City, and in 1902 became permanent rector of St. Gabriel's Church, where he died on January 1st, 1906, Archbishop Farley pontificating at his funeral on January 4th. His lifelong friend, Monsignor Mooney, Vicar-General, preached the eulogy. His remains were brought to Kingston, where a funeral service was held in St. Joseph's Church, filled to its utmost capacity by the most distinguished citizens of the city. Very Rev. Dr. Burtsell preached on the occasion, and the interment was made in St. Mary's Cemetery, Kingston. He had been succeeded in St. Joseph's by the Rev. Edward J. Conroy, who while administering the parish successfully for three years, yet found the work of the out-mission of Jockey Hill irksome, and was therefore transferred to St. Mary's, Poughkeepsie, where he had to face an enormous debt, the burden of which shortened his days.

The Rev. Edwin M. Sweeny, in May, 1891, took hold at St. Joseph's, Kingston, with great energy, and by his assiduous work did much to improve its appearance, while at the same time securing a decrease of the debt. He in 1893 was appointed Vicar-Forane, or Dean of Ulster and

Sullivan Counties. His administration was successful, both from the material and the spiritual standpoints; he in turn was transferred to New York as pastor of the Church of the Ascension, where he, too, found a very large debt, which he quickly reduced, and obtained proof of his influence with his new people by their co-operation in improvements on a large scale. The Rev. Edward McCue, who had been Father Conroy's assistant in 1889-90, at St. Joseph's, and then had gone to New Brighton, S. I., and afterwards as assistant of Bishop Farley, at St. Gabriel's, New York, now returned in October, 1901, to Kingston to begin an active career as pastor of St. Joseph's. At once he undertook a complete renovation of the rectory, and then put in new marble altars in the church, with fine interior decorations of the whole building. His congregation co-operated with his untiring activity and aided him in his new projects, whilst he did not fail to meet the past indebtedness. His latest successful work was to secure, at the moderate sum of $10,000, the substantial mansion, formerly owned by Judge Alton B. Parker, for a convent of the Sisters of Charity, and a parochial school, on the corner of Pearl and Clinton Avenue, opposite the Kingston Academy. The former school has been turned into a parish hall. With these outward or material signs of improvement, the spiritual advancement of the congregation has kept pace through the good work of those who have had charge of St. Joseph's Church. Father McCue, at the mission given in his church in 1905, by the Diocesan Apostolic Band of Missionaries gave the opportunity to the non-Catholics to obtain a thorough knowledge of the teachings and practices of the Catholic Church, through the series of lectures which the missionaries gave during the week after they had given a two weeks' mission directly intended for the Catholics of the Parish.

WILBUR.

Wilbur, as forming part of the city of Kingston, now merits our attention. The Rev. James Dougherty had, as early as 1884, planned to give facilities for its people to hear mass without having to make the long journey up the hill. Wilbur was a centre of fairly numerous families, attracted there by the extensive stone-cutting, which came from its being the terminus of the stone road from the bluestone quarries at West Hurley. There the stone, too, was laden on the canal boats for transportation to New York and elsewhere. The corner-stone of the church was laid on July 17th, 1884, by Archbishop Corrigan. Its title was to be the Church of the Holy Name of Jesus. Rev. Joseph Mooney, then pastor of St. Patrick's in Newburg, gave an able address on the occasion. In spite of the rain a large number of people, Catholics and non-Catholics, were present. The site chosen was eminently picturesque and beautiful, overlooking the creek for a long distance either way. The work of building advanced so rapidly that mass could be said in it late in the fall of the same year, and its dedication took place with solemn ceremonies. It was attended as a mission from St. Joseph's until August, 1887, under the pastorate of the Rev. James Dougherty, but then Wilbur was erected into a separate mission under the care of the Rev. Wm. J. Boddy, with Eddyville as a mission. He was a convert to the Catholic Church, and had been ordained to the priesthood at St. Joseph's Seminary on December 22nd, 1876. His health was not strong, and he died at Wilbur on June 4th, 1890. He was succeeded by the Rev. Michael J. Feely, whose ill health required him to resign early in January of 1892; he is chaplain at the House of the Good Shepherd in New York. The Rev. Daniel P. Ward was appointed pastor of Wilbur in January, 1892. A native of New York, he was ordained to the priesthood in St. Joseph's Seminary, Troy, on December 22nd, 1877. For a short time he was assistant at St. Columba's New York, then St. Patrick's, Newburg, and for more than ten years at St. Bridget's, New York. His pastorate continued till his death in Wilbur on January 12th, 1901. The Rev. Hugh Cullum, ordained in December, 1886, and transferred from the pastorate of Barrytown, did excellent work in his three years, both in renovating the two churches in Wilbur and Eddyville, and in reducing the debt. At present the genial Father Michael Cunniff, ordained in May, 1891, is the active pastor, as far as the decreasing population permits activity. Since his ordination he had been assistant at St. Monica's, New York, to the Rev. James Dougherty. On Father Cullum's transfer to Suffern, Father Cunniff received his appointment to Wilbur on June 16th, 1904. Since then he has reduced the debt on the two churches, so that now it is almost insignificant, and he has been able to renovate the rectory.

PORT EWEN, ESOPUS TOWNSHIP.

The Rev. M. C. O'Farrell, pastor of St. Mary's, Rondout, had in 1873, promoted the erection of a church in Port Ewen, for the large number of boatmen who had fixed their residence on the other side of Rondout

Creek. The new mission was in this year separated from Rondout and placed in charge of the Rev. Michael Phelan. There were given by Father O'Farrell, as donations and collections, $3,151, for the Church of the Presentation of the Blessed Virgin, a handsome brick edifice, having a pleasant location overlooking the Hudson. It was dedicated by Archbishop McCloskey on June 14th, 1874. Father Phelan had been ordained at St. Joseph's Seminary, Troy, on June 3rd, 1871. He was afterward pastor of St. Mary's, Newburg, and at present of St. Cecilia's, New York. His successor at Port Ewen, in 1875, was the Rev. Wm. F. Brady, who had been ordained at the Troy Seminary in November, 1869. His pastorate was of two years, and he was succeeded by the Rev. Thomas O'Hanlon in 1877, though ordained only the June of the preceding year at Troy. He also built and kept charge of the Church of the Sacred Heart at Eddyville. He died in 1883, and his remains were interred in front of the church in Port Ewen. His successor was the Rev. Philip Ahern, ordained at the Troy Seminary in May, 1877, who started the mission at Esopus, and about 1889, as a consequence, the Eddyville church was united to Wilbur. Father Ahern, in 1892, was sent to Cornwall, and later was Chaplain at the Home of the Good Shepherd, where he died in 1904.

Revs. Eugene Smith and Thomas, twins, successively were pastors at Port Ewen, from 1892 till 1899; both suffered from ill health, and died at Mt. Hope in Baltimore. The present pastor, the Rev. Leo C. Beaudet, is a Canadian by birth, but was ordained at the Provincial Seminary of St. Joseph at Troy, on December 17th, 1887, and was for many years assistant at St. Joseph's, in New York. The stoppage of the Hudson and Delaware Canal and other consequent industries has decreased the population of the parish considerably. Port Ewen, once thriving, has become a poor and difficult mission, yet Father Beaudet had the courage to erect a convenient hall for social gatherings.

EAST KINGSTON, ULSTER TOWNSHIP.

A minor offshoot of Rondout, sprouting at the same time as Port Ewen, is the mission of East Kingston, formerly known as Flatbush, where a small brick church was built by the efforts of Rev. M. C. O'Farrell in 1873, at a cost of $2,500. Father Coyle had begun to take an earnest interest in the welfare of its Catholic people as early as 1871. Since then the priests of Rondout had celebrated mass there on Sundays to 1890, when Rev. Dr. Burtsell came to Rondout. He, finding that the congregation had considerably increased, had at a cost of $2,000 a large addition put to the Church of St. Colman in 1891, and the now fairly extensive building was dedicated anew by Bishop Conroy, of Curium, formerly of Albany, the people having been so in earnest that it was out of debt for the occasion. Since 1890, whenever there was a mission at St. Mary's, about every three years, some of the missionaries stayed several days at East Kingston, to give the people the same aid as was given to the Rondouters. About 1900 a large number of Italians began to work in the brickyards in the neighborhood and not a few Italian families settled along the shore. For the benefit of these Dr. Burtsell called several Italian priests to give them due religious instruction with no little success. The church customs in the United States are very different from those to which they were accustomed in Italy, where religion sustained by donations of former generations is to the present as free as water, no demand ever being made for the support of religion. Hence, they find it difficult to realize why they should be called upon here for the erection and support of churches. As this becomes impressed upon them they are inclined to do what is necessary. As they are a people of more demonstrative habits, perhaps even more artistic than the Catholics found here, they are surprised at the lack of outward show, of processions, of statuary, and they need to be convinced of the reasons of the differences, which is the more difficult because of their previous absence of knowledge of any other world than their own small home villages. The immigrations on a vast scale, always involve emancipation from family ties, and moral environments, especially for young and unmarried men, who are liable to think that the land of liberty opens the way to license and consequent relaxation of religious restraints. The present pastor, Rev. Robert A. Weir, finds it difficult to provide for their spiritual needs at East Kingston, because of his lack of knowledge of their language and characteristics. In July, 1904, St. Colman's was erected into a separate parish, entirely free from debt. To erect a pastoral residence, Father Weir purchased a lot near the church and placed a mortgage of $6,000 on the church property.

ELLENVILLE.

From 1828 to 1840 several Catholic families, attracted by the building of the Delaware and Hudson Canal, had settled in Ellenville and neighborhood. The Rev. Father Gilbride, who had been at Saugerties, is known to have paid visits there in 1844, celebrating mass at the residence of Michael Sheridan for several years. In 1842, the Rev. Edward Briody, educated in Montreal, was ordained by Bishop Hughes and appointed to the charge of Port Jervis, and other places within reach. Following the canal, Father Briody reached Ellenville, where under his management the old meeting house of the Reformed Church was purchased and removed to its present site, repaired and fitted up for Catholic service. This was done at an expense of $3,500. This building is still retained looking fairly neat. Father Briody was kept very busy by the large extent of territory attached to Port Jervis, where he also built a fairly large church. He had under his charge, in 1851, Port Jervis and Ellenville, Bridgeville, Fallsburgh, Mongaup Valley, Forestburgh, Callicoon, Liberty, Neversink, Claraville, Grahamsville, Monticello, Parkville and Lackawack. Father Callan had care of Ellenville for a few months, and then, in 1852, the Rev. Daniel Mugan, educated at Mt. St. Mary's, Emittsburgh, and ordained in August, 1856, by Archbishop Hughes, took charge of Ellenville with Liberty and Wurtsboro as missions. He had been stationed at St. Peter's, New York, for a year, and his pastorate at Ellenville of nineteen years continued till his death in 1872. He had his residence near the church. His work was successful, though wearisome. Access was so difficult to Ellenville that the notification of his last illness did not reach any priest in time to administer to him the last Sacraments.

He was succeeded by the Rev. Peter J. Prendergrast, who had within two years come from Ireland. He was assistant for six months at St. Patrick's, Newburg, and another six months at the Church of the Epiphany, New York. He worked earnestly for three years at Ellenville, and then was transferred, in 1875, to Middletown, in 1888, to Rondout, and in 1890 to the Church of the Epiphany, New York, where for a variety of reasons he felt uncomfortable, regretting having given up the country parish of Middletown, where he had done his best work, and where his remains were taken for interment. The Rev. James F. Westerman succeeded him in Ellenville for a year, and in 1876, the Rev. Bernard A. Goodwin, who had been ordained in June, 1871, became pastor, remaining there fully ten years. The Rev. Joseph H. Hayne became pastor in 1887, who worked indefatigably till he had placed the parish in good shape. His successor, in 1894, was the Rev. John Weir, for seven years, who attended Mountaindale and Lackawack, Liberty and Wurtsboro, having been made for many years independent missions.

The present pastor, Rev. Michael Montgomery, ordained at the Troy Seminary in 1875, had been assistant at St. Columba's, New York, and pastor of West Hurley. In 1903 a dam above the village burst, and there was quite an inundation, apparently on the verge of carrying away St. Mary's Church, when providentially a floating barn was thrown against a tree in the rear. This diverted the waters from the church, which thus escaped sure destruction.

MILTON AND MARLBOROUGH.

The pastors of St. Peter's, Poughkeepsie, from an early day, gave attention to the scattered Catholics along the banks of the Hudson River, from Saugerties to Marlborough, and probably through Highland to the interior, as far as Rosendale, though later the Rondout Valley was found more accessible for this. As early as 1842, the Rev. John N. Smith, and again in 1844, the Rev. Joseph Burke, then at Poughkeepsie, had penetrated to Rosendale. Their successors, Father Reardon, Rev. Dr. P. F. McSweeney and Father Nilan, kept up the good work by the assiduous administration of the sacraments to all who called for them, though in 1868, the Rev. Patrick Brady pastor of Rosendale, had in charge Modena, Milton, Esopus and Galesville.

The Rev. James Mee, in 1880, was the first resident pastor of Milton and Marlborough. He had been ordained to the priesthood at the Troy Seminary in June, 1870. He built a neat frame church in Milton, with an adjoining residence. At Marlborough he purchased a Methodist meeting house, which he turned into a church. He celebrated mass every Sunday in both places. He also attended Ireland Corners, better known as Gardiner, where in 1882 ground was secured and plans made for a church. In 1884, this was made a separate mission, with Wallkill and New Paltz attached, under the care of an English priest, the Rev. Charles Browne. The Church of St. Charles Borromeo was dedicated at Gardiner. In 1886, the Rev. Joseph L. Hoey, ordained in 1877, who had for seven years been an active assistant at Rondout, was made pastor of Gardiner, and on the transfer in 1887 of Father Mee to Rosebank, Staten Island, was appointed to the pastorate of Milton, with charge of Marlborough, Gardiner and New Paltz. In 1889 a church was built at Roseton, under the title of Our Lady of Lourdes, by the generosity of Mr. and Mrs. Vatable, and was placed under the care of the pastor of Milton. This entailed speedily a new division of these missions. The Rev. W. P. Kenny was given charge in 1894 of Milton, Marlborough and Roseton, till 1897, when he was succeeded by the Rev. E. J. A. Kenny, who, ordained in Rome, had been an assistant at St. Gabriel's, in New York. He soon (in 1900) found it convenient for the better care of the people to remove to Marlborough and Roseton, and give the opportunity for the appointment to Milton of the Rev. James P. Dooley, with charge of Highland. Here he built a church, under the title of St. Augustine.

GARDINER AND NEW PALTZ.

Meanwhile, in 1892, the Rev. Bernard Duffy had taken charge of Gardiner and New Paltz. Here he was succeeded by the Rev. John B. McGrath, ordained at St. Sulpice in Paris. He in 1894, especially in view of the many Catholics studying at the Normal College, built the Church of St. Joseph in New Paltz. When appointed to the parish of City Island, he was succeeded in 1899 by the Rev. John J. Morris, who since his ordination, in 1877, had been assistant at St. Joseph's, New York. An interesting feature of his pastorate was the advent to the Normal College at New Paltz of about thirty Cuban lady teachers, who had been invited by the United States Government to prepare themselves better for their calling by the training in American methods of education, that they might adapt them to their schools in Cuba. These teachers gave clear evidence of their practical catholicity by their assiduous attendance at all the services of St. Joseph's Church in New Paltz. Father Morris also on several occasions procured for them the services of a priest familiar with Spanish. In 1905 he was transferred to the larger field of Port Jervis, and the present pastor of Gardiner is the Rev. Wm. J. Stewart, who in a short time has by his energy considerably reduced the indebtedness of the mission and made important improvements.

GERMAN CATHOLICS IN ULSTER COUNTY.—ELLENVILLE.

The Very Rev. John Raffeiner, a German priest of great zeal, was recognized as the Apostle of German Catholics in the East. He was from the Diocese of Brixia, in the Tyrol, and came to the United States in 1833. This is the eulogy which Archbishop Hughes made of him at his funeral: "Many of you have no recollection of the spiritual destitution that prevailed in New York when the now populous Dioceses (1862) of Brooklyn, New York, Buffalo, Albany and Newark, were comprised in one. The German Catholics were then but few and totally devoid of spiritual aid. It was the good providence of God that at this particular period (1834) directed the steps of Father Raffeiner hither, where he entered most faithfully and earnestly on the work assigned him in supplying spiritual comfort to his needy countrymen."

Wherever there were German Catholics there would Father Raffeiner seek them out, and minister to them, being prevented neither by the winter's snows, the summer's sun, nor the inconvenience of travel in that day, from fulfilling the duties assigned him. He was appointed Vicar-General for the Germans by Bishop DuBois, and continued in the position by Bishop Hughes. Among the many places visited by him, Ellenville was one of the most difficult of access; yet he undertook the formation of a congregation there in 1850, and was able to assign to it a pastor in the person of Rev. John Raufeisen, educated in St. Joseph's, Fordham, and ordained on October 3rd, 1849, by Bishop Hughes. A small frame structure, at a cost of about $1,200, was built by him, and known as St. Mary's. He established a church at Ulster Heights, under the invocation of St. Michael and Wendelinus, and one under title of the Immaculate Conception at Woodbourne, where quite a number of Bavarians had settled. Father Raufeisen's pastorate in Ellenville extended until 1861, though meanwhile his zeal had brought him to visit, in search of German Catholics in 1850, Rondout, Bridgeville, Calicoon, Fallsburgh, Grahamsville, Lackawack, Neversink, North Branch, Otisville, Stephen's Factories and Woodbourne. He constantly preached at St. Mary's, Rondout, from 1857 to 1860, when he was able to establish a church for the Germans in Rondout. In 1860, a Benedictine, Father Moosmueller, served the German church in Rondout, but Father Raufeisen, from 1861 until 1878, resided in Rondout, where the needs were much greater, though he continued to visit Ellenville till it received a new pastor in the person of Rev. George J. Veith, who attended Ellenville from 1864, though he resided in Jeffersonville, till he was succeeded by the Rev. Ferdinand Raes, in 1867. Not till 1871 did Ellenville again have a resident pastor for the

Germans. Then the Rev. Constantine Van Droste was pastor from 1871 to 1873. Again for a year there was no resident pastor, till the coming in May, 1874, of the Rev. Franz Siegelack, who was succeeded in 1877 by the Rev. E. Henzel. In 1878, Ellenville and stations for the Germans were once more attended from Jeffersonville by the Rev. G. Huntman. Rev. Andrew J. Sauer became resident pastor in 1878, and under his administration a new church was erected in 1881, under the invocation of St. Andrew. His pastorate continued till 1891. Father Sauer had arranged with the public cemetery corporation to set aside a portion for Catholics to be blessed, a deed to be given when $1,000 had been contributed by Catholics. At each burial the pastor is to pay $5 to the cemetery from which he gets a deed for that grave, and gives a deed to the family of the deceased. The cemetery is kept in good order.

Rev. William Eckerth was pastor from 1891 to 1897, when Rev. John S. Braun, a native of New York, ordained at St. Joseph's, Troy, December 22nd, 1888, was appointed pastor. Not far from Ellenville is the Napanoch prison, where Father Braun's zeal prompted him to go frequently to preach to the prisoners. On these occasions he took his choir with him. On other occasions he brought his phonograph, which was a source of great amusement to the prisoners. The piece most encored was one "of a negro kicked by a mule."

Father Braun was very tactful, having to meet at times murmurings that not rarely occur in German congregations made up from different states of Germany. The Rev. John Braun was called in 1905 to the charge of St. Boniface's, in New York, and was succeeded by the Rev. Dr. Edward J. Heinlein, who made but a year's stay, and the present pastor is the Rev. Theodore J. Bamberg.

ST. PETER'S CHURCH, RONDOUT.

In 1850, the Rev. John Raufeisen, immediately after his ordination being assigned to Ellenville, was also given charge of the German Catholics at Rondout. The Redemptorist Fathers from the Church of the Holy Redeemer in New York, paid several visits in the following years to Rondout. After 1857, and following years, Father Raufeisen made regular visits to attend to the spiritual needs of his fellow countrymen, and he was welcomed at St. Mary's, where a collection was regularly taken to meet his expenses. He purchased a lot on the corner of Adams and Pierpont Streets, on which in 1860 was erected a fine brick church. A young Benedictine priest, Father Oswald Moosmueller, was sent from St. Vincent's Abbey, at Latrobe, Pennsylvania, to take charge. Though he remained but one year in Rondout, he always showed great interest in its welfare till his death, which occurred about 1900. Father Raufeisen concluded that he would do more good for the German Catholics by fixing his abode in Rondout, which he did in 1861, and then he continued to look after the German Catholics throughout the County of Ulster, and began to attend them at Plattekill. The desire of the Germans to have a school prompted him to erect, in 1871, the fine church on the corner of Wurts and Pierpont Streets, which under the invocation of St. Peter, was dedicated by Archbishop McCloskey on the Feast of Sts. Peter and Paul, June 29th, 1873. Rev. Oswald Moosmueller was interested in the new church, and had sent a Benedictine Brother, an artist, to make the altar in St. Peter's a facsimile of that of the Benedictine Chapel at Latrobe. The former church was turned into a school, which was placed for ten years in charge of German Sisters of Charity from Mt. St. Vincent. They were succeeded by others of the order, known as Sisters of Christian Charity. Father Raufeisen for twenty years remained pastor till 1878. He died in May, 1880, as Chaplain of a hospital in Jersey City. He was succeeded by the Rev. Franz Siegelack, who had been for some years pastor at Ellenville. He in turn was succeeded in 1887 by the present pastor, Rev. M. Kuhnen, who was ordained at St. Joseph's Seminary, Troy, in December, 1877, and had been pastor at Blauvelt. Father Kuhnen purchased the residence for the Sisters in the rear of the church. He also started the German cemetery, near the Wiltwyck Cemetery. The German Catholic congregation numbers about 1,500 souls. The debt on the church property is about $30,000.

POLISH CATHOLICS IN RONDOUT.

In 1893, Archbishop Corrigan appointed the Rev. Francis Fremel to start a church for the Polish Catholics of Rondout. Father Fremel was a Lithuanian Pole, who had been ordained in December, 1890, and after some months passed in New York, had been made assistant to Father Kuhnen at St. Peter's Church, which the Polish Catholics had been accustomed to attend, as many of them know or understand German. A discarded synagogue in Abeel Street was used for a church for some years, and property secured in North Rondout. Dissensions, not unusual among the Poles, occurred, perhaps because those not Lithuanians did not consider themselves duly considered, and Father Fremel, really a zealous but not diplomatic man, retired, and the present pastor, Rev. Francis Fabian, was appointed to direct the spiritual interests of the Poles. He worked so well that in the fall of 1899, the corner-stone was laid of a church in a very eligible part of the town. The Poles co-operated earnestly, and there are now a fine church and rectory. There are about 350 Polish Catholics in the vicinity of Kingston.

CATHOLIC INSTITUTIONS IN ULSTER COUNTY.

JESUITS' NOVITIATE—HOME FOR ITALIAN CHILDREN—BENEDICTINE SANITARIUM.

The English Jesuits had come to Maryland under the wing of Lord Baltimore about 1632, and again through James Duke of York some English Jesuits came to New York about 1685 to Governor Dongan; these affiliated with those of the Maryland Province, and retired there in 1700, when the law was enacted condemning "Polish priests and Jesuits" to perpetual imprisonment if found in the province of New York. Yet there are evidences that some of the Jesuits did continue now and again to come to New York, even before that law was repealed. Thus we saw Father Farmer saying mass in New York in 1781-82, even during the British occupation. However, the Jesuits of New York had from an early day been under the jurisdiction of the French Province of A———, through the sub-province of Canada. From Canada had come the missionaries to the various Indian tribes which inhabited New York. Hence though the Jesuits who first were called by Archbishop Hughes to New York in 1846, were from Kentucky, there was speedily formed a direct union with Canada, whither American young men wishing to join their community went for their novitiate and studies.

About 1870, the Jesuits of New York obtained a special arrangement whereby there was opened a novitiate near West Park in Ulster County, under the name of Mauresa. A Novitiate for the Jesuits is similar to that of the other Religious Orders in the Catholic Church, that is, a course of probation of candidates for their community. The Jesuits have a special advantage through their colleges of picking out the best and cleverest young men who give signs of a disposition for the Religious life. But this is not enough—they must be tried especially in that rule of obedience to their superiors, which is made such an important characteristic of their society. It is easily understood that this obedience implies giving up the exercise of their own will in those things which are of themselves lawful. It would be absurd in the name of Religion to claim obedience to commands in any degree contrary to the law of nature, of God or of the Church of Christ. The obedience to their superiors in all things else is regulated by the clear written constitution of the Order which is placed in their hands, and may be easily obtained by any one else. A special feature of the Jesuits' Novitiate is to rest from their direct studies and give themselves wholly for two years to the study of the spiritual life as laid down by their founder, St. Ignatius of Loyola. During this novitiate they are obliged to give themselves up to the menial duties of life, even to take part in cooking and other tasks of the kitchen, the scouring of rooms. No one of whatever rank he may have been, is exempt from this kind of humiliation.

This Novitiate remained till the New York Province was united with the Maryland Province, when it was removed to Frederick, Md. Lately the Jesuits have brought back their novitiate even on a much larger scale to Dutchess County, between Hyde Park and Poughkeepsie. They sold their place at West Park to the missionary Sisters of the Sacred Heart, who came from Italy to take care of Italian waifs, and orphans, and to do other good works in behalf of their country people. They have branched out to the care of others also. In West Park their institution houses a dozen Sisters and about 100 children, especially from New York City, who receive thorough care and a fair education.

An important work undertaken by other Sisters, known as the Order of St. Benedict, is the excellent sanitarium in the City of Kingston, which has been the means of relieving great suffering and distress among the sick of Ulster and neighboring counties. Its official title is "Our Lady of Victory Sanitarium," but is more easily designated the Benedictine Sanitarium. Its erection is due to the earnestness of a native of Rondout, a Miss Molloy, known in the sisterhood as Sister Aloysia. First established in two private houses on the summit of West Chestnut Street, it is now in a most eligible site towards the centre of the city, upon a hill whence there is a delightful view of all the surrounding country. The sick of all denominations find it a most healthful and hospitable resort.

Eng. by F. G. Williams & Bro. NY

Charles G. Ellis.

CHAPTER XXXVII.

THE PRESBYTERIAN CHURCH.

By Rev. Charles G. Ellis, D.D.

PRESBYTERIANISM in its growth and influence in Ulster County can only be understood when we consider with it the growth and influence of the Dutch Reformed Church. For while differing in name they are practically one in the essentials of policy and theological standards. The Dutch Reformed is in reality the Dutch Presbyterian Church. The Presbyterian Church in the United States of America being that part of the Presbyterian Church in which the English, Scotch and North of Ireland people predominate. Since the early settlers in Ulster were Dutch, their's was the prevailing type, and, in the interior of the county, is still the only type of Presbyterianism. The documentary records of those years which immediately followed the revocation of the edict of Nantes show how kindly the French Presbyterians, commonly known as Huguenots, who settled in Kingston and vicinity, were welcomed, with what assiduity they were instructed in Dutch, and how readily they were received into the Dutch church. Early records also show that the Dutch governors, in their reports on the state of religion in the colony, held the Independents and Presbyterians from New England who settled in New Amsterdam, in high esteem.

The Presbyterian Church as it is known in Ulster County to-day is the outgrowth of those later immigrations of English speaking peoples which took place in the eighteenth and first half of the nineteenth centuries. It is the history of a denomination cognate with the Dutch Church, supplementing its work, and not of a rival crowding into a field already occupied.

During the fifty years immediately preceding the Revolution, many Presbyterians and Independents from Long Island and New England, as well as others from the old countries, settled in Southeastern Ulster and along the shores of the Hudson. The opening of the Delaware and Hudson Canal, and the development of the blue stone and cement industries in the early part of the nineteenth century brought to the upper part of the county many more immigrants, particularly numbers of Presbyterian Scotch and Irish. The result was that where the ground was not already fully occupied by the Dutch Church, the newer congregations organized were Presbyterian.

The Presbyterian Church of Marlborough, the first church organized in the town and the first Presbyterian Church organized in the County, was established January 1st, 1764. The first entry on its records reads, "A register of the proceedings of Stephen Case and John Woolsey, first trustees of the Marlborough Society and of their successors begun the first day of January, 1764." The subscription for building a house of worship is dated the 8th day of August, 1763, and reads, "We the subscribers for an encouragement towards building a meeting house for worship of God near the old Man's Creek in Ulster County, to be founded on the Presbyterian formation of government of the Kirk of Scotland, do promise for ourselves and assigns to pay on demand the following sums annexed to our names, to those who are trustees of said building, provided that Lewis Dubois does give two acres of land to remain for that use forever." This subscription has the signatures of fifty-one names in sums from 15 pounds to 4 shillings. The condition upon which the land was deeded was that the society "do from this time and at all times forever hereafter call, choose, appoint and settle a minister of the gospel whose principles shall be to maintain and fulfil and keep the articles of the Kirk of Scotland agreeable to their confession of faith."

The building erected the ensuing summer, at a cost of about 117 pounds, was thirty-five by twenty-five feet in dimensions, and remained in use through successive alterations and enlargements until destroyed by fire in 1869, when the present commodious brick structure was erected at a cost of $33,000.

The first sermon was preached in the church by Rev. Charles Jeffrey Smith of Long Island on the 26th of August, 1764. For nearly ten years the church was more or less regularly supplied with preaching, though no regular ecclesiastical organization had as yet been formed. "The Lord's Supper" was first administered April 23d, 1775, when six communicants participated in the rite. The sacrament of Baptism had already been administered to about thirty infants. Samson Occoni, the celebrated Indian preacher, baptized two children here January 22nd, 1775. For ten years following this date, because of the unsettled condition arising from the Revolutionary War, the church was without a settled preacher, and was from time to time supplied by such Presbyterian and Reformed clergymen as they could secure in the neighborhood. Marlborough, being the resort of an unusual number of Whigs, felt those stormy days more than many other places.

Taking advantage of a statute passed in 1784, the congregation met April 8th, 1785, to elect trustees and take steps toward incorporation. The certificate of corporation being filed June 27th, 1785. From 1792, for a number of years, the church was supplied by a Congregational minister, as the congregation had become independent. Though the whole number admitted to membership up to 1808 was but 71, 53 of whom being still on the list, the church was exceedingly influential in all that region, and numbered a host of adherents not communicants.

Wearied and discouraged by the difficulties attending their independent condition, in 1809 they turned again to the Presbyterian Church and secured Rev. James I. Ostrom as supply. In 1810 the church was taken under the care of the Presbytery of Hudson, which thereupon licensed Mr. Ostrom and installed him as pastor. The advent of Mr. Ostrom evidently meant much for Presbyterianism in Ulster County, as his name is associated with the organization and supply of the majority of its churches. His work at Marlborough was signalized at once by what the chronicler describes as a "special season of divine influences," which began in October, 1811, and continued until the following spring, adding to the church 115 members. It was remarkable, and commented on at the time as a peculiar manifestation of divine sovereignty, that though Mr. Ostrom preached also at the Paltz during this awakening, there was no special interest aroused in that place.

About the middle of 1820 the church was visited with another awakening when 150 were added, 90 in a single day, of whom 60 had not before been baptized. This Marlborough Church has experienced a number of revivals. In 1830, when more than 40 members were received; and in 1832, when 40 more were added. Again in 1839, there was an accession of 40, and about 100 in 1860, and during the past year another gracious awakening has taken place.

In 1839 the church took its place with the New School body, but in 1841 there was a division. Those who sympathized most strongly with the New School withdrew and organized the church of Milton, while the remainder reunited themselves with the Old School Presbytery of North River. In 1861 eighteen members withdrew to form the church of Middle Hope.

The church of Marlborough is now one of the strongest in the Presbytery and is splendidly manned and equipped. The property consists of a large and attractive brick edifice and a modern commodious manse, the whole beautifully and conveniently situated in the midst of ample grounds in the village of Marlborough. The pastor is the Rev. William Coombe.

The second Presbyterian church organized in Ulster County is the flourishing congregation of Lloyd at Highland, formerly New Paltz Landing. The organization was effected in 1808 through the efforts of Rev. James I. Ostrom of Marlborough. A building was erected at once, to be superseded by a larger structure in 1840, which was in turn rebuilt in 1871, and has been recently repaired and redecorated. The pastor is the Rev. George Allen.

Another church organized by the Rev. Jas. I. Ostrom, was that of Plattekill, of Pleasant Valley West. When organized, April 12th, 1814, it had only four members, two of whom were elected elders. For many years the church made little progress. In 1834, as a result of protracted meetings conducted by Rev. Leonard Johnson of Marlborough, and Rev. Isaac Beach of New Paltz, nearly 20 were added to the church, when the membership reached the number of 58. A building was erected in 1838. The church had only one settled pastor, and no regular supply after 1848, yet it did not cease to exist as an organization until 1868, a testimony to the staying powers of a Presbyterian church even when injudiciously placed.

Next in the order of time, and the strongest Presbyterian Church in the County, is the Rondout Church, of Kingston. Two young men, George W. Endicott, from near Salem, Mass., and Walter B. Crane of South East, Putnam County, N. Y., kneeling together in an upper chamber of the old Mansion House, to dedicate themselves to the work of the Great Master, conceived the purpose of rearing a church in Rondout. The plan was talked over with others, particularly with Richard Bolton, Benjamin J. Seward and Maurice Wurts. The outcome was a Sabbath School, organized in 1829; held first in a boarding house in Ferry street, then in the stone farm house of Abram Hasbrouck, next in the school house on the rocks near Abeel street, and finally in the basement of the incomplete Presbyterian Church.

The Rev. John Mason came from New York and preached in the school the third Sunday of June, 1833. He was invited to remain and organize the people into a religious society, which he did. A Congregational meeting was called July 9th, 1833, at which Maurice Wurts presided. The organization was effected and seven men were elected trustees and appointed as a building committee. Just five weeks later they signed articles of agreement for the erection of a suitable building for a Presbyterian Church. Its dimensions were 56 by 40 and twenty-five feet posts, which, with the exception of the tower, afterward added, was completed at a cost of $5,000, and dedicated June 19th, 1834. The church was formally organized under the Presbyterian form of government with sixteen members, November 1st, 1833, and the Rev. John Mason was ordained and installed as pastor November 13th, 1833. During the pastorate of the Rev. Benjamin T. Phillips, from 1847 to 1861, the village grew with great rapidity, and under his successful leadership the church increased in numbers and spiritual strength. A manse was erected and the church was enlarged and beautified. Under the pastorate of Dr. William Irwin, 1862-7 and Dr. Edward D. Ledyard from 1867 to 1874, the church still increasing in strength, it was decided to erect a new and more modern house of worship. Thus the corner stone of the present structure was laid June 4th, 1873, and in April, 1874, the church was occupied for divine worship; the cost of the church and furnishings being over $60,000.

This, the mother of Protestant churches in Rondout, is now one of the strongest in the county. It has a membership of nearly 500. Its property consists of a fine large auditorium, a beautiful chapel, and a modern and commodious manse. The present pastor is the Rev. Charles G. Ellis.

The First Presbyterian Church of Malden was incorporated February 17th, 1834. The building and manse were erected before 1833. A chapel was added in later years. During the prosperous days of the bluestone business at Malden this church did excellent work. The decay of business with the consequent loss of population, and the disappearance of old families has rendered the church now nearly extinct.

The Presbyterian Church at Milton was organized July 12th, 1841, and was incorporated August 23d of the same year, the Rev. Jas. I. Ostrom assisting in its organization. The limitations of the field have circumscribed the growth of the church; nevertheless, there has been developed a thrifty congregation. A tasteful modern building has been erected, and the church is prospering under the ministry of the Rev. Wm. Hogarth Tower.

The First Presbyterian Church of Kingston was organized by the Presbytery of North River in the Kingston Court House, December 12th, 1853, and was incorporated January 4th, 1854. Twenty-seven persons constituted its original membership, of whom all but two had been members of the Second Reformed Church of Kingston. The first house of worship, which was situated at the corner of Clinton avenue and Maiden lane, was dedicated April 17th, 1855. It was destroyed by fire October 12th, 1875. For a time the congregation worshipped in a tabernacle on Elmendorf street. The present building at the corner of Elmendorf street and Tremper avenue was dedicated February 24th, 1885. The location of this church, in a growing section of the city, promises, under the capable leadership of the Rev. R. C. Dodds, D.D., an increasingly prosperous future.

It is not likely that there will be more Presbyterian churches organized in Ulster County, but it is possible that the present movement toward the union of Presbyterianism will, in the not distant future, include the Reformed and Presbyterian churches in one denomination.

Charles Mercer Hall.

CHAPTER XXXVIII.

THE EPISCOPAL CHURCH.

By Rev. Charles Mercer Hall, M.A.,

("*I believe one Catholic and Apostolic Church.*"—Nicene Creed.)

THE Episcopal Church is the ancient Catholic Church of the English-speaking people, more often known as the Anglican Communion. In the summer of A. D. 1579, when Admiral Sir Francis Drake was circumnavigating the globe in the "Golden Hind," the first Prayer Book service on the Pacific Coast was held at Point Reye's Head in Drake's Bay. On August 13, 1587, at Raleigh's colony at Roanoke, Va., occurred the baptism of the Indian chieftain Manteo; and the Sunday following that of Virginia Dare, "the first Christian born in Virginia." On Sunday, June 21, 1607, the Holy Communion was first celebrated in English, at Jamestown, Virginia. At Fort St. George in Maine, thirteen years before the landing of the Pilgrim Fathers on Plymouth Rock the services of the Church were begun in New England. Owing to the connection between Church and State and the events connected with 1776, the securing of the episcopate for the American Church was a difficult matter, but on November 14, 1784, at Aberdeen, Scotland, the Rev. Samuel Seabury, D.D., Oxon., was consecrated the first American Catholic bishop by the bishops of the Catholic remainder of the Church of Scotland—just six years before the Rev. Dr. John Carroll was (irregularly) consecrated first Roman Catholic Bishop of Baltimore, in the private chapel of Lullworth Castle, Dorsetshire, England, by Dr. Charles Walmesly, titular Bishop of Rama and senior vicar-apostolic of the Roman mission in England.

On February 4, 1787, at the chapel of Lambeth Palace, the London residence of the Archbishops of Canterbury, Dr. Samuel Provoost was duly consecrated by the Archbishops of Canterbury and York, and the Bishops of Bath and Wells, and Peterborough, as first Bishop of New York. Bishop Provoost died September 6, 1815, and has been succeeded by The Rt. Rev. Benjamin Moore, D.D., 1801-1816, The Rt. Rev. John Henry Hobart, D.D., 1811-1830, the Rt. Rev. Benj. T. Onderdonk, D.D., 1830-1861, The Rt. Rev. Jonathan M. Wainwright, 1852-1854, The Rt. Rev. Horatio Potter, D.D., 1854-1887, The Rt. Rev. Henry C. Potter, D.D., consecrated in 1883, and The Rt. Rev. David H. Greer, D.D., (coadjutor), consecrated in 1904.

TRINITY CHURCH, SAUGERTIES, was built during the year 1831, and the parochial organization was effected the same year. A rectory was built in 1831, but was replaced with a more commodious building in 1884. A Sunday-school building was erected in 1875. The succession of rectors has been as follows: Rev. Reuben Sherwood, 1831-1835; Rev. Cicero S. Hawks, 1835-1837; Rev. Ravaud Kearney, 1837-1838; Rev. Hiram Adams, 1838-1848; Rev. Edwin A. Nichols, 1848-1856; Rev. Wm. J. Lynd, 1856-1859; Rev. John J. Robertson, 1859-1880; Rev. Thomas Cole, 1880.

ST. JOHN'S CHURCH, KINGSTON, was incorporated August 6, 1832, after several years' services held, first in private houses in Rondout and in the Court House, Kingston, by the Rector of Trinity Church, Ulster (Saugerties). The first rector was the Rev. Reuben Sherwood, also rector of Trinity, Ulster, and under his care bi-weekly services were held. The first wardens were, William Kerr, of Kingston, and John Adams, of Rondout. In 1833 a lot was purchased; and Confirmation was administered by Bishop Onderdonk. November 24, 1835, the church was consecrated by Bishop Onderdonk. In 1849 the Church of the Holy Spirit, Rondout, was organized, 42 communicants being set off for it, leaving 30 for the mother parish. From 1854 to 1860 on petition, this new parish, which had no rector, was served on Sunday afternoons by the rector of St. John's. In 1860 St. John's was considerably enlarged, and in 1870 the rectory was purchased. In 1898 the Parish House was erected. The several rectors have been: 1832-1835, Rev. Reuben Sherwood; 1835-1839, Rev. John Downey; 1839-1840, Rev. Henry M. Davis; 1841-1844, Rev. William A. Curtis; 1844-1849, Rev. George Sayres; 1849-1869, Rev. George Waters, D.D.; 1869-1873, Rev. F. Marion McAllister, D.D.; 1873-1874, Rev. Walter Delafield, D.D.; 1875-1885, Rev. C. William Camp; 1886-1895, Rev. Lewis T. Wattson; 1896-1897, Rev. John Henry

Wattson; 1897-1898, Rev. Edgar Gardner Murphy; 1899, Rev. Octavius Applegate, Jr., M. A.

About the year 1701 the Rev. Mr. Hepburn, priest of the Church of England, was, on a vacancy in the Dutch Church of Kingston, forced into that cure by the Governor, Lord Cornbury, but his tenure was of brief duration.

CHRIST CHURCH, MARLBOROUGH. This was the third church organized in Ulster County. The first service was held in the school house, February 12, 1837. An organization was effected February 27, 1837, and in the September following, the new parish was admitted to the convention. The church, erected on land donated by Dennis H. Doyle, was consecrated by Bishop Onderdonk, September 10, 1839. On December 27, 1857, the building was burned to the ground. On May 10, 1858, the foundation of the new church, after designs by Richard M. Upjohn, the noted architect, was begun. The new edifice was consecrated by Bishop Horatio Potter, October 26, 1858. A rectory, erected on ground donated by Mrs. Hester Doyle, was completed in October, 1863. The rectors of this parish have been: Rev. Robert Shaw, 1837; Rev. Geo. W. Fash, 1840; Rev. Samuel Hawksley, 1847; Rev. Samuel M. Ackerley, 1861; Rev. George Waters, D.D., 1875; Rev. John W. Buckmaster, 1876; Rev. Hugh P. Hobson, 1893; Rev. Charles A. Tibbals, 1899; Rev. Harold Morse, 1903-1906.

ALL SAINTS', MILTON, organized in 1850 by the Rev. Samuel Hawksley, has been served by the rectors of Marlborough. The corner stone was laid May 30, 1854, and the church was consecrated by Bishop Horatio Potter in October, 1859.

CHURCH OF THE ASCENSION, ESOPUS (West Park Station). This quaint little country church was admitted into union with the diocese in the year 1842. The rectory was built in 1860. Among a scattered community of summer residences this parish has done a quiet, almost unnoticed work. The incumbents have been, the Rev. Philip Berry, Rev. Wm .T. Smithett, Rev. Richard Temple, Rev. Henry B. Sherman, Rev. Alexander Capron. The present venerable rector is the Rev. Legh R. Dickinson.

CHURCH OF THE HOLY SPIRIT, KINGSTON (Rondout). The first edifice for this parish was built by Miss Verplanck in 1845. A parochial organization was effected in 1849. The present stone church was erected in

1861 and consecrated in 1863. A rectory adjoining the church was built a few years later. The clergy serving this parish have been, the Rev. Wm. T. Smithett, 1849-1854; the Rev. George Waters, D.D., 1854-1861; the Rev. Richard Temple, 1861; the Rev. A. H. Gesner, 1861-1863; the Rev. David Margot, 1864-1865; the Rev. A. F. Olmstead, D.D., 1865-1866; the Rev. Foster Ely, D.D., 1867-1870; the Rev. J. B. Murray, 1870-1875; the Rev. A. Sidney Dealey, 1876-1877; the Rev. F. M. S. Taylor, D.D., 1877-1881; the Rev. Francis Washburn, 1882-1892; the Rev. Charles Josiah Adams, D.D., 1892-1896; the Rev. Thomas Burrows, 1896-1903. The present rector, the Rev. Paul Rogers Fish, entered into this cure in 1904.

St. Peter's Church, Stone Ridge, was organized April 13, 1846, as the Church of the Good Shepherd. The name was changed to St. Peter's about 1860.

St. John's Memorial Church, High Falls, was erected in 1885 by the late Mrs. Richard K. Delafield. The Rev. Ephriam DeGruy became rector in 1860. For several years after his resignation the parish was served irregularly. The Rev. G. W. West became rector in 1874 and has been succeeded by the Rev. Alfred E. Johnson, 1875; the Rev. C. H. Tomlins, 1876-1879; the Rev. W. C. Maguire, 1879-1881; the Rev. Francis J. Clayton, 1881-1882; the Rev. George C. Hepburn, 1882; the Rev. J. J. Rowan Spone, 1883; the Rev. Nelson Ayres, 1884; the Rev. Edward Ransford, 1885; the Rev. S. B. Rathburn, 1885-1887; the Rev. S. Borden Smith, 1887-1890; the Rev. W. J. Clarke Agnew is the present incumbent, and occupies the rectory at High Falls, where also a parish house was built in memory of Eliza Bard Delafield, in 1890.

Saint Paul's Church, Ellenville. The Rev. Samuel Hawksley, rector of Christ Church, Marlborough, was a true missionary. He traveled on foot, preaching the Gospel at Middle Hope, Milton, Highland, Stone Ridge and Ellenville, where he held the first services of the Church in a hall, A. D. 1849. From 1855 to 1865, there was an interim. In October, 1865, the Rev. James E. Kenny was appointed missionary, and services were again resumed in a hall on October 7th. On May 8, 1866, ground given by Mrs. Kniller, of Poughkeepsie, was broken, and on June 27, the corner stone of Saint Paul's Church was laid by the missionary-in-charge.

On August 27 the first service was held. In 1869 the Rev. M. E. Willing succeeded to the cure and was followed in 1870 by the Rev. Chas. C. Edmunds. In 1873 the corner stone of a new edifice, erected by E. C. Humbert, in memory of his son, Cornelius Chandler Humbert, was laid by Dean Capron of the Western Convocation, and on August 18, 1874, the church was duly consecrated by Bishop Horatio Potter. The cost of building and furniture was about $42,000. The Rev. C. C. Edmunds was succeeded by the Rev. Obadiah Valentine in 1875, and the Rev. C. K. Capron in 1881. The certificate of incorporation of the parish was filed July 24, 1884. On September 1, 1884, the Rev. Peter Claude Creveling became rector, resigning in 1889 and leaving behind him a memorial in the shape of a rectory, erected at a cost of $1,600. The incumbents since then have been: Rev. W. H. Brown, 1889-1890; Rev. S. H. S. Gallandet, 1890-1891; Rev. Octavius Applegate, Jr., M.A., 1891-1896; Rev. F. N. Strader, 1896-1899; Rev. C. R. D. Crittenten; Rev. Robert H. Locke; Rev. Aug. Warner Merrick, 1902-1906; Rev. Hugh P. Hobson.

All Saints', Rosendale. The services of the Church were first held in this town at Rocklock School, by the Rev. Walter Delafield, D.D., rector of St. John's, Kingston. Permanent work was begun by the Rev. George W. West, prior to 1872, as a layman, and was carried on by him after his ordination, in 1874, until September 21, 1875. Until 1879 the work was carried on by the Rev. Alfred Evan Johnson and the Rev. William H. Tomlins, rector of the parish at Stone Ridge. The corner stone of All Saints' Church was laid in 1876, and the first service in the new church was held on Easter Day, April 1, 1877. The rectors of Stone Ridge succeeding were: Rev. Wm. Cuffe Maguire, 1879-1882; Rev. G. G. Hepburn, 1882-1883; Rev. J. J. Rowan Spong, 1883-1884; Rev. Nelson Ayers, 1884; Rev. Edward Ransford, 1885-1886; Rev. Scott B. Rathburn, 1886-1887; Rev. S. Borden Smith, 1887-1890.

The church was consecrated Sept. 20, 1885, by the Rt. Rev. H. C. Potter, Assistant Bishop of New York. The missionaries resident from 1889, were: Rev. Wm. H. Brown, 1889; Rev. Horatio Nelson Traggitt, 1889-1892. The Rev. Henry Barker succeeded, July 31, 1892. The parish was duly incorporated February 24, 1893, and the Rev. Henry Barker was elected first rector on February 28th of the same year, from which time he has served the parish with unflagging energy and untiring devotion. Entirely through his personal efforts the chapel of St. Thomas, at

Rifton, was organized. The corner stone was laid September 9, 1899, and the chapel was dedicated December 31, 1899. Land adjoining the church, with a small house, has been purchased. The rector of Rosendale also maintains a Sunday-school and regular services in a hired house at Bloomington, near by.

Church of the Holy Trinity, Highland. This parish was organized in 1872, the corner stone was laid the same year, and the church consecrated in 1873. Various priests served this parish until 1885, when the Rev. Henry Tarrant, D.D., became its first rector. He has been succeeded by various priests who have served the parish for brief terms of missionary work.

The Mission Church of the Holy Cross, at Clintondale, begun by the Rt. Rev. Joseph H. Johnson, D.D., now Bishop of Los Angeles, during his incumbency of Holy Trinity, Highland, was completed through the efforts of the Rev. Henry Tarrant, and was consecrated November 28, 1885, by Bishop Henry C. Potter.

The Mission Church of the Holy Cross, Kingston, was incorporated under the Free Church Act, March 22, 1892. The corner stone was laid on St. James' Day, July 25, 1891, and on St. Paul's Day, January 25, 1892, the church edifice was dedicated by the Venerable Wm. Reed Thomas, D.D., Archdeacon of Orange. The Rev. Lewis T. Watson, B.D., then rector of St. John's Church, was first president of the Board of Trustees and priest-in-charge. It was entirely owing to his missionary zeal and efforts that this work was started and the church built. The Rev. Charles Mercer Hall succeeded Father Wattson, and entered upon his duties as vicar March 11, 1894. An organization under the ordinary diocesan regulations was effected January 11, 1896, and the present incumbent was elected first rector of the new parish, and instituted on St. Patrick's Day, March 17. The church was enlarged to its present size in 1897. A parish house was erected, largely through the generosity of the late Mrs. Wm. B. Fitch and Mr. and Mrs. Ezra Hasbrouck Fitch, and formally opened May 10, 1899. The rectory adjoining was acquired in 1899.

Occasional services are held at St. Bartholomew's Chapel, in the Big Indian Valley, and at the summer Chapel of the Transfiguration at Pine Hill.

The churches in Ulster County are in the Archdeaconry of Orange. The present Archdeacon is the Venerable Wm. Reed Thomas, D.D., Rector of the Church of the Holy Innocents, Highland Falls.

The revival of the Monastic Life in this American Catholic Church is witnessed by the Monastery of the Holy Cross at West Park. The Order of the Holy Cross was organized and the Rev. James O. S. Huntington became its first Superior. The members of the Order engage in the OPUS DEI, conduct spiritual retreats, conferences, parochial missions and other missionary work, in all parts of America and Canada. The monastery was built for the permanent home of the Order and dedicated May 19, 1904, by the Right Rev. Cortland Whitehead, D.D., LL.D., Bishop of Pittsburgh, acting for the Bishop of New York.

CHAPTER XXXIX.

THE LUTHERAN CHURCH.

By Rev. Chester H. Traver, D.D.

THE Lutheran Church in Ulster County dates from October 4th, 1710, when 786 Palatines landed and settled in three villages, Elisabethtown, Georgetown and Newtown. The last is what is now known as West Camp, and perhaps the others were Evesport and Smith's Landing. John Christopher Gerlack was listmaster for 146 in Elisabethtown, while 128 in Georgetown were under Jacob Manck, and 512 in Newtown under Peter Grauberg. As winter was fast approaching they erected huts as temporary homes, so that they were settled by Nov. 14, and clearing the ground. Their food was provided by Robert Livingston at East Camp. The agreement was "Each person each day should receive a quantity of Bread equal to one-third of a Loaf of Bread of such sort and assize which is commonly at the price of four pence half penny in the Citty of New York in weight and finenesse according to the assize of Bread in said city for the time being, and one quart of Beer, such as is commonly called ships Beer of the Price of Three Pounds for each Tun."

This bread and beer was to be delivered to them at the manorhouse at the rate of six pence per diem for adults and four pence for children. The shelter and food proved insufficient, and March 8, 1711, Lord Clarendon wrote: "It is a great mistake." By May 1, 1711, they resolved not to work at tar-making nor remain upon the tract, but remove to Scorie, and use force if necessary.

Others will follow the history of their political and social depression and distribution. We will present briefly their church history as Lutherans.

The first Lutheran Church at West Camp was built in a valley just back of the river ridge. Their first Pastor was Rev. Joshua Kocherthal, who came over with them, not as refugees, but as honest citizens ready to endure for Christ's sake, who brought their religious convictions with them, and set up their spiritual altar at once. Pastor Kocherthal served all, not only in the Hudson Valley, but also in Schoharie County. He

Rev. Chester H. Traver.

lived at West Camp from May, 1711, until he entered into rest December 27, 1719, and was buried under the church. After this was abandoned the loving hands of his daughters placed a tablet over his grave, where it remained until 1895, when the Luther League put it in the front wall of the present church and placed the remains under the same.

The following is a translation of its quaint inscription:

"Know, Traveler, under this stone rests, beside his Sibylla Charlotta, a real traveler, of the High Dutch in North America, their Joshua, and a pure Lutheran preacher of the same on the east and west side of the Hudson river. His first arrival was with Lord Lovelace, in 1709, the first of January. His second with Colonel Hunter, 1710, the fourteenth of June. The journey of his soul to Heaven, on St. John's Day, 1719, interrupted his return to England. Do you wish to know more? Seek in Melanchthous Fatherland, who was Kocherthal, who Harschias, who Winchenback. B. Berkenmeyer. S. Huertin. L. Brevort.

MDCCXLII.

B. is Benigna Sibylla Kocherthal, who married Rev. Wm. C. Berkenmyer, Pastor at Athens, but his pastorate extended from New York to Albany.

S. is Susanna Sibylla Kocherthal, who married William Huertin, goldsmith of Bergen County, N. J., and has descendants in the Town of Wallkill.

L. is Louisa Abigail Kocherthal, who married John Brevort, goldsmith, of New York.

In 1732 the Lutherans of this section helped build the oldest part of the present Katsbaan Reformed Church. The pastors who for over a century served this congregation did not live in this section, but visited them as opportunity offered. After Pastor Kocherthal we find the following: Rev. Justus Falckner, 1719-1723; Rev. Daniel Falckner, 1724; Rev. William C. Berkenmeyer, 1725-1750; Rev. Michael C. Knoll, 1751; Rev. J. T. Reis, 1769; Rev. J. C. Leps, 1774; Rev. Philip Grotz, 1775-1787; Rev. Henry Moeller, 1788-1789; Rev. Dr. F. H. Quitman, 1800-1809; Rev. Joseph Prentice, 1809-1814; Rev. Dr. Augustus Wackerhagen, 1816-1822; Rev. Perry G. Cole, 1829-1835. A Church building was erected in 1791, but never completed. A third Church was consecrated June 17, 1832, which stood until 1871, and the following were Pastors: Rev. Thomas Lape, 1835-1838; Rev. A. Rumph, 1838-1843; Rev. Reuben Dedrick, 1844-1846; Rev. N. H. Cornell, 1847-1850; Rev. David Kline, 1851-1853; Rev. Thomas Lape, 1854-1857; Rev. D. F. Heller, 1858-1864; Rev. Joseph D. Wert, 1865-1869; Rev. W. H. Emerick, 1870-1871.

The present church edifice was dedicated in 1871. The following have been pastors to date: Rev. P. M. Rightmeyer, 1871-1873; Rev. Levi Schell, 1873-1878; Rev. D. W. Lawrence, 1879-1880; Rev. A. N. Daniels,

1880-1886; Rev. C. L. Barringer, 1887-1891; Rev. J. J. Hill, 1891-1893; Rev. W. F. Whittaker, 1893-1895; Rev. L. W. H. Kline, 1896-1897; Rev. R. C. Wright, 1897-1899; Rev. A. S. Hain, 1899-1904; Rev. C. H. Traver, 1905. The first parsonage was built for Rev. A. Rumph and stood near the present church, but was moved to its present site in 1871.

The next oldest Lutheran Church in the County is the Evangelical Lutheran Church, Woodstock, near the base of Overlook Mountain. It is about 14 miles southwest from West Camp. A number of families from Rhinebeck and West Camp moved into the neighborhood. Some time not long after the Revolution they built a church which was standing, but unused when the congregation was reorganized in 1805, and incorporated May 21, 1806, under Rev. Dr. F. H. Quitman. He served them as time allowed from 1805 to 1809, during which period he cared for seven other fields. The following filled out the century: Rev. Joseph Prentice, 1809-1814; Rev. George Wichtman, 1814-1816; Rev. A. Wackerhagen, 1816-1822; Rev. W. J. Eyer, 1822-1827; Rev. John Crawford in 1827 and again in 1829; Rev. Perry E. Cole, 1829-1837; Rev. A. Rumph, 1837-1842; Rev. E. DeYoe, 1824-1845; Rev. W. H. Emerick, 1845-1848; Rev. H. Wheeler, 1848-1850; Rev. Thomas Lape, 1850-1856; Rev. W. I. Cutter, 1856-1858; Rev. Thomas Lape, 1859-1863; Rev. W. H. Emerick, 1863-1868; Rev. H. Wheeler, 1868-1870; Rev. W. I. Cutter, 1870-1872; Rev. Wm. Sharts, 1872-1887; Rev. M. J. Stover, 1887-1893; Rev. B. Q. Hallenbeck, 1893-1895; Rev. I. J. Delo, 1895-1901; Rev. Walter Frederick, 1902.

The site for the second church was on leased land donated by Henry Bonesteel and bought absolutely October, 1847. The corner stone of their present edifice was laid June 12th, 1894, and dedicated November 14th, 1895. They have a commodious and modern parsonage built in 1905, worth $3,000.

The Evangelical Lutheran Church, of Pine Grove, was the fruit of special services held by Rev. W. H. Emerick, just after leaving Woodstock. It is on the State road midway between Woodstock and Saugerties. The building cost $3,000, and was dedicated January 13th, 1869. The Society was organized May 27th, 1869. In 1873, Rev. W. I. Cutter preached for them, but requested them to unite with Woodstock, which they did in 1878.

THE GERMAN EVANGELICAL LUTHERAN CHURCH, of Rondout, was fostered by Rev. A. Rumph, who learned that many Germans were setling there. He began preaching in 1840, and supplied them eight times a year. On June 13th, 1841, Mr. G. F. Von Beck, Secretary of the Delaware and Hudson Coal Company, called the congregation together. Pastor Rumph was present and an organization was effected as Holy Trinity. Rev. C. H. Siebke became pastor in 1849, and labored among them until 1861. They built a frame church and established a parochial school in which English and German were taught. Rev. E. Lubkey was installed July 21st, 1861. The following year a lot was purchased and a brick parsonage erected, costing $3,000. He resigned March 19th, 1863, followed by Rev. P. Krug four years, and Rev. Reichenbecker two years. During the pastorate of Rev. J. M. Steener, 1869-1878, their church and school were burned, September, 1871, when they built on Spring street a beautiful Gothic structure, 105 x 98. Rev. J. Steinhauser was pastor, 1878-1888, and Rev. A. Schmidtkonz, 1888 to date.

THE GERMAN EVANGELICAL LUTHERAN IMMANUEL CHURCH filed their Certificate of Incorporation March 31st, 1870. It was organized by dissatisfied members of Holy Trinity, Rondout. They built between the two villages in what was then known as Wiltwyck, and called Rev. G. F. Stutz as Pastor, who remained until 1881. This Church is connected with the Missouri Synod and has had but three Pastors in 36 years—Rev. G. F. Stutz, 1870-1881; Rev. Fred Tranum, 1881-1888; Rev. G. A. Henkel, 1888 to date.

CHRIST'S EVANGELICAL LUTHERAN CHURCH, Ellenville, N. Y., was organized November 27th, 1850, but was unable to support a pastor. It was reorganized November 23rd, 1861, by Rev. E. Lubkey, of Kingston, and incorporated June 3d, 1863. The Church edifice was consecrated October 19th, 1862, and a parsonage built later. In 1863 they called Rev. C. Kuhn, whom the N. Y. Ministerium would not recognize. He left in 1864, and was followed by Rev. J. Krauss, 1864-1866; Rev. C. Turk, 1867-1869; Rev. J. Goetz, 1869-1874; Rev. F. B. Canz, 1874-1876; Rev. C. Rock, 1876-1877; Rev. G. L. Rau, 1877-1878; Rev. H. Dorn, 1878-1881; Rev. H. B. Kuhn, 1881-1882; Rev. G. A. Batz, 1882-1888. They were served several years by the pastor at Liberty, N. Y. Rev. J. S. Braren was installed July 26th, 1896, and remained to 1900. In 1900, under Rev. P. Leddin, it withdrew from the N. Y. Ministerium and joined the N. Y. and N. J. Synod. He resigned December 26th, 1901, and was followed in 1902 by Rev. H. C. Fultz. Rev. G. A. Neef, D.D., has been pastor since 1904.

THE ENGLISH LUTHERAN CHURCH, of Saugerties, was organized by Rev. A. Rumph, pastor at West Camp, 1837-1842. They purchased the Church property now owned by the German Lutheran Church. Revs. Reuben Dederick, N. H. Cornell and David Kline of West Camp held an afternoon service. A division in 1852 in the Dutch Reformed Church led to the organization of a Congregational Church, into which the most of the influential Lutheran families were drawn, and the Lutheran Society disbanded. It failed to pay for its property, and its owner sold it to the German Methodists. They in turn failed and sold out to the German Evangelical Lutheran Church, organized June 18th, 1859. This joined the N. Y. Ministerium at Wurtenburg, N. Y., September, 1859. This society worshipped in the old Academy on Livingston street until it purchased property on the corner of Ulster Avenue and Elisabeth streets, which it occupied until 1896, when the present building on Market street was erected and dedicated under the pastorate of Rev. Theodore Bauck, 1895-1898. The following pastors served it: Rev. R. Adelberg, 1859-1861; Rev. W. Jahn, 1861-1863; Rev. Herman Fischer, 1863-1865; Rev. J. D. Haeger, 1866-1869; Rev. J. P. Lichtenberg, 1869-1871; Rev. F. C. Kaehler, 1871-1874; Rev. J. P. Lichtenberg, 1874-1879; Rev. C. Kuehn, 1879-1882; Rev. H. Beiderbecke, 1882-1883; Rev. J. J. Roesch, 1883-1885; Rev. B. H. Warnke, 1885-1886; Rev. F. Leddin, 1886-1894; Rev. Oscar Krauch, 1898-1901; Rev. C. Krahmer, 1901. It has 230 communicants.

The corner stone of the PLATTEKILL LUTHERAN CHURCH was laid March 17th, 1863, by Rev. W. Jahn, of Saugerties, and it was dedicated November 15th, 1863. It is supplied as an afternoon service by the pastor at Saugerties.

THE EVANGELICAL LUTHERAN CHURCH OF THE REDEEMER, Rondout, was organized in 1896, as an English church. It called Rev. W. F. Bacher, whose work is growing. He has nearly 500 members. The present building serves as church and parsonage, and is on the corner of Wurtz and Roger streets. The pastor occupies the second and third floors.

CHAPTER XL.

SOCIETY OF FRIENDS.

By Dewitt W. Ostrander.

THE members of this religious society were among the first settlers of the southern part of Ulster County, and came mostly from Long Island and Westchester County. In the month of December, 1760, Edward Hallock, a Friend from Chatauqua, Long Island, sailed up the Hudson river in his own vessel, with his family, which consisted of his wife, two sons and ten daughters, settled upon a farm about one-half mile southerly from the present village of Milton, in what was then known as New Marlborough, and erected a grist mill on a small stream running through the farm. He lived there until his death in 1809, in the ninety-third year of his age.

About the time he settled at New Marlborough a family named Sands, with three sons, one of whom was David, moved from Long Island and settled upon a farm at Cornwall, Orange County.

A short time after the Sands family settled at Cornwall, Samuel Nottingham, a minister of the Friends' Church, from England, came to Cornwall and held meetings, in which young David Sands, who was a Presbyterian, took part. Having learned of Edward Hallock at New Marlborough, he called on him and inquired of Hallock if a Friends' meeting was held in the place, to which Hallock replied, "Yes, my house is open every first day at 11 A. M. for meeting." This is the first account of a Friends' meeting being held in Ulster County.

David Sands afterward attended both monthly and quarterly meetings of the society with Edward Hallock at Nine Partners, Dutchess County, and finally joined the Society of Friends at a Nine Partners monthly meeting.

In the early part of the year 1772, David Sands married Clementine, one of the daughters of Edward Hallock, at a special meeting of the society called for that purpose, at Nine Partners, and, in the spring following, settled at Cornwall, where he opened his dwelling house every

Sunday morning for public worship. This is the first account of a regular Friends' meeting being held in Orange County. At this time the Friends residing at Cornwall and New Marlborough (Milton) were members of the Nine Partners monthly and quarterly meetings, but as their membership increased they desired a monthly meeting on the westerly side of the river, and hence the Cornwall monthly meeting was established or set off from the Nine Partners monthly meeting some time previous to 1798. There is no account of the exact date, but in that year the Cornwall monthly meeting authorized William Thorn, Jacob Wright, Edward Hallock and Alexander Young, as trustees, to purchase from Daniel Knowlton seven acres of land situated about one and a half miles southerly from the present village of Milton, adjoining the post-road, for the Society of Friends at New Marlborough. This is the first purchase of land by the Society of Friends in Ulster County, but there is no record or tradition that the society occupied this land for more than fifteen years.

On December 23, 1793, Joseph Cornwall, in consideration of twelve pounds, conveyed to Daniel Cornwall and William Titus, trustees, appointed at the monthly meeting held at Cornwall, two acres of land situated at Plattekill, then in the town of Marlborough, and known as "The Valley," upon which a meeting house was erected; and having been repaired and enlarged from time to time, meetings have been regularly held there to the present, and it is still known as "The Valley Meeting House."

The Cornwall monthly meeting was held by adjournment at Marlborough (Milton) May 24, 1804, at which extracts from the minutes of the Nine Partners quarterly meeting were received, allowing the Cornwall monthly meeting to establish or set off a new monthly meeting to be known as the Marlborough monthly meeting; the first meeting to be held at the meeting house at Marlborough (Milton), 6 mo. 27th day, 1804, and thereafter at "The Valley" (Plattekill) and Marlborough (Milton) alternately on the day previous to the monthly meeting to be held at Cornwall.

August 20, 1804, Joseph Sutton conveyed to James Hallock, John Wood and Samuel Adams, trustees, appointed at the monthly meeting held at Cornwall, one and one-half acres of land situated about one-third of a mile southerly from the present village of Milton, on the easterly side of the post-road, upon which a meeting house was erected, and occupied until 1828, when the church "divided," and that branch of the church known as "Hicksites" continued to hold meetings in the meeting house, while that branch of the church known as "Orthodox" held meetings for two years at the house of Foster Hallock.

In 1830, the orthodox Friends at Milton purchased a lot of land from Foster Hallock and erected a new meeting house, which was occupied for fifty years, when it was sold and a new site purchased from the estate of James H. Bennett and a large and substantial meeting house erected thereon in 1886, and opened for worship 22nd of 5th month, 1887.

The Friends' Church of Greenfield, in the town of Wawarsing, was organized in 1808, by Zadock Southern, Catharine Billew, and the Washburn and Holmes families, with a membership of about twenty-five. The meeting house was erected in 1818, and the first "approved minister" was Catharine Billew.

In the year 1807, Samuel Adams, Zephaniah Birdsall, James Pine, Merritt Moore and Tristrain Russel were appointed a committee by the Marlborough monthly meeting to establish a meeting at Clintondale in the town of Plattekill, and on August 20, 1811, John Underhill conveyed to Daniel Birdsall and Zephaniah Birdsall, trustees, in consideration of $34.41, one acre and thirty-nine perches of land in Plattekill (now in the village of Clintondale), upon which a meeting house was erected and used until 1889, when the present substantial meeting house was erected.

The Friends' Church at Butterville, in the town of New Paltz, was established in 1807, and in 1812 Friends' meetings were organized at Rosendale Plains in the present town of Rosendale, and at Esopus, and in 1813 the Friends' churches at Rosendale Plains and Esopus were erected.

By the approval of the Nine Partners quarterly meeting the Rosendale Plains monthly meeting was organized 8 mo. 25th day, 1813, composed of the Butterville, Esopus and Rosendale Plains preparative meetings.

In 1813 a new quarterly meeting was established or set off from the Nine Partners quarterly meeting, to be known as the Cornwall quarterly meeting and to be composed of all the monthly meetings on the west side of the Hudson River. The Cornwall monthly meeting, when established, consisted of three monthly meetings, each of which was composed of three preparative meetings. The first quarterly meeting to be held at "Cornwall on the 5th day preceding the two last first days in 10th month, 1813."

The meeting house at Butterville had not been in use by the Friends for many years, and on the 27th of 10th mo., 1900, it was sold, and the proceeds applied towards building a new meeting house at Rosendale Plains, on the site of the one erected in 1813. The new meeting house is a neat frame structure which will seat a large congregation, and is at present the second largest in the county. In re-establishing this meeting, the church owes much to the earnestness and zeal of Violetta M. Ostrander, wife of Zina C. Coutant, since deceased, who was one of the brightest lights that ever adorned the Rosendale Plains meeting.

The Friends' Society in Ulster County at this time nnmbers 514 members.

John J. Linson

CHAPTER XLI.

THE BENCH AND BAR.

By Hon. John J. Linson.

THE first court of which we have record that ever sat within the bounds of the County of Ulster, was held at Wiltwyck, on the 12th day of July, 1661. It was presided over by Roeloff Swartwout, as schout, with whom were associated Everet Pels, Cornelis Barentse Schlecht and Elbert Hymans Roos as schepens. Under the judicial system as it existed in New Netherland the functions of the schout were not merely those of a sheriff, as has been sometimes supposed. The schout-fiscal of the province was also a prosecuting officer. He made arrests and conducted criminal cases. He could apply the torture in the presence of a magistrate, but only once if the prisoner did not confess. So, too, the local schout made arrests, presided in civil cases and prosecuted criminals.

Swartwout was not a native of the colony. He had resided therein but a short time prior to his appointment, which was resented by Stuyvesant, who was compelled, however, to recognize and submit to it by the directors of the West India Company. His appointment was probably secured by family influence. His career was somewhat checquered and he died a resident of Hurley.

During the brief Dutch occupation litigation was, of course, trivial. Nothing of general interest is to be found in the meager archives which we possess.

When the English took possession of the colony the judicial power was vested in the Governor and Council. The Court of Assizes, established under the "Duke's Laws" (A. D. 1665), was composed of the Governor, High Sheriff and certain justices of the peace. This court had original jurisdiction in criminal cases and in civil matters where the amount in dispute was of the value of twenty pounds. A court of Oyer and Terminer, possessing the power of general gaol delivery, was to be held in each county by a judge, whose commission was issued by the governor and who was assisted by four justices of the peace.

The Supreme Court was established by an act of the Colonial Legislature, passed May 6th, 1691. It consisted of five justices and was "fully Impowered and Authorized to have Cognizance of all pleas, Civill, Criminall and Mixt, as fully and amply to all Intents and purposes whatsoever as the Courts of Kings Bench, Common Pleas and Exchequer within their Majestyes Kingdome of England have or ought to have," provided the amount in dispute was at least twenty pounds. It could also remove into itself any action pending in an inferior court where as great a sum as that of its minimum original jurisdiction was in controversy. It sat "at the City of New Yorke and not Elsewhere." It was this court which was recognized and continued in existence by the first constitution of the State.

A court of Common Pleas, to consist of one judge with three justices in each county, was established by the same act. It had civil jurisdiction up to twenty pounds. It could sit but twice a year and "Noe Longer" than two days. It began its terms at the close of those of the Court of Sessions held by three justices, which had been established in 1683, with which it was closely allied. A justice of the peace had jurisdiction in debt or trespass to the amount of forty shillings.

The sparsity of the population, the small financial interests involved and the organization of the courts above outlined provided little incentive for local legal talent during the term of British supremacy. The records that have come down to us show an occasional indictment for assault and battery or petit larceny; misdemeanors on the part of negro slaves who were sentenced to be whipped around the town; an occasional civil action growing out of a controversy as to the title to or possession of real property; probate; apportionment of taxes among the towns and manors, and negotiations with the Indians. The magistrates were generally laymen, and causes were usually conducted by the parties in person. The aid of the Supreme Court seems to have been invoked but seldom; the litigant from Ulster which appeared there most frequently being the corporation known as "The Trustees of the Freeholders and Commonalty of the town of Kingston," which was involved in much litigation over the boundaries of the patent. The trustees were also compelled from time to time to defend actions brought against the inhabitants of the town by the attorney general for quit-rents accruing before the patent was granted. These suits were brought in the Court of Chancery, which was established by

Governor Hunter, illegally, as claimed by the General Assembly. On some occasions, at least, the trustees were represented in this litigation by John Crooke, a lawyer residing at Kingston, who appears to have been a man of ability, but of whom we know little.

On the 3rd day of May, 1777, the convention which had adopted the republican constitution, reorganized the Supreme Court; and on the eighth of the same month, by ordinance, it appointed John Jay, Chief Justice, and Robert Yates and John Sloss Hobart, puisne justices. The first term of court was held under the new government opened at the Court House in Kingston on the 9th day of the following September, with Chief Justice Jay presiding. In his charge to the grand jury he congratulated that body on the dawn of free government, and remarked with satisfaction that the first fruits of the new constitution appeared in a part of the State, the inhabitants of which had "distinguished themselves by having unanimously endeavored to deserve them."

The public services of Justice Jay occupy an important place in the history of the young commonwealth and of the nation. In addition to his other honors he became Chief Justice of the Supreme Court of the United States. Among the many others of our honored dead who have held terms of the State Supreme Court in the Court House at Kingston and who are deserving of mention, were Smith Thompson and Brockholst Livingston, who also attained the Federal Supreme bench; and James Kent, Chancellor and Chief Justice, whose official titles, honorable as they were, appear almost insignificant when compared with the splendor of his fame as the author of the "Commentaries on American Law."

Notwithstanding the unfavorable conditions heretofore referred to, the revolutionary period found an active and able bar in the county. Foremost, of course, in point of official prominence, was George Clinton, a member—and the leader—of the patriotic minority of the Colonial Assembly; member of the Congress which adopted the Declaration of Independence, for which he votes, although his signature is not appended; Brigadier General in the Continental army; first Governor of the State; president of the State Convention which ratified the Federal constitution, and vice-president of the United States. For many years he was clerk of the county.

Associated with Governor Clinton, and ranking high among the lawyers and statesmen of the period, was Charles DeWitt, who, with Clinton, had, in the assembly, opposed the royalists, and supported the proposition to send delegates to Congress; who was chairman of the committee of safety, a member of the Provincial Convention; helped to draft the first State constitution, and subsequently sat in the Assembly of the State and in Congress.

It would not be possible within the limits of this paper to even enumerate all the worthy contemporaries of Clinton and DeWitt. Among the First Judges of the county were Dirck Wynkoop and Lucas Elmendorf. The former was a member of the Committee of Safety, of the Provincial Congress of 1775, of the Assembly in 1780-81, and the State Convention of 1788. The latter served in the Federal Congress from 1797 to 1803, and was particularly prominent in the profession.

John Addison was a leading lawyer of that day, who appears to have contented himself with the practice of his profession, without seeking political preferment. Conrad Edmund Elmendorf lived and practiced at the same time and was one of the prosecuting officers who were then known as Assistants Attorney General, appointed for a district made up of several counties. A relic of the system survives in the title of the officer whom we call District Attorney. Berent Gardinier, who served in the tenth and eleventh congresses, and who had much reputation for eloquence, conducted a long and bitter newspaper controversy with Gen. John Armstrong, Secretary of War, Gardinier claiming that Gen. Armstrong was and had confessed to being the author of the "New Burgh army letters."

Note that when the lines were drawn and the issue was made up, almost every Ulster County lawyer of position was found on the side of the colonies. There was hardly a Tory upon the roll.* These lawyers of the Revolution were versed in the lore of the common law. They had imbibed the learning of Coke and the Whig jurists of the mother country. They knew the importance of eternal vigilance; that seemingly slight departures from correct principles of government are dangerous; that the exercise of the power of taxation without the consent of the representatives of the taxed spells despotism. They were aware that the guarantees of freedom, imbedded in the great charter and soon to be re-enacted in the bills of

* Conspicuous, however, as an exception was Cadwallader Colden, Jr., the presiding judge of the last court held within the county whose writs ran in the name of George the Third. He was arrested at the instance of Governor Clinton and confined within his own county jail, but was soon released on parol. Levi Pawling was appointed to his place by an ordinance of the Provincial Convention. Judge Pawling was the first citizen of the county who sat in the State Senate.

Reuben Bernard.

rights, were absolutely essential to the preservation of the liberties of the people. They saw such guarantees threatened by the action of the king and his parliament; and they unhesitatingly risked their lives and fortunes in defense of the great principles which have kept us free.

The laity followed willingly the leadership of the bar. Indeed, there was never much love for the British throne or loyalty towards its occupants among the descendants of the early settlers. Naturally enough, Dutch William, for a time, was popular in Ulster; but the enthusiasm which he evoked was never extended to his stupid though respectable sister-in-law, nor to the equally stupid and generally less respectable heirs of the body of the Electress Sophia. From the standpoint of an English Officer, General Vaughan wrote truth when he characterized Esopus as "a nursery for almost every villain in the country."

Between the lawyers of revolutionary times and those who belong properly to the latter half of the nineteenth century stretched an unbroken line containing many names of good repute. Abraham Bruyn Hasbrouck was Representative in Congress in 1826 and 1827, and President of Rutgers College from 1840 to 1850. Charles H. Ruggles was in the State Assembly in 1820, and was afterwards Vice Chancellor, Circuit Judge and Judge of the Court of Appeals under the Constitution of 1846. John Sudam attained great eminence professionally and served with equal distinction in the State Senate. Charles G. DeWitt represented the district in Congress in 1830-31, and was *charge d'affaires* of the United States in Central America from 1833 to 1839. As a writer on political questions he was known throughout the country. Herman M. Romeyn, whose reputation as an advocate has never been surpassed by any member of the Ulster County Bar, held no office, except in 1836, when he sat in the Assembly, and in 1840, when he was a member of the Electoral College and its messenger to Washington. John Van Buren was a member of Assembly in 1831 and of Congress in 1842-43. John Cole was the leading lawyer of Southern Ulster.

Connected somewhat with these names, and reaching over among those that follow, was William B. Wright who, having with signal ability represented Sullivan County, of which he was then a resident, in the Constitutional Convention of 1846, was elected, in 1847, to the Supreme Court. He removed to Kingston in 1852 and was twice re-elected to the Supreme bench. In 1861 he was promoted by the people to the Court of Appeals, of which he became chief judge. His powerful mind and massive common sense are best evidenced by his many opinions while a member of the court of last resort.

Marius Schoonmaker was State Senator in 1850-51; Representative in the Thirty-second Congress; auditor of the Canal Department in 1854; Superintendent of the Bank Department in 1855; and a member of the Constitutional Convention of 1867. He also held office for many years in the old village of Kingston. In 1888, at the age of seventy-seven, he published his history of Kingston, which is, and will doubtless ever remain, the standard work on the subject. Mr. Schoonmaker was a lawyer of the old school, particularly well versed in the law of real property and inclined strongly to equity as against purely legal remedies.

John B. Steele sat in the Thirty-seventh and Thirty-eighth Congresses as the Representative of the Eleventh New York district, of which Ulster County was a part. He was a strong man at the trial bar, of great personal popularity and high character. His temperament, however, led him to prefer a political life, even in times of stress and peril, to a career at the bar.

Erastus Cooke was one of the leaders of the bar while in Kingston, and subsequently served on the bench of the Supreme Court in the Second District.

Severyn Bruyn, Charles R. Westbrook, Nicholas Sickles, County Judges James O. Linderman, Henry Brodhead, Jr., Gabriel W. Ludlum and James C. Forsyth belong to the same era. With them should be mentioned Egbert Whitaker, who, surviving many younger men, lived almost to the time these lines were written.

This was the golden age of the village lawyer. His income would appear small to-day. The majority of his cases involved trifling amounts and they were not great in number. But he had a code of professional ethics, adherence to which was to be preferred to riches. He was a gentleman at heart and in conduct; he had the respect and confidence of his neighbors; he tried patiently to keep people out of trouble instead of enticing them in; when important questions divided opinion and agitated the public, his judgment was asked and freely given, and it exerted an influence unequalled by pulpit or press.

As the nineteenth century approached its last quarter, the bar which assembled in Kingston at the sound of the Court House bell, preserved

Hector Sears.

well the traditions of the past and added to the reputation of the fraternity. In what follows, the mention of certain names which became prominent in civil life is not to be taken to the disparagement of others, perforce omitted. The law of the survival of the fittest holds good not always among lawyers' reputations. The soundest reasoner, the strongest advocate, is by no means, necessarily, the most successful politician. But the memory of those who have served the State is best preserved and the limitations of space are inexorable.

Theodoric R. Westbrook was chosen to Congress in 1852 and to the bench of the Supreme Court in 1873; he remained a judge of that court until his death in 1885. When at the bar he had a very extensive experience in the trial of cases—a branch of the profession in which he took delight. His trial practice made him a ready judge. His command of English was remarkable, and his charges to juries were models of diction. He was a man of kind heart, of quick perception and of indefatigable industry.

Jacob Hardenbergh was a delegate to the Constitutional Convention of 1867 and a member of the State Senate in 1870, 1871 and 1872. In both bodies he took high rank. At the bar he was noted for the almost unerring skill with which he selected the strong central point of the case, about which to make his fight, leaving minor issues and complications to take care of themselves. It was, perhaps, not too much to say of him, as has been said, that he "was for several years the most conspicuous and popular citizen of Ulster County."

William S. Kenyon represented Ulster and Greene counties in the exciting Thirty-sixth Congress, which sat for the two years preceding the Civil War. From 1884 to 1899 he was County Judge. He was a courtly gentleman, reminiscent of an older school than ours. His integrity was of the highest order, and his knowledge of the science of law was profound. For many years in the latter part of his life he confined his professional activities mainly to office practice.

Augustus Schoonmaker filled the office of County Judge from 1863 to 1871; that of State Senator in 1876-77; Attorney General in 1878-79; State Civil Service Commissioner from 1883 to 1887, and member of the Federal Interstate Commerce Commission thereafter until 1891. His long public service attests the contemporary estimate of his character and ability. He had a large practice, particularly in litigated cases, and his great strength with a jury of the county was equalled only by his standing in the appellate courts.

George H. Sharpe engaged but little in the active practice of the profession after the outbreak of the Civil War. He was the Colonel of the 120th Regiment, N. Y. S. V., and brevetted Brigadier and Major General. He was afterwards, successively, Special Agent of the State Department in Europe, Marshal for the Southern District of New York, and Surveyor of Customs at the Port of New York. He served in the Assembly in 1879, 1880, 1881 and 1882, being speaker in 1880 and 1881. General Sharpe enjoyed the personal friendship and confidence of at least two presidents of the United States, Generals Grant and Arthur.

William Lawton was County Judge from 1872 to 1883. Together with Seymour L. Stebbins, who was his partner, he had a large practice. Judge Lawton was a man of singularly even temper, judicial and fair to the tips of his fingers. He was no mean antagonist in the court room, and his absolute rectitude was axiomatic with his professional brethren.

The name of Seymour L. Stebbins falls naturally in line after that of his partner. They were associates in business for more than a quarter of a century. Mr. Stebbins held no office other than some of a local nature, but he was a lawyer of subtile mind and clear reasoning faculty, a wit of a high order, whose humor was pleasing and without malice; the master of a fine literary style and the possessor of much literary knowledge, and a companionable, agreeable and honorable man.

Frederick L. Westbrook was Special County Judge and District Attorney. He was best known, however, as counsel in litigated cases, in which capacity, either at *nisi prius* or in the Appellate Courts, he had few superiors anywhere. His professional experience was large. He was a man of noticeable presence. In addition to his multifarious and pressing business engagements he found time to interest himself in local matters of moment, notably in the cause of education.

Peter Cantine was Surrogate from 1872 to 1877. He had a very large practice, representing, perhaps, at one time, more important interests than any other member of the bar of the county. He possessed extraordinary capacity for labor, was never satisfied until he had probed the subject under consideration to the very depths, and he was considered by every other leader of the bar as a dangerous and honorable antagonist.

Charles A. Fowler was elected Surrogate in 1867 and State Senator in

Charles W. Walton.

1879. He served in the legislature with distinguished ability. As a lawyer he was noted for his grasp of legal principles and his remarkable command of apt language in argument. An address of his to a jury or a court, even a speech from the hustings, would have required no revision for publication. He was a genial companion and a kindly man.

William Lounsbery represented the first district of the county in the Assembly of 1868; in 1878-79 he was Mayor of the City of Kingston, and in 1879-80 Representative in Congress. In both the Legislature and in Congress—taking into consideration the fact that he served but a single term in each—he occupied very prominent positions. He wrote with much ability, contributed frequent articles to the press, including occasional poems of considerable merit. He possessed unusual powers of condensation, and his legal papers present in that respect a sharp contrast to the precedents of the olden time.

John E. Van Etten was a lawyer of large practice who held no office. In his leisure moments he relieved the professional strain by oversight of his farms, of which he possessed several, and by versification—an art of which he was fond. He was a man of great industry and he had many devoted clients.

A sketch of the bench and bar of Ulster compressed within the limits required by a work of this character, must necessarily be desultory and incomplete. The writer has tried to forestall two kinds of criticism; the one that his paper is a panegyric, imaginative, rhetorical; the other that it is a brief biographical dictionary of the dry-as-dust order. He has preferred the middle way. Whether he has succeeded is for others to decide. Reference to specific professional work has been manifestly impossible. To even allude to the important questions which have been determined by the court of last resort in cases originating in the county would require a paper as long as this. To catalogue and comment on the interesting causes which have been tried within the walls of Kingston Court House would fill a volume. It has seemed imperative, too, that all reference to persons now living be omitted. Let those who follow us write a supplement if they will; and may the Judge of judges grant that the successors of the giants of the past prove worthy of their professional heritage.

The panorama is a long one. The figures upon the canvas are sometimes blurred; again, they appear in full relief. As one contemplates the prodigious amount of work accomplished by those who have gone before, and contrasts it with the rewards which have accrued to the laborers, it seems, perchance, their message may be this:

"Do what thy manhood bids thee do; from none but self expect applause;
He noblest lives and noblest dies who makes and keeps his self-made laws;
All other life is living death, a world where none but phantoms dwell,
A breath, a wind, a sound, a voice, a tinkling of the camel bell."

H. van Hoevenberg M.D.

CHAPTER XLII.

THE MEDICAL PROFESSION.

By Henry Van Hoevenberg, M.D.

AT the time of the settlement of Ulster County in the early part of the seventeenth century, the profession of medicine was in a condition which, to this age, seems that of the Dark Ages, for the members of the profession were just beginning clinical observation and study. The books in use were, many of them, of no value so far as giving the physician any actual aid in the treatment of disease. The works of Hippocrates, who wrote in the second century before Christ, and Galen, seven centuries later, were still the standard authorities. The armamentarium of that day consisted of simples and compounds with the addition of mineral preparations in a crude form. These were administered in powders, pills and decoctions, or applied locally as ointments, plasters or linaments. The time for gathering the herbs, of which many remedies were composed, was regulated by the phases of the moon or conjunctions of the planets. Above all was the lancet, and on it the physician placed the most reliance in his efforts to overcome ailments. Practically nothing was known of the cause of disease, and its treatment was almost entirely empirical.

The earlier physicians who practiced physic and surgery in the colonies, received their degree in medicine from the Universities of Europe, but as time passed, laws were enacted providing for the licensing of persons to practice physic or surgery, or both, after having passed an examination as to their qualifications. This condition was necessary by the fact that there were no medical schools in this country. The first medical school was founded in 1765 in Philadelphia and was followed in 1768 by the organization of a medical department in Kings College, now Columbia University, in New York City, and to the latter belongs the honor of conferring the first degree of Doctor of Medicine in this country. The seventeenth century doctors, while not the equals of the physicians of the present day in qualifications and training for their professional duties. were very much in advance of those of the previous century, and included in their ranks many men of marked ability. The physician was the guide, counsellor and friend of all his neighbors, wielding an influence second only, if at all, to that of the pastor of the church. This caused him to be frequently called upon to perform public duties other than those arising from his profession, and he was consequently one of the most potent factors in the political as well as the social life of the community.

As the result of conferences between members of the medical profession in Saratoga County held in the latter part of the eighteenth and early part of the nineteenth centuries, it was decided to ask for the passage of an Act to regulate admission to the practice of medicine in this State, by the establishment of a State Medical Society, which was to be composed of representatives of the profession in the different counties, this body to have the power to grant or refuse licenses to practice medicine. This resulted in the passage, on April 4th, 1806, of "an Act to Incorporate Medical Societies for the Purpose of Regulating the Practice of Physic and Surgery in the State." This Act directed how the societies in the counties should be formed and that one representative from each society should meet in the city of Albany on the first Tuesday of February following and there organize the Medical Society of the State.

In accordance with the provisions of this Act, meetings were held and the organization of both County and State Societies effected, the centennial of which event has this year been celebrated by the Medical Society of the County of Ulster with appropriate ceremonies.

The meeting of the physicians of Ulster County was called for July 1st, 1806, at the Court House in the village of Kingston, and the original record book of the Medical Society of the County of Ulster is now on file in the office of the County Clerk at Kingston. The first entry is a copy of the Act of April 4th, 1806, giving detailed directions as to where, when and how the organization should be effected; then follow amendments to the law made in 1807 and 1813. The following extract is taken from the minutes of the first meeting:

"KINGSTON, ULSTER COUNTY, July 1st, 1806.

In pursuance of an Act of the Legislature of the State of New York entitled "an Act to incorporate Medical Societies for the purpose of regulating the practice of Physic and Surgery in said State," passed April 4th, 1806, Thirteen Physicians and Surgeons, To Wit, James Oliver, Luke Kiersted, Benj. R. Bevier, James Houghtaling, Peter Vanderlyn, Andrew Snyder, James J. Hasbrouck, John Bakeman, Conrad Newkirk, Abraham Fieroe, Jr., Ezekiel Webb, George W. Bancker, and Abraham T. E. DeWitt, all of whom, now authorized by law to practice in their several professions, convened, ("pursuant to adjournment from the Court-house where the last term of the Court of Common Pleas, next previous to such meeting was last held,") at the house of Cornelius C. Elmendorf in the village of Kingston, Ulster County, on Tuesday, the first day of July, in the year of our Lord one thousand eight hundred and six and made choice of the following officers, To Wit—James Oliver, President, Luke Kiersted, Vice President, Benjamin R. Bevier, Secretary, and James Houghtaling, Treasurer, as proper for the conduct and regulation of the Medical Society of the County of Ulster, now hereby established, to continue in office for the term of one year and until others are chosen in their Place.

Resolved that this Society will proceed to the Election of three proper Persons as Censors to said Society and one other proper Person to represent Said Society in the Medical Society of the State of New York."

Drs. Abraham T. E. DeWitt, Benj. R. Bevier and Peter Vanderlyn were chosen Censors, and Dr. James G. Graham, representative to the State Society. The dues of members were fixed at fifty cents, and a committee, consisting of Drs. James Oliver, Luke Kiersted and Benjamin R. Bevier, was appointed, "to prepare and report to this Society at the next meeting thereof, a suitable code, or form of rules and regulations for the further conduct of the same."

The Society was soon called upon to take an active part in State Medicine, as is shown by the following communication received at its second meeting, held September 2d, 1806, which was referred to a committee and a reply drafted by them was adopted unanimously:

"KINGSTON, September 2d, 1806.

Gentlemen,—

The Village of Kingston is at present afflicted very generally with a Bilious Fever. Many Persons have an opinion that the Cause exists in the Stagnant Waters in Mr. Benjamin Bogardus' Mill Pond, others entertain a different opinion, but do not attempt to assign any cause for it.—The ideas of so large and respectable a Body of Physicians as are now assembled in the Village, would be entitled to great weight, and we do therefor take the Liberty of earnestly entreating you to communicate to us Your Opinion upon this very serious and important Subject.

With much Respect, Gentlemen, Your Obedt. Servt.

In behalf of the Directors of the Village,

JOSEPH CHIPP,
Presdt.

To the Gentlemen composing
the Medical Society of the
County of Ulster."

REPLY.

"To the Directors of the Village of Kingston:—

Gentlemen,—

The Medical Society of the County of Ulster have, agreeable to your request, deliberately taken into Consideration the Communication Which You were pleased to present to us this day, as far as Time and opportunity would permit. They are of opinion that the noxious Exhalations arising from the Mill Pond and adjacent Sources of Filth annexed to your Village, in a great measure contribute to the Prevalence and progress of that Species of Fever Which is so severely experienced therein.

Time will not permit at present for us to give you that General Satisfaction on this Subject which its importance demands and which you are perhaps induced to desire. By Order of the Society,

B. R. Bevier, Sec'y."

At a meeting held on December 2d, 1806, the following resolution was passed:

"Resolved, That the Seal which is now suspended by the chain of the President's watch be the proper Seal of this Society until another one Shall be procured and admitted of."

Meetings of the Society were held, usually semi-annually, until 1833. Discussions on medical subjects took place at these meetings and the records show that an active part was taken by the members in the various matters affecting the public health. After 1837 no meetings were held until June 1st, 1858, when a call was issued for a meeting at the Court House in Kingston. The physicians present were Drs. Peter Crispell, Jr., John Wales, Josiah Hasbrouck, Barnett McClelland, E. M. Secor, Jacob Vreeland, Thomas J. Nelson, James Oliver Van Hoevenberg, Levi Lounsbery, Abram Crispell, Charles D. DeWitt, Edgar Elting, William B. Davis, Edmund Brink, Philip D. B. Hoornbeck.

The following were elected officers:

Peter Crispell, Jr., President; Barnett McClelland, Vice-President; Edgar Elting, Secretary; Levi Lounsbery, Corresponding Secretary; Charles D. DeWitt, Treasurer; Thomas J. Nelson, John Wales, Levi Lounsbery, James O. Van Hoevenberg and Josiah Hasbrouck, Censors; Abram Crispell, James O. Van Hoevenberg and Thomas J. Nelson, Delegates to the State Society.

The meetings of the Society were continued regularly until 1861. The war of 1861-5 caused a suspension of the meetings until 1864, when they were resumed and have been held regularly since that date.

In 1901 the Ulster County Medical Association, in affiliation with the New York State Medical Association, organized and continued until 1906, when the two State organizations were consolidated under the name of the Medical Society of the State of New York. Quarterly meetings were held regularly and the scientific program was a feature of each.

The roll of membership in the medical profession of Ulster County contains the names of many who ranked high as physicians and surgeons; whose names are to be found in the public records not only of the County, but of the State, as giving freely their services to their country. It was not an unusual thing to find physicians in several generations of a family,

Josiah Hasbrouck M.D.

notably the Kiersteds, Olivers, Crispells, DeWitts, Van Hoevenbergs, Hasbroucks and others, and many of them attained prominence in other branches of public activity.

It is in times of distress and danger, and when men are in mortal agony and suffering from wounds or disease, that the services of a physician are in greatest demand, and well did the physicians and surgeons of Ulster County live up to the high calling of their profession in the troublous times of the Civil War. Alike in the hospitals at home attending the wounded and invalid, in the sanitary departments of the great armies and at the front on the fighting line, incurring the risks of battle and relieving the agonies of those who had fallen beneath the shot and shell of the enemy, the physician could be found with his message of comfort and aid to the afflicted. Ulster County was well represented at the front, among others, by Dr. Joseph D. Keyser, who enlisted while a medical student as hospital steward in the 120th N. Y. Volunteers, was taken prisoner early in his service and after a long imprisonment was exchanged. At the close of the war he resumed his studies and was admitted to the practice of medicine. He died at the age of thirty-five, a victim to disabilities contracted in the service.

In the latter part of the nineteenth century several efforts were made to organize a hospital in Kingston, but they were not successful until July, 1893, when the City of Kingston Hospital was incorporated. Funds for building were raised by subscription, and on November 27th, 1894, the hospital was opened for the reception of patients, since which time it has been in successful operation and proved a boon to the sick and injured, not only of the city of Kingston, but of the surrounding country, receiving patients from the adjoining counties in addition to those from Ulster.

At the time of its organization the Board of Managers was as follows: Dr. George C. Smith, President; Rev. Dr. R. L. Burtsell, Vice-President; William M. Hayes, Secretary; Dr. Jacob Chambers, Treasurer; Messrs. John E. Kraft, P. J. Flynn, James A. Betts, John McEntee and Frederick J. R. Clarke. Previous to the formal opening these physicians of the city were selected by the Board of Managers to compose the medical staff: Surgeons, Drs. Henry Van Hoevenberg, Secretary of Staff; Jacob Chambers, Charles W. Crispell, Charles A. Munn, Alexander A. Stern and James L. Preston. Physicians, Drs. Elbert H. Loughran, A. H.

Mambert, Daniel Connolly, R. R. Thompson, E. E. Norwood, Eugene J. Gallagher, C. F. Keefe, A. P. Chalker, William M. Decker.

The following sketches of some of the more prominent physicians of the past are taken from the files of the Medical Society of Ulster County and various public records of the county, as well as private biographies.

Dr. Gysbert Van Imbroch.—The first physician and surgeon of whom there is any record in the Esopus was Dr. Gysbert Van Imbroch. Governor Stuyvesant, having recognized the necessity for a physician in the new settlement, had induced him to come from New Amsterdam and settle here. Dr. Van Imbroch was prominent in the civil affairs of Esopus and his name appears frequently in the records of his time. He served as Schepen, or Justice, from 1663 to 1665, and was one of the delegates from the Esopus to the first representative body in New Netherlands, which met in New Amsterdam in 1664. He married, before coming here, Rachel, daughter of Dr. Johannes de la Montagne, a prominent physician of New Amsterdam and also Vice-Director under Governor Stuyvesant. She was taken captive by the Indians in 1663 at the burning of Wiltwyck, but escaped sometime afterward and died in October, 1664, soon after the birth of her last child.

Dr. Van Imbroch died on the 29th of August, 1665, less than one year after the death of his wife, leaving three minor children, Lysbert, born 1659; Johannes, born 1661, and Gysbert, born August 24th, 1664, for whom guardians were appointed. An inventory of the estate filed in the Schouts Court shows that his medical library consisted of fourteen volumes, viz.: Folios—Medicine Book of Christopher Wirtungh; Medicine Book of Ambrocius Paree; Medicine Book of Johannes de Vega; a Vessaly and Valuerda Anatomy. Quartos—Bernard van Zutphen, Practice; a German work on Medicine; three written medicine books; Medical Remarks by Nicholæs Tulp; German Medical Manual by Q. Apollinare; Examination of Surgery by Mr. Cornelis Herbs, a written medicine and Sudent Book; a book on surgery without a title.

This list shows that, for his day, he was a man well read in the literature of his profession.

Benjamin Helm was one of the earliest and most distinguished physicians and surgeons who practiced in Ulster. Educated in Holland, a follower of Boerhaave, and a firm believer in the great law that Nature had provided in each locality a specific for the diseases peculiarly incident to the place, he devoted much attention to the curative properties of herbs, roots and barks. He was much interested in the knowledge of their medicinal qualities possessed by the North American Indians, and after submitting the vegetable remedies known to them to many tests, he came to the conclusion that the Indians had a far more accurate and comprehensive knowledge of the effect of simple remedies upon the human system than did many civilized people. He embodied the results of his observations and experiments in a paper which he transmitted to the Guild of the Physicians of Holland, by whom it was printed and distributed among the medical schools of that country. Dr. Helm was a surgeon in the Continental Army, and was the medical attendant and personal friend of Washington during the latter's residence in the City of New York. He married a daughter of Abraham Klaarwater, of Bontecoe, first meeting his wife at Tarrytown, where she was visiting a relative who had married one of the VanTasells of Westchester. After the close of the Revolution he came to Kingston, frequently visiting Bontecoe and the neighborhood thereabouts. He died in the City of New York, where he owned a large amount of valuable property.

James Oliver, First, resided in Marbletown, Ulster County. Born in 1745, died 1826. Married Margaret, daughter of Matthew Newkirk. Was surgeon of an Ulster County regiment in the War of the Revolution, and was at the battle of Saratoga. Appointed Judge of the County Court, 1800. He was the first President of the Medical Society of Ulster County from its organization in 1806 to 1809. He had an extensive practice over the county and was a well-known and able physician. His son,

James Oliver, Second, was born December 24th, 1806, died October 12th, 1893. Married Gitty, daughter of Cornelius C. Cole and lived in Marbletown. He combined the life of a farmer with the practice of medicine.

Dr. Hans Kiersted, born June 17th, 1677. Godfather, Peter Bayard; godmother, Blandina Kiersted. He married Arrantje Tappen on November 19th, 1701, and died April 6th, 1737. He was famous for his knowledge of the Indian dialects. It is recorded of him that upon being addressed in Latin by a learned doctor in the course of a consultation, he replied in the Indian tongue. He practiced in Kingston, living either in Wall or Green street. His son, Dr. Christopher Kiersted, married Catherine DeMyer, and died in Rhinebeck in consequence of a fall from his horse while visiting his son, Dr. Hans Kiersted. This Dr. Hans Kiersted married Janetje Hoffman, daughter of Anthony Hoffman of Kingston. He had been educated in Kingston, but afterward settled in Dutchess County. Major Van Gaasbeek visited him in Rhinebeck and describes him as "a large, portly man, six feet high, broad shouldered and good looking, with light hair, blue eyes, and a benevolent countenance." He was born May 10th, 1743, died Sept. 29, 1811. Jane Hoffman, consort of Dr. Kiersted, was born in Kingston also, April 10, 1743, died, Jan. 18, 1808. They had but one child, Sally, born July 14th, 1773.

Dr. Henry Van Hoevenberg was born at Staatsburg, Dutchess County, N. Y., November 3d, 1790, and died in Kingston, July 29th, 1868, aged seventy-eight years. His youth was spent on his father's farm, having but a short time yearly to attend the common school. Slight as were his opportunities, they created a desire for a more liberal education and, after some months in the Academy at Ellsworth, Conn., he entered upon the study of medicine in 1810 with Dr. Joshua E. R. Birch in the City of New York. In 1811-12 he attended a course of medical lectures in the City of Philadelphia, obtained his diploma in 1812, and immediately entered the army of the United States as Assistant Surgeon of the Thirteenth Regiment of U. S. Infantry, commanded by Col. Peter B. Schuyler, and was ordered to the Niagara Frontier, where, after the battle of Queenstown, he organized the first military hospital. He continued in charge until the general hospital was removed to Buffalo, and at this post acted as Assistant Hospital Surgeon. Here he was obliged to resign his commission in the spring of 1814 because of ill-health. During his term of service in the army, in 1813, he married Jane Catherine Heermance, eldest daughter of General Martin Heermance of Rhinebeck, Dutchess County. His health improving, he shipped as surgeon on board the privateer *Whig*, commanded by Captain Clark, and served until the close of the war, when he settled in Marbletown in the County of Ulster. He remained there until July, 1817, when he removed to Kingston, where he continued until 1827, when he moved to New York. During his residence in the County of Ulster he was a member of, and held several offices in, the Ulster County Medical Society.

In 1835 he was appointed, by the Common Council of New York City, Resident Physician of Bellevue Hospital, Supervisor of the Alms House,

Abraham Crispell, M.D.

Penitentiary, Bridewell's, etc. In 1838 he was appointed Deputy Health Officer of the Port of New York, and in 1843 was appointed Health Officer of the Port, which office he held until 1848. This closed his professional career, and after eight years' residence on Staten Island, he returned to Kingston and lived a retired life until his death. During his whole life he maintained a high standard, both professionally and as a citizen. He attained high rank as a physician and surgeon, always giving thorough satisfaction in the discharge of his duties, both as a public official and private practitioner, in the latter capacity being much in demand in consultation. One daughter and three sons survived him, one of the sons, James Oliver Van Hoevenberg, being a prominent physician of Kingston at the time of his father's death.

Dr. James Oliver Van Hoevenberg, son of Dr. Henry Van Hoevenberg, was born in Kingston, July 16th, 1821. He received a common school education and at the age of nineteen decided to enter the profession of medicine. He thus followed in the footsteps, not only of his father, but of a long line of ancestors, being descended through his maternal grandmother from Dr. Hans Kiersted, who came to New Amsterdam in 1638 as surgeon to the Dutch West India Company, and was the first physician to practice medicine in New Amsterdam, and whose descendants for the next four generations were also physicians and surgeons. After preliminary studies with a physician, as was the custom in those days, he received his degree of Doctor of Medicine from the New York University in 1844. After graduation he served on the staff of Bellevue and Blackwell's Island Hospitals in the City of New York. He was then appointed Deputy Health Officer of the Port of New York and was stationed at the Quarantine on Staten Island. In 1846 he received his commission as Assistant Surgeon of New York Volunteers under Col. J. D. Stevenson. After leaving the Quarantine he practiced his profession on Staten Island until 1856, when he came to Kingston, where he remained until 1877. In 1857 he was commissioned Surgeon of the 20th N. Y. State Militia, and in 1862 went to the Civil War as Surgeon of the 120th N. Y. Volunteers (one of the three hundred fighting regiments), with the rank of Major. Being compelled to resign his commission on account of disabilities contracted in the service, he returned to Kingston and practiced there until 1877, when he was appointed Physician at Sing Sing State Prison. Upon leaving this office he returned to Staten Island and practiced his profession until his death, December 7th, 1897. He married, June 14th, 1849, his cousin Esther Maria, daughter of Colonel James Dumond Van Hoevenberg and Alma Rogers. They had three daughters and two sons, one of the latter, Henry, becoming a physician, and the other, James Dumond, a lawyer.

Dr. Van Hoevenberg became one of the most prominent physicians and surgeons of this part of the State, his practice extending throughout Ulster and the adjoining counties, and his services and advice were sought by both professional brethren and laymen. He was a man of wide reading and general education, having a splendid mind with the poetical temperament, and was a great lover of nature. He held no political office, though always active in any movement for bettering the affairs of the community in which he lived. He was an active member of the State and County Societies, and was frequently called upon to serve them in official capacities.

Dr. Peter Crispell, Jr., was born in August, 1794, at Hurley, Ulster County. His great-grandfather, Anthony Crispell, a Huguenot, came from Artois, France, 1660, and was one of the original patentees of New Paltz. His great-grandmother, Maria Blanshan, was sister-in-law of Louis Bevier, the leader of the New Paltz immigrants, and also a patentee. Peter Crispell was in succession student, tutor and trustee of the Kingston Academy. He attended medical lectures in New York City and was licensed by the Medical Society of Ulster County. He practiced a short time in Esopus, then went to Marbletown until 1837, when he moved to his farm on the Hurley Flats and continued to practice until his death in December, 1878. He enjoyed a large practice, which extended over a great portion of the county. He was also a successful farmer, at one time being awarded a prize for having the best conducted farm in the State.

In 1849 he was a Member of Assembly and was afterward nominated for Congress, but defeated. He was Presidential Elector in 1828, and was a delegate to the National Convention in Chicago which nominated Abraham Lincoln for the Presidency. He married Catherine, daughter of Cornelius Eltinge of Hurley, by whom he had one daughter and five sons, two of whom were professional men, Abraham Crispell, M. D., of Kingston, and Cornelius Elting Crispell, D. D., who became a Professor in Rutgers College, N. J., and afterwards in Hope College, Michigan.

Dr. Abraham Crispell, son of Dr. Peter Crispell, Jr., was born in Marbletown June 22d, 1823, and died in Kingston November 4th, 1881. He was educated in Kingston Academy and Peekskill (N. Y.) Academy, now Peekskill Military Academy. He then began the study of medicine, attending first the Berkshire Medical College at Pittsfield, Mass., and graduated from the University of the City of New York in 1849. He came at once to Kingston, where he attained high rank among the physicians of his time. He enjoyed a large practice throughout the county and was frequently called upon in consultation. At the beginning of the Civil War he was appointed Surgeon of the 20th N. Y. State Militia, and was with them through the three months' service. He was appointed Brigade-Surgeon of Volunteers on April 4th, 1862, by President Lincoln and was stationed at various points in the South. He acted as Health Officer at Hilton Head, S. C., for some time, and was afterward in charge of a large hospital at Buffalo, N. Y.

At the close of the war he resumed practice in Kingston, where he died while still active in his profession. He was an active member of both the State and County Societies and several times served as Health Officer of the city. Although he took a prominent part in the politics of the county, he never held public office outside the profession. His first wife was Adeline Barber of Roxbury, Delaware County, N. Y., who left two children, one of them, Kate A., having married Dr. George C. Smith of Kingston. His second wife was Jane Ann Catlin, by whom he had three children, two of whom, Harry S. and Dr. Charles W. Crispell, are still living.

Richard Elting, M. D., was a descendant of Rollif Elting, who came from Holland and settled at Wiltwyck early in the seventeenth century. He was the son of Josiah Elting and Hester Brodhead, born at New Paltz, May 8th, 1795. He received a common school education and when a young man came to Kingston and commenced the study of medicine with Dr. Henry Van Hoevenberg, an eminent physician of that place. He later attended medical lectures in New York City, and began practice in the town of Esopus, residing near Port Ewen until 1859. From there he removed to Rondout, where he practiced until shortly before his death on October 28th, 1878. His practice extended over a large section of country and he became familiarly known to all as "Dr. Dick Elting." His professional skill gave him an extended reputation and his aid was sought by his professional brethren as well as laymen. He was a man of decided characteristics, being very positive in his likes and dislikes. In March, 1818, he married Elizabeth, daughter of Hon. Abraham Hasbrouck, of Kingston, by whom he had four daughters.

Dr. George Clark Smith was born at Salem, Rockingham County, New Hampshire, August 2d, 1833; died in Kingston, April 14th, 1893. He graduated from Oliver High School, Lawrence, Mass., 1852, and then prepared to enter Amherst College. He abandoned this intention, however, and began the study of medicine at the University of the City of New York, and in 1862 came to Kingston to practice. In August, 1862, he was appointed Assistant Surgeon of the 156th New York Volunteer Infantry, and in January, 1864, was promoted to Surgeon. He served until the close of the war in 1865 and then resumed the practice of medicine in Kingston. He became one of the best known and respected physicians and surgeons of his day, being noted for his rugged honesty and great kindness of heart. His fellow-practitioners were always pleased to meet him in consultation, knowing that they would be treated courteously and would receive the best advice his large experience and knowledge could give. He was the first President of the Board of Managers of the City of Kingston Hospital, but did not live to see the consummation of his hopes and labors in the completion of the hospital, dying only a few days before the laying of the cornerstone. He took an active interest in the public affairs of the city and served in the Board of Supervisors. He was an active member of both the State and County Medical Societies.

In 1873 he married Kate A., daughter of Dr. Abraham Crispell of Kingston, and left three children.

Dr. Robert Loughran was born in Hancock, Delaware County, New York, August 30th, 1834, of Scotch parentage and received a common school education. He studied medicine with Drs. A. B. and W. C. DeWitt of Saugerties, N. Y., and graduated from the Albany Medical College in 1857. He was elected to the Assembly in 1860 and at the opening of the Civil War was appointed Assistant Surgeon of the 20th N. Y. State Militia (one of the three hundred fighting regiments), commanded by Col. George W. Pratt. After the expiration of their three months' service, the regiment was reorganized for three years' service, Dr. Loughran being appointed Surgeon. He served until the close of the war, part of the time being in charge of the Military General Hospital at City Point,

F. W. Ingalls, M.D.

Va. At the end of the war, after being breveted Lieutenant-Colonel for meritorius service, he returned to Kingston and resumed the practice of his profession, becoming one of the most prominent physicians and surgeons of his time. He died in Kingston April 11th, 1899, at the age of sixty-four years, having faithfully served his city and county as Member of Assembly, Supervisor, Health Officer and Alderman, and noted for his honesty and fearlessness in upholding what he considered the best interests of his constituents. He was a member of the First Class of the Legion of Honor of the Grand Army of the Republic, Surgeon of the Fifth Division, N. G. S. N. Y., and member of the Medical Societies of the State and County.

His first wife was Mary, daughter of Edwin W. Budington, who died one year later, leaving no children. His second wife was Helen, daughter of Christopher L. Kiersted, by whom he had five children, one daughter and four sons, two of the latter becoming professional men, Robert L. studying medicine and Christopher K. law.

Dr. Jacob Chambers, born in Marbletown, February 6th, 1852, was a son of Dr. George Chambers, who for many years was a prominent physician of that part of the county. He graduated from Monticello (N. Y.) Academy in 1869, and afterwards attended Phillips Academy at Andover, Mass., and Fort Edward (N. Y.) Institute. He studied medicine and graduated from the University of Buffalo, 1875, practiced in Marbletown until 1882, when he removed to Kingston, where he resided until his death, September 16th, 1904. He served the city as Health Officer and was also a member of the first Board of Police Commissioners. He took an active part in organizing the City of Kingston Hospital, was a member of the Board of Managers and of the Medical Staff. He was affiliated with the Medical Society of the County of Ulster, and had served it in various official positions. Dr. Chambers was one of the best known physicians of the county and was frequently called in consultation.

He married Florence, daughter of Ex-Sheriff John W. Kerr, by whom he had two children; one daughter died in infancy, and one son, Donald, survived him.

CHAPTER XLIII.

THE NEWSPAPERS OF ULSTER.

By Jay E. Klock.

IN these days when a man starts a newspaper, he asserts in his "salutatory," and sometimes really believes, that he is responding to a popular demand. This was not the case, however, with John Holt, the pioneer editor of Ulster County. He had no illusions and was aware that the people cared not a farthing whether he came here or not. Newspapers were not a necessity at a time when it was impossible to gather news promptly and when most men relied upon the Bible and commentaries thereon for their mental guidance. Holt was a native of Virginia. He thought in his youth that a business career would suit him, but changed his mind after going to smash in venture after venture. At length he drifted into journalism, beginning in 1766 the publication of the *New York Journal and General Advertiser* in the city of New York. He seems to have prospered, for he continued the paper in the Metropolis for more than a decade. In 1774 he came out boldly as an uncompromising patriot and removed the king's arms from the heading of his paper. Consequently, when the British took possession of New York, it became unhealthy there for Holt. First he fled to Fishkill, and later to Kingston, where he resumed the publication of his paper under the same name on July 7, 1777. At that time Kingston was the third town in the State in population, wealth and importance, yet it consisted of not more than 300 buildings, of which only about one-third were dwelling houses. The telegraph, the telephone and the railroad were undreamed of. The coming of the steamboat was a generation in the future. Half a generation must elapse before the establishment of a stage line between New York and Albany. Considering everything, the prospect of making a success of the enterprise was poor. Holt admitted editorially that the sheet was not of much account and explained that as yet he had had no opportunity to place himself in communication with public officers throughout the country. He urged his countrymen who heard of anything interest-

Eng by E. G. Williams & Bro. N.Y.

Jay E. Klock.

ing to send him word. The contents of the paper were literary and political, and there is a poem upon the erection of the printing press. Mr. Holt could afford to burst into song in spite of circumstances which would have discouraged a modern printer. He had a contract to do the State printing for the government, lately located in Kingston, and the very highest price charged for board was twenty shillings a week. The State printing was a good thing, since as many as 500 copies of important public documents were occasionally ordered. Holt continued his business until the following October, when Kingston was burned, and he removed to Poughkeepsie.

PROGRESS IN NEWSPAPER MAKING.

Since that time, something like one hundred newspapers have existed in Ulster County. It is not the purpose of this article to enumerate them all. A large proportion of them died in their first year, and the mourners were few. Others merged and experienced changes in title. It is sufficient to sketch those which have strongly influenced the history of the county or which are now living. In order to understand the progress of local journalism, it is necessary to bear in mind a few general facts. Attention has been called already to the date of establishment of modern methods of transportation and communication. It was between 1830 and 1840 when cylinder presses were first used, before which time cumbersome modifications of the hand cider press were in vogue. The perfecting press of the style used to-day first became known to the general public at the Centennial Exposition in Philadelphia. It is only a quarter of a century since practical type-setting machines have been obtainable. It is obvious that before the invention of all these facilities the newspaper, in everything but editorial ability, was trivial in comparison with what it is to-day. There is scarcely a paper in Ulster County which does not surpass, in its budget of news, the great papers in the great cities a century ago.

THE GAZETTE.

For fifteen years after Holt's departure, Ulster County struggled along without a local newspaper. In 1792 one William Copp started the *Farmers' Register,* but soon abandoned it for lack of patronage. Shortly afterward, plucking up fresh courage, he secured Samuel Freer as a partner and began publishing the *Rising Star,* which very quickly turned into a falling star, and Copp drops out of the story. Freer was considered rich as fortunes went in those days, and he had an ambitious son, Samuel S. Freer, who was destined to be Ulster County's first editor of importance. In 1798, these two men founded the *Ulster County Gazette*, which continued until 1822. The elder Freer died a few years after the establishment of the paper, but the son carried on the enterprise until he had exhausted the family fortune, and retired to die in poverty. It is hardly necessary to remark that men did not enter the newspaper business in those days to make money. Their motives were a mixture of that strange vanity which yearns to see its thoughts in print, and of that nobler emotion which leads men to abandon hope of material prosperity in order to advocate the political and religious principles they hold dear. The *Gazette* was from first to last an organ of the Federal party. The younger Freer was one of the most vigorous writers of his day—so vigorous that he was fined upon one occasion for expressing his inmost sentiments regarding the Supreme Court. The first half of the week he spent in getting out his paper, and during the latter half he distributed it through Ulster and the adjoining counties, traveling on horseback and stopping wherever he had a chance to argue with anti-Federalists. In spite of his being so bellicose politically, he was extremely agreeable in business matters, as is shown by the fact that he delivered the out-of-town circulation of his rival, the *Plebeian*, along with his own, until both papers hired a post-rider in common. The issue of the *Gazette* containing the news of the death of George Washington was carefully preserved by the subscribers, and copies, or at least reproductions thereof, may be found in every State of the Union. No other issue of an Ulster County paper has been duplicated by a later generation.

THE PLEBEIAN AND ARGUS.

The second important county paper was the *Ulster Plebeian*, established in Kingston by Jesse Buell in 1802. It was anti-Federal in its politics, and was edited, almost if not quite, as ably as the *Gazette*. These two papers were small in size and poor in news, but have not been surpassed much by later journals in their editorial and literary features. In 1814 Buell, having left town and founded the *Albany Argus*, sold the paper to John Tappen, who conducted it until 1831, when he died. The paper changed hands many times during the succeeding years, its various owners being John J. Tappen, Alonzo P. Stewart, Rodney A. Chipp, Solomon S. Hommel and William Lounsbery. Meanwhile, the name of the paper had been changed twice—first to the *Ulster Republican*, and then to the *Kingston Argus*. On May 1, 1864, the *Argus* became the property of Henry G. Crouch, who conducted it until his death, August 6, 1905, when it passed into the hands of the Kingston Argus Company, of which Leonard C. Crouch is president, Oliver Van Steenburgh vice-president, and Walter Van Steenburgh secretary and treasurer. The *Argus* is to-day, as it has been always, an advocate of old-fashioned Democratic principles. Mr. Crouch had the distinction of occupying the same editorial chair longer than any other man in this region.

THE JOURNAL.

The next important paper to appear was the *Kingston Democratic Journal*, from which title the word "Democratic" was soon dropped. Its editor, William H. Romeyn, was a Whig, and afterward a Republican. In 1837 he came to Kingston and started the *Political Reformer*, and in 1840 bought the *Ulster Sentinel*, a paper which began in 1826, as a rival to the *Plebeian*, but which had recently come over to the Whig side. The two papers were consolidated and continued as the *Journal*. Mr. Romeyn was a strong political writer, of the same school as Messrs. Freer, Buell, Tappen, Hommel, Lounsbery and Crouch. He continued in the harness until 1878, when Charles Marseilles purchased his paper and consolidated it with the *Kingston Weekly Freeman*, which has since continued to be published under the title, *Kingston Weekly Freeman and Journal*.

THE FREEMAN.

In 1845 Daniel Bradbury and E. S. Wells started the *Rondout Freeman*. Bradbury sold out his interest to Robert Gosman in 1846. In 1847 J. P. Hageman bought the plant and changed its name to the *Rondout Courier*. Mr. Hageman conducted the paper until 1868, when he sold it to W. H. and J. C. Romeyn, who in turn sold it to Horatio Fowkes in 1877. In October of that year Mr. Fowkes commenced issuing a daily edition called the *Morning Courier*, but both editions were short lived. Meanwhile, in 1858, the name *Freeman* was revived by Van Keuren and Gildersleeve in a weekly paper at Rondout. In 1865 Horatio Fowkes bought the property and continued it until 1876, having added a daily edition in 1871—the *Kingston Daily Freeman*. In 1876 the Freeman Printing and Publishing Association, consisting of members of the business and editorial departments of the paper, secured control of the property and put in a double cylinder newspaper press with a capacity of about 3,500 impressions an hour, which was considered a great stroke of enterprise at that time. The Association, however, did not succeed financially, and soon turned the business over to Samuel D. Coykendall. The latter, in 1878, sold the business to Charles Marseilles, of Exeter, N. H., who also failed to achieve success, although he effected a consolidation with the *Kingston Journal*, as previously noted. Mr. Coykendall resumed the management of the *Freeman* in 1880, continuing until 1891, when he leased and later sold it to Jay E. Klock, who has since been the publisher. *The Freeman* became a member of the New York Associated Press in 1871, paying a fee of over $9,000, and has had its own leased telegraph wire ever since. The membership fee was over $9,000. In 1894 the paper purchased a Mergenthaler linotype, which does the work of five hand compositors. Since that time two other linotypes have been added. In 1896 a Web perfecting press was added, which uses stereotyped forms and prints and folds an eight-page, seven-column newspaper at the rate of 200 copies per minute. The *Freeman* has developed an extensive job printing business and has about fifty persons on its payroll. It has been the official paper of the city and county for more than a generation. Its politics are and have been consistently Republican. Its weekly edition, as already noted, is called the *Kingston Weekly Freeman and Journal.*

THE KINGSTON LEADER.

The first issue of the *Kingston Daily Leader*, a Democratic newspaper, was dated October 11, 1881. The owners of the paper at that time were William H. Fredenburgh, John E. VanEtten, Walter S. Fredenburgh and Rev. John T. Hargraves. After a few weeks Mr. Hargraves' interest in the concern was purchased by the other three gentlemen named, Walter S. Fredenburgh becoming editor of the paper. After three months, John E. VanEtten and William H. Fredenburgh made a bill of sale of the establishment to Walter S. Fredenburgh, who conducted it until May 17, 1886, when, because of ill health, he sold the establishment to John E. Kraft and John W. Searing. Kraft and Searing continued the publication of the *Leader* until November 1, 1897, when Mr. Kraft purchased the interest of Mr. Searing and organized The Leader Company, Mr. Kraft continuing as the publisher and editor. The *Kingston Weekly Leader* was established during the winter following the establishment of the *Daily Leader*. The *Leader* also uses the Mergenthaler linotype.

THE EXPRESS.

The *Kingston Daily Express* was established June 21, 1891, by Jesse M. Decker, Urban G. Edinger and Isaac T. Mesereau, under the firm name of Decker, Edinger & Mesereau. In 1897, Mr. Mesereau sold his one-third interest in the *Express* to Louis M. Hoysradt and the firm name was then changed to Decker, Edinger & Hoysradt. In 1903, Mr. Hoysradt sold his interest to Floyd G. Edinger, a son of Urban G. Edinger, and the name of the firm was then changed to Decker, Edinger & Edinger. The *Express* plant is equipped with electric motors, a steam engine, a double cylinder press and a Mergenthaler linotype machine. It also has a well equipped job printing plant. The *Express* is independent in politics.

VILLAGE NEWSPAPERS.

The *Saugerties Telegraph* was founded in 1846 by Solomon S. Hommel, who afterward edited the *Kingston Argus*. Mr. Hommel sold the *Telegraph* in the early '50's to Freligh & Gates, who sold out to William Hull about the year 1855, and about 1859 or 1860 Mr. Hull sold to Elting & Rosepaugh, who continued the partnership a few years, when Mr. Elting purchased Mr. Rosepaugh's interest and continued its publication until September 16, 1897, when he sold the paper to James T. Maxwell, who organized a stock company known as the Saugerties Telegraph Printing and Publishing Company, who are the present owners.

The *Saugerties Post*, a daily paper, was founded February 21, 1877, by Edward Jernegan, who continued sole owner until 1880, when he formed a partnership with Arthur L. Hale, who continued with him under the firm name of Jernegan and Hale until 1890, when Mr. Hale sold his interest to Irwin Ronk of Kingston. Mr. Jernegan continued with Mr. Ronk until 1896, when he disposed of his interest to James R. Wood, of Kingston, who remained with Mr. Ronk until 1901, when the *Post* was purchased by J. W. Frankel, who soon after sold it to the Saugerties Telegraph Printing and Publishing Company, who are the present owners. The president of the company is James T. Maxwell, the vice-president Robert A. Snyder, the secretary Joseph W. Frankel, and the treasurer and business manager, Edward Jernegan.

The *Saugerties Telegraph* issued a daily paper, called the *Daily Telegraph,* with Mr. Jernegan as editor, from September 16, 1897, to April 15, 1901, when it was discontinued to be consolidated with the *Daily Post.* Both the *Telegraph* and *Post* are independent in politics.

The *Ellenville Journal* was founded in 1849 by Robert Denton. It was purchased in 1857 by S. M. Taylor, who sold it in 1859, but re-purchased it in 1861, since which time, with a few temporary changes, he has conducted it. It is Republican in politics.

The *South Ulster Press,* now the *Ellenville Press,* was begun in 1870 by Thomas E. Benedict and Brother. When President Cleveland appointed Mr. Benedict Public Printer, these two brothers went to Washington, turning over their paper to their younger brother, Louis R. Benedict, who sold it in 1893 to W. C. McNally, a gentleman who had been prominent in Orange, Wyoming and Delaware county journals for many years. The *Press* is Democratic in politics and is exceedingly prosperous.

The *New Paltz Independent* was started in 1868 by the Independent Association, of which Easton Van Wagenen was secretary. The Association consisted of about 80 stockholders. Ralph Le Fevre became editor of the paper in 1869, purchasing it of the Association about two years afterward, and has since remained the editor and proprietor. Mr. Le Fevre has won a wide reputation as the historian of the Ulster County Huguenots. The *Independent* is Republican.

The *New Paltz Times* has been from its beginning a Democratic newspaper. It was founded in 1860 by Charles J. Ackert, who conducted it until his death in 1900, except while he served in the army during the Civil War, when it was managed by his wife, who is now the proprietress.

The *Pine Hill Sentinel* was founded in 1886 by Wilson Bertrand, who sold it in 1890 to U. S. Grant Cure, who has since been its publisher. It is a Republican paper.

The *Pine Hill Optic* was started in 1892 by E. S. Tompkins, who has conducted it since that time as a Democratic paper.

The *Marlborough Record,* first called the *Pegasus* and later the *Progress,* was started in 1885 by Charles H. Cochrane and E. H. Bulkeley. In 1887 it was purchased by Egbert E. Carr, who conducted it for five years, when he sold a half interest to Charles E. Westervelt, who purchased Mr. Carr's remaining interest in 1902, and has conducted it up to date. The *Record* is independent politically.

The *Highland Independent*, an independent newspaper, founded in 1887, is conducted by Hector and Miss C. W. Sears.

The *Gardiner Weekly*, independent, was founded in 1882, and, until a few years ago, was conducted by Hector Sears, who sold it to Charles Slater, the present publisher.

The *Rosendale Journal*, independent, was started by Marvin E. Parrott in 1899. It was afterward purchased by Isaac T. Mesereau, who has since continued as proprietor.

CHAPTER XLIV.

THE MASONIC FRATERNITY.

By Hon. John E. Kraft.

KINGSTON LODGE, NO. 10, F. & A. M.

WHEN Kingston was burned by the British Army in 1777, the records of the Masonic Fraternity in Ulster County were destroyed. Consequently there is no written history of the craft in Ulster before that date. A Masonic Lodge existed in Kingston long before the War of the Revolution under a dispensation of the Country Grand Lodge, and was visited by many distinguished brethren from other jurisdictions. When Washington visited Kingston in 1782 the members of the lodge, then known as Livingston Lodge, No. 23, called upon him in a body at the house of General Wynkoop on Green street, and requested him to open a communication of the lodge in due and ancient form, he being a past master of his own lodge at Alexandria, Virginia. The great General complied with their request, and opened the lodge, after which he went to the First Dutch Church, the Consistory of which presented to him their address of welcome, his reply to which, in his own handwriting, is in the vestibule of the present church edifice. During the anti-Masonic excitement which prevailed in this State early in the last century, the copper plate from which was engraved upon parchment the certificates of membership in Livingston Lodge, was buried in the First Dutch Churchyard for safe-keeping, and remained there until about twenty years ago, when it was dug up and presented to Judge Clearwater. It now has a place with other relics of pre-revolutionary Kingston in the Judge's residence on Albany avenue. It is understood that it is his intention eventually to present it to Kingston Lodge, No. 10.

Unfortunately the minutes of the meetings of the Fraternity up to the year 1790 are lost, and therefore Kingston Lodge, No. 10, took the latter date as that of its own organization, with Brother John Addison as its first Master. Records of the regular meetings of Livingston Lodge,

No. 23, however, up to the 26th day of December, 1805, are still in existence. For some reason, not known, the charter of the lodge was surrendered until the 28th of August, 1808, when it was reorganized under the name of Kingston Lodge, No. 23, with Brother Moses Cantine as Master. At that time the Hon. DeWitt Clinton was Grand Master of the State of New York, and had on various occasions visited with the brethren in Kingston.

The regular communications of the lodge were held every full moon in a room in the old Court House. It was the rule in those days to have a grand celebration on the 24th day of June, being St. John's Day. The brethren would march to the First Dutch Church, and listen to an eloquent discourse by the minister, and then march over to one of the taverns, where a grand banquet would be spread, after which toasts would be responded to by various brethren.

On the first day of December, 1821, Kingston Lodge proceeded to the house of Isaac L. Hasbrouck, in the town of Marbletown, and instituted Rising Sun Lodge, No. 336, which existed a few years, and then surrendered its charter.

On the 17th of September, 1824, a large number of brethren of Kingston Lodge, upon special invitation, visited Red Hook and took part with the brethren of that village in welcoming the illustrious Gen. Marquis De Lafayette, who stopped there on his memorable trip up the Hudson River.

Kingston and Rondout were naturally much exercised over the building of the waterway that was to connect the Delaware and Hudson rivers. In the old lodge record of 1826 is the following interesting account: "The Lodge was invited by the managers of the Delaware and Hudson Canal Company to take part in their canal completion celebration. The invitation was accepted, and the brethren proceeded to Eddyville in carriages, formed in procession after arriving (headed by the Master), proceeded to the tide-water lock, and there laid the cap-stone in due Masonic form, which completed this great artificial channel from the Delaware to the Hudson River. Brother Myer delivered the address upon this occasion, which was extremely able, and listened to by the vast crowd of spectators with marked attention. At the conclusion of these services the members of the lodge and other guests were invited by the managers of the canal on board of a float fitted up expressly for the occasion, and proceeded several miles up the canal. A band accompanied the party and discoursed sweet music for the excursionists, and upon their return to tide-water the whole party partook of a bountiful repast provided at the house of Mr. H. Radcliff." This latter entertainment, we think, must have been at the expense of the lodge, as we find by their proceedings the "full moon" following that $75.96 was appropriated from the lodge fund to pay for dinners at Eddyville, written in the bold, legible handwriting of John Van Buren, then secretary of Kingston Lodge.

From 1808 to 1829 the work and transactions of the lodge were carefully transcribed. On the minutes in the latter year, Brother John Van Buren was elected Master. For three or four years, no work was done by the lodge. A few members met each year and re-elected the old officers to their various positions. Although these devoted brethren met secretly and kept the organization of the lodge intact, they kept no record from 1833 to 1850, on account of the anti-Masonic sentiment prevailing throughout the country, because of the Morgan trouble. When the unpopularity of Freemasonry died out, the brethren got together on the 13th of November, 1850, and accepted a new charter that had been granted by the Grand Lodge to Kingston Lodge, No. 10, with the Venerable Brother John Van Buren still its master. Since that time Freemasonry has prospered in Ulster County, Kingston Lodge becoming one of the leading lodges in the State, and several other lodges being organized from it.

In 1854 consent was granted by Kingston Lodge to establish Rondout Lodge, No. 343, fifteen members of Kingston Lodge having signed the application.

On the 19th of June, 1855, a number of brethren of Kingston Lodge who lived in the western section of Ulster County, and eastern portion of Delaware County, were granted a dispensation to organize Margaretville Lodge, No. 389.

During the dark days of the Civil War, Kingston Lodge mourned the death of a number of its members. On the 14th of September, 1862, the lodge in a body attended the funeral at Albany of its illustrious Brother George W. Pratt, Colonel of the 20th N. Y. S. M. He died at Albany from the effects of a wound received at Bull Run, Virginia, while nobly leading his regiment to battle.

In 1863 was celebrated in Kingston one of the greatest Masonic events that had ever occurred along the Hudson River. The brethren had resolved to celebrate the anniversary of St. John the Baptist. Application was made for the use of the First Reformed Church of Kingston, in which to have the address delivered, but objection being made by certain ones having control of the church, the matter was not urged, and the brethren determined to erect the speaker's stand in the open air. On the day in question, a large body of Masons, numbering about 450, who had come from Saugerties, Rhinebeck, Poughkeepsie and other river towns, assembled with the Masons of Kingston and Rondout on the Strand, near the Mansion House, formed in procession, and headed by the Rondout band, marched through the upper streets, and halted at the Academy Green. The ceremonies here were impressive. Rev. J. C. Edmunds, acting as chaplain, addressed the Throne of Grace, which was followed by the entire body singing. The orator of the day was the Hon. Darius A. Ogden of Penn Yan, one of the most eloquent and forceful speakers of the times. At the close of the exercises the procession re-formed and marched to the old Armory (now St. Joseph's Roman Catholic Church), where a bountiful repast had been spread. Tables had been set the entire length of the building, and there were seated nearly five hundred persons, who participated in the banquet. Toasts were drank, and many eloquent speeches were made.

On the 21st of June, 1864, Kingston Lodge granted permission to the brethren at Ellenville to organize Wawarsing Lodge, No. 582.

While Rev. Charles W. Camp was Master of the lodge, in 1883, a trained band of craftsmen was organized for the purpose of beautifying the interesting ceremony of the third degree. The success of this feature of the work has attracted the attention of Freemasons all over the country, and has been the means of leading many lodges to imitate the same; in fact there is scarcely a Masonic lodge of any pretense that does not now have such a band of craftsmen.

When it became positively known in 1883 that the crew of the Arctic exploring steamer *Jeanette* must have perished, and the whole world was stunned with the news, Kingston Lodge mourned the loss of a distinguished brother, and placed the following memorial in the archives of the lodge:

THIS MEMORIAL

Is entered in the Records of Kingston Lodge in fraternal memory of our late Brother,

LIEUT. CHARLES WINANS CHIPP, U. S. N.

He was initiated an Entered Apprentice, passed to the degree of Fellow Craft, and raised to the sublime degree of Master Mason at Shanghai, in the Empire of China, in Naval Lodge, and affiliated in Kingston Lodge, No. 10, October 29, 1872.

He entered the United States Naval Academy at Newport, Rhode Island, in 1863, and was attached to the Arctic exploring steamer *Jeanette*, as Executive Officer, in June, 1879.

HE PERISHED AT SEA,

Probably on the night of September 12, 1881, aged 33 years.

"Palmam qui meruit ferat."

His services and history are recorded in the archives of the Nation

"WE CHERISH HIS MEMORY HERE."

Several times during the existence of Kingston Lodge its beautiful rooms have been thrown open for social intercourse and entertainment, one of the most popular being the grand Masonic fair, that was held in May, 1888, which added to the funds of the lodge upwards of $4,000.

A dispensation from the Grand Master authorizing and appointing Worshipful Brother Christopher N. DeWitt Master of the lodge, at that time to act in his stead, proceeded with the members of the lodge to Rosendale, and in due Masonic form laid the cornerstone of the Reformed Church in that village on the 7th day of December, 1895.

The following named lodges, now out of existence, were located, according to Grand Lodge records, in the County of Ulster, Newburgh and Middletown being formerly in Ulster County:

Steuben—Newburgh, September 27th, 1788.
James, No. 85—Middletown, January 6th, 1798.
Moriah, No. 67—Marbletown, January 8th, 1798.
Rising Sun, No. 336—Marbletown, December 1st, 1821.
United—Marlborough, April 3d, 1804.
Columbia, No. 207—New Paltz, July 10th, 1812.

The Lodges in Ulster County, now in existence, are:

Kingston, No. 10—Kingston, December 8th, 1790.
Ulster, No. 193—Saugerties, December 27th, 1850.
Rondout, No. 343—Rondout, July 8th, 1854.
Wawarsing, No. 582—Ellenville, June 13th, 1864.
Adonai, No. 718—Highland, June 11th, 1872.

Sylvester R. Shaw

CHAPTER XLV.

THE SCHOOLS OF THE COUNTY.

By Professor S. R. Shear.

THE chief object of the English settler in America was to found a Christian State; this thought was paramount to every other consideration. At home he had been persecuted by bigots; he had suffered for his religious belief; now he would have a home where he could worship God according to the dictates of his conscience.

The Englishman knew nothing of common schools, and there was no reason why he should be particularly concerned about them after he came to America. In 1671 Sir William Berkeley wrote: "I thank God there are no free schools nor printing, and I hope we shall not have these for a hundred years; for learning has brought disobedience and heresy and sects into the world, and printing has divulged them and libels against the best government. God keep us from both!"

Although hostility to the common schools was greater in Virginia than elsewhere in the English colonies, we find throughout all the colonies a larger interest in higher education for the privileged few than in a general education for all.

The Dutch settlers inherited different customs and different ideals. Taine says that in culture and instruction, the Dutch are two centuries ahead of the rest of Europe. If that is true to-day, it must have been more so 275 years ago. The Dutchman was a trader; and while he was not less religious than his English neighbors, Holland had been too long a home for the persecuted of all Europe, for the Dutch settler in America to give great concern to religious freedom. He had enjoyed it at home, and he expected as a matter of course, that those privileges would be continued to him in a new world. He was, however, largely interested in general education, and we are not surprised to find provision for schools in the "Charter of Freedoms and Exemptions" granted the settlement of New Netherlands in 1629, and we find the first public school in America was opened in New Amsterdam in 1633; the teacher of this school was Adam Roelandson. In 1652, New Amsterdam obtained a municipal charter and a second school was opened.

In 1664 the English assumed control of New Netherlands and continued in control with the exception of one year, until the Revolution. After the English occupation, elementary education declined in New York, and it would have died out altogether had it not been for the existence of certain Dutch communities where schools were maintained by public taxation. From 1664 to 1775, the colonial legislature of New York passed but three acts concerning education, none of which related to common schools. It is a fair inference, therefore, that to the Dutch we owe the origin, the preservation and development of the common school idea in New York.

Higher education was encouraged by the English, but it was not until 1795 that any action was taken toward an appropriation for common schools; from that time forward, educational activities were continuous and fruitful.

The history of the schools of Ulster County is a part of the annals of legislation affecting all the State. We have found that the first public schools were established in New Amsterdam. As towns were erected along the Hudson, it was the uniform practice to reserve lots for school sites, and houses were built thereon; thus at the close of the eighteenth century, there were public schools at Esopus, Albany and other places along the river.

In 1812, the Legislature passed a law providing that each town in the State be divided into districts, by three commissioners elected by the voters of that town. The law further provided that three school trustees be elected in each district. Under this act, the towns of New Paltz, Saugerties, Marlborough, Shawangunk, Plattekill, Esopus, Hurley, Marbletown, Rochester, Wawarsing, Shandaken, Woodstock and Kingston were divided into districts and local officers elected. Later on, as Lloyd, Rosendale, Gardiner, Olive, Denning, Hardenburgh and Ulster were incorporated as towns, they were divided into districts according to law.

About this early period of the district schools, little is known. The school buildings were primitve; the teachers were in the main, poorly prepared for their work and illy paid, and the school year for the older pupils at least, was very short. The early school rooms were unique; on either side were rows of desks facing the middle of the room; injured dignity breathed from every desk. Severely plain were they, yet upon their faces were the monograms of generations; drawing and carving had never been taught, but both were practiced by every boy and by many girls. As the children sat in their seats, they resembled partly closed jack-knives; the angle between the seat and its back being keenly acute. From the teacher would come the order: "Sit up straight and give attention"; the order was obeyed as fully as possible, as are all such orders. Down the middle of the room were three objects of peculiar interest. In the center stood the stove which roared and crackled like some creature chained against his will; while those nearest it squirmed and writhed beneath its fervid heat, those in distant parts of the room shivered and beheld the suffering of the favored few with mingled feelings of envy and dread. Near the door stood the teacher's desk, while behind it stood the teacher.

Such were the schools of a century ago, but from those schools came boys and girls trained in adversity, inured to hardship, habituated to persistence, accustomed to work out difficulties; boys and girls who would scorn to do a mean thing; who were afraid to be cowardly. From those schools came the founders of our nation; men and women whom the world learned to respect.

In 1840 an act was passed by the Legislature providing for the biennial appointment of county superintendents by the Board of Supervisors; this act was very unpopular and it was repealed in 1847. Four years after the act providing for county superintendents, the office of town superintendent was created, and continued until 1856, at which time the office of school commissioner was created practically as it exists at present.

Ulster County was divided into three commissioner districts. Some of the most prominent men of the different towns served as town commissioners, town superintendents and school commissioners. Among the most successful school commissioners may be mentioned William H. Dederick, Cornelius Van Santvoord, H. H. Holden, John J. Moran, of the first district; Frank Willigan, M. W. Baldwin, George Terwilliger, Peter LeFevre, of the second district; Leonard Davis, E. C. Douglas and John Schoonmaker of the third district. The commissioners serving at present are: Edmund M. Wilbur, Melvin G. Rhodes and Thomas C. Perry.

The following table gives a synopsis of the schools in 1880:

	No. District.	No. of Pupils in District.	Average Attendance.
New Paltz	6	641	173
Saugerties	24	4012	1126
Marlborough	8	1034	332
Esopus	16	1653	475
Lloyd	9	....	...
Hurley	9	1087	345
Shawangunk	13	996	302
Plattekill	10	....	...
Marbletown	14	1499	404
Rochester	15	1445	396
Rosendale	7	1502	420
Wawarsing	31	3144	1071
Gardiner	9	643	177
Olive	15	1096	287
Shandaken	15	889	252
Woodstock	28	611	163
Hardenburgh	9	296	86
Denning	9	399	117
Ulster	6	....	...

The following table was prepared from the last report of the school commissioners in the three districts of the county.

	No. District.	No. of Pupils in District.	Average Attendance.
New Paltz	6	449	290
Saugerties	21	1717	1167
Marlborough	7	698	436
Esopus	16	877	589
Lloyd	8	463	299
Hurley	7	341	195
Shawangunk	13	475	274
Plattekill	11	420	249
Marbetown	13	611	380
Rochester	16	598	381
Rosendale	7	853	498
Wawarsing	30	1434	969
Gardiner	9	311	182
Olive	13	534	312
Shandaken	12	659	389
Woodstock	7	314	215
Hardenburgh	10	194	103
Denning	10	166	96
Ulster	8	681	356
Kingston	2	76	46

A comparison of the tables will indicate something of the educational tendencies. Data with reference to the value of property in 1880 is not available, but there has been a gradual improvement in school buildings and school equipment. There has been a gradual diminution in the number of pupils assigned to a given teacher, hence a gradual increase in the number of teachers in the county. It will be seen also that there are less districts at present than in 1880. There is a gradual tendency toward consolidation for the benefit of weaker districts. It will be observed also that the average daily attendance as compared with the number of pupils of school age is very much greater than was true twenty-six years ago. This is due to the beneficial effects of a wise compulsory education law thoroughly administered. The total expenses for all school purposes has been very greatly increased, which means better remuneration for teachers, and consequently a better grade of instruction.

At present the rural schools of Ulster County compare favorably with those of any county in the State. There is increased interest on the part of all concerned, and a strong effort is being made to secure value received for every dollar spent for educational purposes.

Four chief educational centers of the county are worthy of especial note: Ellenville, Kingston, New Paltz and Saugerties.

KINGSTON.

The first school teacher in Esopus, afterward Kingston, was Andries VanderSluys, who obtained his authority from director-general Peter Stuyvesant. This was soon after the municipal charter of New Amsterdam was granted, or about 1652. During the next seventy-five years, the Dutch inhabitants of Kingston, despite the negative influence of the English authorities, maintained free schools by taxation.

The legislative act requiring a State to be divided into school districts and providing for a superintendent of common schools, was passed in 1812. At this time there were within the present corporate limits of the city of Kingston an Academy and several private English schools. The most famous of these schools was held in a frame house on Green street; this school was taught for more than thirty years by Solomon Hasbrouck.

Agreeable to the provisions of the law, the territory comprising the present city, together with considerable adjacent territory, became districts Nos. 7 and 8. District No. 7 was the easterly or Rondout portion, and No. 8 was the westerly or Kingston section. As the population increased, more accommodations became necessary, and other districts were set off from time to time from the two original districts. In 1839, districts Nos. 11 and 12 were taken from No. 8; later districts Nos. 5 and

15 were set off also. In 1850, No. 10 was set off from No. 7, and in 1853, No. 13 became a separate district.

The first public school building in the original district No. 8 was the building on Green street in which Solomon Hasbrouck had conducted a private school. The first building occupied for school purposes in No. 7 was the frame building near the junction of Wurts and Abeel streets.

In 1854, the value of all public school property in Kingston was approximately $21,000. There were eight buildings containing accommodations for 800 pupils. The population of the districts was about 8,000, and the school population about 2,000. In 1862, districts Nos. 5, 8, 11 and 15 were united into one union free school district, to be known as the Kingston School District, and Charles R. Abbott became the first superintendent of schools. In 1864, Kingston Academy was transferred in trust to the Kingston Board of Education, on condition that it should be forever maintained as a free public high school, fitting pupils for the various colleges of the land. In 1864, No. 13 became a union free school district. During the principalship of William A. McConnell, the building was enlarged, the library facilities greatly increased, the curriculum enriched, and a high school department was chartered by the Regents of the University.

KINGSTON ACADEMY.

On April 19th, 1769, Charles DeWitt received a letter from Chauncey Graham of Fishkill, proposing to open an academy in either Albany or Kingston. This matter was under discussion for some years, but definite action was deferred until October 11th, 1773. At that time it was decided to secure accommodations and hire two teachers to instruct students in the classics, sciences, mathematics and English; thus was planted the germ from which Kingston Academy sprang.

The next year, 1774, "The Trustees of the Freeholders and Commonalty of the Town of Kingston" purchased a house and lot on the southwest corner of John and Crown streets, and selected John Addison as the first principal of Kingston Academy. The names of the founders were Derick Wynkoop, Joseph Gasherie, Johannis Persen, Silvester Salisbury, Christopher Tappen, Adam Persen, Johannis DuBois, Abraham VanGaasbeek, Johannis Sleight, Ezekiel Masten and Wilhelmus Houghtaling.

The history of this time-honored institution for the succeeding century is fraught with interest. The school took high rank despite many adverse circumstances. On October 16th, 1777, the building was burned by the British Army, in command of General John Vaughan, but in less than five months it was rebuilt, and the students continued their work as though nothing had happened. A copy of an old rate bill of that period bears the names of ninety-three students who were members of the English department. The first commencement exercises of the Academy were held in the spring of 1778 at the Bogardus tavern.

In November, 1779, John McMillan succeeded Principal Addison. In October, 1788, George B. Ewart was engaged to teach Greek, Latin and the higher English branches, but Mr. Ewart's work was unsatisfactory; the students made slow progress and the school began to decline. In January, 1791, it was resolved by the Trustees that the corporation become a member of the University of the State of New York. At this time the Academy was closed for a year on account of the small attendance.

In December, 1792, Timothy T. Smith was elected principal, and the Academy entered upon a new era of success. After several applications it was finally incorporated by the Regents of the University, February 3d, 1795. At that time the curriculum included ancient languages, mathematics, philosophy, history and civil government. In addition to the regular tuition fees, each student was required to furnish two loads of fire wood, or its cash equivalent. Some of the early principals suggested increasing their stipend by taking a portion of the tuition, but for a long time the Trustees opposed this plan as tending to lower the standard of the Academy.

During the early days of the Academy one of the most pleasing practices was the semi-annual examination by the Trustees. On these occasions the village was in holiday attire; hospitality was free and bountiful; public dinners were held, followed by literary exercises, and in the evening the young people enjoyed the dance.

From funds received from the Regents of the University, and secured through other means, an Academy library was established in 1795. This library contained 103 volumes of standard literature, most of which are still on the present library shelves. A perusal and appreciation of these books would require the mature mind of an adult, but they indicate the scholarly habits of those early days. A part of the original equipment of the library was a pair of valuable globes, which long since disappeared.

Soon after the act of incorporation a room was set apart for the teaching of reading, writing and arithmetic. In February, 1804, the Trustees applied to the legislature for permission to found a college, but this was denied, and the fund in hand for the purpose was deeded to the Academy; this deed conveyed 800 acres of land, including the present academy site.

Up to 1800, the school had been devoted almost entirely to the classical department; the rooms in which the English branches were taught were regarded outside of the Academy proper. This branch of the school was abolished altogether in 1812, and rented to other parties until 1817. Up to 1809 the Academy was devoted to boys and young men exclusively, no women being admitted. Then for nearly three years a woman teacher was employed for a class of girls. This class also was discontinued from 1812 to 1817. At that time Rev. Malbone Kenyon took charge, and he was permitted to open a room for young ladies, but this permission was discontinued in 1820. From 1820 to 1823 the Academy declined until scarcely a dozen students could be gathered. Rev. Daniel Parker was then engaged as principal; coeducation was introduced and some elementary subjects were allowed. A resolution adopted April 21, 1837, indicates the complete satisfaction with both measures. In 1830 a small building was erected on the present site, and to this, additions have been made from time to time.

As early as 1862 the matter of adopting the graded school system was discussed. This question continued to be agitated until 1864, when the Academy was formally turned over to the Kingston Board of Education.

In 1865, Francis Wynkoop gave $5,000, the income of which was to be forever devoted to the instruction of a French class in Kingston free high school. Membership to this class was to be determined by exemplary conduct.

During the 132 years since its organization there have been educated in Kingston Academy thousands of men and women, many of whom have taken front rank in higher institutions of learning, and many afterwards became prominent in political, professional and commercial lines, while many have rendered notable service to their country.

Among the principals may be mentioned Rev. Daniel Parker, Charles L. Hungerford, Rev. John Van Vleck, John Norton Pomeroy, Joseph C. Wyckoff, Francis J. Cheney and Henry W. Callahan. The present principal is Myron J. Michael, who has served in that capacity for the past ten years.

Some of the most distinguished citizens of Kingston have served on the Board of Trustees, notably the Rev. Dr. Gosman, Rev. Mr. Lillie, Marius Schoonmaker, and Rev. J. C. F. Hoes.

ULSTER ACADEMY.

In 1870, Charles M. Ryon, principal of No. 13, was elected principal in district No. 7, and then began a most vigorous campaign of improvement. The old school building and site, corner of Wurts and Pierpont streets, were sold to the present owners, and all but six rooms and the tower of the present building were constructed and furnished at a cost of over $36,000. At that time less than 150 pupils were enrolled in this school. The new building opened with an attendance of over 300 pupils, and at the end of three years the enrollment was 800. Thorough organization and discipline prevailed; the course of study was systematized; trained teachers were employed, and excellent results obtained.

In 1879, under the principalship of Mr. L. M. Edwards, it was changed to a union free school district, and in 1880 a high school department was chartered by the Regents of the University. In 1898, Ulster Academy was chartered as a high school. Under the principalship of the late William E. Bunten the building was enlarged, and it now contains twenty-five well-lighted, thoroughly heated and ventilated rooms.

During the past twenty-five years, Ulster Academy has maintained a high standard of scholarship. Since its incorporation as a high school its graduates have taken high rank in our colleges, technical schools and normal schools. One of the important means by which this school has conserved its usefulness is its library of nearly 4,000 well selected and thoroughly classified books.

The present principal is John E. Shull, who has served since 1898.

CONSOLIDATION.

In 1876, school commissioner Edward Ryer ordered that the school districts in Kingston City should be designated as follows: No. 12 should be No. 1; No. 7 should be No. 2; No. 10 should be No. 3; No. 13 should be No. 4; and Kingston School district, comprising Nos. 5, 8, 11 and 15, should be called No. 5. In 1902, by act of the legislature, all these schools were consolidated under one system. The original Board of Education named in the act were Conrad Hiltebrant, for a long time prominent as a trustee of Ulster Academy; Walter N. Gill, who had rendered signal service in school No. 4; W. Scott Gillespie, Henry C. Connelly, Walter C. Dolson and DuBois G. Atkins, all of whom had been for a long time prominently identified with the schools of Kingston school district; Isaac N. Weiner, Henry R. Brigham and Bernard Loughran. The Board so named organized and elected officers as follows: President, DuBois G. Atkins; Vice-President, Walter N. Gill; Superintendent of Schools, S. R. Shear.

The Board remains intact as to members and officers, with two exceptions—Mr. Weiner was succeeded by A. Wesley Thompson, who resigned to accept the office of Mayor, and his place was filled by the election of Dr. Walter D. Hasbrouck, and John J. Campbell has taken the place of Bernard Loughran, deceased.

Among the distinguished men who have served the schools of the city as trustees, are Hon. Marius Schoonmaker and Elisha M. Brigham, each of whom was president of the Kingston Board of Education for many years; D. B. Abbey and John N. Cordts in district No. 4, Mr. William Winter in district No. 2.

The most notable teacher and executive who has been connected with the Kingston schools is Charles M. Ryon. He reorganized district No. 4; he placed district No. 2 in a prominent position in the educational field; he was superintendent of Kingston school district for nearly thirty years, placing these schools in the forefront, and he is at present the efficient supervisor of penmanship for all the schools of the city. Mr. Ryon is a scholar, a gentleman, an executive and a thorough educator. The recent history of Kingston Public Schools is largely the history of this man's life.

There are at present ten public school buildings in the city; the buildings and sites together with equipment are valued at $367,903.86. The school population is 5,650, of which 4,355 are enrolled in the public schools. There are 105 teachers and supervisors beside various other employees. The annual expenditures are about $100,000. Every effort is made by the citizens to maintain a thoroughly progressive, practical and efficient school administration.

NEW PALTZ.

New Paltz has been for over 200 years one of the chief educational centers of Ulster County. To the Huguenots is due the credit of organizing and maintaining schools during the early period of settlement of this section of the county. The French language prevailed not only in the home and in the church, but in the school from 1677 to 1735, being gradually supplanted by the Dutch language. History has preserved the names of two early French schoolmasters, Jean Tebenin, who wielded the birchen scepter from 1696 to 1700, and Jean Cottin, who taught at probably an earlier period.

In this connection it is worthy of mention that the stones from the building used as a church from 1717 to 1773 were used to construct the building occupied for school purposes from 1773 to 1874, a period of 101 years. This building was afterward remodeled, and is now (1906) occupied by John Drake as a dwelling. In 1874, a brick school building with two large rooms was erected, which structure still remains intact.

True to the spirit of the age, the people of New Paltz in 1828 established a classical school for the benefit of the well favored, and for those fitting for the professions. The sessions of this organization were held in the upper story of the public school. Among the principal organizers of this forerunner of New Paltz Academy may be mentioned Dr. Jacob Wurts, Rev. William R. Bogardus, Peter Eltinge, Solomon Eltinge, Jacob Eltinge, Zachariah Freer, Philip Deyo, Mary DuBois, Nathaniel LeFevre, Jacob I. Schoonmaker, Roeliff Hasbrouck, Jacob J. Hasbrouck, Maurice Hasbrouck, Josiah R. Eltinge, Dr. John Bogardus and Daniel DuBois. The first president was William R. Bogardus and the first secretary was Benjamin Van Wagenen.

So great was the demand for higher education that the organizers of the classical school saw the necessity for enlarged accommodations and a broader curriculum. As a result, the New Paltz Academy was incorporated in 1833 with the following Board of Trustees: Rev. Dow Van Olinda, Jacob J. Hasbrouck, Dr. John Bogardus, Benjamin Van Wagenen, Levi Hasbrouck, Solomon E. Eltinge, Peter Eltinge, Josiah DuBois, and Jesse Eltinge. The original capital was $2,500, but that sum was afterward greatly increased. The first president of the Board of Trustees of New Paltz Academy was Rev. Dow Van Olinda. Among his successors were Solomon E. Eltinge, Derick W. Eltinge, Alfred Deyo and Ralph LeFevre; Mr. LeFevre became president in 1881, and he still serves in that capacity, though the organization has now only a nominal existence.

The first principal of the New Paltz Academy was Eliphaz Fay, a man of broad scholarship, large executive ability and manifold talents. Under his efficient management the school grew and prospered; its membership came from far and near. An all-round education was Mr. Fay's motto, and the work done in the Academy at that time would compare favorably with that done in many of our best secondary schools to-day.

In 1841, Principal Fay resigned to accept the presidency of an Eastern college. He remained in that position for three years, during which time William Parker served as principal. In 1844, Mr. Fay returned to New Paltz as principal, and remained until 1847. Following that year, Mr. Munsell, Mr. Butler, Mr. Steele, Rev. J. Sinclair, Frederick R. Brace, John H. Post and Mr. Walsh served in the order named. In 1861, Principal Walsh resigned to enter the army, and D. M. DeWitt was elected principal. In 1862, Mr. DeWitt's election as District Attorney of the County necessitated his resignation. Charles H. Hayward, Henry Gallup, Jared Hasbrouck and Dr. H. M. Bauscher served during the time from 1862 to 1881.

The administration of Dr. Bauscher from 1867 to 1881 was notable in many ways. He was a German, and a thorough student; possessed of much energy, he imparted enthusiasm to all with whom he came in contact; his theory of discipline was firm kindness, and his success is attested by all who were fortunate enough to be his students. Previous to Dr. Bauscher's time there had been no regular graduating class; he systematized the course, graded the school, and from that time regular graduating exercises were annually held.

In 1881, Frederick E. Partington was elected principal. In 1884, the Academy was burned to the ground, and Principal Partington resigned to accept the principalship of Staten Island Academy. Previous, however, to leaving New Paltz, Mr. Partington was very active and successful in the effort to raise funds for rebuilding the Academy. Others specially active in the work were Rev. Ame Vennema and Jacob LeFevre. To raise $25,000 was no small task, but the townspeople responded nobly, as did many people from other towns. Major Thomas Cornell of Kingston may be mentioned as one of the most liberal contributors. Mr. and Mrs. Lambert Jenkins paid $1,250 in all toward the work. Members of the alumni came promptly forward at this critical time, not only with their own money, but with that given by their friends. The task of collection being completed, it remained to construct a new building. This work finished, the Academy Trustees met on January 22d, 1885, to take account of stock and to discuss the future. The new principal, Henry A. Balcom, was much interested in Normal schools. The matter was discussed at some length with the result that Dr. Balcom and Ralph LeFevre were appointed a committee to determine upon the practicability of turning over the Academy to the State for Normal school purposes, and to secure needed legislation to that end if deemed practicable. The committee promptly commenced the work.

All the normal schools of the State at that time, with the exception of the Albany Normal, were in the western and northern counties, and there was a demand for a training school in the southeastern section. Petitions favorable to the New Paltz plan were secured from Poughkeepsie, Goshen, Kingston, Montgomery, Yonkers, Saugerties, Newburgh and other towns. The leading men of the county were enlisted, and finally near the close of the legislative session in 1885, the bill was passed and signed by Governor David B. Hill, who showed a friendly feeling. The Committee, the Board of Academy Trustees and others who had assisted in the work, had encountered various obstacles and overcome much opposition, but they had achieved a splendid victory not only for New Paltz, but for Ulster County and for education in general. In this connection special mention should be made of the services rendered by Messrs. Jacob LeFevre and Josiah J. Hasbrouck, while outside of New Paltz very great assistance was rendered by Thomas E. Benedict of Ellenville, Dewitt Peltz of Albany, and Gen. George H. Sharpe and Judge Alton B. Parker of Kingston.

The first Local Board of the New Paltz Normal school consisted of Alton B. Parker, George H. Sharpe and Jacob D. Wurts of Kingston, Albert K. Smiley of Lake Mohonk, Jacob LeFevre, Josiah J. Hasbrouck, Solomon Deyo, Charles W. Deyo and Lambert Jenkins of New Paltz.

Dr. Eugene Bouton, with six assistants, constituted the first faculty. At that time there were less than 100 students. Principal Bouton was succeeded by Dr. Frank S. Capen,who served from 1889 to 1900. He was a man of great energy and the number of students rapidly increased.

The present principal is Myron T. Scudder, who, with nineteen assistants, is conducting one of the most progressive and successful Normal schools in the country. At the World's Fair in St. Louis in 1904 the gold medal was awarded to New Paltz for the best educational exhibit from the Normal schools of New York State. This school has taken an advanced position in regard to manual training, domestic science and such subjects as tend to correlate the public schools with real life. The system of student participation in government, known as the School City, is of special importance to all who are interested in the development of civic reforms and social service. The New Paltz Normal School attracts many visitors from other schools and colleges throughout the country, as well as from Alaska, Cuba and Mexico, and has received delegations from Teachers' College, New York University, and many city school systems. Also from such bodies as the Federation of Women's Clubs of New York City and the Federated Clubs of Massachusetts, besides a number of other associations devoted to the study of educational problems. After carefully looking over the normal schools in the East, the United States Government during the temporary occupation of Cuba, sent sixty Cuban young ladies to New Paltz for normal training. These young ladies are now reported as being among the most efficient teachers in the schools of Cuba. Nearly 1,000 teachers have been trained in this school to take positions in the schools of the State, and besides the New Paltz Normal furnishes instruction to all New Paltz pupils of whatever grade.

During the past winter the building was destroyed by fire. However, through prompt action by the Commissioner of Education and the legislature, the insurance money was reappropriated for building purposes, together with a sufficient amount additional to construct a larger building on a larger and commanding site. In placing the matter in its proper light before the legislature, in order to secure the necessary appropriation to rebuild, a great amount of labor was performed by Assemblymen Cunningham and Fowler and Senator Cordts of this county; likewise by Hon. Frank J. LeFevre, Judge G. D. B. Hasbrouck and Bruyn Hasbrouck. The future of the Normal school now seems assured.

SAUGERTIES.

We have shown that common schools for Ulster County were introduced and fostered by the Dutch. However, the early settlement of the county was somewhat unique. The Dutch settled in Esopus, the French in New Paltz, and the Palatines in Saugerties. Thus the efforts of the Dutch in educational matters were supplemented on either side.

History tells us that the Palatine colony, founded in 1710, built a school house within a few months. Another school house was built at Katsbaan. The history of these schools was not unlike that of the other schools of the county. They met the same difficulties, overcame the same obstacles, and gave the young people of those early days the rudiments of an education and a thorough training for the hard pioneer life they were to live. The discipline of those schools was of such a character as to restrain any tendency to convert into license their newly found liberty. Instead of being helped over every difficulty, the pupils were obliged to work out their own salvation, thus fitting them for the stern realities of their primitive life.

The schools of Saugerties passed through the various changes incident to an increasing population and changing laws. The school commissioners, elected under the law of 1812, divided the town into twelve districts, which number has been increased to twenty-one. Ludwig Roesle (now Russell) was a noted teacher before the Revolution. In 1768 he prepared a manuscript arithmetic which is preserved to this day. Efforts were made from time to time to secure the advantages of higher education. The Saugerties Academy flourished for a number of years, but it finally declined and the school was closed. In 1866 the Saugerties Institute was founded; this institution was for a number of years a strong conservator of educational interests in this town.

On January 13th, 1893, Saugerties Union Free School district No. 10 was formed from what were then known as districts Nos. 10, 15 and 21. A provisional charter for the establishment of an academic department was granted by the Regents of the University on the 5th day of June, 1894, and on June 28, 1897, a permanent High School charter was granted. Since that date, the Board of Education has maintained a thoroughly equipped and up-to-date school system. The graduates of the Saugerties High School rank well in higher institutions of learning, and the teachers employed have been thoroughly trained and competent. The present members of the Board of Education are R. B. Overbaugh, President; George Seamon, Samuel M. Gray, William L. Darbee, John T. Washburn, Jr., Edward J. Lewis, John A. Snyder, William Ziegler and James T. Maxwell. They have under their supervision four school buildings, an enrollment of 510 students, and they employ fifteen teachers and a superintendent. The citizens of Saugerties have a commendable degree of interest in their schools, and every effort is made to provide the children of the town with the best educational advantages. The district has just voted to erect a new school building at a cost of $55,000.

ELLENVILLE.

The first authentic record of the Ellenville schools is of a meeting held at the house of Nathan Hoornbeek in district No. 13, of Wawarsing, on November 11th, 1828. Elisha Sheldon was chairman of this meeting. The village was but a small hamlet with buildings scattered here and there amid the corn and wheat fields, and it is quite probable that district No. 13 served for the schooling of the children of a large territory. Annual school meetings, according to the minutes, seem to have been held either at the tavern of Nathan Hoornbeek, or in Patchens' Hall until the year 1833, when, for the first time, it is recorded that a meeting was held in the school house. This school house, called by way of distinction for some years afterward, the "Brick School House," is still standing, and it forms a part of a tenement on the corner of Main and Warren streets, opposite the old pottery site.

On July 8th, 1837, a special meeting was held. The records of this meeting show a broadening of school sentiment. After the routine business had been dispatched, the following resolution was passed:

Resolved, That the school house be enlarged by building an additional story of brick on the top of the present house. That $200 be raised by assessment on the district for above purpose. That if there be an overplus, it shall be used for fencing the lot and for such other improvements as the trustees deem proper.

During the year 1839, district No. 15 was probably created, and the records show that district No. 13 divided and turned over certain public moneys to the newly formed district.

On April 28th, 1845, it is recorded that by order of the town Superintendent, districts Nos. 13 and 15 were united, to be known thereafter as district No. 13. In the same minutes the "White School House" is mentioned for the first time to distinguish it from the "Brick School House" of the old district. The "White School House," located on Canal Street, was enlarged and transformed into a dwelling now occupied by F. W. Campbell. At the annual meeting, Dec. 31st, 1845, some of the progressive men of the village began to agitate the question of a new building which should be sufficiently commodious to accommodate all the school children. This movement was bitterly opposed by certain taxpayers, but on November 13th, 1846, it was voted to commence the building. This building was termed by the opposition the "Mammoth School House," though according to the report twenty years after it was stated that its utmost seating capacity was only 200. The Trustees who were instrumental in bringing about this change were George A. Dudley, Alvah B. Preston and Ditmus Hardenburgh. These men deserve special mention as pioneers in the educational advancement of the town. Through their efforts, and through the efforts of Willet S. Northrop and John H. Van Wagenen, the first principals of the new school, Ellenville took first rank in the county in educational matters. These two principals were disciples and followers of that distinguished educator, David P. Page, the first principal of the Albany State Normal School.

At that time the public school curriculum was simple and unpretending, requiring only spelling, reading, writing, arithmetic, geography and grammar. The school apparatus was limited to a Globe, Outline Maps, Blocks to illustrate the extraction of square and cube roots, a Normal Chart and a rickety Orrery. Scant as were these appliances, they were obtained chiefly by filching from the annual library appropriation. The teaching was characterized by patient, painstaking effort; exposition and demonstration were rigidly required. The ability of a pupil to explain his lesson so that it could be understood by others was held to be first proof that he himself had mastered it; hence blackboard work was regarded as highly essential.

Spelling was either oral or written; the reading classes were trained in modulation and enunciation; during those days the teachers believed that pupils learned by imitation, and some of the most difficult passages were read over and over again by the teachers. Pupils were required to watch for error on the part of their classmates, thus insuring better attention and increased interest in the lesson. Geography was studied and recited in the usual manner, except that more map drawing was required; for this purpose, the large blackboards were utilized. Students in arithmetic were required to place problems upon the blackboard, after which they were expected to pass again to the board, and with the aid of a pointer explain their work step by step. Each student so reciting was subject to criticism by the teacher and by any member of the class.

Mental arithmetic was all that the title implies; the schools usually had but one copy of the text book, and this was in possession of the teacher. The mental arithmetic of those days developed concentration, attention, memory and reason; it also developed ease and correctness of expression. At first Colburn's text book was used; this was afterwards supplanted by a book, the author of which was John F. Stoddard of the town of Wawarsing. Singing and elementary algebra were taught, and composition and declamation were weekly exercises. Not infrequently the teacher gave short talks on various subjects of interest; lessons in astronomy were illustrated by the orrery, which was wont to move in a mysterious way. Altogether, the school maintained a high standard for those days.

The year 1853 was memorable in the school history of Ellenville. Several of the progressive and leading citizens desiring better school privileges than could be furnished by the common school, organized a stock company and built an academy. Some years after, this same company built a residence for the teachers, and boarding accommodations for out of town pupils. The first principal of this academy was John H. Van Wagenen, who had demonstrated his ability and fitness by his successful management of the district school. After several years of service, Mr. Van Wagenen resigned, and was succeeded by S. A. Law Post. Mr. Post, a graduate of Yale, proved to be not only a competent teacher, but a successful business manager as well. After some years, Mr. Post purchased the property, improved and embellished it, reorganized the school and caused it, by act of legislature, to be placed under the visitations of the Regents. These changes resulted in giving it a wider reputation, increased patronage, and a standing among the high schools and seminaries of the State. In 1866, the district school was made a union free school and a Board of Education was elected to have charge of common school matters. At this time, the "Mammoth School House," although greatly relieved by the Academy and private schools, was taxed to its utmost capacity. In 1867, a larger school house was built, in the eastern part of the town, and seven years later a still larger one was erected on the corner of Main and Warren streets. Nine years after, the Board of Education, desirous of establishing an academic department, purchased the old academy property, which had been closed for some years on account of Mr. Post's death. This building has been refitted and enlarged from time to time as requirements have been increased. The revival and restoration of high school privileges, and the incorporation of a union free school have proved of great advantage in many ways.

The school is under the supervision of the Regents, is well equipped with books and apparatus, and its curriculum enables students to prepare for entrance to the Normal schools and colleges. A teachers' training class is also carried on with great success, and a large number of non-resident students are enrolled each year. The largely increased attendance and the corresponding increase in the teaching force led to the election of a superintendent in 1883. Mr. Ira H. Lawton was the first superintendent, followed in succession by Rev. F. W. Woodward, Dr. John W. Chandler, and the present vigorous and efficient incumbent, Mr. E. C. Hocmer. Besides the working libraries in the several schools, aggregating 1,200 volumes, there is also in the district a well equipped Free Public Library of over 5,000 volumes.

The schools of Ellenville were never in a more prosperous condition than at present; 638 resident pupils and 77 non-resident pupils were reported in 1906. The annual expenditure for school purposes is over $12,000. The teaching force consists of eighteen teachers and a superintendent.

CHAPTER XLVI.

THE SHIPPING OF TWAALFSKILL.

By Henry H. Pitts.

THE old North or Hudson River Sloops were of a peculiar model and construction, and were specially planned and adapted to navigate smooth inland waters, with broad full bows shaped somewhat like the head of a huge fish, and great breadth of beam for their length. With masts 90 to 110 feet long, a main boom 75 to 85 feet, a top mast 60 to 85 feet and a jib, they could spread from 3,000 to 5,000 yards of canvas, and sail closer to the wind than vessels of any other rig or model.

Some of them were fleet and could outsail the smartest yachts of their time; they were known among all sailors and boatmen, and their peculiar type and model was not to be seen elsewhere. Most of them carried a crew of 5 men, Captain, 1st, 2nd and 3rd hand, and a first-class cook. All of them set good tables and were furnished with the best food, for all were hearty eaters. The Captain did no work. On account of their great spread of canvas and lofty masts, the sloops presented a beautiful appearance when under full sail. On a bright day in summer with a free wind the Hudson would often be dotted with them for miles.

The good sloop Dollie was owned and sailed by Captain Gurnee of South Rondout. She was the pet of all the Hudson River boatmen, and was believed by them to be almost human, and to know her way on the river as well as the crew, and to be able to find her way in the Rondout Creek in the darkest nights alone. Captain Gurnee related to the writer this story. He was on his way home from Albany to Rondout, but just off the mouth of the Saugerties Creek the wind and tide gave out, and he was compelled to anchor. There being no wind he left all sails standing, and told the crew they could turn in and he would keep anchor watch. After a while the Captain became sleepy and lay down on the locker in the cabin, and fell asleep. How long he slept he does not know, but he was awakened by the noise of the sheet block dragging across the deck on the traveler. Thinking the wind was coming up he dozed off again, when he was again awakened by the same noise. Thinking it was now time to call the crew and get up anchor, he went on deck and to his surprise found the Dolly fast at her regular dock at Rondout. Captain Gurnee explains this as follows: When the tide rose she tripped the anchor and the Dolly was free. The sails being all set and the wind just right she stood off for the east shore. When near the east shore the wind again changed, the boom went over and she stood off for the Rondout Creek, which she made, having just headway enough to carry her to her regular dock in the creek.

The old sloop Hoaxer, built in the year 1832, and owned by Cox and Company at Eddyville, had the name of always being unlucky. She had many owners and captains who always had bad luck. Her last owners were the Booth Brothers, who being practical men and very skeptical, bought her for a song, and placed her in command of Captain Theodore Bush, a young and skilled boatmen. Her first cargo was a load of Wilbur ground lime in barrels. Before she left the dock Mr. Rand of the firm of Smith and Rand, powder manufacturers at Rifton, came to the office of Booth Brothers and begged them to put on 100 kegs of powder for a special hurried order. Captain Bush gave his consent, and the powder was put on on Saturday afternoon in July, 1862. That night the tide was so low that the vessel grounded and could not leave her dock; the crew all went ashore, leaving Captain Bush in charge. The Captain was awakened late Sunday morning by smoke coming through the bulkhead in the cabin. A few springs, and he was on deck and gave the alarm. The hatches were taken off, and the Booths were the first to jump in the hold and pass out the heated kegs of powder to the men on the dock. Twice the owners had to be taken out of the hold in a suffocating condition caused by the heat and fumes from the slacking lime. Finally, all the powder was taken out but one keg, which being fast between the swelling lime barrels, could not be moved. A hole was broken in this keg and water poured in until thoroughly saturated. The hatches were put on and the fire smothered.

During the removal of the powder a panic existed among the residents of Wilbur, most of whom fled to the adjoining hills for safety.

The old sloop Martin Wynkoop had many owners and captains, and the name of always being unlucky. She was believed by all boatmen to be bewitched. Every one who owned her had bad luck while she was in their possession, and every Captain who sailed her was always doing damage. It is said that at the time she was launched a young man was killed and the vessel was cursed by his mother. Captain Edwin Young once sailed her. He was a first-class boatman, a man of good common sense who did not believe in ghosts, witches or anything supernatural; a man of great courage. Captain Young told the writer that this old hulk defied all natural laws, that he had known her to drift and drag her anchor and foul another vessel against both wind and tide. He said he never had a day's luck while sailing her, and gave up his command in disgust. The different crews of this old sloop would tell her that she was at anchor in the river; they would go ashore at night to enjoy themselves, and on returning would find her lighted from stem to stern, and merry music and witches dancing to ghost time, and that all would vanish in darkness as soon as their boat touched the vessel's side.

One of the largest vessels built on the Rondout was the two-masted schooner Henry H. Pitts, built at New Salem at the ship yard of Frank Haber by Henry H. Pitts. She was 165 feet long, 30 feet 6 inches beam, drew 9 feet, loaded, 4 feet light, and carried 500 gross tons. She was launched during a violent thunder storm in the summer of 1872. Old boatmen said that the thunder storm was a bad omen for the vessel. She was fitted out for the deep sea and coast trade, and was chartered for her first voyage to the lower coast of Mexico to bring home a cargo of mahogany logs. On her first outward trip from New York she encountered a heavy northeast gale, which lasted ninety hours, and was so badly damaged that she was compelled to put into the port of Kingston, Jamaica, in distress. On her return from Mexico loaded with mahogany, she encountered a fierce gale in the Straits of Florida, the Captain lost his reckoning and ran on the Bahama rocks. The Captain proceeded on his voyage to New York, but when off Cape Hatteras encountered a terrible northwest hurricane, and after trying to round the Cape was compelled to put off before the gale and did not stop until he made Tybe light at the mouth of the Savannah River, in distress. After a stormy passage up the coast she arrived safe in New York. She was commanded by Captain S. B. Fletcher of Islesboro, Me., who never had a day's luck while on her, and the owner sold her to the firm of C. W. Alcot and Company of New York, who made money with her. She is still running and has had good luck ever since.

The Addison, the Henry Clay and the Greene County Tanner were all famous vessels in their day, and all hailed from Wilbur. The advent of the fast steamer Alida and the propeller Nicholas Elmendorf, in the summer of 1852-53, started a business boom in Wilbur. A company was formed composed of Nicholas Elmendorf, Philip V. D. Lockwood and William Masten of Kingston, who purchased the Alida and placed her on the route as a day boat from Wilbur to New York, returning the same day. The Alida made her first trip in the spring of 1854, and left the Rondout Creek with the largest number of passengers she ever carried. She rolled so that a panic prevailed, women fainted and men were unnerved, so that when she landed at Rondout hundreds left her and could not be induced to return. After leaving the creek and getting under good headway in the river she stopped rolling and made the trip to New York and return quickly and safely. The owners then purchased the propeller Nicholas Elmendorf, and placed her on the route as a freight boat. After running about one year the company failed, all its members lost every dollar they had. The Alida could make the trip from New York to Wilbur in less than five hours, and her time has never been beaten.

She was commanded by Captain William Masten. Her first pilot was Captain Judson Morey, and her second Pilot Mortimer Van Etten, all of Kingston.

The propeller Elmendorf was commanded by Captain DuBois Lowe of Eddyville.

The following vessels commanded as stated, also sailed from Twaalfskill:

Sloop Gideon Lee. Captain James Smith.

Schooner Everett, built at South Rondout by Captain William Gurnee.

Sloop Beckey Ford, South Rondout. Captain David Houghtaling.

Sloop Robert North, Mingo Hollow. Owned and sailed by Captain Adam Beam.

Sloop Dollie, of South Rondout. Owned and sailed by Captain William Gurnee.

Sloop Victor. Captain Steve Schoonmaker.

Sloop Henry Clay, 185 years old, had many captains and owners, is still running in the Creek.

Sloop Milan. Sailed by Captain Alfred Hyde.

Sloop John Leach. Sailed by Captain John Myers, Hyde.

Sloop Hannah Ann. Owned and sailed by Captain Abe Hyde.

Sloop Ambassador, of South Rondout. Owned and sailed by Captain Dick Hamilton.

Old Sloop Canfield. Owned and sailed by Captain Thomas Requa, of Eddyville, one of the veterans of the Hudson.

Sloop Martin Wynkoop. Sailed by Captain James Smith, Edwin Young and many others.

Old Sloop Kemmannah. A fast sailor. Sailed and owned by Captain Edwin Young.

Schooner Kate and Mary, built at South Rondout. Built, sailed and owned by Captain James Cogswell.

Captain William Gurnee, big and fearless, built and owned the Sloop Sarah Gurnee, and the I. & W. Gurnee. Captain Isaac Houghtaling, the strong man, carried anchor to blacksmiths for repair. Owned and sailed many of the old Sloops.

Sloop Dutchess. Captain Cottrell.

Sloop Venus. Owned and sailed by Captain Thomas Martain.

Sloop Josephine. Owned and sailed by Captain Thomas Martain.

Sloop Congress. Big Sloop. Captain Thomas Martain.

Sloop James Lawrence. Captain Sam Van Aken.

Sloop Bell. Owned and sailed by Captain William DeLanoye, of South Rondout.

Sloop John Beveridge, a fast sailor. Captain William Hopkins.

Schooner John H. Gould. Captain William Myers.

Sloop Hoaxer. Sailed by Captain Tom Cherrytree Cox. Always unlucky. Captain Theodore Bush. Carried lime and powder.

Sloop John Jay. Sunk, and raised. Owned and sailed by Captain John Forsyth.

Sloop Lafayette. Owned by H. H. Pitts. Sailed by Captain Philip Kelly, Captain John Forsyth. Rebuilt.

Sloop Ohio. Captain Dennis Donovan.

Sloop Canal. Captain Timothy Donovan.

Sloop Congress. Owned by Edward Kearney. Sailed by Captain Mat Kavanaugh.

Sloop Nellie Wales. Sailed by Captain Mat Cavanagh.

Sloop Holbrook. Rebuilt. Captain Joseph Lynch.

Sloop George W. Hurst. Sailed by Captain William Quinn.

Sloop Hadden. Captain John Quinn, Captain Thomas Bouls.

Sloop Milan. Captain James Henry, Captain Hyde.

Sloop Hellen Brown, of Rondout. Owned and sailed by Captain John Quinn.

Sloop Will Mail. Owned and sailed by Captain Charles Felton, a Frenchman.

Sloop Quackenbush. Owned and sailed by Captain Richard Degraff, who was killed aboard her.

S. & W. B. FITCH LINE.

Sloop Addison. Captains Louis Shultis, Peter Ball, Edwin Young and Jas. Smith.

Schooner Green County Tanner. Captain Alfred Hyde.

Schooner Bride. Sailed by Captain William Hyde.

Sloop William H. Bridger. Sailed by Captain Robert Henry.

Sloop Thomas Colyer. Sailed by Captain Philip Shultus.

Big Sloop Canal. Captain Mauric Lahey and Captain Peter Ball.

Sloop Iowa. Sailed by Captain William Hyde.

Sloop Asa Biglow. Sailed by Captain Peter Bell.

Sloop Jacob Lorilard. Owned and sailed by Captain Ben Simmons.

Big Sloop Othelo, of Wilbur. Captain Aeris Johnson.

Sloop Thomas Adams. Captain Lou Van Aken, of New Salem.

Sloop Missouri. Captain Alfred Hyde.

CHAPTER XLVII.

BLUESTONE.

By CHARLES E. FOOTE.

THIS species of sandstone has for many years formed a foremost industry in Ulster, as well as in other sections of the State. As briefly mentioned in an early chapter of this work, this stratum belongs to the Upper Devonian period. Beginning at a point near Albany, the boundary of the productive region extends southward, from five to twenty miles west of the Hudson, to the vicinity of Hurley, when it turns to the southwest along Rondout Creek. The northern boundary of the formation stretches westward across the State on about an east and west line, beginning about fifteen or twenty miles south of the Mohawk and ending near the shore of Lake Erie, the district thus covering the principal portion of the southern and southeastern part of the State. The most prolific regions are in Ulster, the southeastern portion of Greene County, and a strip along the Delaware River.

As nearly as can be ascertained, the first quarry of bluestone was opened by Silas Brainerd, near Saugerties, in 1832. While others are said to have preceded him, authentic data thereof is lacking. In any event the quarries were not worked to an extent which would make them commercially historical.

Bluestone is a peculiarly hard, fine-grained quality of sandstone. The name was originally applied to the blue colored stone quarried in Ulster County, but its commercial application of recent years has been extended to cover most of the flagstone produced in the State, some of which is green and some of a reddish color. The beds are generally horizontal, or dip at gentle angles, so that the working is comparatively easy.

This district, which comprises Greene, Ulster, Delaware, Sullivan and Broome Counties, according to the division made by the State Geologist, is composed of a large number of quarries, most of which are small and short lived. To offset this, however, is the further fact that there are thousands of them known, but still under cover, and presumably other thousands which have not yet been looked for. It may be safely said that there is enough bluestone in Ulster County alone to keep the quarrying portion of its population busy for centuries to come.

Most of the stone quarried in Ulster is subjected to mill-treatment, known commercially as quarry-dressed at the mills in the vicinity of the quarries. The balance, probably twenty-five per cent of the whole, is treated at the mills along the Hudson River.

Commercially the Ulster bluestone is divided into three classes as follows:

No. 1. Flagstone. No. 2. Edge. No. 3. Rock. No. 1 includes the stone used for sidewalks, and requires little dressing. Stone an inch and a half thick or over, with a smooth surface and edges at right angles, fulfil the requirements. Its density is so great as to absorb little moisture, and this renders it almost impervious to wear, while its character is such that it never becomes smooth and slippery with the moisture as does clay slate.

No. 2 includes such stone as curb, window and door-sills, lintels and other house trimmings. This stone requires dressing; curb requires "axing" on the face and edge. All this class of stone requires one or more perfect edges for market.

No. 3 includes the stone sold in the rough to dealers for mill-treatment. It ranges from four inches to as many feet or more in thickness, and is sawed or planed in the mills for platforms, steps, and building-stone. The first two classes are often treated in the mills when finished work is required.

The beds of stone in the Ulster quarries are divided naturally by vertical joints at right angles, one system running north and south and the other east and west. The east and west joints are known to the quarrymen as the "heads," or "headers," while those running north and south are called "side seams." These seams are five to seventy-five feet apart, and the distance determines the maximum size of the stone that can be taken from them. The layers into which a ledge is divided by horizontal seams are known as "lifts." These are split apart by means of thin wedges, driven to make a practically uniform pressure along the entire front, so as to raise the layer back to the next joint. If the joint be too far back, so that the stone would be too large for handling, a place of cleavage, or breaking point, is made by drilling holes in a line across it, thus dividing it into sections. It sometimes occurs that the stone is brittle, or that for some other reason the stone refuses to split, and breaks into fragments at the introduction of the wedges; this destroys the value of the quarry, so far as that particular lift is concerned. More loss may be incurred by following it up in search for better results, or the very next lift may be a perfect one. Judgment and experience seem to have no place in the determination of "when to stop" under these circumstances. To proceed may mean to add to the loss already incurred by "stripping," (uncovering the top) or it may mean to develop a fine and profitable quarry which will repay many fold the time and labor spent upon it. This feature constitutes the "miner's gamble," and no unlucky gold miner ever saw a fine prospect "pinch out," with feelings of more acute regret, than have Ulster County bluestone quarrymen watched the continuation of the breaking and crumbling of the stone as the wedges tried to cleave it from its bed.

In addition to the open seams which separate the lifts, and which are often filled with a thin stratum of shale called "pencil," there are often numerous closed seams, sometimes very close together, which show where the stone may be split if care is exercised. These are called "reeds," and frequently indicate that very thin layers may be produced if desired. These "reeds" do not detract from the durability or excellence of the stone, but rather add to them, by giving it a condition of comparative elasticity, which better enables it to resist the extremes of weather.

When a quarry is first opened the lifts are usually thin, but they become thicker as each successive tier is removed. Sometimes the thicker lifts are at the bottom, at other times at the top. Quarries which run principally to flagstone may be operated by hand or horse-power. The "stripping," by which is meant the removal of the soil covering, clay or hardpan, and sometimes rocks, from the top of the bluestone ledge, is usually done in winter, when the ground is frozen, as it may then be blasted and removed more readily. Most of the quarrying is done during eight or nine months of the year, few quarries are operated in the very cold weather of winter.

After the stone is taken from its bed, it is turned over to the stonecutter, who prepares it for the market. Flagstone is cut to commercial sizes and irregularities of the surface are chiseled down. Curb or other "edge" stones must be broken or split to the proper dimensions, "axed" on the face, and the top edge pitched to the proper angle. Rock and platform stone require no dressing at the quarry, the finer dressing being done at the docks. At many of these docks, stone mills are in operation. The mill-treatment consists of sawing the large blocks, planing and rubbing the house trimmings, steps, platforms, etc., and boring sewer heads.

A planer consists of a stationary base and upper frame, with an oscillating carriage on which the stone is firmly fastened. In the upper frame the plane-bits are firmly fixed, which take off the irregularities of the surface of the stone as it passes under them on the carriage. "Rubbing" is done by a circular cast-iron plate, which is made to revolve swiftly against the surface of the stone. Sand and water are fed to facilitate this work.

Most of the quarries in Ulster are worked by from two to five men; sometimes in partnership, sometimes as employer and helpers. The quarryman rarely owns the land on which the quarry is located, but usually leases it at a rental of five per cent. of the value of the product. Many of the larger quarries are owned by the wholesale dealers, who lease to the quarrymen, and maintain mills for preparing the product for market. One of the difficulties under which the quarryman labors, is the transportation of the stone to the dock of the dealer to whom he sells. In some cases the cost of this is equal to half the value of the load hauled; in other, and more favorable locations, it runs as low as eight or ten per cent. Settlements are made weekly or monthly as may be agreed upon.

Flagstone is sold by the square foot. Curbing and crosswalk by the linear foot. Rock, the thick large stone, is sold by a sort of inverted lumber measure, per inch, by the square foot. For instance, a stone 10 by 10, containing one hundred square feet of surface, would, if ten inches thick, at two and a half cents an inch, bring twenty-five dollars. The same stone, sixteen inches thick, would bring forty dollars.

37597729R10401

Made in the USA
Charleston, SC
11 January 2015